TREATY SUPPLEMENT

INTERNATIONAL ENVIRONMENTAL LAW AND POLICY

2011 EDITION

by

DAVID HUNTER
Associate Professor of Law
Director, Program on International and Comparative Environmental Law
Director, International Legal Studies Program
Washington College of Law, American University

JAMES SALZMAN
Professor of Law, Nicholas Institute Professor of Environmental Policy
School of Law, Nicholas School of the Environment and Earth Sciences
Duke University

DURWOOD ZAELKE
President, Institute for Governance and Sustainable Development
Director, International Network for Environmental Compliance and
Enforcement
Adjunct Professor of Law
Washington College of Law, American University
Co–Director, Program on Governance for Sustainable Development
University of California, Santa Barbara

FOUNDATION PRESS
2011

THOMSON REUTERS™

This publication was created to provide you with accurate and authoritative information concerning the subject matter covered; however, this publication was not necessarily prepared by persons licensed to practice law in a particular jurisdiction. The publisher is not engaged in rendering legal or other professional advice and this publication is not a substitute for the advice of an attorney. If you require legal or other expert advice, you should seek the services of a competent attorney or other professional.

Nothing contained herein is intended or written to be used for the purposes of 1) avoiding penalties imposed under the federal Internal Revenue Code, or 2) promoting, marketing or recommending to another party any transaction or matter addressed herein.matter addressed herein.

© 2002 FOUNDATION PRESS
© 2007 THOMSON REUTERS/FOUNDATION PRESS
© 2011 By THOMSON REUTERS/FOUNDATION PRESS
1 New York Plaza, 34th Floor
New York, NY 10004
Phone Toll Free 1–877–888–1330
Fax 646–424–5201
foundation–press.com
Printed in the United States of America

ISBN 978–1–59941–536–9

Mat #40743662

Table of Contents

Protection of Habitat and Natural Places

International Trade

Preface

This supplement accompanies the fourth edition of the course book, *International Environmental Law and Policy* (Foundation Press, 2011). The course book contains excerpts from the most significant international environmental agreements and declarations. This supplement is directed at professors, students and practitioners who wish to study the complete texts. Each document reprinted in this supplement contains information on its date of signing, date entered into force, and citation. We have also included, where relevant, the internet homepage of the treaty secretariat.

While dozens of agreements have played an important role in the development and application of international environmental law, we have strived to keep this supplement at a manageable size and an affordable price. Thus we have reprinted only the most influential agreements and, out of concern over space constraints, a number of the agreements have not been fully reproduced. In some instances (*e.g.,* GATT, UN Convention on the Law of the Sea) we have excerpted relevant provisions from the main text of the treaty, while in others (*e.g.,* MARPOL, Desertification Convention) we have not included all the annexes.

All the agreements reprinted in the supplement have been proofread against the official versions to verify accuracy, but some typographic errors from the transcription and formatting of texts for the supplement could remain. Thus if using the documents for other than teaching purposes, it is essential that you verify these texts against the official version noted in the citations (*i.e.,* the International Legal Materials series, UN Treaty series, or secretariat homepage) to ensure complete accuracy of the text.

David Hunter
James Salzman
Durwood Zaelke

VIENNA CONVENTION ON THE LAW OF TREATIES

1155 U.N.T.S. 331
Signed: 23 May 1969
Entered into Force: 27 January 1980

The States Parties to the present Convention,

Considering the fundamental role of treaties in the history of international relations,

Recognizing the ever-increasing importance of treaties as a source of international law and as a means of developing peaceful co-operation among nations, whatever their constitutional and social systems,

Noting that the principles of free consent and of good faith and the *pacta sunt servanda* rule are universally recognized,

Affirming that disputes concerning treaties, like other international disputes, should be settled by peaceful means and in conformity with the principles of justice and international law,

Recalling the determination of the peoples of the United Nations to establish conditions under which justice and respect for the obligations arising from treaties can be maintained,

Having in mind the principles of international law embodied in the Charter of the United Nations, such as the principles of the equal rights and self-determination of peoples, of the sovereign equality and independence of all States, of non-interference in the domestic affairs of States, of the prohibition of the threat or use of force and of universal respect for, and observance of, human rights and fundamental freedoms for all,

Believing that the codification and progressive development of the law of treaties achieved in the present Convention will promote the purposes of the United Nations set forth in the Charter, namely, the maintenance of international peace and security, the development of friendly relations and the achievement of co-operation among nations,

Affirming that the rules of customary international law will continue to govern questions not regulated by the provisions of the present Convention,

Have agreed as follows:

PART I: INTRODUCTION

Article 1   Scope of the present Convention

The present Convention applies to treaties between States.

Article 2   Use of terms

1. For the purposes of the present Convention:

    (a) 'treaty' means an international agreement concluded between States in written form and governed by international law, whether embodied in a single instrument or in two or more related instruments and whatever its particular designation;

    (b) 'ratification', 'acceptance', 'approval' and 'accession' mean in each case the international act so named whereby a State establishes on the international plane its consent to be bound by a treaty;

    (c) 'full powers' means a document emanating from the competent authority of a State designating a person or persons to represent the State for negotiating, adopting or authenticating the text of a treaty, for expressing the consent of the State to be bound by a treaty, or for accomplishing any other act with respect to a treaty;

(d) 'reservation' means a unilateral statement, however phrased or named, made by a State, when signing, ratifying, accepting, approving or acceding to a treaty, whereby it purports to exclude or to modify the legal effect of certain provisions of the treaty in their application to that State;

(e) 'negotiating State' means a State which took part in the drawing up and adoption of the text of the treaty;

(f) 'contracting State' means a State which has consented to be bound by the treaty, whether or not the treaty has entered into force;

(g) 'party' means a State which has consented to be bound by the treaty and for which the treaty is in force;

(h) 'third State' means a State not a party to the treaty;

(i) 'international organization' means an intergovernmental organization.

2. The provisions of paragraph 1 regarding the use of terms in the present Convention are without prejudice to the use of those terms or to the meanings which may be given to them in the internal law of any State.

Article 3   International agreements not within the scope of the present Convention

The fact that the present Convention does not apply to international agreements concluded between States and other subjects of international law or between such other subjects of international law, or to international agreements not in written form, shall not affect:

(a) the legal force of such agreements;

(b) the application to them of any of the rules set forth in the present Convention to which they would be subject under international law independently of the Convention;

(c) the application of the Convention to the relations of States as between themselves under international agreements to which other subjects of international law are also parties.

Article 4   Non-Retroactivity of the Present Convention

Without prejudice to the application of any rules set forth in the present Convention to which treaties would be subject under international law independently of the Convention, the Convention applies only to treaties which are concluded by States after the entry into force of the present Convention with regard to such States.

Article 5   Treaties constituting international organizations and treaties adopted within an international organization

The present Convention applies to any treaty which is the constituent instrument of an international organization and to any treaty adopted within an international organization without prejudice to any relevant rules of the organization.

PART II: CONCLUSION AND ENTRY INTO FORCE OF TREATIES

SECTION 1. CONCLUSION OF TREATIES

Article 6   Capacity of States to conclude treaties

Every State possesses capacity to conclude treaties.

Article 7   Full powers

1. A person is considered as representing a State for the purpose of adopting or authenticating the text of a treaty or for the purpose of expressing the consent of the State to be bound by a treaty if:

(a) he produces appropriate full powers; or

(b) it appears from the practice of the States concerned or from other circumstances that their intention was to consider that person as representing the State for such purposes and to dispense with full powers.

2. In virtue of their functions and without having to produce full powers, the following are considered as representing their State:

(a) Heads of State, Heads of Government and Ministers for Foreign Affairs, for the purpose of performing all acts relating to the conclusion of a treaty;
(b) heads of diplomatic missions, for the purpose of adopting the text of a treaty between the accrediting State and the State to which they are accredited;
(c) representatives accredited by States to an international conference or to an international organization or one of its organs, for the purpose of adopting the text of a treaty in that conference, organization or organ.

Article 8   Subsequent confirmation of an act performed without authorization

An act relating to the conclusion of a treaty performed by a person who cannot be considered under article 7 as authorized to represent a State for that purpose is without legal effect unless afterwards confirmed by that State.

Article 9   Adoption of the text

1. The adoption of the text of a treaty takes place by the consent of all the States participating in its drawing up except as provided in paragraph 2.

2. The adoption of the text of a treaty at an international conference takes place by the vote of two-thirds of the States present and voting, unless by the same majority they shall decide to apply a different rule.

Article 10   Authentication of the text

The text of a treaty is established as authentic and definitive:

(a) by such procedure as may be provided for in the text or agreed upon by the States participating in its drawing up; or
(b) failing such procedure, by the signature, signature *ad referendum* or initialling by the representatives of those States of the text of the treaty or of the Final Act of a conference incorporating the text.

Article 11   Means of expressing consent to be bound by a treaty

The consent of a State to be bound by a treaty may be expressed by signature, exchange of instruments constituting a treaty, ratification, acceptance, approval or accession, or by any other means if so agreed.

Article 12   Consent to be bound by a treaty expressed by signature

1. The consent of a State to be bound by a treaty is expressed by the signature of its representative when:

(a) the treaty provides that signature shall have that effect;
(b) it is otherwise established that the negotiating States were agreed that signature should have that effect; or
(c) the intention of the State to give that effect to the signature appears from the full powers of its representative or was expressed during the negotiation.

2. For the purposes of paragraph 1:

     (a) the initialling of a text constitutes a signature of the treaty when it is established that the negotiating States so agreed;

     (b) the signature ad referendum of a treaty by a representative, if confirmed by his State, constitutes a full signature of the treaty.

Article 13	**Consent to be bound by a treaty expressed by an exchange of instruments constituting a treaty**

The consent of States to be bound by a treaty constituted by instruments exchanged between them is expressed by that exchange when:

     (a) the instruments provide that their exchange shall have that effect; or

     (b) it is otherwise established that those States were agreed that the exchange of instruments should have that effect.

Article 14	**Consent to be bound by a treaty expressed by ratification, acceptance or approval**

1. The consent of a State to be bound by a treaty is expressed by ratification when:

     (a) the treaty provides for such consent to be expressed by means of ratification;

     (b) it is otherwise established that the negotiating States were agreed that ratification should be required;

     (c) the representative of the State has signed the treaty subject to ratification; or

     (d) the intention of the State to sign the treaty subject to ratification appears from the full powers of its representative or was expressed during the negotiation.

2. The consent of a State to be bound by a treaty is expressed by acceptance or approval under conditions similar to those which apply to ratification.

Article 15	**Consent to be bound by a treaty expressed by accession**

The consent of a State to be bound by a treaty is expressed by accession when:

     (a) the treaty provides that such consent may be expressed by that State by means of accession;

     (b) it is otherwise established that the negotiating States were agreed that such consent may be expressed by that State by means of accession; or

     (c) all the parties have subsequently agreed that such consent may be expressed by that State by means of accession.

Article 16	**Exchange or deposit of instruments of ratification, acceptance, approval or accession**

Unless the treaty otherwise provides, instruments of ratification, acceptance, approval or accession establish the consent of a State to be bound by a treaty upon:

     (a) their exchange between the contracting States;

     (b) their deposit with the depositary; or

     (c) their notification to the contracting States or to the depositary, if so agreed.

Article 17	**Consent to be bound by part of a treaty and choice of differing provisions**

1. Without prejudice to articles 19 to 23, the consent of a State to be bound by part of a treaty is effective only if the treaty so permits or the other contracting States so agree.

2. The consent of a State to be bound by a treaty which permits a choice between differing provisions is effective only if it is made clear to which of the provisions the consent relates.

Article 18	**Obligation not to defeat the object and purpose of a treaty prior to its entry into force**

A State is obliged to refrain from acts which would defeat the object and purpose of a treaty when:

(a) it has signed the treaty or has exchanged instruments constituting the treaty subject to ratification, acceptance or approval, until it shall have made its intention clear not to become a party to the treaty; or

(b) it has expressed its consent to be bound by the treaty, pending the entry into force of the treaty and provided that such entry into force is not unduly delayed.

SECTION 2. RESERVATIONS

Article 19	**Formulation of reservations**

A State may, when signing, ratifying, accepting, approving or acceding to a treaty, formulate a reservation unless:

(a) the reservation is prohibited by the treaty;

(b) the treaty provides that only specified reservations, which do not include the reservation in question, may be made; or

(c) in cases not falling under sub-paragraphs (a) and (b), the reservation is incompatible with the object and purpose of the treaty.

Article 20	**Acceptance of and objection to reservations**

1. A reservation expressly authorized by a treaty does not require any subsequent acceptance by the other contracting States unless the treaty so provides.

2. When it appears from the limited number of the negotiating States and the object and purpose of a treaty that the application of the treaty in its entirety between all the parties is an essential condition of the consent of each one to be bound by the treaty, a reservation requires acceptance by all the parties.

3. When a treaty is a constituent instrument of an international organization and unless it otherwise provides, a reservation requires the acceptance of the competent organ of that organization.

4. In cases not falling under the preceding paragraphs and unless the treaty otherwise provides:

(a) acceptance by another contracting State of a reservation constitutes the reserving State a party to the treaty in relation to that other State if or when the treaty is in force for those States;

(b) an objection by another contracting State to a reservation does not preclude the entry into force of the treaty as between the objecting and reserving States unless a contrary intention is definitely expressed by the objecting State;

(c) an act expressing a State's consent to be bound by the treaty and containing a reservation is effective as soon as at least one other contracting State has accepted the reservation.

5. For the purposes of paragraphs 2 and 4 and unless the treaty otherwise provides, a reservation is considered to have been accepted by a State if it shall have raised no objection to the reservation by the end of a period of twelve

months after it was notified of the reservation or by the date on which it expressed its consent to be bound by the treaty, whichever is later.

| Article 21 | Legal effects of reservations and of objections to reservations |

1. A reservation established with regard to another party in accordance with articles 19, 20 and 23:

(a) modifies for the reserving State in its relations with that other party the provisions of the treaty to which the reservation relates to the extent of the reservation; and

(b) modifies those provisions to the same extent for that other party in its relations with the reserving State.

2. The reservation does not modify the provisions of the treaty for the other parties to the treaty *inter se*.

3. When a State objecting to a reservation has not opposed the entry into force of the treaty between itself and the reserving State, the provisions to which the reservation relates do not apply as between the two States to the extent of the reservation.

| Article 22 | Withdrawal of reservations and of objections to reservations |

1. Unless the treaty otherwise provides, a reservation may be withdrawn at any time and the consent of a State which has accepted the reservation is not required for its withdrawal.

2. Unless the treaty otherwise provides, an objection to a reservation may be withdrawn at any time.

3. Unless the treaty otherwise provides, or it is otherwise agreed:

(a) the withdrawal of a reservation becomes operative in relation to another contracting State only when notice of it has been received by that State;

(b) the withdrawal of an objection to a reservation becomes operative only when notice of it has been received by the State which formulated the reservation.

| Article 23 | Procedure regarding reservations |

1. A reservation, an express acceptance of a reservation and an objection to a reservation must be formulated in writing and communicated to the contracting States and other States entitled to become parties to the treaty.

2. If formulated when signing the treaty subject to ratification, acceptance or approval, a reservation must be formally confirmed by the reserving State when expressing its consent to be bound by the treaty. In such a case the reservation shall be considered as having been made on the date of its confirmation.

3. An express acceptance of, or an objection to, a reservation made previously to confirmation of the reservation does not itself require confirmation.

4. The withdrawal of a reservation or of an objection to a reservation must be formulated in writing.

SECTION 3.   ENTRY INTO FORCE AND PROVISIONAL APPLICATION OF TREATIES

| Article 24 | Entry into force |

1. A treaty enters into force in such manner and upon such date as it may provide or as the negotiating States may agree.

2. Failing any such provision or agreement, a treaty enters into force as soon as consent to be bound by the treaty has been established for all the negotiating States.

3. When the consent of a State to be bound by a treaty is established on a date after the treaty has come into force, the treaty enters into force for that State on that date, unless the treaty otherwise provides.

4. The provisions of a treaty regulating the authentication of its text, the establishment of the consent of States to be bound by the treaty, the manner or date of its entry into force, reservations, the functions of the depositary and other matters arising necessarily before the entry into force of the treaty apply from the time of the adoption of its text.

Article 25   Provisional application

1. A treaty or a part of a treaty is applied provisionally pending its entry into force if:

> (a) the treaty itself so provides; or
> (b) the negotiating States have in some other manner so agreed.

2. Unless the treaty otherwise provides or the negotiating States have otherwise agreed, the provisional application of a treaty or a part of a treaty with respect to a State shall be terminated if that State notifies the other States between which the treaty is being applied provisionally of its intention not to become a party to the treaty.

PART III OBSERVANCE, APPLICATION AND INTERPRETATION OF TREATIES

SECTION 1. OBSERVANCE OF TREATIES

Article 26   *Pacta sunt servanda*

Every treaty in force is binding upon the parties to it and must be performed by them in good faith.

Article 27   Internal law and observance of treaties

A party may not invoke the provisions of its internal law as justification for its failure to perform a treaty. This rule is without prejudice to article 46.

SECTION 2. APPLICATION OF TREATIES

Article 28   Non-retroactivity of treaties

Unless a different intention appears from the treaty or is otherwise established, its provisions do not bind a party in relation to any act or fact which took place or any situation which ceased to exist before the date of the entry into force of the treaty with respect to that party.

Article 29   Territorial scope of treaties

Unless a different intention appears from the treaty or is otherwise established, a treaty is binding upon each party in respect of its entire territory.

Article 30   Application of successive treaties relating to the same subject-matter

1. Subject to Article 103 of the Charter of the United Nations, the rights and obligations of States parties to successive treaties relating to the same subject-matter shall be determined in accordance with the following paragraphs.

2. When a treaty specifies that it is subject to, or that it is not to be considered as incompatible with, an earlier or later treaty, the provisions of that other treaty prevail.

3. When all the parties to the earlier treaty are parties also to the later treaty but the earlier treaty is not terminated or suspended in operation under article 59, the earlier treaty applies only to the extent that its provisions are compatible with those of the later treaty.

4. When the parties to the later treaty do not include all the parties to the earlier one:

    (a) as between States parties to both treaties the same rule applies as in paragraph 3;
    (b) as between a State party to both treaties and a State party to only one of the treaties, the treaty to which both States are parties governs their mutual rights and obligations.

5. Paragraph 4 is without prejudice to article 41, or to any question of the termination or suspension of the operation of a treaty under article 60 or to any question of responsibility which may arise for a State from the conclusion or application of a treaty, the provisions of which are incompatible with its obligations towards another State under another treaty.

SECTION 3.   INTERPRETATION OF TREATIES

Article 31   General rule of interpretation

1. A treaty shall be interpreted in good faith in accordance with the ordinary meaning to be given to the terms of the treaty in their context and in the light of its object and purpose.

2. The context for the purpose of the interpretation of a treaty shall comprise, in addition to the text, including its preamble and annexes:

    (a) any agreement relating to the treaty which was made between all the parties in connection with the conclusion of the treaty;
    (b) any instrument which was made by one or more parties in connection with the conclusion of the treaty and accepted by the other parties as an instrument related to the treaty.

3. There shall be taken into account, together with the context:

    (a) any subsequent agreement between the parties regarding the interpretation of the treaty or the application of its provisions;
    (b) any subsequent practice in the application of the treaty which establishes the agreement of the parties regarding its interpretation;
    (c) any relevant rules of international law applicable in the relations between the parties.

4. A special meaning shall be given to a term if it is established that the parties so intended.

Article 32   Supplementary means of interpretation

Recourse may be had to supplementary means of interpretation, including the preparatory work of the treaty and the circumstances of its conclusion, in order to confirm the meaning resulting from the application of article 31, or to determine the meaning when the interpretation according to article 31:

    (a) leaves the meaning ambiguous or obscure; or
    (b) leads to a result which is manifestly absurd or unreasonable.

Article 33   Interpretation of treaties authenticated in two or more languages

1. When a treaty has been authenticated in two or more languages, the text is equally authoritative in each language, unless the treaty provides or the parties agree that, in case of divergence, a particular text shall prevail.

2. A version of the treaty in a language other than one of those in which the text was authenticated shall be considered an authentic text only if the treaty so provides or the parties so agree.

3. The terms of the treaty are presumed to have the same meaning in each authentic text.

4. Except where a particular text prevails in accordance with paragraph 1, when a comparison of the authentic texts discloses a difference of meaning which the application of articles 31 and 32 does not remove, the meaning which best reconciles the texts, having regard to the object and purpose of the treaty, shall be adopted.

SECTION 4. TREATIES AND THIRD STATES

Article 34   General rule regarding third States

A treaty does not create either obligations or rights for a third State without its consent.

Article 35   Treaties providing for obligations for third States

An obligation arises for a third State from a provision of a treaty if the parties to the treaty intend the provision to be the means of establishing the obligation and the third State expressly accepts that obligation in writing.

Article 36   Treaties providing for rights for third States

1. A right arises for a third State from a provision of a treaty if the parties to the treaty intend the provision to accord that right either to the third State, or to a group of States to which it belongs, or to all States, and the third State assents thereto. Its assent shall be presumed so long as the contrary is not indicated, unless the treaty otherwise provides.

2. A State exercising a right in accordance with paragraph 1 shall comply with the conditions for its exercise provided for in the treaty or established in conformity with the treaty.

Article 37   Revocation or modification of obligations or rights of third States

1. When an obligation has arisen for a third State in conformity with article 35, the obligation may be revoked or modified only with the consent of the parties to the treaty and of the third State, unless it is established that they had otherwise agreed.

2. When a right has arisen for a third State in conformity with article 36, the right may not be revoked or modified by the parties if it is established that the right was intended not to be revocable or subject to modification without the consent of the third State.

Article 38   Rules in a treaty becoming binding on third States through international custom

Nothing in articles 34 to 37 precludes a rule set forth in a treaty from becoming binding upon a third State as a customary rule of international law, recognized as such.

PART IV   AMENDMENT AND MODIFICATION OF TREATIES

Article 39   General rule regarding the amendment of treaties

A treaty may be amended by agreement between the parties. The rules laid down in Part II apply to such an agreement except in so far as the treaty may otherwise provide.

Article 40   **Amendment of multilateral treaties**

1. Unless the treaty otherwise provides, the amendment of multilateral treaties shall be governed by the following paragraphs.

2. Any proposal to amend a multilateral treaty as between all the parties must be notified to all the contracting States, each one of which shall have the right to take part in:

     (a) the decision as to the action to be taken in regard to such proposal;
     (b) the negotiation and conclusion of any agreement for the amendment of the treaty.

3. Every State entitled to become a party to the treaty shall also be entitled to become a party to the treaty as amended.

4. The amending agreement does not bind any State already a party to the treaty which does not become a party to the amending agreement; article 30, paragraph 4(b), applies in relation to such State.

5. Any State which becomes a party to the treaty after the entry into force of the amending agreement shall, failing an expression of a different intention by that State:

     (a) be considered as a party to the treaty as amended; and
     (b) be considered as a party to the unamended treaty in relation to any party to the treaty not bound by the amending agreement.

Article 41   **Agreements to modify multilateral treaties between certain of the parties only**

1. Two or more of the parties to a multilateral treaty may conclude an agreement to modify the treaty as between themselves alone if:

     (a) the possibility of such a modification is provided for by the treaty; or
     (b) the modification in question is not prohibited by the treaty and:
         (i) does not affect the enjoyment by the other parties of their rights under the treaty or the performance of their obligations;
         (ii) does not relate to a provision, derogation from which is incompatible with the effective execution of the object and purpose of the treaty as a whole.

2. Unless in a case falling under paragraph 1(a) the treaty otherwise provides, the parties in question shall notify the other parties of their intention to conclude the agreement and of the modification to the treaty for which it provides.

PART V
INVALIDITY, TERMINATION AND SUSPENSION OF THE OPERATION OF TREATIES

SECTION 1. GENERAL PROVISIONS

Article 42   **Validity and continuance in force of treaties**

1. The validity of a treaty or of the consent of a State to be bound by a treaty may be impeached only through the application of the present Convention.

2. The termination of a treaty, its denunciation or the withdrawal of a party, may take place only as a result of the application of the provisions of the treaty or of the present Convention. The same rule applies to suspension of the operation of a treaty.

| Article 43 | Obligations imposed by international law independently of a treaty |

The invalidity, termination or denunciation of a treaty, the withdrawal of a party from it, or the suspension of its operation, as a result of the application of the present Convention or of the provisions of the treaty, shall not in any way impair the duty of any State to fulfill any obligation embodied in the treaty to which it would be subject under international law independently of the treaty.

| Article 44 | Separability of treaty provisions |

1. A right of a party, provided for in a treaty or arising under article 56, to denounce, withdraw from or suspend the operation of the treaty may be exercised only with respect to the whole treaty unless the treaty otherwise provides or the parties otherwise agree.

2. A ground for invalidating, terminating, withdrawing from or suspending the operation of a treaty recognized in the present Convention may be invoked only with respect to the whole treaty except as provided in the following paragraphs or in article 60.

3. If the ground relates solely to particular clauses, it may be invoked only with respect to those clauses where:

   (a) the said clauses are separable from the remainder of the treaty with regard to their application;
   (b) it appears from the treaty or is otherwise established that acceptance of those clauses was not an essential basis of the consent of the other party or parties to be bound by the treaty as a whole; and
   (c) continued performance of the remainder of the treaty would not be unjust.

4. In cases falling under articles 49 and 50, the State entitled to invoke the fraud or corruption may do so with respect either to the whole treaty or, subject to paragraph 3, to the particular clauses alone.

5. In cases falling under articles 51, 52 and 53, no separation of the provisions of the treaty is permitted.

| Article 45 | Loss of a right to invoke a ground for invalidating, terminating, withdrawing from or suspending the operation of a treaty |

A State may no longer invoke a ground for invalidating, terminating, withdrawing from or suspending the operation of a treaty under articles 46 to 50 or articles 60 and 62 if, after becoming aware of the facts:

   (a) it shall have expressly agreed that the treaty is valid or remains in force or continues in operation, as the case may be; or
   (b) it must by reason of its conduct be considered as having acquiesced in the validity of the treaty or in its maintenance in force or in operation, as the case may be.

SECTION 2. INVALIDITY OF TREATIES

| Article 46 | Provisions of internal law regarding competence to conclude treaties |

1. A State may not invoke the fact that its consent to be bound by a treaty has been expressed in violation of a provision of its internal law regarding competence to conclude treaties as invalidating its consent unless that violation was manifest and concerned a rule of its internal law of fundamental importance.

2. A violation is manifest if it would be objectively evident to any State conducting itself in the matter in accordance with normal practice and in good faith.

Article 47	Specific restrictions on authority to express the consent of a State

If the authority of a representative to express the consent of a State to be bound by a particular treaty has been made subject to a specific restriction, his omission to observe that restriction may not be invoked as invalidating the consent expressed by him unless the restriction was notified to the other negotiating States prior to his expressing such consent.

Article 48	Error

1. A State may invoke an error in a treaty as invalidating its consent to be bound by the treaty if the error relates to a fact or situation which was assumed by that State to exist at the time when the treaty was concluded and formed an essential basis of its consent to be bound by the treaty.

2. Paragraph 1 shall not apply if the State in question contributed by its own conduct to the error or if the circumstances were such as to put that State on notice of a possible error.

3. An error relating only to the wording of the text of a treaty does not affect its validity; article 79 then applies.

Article 49	Fraud

If a State has been induced to conclude a treaty by the fraudulent conduct of another negotiating State, the State may invoke the fraud as invalidating its consent to be bound by the treaty.

Article 50	Corruption of a representative of a State

If the expression of a State's consent to be bound by a treaty has been procured through the corruption of its representative directly or indirectly by another negotiating State, the State may invoke such corruption as invalidating its consent to be bound by the treaty.

Article 51	Coercion of a representative of a State

The expression of a State's consent to be bound by a treaty which has been procured by the coercion of its representative through acts or threats directed against him shall be without any legal effect.

Article 52	Coercion of a State by the threat or use of force

A treaty is void if its conclusion has been procured by the threat or use of force in violation of the principles of international law embodied in the Charter of the United Nations.

Article 53	Treaties conflicting with a peremptory norm of general international law (jus cogens)

A treaty is void if, at the time of its conclusion, it conflicts with a peremptory norm of general international law. For the purposes of the present Convention, a peremptory norm of general international law is a norm accepted and recognized by the international community of States as a whole as a norm from which no derogation is permitted and which can be modified only by a subsequent norm of general international law having the same character.

SECTION 3. TERMINATION AND SUSPENSION OF THE OPERATION OF TREATIES

Article 54   **Termination of or withdrawal from a treaty under its provisions or by consent of the parties**

The termination of a treaty or the withdrawal of a party may take place:

    (a) in conformity with the provisions of the treaty; or
    (b) at any time by consent of all the parties after consultation with the other contracting States.

Article 55   **Reduction of the parties to a multilateral treaty below the number necessary for its entry into force**

Unless the treaty otherwise provides, a multilateral treaty does not terminate by reason only of the fact that the number of the parties falls below the number necessary for its entry into force.

Article 56   **Denunciation of or withdrawal from a treaty containing no provision regarding termination, denunciation or withdrawal**

1. A treaty which contains no provision regarding its termination and which does not provide for denunciation or withdrawal is not subject to denunciation or withdrawal unless:

    (a) it is established that the parties intended to admit the possibility of denunciation or withdrawal; or
    (b) a right of denunciation or withdrawal may be implied by the nature of the treaty.

2. A party shall give not less than twelve months' notice of its intention to denounce or withdraw from a treaty under paragraph 1.

Article 57   **Suspension of the operation of a treaty under its provisions or by consent of the parties**

The operation of a treaty in regard to all the parties or to a particular party may be suspended:

    (a) in conformity with the provisions of the treaty; or
    (b) at any time by consent of all the parties after consultation with the other contracting States.

Article 58   **Suspension of the operation of a multilateral treaty by agreement between certain of the parties only**

1. Two or more parties to a multilateral treaty may conclude an agreement to suspend the operation of provisions of the treaty, temporarily and as between themselves alone, if:

    (a) the possibility of such a suspension is provided for by the treaty; or
    (b) the suspension in question is not prohibited by the treaty and:
        (i) does not affect the enjoyment by the other parties of their rights under the treaty or the performance of their obligations;
        (ii) is not incompatible with the object and purpose of the treaty.

2. Unless in a case falling under paragraph 1(a) the treaty otherwise provides, the parties in question shall notify the other parties of their intention to conclude the agreement and of those provisions of the treaty the operation of which they intend to suspend.

Article 59	Termination or suspension of the operation of a treaty implied by conclusion of a later treaty

1. A treaty shall be considered as terminated if all the parties to it conclude a later treaty relating to the same subject-matter and:

      (a) it appears from the later treaty or is otherwise established that the parties intended that the matter should be governed by that treaty; or

      (b) the provisions of the later treaty are so far incompatible with those of the earlier one that the two treaties are not capable of being applied at the same time.

2. The earlier treaty shall be considered as only suspended in operation if it appears from the later treaty or is otherwise established that such was the intention of the parties.

Article 60	Termination or suspension of the operation of a treaty as a consequence of its breach

1. A material breach of a bilateral treaty by one of the parties entitles the other to invoke the breach as a ground for terminating the treaty or suspending its operation in whole or in part.

2. A material breach of a multilateral treaty by one of the parties entitles:

      (a) the other parties by unanimous agreement to suspend the operation of the treaty in whole or in part or to terminate it either:

            (i) in the relations between themselves and the defaulting State, or

            (ii) as between all the parties;

      (b) a party specially affected by the breach to invoke it as a ground for suspending the operation of the treaty in whole or in part in the relations between itself and the defaulting State;

      (c) any party other than the defaulting State to invoke the breach as a ground for suspending the operation of the treaty in whole or in part with respect to itself if the treaty is of such a character that a material breach of its provisions by one party radically changes the position of every party with respect to the further performance of its obligations under the treaty.

3. A material breach of a treaty, for the purposes of this article, consists in:

      (a) a repudiation of the treaty not sanctioned by the present Convention; or

      (b) the violation of a provision essential to the accomplishment of the object or purpose of the treaty.

4. The foregoing paragraphs are without prejudice to any provision in the treaty applicable in the event of a breach.

5. Paragraphs 1 to 3 do not apply to provisions relating to the protection of the human person contained in treaties of a humanitarian character, in particular to provisions prohibiting any form of reprisals against persons protected by such treaties.

Article 61	Supervening impossibility of performance

1. A party may invoke the impossibility of performing a treaty as a ground for terminating or withdrawing from it if the impossibility results from the permanent disappearance or destruction of an object indispensable for the execution of the treaty. If the impossibility is temporary, it may be invoked only as a ground for suspending the operation of the treaty.

2. Impossibility of performance may not be invoked by a party as a ground for terminating, withdrawing from or suspending the operation of a treaty if the impossibility is the result of a breach by that party either of an obligation under the treaty or of any other international obligation owed to any other party to the treaty.

Article 62   Fundamental change of circumstances

1. A fundamental change of circumstances which has occurred with regard to those existing at the time of the conclusion of a treaty, and which was not foreseen by the parties, may not be invoked as a ground for terminating or withdrawing from the treaty unless:

> (a) the existence of those circumstances constituted an essential basis of the consent of the parties to be bound by the treaty; and
> (b) the effect of the change is radically to transform the extent of obligations still to be performed under the treaty.

2. A fundamental change of circumstances may not be invoked as a ground for terminating or withdrawing from a treaty:

> (a) if the treaty establishes a boundary; or
> (b) if the fundamental change is the result of a breach by the party invoking it either of an obligation under the treaty or of any other international obligation owed to any other party to the treaty.

3. If, under the foregoing paragraphs, a party may invoke a fundamental change of circumstances as a ground for terminating or withdrawing from a treaty it may also invoke the change as a ground for suspending the operation of the treaty.

Article 63   Severance of diplomatic or consular relations

The severance of diplomatic or consular relations between parties to a treaty does not affect the legal relations established between them by the treaty except in so far as the existence of diplomatic or consular relations is indispensable for the application of the treaty.

Article 64   Emergence of a new peremptory norm of general international law (*jus cogens*)

If a new peremptory norm of general international law emerges, any existing treaty which is in conflict with that norm becomes void and terminates.

SECTION 4. PROCEDURE

Article 65   Procedure to be followed with respect to invalidity, termination, withdrawal from or suspension of the operation of a treaty

1. A party which, under the provisions of the present Convention, invokes either a defect in its consent to be bound by a treaty or a ground for impeaching the validity of a treaty, terminating it, withdrawing from it or suspending its operation, must notify the other parties of its claim. The notification shall indicate the measure proposed to be taken with respect to the treaty and the reasons therefor.

2. If, after the expiry of a period which, except in cases of special urgency, shall not be less than three months after the receipt of the notification, no party has raised any objection, the party making the notification may carry out in the manner provided in article 67 the measure which it has proposed.

3. If, however, objection has been raised by any other party, the parties shall seek a solution through the means indicated in article 33 of the Charter of the United Nations.

4. Nothing in the foregoing paragraphs shall affect the rights or obligations of the parties under any provisions in force binding the parties with regard to the settlement of disputes.

5. Without prejudice to article 45, the fact that a State has not previously made the notification prescribed in paragraph 1 shall not prevent it from making such notification in answer to another party claiming performance of the treaty or alleging its violation.

Article 66	**Procedures for judicial settlement, arbitration and conciliation**

If, under paragraph 3 of article 65, no solution has been reached within a period of 12 months following the date on which the objection was raised, the following procedures shall be followed:

(a) any one of the parties to a dispute concerning the application or the interpretation of articles 53 or 64 may, by a written application, submit it to the International Court of Justice for a decision unless the parties by common consent agree to submit the dispute to arbitration;

(b) any one of the parties to a dispute concerning the application or the interpretation of any of the other articles in Part V of the present Convention may set in motion the procedure specified in the Annex to the Convention by submitting a request to that effect to the Secretary-General of the United Nations.

Article 67	**Instruments for declaring invalid, terminating, withdrawing from or suspending the operation of a treaty**

1. The notification provided for under article 65 paragraph 1 must be made in writing.

2. Any act declaring invalid, terminating, withdrawing from or suspending the operation of a treaty pursuant to the provisions of the treaty or of paragraphs 2 or 3 of article 65 shall be carried out through an instrument communicated to the other parties. If the instrument is not signed by the Head of State, Head of Government or Minister for Foreign Affairs, the representative of the State communicating it may be called upon to produce full powers.

Article 68	**Revocation of notifications and instruments provided for in articles 65 and 67**

A notification or instrument provided for in articles 65 or 67 may be revoked at any time before it takes effect.

SECTION 5. CONSEQUENCES OF THE INVALIDITY, TERMINATION OR SUSPENSION OF THE OPERATION OF A TREATY

Article 69	**Consequences of the invalidity of a treaty**

1. A treaty the invalidity of which is established under the present Convention is void. The provisions of a void treaty have no legal force.

2. If acts have nevertheless been performed in reliance on such a treaty:

(a) each party may require any other party to establish as far as possible in their mutual relations the position that would have existed if the acts had not been performed;

(b) acts performed in good faith before the invalidity was invoked are not rendered unlawful by reason only of the invalidity of the treaty.

3. In cases falling under articles 49, 50, 51 or 52, paragraph 2 does not apply with respect to the party to which the fraud, the act of corruption or the coercion is imputable.

4. In the case of the invalidity of a particular State's consent to be bound by a multilateral treaty, the foregoing rules apply in the relations between that State and the parties to the treaty.

Article 70   **Consequences of the termination of a treaty**

1. Unless the treaty otherwise provides or the parties otherwise agree, the termination of a treaty under its provisions or in accordance with the present Convention:

   (a) releases the parties from any obligation further to perform the treaty;
   (b) does not affect any right, obligation or legal situation of the parties created through the execution of the treaty prior to its termination.

2. If a State denounces or withdraws from a multilateral treaty, paragraph 1 applies in the relations between that State and each of the other parties to the treaty from the date when such denunciation or withdrawal takes effect.

Article 71   **Consequences of the invalidity of a treaty which conflicts with a peremptory norm of general international law**

1. In the case of a treaty which is void under article 53 the parties shall:

   (a) eliminate as far as possible the consequences of any act performed in reliance on any provision which conflicts with the peremptory norm of general international law; and
   (b) bring their mutual relations into conformity with the peremptory norm of general international law.

2. In the case of a treaty which becomes void and terminates under article 64, the termination of the treaty:

   (a) releases the parties from any obligation further to perform the treaty;
   (b) does not affect any right, obligation or legal situation of the parties created through the execution of the treaty prior to its termination; provided that those rights, obligations or situations may thereafter be maintained only to the extent that their maintenance is not in itself in conflict with the new peremptory norm of general international law.

Article 72   **Consequences of the suspension of the operation of a treaty**

1. Unless the treaty otherwise provides or the parties otherwise agree, the suspension of the operation of a treaty under its provisions or in accordance with the present Convention:

   (a) releases the parties between which the operation of the treaty is suspended from the obligation to perform the treaty in their mutual relations during the period of the suspension;
   (b) does not otherwise affect the legal relations between the parties established by the treaty.

2. During the period of the suspension the parties shall refrain from acts tending to obstruct the resumption of the operation of the treaty.

PART VI   MISCELLANEOUS PROVISIONS

Article 73   **Cases of State succession, State responsibility and outbreak of hostilities**

The provisions of the present Convention shall not prejudge any question that may arise in regard to a treaty from a succession of States or from the international responsibility of a State or from the outbreak of hostilities between States.

Article 74	Diplomatic and consular relations and the conclusion of treaties

The severance or absence of diplomatic or consular relations between two or more States does not prevent the conclusion of treaties between those States. The conclusion of a treaty does not in itself affect the situation in regard to diplomatic or consular relations.

Article 75	Case of an aggressor State

The provisions of the present Convention are without prejudice to any obligation in relation to a treaty which may arise for an aggressor State in consequence of measures taken in conformity with the Charter of the United Nations with reference to that State's aggression.

PART VII   DEPOSITARIES, NOTIFICATIONS, CORRECTIONS AND REGISTRATION

Article 76	Depositaries of treaties

1. The designation of the depositary of a treaty may be made by the negotiating States, either in the treaty itself or in some other manner. The depositary may be one or more States, an international organization or the chief administrative officer of the organization.

2. The functions of the depositary of a treaty are international in character and the depositary is under an obligation to act impartially in their performance. In particular, the fact that a treaty has not entered into force between certain of the parties or that a difference has appeared between a State and a depositary with regard to the performance of the latter's functions shall not affect that obligation.

Article 77	Functions of depositaries

1. The functions of a depositary, unless otherwise provided in the treaty or agreed by the contracting States, comprise in particular:

    (a) keeping custody of the original text of the treaty and of any full powers delivered to the depositary;
    (b) preparing certified copies of the original text and preparing any further text of the treaty in such additional languages as may be required by the treaty and transmitting them to the parties and to the States entitled to become parties to the treaty;
    (c) receiving any signatures to the treaty and receiving and keeping custody of any instruments, notifications and communications relating to it;
    (d) examining whether the signature or any instrument, notification or communication relating to the treaty is in due and proper form and, if need be, bringing the matter to the attention of the State in question;
    (e) informing the parties and the States entitled to become parties to the treaty of acts, notifications and communications relating to the treaty;
    (f) informing the States entitled to become parties to the treaty when the number of signatures or of instruments of ratification, acceptance, approval or accession required for the entry into force of the treaty has been received or deposited;
    (g) registering the treaty with the Secretariat of the United Nations;
    (h) performing the functions specified in other provisions of the present Convention.

2. In the event of any difference appearing between a State and the depositary as to the performance of the latter's functions, the depositary shall bring the question to the attention of the signatory States and the contracting States or, where appropriate, of the competent organ of the international organization concerned.

Article 78	Notifications and communications

Except as the treaty or the present Convention otherwise provide, any notification or communication to be made by any State under the present Convention shall:

(a) if there is no depositary, be transmitted direct to the States for which it is intended, or if there is a depositary, to the latter;

(b) be considered as having been made by the State in question only upon its receipt by the State to which it was transmitted or, as the case may be, upon its receipt by the depositary;

(c) if transmitted to a depositary, be considered as received by the State for which it was intended only when the latter State has been informed by the depositary in accordance with article 77, paragraph 1(e).

Article 79   **Correction of errors in texts or in certified copies of treaties**

1. Where, after the authentication of the text of a treaty, the signatory States and the contracting States are agreed that it contains an error, the error shall, unless they decide upon some other means of correction, be corrected:

(a) by having the appropriate correction made in the text and causing the correction to be initialled by duly authorized representatives;

(b) by executing or exchanging an instrument or instruments setting out the correction which it has been agreed to make; or

(c) by executing a corrected text of the whole treaty by the same procedure as in the case of the original text.

2. Where the treaty is one for which there is a depositary, the latter shall notify the signatory States and the contracting States of the error and of the proposal to correct it and shall specify an appropriate time-limit within which objection to the proposed correction may be raised. If, on the expiry of the time-limit:

(a) no objection has been raised, the depositary shall make and initial the correction in the text and shall execute a *procés-verbal* of the rectification of the text and communicate a copy of it to the parties and to the States entitled to become parties to the treaty;

(b) an objection has been raised, the depositary shall communicate the objection to the signatory States and to the contracting States.

3. The rules in paragraphs 1 and 2 apply also where the text has been authenticated in two or more languages and it appears that there is a lack of concordance which the signatory States and the contracting States agree should be corrected.

4. The corrected text replaces the defective text *ab initio*, unless the signatory States and the contracting States otherwise decide.

5. The correction of the text of a treaty that has been registered shall be notified to the Secretariat of the United Nations.

6. Where an error is discovered in a certified copy of a treaty, the depositary shall execute a *procés-verbal* specifying the rectification and communicate a copy of it to the signatory States and to the contracting States.

Article 80   **Registration and publication of treaties**

1. Treaties shall, after their entry into force, be transmitted to the Secretariat of the United Nations for registration or filing and recording, as the case may be, and for publication.

2. The designation of a depositary shall constitute authorization for it to perform the acts specified in the preceding paragraph.

PART VIII   FINAL PROVISIONS

(Omitted)

ANNEX

1. A list of conciliators consisting of qualified jurists shall be drawn up and maintained by the Secretary-General of the United Nations. To this end, every State which is a Member of the United Nations or a party to the present Convention shall be invited to nominate two conciliators, and the names of the persons so nominated shall constitute the list. The term of a conciliator, including that of any conciliator nominated to fill a casual vacancy, shall be five years and may be renewed. A conciliator whose term expires shall continue to fulfil any function for which he shall have been chosen under the following paragraph.

2. When a request has been made to the Secretary-General under article 66, the Secretary-General shall bring the dispute before a conciliation commission constituted as follows:

The State or States constituting one of the parties to the dispute shall appoint:
    (a) one conciliator of the nationality of that State or of one of those States, who may or may not be chosen from the list referred to in paragraph 1; and
    (b) one conciliator not of the nationality of that State or of any of those States, who shall be chosen from the list.

The State or States constituting the other party to the dispute shall appoint two conciliators in the same way. The four conciliators chosen by the parties shall be appointed within sixty days following the date on which the Secretary-General receives the request.

The four conciliators shall, within sixty days following the date of the last of their own appointments, appoint a fifth conciliator chosen from the list, who shall be chairman.

If the appointment of the chairman or of any of the other conciliators has not been made within the period prescribed above for such appointment, it shall be made by the Secretary-General within sixty days following the expiry of that period. The appointment of the chairman may be made by the Secretary-General either from the list or from the membership of the International Law Commission. Any of the periods within which appointments must be made may be extended by agreement between the parties to the dispute.

Any vacancy shall be filled in the manner prescribed for the initial appointment.

3. The Conciliation Commission shall decide its own procedure. The Commission, with the consent of the parties to the dispute, may invite any party to the treaty to submit to it its views orally or in writing. Decisions and recommendations of the Commission shall be made by a majority vote of the five members.

4. The Commission may draw the attention of the parties to the dispute to any measures which might facilitate an amicable settlement.

5. The Commission shall hear the parties, examine the claims and objections, and make proposals to the parties with a view to reaching an amicable settlement of the dispute.

6. The Commission shall report within twelve months of its constitution. Its report shall be deposited with the Secretary-General and transmitted to the parties to the dispute. The report of the Commission, including any conclusions stated therein regarding the facts or questions of law, shall not be binding upon the parties and it shall have no other character than that of recommendations submitted for the consideration of the parties in order to facilitate an amicable settlement of the dispute.

7. The Secretary-General shall provide the Commission with such assistance and facilities as it may require. The expenses of the Commission shall be borne by the United Nations.

STOCKHOLM DECLARATION OF THE
UNITED NATIONS CONFERENCE ON THE HUMAN ENVIRONMENT

11 I.L.M. 1416 (1972)
Signed: June 16, 1972

THE UNITED NATIONS CONFERENCE ON THE HUMAN ENVIRONMENT,

Having Met at Stockholm from 5 to 16 June 1972,

Having Considered the need for a common outlook and for common principles to inspire and guide the peoples of the world in the preservation and enhancement of the human environment.

I.

PROCLAIMS THAT:

1. Man is both creature and molder of his environment, which gives him physical sustenance and affords him the opportunity for intellectual, moral, social and spiritual growth. In the long and tortuous evolution of the human race on this planet a stage has been reached when, through the rapid acceleration of science and technology, man has acquired the power to transform his environment in countless ways and on an unprecedented scale. Both aspects of man's environment, the natural and the man-made, are essential to his well-being and to the enjoyment of basic human rights—even the right to life itself.

2. The protection and improvement of the human environment is a major issue which affects the well-being of peoples and economic development throughout the world; it is the urgent desire of the peoples of the whole world and the duty of all Governments.

3. Man has constantly to sum up experience and go on discovering, inventing, creating and advancing. In our time, man's capability to transform his surroundings, if used wisely, can bring to all peoples the benefits of development and the opportunity to enhance the quality of life. Wrongly or heedlessly applied, the same power can do incalculable harm to human beings and the human environment. We see around us growing evidence of man-made harm in many regions of the earth: dangerous levels of pollution in water, air, earth and living beings, major and undesirable disturbances to the ecological balance of the biosphere; destruction and depletion of replaceable resources; and gross deficiencies harmful to the physical, mental and social health of man, in the man-made environment, particularly in the living and working environment.

4. In the developing countries most of the environmental problems are caused by under-development. Millions continue to live far below the minimum levels required for a decent human existence, deprived of adequate food and clothing, shelter and education, health and sanitation. Therefore, the developing countries must direct their efforts to development, bearing in mind their priorities and the need to safeguard and improve the environment. For the same purpose, the industrialized countries should make efforts to reduce the gap between themselves and the developing countries. In the industrialized countries, environmental problems are generally related to industrialization and technological development.

5. The natural growth of population continuously presents problems on the preservation of the environment, and adequate policies and measures should be adopted, as appropriate, to face these problems. Of all things in the world, people are the most precious. It is the people that propel social progress, create social wealth, develop science and technology and, through their hard work, continuously transform the human environment. Along with social progress and the advance of production, science and technology, the capability of man to improve the environment increases with each passing day.

6. A point has been reached in history when we must shape our actions throughout the world with a more prudent care for their environmental consequences. Through ignorance or indifference we can do massive and irreversible

harm to the earthly environment on which our life and well-being depend. Conversely, through fuller knowledge and wiser action, we can achieve for ourselves and our posterity a better life in an environment more in keeping with human needs and hopes. There are broad vistas for the enhancement of environmental quality and the creation of a good life. What is needed is an enthusiastic but calm state of mind and intense but orderly work. For the purpose of attaining freedom in the world of nature, man must use knowledge to build, in collaboration with nature, a better environment. To defend and improve the human environment for present and future generations has become an imperative goal for mankind -- a goal to be pursued together with, and in harmony with, the established and fundamental goals of peace and of worldwide economic and social development.

7. To achieve this environmental goal will demand the acceptance of responsibility by citizens and communities and by enterprises and institutions at every level, all sharing equitably in common efforts. Individuals in all walks of life as well as organizations in many fields, by their values and the sum of their actions, will shape the world environment of the future. Local and national governments will bear the greatest burden for large-scale environmental policy and action within their jurisdictions. International cooperation is also needed in order to raise resources to support the developing countries in carrying out their responsibilities in this field. A growing class of environmental problems, because they are regional or global in extent or because they affect the common international realm, will require extensive cooperation among nations and action by international organizations in the common interest. The Conference calls upon Governments and peoples to exert common efforts for the preservation and improvement of the human environment, for the benefit of all the people and for their posterity.

II.   Principles

STATES THE COMMON CONVICTION THAT:

Principle 1

Man has the fundamental right to freedom, equality and adequate conditions of life, in an environment of a quality that permits a life of dignity and well-being, and he bears a solemn responsibility o protect and improve the environment for present and future generations. In this respect, policies promoting or perpetuating apartheid, racial segregation, discrimination, colonial and other forms of oppression and foreign domination stand condemned and must be eliminated.

Principle 2

The natural resources of the earth including the air, water, land, flora and fauna and especially representative samples of natural ecosystems must be safeguarded for the benefit of present and future generations through careful planning or management, as appropriate.

Principle 3

The capacity of the earth to produce vital renewable resources must be maintained and, wherever practicable, restored or improved.

Principle 4

Man has a special responsibility to safeguard and wisely manage the heritage of wildlife and its habitat which are now gravely imperilled by a combination of adverse factors. Nature conservation, including wildlife, must therefore receive importance in planning for economic development.

Principle 5

The non-renewable resources of the earth must be employed in such a way as to guard against the danger of their future exhaustion and to ensure that benefits from such employment are shared by all mankind.

Principle 6

The discharge of toxic substances or of other substances and the release of heat, in such quantities or concentrations as to exceed the capacity of the environment to render them harmless, must be halted in order to ensure that serious or irreversible damage is not inflicted upon ecosystems. The just struggle of the peoples of all countries against pollution should be supported.

Principle 7

States shall take all possible steps to prevent pollution of the seas by substances that are liable to create hazards to human health, to harm living resources and marine life, to damage amenities or to interfere with other legitimate uses of the sea.

Principle 8

Economic and social development is essential for ensuring a favorable living and working environment for man and for creating conditions on earth that are necessary for the improvement of the quality of life.

Principle 9

Environmental deficiencies generated by the conditions of underdevelopment and natural disasters pose grave problems and can best be remedied by accelerated development through the transfer of substantial quantities of financial and technological assistance as a supplement to the domestic effort of the developing countries and such timely assistance as may be required.

Principle 10

For the developing countries, stability of prices and adequate earnings for primary commodities and raw material are essential to environmental management since economic factors as well as ecological processes must be taken into account.

Principle 11

The environmental policies of all States should enhance and not adversely affect the present or future development potential of developing countries, nor should they hamper the attainment of better living conditions for all, and appropriate steps should be taken by States and international organizations with a view to reaching agreement on meeting the possible national and international economic consequences resulting from the application of environmental measures.

Principle 12

Resources should be made available to preserve and improve the environment, taking into account the circumstances and particular requirements of developing countries and any costs which may emanate from their incorporating environmental safeguards into their development planning and the need for making available to them, upon their request, additional international technical and financial assistance for this purpose.

Principle 13

In order to achieve a more rational management of resources and thus to improve the environment, State should adopt an integrated and co-ordinated approach to their development planning so as to ensure that development is compatible with the need to protect and improve the human environment for the benefit of their population.

Principle 14

Rational planning constitutes an essential tool for reconciling any conflict between the needs of development and the need to protect and improve the environment.

Principle 15

Planning must be applied to human settlements and urbanization with a view to avoiding adverse effects on the environment and obtaining maximum social, economic and environmental benefits for all. In this respect projects which are designed for colonialist and racist domination must be abandoned.

Principle 16

Demographic policies, which are without prejudice to basic human rights and which are deemed appropriate by Governments concerned, should be applied in those regions where the rate of population growth or excessive population concentrations are likely to have adverse effects on the environment or development, or where low population density may prevent improvement of the human environment and impede development.

Principle 17

Appropriate national institutions must be entrusted with the task of planning, managing or controlling the environmental resources of States with the view to enhancing environmental quality.

Principle 18

Science and technology, as part of their contribution to economic and social development, must be applied to the identification, avoidance and control of environmental risks and the solution of environmental problems and for the common good of mankind.

Principle 19

Education in environmental matters, for the younger generation as well as adults, giving due consideration to the underprivileged, is essential in order to broaden the basis for an enlightened opinion and responsible conduct by individuals, enterprises and communities in protecting and improving the environment in its full human dimension. It is also essential that mass media of communications avoid contributing to the deterioration of the environment, but, on the contrary, disseminate information of an educational nature, on the need to protect and improve the environment in order to enable man to develop in every respect.

Principle 20

Scientific research and development in the context of environmental problems, both national and multinational, must be promoted in all countries, especially the developing countries. In this connection, the free flow of up-to-date scientific information and transfer of experience must be supported and assisted, to facilitate the solution of environmental problems; environmental technologies should be made available to developing countries on terms which would encourage their wide dissemination without constituting an economic burden on the developing countries.

Principle 21

States have, in accordance with the Charter of the United Nations and the principles of international law, the sovereign right to exploit their own resources pursuant to their own environmental policies, and the responsibility to ensure that activities within their jurisdiction or control do not cause damage to the environment of other States or of areas beyond the limits of national jurisdiction.

Principle 22

States shall cooperate to develop further the international law regarding liability and compensation for the victims of pollution and other environmental damage caused by activities within the jurisdiction or control of such States to areas beyond their jurisdiction.

Principle 23

Without prejudice to such criteria as may be agreed upon by the international community, or to standards which will have to be determined nationally, it will be essential in all cases to consider the systems of values prevailing in each country, and the extent of the applicability of standards which are valid for the most advanced countries but which may be inappropriate and of unwarranted social cost for the developing countries.

Principle 24

International matters concerning the protection and improvement of the environment should be handled in a cooperative spirit by all countries, big or small, on an equal footing. Cooperation through multilateral or bilateral arrangements or other appropriate means is essential to effectively control, prevent, reduce and eliminate adverse environmental effects resulting from activities conducted in all spheres, in such a way that due account is taken of the sovereignty and interests of all States.

Principle 25

States shall ensure that international organizations play a coordinated, efficient and dynamic role for the protection and improvement of the environment.

Principle 26

Man and his environment must be spared the effects of nuclear weapons and all other means of mass destruction. States must strive to reach prompt agreement, in the relevant international organs, on the elimination and complete destruction of such weapons.

WORLD CHARTER FOR NATURE

U.N.G.A. RES 37/7;
22 I.L.M.455 (1983)
Signed: October 28, 1982

The General Assembly,

Reaffirming the fundamental purposes of the United Nations, in particular the maintenance of international peace and security, the development of friendly relations among nations and the achievement of international cooperation in solving international problems of an economic, social, cultural, technical, intellectual or humanitarian character,

Aware that:

(a) Mankind is a part of nature and life depends on the uninterrupted functioning of natural systems which ensure the supply of energy and nutrients,

(b) Civilization is rooted in nature, which has shaped human culture and influenced all artistic and scientific achievements, and living in harmony with nature gives man the best opportunities for the development of his creativity, and for rest and recreation,

Convinced that:

(a) Every form of life is unique, warranting respect regardless of its worth to man, and, to accord other organisms such recognition, man must be guided by a moral code of action,

(b) Man can alter nature and exhaust natural resources by his action or its consequences and, therefore, must fully recognize the urgency of maintaining the stability and quality of nature and of conserving natural resources,

Persuaded that:

(a) Lasting benefits from nature depend upon the maintenance of essential ecological processes and life support systems, and upon the diversity of life forms, which are jeopardized through excessive exploitation and habitat destruction by man,

(b) The degradation of natural systems owing to excessive consumption and misuse of natural resources, as well as to failure to establish an appropriate economic order among peoples and among States, leads to the breakdown of the economic, social and political framework of civilization,

(c) Competition for scarce resources creates conflicts, whereas the conservation of nature and natural resources contributes to justice and the maintenance of peace and cannot be achieved until mankind learns to live in peace and to forsake war and armaments,

Reaffirming that man must acquire the knowledge to maintain and enhance his ability to use natural resources in a manner which ensures the preservation of the species and ecosystems for the benefit of present and future generations,

Firmly convinced of the need for appropriate measures, at the national and international, individual and collective, and private and public levels, to protect nature and promote international co-operation in this field,

Adopts, to these ends, the present World Charter for Nature, which proclaims the following principles of conservation by which all human conduct affecting nature is to be guided and judged.

I.   GENERAL PRINCIPLES

1. Nature shall be respected and its essential processes shall not be impaired.

2. The genetic viability on the earth shall not be compromised; the population levels of all life forms, wild and domesticated, must be at least sufficient for their survival, and to this end necessary habitat shall be safeguarded.

3. All areas of the earth, both land and sea, shall be subject to these principles of conservation; special protection shall be given to unique areas, to representative samples of all the different types of ecosystems and to the habitat of rare or endangered species.

4. Ecosystems and organisms, as well as the land, marine and atmospheric resources that are utilized by man, shall be managed to achieve and maintain optimum sustainable productivity, but not in such a way as to endanger the integrity of those other ecosystems or species with which they coexist.

5. Nature shall be secured against degradation caused by warfare or other hostile activities.

II.   FUNCTIONS

6. In the decision-making process it shall be recognized that man's needs can be met only by ensuring the proper functioning of natural systems and by respecting the principles set forth in the present Charter.

7. In the planning and implementation of social and economic development activities, due account shall be taken of the fact that the conservation of nature is an integral part of those activities.

8. In formulating long-term plans for economic development, population growth and the improvement of standards of living, due account shall be taken of the long-term capacity of natural systems to ensure the subsistence and settlement of the populations concerned, recognizing that this capacity may be enhanced through science and technology.

9. The allocation of areas of the earth to various uses shall be planned and due account shall be taken of the physical constraints, the biological productivity and diversity and the natural beauty of the areas concerned.

10. Natural resources shall not be wasted, but used with a restraint appropriate to the principles set forth in the present Charter, in accordance with the following rules:

    (a) Living resources shall not be utilized in excess of their natural capacity for regeneration;

    (b) The productivity of soils shall be maintained or enhanced through measures which safeguard their long-term fertility and the process of organic decomposition, and prevent erosion and all other forms of degradation;

    (c) Resources, including water, which are not consumed as they are used shall be reused or recycled;

    (d) Non-renewable resources which are consumed as they are used shall be exploited with restraint, taking into account their abundance, their rational possibilities of converting them for consumption, and the compatibility of their exploitation with the functioning of natural systems.

11. Activities which might have an impact on nature shall be controlled, and the best available technologies that minimize significant risks to nature or other adverse effects shall be used; in particular:

    (a) Activities which are likely to cause irreversible damage to nature shall be avoided;

    (b) Activities which are likely to pose a significant risk to nature shall be preceded by an exhaustive examination; their proponents shall demonstrate that expected benefits outweigh potential damage to nature, and where potential adverse effects are not fully understood, the activities should not proceed;

    (c) Activities which may disturb nature shall be preceded by assessment of their consequences, and environmental impact studies of development projects shall be conducted sufficiently in advance, and if they are to be undertaken, such activities shall be planned and carried out so as to minimize potential adverse effects;

    (d) Agriculture, grazing, forestry and fisheries practices shall be adapted to the natural characteristics and constraints of given areas;

    (e) Areas degraded by human activities shall be rehabilitated for purposes in accord with their natural potential and compatible with the well-being of affected populations.

12. Discharge of pollutants into natural systems shall be avoided and:

    (a) Where this is not feasible, such pollutants shall be treated at the source, using the best practicable means available;

    (b) Special precautions shall be taken to prevent discharge of radioactive or toxic wastes.

13. Measures intended to prevent, control or limit natural disasters, infestations and diseases shall be specifically directed to the causes of these scourges and shall avoid averse side-effects on nature.

III.   IMPLEMENTATION

14. The principles set forth in the present Charter shall be reflected in the law and practice of each State, as well as at the international level.

15. Knowledge of nature shall be broadly disseminated by all possible means, particularly by ecological education as an integral part of general education.

16. All planning shall include, among its essential elements, the formulation of strategies for the conservation of nature, the establishment of inventories of ecosystems and assessments of the effects on nature of proposed policies and activities; all of these elements shall be disclosed to the public by appropriate means in time to permit effective consultation and participation.

17. Funds, programmes and administrative structures necessary to achieve the objective of the conservation of nature shall be provided.

18. Constant efforts shall be made to increase knowledge of nature by scientific research and to disseminate such knowledge unimpeded by restrictions of any kind.

19. The status of natural processes, ecosystems and species shall be closely monitored to enable early detection of degradation or threat, ensure timely intervention and facilitate the evaluation of conservation policies and methods.

20. Military activities damaging to nature shall be avoided.

21. States and, to the extent they are able, other public authorities, international organizations, individuals, groups and corporations shall:

(a) Co-operate in the task of conserving nature through common activities and other relevant actions, including information exchange and consultations;

(b) Establish standards for products and other manufacturing processes that may have adverse effects on nature, as well as agreed methodologies for assessing these effects;

(c) Implement the applicable international legal provisions for the conservation of nature and the protection of the environment;

(d) Ensure that activities within their jurisdictions or control do not cause damage to the natural systems located within other States or in the areas beyond the limits of national jurisdiction;

(e) Safeguard and conserve nature in areas beyond national jurisdiction.

22. Taking fully into account the sovereignty of States over their natural resources, each State shall give effect to the provisions of the present Charter through its competent organs and in co-operation with other States.

23. All persons, in accordance with their national legislation, shall have the opportunity to participate, individually or with others, in the formulation of decisions of direct concern to their environment, and shall have access to means of redress when their environment has suffered damage or degradation.

24. Each person has a duty to act in accordance with the provisions of the present Charter, acting individually, in association with others or through participation in the political process, each person shall strive to ensure that the objectives and requirements of the present Charter are met.

RIO DECLARATION ON ENVIRONMENT AND DEVELOPMENT

U.N. Doc.A/CONF.151/26;3II.L.M.874 (1992)
Signed: June 13, 1992

Preamble

The United Nations Conference on Environment and Development

Having met at Rio de Janeiro from 3 to 14 June 1992,

Reaffirming the Declaration of the United Nations Conference on the Human Environment, adopted at Stockholm on 16 June 1972, and seeking to build upon it,

With the goal of establishing a new and equitable global partnership through the creation of new levels of cooperation among States, key sectors of societies and people,

Working towards international agreements which respect the interests of all protect the integrity of the global environmental and developmental system,

Recognizing the integral and interdependent nature of the Earth, our home,

Proclaims that:

Principle 1

Human beings are at the centre of concerns for sustainable development. They are entitled to a healthy and productive life in harmony with nature.

Principle 2

States have, in accordance with the Charter of the United Nations and the principles of international law, the sovereign right to exploit their own resources pursuant to their own environmental and developmental policies, and the responsibility to ensure that activities within their jurisdiction or control do not cause damage to the environment of other States or of areas beyond the limits of national jurisdiction.

Principle 3

The right to development must be fulfilled so as to equitably meet developmental and environmental needs of present and future generations.

Principle 4

In order to achieve sustainable development, environmental protection shall constitute an integral part of the development process and cannot be considered in isolation from it.

Principle 5

All States and all people shall cooperate in the essential task of eradicating poverty as an indispensable requirement for sustainable development, in order to decrease the disparities in standards of living and better meet the needs of the majority of the people of the world.

Principle 6

The special situation and needs of developing countries, particularly the least developed and those most environmentally vulnerable, shall be given special priority. International actions in the field of environment and development should also address the interests and needs of all countries.

Principle 7

States shall cooperate in a spirit of global partnership to conserve, protect and restore the health and integrity of the Earth's ecosystem. In view of the different contributions to global environmental degradation, States have common but differentiated responsibilities. The developed countries acknowledge the responsibility that they bear in the international pursuit of sustainable development in view of the pressures their societies place on the global environment and of the technologies and financial resources they command.

Principle 8

To achieve sustainable development and a higher quality of life for all people, States should reduce and eliminate unsustainable patters of production and consumption and promote appropriate demographic policies.

Principle 9

States should cooperate to strengthen endogenous capacity-building for sustainable development by improving scientific understanding through exchanges of scientific and technological knowledge, and by enhancing the development, adaptation, diffusion and transfer of technologies, including new and innovative technologies.

Principle 10

Environmental issues are best handled with the participation of all concerned citizens, at the relevant level. At the national level, each individual shall have appropriate access to information concerning the environment that is held by public authorities, including information on hazardous materials and activities in their communities, and the opportunity to participate in decision-making processes. States shall facilitate and encourage public awareness and participation by making information widely available. Effective access to judicial and administrative proceedings, including redress and remedy, shall be provided.

Principle 11

States shall enact effective environmental legislation. Environmental standards, management objectives and priorities should reflect the environmental and developmental context to which they apply. Standards applied by some countries may be inappropriate and of unwarranted economic and social cost to other countries, in particular developing countries.

Principle 12

States should cooperate to promote a supportive and open international economic system that would lead to economic growth and sustainable development in all countries, to better address the problems of environmental degradation. Trade policy measures for environmental purposes should not constitute a means of arbitrary or unjustifiable discrimination or a disguised restriction on international trade. Unilateral actions to deal with environmental challenges outside the jurisdiction of the importing country should be avoided. Environmental measures addressing transboundary or global environmental problems should, as far as possible, be based on an international consensus.

Principle 13

States shall develop national law regarding liability and compensation for the victims of pollution and other environmental damage. States shall also cooperate in an expeditious and more determined manner to develop further international law regarding liability and compensation for adverse effects of environmental damage caused by activities within their jurisdiction or control to areas beyond their jurisdiction.

Principle 14

States should effectively cooperate to discourage or prevent the relocation and transfer to other States of any activities and substances that cause severe environmental degradation or are found to be harmful to human health.

Principle 15

In order to protect the environment, the precautionary approach shall be widely applied by States according to their capabilities. Where there are threats of serious or irreversible damage, lack of full scientific certainty shall not be used as a reason for postponing cost-effective measures to prevent environmental degradation.

Principle 16

National authorities should endeavour to promote the internalization of environmental costs and the use of economic instruments, taking into account the approach that the polluter should, in principle, bear the cost of pollution, with due regard to the public interest and without distorting international trade and investment.

Principle 17

Environmental impact assessment, as a national instrument, shall be undertaken for proposed activities that are likely to have a significant adverse impact on the environment and are subject to a decision of a competent national authority.

Principle 18

States shall immediately notify other States of any natural disasters of other emergencies that are likely to produce sudden harmful effects on the environment of those States. Every effort shall be made by the international community to help States so afflicted.

Principle 19

States shall provide prior and timely notification and relevant information to potentially affected States on activities that may have a significant adverse transboundary environmental effect and shall consult with those States at an early stage and in good faith.

Principle 20

Women have a vital role in environmental management and development. Their full participation is therefore essential to achieve sustainable development.

Principle 21

The creativity, ideals and courage of the youth of the world should be mobilized to forge a global partnership in order to achieve sustainable development and ensure a better future for all.

Principle 22

Indigenous people and their communities, and other local communities, have a vital role in environmental management and development because of their knowledge and traditional practices. States should recognize and duly support their identity, culture and interests and enable their effective participation in the achievement of sustainable development.

Principle 23

The environment and natural resources of people under oppression, domination and occupation shall be protected.

Principle 24

Warfare is inherently destructive of sustainable development. States shall therefore respect international law providing protection for the environment in times of armed conflict and cooperate in its further development, as necessary.

Principle 25

Peace, development and environmental protection are interdependent and indivisible.

Principle 26

States shall resolve all their environmental disputes peacefully and by appropriate means in accordance with the Charter of the United Nations.

Principle 27

States and people shall cooperate in good faith and in a spirit of partnership in the fulfillment of the principles embodies in this Declaration and in the further development of international law in the field of sustainable development.

JOHANNESBURG DECLARATION ON SUSTAINABLE DEVELOPMENT: FROM OUR ORIGINS TO THE FUTURE

1.   We, the representatives of the peoples of the world, assembled at the World Summit on Sustainable Development in Johannesburg, South Africa, from 2 to 4 September 2002, reaffirm our commitment to sustainable development.

2.   We commit ourselves to building a humane, equitable and caring global society, cognizant of the need for human dignity for all.

3.   At the beginning of this Summit, the children of the world spoke to us in a simple yet clear voice that the future belongs to them, and accordingly challenged all of us to ensure that through our actions they will inherit a world free of the indignity and indecency occasioned by poverty, environmental degradation and patterns of unsustainable development.

4.   As part of our response to these children, who represent our collective future, all of us, coming from every corner of the world, informed by different life experiences, are united and moved by a deeply felt sense that we urgently need to create a new and brighter world of hope.

5.   Accordingly, we assume a collective responsibility to advance and strengthen the interdependent and mutually reinforcing pillars of sustainable development — economic development, social development and environmental protection — at the local, national, regional and global levels.

6.   From this continent, the cradle of humanity, we declare, through the Plan of Implementation of the World Summit on Sustainable Development and the present Declaration, our responsibility to one another, to the greater community of life and to our children.

7.   Recognizing that humankind is at a crossroads, we have united in a common resolve to make a determined effort to respond positively to the need to produce a practical and visible plan to bring about poverty eradication and human development.

From Stockholm to Rio de Janeiro to Johannesburg

8.   Thirty years ago, in Stockholm, we agreed on the urgent need to respond to the problem of environmental deterioration.[1] Ten years ago, at the United Nations Conference on Environment and Development, held in Rio de Janeiro,[2] we agreed that the protection of the environment and social and economic development are fundamental to sustainable development, based on the Rio Principles. To achieve such development, we adopted the global programme entitled Agenda 21[3] and the Rio Declaration on Environment and Development,[3] to which we reaffirm our commitment. The Rio Conference was a significant milestone that set a new agenda for sustainable development.

9.   Between Rio and Johannesburg, the world's nations have met in several major conferences under the auspices of the United Nations, including the International Conference on Financing for Development,[4] as well as the Doha Ministerial Conference.[5] These conferences defined for the world a comprehensive vision for the future of humanity.

10.   At the Johannesburg Summit, we have achieved much in bringing together a rich tapestry of peoples and views in a constructive search for a common path towards a world that respects and implements the vision of sustainable development. The Johannesburg Summit has also confirmed that significant progress has been made towards achieving a global consensus and partnership among all the people of our planet.

The challenges we face

11.   We recognize that poverty eradication, changing consumption and production patterns and protecting and managing the natural resource base for economic and social development are overarching objectives of and essential requirements for sustainable development.

12.   The deep fault line that divides human society between the rich and the poor and the ever-increasing gap between the developed and developing worlds pose a major threat to global prosperity, security and stability.

13.   The global environment continues to suffer. Loss of biodiversity continues, fish stocks continue to be depleted, desertification claims more and more fertile land, the adverse effects of climate change are already evident, natural disasters are more frequent and more devastating, and developing countries more vulnerable, and air, water and marine pollution continue to rob millions of a decent life.

14.   Globalization has added a new dimension to these challenges. The rapid integration of markets, mobility of capital and significant increases in investment flows around the world have opened new challenges and opportunities for the pursuit of sustainable development. But the benefits and costs of globalization are unevenly distributed, with developing countries facing special difficulties in meeting this challenge.

15.   We risk the entrenchment of these global disparities and unless we act in a manner that fundamentally changes their lives the poor of the world may lose confidence in their representatives and the democratic systems to which we remain committed, seeing their representatives as nothing more than sounding brass or tinkling cymbals.

Our commitment to sustainable development

16.   We are determined to ensure that our rich diversity, which is our collective strength, will be used for constructive partnership for change and for the achievement of the common goal of sustainable development.

17.   Recognizing the importance of building human solidarity, we urge the promotion of dialogue and cooperation among the world's civilizations and peoples, irrespective of race, disabilities, religion, language, culture or tradition.

18.   We welcome the focus of the Johannesburg Summit on the indivisibility of human dignity and are resolved, through decisions on targets, timetables and partnerships, to speedily increase access to such basic requirements as clean water, sanitation, adequate shelter, energy, health care, food security and the protection of biodiversity. At the same time, we will work together to help one another gain access to financial resources, benefit from the opening of markets, ensure capacity-building, use modern technology to bring about development and make sure that there is technology transfer, human resource development, education and training to banish underdevelopment forever.

19.   We reaffirm our pledge to place particular focus on, and give priority attention to, the fight against the worldwide conditions that pose severe threats to the sustainable development of our people, which include: chronic hunger; malnutrition; foreign occupation; armed conflict; illicit drug problems; organized crime; corruption; natural disasters; illicit arms trafficking; trafficking in persons; terrorism; intolerance and incitement to racial, ethnic, religious and other hatreds; xenophobia; and endemic, communicable and chronic diseases, in particular HIV/AIDS, malaria and tuberculosis.

20.   We are committed to ensuring that women's empowerment, emancipation and gender equality are integrated in all the activities encompassed within Agenda 21, the Millennium development goals[6/] and the Plan of Implementation of the Summit.

21.   We recognize the reality that global society has the means and is endowed with the resources to address the challenges of poverty eradication and sustainable development confronting all humanity. Together, we will take extra steps to ensure that these available resources are used to the benefit of humanity.

22.   In this regard, to contribute to the achievement of our development goals and targets, we urge developed countries that have not done so to make concrete efforts reach the internationally agreed levels of official development assistance.

23.   We welcome and support the emergence of stronger regional groupings and alliances, such as the New Partnership for Africa's Development, to promote regional cooperation, improved international cooperation and sustainable development.

24.   We shall continue to pay special attention to the developmental needs of small island developing States and the least developed countries.

25.   We reaffirm the vital role of the indigenous peoples in sustainable development.

26.   We recognize that sustainable development requires a long-term perspective and broad-based participation in policy formulation, decision-making and implementation at all levels. As social partners, we will continue to work for stable partnerships with all major groups, respecting the independent, important roles of each of them.

27.   We agree that in pursuit of its legitimate activities the private sector, including both large and small companies, has a duty to contribute to the evolution of equitable and sustainable communities and societies.

28.   We also agree to provide assistance to increase income-generating employment opportunities, taking into account the Declaration on Fundamental Principles and Rights at Work of the International Labour Organization.[7]

29.   We agree that there is a need for private sector corporations to enforce corporate accountability, which should take place within a transparent and stable regulatory environment.

30.   We undertake to strengthen and improve governance at all levels for the effective implementation of Agenda 21, the Millennium development goals and the Plan of Implementation of the Summit.

Multilateralism is the future

31.   To achieve our goals of sustainable development, we need more effective, democratic and accountable international and multilateral institutions.

32.   We reaffirm our commitment to the principles and purposes of the Charter of the United Nations and international law, as well as to the strengthening of multilateralism. We support the leadership role of the United Nations as the most universal and representative organization in the world, which is best placed to promote sustainable development.

33.   We further commit ourselves to monitor progress at regular intervals towards the achievement of our sustainable development goals and objectives.

Making it happen!

34.   We are in agreement that this must be an inclusive process, involving all the major groups and Governments that participated in the historic Johannesburg Summit.

35.   We commit ourselves to act together, united by a common determination to save our planet, promote human development and achieve universal prosperity and peace.

36.   We commit ourselves to the Plan of Implementation of the World Summit on Sustainable Development and to expediting the achievement of the time-bound, socio-economic and environmental targets contained therein.

37.   From the African continent, the cradle of humankind, we solemnly pledge to the peoples of the world and the generations that will surely inherit this Earth that we are determined to ensure that our collective hope for sustainable development is realized.

*   Adopted at the 17th plenary meeting of the World Summit on Sustainable Development, on 4 September 2002; for the discussion, see chap. VIII of the Summit Report.

Notes

1/ *Report of the United Nations Conference on the Human Environment, Stockholm, 5-16 June 1972* (United Nations publication, Sales No. E.73.II.A.14 and corrigendum), chap. I.

2/ *Report of the United Nations Conference on Environment and Development, Rio de Janeiro, 3-14 June 1992* (United Nations publication, Sales No. E.93.I.8 and corrigenda), vols. I-III.

3/ Ibid., vol. I: *Resolutions adopted by the Conference*, resolution 1, annexes I and II.

4/ *Report of the International Conference on Financing for Development, Monterrey, Mexico, 18-22 March 2002* (United Nations publication, Sales No. E.02.II.A.7), chap. I, resolution 1, annex.

5/ See A/C.2/56/7, annex.

6/ See General Assembly resolution 55/2.

7/ See *ILO Declaration on Fundamental Principles and Rights at Work and its Follow-up Adopted by the International Labour Conference at its Eighty-sixth Session, Geneva, 18 June 1998* (Geneva, International Labour Office, 1998).

NEW DELHI DECLARATION OF PRINCIPLES OF INTERNATIONAL LAW
RELATING TO SUSTAINABLE DEVELOPMENT

The 70th Conference of the International Law Association, held in New Delhi, India, 2-6 April 2002,

Noting that sustainable development is now widely accepted as a global objective and that the concept has been amply recognized in various international and national legal instruments, including treaty law and jurisprudence at international and national levels,

Emphasizing that sustainable development is a matter of common concern both to developing and industrialized countries and that, as such, it should be integrated into all relevant fields of policy in order to realize the goals of environmental protection, development and respect for human rights, emphasizing the critical relevance of the gender dimension in all these areas and recognizing the need to ensure practical and effective implementation,

Taking the View that there is a need for a comprehensive international law perspective on integration of social, economic, financial and environmental objectives and activities and that enhanced attention should be paid to the interests and needs of developing countries, particularly least developed countries, and those adversely affected by environmental, social and developmental considerations,

Recalling that in its Report on *Our Common Future* (1987), the World Commission on Environment and Development identified the objective of sustainable development as being '...to ensure that it meets the needs of the present without compromising the ability of future generations to meet their own needs',

Concerned about growing economic and social inequalities between and within States as well as about the ability of many developing countries, particularly least developed countries, to participate in the global economy,

Recognizing the need to further develop international law in the field of sustainable development, with a view to according due weight to both the developmental and environmental concerns, in order to achieve a balanced and comprehensive international law on sustainable development, as called for in Principle 27 of the Rio Declaration and Chapter 39 of Agenda 21 of the UN Conference on Environment and Development as well as in the various resolutions on legal aspects of sustainable development of the International Law Association,

Affirming that consideration should be given to the interaction of States, intergovernmental organizations, peoples and individuals, industrial concerns and other non-governmental organizations as participants in multilateral development co-operation,

Aware of the concern expressed by the UN General Assembly during its 19th Special Session in 1997 to review progress achieved since the 1992 UN Conference on Environment and Development that 'the overall trends for sustainable development are worse today than they were in 1992'; and of the General Assembly's call 'to continue the progressive development and, as and where appropriate, codification of international law related to sustainable development',

Recognizing that the forthcoming World Summit on Sustainable Development, convened by the United Nations General Assembly in Johannesburg, South Africa, 26 August-4 September 2002, provides an important opportunity for addressing the role of international law in the pursuance of sustainable development,

Reaffirming the ILA's Seoul Declaration on Progressive Development of Principles of Public International Law Relating to a New International Economic Order, as adopted by the 62nd Conference of the International Law Association held in Seoul in 1986,

Taking into account the United Nations General Assembly Declaration on the Right to Development of 1986,

Taking further into account the Rio Declaration on Environment and Development and related documents ensuing from the 1992 UN Conference on Environment and Development, as well as the final documents resulting from the series of world conferences on social progress for development (Copenhagen, 1993), human rights (Vienna, 1993), population and development (Cairo, 1994), small islands states and sustainable development (Barbados, 1994), women and development (Beijing, 1995), least-developed countries (Brussels, 2001) and financing for development (Monterrey, 2002), respectively,

Expresses the view that the objective of sustainable development involves a comprehensive and integrated approach to economic, social and political processes, which aims at the sustainable use of natural resources of the Earth and the protection of the environment on which nature and human life as well as social and economic development depend and which seeks to realize the right of all human beings to an adequate living standard on the basis of their active, free and meaningful participation in development and in the fair distribution of benefits resulting therefrom, with due regard to the needs and interests of future generations,

Is of the opinion that the realization of the international bill of human rights, comprising economic, social and cultural rights, civil and political rights and peoples' rights, is central to the pursuance of sustainable development,

Considers that the application and, where relevant, consolidation and further development of the following principles of international law relevant to the activities of all actors involved would be instrumental in pursuing the objective of sustainable development in an effective way:

1. The duty of States to ensure sustainable use of natural resources

1.1 It is a well-established principle that, in accordance with international law, all States have the sovereign right to manage their own natural resources pursuant to their own environmental and developmental policies, and the responsibility to ensure that activities within their jurisdiction or control do not cause significant damage to the environment of other States or of areas beyond the limits of national jurisdiction.

1.2 States are under a duty to manage natural resources, including natural resources within their own territory or jurisdiction, in a rational, sustainable and safe way so as to contribute to the development of their peoples, with particular regard for the rights of indigenous peoples, and to the conservation and sustainable use of natural resources and the protection of the environment, including ecosystems. States must take into account the needs of future generations in determining the rate of use of natural resources. All relevant actors (including States, industrial concerns and other components of civil society) are under a duty to avoid wasteful use of natural resources and promote waste minimization policies.

1.3 The protection, preservation and enhancement of the natural environment, particularly the proper management of climate system, biological diversity and fauna and flora of the Earth, are the common concern of humankind. The resources of outer space and celestial bodies and of the sea-bed, ocean floor and subsoil thereof beyond the limits of national jurisdiction are the common heritage of humankind.

2. The principle of equity and the eradication of poverty

2.1 The principle of equity is central to the attainment of sustainable development. It refers to both *inter-generational equity* (the right of future generations to enjoy a fair level of the common patrimony) and *intra-generational equity* (the right of all peoples within the current generation of fair access to the current generation's entitlement to the Earth's natural resources).

2.2 The present generation has a right to use and enjoy the resources of the Earth but is under an obligation to take into account the long-term impact of its activities and to sustain the resource base and the global environment for the benefit of future generations of humankind. 'Benefit' in this context is to be understood in its broadest meaning as including, *inter alia*, economic, environmental, social and intrinsic benefit.

2.3 The right to development must be implemented so as to meet developmental and environmental needs of present and future generations in a sustainable and equitable manner. This includes the duty to co-operate for the eradication of poverty in accordance with Chapter IX on International Economic and Social Co-operation of the Charter of the United Nations and the Rio Declaration on Environment and Development as well as the duty to co-operate for global sustainable development and the attainment of equity in the development opportunities of developed and developing countries.

2.4 Whilst it is the primary responsibility of the State to aim for conditions of equity within its own population and to ensure, as a minimum, the eradication of poverty, all States which are in a position to do so have a further responsibility, as recognized by the Charter of the United Nations and the Millennium Declaration of the United Nations, to assist States in achieving this objective.

3. The principle of common but differentiated responsibilities

3.1 States and other relevant actors have common but differentiated responsibilities. All States are under a duty to co-operate in the achievement of global sustainable development and the protection of the environment. International organizations, corporations (including in particular transnational corporations), non-governmental organizations and civil society should co-operate in and contribute to this global partnership. Corporations have also responsibilities pursuant to the polluter-pays principle.

3.2 Differentiation of responsibilities, whilst principally based on the contribution that a State has made to the emergence of environmental problems, must also take into account the economic and developmental situation of the State, in accordance with paragraph 3.3.

3.3 The special needs and interests of developing countries and of countries with economies in transition, with particular regard to least developed countries and those affected adversely by environmental, social and developmental considerations, should be recognized.

3.4 Developed countries bear a special burden of responsibility in reducing and eliminating unsustainable patterns of production and consumption and in contributing to capacity-building in developing countries, *inter alia* by providing financial assistance and access to environmentally sound technology. In particular, developed countries should play a leading role and assume primary responsibility in matters of relevance to sustainable development.

4. The principle of the precautionary approach to human health, natural resources and ecosystems

4.1 A precautionary approach is central to sustainable development in that it commits States, international organizations and the civil society, particularly the scientific and business communities, to avoid human activity which may cause significant harm to human health, natural resources or ecosystems, including in the light of scientific uncertainty.

4.2 Sustainable development requires that a precautionary approach with regard to human health, environmental protection and sustainable utilization of natural resources should include:

      (a) accountability for harm caused (including, where appropriate, State responsibility);
      (b) planning based on clear criteria and well-defined goals;
      (c) consideration in an environmental impact assessment of all possible means to achieve an objective (including, in certain instances, not proceeding with an envisaged activity); and
      (d) in respect of activities which may cause serious long-term or irreversible harm, establishing an appropriate burden of proof on the person or persons carrying out (or intending to carry out) the activity.

4.3 Decision-making processes should always endorse a precautionary approach to risk management and in particular should include the adoption of appropriate precautionary measures.

4.4 Precautionary measures should be based on up-to-date and independent scientific judgment and be transparent. They should not result in economic protectionism. Transparent structures should be established which involve all interested parties, including non-state actors, in the consultation process. Appropriate review by a judicial or administrative body should be available.

5. The principle of public participation and access to information and justice

5.1 Public participation is essential to sustainable development and good governance in that it is a condition for responsive, transparent and accountable governments as well a condition for the active engagement of equally responsive, transparent and accountable civil society organizations, including industrial concerns and trade unions. The vital role of women in sustainable development should be recognized.

5.2 Public participation in the context of sustainable development requires effective protection of the human right to hold and express opinions and to seek, receive and impart ideas. It also requires a right of access to appropriate, comprehensible and timely information held by governments and industrial concerns on economic and social policies regarding the sustainable use of natural resources and the protection of the environment, without imposing undue financial burdens upon the applicants and with due consideration for privacy and adequate protection of business confidentiality.

5.3 The empowerment of peoples in the context of sustainable development requires access to effective judicial or administrative procedures in the State where the measure has been taken to challenge such measure and to claim compensation. States should ensure that where transboundary harm has been, or is likely to be, caused, individuals and peoples affected have non-discriminatory access to the same judicial and administrative procedures as would individuals and peoples of the State in which the harm is caused.

6. The principle of good governance

6.1 The principle of good governance is essential to the progressive development and codification of international law relating to sustainable development. It commits States and international organizations:
   (a) to adopt democratic and transparent decision-making procedures and financial accountability;
   (b) to take effective measures to combat official or other corruption;
   (c) to respect the principle of due process in their procedures and to observe the rule of law and human rights; and
   (d) to implement a public procurement approach according to the WTO Code on Public Procurement.

6.2 Civil society and non-governmental organizations have a right to good governance by States and international organizations. Non-state actors should be subject to internal democratic governance and to effective accountability.

6.3 Good governance requires full respect for the principles of the 1992 Rio Declaration on Environment and Development as well as the full participation of women in all levels of decision-making. Good governance also calls for corporate social responsibility and socially responsible investments as conditions for the existence of a global market aimed at a fair distribution of wealth among and within communities.

7. The principle of integration and interrelationship, in particular in relation to human rights and social, economic and environmental objectives

7.1 The principle of integration reflects the interdependence of social, economic, financial, environmental and human rights aspects of principles and rules of international law relating to sustainable development as well as of the interdependence of the needs of current and future generations of humankind.

7.2 All levels of governance – global, regional, national, sub-national and local – and all sectors of society should implement the integration principle, which is essential to the achievement of sustainable development.

7.3 States should strive to resolve apparent conflicts between competing economic, financial, social and environmental considerations, whether through existing institutions or through the establishment of appropriate new institutions.

7.4 In their interpretation and application, the above principles are interrelated and each of them should be construed in the context of the other principles of this Declaration. Nothing in this Declaration shall be construed as prejudicing in any manner the provisions of the Charter of the United Nations and the rights of peoples under that Charter.

INTERNATIONAL LAW COMMISSION'S DRAFT PRINCIPLES ON INTERNATIONAL LIABILITY IN CASE OF LOSS FROM TRANSBOUNDARY HARM ARISING OUT OF HAZARDOUS ACTIVITIES

International Law Commission
A/CN.4/L.686,
26 May 2006

**Draft principles on the allocation of loss in the case of
transboundary harm arising out of hazardous activities**

The General Assembly,

Reaffirming principles 13 and 16 of the Rio Declaration on Environment and Development,

Recalling the Draft articles on the Prevention of Transboundary Harm from Hazardous Activities,

Aware that incidents involving hazardous activities may occur despite compliance by the relevant State with its obligations concerning prevention of transboundary harm from hazardous activities,

Noting that as a result of such incidents other States and/or their nationals may suffer harm and serious loss,

Emphasizing that appropriate and effective measures should be in place to ensure that those natural and legal persons, including States, that incur harm and loss as a result of such incidents are able to obtain prompt and adequate compensation,

Concerned that prompt and effective response measures should be taken to minimize the harm and loss which may result from such incidents,

Noting that States are responsible for infringements of their obligations of prevention under international law,

Recalling the significance of existing international agreements covering specific categories of hazardous activities and stressing the importance of the conclusion of further such agreements,

Desiring to contribute to the further development of international law in this field,

Principle 1
Scope of application

The present draft principles apply to transboundary damage caused by hazardous activities not prohibited by international law.

Principle 2
Use of terms

For the purposes of the present draft principles:

(a)   "damage" means significant damage caused to persons, property or the environment; and includes:
     (i)   loss of life or personal injury;
     (ii)   loss of, or damage to, property, including property which forms part of the cultural heritage;
     (iii)   loss or damage by impairment of the environment;
     (iv)   the costs of reasonable measures of reinstatement of the property, or
environment, including natural resources;
     (v)   the costs of reasonable response measures;

(b)   "environment" includes: natural resources, both abiotic and biotic, such as air, water, soil, fauna and flora and the interaction between the same factors; and the characteristic aspects of the landscape;

(c)   "hazardous activity" means an activity which involves a risk of causing significant harm;

(d)   "State of origin" means the State in the territory or otherwise under the jurisdiction or control of which the hazardous activity is carried out;

(e)   "transboundary damage" means damage caused to persons, property or the environment in the territory or in other places under the jurisdiction or control of a State other than the State of origin;

(f)   "victim" means any natural or legal person or State that suffers damage;

(g)   "operator" means any person in command or control of the activity at the time the incident causing transboundary damage occurs.

Principle 3
Purposes

The purposes of the present draft principles are:

(a)   to ensure prompt and adequate compensation to victims of transboundary damage; and
(b)   to preserve and protect the environment in the event of transboundary damage, especially with respect to mitigation of damage to the environment and its restoration or reinstatement.

Principle 4
Prompt and adequate compensation

1.   Each State should take all necessary measures to ensure that prompt and adequate compensation is available for victims of transboundary damage caused by hazardous activities located within its territory or otherwise under its jurisdiction or control.

2.   These measures should include the imposition of liability on the operator or, where appropriate, other person or entity. Such liability should not require proof of fault. Any conditions, limitations or exceptions to such liability shall be consistent with draft principle 3.

3.   These measures should also include the requirement on the operator or, where appropriate, other person or entity, to establish and maintain financial security such as insurance, bonds or other financial guarantees to cover claims of compensation.

4.   In appropriate cases, these measures should include the requirement for the establishment of industry wide funds at the national level.

5.   In the event that the measures under the preceding paragraphs are insufficient to provide adequate compensation, the State of origin should also ensure that additional financial resources are made available.

Principle 5
Response measures

Upon the occurrence of an incident involving a hazardous activity which results or is likely to result in transboundary damage:

(a)   the State of origin shall promptly notify all States affected or likely to be affected of the incident and the possible effects of the transboundary damage;

(b)   the State of origin, with the appropriate involvement of the operator, shall ensure that appropriate response measures are taken and should, for this purpose, rely upon the best available scientific data and technology;

(c)   the State of origin, as appropriate, should also consult with and seek the cooperation of all States affected or likely to be affected to mitigate the effects of damage and if possible eliminate them;

(d)   the States affected or likely to be affected by the damage shall take all feasible measures to mitigate and if possible to eliminate the effects of damage;

(e)   the States concerned should, where appropriate, seek the assistance of competent international organizations and other States on mutually acceptable terms and conditions.

Principle 6
International and domestic remedies

1.   States shall provide their domestic judicial and administrative bodies with the necessary jurisdiction and competence and ensure that these bodies have prompt, adequate and effective remedies available in the event of transboundary damage caused by hazardous activities located within their territory or otherwise under their jurisdiction or control.

2.   Victims of transboundary damage should have access to remedies in the State of origin that are no less prompt, adequate and effective than those available to victims that suffer damage, from the same incident, within the territory of that State.

3.   Paragraphs 1 and 2 are without prejudice to the right of the victims to seek remedies other than those available in the State of origin.

4.   States may provide for recourse to international claims settlement procedures that are expeditious and involve minimal expenses.

5.   States should guarantee appropriate access to information relevant for the pursuance of remedies, including claims for compensation.

Principle 7
Development of specific international regimes

1.   Where, in respect of particular categories of hazardous activities, specific global, regional or bilateral agreements would provide effective arrangements concerning compensation, response measures and international and domestic remedies, all efforts should be made to conclude such specific agreements.

2.   Such agreements should, as appropriate, include arrangements for industry and/or State funds to provide supplementary compensation in the event that the financial resources of the operator, including financial security measures, are insufficient to cover the damage suffered as a result of an incident. Any such funds may be designed to supplement or replace national industry based funds.

Principle 8
Implementation

1.   Each State should adopt the necessary legislative, regulatory and administrative measures to implement the present draft principles.

2.   The present draft principles and the measures adopted to implement them shall be applied without any discrimination such as that based on nationality, domicile or residence.

3.   States should cooperate with each other to implement the present draft principles.

UNITED NATIONS DECLARATION ON THE RIGHTS OF
INDIGENOUS PEOPLES

Adopted by General Assembly Resolution 61/295 on 13 September 2007

The General Assembly,

Guided by the purposes and principles of the Charter of the United Nations, and good faith in the fulfilment of the obligations assumed by States in accordance with the Charter,

Affirming that indigenous peoples are equal to all other peoples, while recognizing the right of all peoples to be different, to consider themselves different, and to be respected as such,

Affirming also that all peoples contribute to the diversity and richness of civilizations and cultures, which constitute the common heritage of humankind,

Affirming further that all doctrines, policies and practices based on or advocating superiority of peoples or individuals on the basis of national origin or racial, religious, ethnic or cultural differences are racist, scientifically false, legally invalid, morally condemnable and socially unjust,

Reaffirming that indigenous peoples, in the exercise of their rights, should be free from discrimination of any kind,

Concerned that indigenous peoples have suffered from historic injustices as a result of, inter alia, their colonization and dispossession of their lands, territories and resources, thus preventing them from exercising, in particular, their right to development in accordance with their own needs and interests,

Recognizing the urgent need to respect and promote the inherent rights of indigenous peoples which derive from their political, economic and social structures and from their cultures, spiritual traditions, histories and philosophies, especially their rights to their lands, territories and resources,

Recognizing also the urgent need to respect and promote the rights of indigenous peoples affirmed in treaties, agreements and other constructive arrangements with States,

Welcoming the fact that indigenous peoples are organizing themselves for political, economic, social and cultural enhancement and in order to bring to an end all forms of discrimination and oppression wherever they occur,

Convinced that control by indigenous peoples over developments affecting them and their lands, territories and resources will enable them to maintain and strengthen their institutions, cultures and traditions, and to promote their development in accordance with their aspirations and needs,

Recognizing that respect for indigenous knowledge, cultures and traditional practices contributes to sustainable and equitable development and proper management of the environment,

Emphasizing the contribution of the demilitarization of the lands and territories of indigenous peoples to peace, economic and social progress and development, understanding and friendly relations among nations and peoples of the world,

Recognizing in particular the right of indigenous families and communities to retain shared responsibility for the upbringing, training, education and well-being of their children, consistent with the rights of the child,

Considering that the rights affirmed in treaties, agreements and other constructive arrangements between States and indigenous peoples are, in some situations, matters of international concern, interest, responsibility and character,

Considering also that treaties, agreements and other constructive arrangements, and the relationship they represent, are the basis for a strengthened partnership between indigenous peoples and States,

Acknowledging that the Charter of the United Nations, the International Covenant on Economic, Social and Cultural Rights and the International Covenant on Civil and Political Rights, as well as the Vienna Declaration and Programme of Action, affirm the fundamental importance of the right to self-determination of all peoples, by virtue of which they freely determine their political status and freely pursue their economic, social and cultural development,

Bearing in mind that nothing in this Declaration may be used to deny any peoples their right to self-determination, exercised in conformity with international law,

Convinced that the recognition of the rights of indigenous peoples in this Declaration will enhance harmonious and cooperative relations between the State and indigenous peoples, based on principles of justice, democracy, respect for human rights, non-discrimination and good faith,

Encouraging States to comply with and effectively implement all their obligations as they apply to indigenous peoples under international instruments, in particular those related to human rights, in consultation and cooperation with the peoples concerned,

Emphasizing that the United Nations has an important and continuing role to play in promoting and protecting the rights of indigenous peoples,

Believing that this Declaration is a further important step forward for the recognition, promotion and protection of the rights and freedoms of indigenous peoples and in the development of relevant activities of the United Nations system in this field,

Recognizing and reaffirming that indigenous individuals are entitled without discrimination to all human rights recognized in international law, and that indigenous peoples possess collective rights which are indispensable for their existence, well-being and integral development as peoples,

Recognizing that the situation of indigenous peoples varies from region to region and from country to country and that the significance of national and regional particularities and various historical and cultural backgrounds should be taken into consideration,

Solemnly proclaims the following United Nations Declaration on the Rights of Indigenous Peoples as a standard of achievement to be pursued in a spirit of partnership and mutual respect:

Article 1

Indigenous peoples have the right to the full enjoyment, as a collective or as individuals, of all human rights and fundamental freedoms as recognized in the Charter of the United Nations, the Universal Declaration of Human Rights and international human rights law.

Article 2

Indigenous peoples and individuals are free and equal to all other peoples and individuals and have the right to be free from any kind of discrimination, in the exercise of their rights, in particular that based on their indigenous origin or identity.

Article 3

Indigenous peoples have the right to self-determination. By virtue of that right they freely determine their political status and freely pursue their economic, social and cultural development.

Article 4

Indigenous peoples, in exercising their right to self-determination, have the right to autonomy or self-government in matters relating to their internal and local affairs, as well as ways and means for financing their autonomous functions.

Article 5

Indigenous peoples have the right to maintain and strengthen their distinct political, legal, economic, social and cultural institutions, while retaining their right to participate fully, if they so choose, in the political, economic, social and cultural life of the State.

Article 6

Every indigenous individual has the right to a nationality.

Article 7

1. Indigenous individuals have the rights to life, physical and mental integrity, liberty and security of person.

2. Indigenous peoples have the collective right to live in freedom, peace and security as distinct peoples and shall not be subjected to any act of genocide or any other act of violence, including forcibly removing children of the group to another group.

Article 8

1. Indigenous peoples and individuals have the right not to be subjected to forced assimilation or destruction of their culture.

2. States shall provide effective mechanisms for prevention of, and redress for:

(a) Any action which has the aim or effect of depriving them of their integrity as distinct peoples, or of their cultural values or ethnic identities;

(b) Any action which has the aim or effect of dispossessing them of their lands, territories or resources;

(c) Any form of forced population transfer which has the aim or effect of violating or undermining any of their rights;

(d) Any form of forced assimilation or integration;

(e) Any form of propaganda designed to promote or incite racial or ethnic discrimination directed against them.

Article 9

Indigenous peoples and individuals have the right to belong to an indigenous community or nation, in accordance with the traditions and customs of the community or nation concerned. No discrimination of any kind may arise from the exercise of such a right.

Article 10

Indigenous peoples shall not be forcibly removed from their lands or territories. No relocation shall take place without the free, prior and informed consent of the indigenous peoples concerned and after agreement on just and fair compensation and, where possible, with the option of return.

Article 11

1. Indigenous peoples have the right to practise and revitalize their cultural traditions and customs. This includes the right to maintain, protect and develop the past, present and future manifestations of their cultures, such as archaeological and historical sites, artefacts, designs, ceremonies, technologies and visual and performing arts and literature.

2. States shall provide redress through effective mechanisms, which may include restitution, developed in conjunction with indigenous peoples, with respect to their cultural, intellectual, religious and spiritual property taken without their free, prior and informed consent or in violation of their laws, traditions and customs.

Article 12

1. Indigenous peoples have the right to manifest, practise, develop and teach their spiritual and religious traditions, customs and ceremonies; the right to maintain, protect, and have access in privacy to their religious and cultural sites; the right to the use and control of their ceremonial objects; and the right to the repatriation of their human remains.

2. States shall seek to enable the access and/or repatriation of ceremonial objects and human remains in their possession through fair, transparent and effective mechanisms developed in conjunction with indigenous peoples concerned.

Article 13

1. Indigenous peoples have the right to revitalize, use, develop and transmit to future generations their histories, languages, oral traditions, philosophies, writing systems and literatures, and to designate and retain their own names for communities, places and persons.

2. States shall take effective measures to ensure that this right is protected and also to ensure that indigenous peoples can understand and be understood in political, legal and administrative proceedings, where necessary through the provision of interpretation or by other appropriate means.

Article 14

1. Indigenous peoples have the right to establish and control their educational systems and institutions providing education in their own languages, in a manner appropriate to their cultural methods of teaching and learning.

2. Indigenous individuals, particularly children, have the right to all levels and forms of education of the State without discrimination.

3. States shall, in conjunction with indigenous peoples, take effective measures, in order for indigenous individuals, particularly children, including those living outside their communities, to have access, when possible, to an education in their own culture and provided in their own language.

Article 15

1. Indigenous peoples have the right to the dignity and diversity of their cultures, traditions, histories and aspirations which shall be appropriately reflected in education and public information.

2. States shall take effective measures, in consultation and cooperation with the indigenous peoples concerned, to combat prejudice and eliminate discrimination and to promote tolerance, understanding and good relations among indigenous peoples and all other segments of society.

Article 16

1. Indigenous peoples have the right to establish their own media in their own languages and to have access to all forms of non-indigenous media without discrimination.

2. States shall take effective measures to ensure that State-owned media duly reflect indigenous cultural diversity. States, without prejudice to ensuring full freedom of expression, should encourage privately owned media to adequately reflect indigenous cultural diversity.

Article 17

1. Indigenous individuals and peoples have the right to enjoy fully all rights established under applicable international and domestic labour law.

2. States shall in consultation and cooperation with indigenous peoples take specific measures to protect indigenous children from economic exploitation and from performing any work that is likely to be hazardous or to interfere with the child's education, or to be harmful to the child's health or physical, mental, spiritual, moral or social development, taking into account their special vulnerability and the importance of education for their empowerment.

3. Indigenous individuals have the right not to be subjected to any discriminatory conditions of labour and, inter alia, employment or salary.

Article 18

Indigenous peoples have the right to participate in decision-making in matters which would affect their rights, through representatives chosen by themselves in accordance with their own procedures, as well as to maintain and develop their own indigenous decision-making institutions.

Article 19

States shall consult and cooperate in good faith with the indigenous peoples concerned through their own representative institutions in order to obtain their free, prior and informed consent before adopting and implementing legislative or administrative measures that may affect them.

Article 20

1. Indigenous peoples have the right to maintain and develop their political, economic and social systems or institutions, to be secure in the enjoyment of their own means of subsistence and development, and to engage freely in all their traditional and other economic activities.

2. Indigenous peoples deprived of their means of subsistence and development are entitled to just and fair redress.

Article 21

1. Indigenous peoples have the right, without discrimination, to the improvement of their economic and social conditions, including, inter alia, in the areas of education, employment, vocational training and retraining, housing, sanitation, health and social security.

2. States shall take effective measures and, where appropriate, special measures to ensure continuing improvement of their economic and social conditions. Particular attention shall be paid to the rights and special needs of indigenous elders, women, youth, children and persons with disabilities.

Article 22

1. Particular attention shall be paid to the rights and special needs of indigenous elders, women, youth, children and persons with disabilities in the implementation of this Declaration.

2. States shall take measures, in conjunction with indigenous peoples, to ensure that indigenous women and children enjoy the full protection and guarantees against all forms of violence and discrimination.

Article 23

Indigenous peoples have the right to determine and develop priorities and strategies for exercising their right to development. In particular, indigenous peoples have the right to be actively involved in developing and determining health, housing and other economic and social programmes affecting them and, as far as possible, to administer such programmes through their own institutions.

Article 24

1. Indigenous peoples have the right to their traditional medicines and to maintain their health practices, including the conservation of their vital medicinal plants, animals and minerals. Indigenous individuals also have the right to access, without any discrimination, to all social and health services.

2. Indigenous individuals have an equal right to the enjoyment of the highest attainable standard of physical and mental health. States shall take the necessary steps with a view to achieving progressively the full realization of this right.

Article 25

Indigenous peoples have the right to maintain and strengthen their distinctive spiritual relationship with their traditionally owned or otherwise occupied and used lands, territories, waters and coastal seas and other resources and to uphold their responsibilities to future generations in this regard.

Article 26

1. Indigenous peoples have the right to the lands, territories and resources which they have traditionally owned, occupied or otherwise used or acquired.

2. Indigenous peoples have the right to own, use, develop and control the lands, territories and resources that they possess by reason of traditional ownership or other traditional occupation or use, as well as those which they have otherwise acquired.

3. States shall give legal recognition and protection to these lands, territories and resources. Such recognition shall be conducted with due respect to the customs, traditions and land tenure systems of the indigenous peoples concerned.

Article 27

States shall establish and implement, in conjunction with indigenous peoples concerned, a fair, independent, impartial, open and transparent process, giving due recognition to indigenous peoples' laws, traditions, customs and land tenure systems, to recognize and adjudicate the rights of indigenous peoples pertaining to their lands, territories and resources, including those which were traditionally owned or otherwise occupied or used. Indigenous peoples shall have the right to participate in this process.

Article 28

1. Indigenous peoples have the right to redress, by means that can include restitution or, when this is not possible, just, fair and equitable compensation, for the lands, territories and resources which they have traditionally owned or otherwise occupied or used, and which have been confiscated, taken, occupied, used or damaged without their free, prior and informed consent.

2. Unless otherwise freely agreed upon by the peoples concerned, compensation shall take the form of lands, territories and resources equal in quality, size and legal status or of monetary compensation or other appropriate redress.

Article 29

1. Indigenous peoples have the right to the conservation and protection of the environment and the productive capacity of their lands or territories and resources. States shall establish and implement assistance programmes for indigenous peoples for such conservation and protection, without discrimination.

2. States shall take effective measures to ensure that no storage or disposal of hazardous materials shall take place in the lands or territories of indigenous peoples without their free, prior and informed consent.

3. States shall also take effective measures to ensure, as needed, that programmes for monitoring, maintaining and restoring the health of indigenous peoples, as developed and implemented by the peoples affected by such materials, are duly implemented.

Article 30

1. Military activities shall not take place in the lands or territories of indigenous peoples, unless justified by a relevant public interest or otherwise freely agreed with or requested by the indigenous peoples concerned.

2. States shall undertake effective consultations with the indigenous peoples concerned, through appropriate procedures and in particular through their representative institutions, prior to using their lands or territories for military activities.

Article 31

1. Indigenous peoples have the right to maintain, control, protect and develop their cultural heritage, traditional knowledge and traditional cultural expressions, as well as the manifestations of their sciences, technologies and cultures, including human and genetic resources, seeds, medicines, knowledge of the properties of fauna and flora, oral traditions, literatures, designs, sports and traditional games and visual and performing arts. They also have the right to maintain, control, protect and develop their intellectual property over such cultural heritage, traditional knowledge, and traditional cultural expressions.

2. In conjunction with indigenous peoples, States shall take effective measures to recognize and protect the exercise of these rights.

Article 32

1. Indigenous peoples have the right to determine and develop priorities and strategies for the development or use of their lands or territories and other resources.

2. States shall consult and cooperate in good faith with the indigenous peoples concerned through their own representative institutions in order to obtain their free and informed consent prior to the approval of any project affecting their lands or territories and other resources, particularly in connection with the development, utilization or exploitation of mineral, water or other resources.

3. States shall provide effective mechanisms for just and fair redress for any such activities, and appropriate measures shall be taken to mitigate adverse environmental, economic, social, cultural or spiritual impact.

Article 33

1. Indigenous peoples have the right to determine their own identity or membership in accordance with their customs and traditions. This does not impair the right of indigenous individuals to obtain citizenship of the States in which they live.

2. Indigenous peoples have the right to determine the structures and to select the membership of their institutions in accordance with their own procedures.

Article 34

Indigenous peoples have the right to promote, develop and maintain their institutional structures and their distinctive customs, spirituality, traditions, procedures, practices and, in the cases where they exist, juridical systems or customs, in accordance with international human rights standards.

Article 35

Indigenous peoples have the right to determine the responsibilities of individuals to their communities.

Article 36

1. Indigenous peoples, in particular those divided by international borders, have the right to maintain and develop contacts, relations and cooperation, including activities for spiritual, cultural, political, economic and social purposes, with their own members as well as other peoples across borders.

2. States, in consultation and cooperation with indigenous peoples, shall take effective measures to facilitate the exercise and ensure the implementation of this right.

Article 37

1. Indigenous peoples have the right to the recognition, observance and enforcement of treaties, agreements and other constructive arrangements concluded with States or their successors and to have States honour and respect such treaties, agreements and other constructive arrangements.

2. Nothing in this Declaration may be interpreted as diminishing or eliminating the rights of indigenous peoples contained in treaties, agreements and other constructive arrangements.

Article 38

States in consultation and cooperation with indigenous peoples, shall take the appropriate measures, including legislative measures, to achieve the ends of this Declaration.

Article 39

Indigenous peoples have the right to have access to financial and technical assistance from States and through international cooperation, for the enjoyment of the rights contained in this Declaration.

Article 40

Indigenous peoples have the right to access to and prompt decision through just and fair procedures for the resolution of conflicts and disputes with States or other parties, as well as to effective remedies for all infringements of their individual and collective rights. Such a decision shall give due consideration to the customs, traditions, rules and legal systems of the indigenous peoples concerned and international human rights.

Article 41

The organs and specialized agencies of the United Nations system and other intergovernmental organizations shall contribute to the full realization of the provisions of this Declaration through the mobilization, inter alia, of financial cooperation and technical assistance. Ways and means of ensuring participation of indigenous peoples on issues affecting them shall be established.

Article 42

The United Nations, its bodies, including the Permanent Forum on Indigenous Issues, and specialized agencies, including at the country level, and States shall promote respect for and full application of the provisions of this Declaration and follow up the effectiveness of this Declaration.

Article 43

The rights recognized herein constitute the minimum standards for the survival, dignity and well-being of the indigenous peoples of the world.

Article 44

All the rights and freedoms recognized herein are equally guaranteed to male and female indigenous individuals.

Article 45

Nothing in this Declaration may be construed as diminishing or extinguishing the rights indigenous peoples have now or may acquire in the future.

Article 46

1. Nothing in this Declaration may be interpreted as implying for any State, people, group or person any right to engage in any activity or to perform any act contrary to the Charter of the United Nations or construed as authorizing or encouraging any action which would dismember or impair, totally or in part, the territorial integrity or political unity of sovereign and independent States.

2. In the exercise of the rights enunciated in the present Declaration, human rights and fundamental freedoms of all shall be respected. The exercise of the rights set forth in this Declaration shall be subject only to such limitations as are determined by law and in accordance with international human rights obligations. Any such limitations shall be non-discriminatory and strictly necessary solely for the purpose of securing due recognition and respect for the rights and freedoms of others and for meeting the just and most compelling requirements of a democratic society.

3. The provisions set forth in this Declaration shall be interpreted in accordance with the principles of justice, democracy, respect for human rights, equality, non-discrimination, good governance and good faith.

CONVENTION ON ENVIRONMENTAL IMPACT ASSESSMENT IN A TRANSBOUNDARY CONTEXT
(Annexes not Included)

30 I.L.M. 800 (1991)
Signed: February 25, 1991
Entry into Force: September 10, 1997
Secretariat Homepage: http://www.unece.org/env/eia/

The Parties to this Convention

Aware of the interrelationship between economic activities and their environmental consequences,

Affirming the need to ensure environmentally sound and sustainable development,

Determined to enhance international co-operation in assessing environmental impact in particular in a transboundary context,

Mindful of the need and importance to develop anticipatory policies and of preventing, mitigating and monitoring significant adverse environmental impact in general and more specifically in a transboundary context

Recalling the relevant provisions of the Charter of the United Nations, the Declaration of the Stockholm Conference on the Human Environment, the Final Act of the Conference on Security and Co-operation in Europe (CSCE) and the Concluding Documents of the Madrid and Vienna Meetings of Representatives of the Participating States of the CSCE,

Commending the ongoing activities of States to ensure that, through their national legal and administrative provisions and their national policies, environmental impact assessment is carried out,

Conscious of the need to give explicit consideration to environmental factors at an early stage in the decision-making process by applying environmental impact assessment, at all appropriate administrative levels, as a necessary tool to improve the quality of information presented to decision makers so that environmentally sound decisions can be made paying careful attention to minimizing significant adverse impact, particularly in a transboundary context,

Mindful of the efforts of international organizations to promote the use of environmental impact assessment both at the national and international levels, and taking into account work on environmental impact assessment carried out under the auspices of the United Nations Economic Commission for Europe, in particular results achieved by the Seminar on Environmental Impact Assessment (September 1987, Warsaw, Poland) as well as noting the Goals and Principles on environmental impact assessment adopted by the Governing Council of the United Nations Environment Programme, and the Ministerial Declaration on Sustainable Development (May 1990, Bergen, Norway),

Have agreed as follows:

Article 1   DEFINITIONS

For the purpose of this Convention,

(i) "Parties" means, unless the text otherwise indicates, the Contracting Parties to this Convention;

(ii) "Party of origin" means the Contracting Party or Parties to this Convention under whose jurisdiction a proposed activity is envisaged to take place;

(iii) "Affected Party" means the Contracting Party or Parties to this Convention likely to be affected by the transboundary impact of proposed activity;

(iv) "Concerned Parties" means the Party of origin and the affected Party of an environmental impact assessment pursuant to this Convention;

(v) "Proposed activity" means any activity or any major change to an activity subject to a decision of a competent authority in accordance with an applicable national procedure;

(vi) "Environmental impact assessment" means a national procedure for evaluating the likely impact of a proposed activity on the environment;

(vii) "Impact" means any effect caused by a proposed activity on the environment including human health and safety, flora, fauna, soil, air, water, climate, landscape and historical monuments or other physical structures or the interaction among these factors; it also includes effects on cultural heritage or socio-economic conditions resulting from alterations to those factors;

(viii) "Transboundary impact" means any impact, not exclusively of a global nature, within an area under the jurisdiction of a Party caused by a proposed activity the physical origin of which is situated wholly or in part within the area under the jurisdiction of another Party;

(ix) "Competent authority" means the national authority or authorities designated by a Party as responsible for performing the tasks covered by this Convention and/or the authority or authorities entrusted by a Party with decision-making powers regarding a proposed activity;

(x) "The Public" means one or more natural or legal persons.

Article 2   GENERAL PROVISIONS

1.   The Parties shall, either individually or jointly, take all appropriate and effective measures to prevent, reduce and control significant adverse transboundary environmental impact from proposed activities.

2.   Each Party shall take the necessary legal, administrative or other measures to implement the provisions of this Convention, including, with respect to proposed activities listed in Appendix I that are likely to cause significant adverse transboundary impact, the establishment of an environmental impact assessment procedure that permits public participation and preparation of the environmental impact assessment documentation described in Appendix II.

3.   The Party of origin shall ensure that in accordance with the provisions of this Convention an environmental impact assessment is undertaken prior to a decision to authorize or undertake a proposed activity listed in Appendix I that is likely to cause a significant adverse transboundary impact.

4.   The Party of origin shall, consistent with the provisions of this Convention, ensure that affected Parties are notified of a proposed activity listed in Appendix I that is likely to cause a significant adverse transboundary impact.

5.   Concerned Parties shall, at the initiative of any such Party, enter into discussions on whether one or more proposed activities not listed in Appendix I is or are likely to cause a significant adverse transboundary impact and thus should be treated as if it or they were so listed. Where those Parties so agree, the activity or activities shall be thus treated. General guidance for identifying criteria to determine significant adverse impact is set forth in Appendix III.

6.   The Party of origin shall provide, in accordance with the provisions of this Convention, an opportunity to the public in the areas likely to be affected to participate in relevant environmental impact assessment procedures regarding proposed activities and shall ensure that the opportunity provided to the public of the affected Party is equivalent to that provided to the public of the Party of origin.

7.   Environmental impact assessments as required by this Convention shall, as a minimum requirement, be undertaken at the project level of the proposed activity. To the extent appropriate, the Parties shall endeavour to apply the principles of environmental impact assessment to policies, plans and programmes.

8.   The provisions of this Convention shall not affect the right of Parties to implement national laws, regulations, administration provisions or accepted legal practices protecting information the supply of which would be prejudicial to industrial and commercial secrecy or national security.

9.   The provisions of this Convention shall not affect the right of particular Parties to implement, by bilateral or multilateral agreement where appropriate, more stringent measures than those of this Convention.

10.   The provisions of this Convention shall not prejudice any obligations of the Parties under international law with regard to activities having or likely to have a transboundary impact.

Article 3   NOTIFICATION

1.   For a proposed activity listed in Appendix I that is likely to cause a significant adverse transboundary impact, the Party of origin shall, for the purpose of ensuring adequate and effective consultations under Article 5, notify any Party which it considers may be an affected Party as early as possible and no later than when informing its own public about that proposed activity.

2.   This notification shall contain, inter alia,

     (a)   Information on the proposed activity, including any available information on its possible transboundary impact;
     (b)   The nature of the possible decision; and
     (c)   An indication of a reasonable time within which a response under paragraph 3 of this Article is required, taking into account the nature of the proposed activity;

and may include the information set out in paragraph 5 of this Article.

3.   The affected Party shall respond to the Party of origin within the time specified in the notification, acknowledging receipt of the notification, and shall indicate whether it intends to participate in the environmental impact assessment procedure.

4.   If the affected Party indicates that it does not intend to participate in the environmental impact assessment procedure, or if it does not respond within the time specified in the notification, the provisions in paragraph 5, 6, 7 and 8 of this Article and in Articles 4 to 7 will not apply. In such circumstances the right of a Party of origin to determine whether to carry out an environmental impact assessment on the basis of its national law and practice is not prejudiced.

5.   Upon receipt of a response from the affected Party indicating its desire to participate in the environmental impact assessment procedure, the Party of origin shall, if it has not already done so, provide to the affected Party:

     (a)   Relevant information regarding the environmental impact assessment procedure, including an indication of the time schedule for transmittal of comments; and
     (b)   Relevant information on the proposed activity and its possible significant adverse transboundary impact.

6.   An affected Party shall, at the request of the Party of origin, provide the latter with reasonably obtainable information relating to the potentially affected environment under the jurisdiction of the affected Party, where such information is necessary for the preparation of the environmental impact assessment documentation. The information shall be furnished promptly and, as appropriate, through a joint body where one exists.

7.   When a Party considers that it would be affected by a significant adverse transboundary impact of a proposed activity listed in Appendix I, and when no notification has taken place in accordance with paragraph 1 of this Article, the concerned Parties shall, at the request of the affected Party, exchange sufficient information for the

purposes of holding discussions on whether there is likely to be a significant adverse transboundary impact. If those Parties agree that there is likely to be a significant adverse transboundary impact, the provisions of this Convention shall apply accordingly. If those Parties cannot agree whether there is likely to be a significant adverse transboundary impact, any such Party may submit that question to an inquiry commission in accordance with the provisions of Appendix IV to advise on the likelihood of significant adverse transboundary impact, unless they agree on another method of settling this question.

8.   The concerned Parties shall ensure that the public of the affected Party in the areas likely to be affected be informed of, and be provided with possibilities for making comments or objections on, the proposed activity, and for the transmittal of these comments or objections to the competent authority of the Party of origin, either directly to this authority or, where appropriate, through the Party of origin.

Article 4   PREPARATION OF THE ENVIRONMENTAL IMPACT ASSESSMENT DOCUMENTATION

1.   The environmental impact assessment documentation to be submitted to the competent authority of the Party of origin shall contain, as a minimum, the information described in Appendix II.

2.   The Party of origin shall furnish the affected Party, as appropriate through a joint body where one exists, with the environmental impact assessment documentation. The concerned Parties shall arrange for distribution of the documentation to the authorities and the public of the affected Party in the areas likely to be affected and for the submission of comments to the competent authority of the Party of origin, either directly to this authority or, where appropriate, through the Party of origin within a reasonable time before the final decision is taken on the proposed activity.

Article 5   CONSULTATION ON THE BASIS OF THE ENVIRONMENTAL IMPACT ASSESSMENT DOCUMENTATION

The Party of origin shall, after completion of the environmental impact assessment documentation, without undue delay enter into consultations with the affected Party concerning, inter alia, the potential transboundary impact of the proposed activity and measures to reduce or eliminate its impact. Consultations may relate to:

(a)   Possible alternatives to the proposed activity, including the no-action alternative and possible measures to mitigate significant adverse transboundary impact and to monitor the effects of such measures at the expense of the Party of origin;

(b)   Other forms of possible mutual assistance in reducing any significant adverse transboundary impact of the proposed activity; and

(c)   Any other appropriate matters relating to the proposed activity.

The Parties shall agree, at the commencement of such consultations, on a reasonable time-frame for the duration of the consultation period.

Article 6   FINAL DECISION

1.   The Parties shall ensure that, in the final decision on the proposed activity, due account is taken of the outcome of the environmental impact assessment, including the environmental impact assessment documentation, as well as the comments thereon received pursuant to Article 3, paragraph 8 and Article 4, paragraph 2, and the outcome of the consultations as referred to in Article 5.

2.   The Party of origin shall provide to the affected Party the final decision on the proposed activity along with the reasons and considerations on which it was based.

3.   If additional information on the significant transboundary impact of a proposed activity, which was not available at the time a decision was made with respect to that activity and which could have materially affected the decision, becomes available to a concerned Party before work on that activity commences, that Party shall immediately inform the other concerned Party or Parties. If one of the concerned Parties so requests, consultations shall be held as to whether the decision needs to be revised.

Article 7   POST-PROJECT ANALYSIS

1.   The concerned Parties, at the request of any such Party, shall determine whether, and if so to what extent, a post-project analysis shall be carried out, taking into account the likely significant adverse transboundary impact of the activity for which an environmental impact assessment has been undertaken pursuant to this Convention. Any post-project analysis undertaken shall include, in particular, the surveillance of the activity and the determination of any adverse transboundary impact. Such surveillance and determination may be undertaken with a view to achieving the objectives listed in Appendix V.

2.   When, as a result of post-project analysis, the Party of origin or the affected Party has reasonable grounds for concluding that there is a significant adverse transboundary impact or factors have been discovered which may result in such an impact, it shall immediately inform the other Party. The concerned Parties shall then consult on necessary measures to reduce or eliminate the impact.

Article 8   BILATERAL AND MULTILATERAL CO-OPERATION

The Parties may continue existing or enter into new bilateral or multilateral agreements or other arrangements in order to implement their obligations under this Convention. Such agreements or other arrangements may be based on the elements listed in Appendix VI.

Article 9   RESEARCH PROGRAMMES

The Parties shall give special consideration to the setting up, or intensification of, specific research programmes aimed at:

(a)   Improving existing qualitative and quantitative methods for assessing the impacts of proposed activities;

(b)   Achieving a better understanding of cause-effect relationships and their role in integrated environmental management;

(c)   Analysing and monitoring the efficient implementation of decisions on proposed activities with the intention of minimizing or preventing impacts;

(d)   Developing methods to stimulate creative approaches in the search for environmentally sound alternatives to proposed activities, production and consumption patterns;

(e)   Developing methodologies for the application of the principles of environmental impact assessment at the macro-economic level.

The results of the programmes listed above shall be exchanged by the Parties.

Article 10   STATUS OF THE APPENDICES

The Appendices attached to this Convention form an integral part of the Convention.

Article 11   MEETING OF PARTIES

1.   The Parties shall meet, so far as possible, in connection with the annual sessions of the Senior Advisers to ECE Governments on Environmental and Water Problems. The first meeting of the Parties shall be convened not later than one year after the date of the entry into force of this Convention. Thereafter, meetings of the Parties shall be held at such other times as may be deemed necessary by a meeting of the Parties, or at the written request of any Party, provided that, within six months of the request being communicated to them by the secretariat, it is supported by at least one third of the Parties.

2.   The Parties shall keep under continuous review the implementation of this Convention, and, with this purpose in mind, shall:

(a)   Review the policies and methodological approaches to environmental impact assessment by the Parties with a view to further improving environmental impact assessment procedures in a transboundary context;

(b)   Exchange information regarding experience gained in concluding and implementing bilateral and multilateral agreements or other arrangements regarding the use of environmental impact assessment in a transboundary context to which one or more of the Parties are party;

(c)   Seek, where appropriate, the services of competent international bodies and scientific committees in methodological and technical aspects pertinent to the achievement of the purposes of this Convention;

(d)   At their first meeting, consider and by consensus adopt rules of procedure for their meetings;

(e)   Consider and, where necessary, adopt proposals for amendments to this Convention;

(f)   Consider and undertake any additional action that may be required for the achievement of the purposes of this Convention.

Article 12   RIGHT TO VOTE

1.   Each Party to this Convention shall have one vote.

2.   Except as provided for in paragraph 1 of this Article, regional economic integration organizations, in matters within their competence, shall exercise their right to vote with a number of votes equal to the number of their member States which are Parties to this Convention. Such organizations shall not exercise their right to vote if their member States exercise theirs, and vice versa.

Article 13   SECRETARIAT

The Executive Secretary of the Economic Commission for Europe shall carry out the following secretariat functions:

(a)   The convening and preparing of meetings of the Parties;

(b)   The transmission of reports and other information received in accordance with the provisions of this Convention to the Parties; and

(c)   The performance of other functions as may be provided for in this Convention or as may be determined by the Parties.

Article 14   AMENDMENTS TO THE CONVENTION

1.   Any Party may propose amendments to this Convention.

2.   Proposed amendments shall be submitted in writing to the secretariat, which shall communicate them to all Parties. The proposed amendments shall be discussed at the next meeting of the Parties, provided these proposals have been circulated by the secretariat to the Parties at least ninety days in advance.

3.   The Parties shall make every effort to reach agreement on any proposed amendment to this Convention by consensus. If all efforts at consensus have been exhausted, and no agreement reached, the amendment shall as a last resort be adopted by a three-fourths majority vote of the Parties present and voting at the meeting.

4.   Amendments to this Convention adopted in accordance with paragraph 3 of this Article shall be submitted by the Depository to all Parties for ratification, approval or acceptance. They shall enter into force for Parties having ratified, approved or accepted them on the ninetieth day after the receipt by the Depositary of notification of their ratification, approval or acceptance by at least three fourths of these Parties. Thereafter they shall enter into force for any other Party on the ninetieth day after that Party deposits its instrument of ratification, approval or acceptance of the amendments.

5.   For the purpose of this Article, "Parties present and voting" means Parties present and casting an affirmative or negative vote.

6.   The voting procedure set forth in paragraph 3 of this Article is not intended to constitute a precedent for future agreements negotiated within the Economic Commission for Europe.

Article 15   SETTLEMENT OF DISPUTES

1.   If a dispute arises between two or more Parties about the interpretation or application of this Convention, they shall seek a solution by negotiation or by any other method of dispute settlement acceptable to the parties to the dispute.

2.   When signing, ratifying, accepting, approving or acceding to this Convention, or at any time thereafter, a Party may declare in writing to the Depositary that for a dispute not resolved in accordance with paragraph 1 of this Article, it accepts one or both of the following means of dispute settlement as compulsory in relation to any Party accepting the same obligation:

(a)   Submission of the dispute to the International Court of Justice;
(b)   Arbitration in accordance with the procedure set out in Appendix VII.

3.   If the parties to the dispute have accepted both means of dispute settlement referred to in paragraph 2 of this Article, the dispute may be submitted only to the International Court of Justice, unless the parties agree otherwise.

Article 16   SIGNATURE

This Convention shall be open for signature at Espoo (Finland) from 25 February to 1 March 1991 and thereafter at United Nations Headquarters in New York until 2 September 1991 by States members of the Economic Commission for Europe as well as States having consultative status with the Economic Commission for Europe pursuant to paragraph 8 of the Economic and Social Council resolution 36 (IV) of 28 March 1947, and by regional economic integration organizations constituted by sovereign States members of the Economic Commission for Europe to which their member States have transferred competence in respect of matters governed by this Convention, including the competence to enter into treaties in respect of these matters.

Article 17   RATIFICATION, ACCEPTANCE, APPROVAL AND ACCESSION

1.   This Convention shall be subject to ratification, acceptance or approval by signatory States and regional economic integration organizations.

2.   This Convention shall be open for accession as from 3 September 1991 by the States and organizations referred to in Article 16.

3.   The instruments of ratification, acceptance, approval or accession shall be deposited with the Secretary-General of the United Nations, who shall perform the functions of Depositary.

4.   Any organization referred to in Article 16 which becomes a Party to this Convention without any of its member States being a Party shall be bound by all the obligations under this Convention. In the case of such organizations, one or more of whose member States is a Party to this Convention, the organization and its member States shall decide on their respective responsibilities for the performance of their obligations under this Convention. In such cases, the organization and the member States shall not be entitled to exercise rights under this Convention concurrently.

5.   In their instruments of ratification, acceptance, approval or accession, the regional economic integration organizations referred to in Article 16 shall declare the extent of their competence with respect to the matters governed by this Convention. These organizations shall also inform the Depositary of any relevant modification to the extent of their competence.

Article 18   WITHDRAWAL

At any time after four years from the date on which this Convention has come into force with respect to a Party, that Party may withdraw from this Convention by giving written notification to the Depositary. Any such withdrawal shall take effect on the ninetieth day after the date of its receipt by the Depositary. Any such withdrawal shall not affect the application of Articles 3 to 6 of this Convention to a proposed activity in respect of which a notification has been made pursuant to Article 3, paragraph 1, or a request has been made pursuant to Article 3, paragraph 7, before such withdrawal took effect.

Article 19   WITHDRAWAL

At any time after four years from the date on which this Convention has come into force with respect to a Party, that Party may withdraw from this Convention by giving written notification to the Depositary. Any such withdrawal shall take effect on the ninetieth day after the date of its receipt by the Depositary. Any such withdrawal shall not affect the application of Articles 3 to 6 of this Convention to a proposed activity in respect of which a notification has been made pursuant to Article 3, paragraph 1, or a request has been made pursuant to Article 3, paragraph 7, before such withdrawal took effect.

Article 20   AUTHENTIC TEXTS

The original of this Convention, of which the English, French and Russian texts are equally authentic, shall be deposited with the Secretary-General of the United Nations.

IN WITNESS WHEREOF the undersigned, being duly authorized thereto, have signed this Convention.

DONE at Espoo (Finland), this twenty-fifth day of February one thousand nine hundred and ninety-one.

CONVENTION ON ACCESS TO INFORMATION, PUBLIC PARTICIPATION IN DECISIONMAKING AND ACCESS TO JUSTICE IN ENVIRONMENTAL MATTERS

Done at Aarhus, Denmark,
Signed: 25 June 1998

The Parties to this Convention,

Recalling principle 1 of the Stockholm Declaration on the Human Environment,

Recalling also principle 10 of the Rio Declaration on Environment and Development,

Recalling further General Assembly resolutions 37/7 of 28 October 1982 on the World Charter for Nature and 45/94 of 14 December 1990 on the need to ensure a healthy environment for the well-being of individuals,

Recalling the European Charter on Environment and Health adopted at the First European Conference on Environment and Health of the World Health Organization in Frankfurt-am-Main, Germany, on 8 December 1989,

Affirming the need to protect, preserve and improve the state of the environment and to ensure sustainable and environmentally sound development,

Recognizing that adequate protection of the environment is essential to human well-being and the enjoyment of basic human rights, including the right to life itself,

Recognizing also that every person has the right to live in an environment adequate to his or her health and well-being, and the duty, both individually and in association with others, to protect and improve the environment for the benefit of present and future generations,

Considering that, to be able to assert this right and observe this duty, citizens must have access to information, be entitled to participate in decision-making and have access to justice in environmental matters, and acknowledging in this regard that citizens may need assistance in order to exercise their rights,

Recognizing that, in the field of the environment, improved access to information and public participation in decision-making enhance the quality and the implementation of decisions, contribute to public awareness of environmental issues, give the public the opportunity to express its concerns and enable public authorities to take due account of such concerns,

Aiming thereby to further the accountability of and transparency in decision-making and to strengthen public support for decisions on the environment,

Recognizing the desirability of transparency in all branches of government and inviting legislative bodies to implement the principles of this Convention in their proceedings,

Recognizing also that the public needs to be aware of the procedures for participation in environmental decision-making, have free access to them and know how to use them,

Recognizing further the importance of the respective roles that individual citizens, non-governmental organizations and the private sector can play in environmental protection,

Desiring to promote environmental education to further the understanding of the environment and sustainable development and to encourage widespread public awareness of, and participation in, decisions affecting the environment and sustainable development,

Noting, in this context, the importance of making use of the media and of electronic or other, future forms of communication,

Recognizing the importance of fully integrating environmental considerations in governmental decision-making and the consequent need for public authorities to be in possession of accurate, comprehensive and up-to- date environmental information,

Acknowledging that public authorities hold environmental information in the public interest,

Concerned that effective judicial mechanisms should be accessible to the public, including organizations, so that its legitimate interests are protected and the law is enforced,

Noting the importance of adequate product information being provided to consumers to enable them to make informed environmental choices,

Recognizing the concern of the public about the deliberate release of genetically modified organisms into the environment and the need for increased transparency and greater public participation in decision-making in this field,

Convinced that the implementation of this Convention will contribute to strengthening democracy in the region of the United Nations Economic Commission for Europe (ECE),

Conscious of the role played in this respect by ECE and recalling, inter alia, the ECE Guidelines on Access to Environmental Information and Public Participation in Environmental Decision-making endorsed in the Ministerial Declaration adopted at the Third Ministerial Conference "Environment for Europe" in Sofia, Bulgaria, on 25 October 1995,

Bearing in mind the relevant provisions in the Convention on Environmental Impact Assessment in a Transboundary Context, done at Espoo, Finland, on 25 February 1991, and the Convention on the Transboundary Effects of Industrial Accidents and the Convention on the Protection and Use of Transboundary Watercourses and International Lakes, both done at Helsinki on 17 March 1992, and other regional Conventions,

Conscious that the adoption of this Convention will have contributed to the further strengthening of the "Environment for Europe" process and to the results of the Fourth Ministerial Conference in Aarhus, Denmark, in June 1998,

Have agreed as follows:

Article 1
OBJECTIVE

In order to contribute to the protection of the right of every person of present and future generations to live in an environment adequate to his or her health and well-being, each Party shall guarantee the rights of access to information, public participation in decision-making, and access to justice in environmental matters in accordance with the provisions of this Convention.

Article 2
DEFINITIONS

For the purposes of this Convention,

1. "Party" means, unless the text otherwise indicates, a Contracting Party to this Convention;

2. "Public authority" means:
    (a) Government at national, regional and other level;
    (b) Natural or legal persons performing public administrative functions under national law, including specific duties, activities or services in relation to the environment;
    (c) Any other natural or legal persons having public responsibilities or functions, or providing public

services, in relation to the environment, under the control of a body or person falling within subparagraphs (a) or (b) above;

(d) The institutions of any regional economic integration organization referred to in article 17 which is a Party to this Convention. This definition does not include bodies or institutions acting in a judicial or legislative capacity;

3. "Environmental information" means any information in written, visual, aural, electronic or any other material form on:

(a) The state of elements of the environment, such as air and atmosphere, water, soil, land, landscape and natural sites, biological diversity and its components, including genetically modified organisms, and the interaction among these elements;

(b) Factors, such as substances, energy, noise and radiation, and activities or measures, including administrative measures, environmental agreements, policies, legislation, plans and programmes, affecting or likely to affect the elements of the environment within the scope of subparagraph (a) above, and cost-benefit and other economic analyses and assumptions used in environmental decision-making;

(c) The state of human health and safety, conditions of human life, cultural sites and built structures, inasmuch as they are or may be affected by the state of the elements of the environment or, through these elements, by the factors, activities or measures referred to in subparagraph (b) above;

4. "The public" means one or more natural or legal persons, and, in accordance with national legislation or practice, their associations, organizations or groups;

5. "The public concerned" means the public affected or likely to be affected by, or having an interest in, the environmental decision-making; for the purposes of this definition, non-governmental organizations promoting environmental protection and meeting any requirements under national law shall be deemed to have an interest.

Article 3
GENERAL PROVISIONS

1. Each Party shall take the necessary legislative, regulatory and other measures, including measures to achieve compatibility between the provisions implementing the information, public participation and access-to-justice provisions in this Convention, as well as proper enforcement measures, to establish and maintain a clear, transparent and consistent framework to implement the provisions of this Convention.

2. Each Party shall endeavour to ensure that officials and authorities assist and provide guidance to the public in seeking access to information, in facilitating participation in decision-making and in seeking access to justice in environmental matters.

3. Each Party shall promote environmental education and environmental awareness among the public, especially on how to obtain access to information, to participate in decision-making and to obtain access to justice in environmental matters.

4. Each Party shall provide for appropriate recognition of and support to associations, organizations or groups promoting environmental protection and ensure that its national legal system is consistent with this obligation.

5. The provisions of this Convention shall not affect the right of a Party to maintain or introduce measures providing for broader access to information, more extensive public participation in decision-making and wider access to justice in environmental matters than required by this Convention.

6. This Convention shall not require any derogation from existing rights of access to information, public participation in decision-making and access to justice in environmental matters.

7. Each Party shall promote the application of the principles of this Convention in international environmental decision-making processes and within the framework of international organizations in matters relating to the environment.

8. Each Party shall ensure that persons exercising their rights in conformity with the provisions of this Convention shall not be penalized, persecuted or harassed in any way for their involvement. This provision shall not affect the powers of national courts to award reasonable costs in judicial proceedings.

9. Within the scope of the relevant provisions of this Convention, the public shall have access to information, have the possibility to participate in decision-making and have access to justice in environmental matters without discrimination as to citizenship, nationality or domicile and, in the case of a legal person, without discrimination as to where it has its registered seat or an effective centre of its activities.

Article 4
ACCESS TO ENVIRONMENTAL INFORMATION

1. Each Party shall ensure that, subject to the following paragraphs of this article, public authorities, in response to a request for environmental information, make such information available to the public, within the framework of national legislation, including, where requested and subject to subparagraph (b) below, copies of the actual documentation containing or comprising such information:

(a) Without an interest having to be stated;
(b) In the form requested unless:
     (i) It is reasonable for the public authority to make it available in another form, in which case reasons shall be given for making it available in that form; or
     (ii) The information is already publicly available in another form.

2. The environmental information referred to in paragraph 1 above shall be made available as soon as possible and at the latest within one month after the request has been submitted, unless the volume and the complexity of the information justify an extension of this period up to two months after the request. The applicant shall be informed of any extension and of the reasons justifying it.

3. A request for environmental information may be refused if:

(a) The public authority to which the request is addressed does not hold the environmental information requested;
(b) The request is manifestly unreasonable or formulated in too general a manner; or
(c) The request concerns material in the course of completion or concerns internal communications of public authorities where such an exemption is provided for in national law or customary practice, taking into account the public interest served by disclosure.

4. A request for environmental information may be refused if the disclosure would adversely affect:

(a) The confidentiality of the proceedings of public authorities, where such confidentiality is provided for under national law;
(b) International relations, national defence or public security;
(c) The course of justice, the ability of a person to receive a fair trial or the ability of a public authority to conduct an enquiry of a criminal or disciplinary nature;
(d) The confidentiality of commercial and industrial information, where such confidentiality is protected by law in order to protect a legitimate economic interest. Within this framework, information on emissions which is relevant for the protection of the environment shall be disclosed;
(e) Intellectual property rights;
(f) The confidentiality of personal data and/or files relating to a natural person where that person has not consented to the disclosure of the information to the public, where such confidentiality is provided for in national law;
(g) The interests of a third party which has supplied the information requested without that party being under or capable of being put under a legal obligation to do so, and where that party does not consent to the release of the material; or

(h) The environment to which the information relates, such as the breeding sites of rare species.

The aforementioned grounds for refusal shall be interpreted in a restrictive way, taking into account the public interest served by disclosure and taking into account whether the information requested relates to emissions into the environment.

5. Where a public authority does not hold the environmental information requested, this public authority shall, as promptly as possible, inform the applicant of the public authority to which it believes it is possible to apply for the information requested or transfer the request to that authority and inform the applicant accordingly.

6. Each Party shall ensure that, if information exempted from disclosure under paragraphs 3 (c) and 4 above can be separated out without prejudice to the confidentiality of the information exempted, public authorities make available the remainder of the environmental information that has been requested.

7. A refusal of a request shall be in writing if the request was in writing or the applicant so requests. A refusal shall state the reasons for the refusal and give information on access to the review procedure provided for in accordance with article 9. The refusal shall be made as soon as possible and at the latest within one month, unless the complexity of the information justifies an extension of this period up to two months after the request. The applicant shall be informed of any extension and of the reasons justifying it.

8. Each Party may allow its public authorities to make a charge for supplying information, but such charge shall not exceed a reasonable amount. Public authorities intending to make such a charge for supplying information shall make available to applicants a schedule of charges which may be levied, indicating the circumstances in which they may be levied or waived and when the supply of information is conditional on the advance payment of such a charge.

Article 5
COLLECTION AND DISSEMINATION OF ENVIRONMENTAL INFORMATION

1. Each Party shall ensure that:
    (a) Public authorities possess and update environmental information which is relevant to their functions;

    (b) Mandatory systems are established so that there is an adequate flow of information to public authorities about proposed and existing activities which may significantly affect the environment;

    (c) In the event of any imminent threat to human health or the environment, whether caused by human activities or due to natural causes, all information which could enable the public to take measures to prevent or mitigate harm arising from the threat and is held by a public authority is disseminated immediately and without delay to members of the public who may be affected.

2. Each Party shall ensure that, within the framework of national legislation, the way in which public authorities make environmental information available to the public is transparent and that environmental information is effectively accessible, inter alia, by:

    (a) Providing sufficient information to the public about the type and scope of environmental information held by the relevant public authorities, the basic terms and conditions under which such information is made available and accessible, and the process by which it can be obtained;

    (b) Establishing and maintaining practical arrangements, such as:
        (i) Publicly accessible lists, registers or files;
        (ii) Requiring officials to support the public in seeking access to information under this Convention; and
        (iii) The identification of points of contact; and
    (c) Providing access to the environmental information contained in lists, registers or files as referred to in subparagraph (b) (i) above free of charge.

3. Each Party shall ensure that environmental information progressively becomes available in electronic databases which are easily accessible to the public through public telecommunications networks. Information accessible in this

form should include:

(a) Reports on the state of the environment, as referred to in paragraph 4 below;

(b) Texts of legislation on or relating to the environment;

(c) As appropriate, policies, plans and programmes on or relating to the environment, and environmental agreements; and

(d) Other information, to the extent that the availability of such information in this form would facilitate the application of national law implementing this Convention, provided that such information is already available in electronic form.

4. Each Party shall, at regular intervals not exceeding three or four years, publish and disseminate a national report on the state of the environment, including information on the quality of the environment and information on pressures on the environment.

5. Each Party shall take measures within the framework of its legislation for the purpose of disseminating, inter alia:

(a) Legislation and policy documents such as documents on strategies, policies, programmes and action plans relating to the environment, and progress reports on their implementation, prepared at various levels of government;

(b) International treaties, Conventions and agreements on environmental issues; and

(c) Other significant international documents on environmental issues, as appropriate.

6. Each Party shall encourage operators whose activities have a significant impact on the environment to inform the public regularly of the environmental impact of their activities and products, where appropriate within the framework of voluntary eco-labelling or eco-auditing schemes or by other means.

7. Each Party shall:

(a) Publish the facts and analyses of facts which it considers relevant and important in framing major environmental policy proposals;

(b) Publish, or otherwise make accessible, available explanatory material on its dealings with the public in matters falling within the scope of this Convention; and

(c) Provide in an appropriate form information on the performance of public functions or the provision of public services relating to the environment by government at all levels.

8. Each Party shall develop mechanisms with a view to ensuring that sufficient product information is made available to the public in a manner which enables consumers to make informed environmental choices.

9. Each Party shall take steps to establish progressively, taking into account international processes where appropriate, a coherent, nationwide system of pollution inventories or registers on a structured, computerized and publicly accessible database compiled through standardized reporting. Such a system may include inputs, releases and transfers of a specified range of substances and products, including water, energy and resource use, from a specified range of activities to environmental media and to on-site and off-site treatment and disposal sites.

10. Nothing in this article may prejudice the right of Parties to refuse to disclose certain environmental information in accordance with article 4, paragraphs 3 and 4.

Article 6
PUBLIC PARTICIPATION IN DECISIONS ON SPECIFIC ACTIVITIES

1. Each Party:

(a) Shall apply the provisions of this article with respect to decisions on whether to permit proposed activities listed in annex I;

(b) Shall, in accordance with its national law, also apply the provisions of this article to decisions on proposed activities not listed in annex I which may have a significant effect on the environment. To this end, Parties shall determine whether such a proposed activity is subject to these provisions; and

(c) May decide, on a case-by-case basis if so provided under national law, not to apply the provisions of this article to proposed activities serving national defence purposes, if that Party deems that such application would have an adverse effect on these purposes.

2. The public concerned shall be informed, either by public notice or individually as appropriate, early in an environmental decision-making procedure, and in an adequate, timely and effective manner, inter alia, of:

(a) The proposed activity and the application on which a decision will be taken;

(b) The nature of possible decisions or the draft decision;

(c) The public authority responsible for making the decision;

(d) The envisaged procedure, including, as and when this information can be provided:

(i) The commencement of the procedure;
(ii) The opportunities for the public to participate;
(iii) The time and venue of any envisaged public hearing;
(iv) An indication of the public authority from which relevant information can be obtained and where the relevant information has been deposited for examination by the public;
(v) An indication of the relevant public authority or any other official body to which comments or questions can be submitted and of the time schedule for transmittal of comments or questions; and
(vi) An indication of what environmental information relevant to the proposed activity is available; and

(e) The fact that the activity is subject to a national or transboundary environmental impact assessment procedure.

3. The public participation procedures shall include reasonable time-frames for the different phases, allowing sufficient time for informing the public in accordance with paragraph 2 above and for the public to prepare and participate effectively during the environmental decision-making.

4. Each Party shall provide for early public participation, when all options are open and effective public participation can take place.

5. Each Party should, where appropriate, encourage prospective applicants to identify the public concerned, to enter into discussions, and to provide information regarding the objectives of their application before applying for a permit.

6. Each Party shall require the competent public authorities to give the public concerned access for examination, upon request where so required under national law, free of charge and as soon as it becomes available, to all information relevant to the decision-making referred to in this article that is available at the time of the public participation procedure, without prejudice to the right of Parties to refuse to disclose certain information in accordance with article 4, paragraphs 3 and 4. The relevant information shall include at least, and without prejudice to the provisions of article 4:

(a) A description of the site and the physical and technical characteristics of the proposed activity, including an estimate of the expected residues and emissions;

(b) A description of the significant effects of the proposed activity on the environment;

(c) A description of the measures envisaged to prevent and/or reduce the effects, including emissions;

(d) A non-technical summary of the above;

(e) An outline of the main alternatives studied by the applicant; and

(f) In accordance with national legislation, the main reports and advice issued to the public authority at the time when the public concerned shall be informed in accordance with paragraph 2 above.

7. Procedures for public participation shall allow the public to submit, in writing or, as appropriate, at a public hearing or inquiry with the applicant, any comments, information, analyses or opinions that it considers relevant to the proposed activity.

8. Each Party shall ensure that in the decision due account is taken of the outcome of the public participation.

9. Each Party shall ensure that, when the decision has been taken by the public authority, the public is promptly informed of the decision in accordance with the appropriate procedures. Each Party shall make accessible to the public the text of the decision along with the reasons and considerations on which the decision is based.

10. Each Party shall ensure that, when a public authority reconsiders or updates the operating conditions for an activity referred to in paragraph 1, the provisions of paragraphs 2 to 9 of this article are applied mutatis mutandis, and where appropriate.

11. Each Party shall, within the framework of its national law, apply, to the extent feasible and appropriate, provisions of this article to decisions on whether to permit the deliberate release of genetically modified organisms into the environment.

Article 7
PUBLIC PARTICIPATION CONCERNING PLANS, PROGRAMMES AND POLICIES RELATING TO THE ENVIRONMENT

Each Party shall make appropriate practical and/or other provisions for the public to participate during the preparation of plans and programmes relating to the environment, within a transparent and fair framework, having provided the necessary information to the public. Within this framework, article 6, paragraphs 3, 4 and 8, shall be applied. The public which may participate shall be identified by the relevant public authority, taking into account the objectives of this Convention. To the extent appropriate, each Party shall endeavour to provide opportunities for public participation in the preparation of policies relating to the environment.

Article 8
PUBLIC PARTICIPATION DURING THE PREPARATION OF EXECUTIVE REGULATIONS AND/OR GENERALLY APPLICABLE LEGALLY BINDING NORMATIVE INSTRUMENTS

Each Party shall strive to promote effective public participation at an appropriate stage, and while options are still open, during the preparation by public authorities of executive regulations and other generally applicable legally binding rules that may have a significant effect on the environment. To this end, the following steps should be taken:

(a) Time-frames sufficient for effective participation should be fixed;

(b) Draft rules should be published or otherwise made publicly available; and

(c) The public should be given the opportunity to comment, directly or through representative consultative bodies.

The result of the public participation shall be taken into account as far as possible.

Article 9
ACCESS TO JUSTICE

1. Each Party shall, within the framework of its national legislation, ensure that any person who considers that his or her request for information under article 4 has been ignored, wrongfully refused, whether in part or in full, inadequately answered, or otherwise not dealt with in accordance with the provisions of that article, has access to a review procedure before a court of law or another independent and impartial body established by law. In the circumstances where a Party provides for such a review by a court of law, it shall ensure that such a person also has access to an expeditious procedure established by law that is free of charge or inexpensive for reconsideration by a public authority or review by an independent and impartial body other than a court of law. Final decisions under this paragraph 1 shall be binding on the public authority holding the information. Reasons shall be stated in writing, at least where access to information is refused under this paragraph.

2. Each Party shall, within the framework of its national legislation, ensure that members of the public concerned

      (a) Having a sufficient interest or, alternatively,

      (b) Maintaining impairment of a right, where the administrative procedural law of a Party requires this as a precondition, have access to a review procedure before a court of law and/or another independent and impartial body established by law, to challenge the substantive and procedural legality of any decision, act or omission subject to the provisions of article 6 and, where so provided for under national law and without prejudice to paragraph 3 below, of other relevant provisions of this Convention. What constitutes a sufficient interest and impairment of a right shall be determined in accordance with the requirements of national law and consistently with the objective of giving the public concerned wide access to justice within the scope of this Convention. To this end, the interest of any non-governmental organization meeting the requirements referred to in article 2, paragraph 5, shall be deemed sufficient for the purpose of subparagraph (a) above. Such organizations shall also be deemed to have rights capable of being impaired for the purpose of subparagraph (b) above. The provisions of this paragraph 2 shall not exclude the possibility of a preliminary review procedure before an administrative authority and shall not affect the requirement of exhaustion of administrative review procedures prior to recourse to judicial review procedures, where such a requirement exists under national law.

3. In addition and without prejudice to the review procedures referred to in paragraphs 1 and 2 above, each Party shall ensure that, where they meet the criteria, if any, laid down in its national law, members of the public have access to administrative or judicial procedures to challenge acts and omissions by private persons and public authorities which contravene provisions of its national law relating to the environment.

4. In addition and without prejudice to paragraph 1 above, the procedures referred to in paragraphs 1, 2 and 3 above shall provide adequate and effective remedies, including injunctive relief as appropriate, and be fair, equitable, timely and not prohibitively expensive. Decisions under this article shall be given or recorded in writing. Decisions of courts, and whenever possible of other bodies, shall be publicly accessible.

5. In order to further the effectiveness of the provisions of this article, each Party shall ensure that information is provided to the public on access to administrative and judicial review procedures and shall consider the establishment of appropriate assistance mechanisms to remove or reduce financial and other barriers to access to justice.

Article 10
MEETING OF THE PARTIES

1. The first meeting of the Parties shall be convened no later than one year after the date of the entry into force of this Convention. Thereafter, an ordinary meeting of the Parties shall be held at least once every two years, unless otherwise decided by the Parties, or at the written request of any Party, provided that, within six months of the request being communicated to all Parties by the Executive Secretary of the Economic Commission for Europe, the said request is supported by at least one third of the Parties.

2. At their meetings, the Parties shall keep under continuous review the implementation of this Convention on the basis of regular reporting by the Parties, and, with this purpose in mind, shall:

(a) Review the policies for and legal and methodological approaches to access to information, public participation in decision-making and access to justice in environmental matters, with a view to further improving them;

(b) Exchange information regarding experience gained in concluding and implementing bilateral and multilateral agreements or other arrangements having relevance to the purposes of this Convention and to which one or more of the Parties are a party;

(c) Seek, where appropriate, the services of relevant ECE bodies and other competent international bodies and specific committees in all aspects pertinent to the achievement of the purposes of this Convention;

(d) Establish any subsidiary bodies as they deem necessary;

(e) Prepare, where appropriate, protocols to this Convention;

(f) Consider and adopt proposals for amendments to this Convention in accordance with the provisions of article 14;

(g) Consider and undertake any additional action that may be required for the achievement of the purposes of this Convention;

(h) At their first meeting, consider and by consensus adopt rules of procedure for their meetings and the meetings of subsidiary bodies;

(i) At their first meeting, review their experience in implementing the provisions of article 5, paragraph 9, and consider what steps are necessary to develop further the system referred to in that paragraph, taking into account international processes and developments, including the elaboration of an appropriate instrument concerning pollution release and transfer registers or inventories which could be annexed to this Convention.

3. The Meeting of the Parties may, as necessary, consider establishing financial arrangements on a consensus basis.

4. The United Nations, its specialized agencies and the International Atomic Energy Agency, as well as any State or regional economic integration organization entitled under article 17 to sign this Convention but which is not a Party to this Convention, and any intergovernmental organization qualified in the fields to which this Convention relates, shall be entitled to participate as observers in the meetings of the Parties.

5. Any non-governmental organization, qualified in the fields to which this Convention relates, which has informed the Executive Secretary of the Economic Commission for Europe of its wish to be represented at a meeting of the Parties shall be entitled to participate as an observer unless at least one third of the Parties present in the meeting raise objections.

6. For the purposes of paragraphs 4 and 5 above, the rules of procedure referred to in paragraph 2 (h) above shall provide for practical arrangements for the admittance procedure and other relevant terms.

Article 11
RIGHT TO VOTE

1. Except as provided for in paragraph 2 below, each Party to this Convention shall have one vote.

2. Regional economic integration organizations, in matters within their competence, shall exercise their right to vote with a number of votes equal to the number of their member States which are Parties to this Convention. Such organizations shall not exercise their right to vote if their member States exercise theirs, and vice versa.

Article 12
SECRETARIAT

The Executive Secretary of the Economic Commission for Europe shall carry out the following secretariat functions:

(a) The convening and preparing of meetings of the Parties;

(b) The transmission to the Parties of reports and other information received in accordance with the provisions of this Convention; and

(c) Such other functions as may be determined by the Parties.

Article 13
ANNEXES

The annexes to this Convention shall constitute an integral part thereof.

Article 14
AMENDMENTS TO THE CONVENTION

1. Any Party may propose amendments to this Convention.

2. The text of any proposed amendment to this Convention shall be submitted in writing to the Executive Secretary of the Economic Commission for Europe, who shall communicate it to all Parties at least ninety days before the meeting of the Parties at which it is proposed for adoption.

3. The Parties shall make every effort to reach agreement on any proposed amendment to this Convention by consensus. If all efforts at consensus have been exhausted, and no agreement reached, the amendment shall as a last resort be adopted by a three-fourths majority vote of the Parties present and voting at the meeting.

4. Amendments to this Convention adopted in accordance with paragraph 3 above shall be communicated by the Depositary to all Parties for ratification, approval or acceptance. Amendments to this Convention other than those to an annex shall enter into force for Parties having ratified, approved or accepted them on the ninetieth day after the receipt by the Depositary of notification of their ratification, approval or acceptance by at least three fourths of these Parties. Thereafter they shall enter into force for any other Party on the ninetieth day after that Party deposits its instrument of ratification, approval or acceptance of the amendments.

5. Any Party that is unable to approve an amendment to an annex to this Convention shall so notify the Depositary in writing within twelve months from the date of the communication of the adoption. The Depositary shall without delay notify all Parties of any such notification received. A Party may at any time substitute an acceptance for its previous notification and, upon deposit of an instrument of acceptance with the Depositary, the amendments to such an annex shall become effective for that Party.

6. On the expiry of twelve months from the date of its communication by the Depositary as provided for in paragraph 4 above an amendment to an annex shall become effective for those Parties which have not submitted a notification to the Depositary in accordance with the provisions of paragraph 5 above, provided that not more than one third of the Parties have submitted such a notification.

7. For the purposes of this article, "Parties present and voting" means Parties present and casting an affirmative or negative vote.

Article 15
REVIEW OF COMPLIANCE

The Meeting of the Parties shall establish, on a consensus basis, optional arrangements of a non-confrontational, non-judicial and consultative nature for reviewing compliance with the provisions of this Convention. These arrangements shall allow for appropriate public involvement and may include the option of considering communications from members of the public on matters related to this Convention.

Article 16
SETTLEMENT OF DISPUTES

1. If a dispute arises between two or more Parties about the interpretation or application of this Convention, they shall seek a solution by negotiation or by any other means of dispute settlement acceptable to the parties to the dispute.

2. When signing, ratifying, accepting, approving or acceding to this Convention, or at any time thereafter, a Party may declare in writing to the Depositary that, for a dispute not resolved in accordance with paragraph 1 above, it accepts one or both of the following means of dispute settlement as compulsory in relation to any Party accepting the same obligation:

(a) Submission of the dispute to the International Court of Justice;

(b) Arbitration in accordance with the procedure set out in annex II.

3. If the parties to the dispute have accepted both means of dispute settlement referred to in paragraph 2 above, the dispute may be submitted only to the International Court of Justice, unless the parties agree otherwise.

Article 17
SIGNATURE

This Convention shall be open for signature at Aarhus (Denmark) on 25 June 1998, and thereafter at United Nations Headquarters in New York until 21 December 1998, by States members of the Economic Commission for Europe as well as States having consultative status with the Economic Commission for Europe pursuant to paragraphs 8 and 11 of Economic and Social Council resolution 36 (IV) of 28 March 1947, and by regional economic integration organizations constituted by sovereign States members of the Economic Commission for Europe to which their member States have transferred competence over matters governed by this Convention, including the competence to enter into treaties in respect of these matters.

Article 18
DEPOSITARY

The Secretary-General of the United Nations shall act as the Depositary of this Convention.

Article 19
RATIFICATION, ACCEPTANCE, APPROVAL AND ACCESSION

1. This Convention shall be subject to ratification, acceptance or approval by signatory States and regional economic integration organizations.

2. This Convention shall be open for accession as from 22 December 1998 by the States and regional economic integration organizations referred to in article 17.

3. Any other State, not referred to in paragraph 2 above, that is a Member of the United Nations may accede to the Convention upon approval by the Meeting of the Parties.

4. Any organization referred to in article 17 which becomes a Party to this Convention without any of its member States being a Party shall be bound by all the obligations under this Convention. If one or more of such an

organization's member States is a Party to this Convention, the organization and its member States shall decide on their respective responsibilities for the performance of their obligations under this Convention. In such cases, the organization and the member States shall not be entitled to exercise rights under this Convention concurrently.

5. In their instruments of ratification, acceptance, approval or accession, the regional economic integration organizations referred to in article 17 shall declare the extent of their competence with respect to the matters governed by this Convention. These organizations shall also inform the Depositary of any substantial modification to the extent of their competence.

Article 20
ENTRY INTO FORCE

1. This Convention shall enter into force on the ninetieth day after the date of deposit of the sixteenth instrument of ratification, acceptance, approval or accession.

2. For the purposes of paragraph 1 above, any instrument deposited by a regional economic integration organization shall not be counted as additional to those deposited by States members of such an organization.

3. For each State or organization referred to in article 17 which ratifies, accepts or approves this Convention or accedes thereto after the deposit of the sixteenth instrument of ratification, acceptance, approval or accession, the Convention shall enter into force on the ninetieth day after the date of deposit by such State or organization of its instrument of ratification, acceptance, approval or accession.

Article 21
WITHDRAWAL

At any time after three years from the date on which this Convention has come into force with respect to a Party, that Party may withdraw from the Convention by giving written notification to the Depositary. Any such withdrawal shall take effect on the ninetieth day after the date of its receipt by the Depositary.

Article 22
AUTHENTIC TEXTS

The original of this Convention, of which the English, French and Russian texts are equally authentic, shall be deposited with the Secretary-General of the United Nations.

IN WITNESS WHEREOF the undersigned, being duly authorized thereto, have signed this Convention.
DONE at Aarhus (Denmark), this twenty-fifth day of June, one thousand nine hundred and ninety-eight.

Annex I
LIST OF ACTIVITIES REFERRED TO IN ARTICLE 6, PARAGRAPH 1 (a)
(Omitted)

Annex II
ARBITRATION
(Omitted)

CONVENTION ON LONG-RANGE TRANSBOUNDARY AIR POLLUTION

18 I.L.M.1442 (1979); 1302 U.N.T.S. 217
Signed: November 13, 1979
Entered Into Force: March 16, 1983
Secretariat Homepage: www.unece.org/env/lrtap/lrtap_h1.htm

The Parties to the present Convention,

Determined to promote relations and cooperation in the field of environmental protection,

Aware of the significance of the activities of the United Nations Economic Commission for Europe in strengthening such relations and co-operation, particularly in the field of air pollution including long-range transport of air pollutants,

Recognizing the contribution of the Economic Commission for Europe to the multilateral implementation of the pertinent provisions of the Final Act of the Conference on Security and Cooperating in Europe,

Cognizant of the references in the chapter on environment of the Final Act of the Conference on Security and Co-operation in Europe calling for co-operation to control air pollution and its effects, including long-range transport of air pollutants, and to the development through international co-operation of an extensive programme for the monitoring and evaluation of long-range transport of air pollutants, starting with sulphur dioxide and with possible extension to other pollutants,

Considering the pertinent provisions of the Declaration of the United Nations Conference on the Human Environment, and in particular principle 21, which expresses the common conviction that States have, in accordance with the Charter of the United Nations and the principles of international law, the sovereign right to exploit their own resources pursuant to their own environmental policies, and the responsibility to ensure that activities within their jurisdiction or control do not cause damage to the environment of other States or of areas beyond the limits of national jurisdiction,

Recognizing the existence of possible adverse effects, in the short and long term, of air pollution including transboundary air pollution,

Concerned that a rise in the level of emission of air pollutants within the region as forecast may increase such adverse effects,

Recognizing the need to study the implications of the long-range transport of air pollutants and the need to seek solutions for the problems identified,

Affirming their willingness to reinforce active international co-operation to develop appropriate national policies and by means of exchange of information, consultation, research and monitoring, to co-ordinate national action for combating air pollution including long-range transboundary air pollution,

Have agreed as follows:

Article 1   **Definitions**

For the purpose of the present Convention:

a) "air pollution" means the introduction by man, directly or indirectly, of substances or energy into the air resulting in deleterious effects of such a nature as to endanger human health, harm living resources and ecosystems and material property and impair or interfere with amenities and other legitimate uses of the environment, and "air pollutants" shall be construed accordingly;

b) "long-range transboundary air pollution" means air pollution whose physical origin is situated wholly or in part within the area under the national jurisdiction of one State and which has adverse effects in the area under the jurisdiction of another State at such a distance that it is not generally possible to distinguish the contribution of individual emission sources or groups of sources.

Article 2   Fundamental Principles

The Contracting Parties, taking due account of the facts and problems involved, are determined to protect man and his environment against air pollution and shall endeavour to limit and, as far as possible, gradually reduce and prevent air pollution including long-range transboundary pollution.

Article 3

The Contracting Parties, within the framework of the present Convention, shall by means of exchanges of information, consultation, research and monitoring, develop without undue delay policies and strategies which shall serve as a means of combating the discharge of air pollutants, taking into account efforts already made at national and international levels.

Article 4

The Contracting Parties shall exchange information on and review their policies, scientific activities and technical measures aimed at combating, as far as possible, the discharge of air pollutants, which may have adverse effects, thereby contributing to the reduction of air pollution including long-range transboundary air pollution.

Article 5

Consultations shall be held, upon request, at an early stage between, on the one hand, Contracting Parties which are actually affected by or exposed to a significant risk of long-range transboundary air pollution and, on the other hand, Contracting Parties within which and subject to whose jurisdiction a significant contribution to long-range transboundary air pollution originates, or could originate, in connection with activities carried on or contemplated therein.

Article 6   Air Quality Management

Taking into account articles 2 to 5, the ongoing research, exchange of information and monitoring and the results thereof, the cost and effectiveness of local and other remedies and, in order to combat air pollution, in particular that originates from new or rebuilt installations, each Contracting Party undertakes to develop the best policies and strategies including air quality management systems, and, as part of them, control measures compatible with balanced development, in particular by using the best available technology which is economically feasible and low- and non-waste technology.

Article 7   Research and Development

The Contracting Parties, as appropriate to their needs, shall initiate and co-operate in the conduct of research into and/or development of:

a) existing and proposed technologies for reducing emissions of sulphur compounds and other major air pollutants, including technical and economic feasibility, and environmental consequences;

b) instrumentation and other techniques for monitoring and measuring emission rates and ambient concentrations of air pollutants;

c) improved models for a better understanding of the transmission of long-range transboundary air pollutants;

d) the effects of sulphur compounds and other major air pollutants on human health and the environment, including agriculture, forestry, materials, aquatic and other natural ecosystems and visibility, with a view to establishing a scientific basis for dose/effect relationships designed to protect the environment;

e) the economic, social and environmental assessment of alternative measures for attaining environmental objectives including the reduction of long-range transboundary air pollution;

f) education and training programmes related to the environmental aspects of pollution by sulphur compounds and other major air pollutants.

Article 8   **Exchange of Information**

The Contracting Parties, within the framework of the Executive Body referred to in article 10 and bilaterally, shall, in their common interests, exchange available information on:

a) data on emission at periods of time to be agreed upon, of agreed air pollutants, starting with sulphur dioxide,

coming from grid-units of agreed size; or on the fluxes of agreed air pollutants, starting with sulphur dioxide, across national borders, at distances and at periods of time to be agreed upon;

b) major changes in national policies and in general industrial development, and their potential impact, which would be likely to cause significant changes in long-range transboundary air pollution;

c) control technologies for reducing air pollution relevant to long-range transboundary air pollution;

d) the projected cost of the emission control or sulphur compounds and other major air pollutants on a national scale;

e) meteorological and physico-chemical data relating to the processes during transmission;

f) physico-chemical and biological data relating to the effects of long-range transboundary air pollution and the extent of the damage which these data indicate can be attributed to long-range transboundary air pollution;

g) national, subregional and regional policies and strategies for the control of sulphur compounds and other major oil pollutants.

Article 9   **Implementation and Further Development of the Cooperative Programme for the Monitoring and Evaluation of the Long-Range Transmission of Air Pollutants in Europe**

The Contracting Parties stress the need for the implementation of the existing "Co-operative programme for the monitoring and evaluation of the long-range transmission of air pollutants in Europe" (hereinafter referred to as EMEP) and with regard to the further development of this programme, agree to emphasize:

a) the desirability of Contracting Parties joining in and fully implementing EMEP which, as a first step, is based on the monitoring of sulphur dioxide and related substances;

b) the need to use comparable or standardized procedures for monitoring whenever possible;

c) the desirability of basing the monitoring programme on the framework of both national and international programmes. The establishment of monitoring stations and the collection of data shall be carried out under the national jurisdiction of the country in which the monitoring stations are located;

d) the desirability of establishing a framework for a co-operative environmental monitoring programme, based on and taking into account present and future national, subregional, regional and other international programmes;

e) the need to exchange data on emissions at periods of time to be agreed upon, of agreed air pollutants, starting with sulphur dioxide, coming from grid-units of agreed size; or on the fluxes of agreed air pollutants, starting with sulphur dioxide, across national borders, at distances and at periods of time to be agreed upon. The method including the model, used to determine the fluxes as well as the method, including the model, used to determine the transmission of air pollutants, based on the emissions per grid-unit, shall be made available and periodically reviewed, in order to improve the methods and the models;

f) their willingness to continue the exchange and periodic updating of national data on total emissions of agreed air pollutants, starting with sulphur dioxide;

g) the need to provide meteorological and physico-chemical data relating to processes during transmission;

h) the need to monitor chemical components in other media such as water, soil and vegetation, as well as a similar monitoring programme to record effects on health and environment;

i) the desirability of extending the national EMEP networks to make them operational for control and surveillance purposes.

Article 10   Executive body

1. The representatives of the Contracting Parties shall, within the framework of the Senior Advisers to ESE Governments on Environmental Problems, constitute the Executive Body of the present Convention, and shall meet at least annually in that capacity.

2. The Executive Body shall:

    a) review the implementation of the present Convention;
    b) establish, as appropriate, working groups to consider matters related to the implementation and development of the present Convention and to this end to prepare appropriate studies and other documentation and to submit recommendations to be considered by the Executive Body;
    c) fulfill such other functions as may be appropriate under the provisions of the present Convention.

3. The Executive Body shall utilize the Steering Body for the EMEP to play an integral part in the operation of the present Convention, in particular with regard to data collection and scientific cooperation.

4. The Executive Body, in discharging its functions, shall, when it deems appropriate, also make use of information from other relevant international organizations.

Article 11   Secretariat

The Executive Secretary of the Economic Commission for Europe shall carry out, for the Executive Body, the following secretariat functions --

    a) to convene and prepare the meetings of the Executive Body;
    b) to transmit to the Contracting Parties reports and other information received in accordance with the provisions of the present Convention;
    c) to discharge the functions assigned by the Executive Body.

Article 12   Amendments to the Convention

1. Any Contracting Party may propose amendments to the present convention.

2. The text of proposed amendments shall be submitted in writing to the Executive Secretary of the Economic Commission for Europe, who shall communicate them to all Contracting Parties. The Executive Body shall discuss proposed amendments at its next annual meeting provided that such proposals have been circulated by the Executive Secretary of the Economic Commission for Europe to the Contracting Parties at least ninety days in advance.

3. An amendment to the present Convention shall be adopted by consensus of the representatives of the Contracting Parties, and shall enter into force for the Contracting Parties which have accepted it on the ninetieth day after the date on which two-thirds of the Contracting Parties have deposited their instruments of acceptance with the depositary. Thereafter, the amendment shall enter into force for any other Contracting Party on the ninetieth day after the date on which that Contracting Party deposits its instrument of acceptance of the amendment.

Article 13   Settlement of Disputes

If a dispute arises between two or more Contracting Parties to the present Convention as to the interpretation or application of the Convention, they shall seek a solution by negotiation or by any other method of dispute settlement acceptable to the parties to the dispute.

Article 14   Signature

1. The present Convention shall be open for signature at the United Nations Office at Geneva from 13 to 16 November 1979 on the occasion of the High-level Meeting within the framework of the Economic Commission for Europe on the Protection of the Environment, by the member States of the Economic Commission for Europe as well as States having consultative status with the Economic Commission for Europe, pursuant to paragraph 8 of

Economic and Social Council resolution 36 (IV) of 28 March 1947, and by regional economic integration organizations, constituted by sovereign States members of the Economic Commission for Europe, which have competence in respect of the negotiation, conclusion and application of international agreements in matters covered by the present Convention.

2. In matters within their competence, such regional economic integration organizations shall, on their own behalf, exercise the rights and fulfill the responsibilities which the present Convention attributes to their member States. In such cases, the member States of these organizations shall not be entitled to exercise such rights individually.

Article 15   Ratification, Acceptance, Approval and Accession

1. The present Convention shall be subject to ratification, acceptance or approval.

2. The present Convention shall be open for accession as from 17 November 1979 by the States and organizations referred to in article 14 paragraph 1.

3. The instruments of ratification, acceptance, approval or accession shall be deposited with the Secretary-General of the United Nations, who will perform the functions of the depositary.

Article 16   Entry into Force

1. The present Convention shall enter into force on the ninetieth day after the date of deposit of the twenty-fourth instrument of ratification, acceptance, approval or accession.

2. For each Contracting Party which ratifies, accepts or approves the present Convention or accedes thereto after the deposit of the twenty-fourth instrument of ratification, acceptance approval or accession, the Convention shall enter into force on the ninetieth day after the date of deposit by such Contracting Party of its instrument of ratification, acceptance, approval or accession.

Article 17   Withdrawal

At any time after five years from the date on which the present Convention has come into force with respect to a Contracting Party, that Contracting Party may withdraw from the Convention by giving written notification to the depositary. Any such withdrawal shall take effect on the ninetieth day after the date of its receipt by the depositary.

Article 18   Authentic Texts

The original of the present Convention of which the English, French and Russian texts are equally authentic, shall be deposited with the Secretary-General of the United Nations.

In witness whereof the undersigned, being duly authorized thereto, have signed the present Convention.

Done at Geneva, this thirteenth day of November, one thousand nine hundred and seventy nine.

———————————————————

Vienna Convention for the Protection of the Ozone Layer

1513 U.N.T.S. 293
Signed: March 22, 1985
Entered into Force: September 22, 1988
Secretariat: http://www.unep.org/unep/ozone/index.shtml

The Parties to this Convention,

Aware of the potentially harmful impact on human health and the environment through modification of the ozone layer,

Recalling the pertinent provisions of the Declaration of the United Nations Conference on the Human Environment, and in particular principle 21, which provides that "States have, in accordance with the Charter of the United Nations and the principles of international law, the sovereign right to exploit their own resources pursuant to their own environmental policies, and the responsibility to ensure that activities within their jurisdiction or control do not cause damage to the environment of other States or of areas beyond the limits of national jurisdiction,"

Taking into account the circumstances and particular requirements of developing countries,

Mindful of the work and studies proceeding within both international and national organizations and, in particular, of the World Plan of Action on the Ozone Layer of the United Nations Environment Programme.

Mindful also of the precautionary measures for the protection of the ozone layer which have already been taken at the national and international levels,

Aware that measures to protect the ozone layer from modifications due to human activities require international co-operation and action, and should be based on relevant scientific and technical considerations,

Aware also of the need for further research and systematic observations to further develop scientific knowledge of the ozone layer and possible adverse effects resulting from its modification.

Determined to protect human health and the environment against adverse effects resulting from modifications of the ozone layer,

HAVE AGREED AS FOLLOWS:

Article 1　　　Definitions

For the purposes of this Convention:

1. "The ozone layer" means the layer of atmospheric ozone above the planetary boundary layer.

2. "Adverse effects" means changes in the physical environment or biota, including changes in climate, which have significant deleterious effects on human health or on the composition, resilience and productivity of natural and managed ecosystems, or on materials useful to mankind.

3. "Alternative technologies or equipment" means technologies or equipment the use of which makes it possible to reduce or effectively eliminate emissions of substances which have or are likely to have adverse effects on the ozone layer.

4. "Alternative substances" means substances which reduce, eliminate or avoid adverse effects on the ozone layer.

5. "Parties" means, unless the text otherwise indicates, Parties to this Convention.

6. "Regional economic integration organization" means an organization constituted by sovereign States of a given region which was competence in respect of matters governed by this Convention or its protocols and has been duly

authorized, in accordance with its internal procedures, to sign, ratify, accept, approve or accede to the instruments concerned.

7. "Protocols" means protocols to this Convention.

Article 2   General Obligations

1. The Parties shall take appropriate measures in accordance with the provisions of this Convention and of those protocols in force to which they are party to protect human health and the environment against adverse effects resulting or likely to result from human activities which modify or are likely to modify the ozone layer.

2. To this end the Parties shall, in accordance with the means at their disposal and their capabilities:

(a) Co-operate by means of systematic observations, research and information exchange in order to better understand and assess the effects of human activities on the zone layer and the effects on human health and the environment from modification of the ozone layer;

(b) Adopt appropriate legislative or administrative measures and co-operate in harmonizing appropriate policies to control, limit, reduce or prevent human activities under their jurisdiction or control should it be found that these activities have or are likely to have adverse effects resulting from modification or likely modification of the ozone layer;

(c) Co-operate in the formulation of agreed measures, procedures and standards for the implementation of this Convention, with a view to the adoption of protocols and annexes;

(d) Co-operate with competent international bodies to implement effectively this Convention and protocols to which they are party.

3. The provisions of this Convention shall in no way affect the right of Parties to adopt, in accordance with international law, domestic measures additional to those referred to in paragraphs 1 and 2 above, nor shall they affect additional domestic measures already taken by a Party, provided that these measures are not incompatible with their obligations under this Convention.

4. The application of this article shall be based on relevant scientific and technical considerations.

Article 3   Research and Systematic Observations

1. The Parties undertake, as appropriate, to initiative and co-operate in, directly or through competent international bodies, the conduct of research and scientific assessments on:

(a) The physical and chemical processes that may affect the ozone layer;

(b) The human health and other biological effects deriving from any modifications of the ozone layer, particularly those resulting from changes in ultra-violet solar radiation having biological effects (UV-B);

(c) Climatic effects deriving from many modifications of the ozone layer;

(d) Effects deriving from any modifications of the ozone layer and any consequent change in UV-B radiation on natural and synthetic materials useful to mankind;

(e) Substances, practices, processes and activities that may affect the ozone layer, and their cumulative effects;

(f) Alternative substances and technologies;

(g) Related socio-economic matters;

and as further elaborated in annexes I and II.

2. The Parties undertake to promote or establish, as appropriate, directly or through competent international bodies and taking fully into account national legislation and relevant ongoing activities at both the national and international levels, joint or complementary programmes for systematic observation of the state of the ozone layer and other relevant parameters, as elaborated in annex I.

3. The Parties undertake to co-operate, directly or through competent international bodies, in ensuring the collection, validation and transmission of research and observational data through appropriate world data centers in a regular and timely fashion.

Article 4	**Co-operation in the Legal, Scientific and Technical Fields**

1. The Parties shall facilitate and encourage of scientific, technical, socio-economic, commercial and legal information relevant to this Convention as further elaborated in annex II. Such information shall be supplied to bodies agreed upon by the Parties. Any such body receiving information regarded as confidential by the supplying Party shall ensure that such information is not disclosed and shall aggregate it to protect its confidentiality before it is made available to all Parties.

2. The Parties shall co-operate, consistent with their national laws, regulations and practices and taking into account in particular the needs of the developing countries, in promoting, directly or through competent international bodies, the development and transfer of technology and knowledge.
Such co-operation shall be carried out particularly through:

 (a) Facilitation of the acquisition of alternative technologies by other Parties:

 (b) Provision of information on alternative technologies and equipment, and supply of special manuals or guides to them;

 (c) The supply of necessary equipment and facilities for research and systematic observations;

 (d) Appropriate training of scientific and technical personnel.

Article 5	**Transmission of Information**

The Parties shall transmit, through the secretariat, to the Conference of the Parties established under article 6 information on the measures adopted by them in implementation of this Convention and of protocols to which they are party in such form and at such intervals as the meetings of the parties to the relevant instruments may determine.

Article 6	**Conference of the Parties**

1. A Conference of the Parties is hereby established. The first meeting of the Conference of the Parties shall be convened by the secretariat designated on an interim basis under article 7 not later than one year after entry into force of this Convention. Thereafter, ordinary meetings of the Conference of the Parties shall be held at regular intervals to be determined by the Conference at its meeting.

2. Extraordinary meetings of the Conference of the Parties shall be held at such other times as may be deemed necessary by the Conference, or at the written request of any party, provided that, within six months of the request being communicated to them by the secretariat, it is supported by at least one third of the Parties.

3. The Conference of the Parties shall by consensus agree upon and adopt rules of procedure and financial rules for itself and for any subsidiary bodies it may establish, as well as financial provisions governing the functioning of the secretariat.

4. The Conference of the Parties shall keep under continuous review the implementation of this Convention, and, in addition, shall:

 (a) Establish the form and the intervals for transmitting the information to be submitted in accordance with article 5 and consider such information as well reports submitted by any subsidiary body;

 (b) Review the scientific information on the ozone layer, on its possible modification and on possible effects of any such modification;

 (c) Promote, in accordance with article 2, the harmonization of appropriate policies, strategies and measures for minimizing the release of substances causing or likely to cause modification of the ozone layer, and make recommendations on any other measure relating to this Convention;

 (d) Adopt, in accordance with articles 3 and 4, programmes for research, systematic observations, scientific and technological co-operation, the exchange of information and the transfer of technology and knowledge;

(e) Consider and adopt, as required, in accordance with articles 9 and 10, amendments of this Convention and its annexes;

(f) Consider amendments to any protocol, as well as to any annexes thereto, and, if so decided, recommend their adoption to the parties to the protocol concerned;

(g) Consider and adopt, as required in accordance with article 10, additional annexes to this Convention;

(h) Consider and adept, as required, protocols in accordance with article 8;

(i) Establish such subsidiary bodies as are deemed necessary for the implementation of this Convention;

(j) Seek, where appropriate, the services of competent international bodies and scientific committees, in particular the World Meteorological Organization and the World Health Organization, as well as the Coordinating Committee on the Ozone Layer, in scientific research, systematic observations and other activities pertinent to the objectives of this Convention, and make use as appropriate of information from these bodies and committees;

(k) Consider and undertake any additional action that may be required for the achievement of the purpose of this Convention.

5. The United Nations, its specialized agencies and the International Atomic Energy Agency, as well as any state not party to this Convention, may be represented at meetings of the Conference of the Parties by observers. Any body or agency, whether national or international, governmental or non-governmental, qualified in fields relating to the protection of the ozone layer which has informed the secretariat of its wish to be represented at a meeting of the Conference of the Parties as an observer may be admitted unless at least one-third of the Parties present object. The admission and participation of observers shall be subject to the rules of procedure adopted by the Conference of the Parties.

Article 7   Secretariat

1. The functions of the secretariat shall be:

(a) To arrange for and service meetings provided for in articles 6, 8, 9 and 10;

(b) To prepare and transmit reports based upon information received in accordance with articles 4 and 5, as well as upon information derived from meetings of subsidiary bodies established under article 6;

(c) To perform the functions assigned to it by any protocols;

(d) To prepare reports on its activities carried out in implementation of its functions under this Convention and present them to the Conference of the Parties;

(e) To ensure the necessary co-ordination with other relevant international bodies, and in particular to enter into such administrative and contractual arrangements as may be required for the effective discharge of its functions;

(f) To perform such other functions as may be determined by the Conference of the Parties.

2. The secretariat functions will be carried out on an interim basis by the United Nations Environment Programme until the completion of the first ordinary meeting of the Conference of the Parties held pursuant to article 6. At its first ordinary meeting, the Conference of the Parties shall designate the secretariat from amongst those existing competent international organizations which has signified their willingness to carry out the secretariat functions under this Convention.

Article 8   Adoption of Protocols

1. The Conference of the Parties may at a meeting adopt protocols pursuant to article 2.

2. The text of any proposed protocol shall be communicated to the Parties by the secretariat at least six months before such a meeting.

Article 9   Amendment of the Convention of Protocols

1. Any Party may propose amendments to this Convention or to any protocol. Such amendments shall take due account, inter alia, of relevant scientific and technical considerations.

2. Amendments to this Convention shall be adopted at a meeting of the Conference of the Parties. Amendments to any protocol shall be adopted at a meeting of the Parties to the protocol in question. The text of any proposed

amendment of this Convention or to any protocol, except as may otherwise be provided in such protocol, shall be communicated to the Parties by the secretariat at least six months before the meeting at which it is proposed for adoption. The secretariat shall also communicate proposed amendments to the signatories to this Convention for information.

3. The Parties shall make every effort to reach agreement on any proposed amendment to this Convention by consensus. If all efforts at consensus have been exhausted, and no agreement reached, the amendment shall as a last resort by adopted by a three-fourth majority vote of the Parties present and voting at the meeting, and shall be submitted by the Depositary to all Parties for ratification, approval or acceptance.

4. The procedure mentioned in paragraph 3 above shall apply to amendments to any protocol, except that a two-thirds majority of the parties to that protocol and voting at the meeting shall suffice for their adoption.

5. Ratification, approval or acceptance of amendments shall be notified to the Depository in writing. Amendments adopted in accordance with paragraphs 3 or 4 above shall enter into force between parties having accepted them on the ninetieth day after the receipt by the Depositary of notification of their ratification, approval or acceptance by at least three-fourths of the Parties to this Convention or by at least two-thirds of the parties to the protocol concerned, except as may otherwise be provided in such protocol. Thereafter the amendments shall enter into force for any other Party on the ninetieth day after that Party deposits its instrument of ratification, approval or acceptance of the amendments.

6. For the purpose of this article, "Parties present and voting" means Parties present and casting an affirmative or negative vote.

Article 10   Adoption and Amendment of Annexes

1. The annexes to this Convention or to any protocol shall form an integral part of this Convention or of such protocol, as the case may be, and, unless expressly provided otherwise, a reference to this Convention or its protocols constitutes at the same time a reference to any annexes thereto. Such annexes shall be restricted to scientific, technical and administrative matters.

2. Except as may be otherwise provided in any protocol with respect to its annexes, the following procedure shall apply to the proposal, adoption and entry into force of additional annexes to this Convention or of annexes to a protocol;

(a) Annexes to this Convention shall be proposed and adopted according to the procedure laid down in article 9, paragraphs 2 and 3, while annexes to any protocol shall be proposed and adopted according to the procedure laid down in article 9, paragraphs 2 and 4;

(b) Any party that is unable to approve an additional annex to this Convention or an annex to any protocol to which it is party so notify the Depository, in writing, within six months from date of the communication of the adoption by the Depository. The Depository shall without delay notify all Parties of any such notification received may at any time substitute an acceptance for a previous declaration of objection and the annexes shall thereupon enter into force for that Party.

(c) On the expiry of six months from the date of the circulation of the communication by the Depositary, the annex shall become effective for all Parties to this Convention or to any protocol concerned which have not submitted a notification in accordance with the provision of subparagraph (b) above.

3. The proposal, adoption and entry into force of amendments to annexes to this Convention or to any protocol shall be subject to the same procedure as for the proposal, adoption and entry into force of annexes to the Convention or annexes to a protocol Annexes and amendments thereto shall take due account, inter alia, of relevant scientific and technical considerations.

4. If an additional annex or an amendment to an annex involves an amendment to this Convention or to any protocol, the additional annex or amended annex shall not enter into force until such time as the amendment to this Convention or to the protocol concerned enters into force.

Article 11   Settlement of Disputes

1. In the event of a dispute between Parties concerning the interpretation or application of this Convention, the parties concerned shall seek solution by negotiation.

2. If the parties concerned cannot reach agreement by negotiation, they may jointly seek the good offices, of, or request mediation by, a third party.

3. When ratifying, accepting, approving or acceding to this Convention, or at any time thereafter, a State or regional economic integration organization may declare in writing to the Depository that for a dispute not resolved in accordance with paragraph 1 or paragraph 2 above, it accepts one or both of the following means of dispute settlement as compulsory:

(a) Arbitration in accordance with procedures to be adopted by the Conference of the Parties at its first ordinary meeting;

(b) Submission of the dispute to the International Court of Justice.

4. If the parties have not, in accordance with paragraph 3 above, accepted the same or any procedure, the dispute shall be submitted to conciliation in accordance with paragraph 5 below unless the parties otherwise agree.

5. A conciliation commission shall be created upon the request of one of the parties to the dispute. The commission shall be composed of an equal number of members appointed by each party concerned and a chairman chosen jointly by the members appointed by each party. The commission shall render a final and recommendatory award, which the parties shall consider in good faith.

6. The provisions of this article shall apply with respect to any protocol except as otherwise provided in the protocol concerned.

Article 12   Signature

This Convention shall be open for signature at the Federal Ministry for Foreign Affairs of the Republic of Austria in Vienna from 22 March 1985 to 21 September 1985, and at United Nations Headquarters in New York from 22 September 1985 to 21 March 1986.

Article 13   Ratification, Acceptance or Approval

1. This Convention and any protocol shall be subject to ratification, acceptance or approval by States and be regional economic integration organizations. Instruments of ratification, acceptance or approval shall be deposited with the Depository.

2. Any organization referred to in paragraph 1 above which becomes a Party to this Convention or any protocol without any of its member States being a Party shall be bound by all the obligations under the Convention or the protocol as the case may be. In the case of such organizations, one or more of whose member States is a Party to the Convention or relevant protocol, the organization and its member States shall decide on their respective responsibilities for the performance or their obligation under the Convention or protocol, as the case may be. In such cases, the organization and the member States shall not be entitled to exercise rights under the Convention or relevant protocol concurrently.

3. In their instruments of ratification, acceptance or approval, the organizations referred to in paragraph 1 above shall declare the extent of their competence with respect to the matters governed by the Convention or the relevant protocol. These organizations shall also inform the Depository of any substantial modification in the extent of their competence.

Article 14   Accession

1. This Convention and any protocol shall be open for accession by States and by regional economic integration organizations from the date on which the Convention or the protocol concerned is closed for signature.   The instruments of accession shall be deposited with the Depository.

2. In their instruments of accession, the organizations referred to in paragraph 1 above shall declare the extent of their competence with respect to the matters governed by the Convention of the relevant protocol.   These organizations shall also inform the Depository of any substantial modification in the extent of their competence.

3.   The provisions of article 13, paragraph 2, shall apply to regional economic integration organizations which acceded to this Convention or any protocol.

Article 15   Right to Vote

1. Each Party to this Convention or to any protocol shall have one vote.

2. Except as provided for in paragraph 1 above, regional economic integration organizations, in matters within their competence, shall exercise their right to vote with a number of votes equal to the number of their member States which are Parties to the Convention or the relevant protocol.   Such organizations shall exercise their right to vote if their member States exercise theirs, and vice versa.

Article 16   Relationship Between the Convention and its Protocols

1.   A State or a regional economic integration organization may not become a party to a protocol unless it is, or becomes at the same time, a Party to the Convention.

2.   Decisions concerning any protocol shall be taken only by the parties to the protocol concerned.

Article 17   Entry into Force

1. This Convention shall enter into force on the ninetieth day after the date of deposit of the twentieth instrument of ratification, acceptance, approval or accession.

2. Any protocol, except as otherwise provided in such protocol, shall enter into force on the ninetieth day after the date of deposit of the eleventh instrument of ratification, acceptance or approval of such protocol or accession thereto.

3.   For each Party which ratifies, accepts or approves this Convention or accedes thereto after the deposit of the twentieth instrument of ratification, acceptance, approval or accession, it shall enter into force on the ninetieth day after the date of deposit by such Party of its instrument of ratification, acceptance, approval or accession.

4. Any protocol, except as otherwise provided in such protocol, shall enter into force for a party that ratifies, accepts or approves the protocol or accedes thereto after its entry into force pursuant to paragraph 2 above, on the ninetieth day after the date on which the party deposits its instrument of ratification, acceptance, approval or accession, or on the date on which the Convention enters into force for that Party, whichever shall be the later.

5. For the purposes of paragraphs 1 and 2 above, any instrument deposited by a regional economic integration organization shall not be counted as additional to those deposited by member States of such organizations.

Article 18   Reservations

No reservations may be made to this Convention.

Article 19   Withdrawal

1. At any time after four years from the date on which this Convention has entered into force for a Party, that Party may withdraw from the Convention by giving written notification to the Depository.

2. Except as may be provided in any protocol, at any time after four years from the date on which such protocol has entered into force for a party, that party may withdraw from the protocol by giving written notification to the Depositary.

3. Any such withdrawal shall take effect upon expiry of one year after the date of its receipt by the Depository, or on such later date as may be specified in the notification of the withdrawal.

4. Any Party which draws from this Convention shall be considered as also having withdrawn from any protocol to which it is party.

Article 20   Depositary

1. The Secretary-General of the United Nations shall assume the functions of depositary of this Convention and any protocols.

2. The Depository shall inform the Parties, in particular of:

(a) The signature of this Convention and of any protocol, and the deposit of instruments of ratification, acceptance, approval or accession in accordance with articles 13 and 14;

(b) The date on which the Convention and any protocol will come into force in accordance with article 17;

(c) Notifications of withdrawal made in accordance with article 19;

(d) Amendments adopted with respect to the Convention and any protocol, their acceptance by the parties and their date of entry into force in accordance with article 9;

(e) All communications relating to the adoption and approval of annexes and to the amendment of annexes in accordance with article 10;

(f) Notifications by regional economic integration organizations of the extent of their competence with respect to matters governed by this Convention and any protocols, and of any modifications thereof.

(g) Declarations made in accordance with article 11, paragraph 3.

Article 21   Authentic Texts

The original of this Convention, of which the Arabic, Chinese, English, French, Russian and Spanish texts are equally authentic, shall be deposited with the Secretary-General of the United Nations. IN WITNESS THEREOF the undersigned, being duly authorized to that effect, have signed this Convention.

Done at Vienna on the 22nd day of March 1985.

Annex I   Research and Systematic Observations

1. The Parties to the Convention recognize that the major scientific issues are:

(a) Modification of the ozone layer which would result in change in the amount of solar ultra-violate radiation having biological effects (UV-B) that reaches the Earth's surface and the potential consequences for human health, for organisms, ecosystems and materials useful to mankind;

(b) Modification of the vertical distribution of ozone, which could change the temperature structure of the atmosphere and the potential consequences for weather and climate.

2. The Parties to the Convention, in accordance with article 3, shall cooperate in conducting research and systematic observations and in formulating recommendations for future research and observations in such areas as:

(a) Research into the physics and chemistry of the atmosphere

(i) Comprehensive theoretical models: further development of models which consider the interaction between radiative, dynamic and chemical processes; studies of the simultaneous effects of various man-made and naturally occurring species upon atmospheric ozone; interpretation of satellite and non-satellite measurement data sets; evaluation of trends in atmospheric and geophysical parameters, and the development of methods for attributing changes in these parameters to specific causes;

(ii) Laboratory studies of: rate coefficients, absorption cross-sections and mechanisms of tropospheric and stratospheric chemical and photochemical processes; spectroscopic data to support field measurements in all relevant spectral regions;

(iii) Field measurements: the concentration and fluxes of key source gases of both natural and anthropogenic origin; atmospheric dynamics studies; simultaneous measurements of photochemically-related species down to the planetary boundary layer, using in situ and remote sensing instruments; inter-comparison of different sensors, including co-ordinated correlative measurements for satellite instrumentation; three-dimensional fields of key atmospheric trace constituents, solar spectral flux and meteorological parameters;

(iv) Instrument development, including satellite and non-satellite sensors for atmospheric trace constituents, solar flux and meteorological parameters;

(b) Research into health, biological and photodegradation effects

(i) The relationship between human exposure to visible and ultra-violet solar radiation and (a) the development of both non-melanoma and melanoma skin cancer and (b) the effects of the immunological system;

(ii) Effects of UV-B radiation, including the wavelength dependence, upon (a) agricultural crops, forests and other terrestrial ecosystems and (b) the aquatic food web and fisheries, as well as possible inhibition of oxygen production by marine phytoplankton;

(iii) The mechanisms by which UV-B radiation acts on biological materials, species and ecosystems, including: the relationship between dose, dose rate, and response; photorepair, adaptation, and protection;

(iv) Studies of biological action spectra and the spectral response using polychromatic radiation in order to include possible interactions of the various wavelength regions;

(v) The influence of UV-B radiation on: the sensitivities and activities of biological species important to the biospheric balance; primary processes such as photosynthesis and biosynthesis;

(vi) The influence of UV-B radiation on the photodegradation of pollutants, agricultural chemicals and other materials;

(c) Research on effects on climate

(i) Theoretical and observational studies of the radiative effects of ozone and other trace species and the impact on climate parameters, such as land and ocean surface temperatures, precipitation patterns, the exchange between the troposphere and stratosphere;

(ii) The investigation of the effects of such climate impacts on various aspects of human activity;

(d) Systematic observations on:

(i) The status of ozone layer (i.e. the spatial and temporal variability of the total column content and vertical distribution) by making the Global Ozone Observing System, based on the integration of satellite and groundbased systems, fully operational;

(ii) The tropospheric and stratospheric concentrations of source gases for the HO_x, NO_x ClO_x and carbon families;

(iii) The temperature from the ground to the mesosphere, utilizing both ground-based and satellite systems;

(iv) Wavelength-resolved solar flux reaching, and thermal radiation leaving, the Earth's atmosphere, utilizing satellite measurements;

(v) Wavelength-resolved solar flux reaching the Earth's surface in the ultra-violet range having biological effects (UV-B);

(vi) Aerosol properties and distribution from the ground to the mesosphere, utilizing ground-based, airborne and satellite systems;

(vii) Climatically important variables by the maintenance of programmes of high-quality meteorological surface measurements;

(viii) Trace species, temperatures, solar flux and aerosols utilizing improved methods for analysing global data.

3. The Parties to the Convention shall co-operate, taking into account the particular needs of the developing countries, in promoting the appropriate scientific and technical training required to participate in the research and systematic observations outlined in this annex. Particular emphasis should be given to the intercalibration of observational instrumentation and methods with a view to generating comparable or standardized scientific data sets.

4. The following chemical substances of natural and anthropogenic origin, not listed in order of priority, are thought to have the potential to modify the chemical and physical properties of the ozone layer.

(a) Carbon substances

(i) Carbon monoxide (CO)

Carbon monoxide has significant natural and anthropogenic sources, and is thought to play a major direct role in tropospheric photochemistry, and an indirect role in stratospheric photochemistry.

(ii) Carbon dioxide (CO_2)

Carbon dioxide has significant natural and anthropogenic sources, and affects stratospheric ozone by influencing the thermal structure of the atmosphere.

(iii) Methane (CH_4)

Methane has both natural and anthropogenic sources, and affects both tropospheric and stratospheric ozone.

(iv) Non-methane hydrocarbon species

Non-methane hydrocarbon species, which consist of a large number of chemical substances, have both natural and anthropogenic sources, and play a direct role in tropospheric photochemistry and an indirect role in stratospheric photochemistry.

(b) Nitrogen substances

(i) Nitrous oxide (N_2O)

The dominant sources of N_2O are natural, but anthropogenic contributions are becoming increasingly important. Nitrous oxide is the primary source of stratospheric NOx, which play a vital role in controlling the abundance of stratospheric ozone.

(ii) Nitrogen oxides (NOx)

Ground-level sources of NOx play a major direct role only in tropospheric photochemical processes and an indirect role in stratosphere photochemistry, whereas injection of NOx close to the tropopause may lead directly to a change in upper tropospheric and stratospheric ozone.

(c) Chlorine substances

(i) Fully halogenated alkanes, e.g., CCl_4, $CFCl_3$ (CFC-11), CF_2Cl_2 (CFC-12), $C_2F_3Cl_3$ (CFC-113), $C_2F_4Cl_2$ (CFC-114)

Fully halogenated alkanes are anthropogenic and act as a source of ClOx, which plays a vital role in ozone photochemistry, especially in the 30-50 km altitude region.

(ii) Partially halogenated alkanes, e.g., CH_3Cl, CHF_2Cl (CFC-22), CH_3CCl_3, $CHFCl_2$ (CFC-21)

d) Bromine substances

Fully halogenated alkanes, e.g., CF_3Br

These gases are anthropogenic and act as a source of BrOx, which behaves in a manner similar to ClOx.

(e) Hydrogen substances

(i) Hydrogen (H_2)

Hydrogen, the source of which is natural and anthropogenic, plays a minor role in stratospheric photochemistry.

(ii) Water (H_2O)

Water, the source of which is natural, plays a vital role in both tropospheric and stratospheric photochemistry. Local sources of water vapour in the stratosphere include the oxidation of methane and, to a lesser extent, of hydrogen.

Annex II   Information Exchange

1. The Parties to the Convention recognize that the collection and sharing of information is an important means of implementing the objectives of this Convention and of assuring that any actions that may be taken are appropriate and equitable. Therefore, Parties shall exchange scientific, technical, socio-economic, business, commercial and legal information.

2. The Parties to the Convention, in deciding what information is to be collected and exchanged, should take into account the usefulness of the information and the costs of obtaining it. The Parties further recognize that co-operation under this annex has to be consistent with national laws, regulations and practices regarding patents, trade secrets, and protection of confidential and proprietary information.

3. Scientific information. This includes information on:

(a) Planned and ongoing research, both governmental and private, to facilitate the co-ordination of research programmes so as to make the most effective use of available national and international resources;

(b) The emission data needed for research;

(c) Scientific results published in peer-reviewed literature on the understanding of the physics and chemistry of the Earth's atmosphere and of its susceptibility to change, in particular on the state of the ozone layer and effects on human health, environment and climate which would result from changes on all time-scales in either the total column content or the vertical distribution of ozone;

(d) The assessment of research results and the recommendations for future research.

4. Technical information. This includes information on:

(a) The availability and cost of chemical substitutes and of alternative technologies to reduce the emissions of ozone-modifying substance and related planned and ongoing research;

(b) The limitations and any risks involved in using chemical or other substitutes and alternative technologies.

5. Socio-economic and commercial information on the substances referred to in annex I. This includes information on:

(a) Production and production capacity;

(b) Use and use patterns;

(c) Imports/exports;

(d) The costs, risks and benefits of human activities which may indirectly modify the ozone layer and of the impacts of regulatory actions taken or being considered to control these activities.

6. Legal information. This includes information on:

(a) National laws, administrative measures and legal research relevant to the protection of the ozone layer;

(b) International agreements, including bilateral agreements, relevant to the protection of the ozone layer;

(c) Methods and terms of licensing and availability of patents relevant to the protection of the ozone layer.

THE MONTREAL PROTOCOL ON SUBSTANCES THAT DEPLETE THE OZONE LAYER
(as either adjusted and/or amended in London 1990; Copenhagen 1992;
Vienna 1995; Montreal 1997; Beijing 1999)

1522 U.N.T.S. 3
Signed: September 16, 1987
Entered into Force: January 1, 1989
Secretariat: http://www.unep.org/ozone/index.shtml

Preamble

The Parties to this Protocol,

Being Parties to the Vienna Convention for the Protection of the Ozone Layer,

Mindful of their obligation under that Convention to take appropriate measures to protect human health and the environment against adverse effects resulting or likely to result from human activities which modify or are likely to modify the ozone layer,

Recognizing that world-wide emissions of certain substances can significantly deplete and otherwise modify the ozone layer in a manner that is likely to result in adverse effects on human health and the environment,

Conscious of the potential climatic effects of emissions of these substances,

Aware that measures taken to protect the ozone layer from depletion should be based on relevant scientific knowledge, taking into account technical and economic considerations,

Determined to protect the ozone layer by taking precautionary measures to control equitably total global emissions of substances that deplete it, with the ultimate objective of their elimination on the basis of developments in scientific knowledge, taking into account technical and economic considerations and bearing in mind the developmental needs of developing countries,

Acknowledging that special provision is required to meet the needs of developing countries, including the provision of additional financial resources and access to relevant technologies, bearing in mind that the magnitude of funds necessary is predictable, and the funds can be expected to make a substantial difference in the world's ability to address the scientifically established problem of ozone depletion and its harmful effects, *Noting* the precautionary measures for controlling emissions of certain chlorofluorocarbons that have already been taken at national and regional levels,

Considering the importance of promoting international co-operation in the research, development and transfer of alternative technologies relating to the control and reduction of emissions of substances that deplete the ozone layer, bearing in mind in particular the needs of developing countries,

HAVE AGREED AS FOLLOWS:

Article 1: Definitions

For the purposes of this Protocol:

1. "Convention" means the Vienna Convention for the Protection of the Ozone Layer, adopted on 22 March 1985.

2. "Parties" means, unless the text otherwise indicates, Parties to this Protocol.

3. "Secretariat" means the Secretariat of the Convention.

4. "Controlled substance" means a substance in Annex A, Annex B, Annex C or Annex E to this Protocol, whether existing alone or in a mixture. It includes the isomers of any such substance, except as specified in the relevant Annex, but excludes any controlled substance or mixture which is in a manufactured product other than a container used for the transportation or storage of that substance.

5. "Production" means the amount of controlled substances produced, minus the amount destroyed by technologies to be approved by the Parties and minus the amount entirely used as feedstock in the manufacture of other chemicals. The amount recycled and reused is not to be considered as "production".

6. "Consumption" means production plus imports minus exports of controlled substances.

7. "Calculated levels" of production, imports, exports and consumption means levels determined in accordance with Article 3.

8. "Industrial rationalization" means the transfer of all or a portion of the calculated level of production of one Party to another, for the purpose of achieving economic efficiencies or responding to anticipated shortfalls in supply as a result of plant closures.

Article 2: Control Measures

1. *Incorporated in Article 2A.*

2. *Replaced by Article 2B.*

3. *Replaced by Article 2A.*

4. *Replaced by Article 2A.*

5. Any Party may, for one or more control periods, transfer to another Party any portion of its calculated level of production set out in Articles 2A to 2F, and Article 2H, provided that the total combined calculated levels of production of the Parties concerned for any group of controlled substances do not exceed the production limits set out in those Articles for that group. Such transfer of production shall be notified to the Secretariat by each of the Parties concerned, stating the terms of such transfer and the period for which it is to apply.

5 *bis*. Any Party not operating under paragraph 1 of Article 5 may, for one or more control periods, transfer to another such Party any portion of its calculated level of consumption set out in Article 2F, provided that the calculated level of consumption of controlled substances in Group I of Annex A of the Party transferring the portion of its calculated level of consumption did not exceed 0.25 kilograms per capita in 1989 and that the total combined calculated levels of consumption of the Parties concerned do not exceed the consumption limits set out in Article 2F. Such transfer of consumption shall be notified to the Secretariat by each of the Parties concerned, stating the terms of such transfer and the period for which it is to apply.

6. Any Party not operating under Article 5, that has facilities for the production of Annex A or Annex B controlled substances under construction, or contracted for, prior to 16 September 1987, and provided for in national legislation prior to 1 January 1987, may add the production from such facilities to its 1986 production of such substances for the purposes of determining its calculated level of production for 1986, provided that such facilities are completed by 31 December 1990 and that such production does not raise that Party's annual calculated level of consumption of the controlled substances above 0.5 kilograms per capita.

7. Any transfer of production pursuant to paragraph 5 or any addition of production pursuant to paragraph 6 shall be notified to the Secretariat, no later than the time of the transfer or addition.

8. (a) Any Parties which are Member States of a regional economic integration organization as defined in Article 1 (6) of the Convention may agree that they shall jointly fulfill their obligations respecting consumption under this Article and Articles 2A to 2I provided that their total combined calculated level of consumption does not exceed the levels required by this Article and Articles 2A to 2I.

(b)   The Parties to any such agreement shall inform the Secretariat of the terms of the agreement before the date of the reduction in consumption with which the agreement is concerned.

(c)   Such agreement will become operative only if all Member States of the regional economic integration organization and the organization concerned are Parties to the Protocol and have notified the Secretariat of their manner of implementation.

9.   (a)   Based on the assessments made pursuant to Article 6, the Parties may decide whether:

        (i)   Adjustments to the ozone depleting potentials specified in Annex A, Annex B, Annex C and/or Annex E should be made and, if so, what the adjustments should be; and

        (ii)   Further adjustments and reductions of production or consumption of the controlled substances should be undertaken and, if so, what the scope, amount and timing of any such adjustments and reductions should be;

    (b)   Proposals for such adjustments shall be communicated to the Parties by the Secretariat at least six months before the meeting of the Parties at which they are proposed for adoption;

    (c)   In taking such decisions, the Parties shall make every effort to reach agreement by consensus. If all efforts at consensus have been exhausted, and no agreement reached, such decisions shall, as a last resort, be adopted by a two-thirds majority vote of the Parties present and voting representing a majority of the Parties operating under Paragraph 1 of Article 5 present and voting and a majority of the Parties not so operating present and voting;

    (d)   The decisions, which shall be binding on all Parties, shall forthwith be communicated to the Parties by the Depositary. Unless otherwise provided in the decisions, they shall enter into force on the expiry of six months from the date of the circulation of the communication by the Depositary.

10.   Based on the assessments made pursuant to Article 6 of this Protocol and in accordance with the procedure set out in Article 9 of the Convention, the Parties may decide:

    (a)   whether any substances, and if so which, should be added to or removed from any annex to this Protocol, and

    (b)   the mechanism, scope and timing of the control measures that should apply to those substances;

11.   Notwithstanding the provisions contained in this Article and Articles 2A to 2I Parties may take more stringent measures than those required by this Article and Articles 2A to 2I.

Article 2A: CFCs

1.   Each Party shall ensure that for the twelve-month period commencing on the first day of the seventh month following the date of entry into force of this Protocol, and in each twelve-month period thereafter, its calculated level of consumption of the controlled substances in Group I of Annex A does not exceed its calculated level of consumption in 1986. By the end of the same period, each Party producing one or more of these substances shall ensure that its calculated level of production of the substances does not exceed its calculated level of production in 1986, except that such level may have increased by no more than ten per cent based on the 1986 level. Such increase shall be permitted only so as to satisfy the basic domestic needs of the Parties operating under Article 5 and for the purposes of industrial rationalization between Parties.

2.   Each Party shall ensure that for the period from 1 July 1991 to 31 December 1992 its calculated levels of consumption and production of the controlled substances in Group I of Annex A do not exceed 150 per cent of its calculated levels of production and consumption of those substances in 1986; with effect from 1 January 1993, the twelve-month control period for these controlled substances shall run from 1 January to 31 December each year.

3.   Each Party shall ensure that for the twelve-month period commencing on 1 January 1994, and in each twelve-month period thereafter, its calculated level of consumption of the controlled substances in Group I of Annex A does not exceed, annually, twenty-five per cent of its calculated level of consumption in 1986. Each Party producing one or more of these substances shall, for the same periods, ensure that its calculated level of production of the substances does not exceed, annually, twenty-five per cent of its calculated level of production in 1986. However, in order to satisfy the basic domestic needs of the Parties operating under

paragraph 1 of Article 5, its calculated level of production may exceed that limit by up to ten per cent of its calculated level of production in 1986.

4.   Each Party shall ensure that for the twelve-month period commencing on 1 January 1996, and in each twelve-month period thereafter, its calculated level of consumption of the controlled substances in Group I of Annex A does not exceed zero. Each Party producing one or more of these substances shall, for the same periods, ensure that its calculated level of production of the substances does not exceed zero. However, in order to satisfy the basic domestic needs of the Parties operating under paragraph 1 of Article 5, its calculated level of production may exceed that limit by a quantity equal to the annual average of its production of the controlled substances in Group I of Annex A for basic domestic needs for the period 1995 to 1997 inclusive. This paragraph will apply save to the extent that the Parties decide to permit the level of production or consumption that is necessary to satisfy uses agreed by them to be essential.

5.   Each Party shall ensure that for the twelve-month period commencing on 1 January 2003 and in each twelve-month period thereafter, its calculated level of production of the controlled substances in Group I of Annex A for the basic domestic needs of the Parties operating under paragraph 1 of Article 5 does not exceed eighty per cent of the annual average of its production of those substances for basic domestic needs for the period 1995 to 1997 inclusive.

6.   Each Party shall ensure that for the twelve-month period commencing on 1 January 2005 and in each twelve-month period thereafter, its calculated level of production of the controlled substances in Group I of Annex A for the basic domestic needs of the Parties operating under paragraph 1 of Article 5 does not exceed fifty per cent of the annual average of its production of those substances for basic domestic needs for the period 1995 to 1997 inclusive.

7.   Each Party shall ensure that for the twelve-month period commencing on 1 January 2007 and in each twelve-month period thereafter, its calculated level of production of the controlled substances in Group I of Annex A for the basic domestic needs of the Parties operating under paragraph 1 of Article 5 does not exceed fifteen per cent of the annual average of its production of those substances for basic domestic needs for the period 1995 to 1997 inclusive.

8.   Each Party shall ensure that for the twelve-month period commencing on 1 January 2010 and in each twelve-month period thereafter, its calculated level of production of the controlled substances in Group I of Annex A for the basic domestic needs of the Parties operating under paragraph 1 of Article 5 does not exceed zero.

9.   For the purposes of calculating basic domestic needs under paragraphs 4 to 8 of this Article, the calculation of the annual average of production by a Party includes any production entitlements that it has transferred in accordance with paragraph 5 of Article 2, and excludes any production entitlements that it has acquired in accordance with paragraph 5 of Article 2.

Article 2B: Halons

1.   Each Party shall ensure that for the twelve-month period commencing on 1 January 1992, and in each twelve-month period thereafter, its calculated level of consumption of the controlled substances in Group II of Annex A does not exceed, annually, its calculated level of consumption in 1986. Each Party producing one or more of these substances shall, for the same periods, ensure that its calculated level of production of the substances does not exceed, annually, its calculated level of production in 1986. However, in order to satisfy the basic domestic needs of the Parties operating under paragraph 1 of Article 5, its calculated level of production may exceed that limit by up to ten per cent of its calculated level of production in 1986.

2.   Each Party shall ensure that for the twelve-month period commencing on 1 January 1994, and in each twelve-month period thereafter, its calculated level of consumption of the controlled substances in Group II of Annex A does not exceed zero. Each Party producing one or more of these substances shall, for the same periods, ensure that its calculated level of production of the substances does not exceed zero. However, in order to satisfy the basic domestic needs of the Parties operating under paragraph 1 of Article 5, its calculated level of production may, until 1 January 2002 exceed that limit by up to fifteen per cent of its calculated level of

production in 1986; thereafter, it may exceed that limit by a quantity equal to the annual average of its production of the controlled substances in Group II of Annex A for basic domestic needs for the period 1995 to 1997 inclusive. This paragraph will apply save to the extent that the Parties decide to permit the level of production or consumption that is necessary to satisfy uses agreed by them to be essential.

3.　Each Party shall ensure that for the twelve-month period commencing on 1 January 2005 and in each twelve-month period thereafter, its calculated level of production of the controlled substances in Group II of Annex A for the basic domestic needs of the Parties operating under paragraph 1 of Article 5 does not exceed fifty per cent of the annual average of its production of those substances for basic domestic needs for the period 1995 to 1997 inclusive.

4.　Each Party shall ensure that for the twelve-month period commencing on 1 January 2010 and in each twelve-month period thereafter, its calculated level of production of the controlled substances in Group II of Annex A for the basic domestic needs of the Parties operating under paragraph 1 of Article 5 does not exceed zero.

Article 2C: Other fully halogenated CFCs

1.　Each Party shall ensure that for the twelve-month period commencing on 1 January 1993, its calculated level of consumption of the controlled substances in Group I of Annex B does not exceed, annually, eighty per cent of its calculated level of consumption in 1989. Each Party producing one or more of these substances shall, for the same period, ensure that its calculated level of production of the substances does not exceed, annually, eighty per cent of its calculated level of production in 1989. However, in order to satisfy the basic domestic needs of the Parties operating under paragraph 1 of Article 5, its calculated level of production may exceed that limit by up to ten per cent of its calculated level of production in 1989.

2.　Each Party shall ensure that for the twelve-month period commencing on 1 January 1994, and in each twelve-month period thereafter, its calculated level of consumption of the controlled substances in Group I of Annex B does not exceed, annually, twenty-five per cent of its calculated level of consumption in 1989. Each Party producing one or more of these substances shall, for the same periods, ensure that its calculated level of production of the substances does not exceed, annually, twenty-five per cent of its calculated level of production in 1989. However, in order to satisfy the basic domestic needs of the Parties operating under paragraph 1 of Article 5, its calculated level of production may exceed that limit by up to ten per cent of its calculated level of production in 1989.

3.　Each Party shall ensure that for the twelve-month period commencing on 1 January 1996, and in each twelve-month period thereafter, its calculated level of consumption of the controlled substances in Group I of Annex B does not exceed zero. Each Party producing one or more of these substances shall, for the same periods, ensure that its calculated level of production of the substances does not exceed zero. However, in order to satisfy the basic domestic needs of the Parties operating under paragraph 1 of Article 5, its calculated level of production may, until 1 January 2003 exceed that limit by up to fifteen per cent of its calculated level of production in 1989; thereafter, it may exceed that limit by a quantity equal to eighty per cent of the annual average of its production of the controlled substances in Group I of Annex B for basic domestic needs for the period 1998 to 2000 inclusive. This paragraph will apply save to the extent that the Parties decide to permit the level of production or consumption that is necessary to satisfy uses agreed by them to be essential.

4.　Each Party shall ensure that for the twelve-month period commencing on 1 January 2007 and in each twelve-month period thereafter, its calculated level of production of the controlled substances in Group I of Annex B for the basic domestic needs of the Parties operating under paragraph 1 of Article 5 does not exceed fifteen per cent of the annual average of its production of those substances for basic domestic needs for the period 1998 to 2000 inclusive.

5.　Each Party shall ensure that for the twelve-month period commencing on 1 January 2010 and in each twelve-month period thereafter, its calculated level of production of the controlled substances in Group I of Annex B for the basic domestic needs of the Parties operating under paragraph 1 of Article 5 does not exceed zero.

Article 2D: Carbon tetrachloride

1. Each Party shall ensure that for the twelve-month period commencing on 1 January 1995, its calculated level of consumption of the controlled substance in Group II of Annex B does not exceed, annually, fifteen per cent of its calculated level of consumption in 1989. Each Party producing the substance shall, for the same period, ensure that its calculated level of production of the substance does not exceed, annually, fifteen per cent of its calculated level of production in 1989. However, in order to satisfy the basic domestic needs of the Parties operating under paragraph 1 of Article 5, its calculated level of production may exceed that limit by up to ten per cent of its calculated level of production in 1989.

2. Each Party shall ensure that for the twelve-month period commencing on 1 January 1996, and in each twelve-month period thereafter, its calculated level of consumption of the controlled substance in Group II of Annex B does not exceed zero. Each Party producing the substance shall, for the same periods, ensure that its calculated level of production of the substance does not exceed zero. However, in order to satisfy the basic domestic needs of the Parties operating under paragraph 1 of Article 5, its calculated level of production may exceed that limit by up to fifteen per cent of its calculated level of production in 1989. This paragraph will apply save to the extent that the Parties decide to permit the level of production or consumption that is necessary to satisfy uses agreed by them to be essential.

Article 2E: 1,1,1-Trichloroethane (Methyl (Methyl-chloroform)

1. Each Party shall ensure that for the twelve-month period commencing on 1 January 1993, its calculated level of consumption of the controlled substance in Group III of Annex B does not exceed, annually, its calculated level of consumption in 1989. Each Party producing the substance shall, for the same period, ensure that its calculated level of production of the substance does not exceed, annually, its calculated level of production in 1989. However, in order to satisfy the basic domestic needs of the Parties operating under paragraph 1 of Article 5, its calculated level of production may exceed that limit by up to ten per cent of its calculated level of production in 1989.

2. Each Party shall ensure that for the twelve-month period commencing on 1 January 1994, and in each twelve-month period thereafter, its calculated level of consumption of the controlled substance in Group III of Annex B does not exceed, annually, fifty per cent of its calculated level of consumption in 1989. Each Party producing the substance shall, for the same periods, ensure that its calculated level of production of the substance does not exceed, annually, fifty per cent of its calculated level of production in 1989. However, in order to satisfy the basic domestic needs of the Parties operating under paragraph 1 of Article 5, its calculated level of production may exceed that limit by up to ten per cent of its calculated level of production in 1989.

3. Each Party shall ensure that for the twelve-month period commencing on 1 January 1996, and in each twelve-month period thereafter, its calculated level of consumption of the controlled substance in Group III of Annex B does not exceed zero. Each Party producing the substance shall, for the same periods, ensure that its calculated level of production of the substance does not exceed zero. However, in order to satisfy the basic domestic needs of the Parties operating under paragraph 1 of Article 5, its calculated level of production may exceed that limit by up to fifteen per cent of its calculated level of production for 1989. This paragraph will apply save to the extent that the Parties decide to permit the level of production or consumption that is necessary to satisfy uses agreed by them to be essential.

Article 2F: Hydrochlorofluorocarbons

1. Each Party shall ensure that for the twelve-month period commencing on 1 January 1996, and in each twelve-month period thereafter, its calculated level of consumption of the controlled substances in Group I of Annex C does not exceed, annually, the sum of:

    (a) Two point eight per cent of its calculated level of consumption in 1989 of the controlled substances in Group I of Annex A; and
    (b) Its calculated level of consumption in 1989 of the controlled substances in Group I of Annex C.

2. Each Party producing one or more of these substances shall ensure that for the twelve-month period commencing on 1 January 2004, and in each twelve-month period thereafter, its calculated level of production of the controlled substances in Group I of Annex C does not exceed, annually, the average of:

    (a) The sum of its calculated level of consumption in 1989 of the controlled substances in Group I of Annex C and two point eight per cent of its calculated level of consumption in 1989 of the controlled substances in Group I of Annex A; and

    (b) The sum of its calculated level of production in 1989 of the controlled substances in Group I of Annex C and two point eight per cent of its calculated level of production in 1989 of the controlled substances in Group I of Annex A.

    However, in order to satisfy the basic domestic needs of the Parties operating under paragraph 1 of Article 5, its calculated level of production may exceed that limit by up to fifteen per cent of its calculated level of production of the controlled substances in Group I of Annex C as defined above.

3. Each Party shall ensure that for the twelve month period commencing on 1 January 2004, and in each twelve-month period thereafter, its calculated level of consumption of the controlled substances in Group I of Annex C does not exceed, annually, sixty-five per cent of the sum referred to in paragraph 1 of this Article.

4. Each Party shall ensure that for the twelve-month period commencing on 1 January 2010, and in each twelve-month period thereafter, its calculated level of consumption of the controlled substances in Group I of Annex C does not exceed, annually, twenty-five per cent of the sum referred to in paragraph 1 of this Article. Each Party producing one or more of these substances shall, for the same periods, ensure that its calculated level of production of the controlled substances in Group I of Annex C does not exceed, annually, twenty-five per cent of the calculated level referred to in paragraph 2 of this Article. However, in order to satisfy the basic domestic needs of the Parties operating under paragraph 1 of Article 5, its calculated level of production may exceed that limit by up to ten per cent of its calculated level of production of the controlled substances in Group I of Annex C as referred to in paragraph 2.

5. Each Party shall ensure that for the twelve-month period commencing on 1 January 2015, and in each twelve-month period thereafter, its calculated level of consumption of the controlled substances in Group I of Annex C does not exceed, annually, ten per cent of the sum referred to in paragraph 1 of this Article. Each Party producing one or more of these substances shall, for the same periods, ensure that its calculated level of production of the controlled substances in Group I of Annex C does not exceed, annually, ten per cent of the calculated level referred to in paragraph 2 of this Article. However, in order to satisfy the basic domestic needs of the Parties operating under paragraph 1 of Article 5, its calculated level of production may exceed that limit by up to ten per cent of its calculated level of production of the controlled substances in Group I of Annex C as referred to in paragraph 2.

6. Each Party shall ensure that for the twelve-month period commencing on 1 January 2020, and in each twelve-month period thereafter, its calculated level of consumption of the controlled substances in Group I of Annex C does not exceed zero. Each Party producing one or more of these substances shall, for the same periods, ensure that its calculated level of production of the controlled substances in Group I of Annex C does not exceed zero. However:

    (a) Each Party may exceed that limit on consumption by up to zero point five per cent of the sum referred to in paragraph 1 of this Article in any such twelve-month period ending before 1 January 2030, provided that such consumption shall be restricted to the servicing of refrigeration and air-conditioning equipment existing on 1 January 2020;

    (b) Each Party may exceed that limit on production by up to zero point five per cent of the average referred to in paragraph 2 of this Article in any such twelve-month period ending before 1 January 2030, provided that such production shall be restricted to the servicing of refrigeration and air-conditioning equipment existing on 1 January 2020.

7.   As of 1 January 1996, each Party shall endeavour to ensure that:

(a)   The use of controlled substances in Group I of Annex C is limited to those applications where other more environmentally suitable alternative substances or technologies are not available;

(b)   The use of controlled substances in Group I of Annex C is not outside the areas of application currently met by controlled substances in Annexes A, B and C, except in rare cases for the protection of human life or human health; and

(c)   Controlled substances in Group I of Annex C are selected for use in a manner that minimizes ozone depletion, in addition to meeting other environmental, safety and economic considerations.

Article 2G: Hydrobromofluorocarbons

Each Party shall ensure that for the twelve-month period commencing on 1 January 1996, and in each twelve-month period thereafter, its calculated level of consumption of the controlled substances in Group II of Annex C does not exceed zero. Each Party producing the substances shall, for the same periods, ensure that its calculated level of production of the substances does not exceed zero. This paragraph will apply save to the extent that the Parties decide to permit the level of production or consumption that is necessary to satisfy uses agreed by them to be essential.

Article 2H: Methyl bromide

1.   Each Party shall ensure that for the twelve-month period commencing on 1 January 1995, and in each twelve-month period thereafter, its calculated level of consumption of the controlled substance in Annex E does not exceed, annually, its calculated level of consumption in 1991. Each Party producing the substance shall, for the same period, ensure that its calculated level of production of the substance does not exceed, annually, its calculated level of production in 1991. However, in order to satisfy the basic domestic needs of the Parties operating under paragraph 1 of Article 5, its calculated level of production may exceed that limit by up to ten per cent of its calculated level of production in 1991.

2.   Each Party shall ensure that for the twelve-month period commencing on 1 January 1999, and in the twelve month period thereafter, its calculated level of consumption of the controlled substance in Annex E does not exceed, annually, seventy-five per cent of its calculated level of consumption in 1991. Each Party producing the substance shall, for the same periods, ensure that its calculated level of production of the substance does not exceed, annually, seventy-five per cent of its calculated level of production in 1991. However, in order to satisfy the basic domestic needs of the Parties operating under paragraph 1 of Article 5, its calculated level of production may exceed that limit by up to ten per cent of its calculated level of production in 1991.

3.   Each Party shall ensure that for the twelve-month period commencing on 1 January 2001, and in the twelve-month period thereafter, its calculated level of consumption of the controlled substance in Annex E does not exceed, annually, fifty per cent of its calculated level of consumption in 1991. Each Party producing the substance shall, for the same periods, ensure that its calculated level of production of the substance does not exceed, annually, fifty per cent of its calculated level of production in 1991. However, in order to satisfy the basic domestic needs of the Parties operating under paragraph 1 of Article 5, its calculated level of production may exceed that limit by up to ten per cent of its calculated level of production in 1991.

4.   Each Party shall ensure that for the twelve-month period commencing on 1 January 2003, and in the twelve-month period thereafter, its calculated level of consumption of the controlled substance in Annex E does not exceed, annually, thirty per cent of its calculated level of consumption in 1991. Each Party producing the substance shall, for the same periods, ensure that its calculated level of production of the substance does not exceed, annually, thirty per cent of its calculated level of production in 1991. However, in order to satisfy the

basic domestic needs of the Parties operating under paragraph 1 of Article 5, its calculated level of production may exceed that limit by up to ten per cent of its calculated level of production in 1991.

5. Each Party shall ensure that for the twelve-month period commencing on 1 January 2005, and in each twelve-month period thereafter, its calculated level of consumption of the controlled substance in Annex E does not exceed zero. Each Party producing the substance shall, for the same periods, ensure that its calculated level of production of the substance does not exceed zero. However, in order to satisfy the basic domestic needs of the Parties operating under paragraph 1 of Article 5, its calculated level of production may, until 1 January 2002 exceed that limit by up to fifteen per cent of its calculated level of production in 1991; thereafter, it may exceed that limit by a quantity equal to the annual average of its production of the controlled substance in Annex E for basic domestic needs for the period 1995 to 1998 inclusive. This paragraph will apply save to the extent that the Parties decide to permit the level of production or consumption that is necessary to satisfy uses agreed by them to be critical uses.

5 *bis*. Each Party shall ensure that for the twelve-month period commencing on 1 January 2005 and in each twelve-month period thereafter, its calculated level of production of the controlled substance in Annex E for the basic domestic needs of the Parties operating under paragraph 1 of Article 5 does not exceed eighty per cent of the annual average of its production of the substance for basic domestic needs for the period 1995 to 1998 inclusive.

5 *ter*. Each Party shall ensure that for the twelve-month period commencing on 1 January 2015 and in each twelve-month period thereafter, its calculated level of production of the controlled substance in Annex E for the basic domestic needs of the Parties operating under paragraph 1 of Article 5 does not exceed zero.

6. The calculated levels of consumption and production under this Article shall not include the amounts used by the Party for quarantine and pre-shipment applications.

Article 2I: Bromochloromethane

Each Party shall ensure that for the twelve-month period commencing on 1 January 2002, and in each twelve-month period thereafter, its calculated level of consumption and production of the controlled substance in Group III of Annex C does not exceed zero. This paragraph will apply save to the extent that the Parties decide to permit the level of production or consumption that is necessary to satisfy uses agreed by them to be essential.

Article 3: Calculation of control levels

For the purposes of Articles 2, 2A to 2I and 5, each Party shall, for each group of substances in Annex A, Annex B, Annex C or Annex E determine its calculated levels of:

(a) Production by:

    (i) multiplying its annual production of each controlled substance by the ozone depleting potential specified in respect of it in Annex A, Annex B, Annex C or Annex E;
    (ii) adding together, for each such Group, the resulting figures;

(b) Imports and exports, respectively, by following, *mutatis mutandis*, the procedure set out in subparagraph (a); and

(c) Consumption by adding together its calculated levels of production and imports and subtracting its calculated level of exports as determined in accordance with subparagraphs (a) and (b). However, beginning on 1 January 1993, any export of controlled substances to non-Parties shall not be subtracted in calculating the consumption level of the exporting Party.

Article 4:   Control of trade with non-Parties

1. As of 1 January 1990, each party shall ban the import of the controlled substances in Annex A from any

State not party to this Protocol.

1 *bis*. Within one year of the date of the entry into force of this paragraph, each Party shall ban the import of the controlled substances in Annex B from any State not party to this Protocol.

1 *ter*. Within one year of the date of entry into force of this paragraph, each Party shall ban the import of any controlled substances in Group II of Annex C from any State not party to this Protocol.

1 *qua*. Within one year of the date of entry into force of this paragraph, each Party shall ban the import of the controlled substance in Annex E from any State not party to this Protocol.

1 *quin*. As of 1 January 2004, each Party shall ban the import of the controlled substances in Group I of Annex C from any State not party to this Protocol.

1 *sex*. Within one year of the date of entry into force of this paragraph, each Party shall ban the import of the controlled substance in Group III of Annex C from any State not party to this Protocol.

2. As of 1 January 1993, each Party shall ban the export of any controlled substances in Annex A to any State not party to this Protocol.

2 *bis*. Commencing one year after the date of entry into force of this paragraph, each Party shall ban the export of any controlled substances in Annex B to any State not party to this Protocol.

2 *ter*. Commencing one year after the date of entry into force of this paragraph, each Party shall ban the export of any controlled substances in Group II of Annex C to any State not party to this Protocol.

2 *qua*. Commencing one year of the date of entry into force of this paragraph, each Party shall ban the export of the controlled substance in Annex E to any State not party to this Protocol.

2 *quin*. As of 1 January 2004, each Party shall ban the export of the controlled substances in Group I of Annex C to any State not party to this Protocol.

2 *sex*. Within one year of the date of entry into force of this paragraph, each Party shall ban the export of the controlled substance in Group III of Annex C to any State not party to this Protocol.

3. By 1 January 1992, the Parties shall, following the procedures in Article 10 of the Convention, elaborate in an annex a list of products containing controlled substances in Annex A. Parties that have not objected to the annex in accordance with those procedures shall ban, within one year of the annex having become effective, the import of those products from any State not party to this Protocol.

3 *bis*. Within three years of the date of the entry into force of this paragraph, the Parties shall, following the procedures in Article 10 of the Convention, elaborate in an annex a list of products containing controlled substances in Annex B. Parties that have not objected to the annex in accordance with those procedures shall ban, within one year of the annex having become effective, the import of those products from any State not party to this Protocol.

3 *ter*. Within three years of the date of entry into force of this paragraph, the Parties shall, following the procedures in Article 10 of the Convention, elaborate in an annex a list of products containing controlled substances in Group II of Annex C. Parties that have not objected to the annex in accordance with those procedures shall ban, within one year of the annex having become effective, the import of those products from any State not party to this Protocol.

4. By 1 January 1994, the Parties shall determine the feasibility of banning or restricting, from States not party to this Protocol, the import of products produced with, but not containing, controlled substances in Annex A. If determined feasible, the Parties shall, following the procedures in Article 10 of the Convention, elaborate in an annex a list of such products. Parties that have not objected to the annex in accordance with those procedures shall ban, within one year of the annex having become effective, the import of those products from any State not party to this Protocol.

4 *bis.*   Within five years of the date of the entry into force of this paragraph, the Parties shall determine the feasibility of banning or restricting, from States not party to this Protocol, the import of products produced with, but not containing, controlled substances in Annex B. If determined feasible, the Parties shall, following the procedures in Article 10 of the Convention, elaborate in an annex a list of such products. Parties that have not objected to the annex in accordance with those procedures shall ban or restrict, within one year of the annex having become effective, the import of those products from any State not party to this Protocol.

4 *ter.*   Within five years of the date of entry into force of this paragraph, the Parties shall determine the feasibility of banning or restricting, from States not party to this Protocol, the import of products produced with, but not containing, controlled substances in Group II of Annex C. If determined feasible, the Parties shall, following the procedures in Article 10 of the Convention, elaborate in an annex a list of such products. Parties that have not objected to the annex in accordance with those procedures shall ban or restrict, within one year of the annex having become effective, the import of those products from any State not party to this Protocol.

5.   Each Party undertakes to the fullest practicable extent to discourage the export to any State not party to this Protocol of technology for producing and for utilizing controlled substances in Annexes A, B, C and E.

6.   Each Party shall refrain from providing new subsidies, aid, credits, guarantees or insurance programmes for the export to States not party to this Protocol of products, equipment, plants or technology that would facilitate the production of controlled substances in Annexes A, B, C and E.

7.   Paragraphs 5 and 6 shall not apply to products, equipment, plants or technology that improve the containment, recovery, recycling or destruction of controlled substances, promote the development of alternative substances, or otherwise contribute to the reduction of emissions of controlled substances in Annexes A, B, C and E.

8.   Notwithstanding the provisions of this Article, imports and exports referred to in paragraphs 1 to 4 *ter* of this Article may be permitted from, or to, any State not party to this Protocol, if that State is determined, by a meeting of the Parties, to be in full compliance with Article 2, Articles 2A to 2I and this Article, and have submitted data to that effect as specified in Article 7.

9.   For the purposes of this Article, the term "State not party to this Protocol" shall include, with respect to a particular controlled substance, a State or regional economic integration organization that has not agreed to be bound by the control measures in effect for that substance.

10.   By 1 January 1996, the Parties shall consider whether to amend this Protocol in order to extend the measures in this Article to trade in controlled substances in Group I of Annex C and in Annex E with States not party to the Protocol.

Article 4A: Control of trade with Parties

1.   Where, after the phase-out date applicable to it for a controlled substance, a Party is unable, despite having taken all practicable steps to comply with its obligation under the Protocol, to cease production of that substance for domestic consumption, other than for uses agreed by the Parties to be essential, it shall ban the export of used, recycled and reclaimed quantities of that substance, other than for the purpose of destruction.

2.   Paragraph 1 of this Article shall apply without prejudice to the operation of Article 11 of the Convention and the noncompliance procedure developed under Article 8 of the Protocol.

Article 4B: Licensing

1.   Each Party shall, by 1 January 2000 or within three months of the date of entry into force of this Article for it, whichever is the later, establish and implement a system for licensing the import and export of new, used, recycled and reclaimed controlled substances in Annexes A, B, C and E.

2.   Notwithstanding paragraph 1 of this Article, any Party operating under paragraph 1 of Article 5 which decides it is not in a position to establish and implement a system for licensing the import and export of controlled

substances in Annexes C and E, may delay taking those actions until 1 January 2005 and 1 January 2002, respectively.

3. Each Party shall, within three months of the date of introducing its licensing system, report to the Secretariat on the establishment and operation of that system.

4. The Secretariat shall periodically prepare and circulate to all Parties a list of the Parties that have reported to it on their licensing systems and shall forward this information to the Implementation Committee for consideration and appropriate recommendations to the Parties.

Article 5: Special situation of developing countries

1. Any Party that is a developing country and whose annual calculated level of consumption of the controlled substances in Annex A is less than 0.3 kilograms per capita on the date of the entry into force of the Protocol for it, or any time thereafter until 1 January 1999, shall, in order to meet its basic domestic needs, be entitled to delay for ten years its compliance with the control measures set out in Articles 2A to 2E, provided that any further amendments to the adjustments or Amendment adopted at the Second Meeting of the Parties in London, 29 June 1990, shall apply to the Parties operating under this paragraph after the review provided for in paragraph 8 of this Article has taken place and shall be based on the conclusions of that review.

1 *bis*. The Parties shall, taking into account the review referred to in paragraph 8 of this Article, the assessments made pursuant to Article 6 and any other relevant information, decide by 1 January 1996, through the procedure set forth in paragraph 9 of Article 2:

   (a) With respect to paragraphs 1 to 6 of Article 2F, what base year, initial levels, control schedules and phase-out date for consumption of the controlled substances in Group I of Annex C will apply to Parties operating under paragraph 1 of this Article;

   (b) With respect to Article 2G, what phase-out date for production and consumption of the controlled substances in Group II of Annex C will apply to Parties operating under paragraph 1 of this Article; and

   (c) With respect to Article 2H, what base year, initial levels and control schedules for consumption and production of the controlled substance in Annex E will apply to Parties operating under paragraph 1 of this Article.

2. However, any Party operating under paragraph 1 of this Article shall exceed neither an annual calculated level of consumption of the controlled substances in Annex A of 0.3 kilograms per capita nor an annual calculated level of consumption of controlled substances of Annex B of 0.2 kilograms per capita.

3. When implementing the control measures set out in Articles 2A to 2E, any Party operating under paragraph 1 of this Article shall be entitled to use:

   (a) For controlled substances under Annex A, either the average of its annual calculated level of consumption for the period 1995 to 1997 inclusive or a calculated level of consumption of 0.3 kilograms per capita, whichever is the lower, as the basis for determining its compliance with the control measures relating to consumption.

   (b) For controlled substances under Annex B, the average of its annual calculated level of consumption for the period 1998 to 2000 inclusive or a calculated level of consumption of 0.2 kilograms per capita, whichever is the lower, as the basis for determining its compliance with the control measures relating to consumption.

   (c) For controlled substances under Annex A, either the average of its annual calculated level of production for the period 1995 to 1997 inclusive or a calculated level of production of 0.3 kilograms per capita, whichever is the lower, as the basis for determining its compliance with the control measures relating to production.

(d) For controlled substances under Annex B, either the average of its annual calculated level of production for the period 1998 to 2000 inclusive or a calculated level of production of 0.2 kilograms per capita, whichever is the lower, as the basis for determining its compliance with the control measures relating to production.

4. If a Party operating under paragraph 1 of this Article, at any time before the control measures obligations in Articles 2A to 2I become applicable to it, finds itself unable to obtain an adequate supply of controlled substances, it may notify this to the Secretariat. The Secretariat shall forthwith transmit a copy of such notification to the Parties, which shall consider the matter at their next Meeting, and decide upon appropriate action to be taken.

5. Developing the capacity to fulfil the obligations of the Parties operating under paragraph 1 of this Article to comply with the control measures set out in Articles 2A to 2E and Article 2I, and any control measures in Articles 2F to 2H that are decided pursuant to paragraph 1 *bis* of this Article, and their implementation by those same Parties will depend upon the effective implementation of the financial co-operation as provided by Article 10 and the transfer of technology as provided by Article 10A.

6. Any Party operating under paragraph 1 of this Article may, at any time, notify the Secretariat in writing that, having taken all practicable steps it is unable to implement any or all of the obligations laid down in Articles 2A to 2E and Article 2I, or any or all obligations in Articles 2F to 2H that are decided pursuant to paragraph 1 *bis* of this Article, due to the inadequate implementation of Articles 10 and 10A. The Secretariat shall forthwith transmit a copy of the notification to the Parties, which shall consider the matter at their next Meeting, giving due recognition to paragraph 5 of this Article and shall decide upon appropriate action to be taken.

7. During the period between notification and the Meeting of the Parties at which the appropriate action referred to in paragraph 6 above is to be decided, or for a further period if the Meeting of the Parties so decides, the non-compliance procedures referred to in Article 8 shall not be invoked against the notifying Party. \

8. A Meeting of the Parties shall review, not later than 1995, the situation of the Parties operating under paragraph 1 of this Article, including the effective implementation of financial co-operation and transfer of technology to them, and adopt such revisions that may be deemed necessary regarding the schedule of control measures applicable to those Parties.

8 *bis.* Based on the conclusions of the review referred to in paragraph 8 above:

(a) With respect to the controlled substances in Annex A, a Party operating under paragraph 1 of this Article shall, in order to meet its basic domestic needs, be entitled to delay for ten years its compliance with the control measures adopted by the Second Meeting of the Parties in London, 29 June 1990, and reference by the Protocol to Articles 2A and 2B shall be read accordingly;

(b) With respect to the controlled substances in Annex B, a Party operating under paragraph 1 of this Article shall, in order to meet its basic domestic needs, be entitled to delay for ten years its compliance with the control measures adopted by the Second Meeting of the Parties in London, 29 June 1990, and reference by the Protocol to Articles 2C to 2E shall be read accordingly.

8 *ter.* Pursuant to paragraph 1 *bis* above:

(a) Each Party operating under paragraph 1 of this Article shall ensure that for the twelve-month period commencing on 1 January 2013, and in each twelve-month period thereafter, its calculated level of consumption of the controlled substances in Group I of Annex C does not exceed, annually, the average of its calculated levels of consumption in 2009 and 2010. Each Party operating under paragraph 1 of this Article shall ensure that for the twelve-month period commencing on 1 January 2013 and in each twelve-month period thereafter, its calculated level of production of the controlled substances in Group

I of Annex C does not exceed, annually, the average of its calculated levels of production in 2009 and 2010;

(b) Each Party operating under paragraph 1 of this Article shall ensure that for the twelve-month period commencing on 1 January 2015, and in each twelve-month period thereafter, its calculated level of consumption of the controlled substances in Group I of Annex C does not exceed, annually, ninety per cent of the average of its calculated levels of consumption in 2009 and 2010. Each such Party producing one or more of these substances shall, for the same periods, ensure that its calculated level of production of the controlled substances in Group I of Annex C does not exceed, annually, ninety per cent of the average of its calculated levels of production in 2009 and 2010;

(c) Each Party operating under paragraph 1 of this Article shall ensure that for the twelve-month period commencing on 1 January 2020, and in each twelve-month period thereafter, its calculated level of consumption of the controlled substances in Group I of Annex C does not exceed, annually, sixty-five per cent of the average of its calculated levels of consumption in 2009 and 2010. Each such Party producing one or more of these substances shall, for the same periods, ensure that its calculated level of production of the controlled substances in Group I of Annex C does not exceed, annually, sixty-five per cent of the average of its calculated levels of production in 2009 and 2010;

(d) Each Party operating under paragraph 1 of this Article shall ensure that for the twelve-month period commencing on 1 January 2025, and in each twelve-month period thereafter, its calculated level of consumption of the controlled substances in Group I of Annex C does not exceed, annually, thirty-two point five per cent of the average of its calculated levels of consumption in 2009 and 2010. Each such Party producing one or more of these substances shall, for the same periods, ensure that its calculated level of production of the controlled substances in Group I of Annex C does not exceed, annually, thirty-two point five per cent of the average of its calculated levels of production in 2009 and 2010;

(e) Each Party operating under paragraph 1 of this Article shall ensure that for the twelve-month period commencing on 1 January 2030, and in each twelve-month period thereafter, its calculated level of consumption of the controlled substances in Group I of Annex C does not exceed zero. Each such Party producing one or more of these substances shall, for the same periods, ensure that its calculated level of production of the controlled substances in Group I of Annex C does not exceed zero. However:

(i) Each such Party may exceed that limit on consumption in any such twelve-month period so long as the sum of its calculated levels of consumption over the ten-year period from 1 January 2030 to 1 January 2040, divided by ten, does not exceed two point five per cent of the average of its calculated levels of consumption in 2009 and 2010, and provided that such consumption shall be restricted to the servicing of refrigeration and air-conditioning equipment existing on 1 January 2030;

(ii) Each such Party may exceed that limit on production in any such twelve-month period so long as the sum of its calculated levels of production over the ten-year period from 1 January 2030 to 1 January 2040, divided by ten, does not exceed two point five per cent of the average of its calculated levels of production in 2009 and 2010, and provided that such production shall be restricted to the servicing of refrigeration and air-conditioning equipment existing on 1 January 2030.

(f) Each Party operating under paragraph 1 of this Article shall comply with Article 2G;

(g) With regard to the controlled substance contained in Annex E:

(i) As of 1 January 2002 each Party operating under paragraph 1 of this Article shall comply with the control measures set out in paragraph 1 of Article 2H and, as the basis for its compliance with these control measures, it shall use the average of its annual calculated level of consumption and production, respectively, for the period of 1995 to 1998 inclusive;

(ii)   Each Party operating under paragraph 1 of this Article shall ensure that for the twelve-month period commencing on 1 January 2005, and in each twelve-month period thereafter, its calculated levels of consumption and production of the controlled substance in Annex E do not exceed, annually, eighty per cent of the average of its annual calculated levels of consumption and production, respectively, for the period of 1995 to 1998 inclusive;

(iii) Each Party operating under paragraph 1 of this Article shall ensure that for the twelve-month period commencing on 1 January 2015 and in each twelve-month period thereafter, its calculated levels of consumption and production of the controlled substance in Annex E do not exceed zero. This paragraph will apply save to the extent that the Parties decide to permit the level of production or consumption that is necessary to satisfy uses agreed by them to be critical uses;

(iv) The calculated levels of consumption and production under this subparagraph shall not include the amounts used by the Party for quarantine and pre-shipment applications.

9.   Decisions of the Parties referred to in paragraph 4, 6 and 7 of this Article shall be taken according to the same procedure applied to decision-making under Article 10.

Article 6:   Assessment and review of control measures

Beginning in 1990, and at least every four years thereafter, the Parties shall assess the control measures provided for in Article 2 and Articles 2A to 2I on the basis of available scientific, environmental, technical and economic information. At least one year before each assessment, the Parties shall convene appropriate panels of experts qualified in the fields mentioned and determine the composition and terms of reference of any such panels. Within one year of being convened, the panels will report their conclusions, through the Secretariat, to the Parties.

Article 7:   Reporting of data

1.   Each Party shall provide to the Secretariat, within three months of becoming a Party, statistical data on its production, imports and exports of each of the controlled substances in Annex A for the year 1986, or the best possible estimates of such data where actual data are not available.

2.   Each Party shall provide to the Secretariat statistical data on its production, imports and exports of each of the controlled substances

   –   in Annex B and Groups I and II of Annex C for the year 1989;
   –   in Annex E, for the year 1991,

or the best possible estimates of such data where actual data are not available, not later than three months after the date when the provisions set out in the Protocol with regard to the substances in Annexes B, C and E respectively enter into force for that Party.

3.   Each Party shall provide to the Secretariat statistical data on its annual production (as defined in paragraph 5 of Article 1) of each of the controlled substances listed in Annexes A, B, C and E and, separately, for each substance,

   –   Amounts used for feedstocks,
   –   Amounts destroyed by technologies approved by the Parties, and
   –   Imports from and exports to Parties and non-Parties respectively,

for the year during which provisions concerning the substances in Annexes A, B, C and E respectively entered into force for that Party and for each year thereafter. Each Party shall provide to the Secretariat statistical data on the annual amount of the controlled substance listed in Annex E used for quarantine and pre-shipment applications. Data shall be forwarded not later than nine months after the end of the year to which the data relate.

3 *bis*. Each Party shall provide to the Secretariat separate statistical data of its annual imports and exports of each of the controlled substances listed in Group II of Annex A and Group I of Annex C that have been recycled.

4.   For Parties operating under the provisions of paragraph 8 (a) of Article 2, the requirements in paragraphs 1, 2, 3 and 3 *bi*s of this Article in respect of statistical data on imports and exports shall be satisfied if the regional economic integration organization concerned provides data on imports and exports between the organization and States that are not members of that organization.

Article 8:   Non-compliance

The Parties, at their first meeting, shall consider and approve procedures and institutional mechanisms for determining noncompliance with the provisions of this Protocol and for treatment of Parties found to be in non-compliance.

Article 9:   Research, development, public awareness and exchange of information

1.   The Parties shall co-operate, consistent with their national laws, regulations and practices and taking into account in particular the needs of developing countries, in promoting, directly or through competent international bodies, research, development and exchange of information on:

    (a)   best technologies for improving the containment, recovery, recycling, or destruction of controlled substances or otherwise reducing their emissions;

    (b)   possible alternatives to controlled substances, to products containing such substances, and to products manufactured with them; and

    (c)   costs and benefits of relevant control strategies.

2.   The Parties, individually, jointly or through competent international bodies, shall co-operate in promoting public awareness of the environmental effects of the emissions of controlled substances and other substances that deplete the ozone layer.

3.   Within two years of the entry into force of this Protocol and every two years thereafter, each Party shall submit to the Secretariat a summary of the activities it has conducted pursuant to this Article.

Article 10:   Financial mechanism

1.   The Parties shall establish a mechanism for the purposes of providing financial and technical co-operation, including the transfer of technologies, to Parties operating under paragraph 1 of Article 5 of this Protocol to enable their compliance with the control measures set out in Articles 2A to 2E and Article 2I, and any control measures in Articles 2F to 2H that are decided pursuant to paragraph 1 *bis* of Article 5 of the Protocol. The mechanism, contributions to which shall be additional to other financial transfers to Parties operating under that paragraph, shall meet all agreed incremental costs of such Parties in order to enable their compliance with the control measures of the Protocol. An indicative list of the categories of incremental costs shall be decided by the meeting of the Parties.

2.   The mechanism established under paragraph 1 shall include a Multilateral Fund. It may also include other means of multilateral, regional and bilateral co-operation.

3.   The Multilateral Fund shall:

(a)   Meet, on a grant or concessional basis as appropriate, and according to criteria to be decided upon by the Parties, the agreed incremental costs;

(b)   Finance clearing-house functions to:

   (i)   Assist Parties operating under paragraph 1 of Article 5, through country specific studies and other technical co-operation, to identify their needs for co-operation;

   (ii)   Facilitate technical co-operation to meet these identified needs;

   (iii)   Distribute, as provided for in Article 9, information and relevant materials, and hold workshops, training sessions, and other related activities, for the benefit of Parties that are developing countries; and

   (iv) Facilitate and monitor other multilateral, regional and bilateral co-operation available to Parties that are developing countries;

(c)   Finance the secretarial services of the Multilateral Fund and related support costs.

4.   The Multilateral Fund shall operate under the authority of the Parties who shall decide on its overall policies.

5.   The Parties shall establish an Executive Committee to develop and monitor the implementation of specific operational policies, guidelines and administrative arrangements, including the disbursement of resources, for the purpose of achieving the objectives of the Multilateral Fund. The Executive Committee shall discharge its tasks and responsibilities, specified in its terms of reference as agreed by the Parties, with the co-operation and assistance of the International Bank for Reconstruction and Development (World Bank), the United Nations Environment Programme, the United Nations Development Programme or other appropriate agencies depending on their respective areas of expertise. The members of the Executive Committee, which shall be selected on the basis of a balanced representation of the Parties operating under paragraph 1 of Article 5 and of the Parties not so operating, shall be endorsed by the Parties.

6.   The Multilateral Fund shall be financed by contributions from Parties not operating under paragraph 1 of Article 5 in convertible currency or, in certain circumstances, in kind and/or in national currency, on the basis of the United Nations scale of assessments. Contributions by other Parties shall be encouraged. Bilateral and, in particular cases agreed by a decision of the Parties, regional co-operation may, up to a percentage and consistent with any criteria to be specified by decision of the Parties, be considered as a contribution to the Multilateral Fund, provided that such co-operation, as a minimum:

(a)   Strictly relates to compliance with the provisions of this Protocol;

(b)   Provides additional resources; and

(c)   Meets agreed incremental costs.

7.   The Parties shall decide upon the programme budget of the Multilateral Fund for each fiscal period and upon the percentage of contributions of the individual Parties thereto.

8.   Resources under the Multilateral Fund shall be disbursed with the concurrence of the beneficiary Party.

9.   Decisions by the Parties under this Article shall be taken by consensus whenever possible. If all efforts at consensus have been exhausted and no agreement reached, decisions shall be adopted by a two-thirds majority vote of the Parties present and voting, representing a majority of the Parties operating under paragraph 1 of Article 5 present and voting and a majority of the Parties not so operating present and voting.

10.   The financial mechanism set out in this Article is without prejudice to any future arrangements that may be

developed with respect to other environmental issues.

Article 10A: Transfer of technology

Each Party shall take every practicable step, consistent with the programmes supported by the financial mechanism, to ensure:

(a)   that the best available, environmentally safe substitutes and related technologies are expeditiously transferred to Parties operating under paragraph 1 of Article 5; and

(b)   that the transfers referred to in subparagraph (a) occur under fair and most favourable conditions.

Article 11: Meetings of the parties

1.   The Parties shall hold meetings at regular intervals. The Secretariat shall convene the first meeting of the Parties not later than one year after the date of the entry into force of this Protocol and in conjunction with a meeting of the Conference of the Parties to the Convention, if a meeting of the latter is scheduled within that period.

2.   Subsequent ordinary meetings of the parties shall be held, unless the Parties otherwise decide, in conjunction with meetings of the Conference of the Parties to the Convention. Extraordinary meetings of the Parties shall be held at such other times as may be deemed necessary by a meeting of the Parties, or at the written request of any Party, provided that within six months of such a request being communicated to them by the Secretariat, it is supported by at least one third of the Parties.

3.   The Parties, at their first meeting, shall:

(a)   adopt by consensus rules of procedure for their meetings;

(b)   adopt by consensus the financial rules referred to in paragraph 2 of Article 13;

(c)   establish the panels and determine the terms of reference referred to in Article 6;

(d)   consider and approve the procedures and institutional mechanisms specified in Article 8; and

(e)   begin preparation of workplans pursuant to paragraph 3 of Article 10.

4.   The functions of the meetings of the Parties shall be to:

(a)   review the implementation of this Protocol;

(b)   decide on any adjustments or reductions referred to in paragraph 9 of Article 2;

(c)   decide on any addition to, insertion in or removal from any annex of substances and on related control measures in accordance with paragraph 10 of Article 2;

(d)   establish, where necessary, guidelines or procedures for reporting of information as provided for in Article 7 and paragraph 3 of Article 9;

(e)   review requests for technical assistance submitted pursuant to paragraph 2 of Article 10;

(f)   review reports prepared by the secretariat pursuant to subparagraph (c) of Article 12;

(g)   assess, in accordance with Article 6, the control measures;

(h)   consider and adopt, as required, proposals for amendment of this Protocol or any annex and for any new annex;

(i)   consider and adopt the budget for implementing this Protocol; and

(j)   consider and undertake any additional action that may be required for the achievement of the purposes of this Protocol.

5.   The United Nations, its specialized agencies and the International Atomic Energy Agency, as well as any State not party to this Protocol, may be represented at meetings of the Parties as observers. Any body or agency, whether national or international, governmental or non-governmental, qualified in fields relating to the protection of the ozone layer which has informed the secretariat of its wish to be represented at a meeting of the Parties as an observer may be admitted unless at least one third of the Parties present object. The admission and participation of observers shall be subject to the rules of procedure adopted by the Parties.

Article 12:   Secretariat

For the purposes of this Protocol, the Secretariat shall:

(a)   arrange for and service meetings of the Parties as provided for in Article 11;

(b)   receive and make available, upon request by a Party, data provided pursuant to Article 7;

(c)   prepare and distribute regularly to the Parties reports based on information received pursuant to Articles 7 and 9;

(d)   notify the Parties of any request for technical assistance received pursuant to Article 10 so as to facilitate the provision of such assistance;

(e)   encourage non-Parties to attend the meetings of the Parties as observers and to act in accordance with the provisions of this Protocol;

(f)   provide, as appropriate, the information and requests referred to in subparagraphs (c) and (d) to such non-party observers; and

(g)   perform such other functions for the achievement of the purposes of this Protocol as may be assigned to it by the Parties.

Article 13:   Financial provisions

1.   The funds required for the operation of this Protocol, including those for the functioning of the Secretariat related to this Protocol, shall be charged exclusively against contributions from the Parties.

2.   The Parties, at their first meeting, shall adopt by consensus financial rules for the operation of this Protocol.

Article 14:   Relationship of this Protocol to the Convention

Except as otherwise provided in this Protocol, the provisions of the Convention relating to its protocols shall apply to this Protocol.

Article 15:   Signature

This Protocol shall be open for signature by States and by regional economic integration organizations in Montreal on 16 September 1987, in Ottawa from 17 September 1987 to 16 January 1988, and at United Nations Headquarters in New York from 17 January 1988 to 15 September 1988.

Article 16: Entry into force

1. This Protocol shall enter into force on 1 January 1989, provided that at least eleven instruments of ratification, acceptance, approval of the Protocol or accession thereto have been deposited by States or regional economic integration organizations representing at least two-thirds of 1986 estimated global consumption of the controlled substances, and the provisions of paragraph 1 of Article 17 of the Convention have been fulfilled. In the event that these conditions have not been fulfilled by that date, the Protocol shall enter into force on the ninetieth day following the date on which the conditions have been fulfilled.

2. For the purposes of paragraph 1, any such instrument deposited by a regional economic integration organization shall not be counted as additional to those deposited by member States of such organization.

3. After the entry into force of this Protocol, any State or regional economic integration organization shall become a Party to it on the ninetieth day following the date of deposit of its instrument of ratification, acceptance, approval or accession.

Article 17:   Parties joining after entry into force

Subject to Article 5, any State or regional economic integration organization which becomes a Party to this Protocol after the date of its entry into force, shall fulfil forthwith the sum of the obligations under Article 2, as well as under Articles 2A to 2I and Article 4, that apply at that date to the States and regional economic integration organizations that became Parties on the date the Protocol entered into force.

Article 18:   Reservations

No reservations may be made to this Protocol.

Article 19:   Withdrawal

Any Party may withdraw from this Protocol by giving written notification to the Depositary at any time after four years of assuming the obligations specified in paragraph 1 of Article 2A. Any such withdrawal shall take effect upon expiry of one year after the date of its receipt by the Depositary, or on such later date as may be specified in the notification of the withdrawal.

Article 20: Authentic texts

The original of this Protocol, of which the Arabic, Chinese, English, French, Russian and Spanish texts are equally authentic, shall be deposited with the Secretary-General of the United Nations.

IN WITNESS WHEREOF THE UNDERSIGNED, BEING DULY AUTHORIZED TO THAT EFFECT, HAVE SIGNED THIS PROTOCOL.

DONE AT MONTREAL THIS SIXTEENTH DAY OF SEPTEMBER, ONE THOUSAND NINE HUNDRED AND EIGHTY SEVEN.

Annex A: Controlled substances

Group	Substance	Ozone-Depleting Potential
Group I		
$CFCl_3$	(CFC-11)	1.0
CF_2Cl_2	(CFC-12)	1.0
$C_2F_3Cl_3$	(CFC-113)	0.8
$C_2F_4Cl_2$	(CFC-114)	1.0
C_2F_5Cl	(CFC-115)	0.6
Group II		
CF_2BrCl	(halon-1211)	3.0
CF_3Br	(halon-1301)	10.0
$C_2F_4Br_2$	(halon-2402)	6.0

* These ozone depleting potentials are estimates based on existing knowledge and will be reviewed and revised periodically.

Annex B: Controlled substances

Group	Substance	Ozone-Depleting Potential
Group I		
CF_3Cl	(CFC-13)	1.0
C_2FCl_5	(CFC-111)	1.0
$C_2F_2Cl_4$	(CFC-112)	1.0
C_3FCl_7	(CFC-211)	1.0
$C_3F_2Cl_6$	(CFC-212)	1.0
$C_3F_3Cl_5$	(CFC-213)	1.0
$C_3F_4Cl_4$	(CFC-214)	1.0
$C_3F_5Cl_3$	(CFC-215)	1.0
$C_3F_6Cl_2$	(CFC-216)	1.0
C_3F_7Cl	(CFC-217)	1.0
Group II		
CCl4	carbon 1.1 tetrachloride	1.1
Group III		
$C_2H_3Cl_3$*	1,1,1-trichloroethane* (methyl chloroform)	0.1

* This formula does not refer to 1,1,2-trichloroethane.

Annex C: Controlled substances

Group	Substance	Number of isomers	Ozone-Depleting Potential
Group I			
$CHFCl_2$	(HCFC-21)**	1	0.04
CHF_2Cl	(HCFC-22)**	1	0.055
CH_2FCl	(HCFC-31)	1	0.02
C_2HFCl_4	(HCFC-121)	2	0.01–0.04
$C_2HF_2Cl_3$	(HCFC-122)	3	0.02–0.08
$C_2HF_3Cl_2$	(HCFC-123)	3	0.02–0.06
$CHCl_2CF_3$	(HCFC-123)**	–	0.02
C_2HF_4Cl	(HCFC-124)	2	0.02–0.04
$CHFClCF_3$	(HCFC-124)**	–	0.022
$C_2H_2FCl_3$	(HCFC-131)	3	0.007–0.05
$C_2H_2F_2Cl_2$	(HCFC-132)	4	0.008–0.05
$C_2H_2F_3Cl$	(HCFC-133)	3	0.02–0.06
$C_2H_3FCl_2$	(HCFC-141)	3	0.005–0.07
CH_3CFCl_2	(HCFC-141b)**	–	0.11
$C_2H_3F_2Cl$	(HCFC-142)	3	0.008–0.07
CH_3CF_2Cl	(HCFC-142b)**	–	0.065
C_2H_4FCl	(HCFC-151)	2	0.003–0.005
C_3HFCl_6	(HCFC-221)	5	0.015–0.07
$C_3HF_2Cl_5$	(HCFC-222)	9	0.01–0.09
$C_3HF_3Cl_4$	(HCFC-223)	12	0.01–0.08
$C_3HF_4Cl_3$	(HCFC-224)	12	0.01–0.09
$C_3HF_5Cl_2$	(HCFC-225)	9	0.02–0.07
$CF_3CF_2CHCl_2$	(HCFC-225ca)**	–	0.025
CF_2ClCF_2CHClF	(HCFC-225cb)**	–	0.033
C_3HF_6Cl	(HCFC-226)	5	0.02–0.10
$C_3H_2FCl_5$	(HCFC-231)	9	0.05–0.09
$C_3H_2F_2Cl_4$	(HCFC-232)	16	0.008–0.10
$C_3H_2F_3Cl_3$	(HCFC-233)	18	0.007–0.23
$C_3H_2F_4Cl_2$	(HCFC-234)	16	0.01–0.28
$C_3H_2F_5Cl$	(HCFC-235)	9	0.03–0.52
$C_3H_3FCl_4$	(HCFC-241)	12	0.004–0.09
$C_3H_3F_2Cl_3$	(HCFC-242)	18	0.005–0.13
$C_3H_3F_3Cl_2$	(HCFC-243)	18	0.007–0.12
$C_3H_3F_4Cl$	(HCFC-244)	12	0.009–0.14
$C_3H_4FCl_3$	(HCFC-251)	12	0.001–0.01
$C_3H_4F_2Cl_2$	(HCFC-252)	16	0.005–0.04
$C_3H_4F_3Cl$	(HCFC-253)	12	0.003–0.03
$C_3H_5FCl_2$	(HCFC-261)	9	0.002–0.02
$C_3H_5F_2Cl$	(HCFC-262)	9	0.002–0.02
C_3H_6FCl	(HCFC-271)	5	0.001–0.03
Group II			
$CHFBr_2$		1	1.00
CHF_2Br	(HBFC-22B1)	1	0.74
CH_2FBr		1	0.73
C_2HFBr_4		2	0.3–0.8
$C_2HF_2Br_3$		3	0.5–1.8
$C_2HF_3Br_2$		3	0.4–1.6
C_2HF_4Br		2	0.7–1.2
$C_2H_2FBr_3$		3	0.1–1.1

$C_2H_2F_2Br_2$		4	0.2–1.5
$C_2H_2F_3Br$		3	0.7–1.6
$C_2H_3FBr_2$		3	0.1–1.7
$C_2H_3F_2Br$		3	0.2–1.1
C_2H_4FBr		2	0.07–0.1
C_3HFBr_6		5	0.3–1.5
$C_3HF_2Br_5$		9	0.2–1.9
$C_3HF_3Br_4$		12	0.3–1.8
$C_3HF_4Br_3$		12	0.5–2.2
$C_3HF_5Br_2$		9	0.9–2.0
C_3HF_6Br		5	0.7–3.3
$C_3H_2FBr_5$		9	0.1–1.9
$C_3H_2F_2Br_4$		16	0.2–2.1
$C_3H_2F_3Br_3$		18	0.2–5.6
$C_3H_2F_4Br_2$		16	0.3–7.5
$C_3H_2F_5Br$		8	0.9–14.0
$C_3H_3FBr_4$		12	0.08–1.9
$C_3H_3F_2Br_3$		18	0.1–3.1
$C_3H_3F_3Br_2$		18	0.1–2.5
$C_3H_3F_4Br$		12	0.3–4.4
$C_3H_4FBr_3$		12	0.03–0.3
$C_3H_4F_2Br_2$		16	0.1–1.0
$C_3H_4F_3Br$		12	0.07–0.8
$C_3H_5FBr_2$		9	0.04–0.4
$C_3H_5F_2Br$		9	0.07–0.8
C_3H_6FBr		5	0.02–0.7

Group III

CH_2BrCl	bromochloromethane	1	0.12

* Where a range of ODPs is indicated, the highest value in that range shall be used for the purposes of the Protocol. The ODPs listed as a single value have been determined from calculations based on laboratory measurements. Those listed as a range are based on estimates and are less certain. The range pertains to an isomeric group. The upper value is the estimate of the ODP of the isomer with the highest ODP, and the lower value is the estimate of the ODP of the isomer with the lowest ODP.

** Identifies the most commercially viable substances with ODP values listed against them to be used for the purposes of the Protocol.

Annex D:*   A list of products** containing controlled substances specified in Annex A

	Products	Customs code number
1.	Automobile and truck air conditioning units (whether incorporated in vehicles or not)	....
2.	Domestic and commercial refrigeration and air conditioning/heat pump equipment***	....
	e.g. Refrigerators	....
	Freezers	....
	Dehumidifiers	....
	Water coolers	....
	Ice machines	....
	Air conditioning and heat pump units	....
3.	Aerosol products, except medical aerosols	....
4.	Portable fire extinguisher	....
5.	Insulation boards, panels and pipe covers	....
6.	Pre-polymers	....

* This Annex was adopted by the Third Meeting of the Parties in Nairobi, 21 June 1991 as required by paragraph 3 of Article 4 of the Protocol.

** Though not when transported in consignments of personal or household effects or in similar non-commercial situations normally exempted from customs attention.

*** When containing controlled substances in Annex A as a refrigerant and/or in insulating material of the product.

Annex E: Controlled substance

Group	Substance	Ozone-Depleting Potential
Group I		
CH_3Br	methyl bromide	0.6

UNITED NATIONS FRAMEWORK CONVENTION ON CLIMATE CHANGE

1771 U.N.T.S. 107
Signed: May 9, 1992
Entered Into Force: March 21, 1994
Secretariat Homepage: http://www.unfccc.de/

The Parties to this Convention,

Acknowledging that change in the Earth's climate and its adverse effects are a common concern of humankind,

Concerned that human activities have been substantially increasing the atmospheric concentrations of greenhouse gases, that these increases enhance the natural greenhouse effect, and that this will result on average in an additional warming of the Earth's surface and atmosphere and may adversely affect natural ecosystems and humankind,

Noting that the largest share of historical and current global emissions of greenhouse gases has originated in developed countries, that per capita emissions in developing countries are still relatively low and that the share of global emissions originating in developing countries will grow to meet their social and development needs,

Aware of the role and importance in terrestrial and marine ecosystems of sinks and reservoirs of greenhouse gases,

Noting that there are many uncertainties in predictions of climate change, particularly with regard to the timing, magnitude and regional patterns thereof,

Acknowledging that the global nature of climate change calls for the widest possible cooperation by all countries and their participation in an effective and appropriate international response, in accordance with their common but differentiated responsibilities and respective capabilities and their social and economic conditions,

Recalling the pertinent provisions of the Declaration of the United Nations Conference on the Human Environment, adopted at Stockholm on 16 June 1972,

Recalling also that States have, in accordance with the Charter of the United Nations and the principles of international law, the sovereign right to exploit their own resources pursuant to their own environmental and developmental policies, and the responsibility to ensure that activities within their jurisdiction or control do not cause damage to the environment of other States or of areas beyond the limits of national jurisdiction,

Reaffirming the principle of sovereignty of States in international cooperation to address climate change,

Recognizing that States should enact effective environmental legislation, that environmental standards, management objectives and priorities should reflect the environmental and developmental context to which they apply, and that standards applied by some countries may be inappropriate and of unwarranted economic and social cost to other countries, in particular developing countries,

Recalling the provisions of General Assembly resolution 44/228 of 22 December 1989 on the United Nations Conference on Environment and Development, and resolutions 43/53 of 6 December 1988, 44/207 of 22 December 1989, 45/212 of 21 December 1990 and 46/169 of 19 December 1991 on protection of global climate for present and future generations of mankind,

Recalling also the provisions of General Assembly resolution 44/206 of 22 December 1989 on the possible adverse effects of sea level rise on islands and coastal areas, particularly low-lying coastal areas and the pertinent provisions of General Assembly resolution 44/172 of 19 December 1989 on the implementation of the Plan of Action to Combat Desertification,

Recalling further the Vienna Convention for the Protection of the Ozone Layer, 1985, and the Montreal Protocol on Substances that Deplete the Ozone Layer, 1987, as adjusted and amended on 29 June 1990,

Noting the Ministerial Declaration of the Second World Climate Conference adopted on 7 November 1990,

Conscious of the valuable analytical work being conducted by many States on climate change and of the important contributions of the World Meteorological Organization, the United Nations Environment Programme and other organs, organizations and bodies of the United Nations system, as well as other international and intergovernmental bodies, to the exchange of results of scientific research and the coordination of research,

Recognizing that steps required to understand and address climate change will be environmentally, socially and economically most effective if they are based on relevant scientific, technical and economic considerations and continually re-evaluated in the light of new findings in these areas,

Recognizing that various actions to address climate change can be justified economically in their own right and can also help in solving other environmental problems,

Recognizing also the need for developed countries to take immediate action in a flexible manner on the basis of clear priorities, as a first step towards comprehensive response strategies at the global, national and, where agreed, regional levels that take into account all greenhouse gases, with due consideration of their relative contributions to the enhancement of the greenhouse effect,

Recognizing further that low-lying and other small island countries, countries with low-lying coastal, arid and semi-arid areas or areas liable to floods, drought and desertification, and developing countries with fragile mountainous ecosystems are particularly vulnerable to the adverse effects of climate change,

Recognizing the special difficulties of those countries, especially developing countries, whose economies are particularly dependent on fossil fuel production, use and exportation, as a consequence of action taken on limiting greenhouse gas emissions,

Affirming that responses to climate change should be coordinated with social and economic development in an integrated manner with a view to avoiding adverse impacts on the latter, taking into full account the legitimate priority needs of developing countries for the achievement of sustained economic growth and the eradication of poverty,

Recognizing that all countries, especially developing countries, need access to resources required to achieve sustainable social and economic development and that, in order for developing countries to progress towards that goal, their energy consumption will need to grow taking into account the possibilities for achieving greater energy efficiency and for controlling greenhouse gas emissions in general, including through the application of new technologies on terms which make such an application economically and socially beneficial,

Determined to protect the climate system for present and future generations,

Have agreed as follows:

ARTICLE 1   DEFINITIONS

For the purposes of this Convention:

1. "Adverse effects of climate change" means changes in the physical environment or biota resulting from climate change which have significant deleterious effects on the composition, resilience or productivity of natural and managed ecosystems or on the operation of socio-economic systems or on human health and welfare.

2. "Climate change" means a change of climate which is attributed directly or indirectly to human activity that alters the composition of the global atmosphere and which is in addition to natural climate variability observed over comparable time periods.

3. "Climate system" means the totality of the atmosphere, hydrosphere, biosphere and geosphere and their interactions.

4. "Emissions" means the release of greenhouse gases and/or their precursors into the atmosphere over a specified area and period of time.

5. "Greenhouse gases" means those gaseous constituents of the atmosphere, both natural and anthropogenic, that absorb and re-emit infrared radiation.

6. "Regional economic integration organization" means an organization constituted by sovereign States of a given region which has competence in respect of matters governed by this Convention or its protocols and has been duly authorized, in accordance with its internal procedures, to sign, ratify, accept, approve or accede to the instruments concerned.

7. "Reservoir" means a component or components of the climate system where a greenhouse gas or a precursor of a greenhouse gas is stored.

8. "Sink" means any process, activity or mechanism which removes a greenhouse gas, an aerosol or a precursor of a greenhouse gas from the atmosphere.

9. "Source" means any process or activity which releases a greenhouse gas, an aerosol or a precursor of a greenhouse gas into the atmosphere.

ARTICLE 2   OBJECTIVE

The ultimate objective of this Convention and any related legal instruments that the Conference of the Parties may adopt is to achieve, in accordance with the relevant provisions of the Convention, stabilization of greenhouse gas concentrations in the atmosphere at a level that would prevent dangerous anthropogenic interference with the climate system. Such a level should be achieved within a time frame sufficient to allow ecosystems to adapt naturally to climate change, to ensure that food production is not threatened and to enable economic development to proceed in a sustainable manner.

ARTICLE 3   PRINCIPLES

In their actions to achieve the objective of the Convention and to implement its provisions, the Parties shall be guided, inter alia, by the following:

1. The Parties should protect the climate system for the benefit of present and future generations of humankind, on the basis of equity and in accordance with their common but differentiated responsibilities and respective capabilities. Accordingly, the developed country Parties should take the lead in combating climate change and the adverse effects thereof.

2. The specific needs and special circumstances of developing country Parties, especially those that are particularly vulnerable to the adverse effects of climate change, and of those Parties, especially developing country Parties, that would have to bear a disproportionate or abnormal burden under the Convention, should be given full consideration.

3. The Parties should take precautionary measures to anticipate, prevent or minimize the causes of climate change and mitigate its adverse effects. Where there are threats of serious or irreversible damage, lack of full scientific certainty should not be used as a reason for postponing such measures, taking into account that policies and measures to deal with climate change should be cost-effective so as to ensure global benefits at the lowest possible cost. To achieve this, such policies and measures should take into account different socio-economic contexts, be comprehensive, cover all relevant sources, sinks and reservoirs of greenhouse gases and adaptation, and comprise all economic sectors. Efforts to address climate change may be carried out cooperatively by interested Parties.

4. The Parties have a right to, and should, promote sustainable development. Policies and measures to protect the climate system against human-induced change should be appropriate for the specific conditions of each Party and should be integrated with national development programmes, taking into account that economic development is essential for adopting measures to address climate change.

5. The Parties should cooperate to promote a supportive and open international economic system that would lead to sustainable economic growth and development in all Parties, particularly developing country Parties, thus enabling them better to address the problems of climate change. Measures taken to combat climate change, including unilateral ones, should not constitute a means of arbitrary or unjustifiable discrimination or a disguised restriction on international trade.

ARTICLE 4   COMMITMENTS

1. All Parties, taking into account their common but differentiated responsibilities and their specific national and regional development priorities, objectives and circumstances, shall:

(a) Develop, periodically update, publish and make available to the Conference of the Parties, in accordance with Article 12, national inventories of anthropogenic emissions by sources and removals by sinks of all greenhouse gases not controlled by the Montreal Protocol, using comparable methodologies to be agreed upon by the Conference of the Parties;

(b) Formulate, implement, publish and regularly update national and, where appropriate, regional programmes containing measures to mitigate climate change by addressing anthropogenic emissions by sources and removals by sinks of all greenhouse gases not controlled by the Montreal Protocol, and measures to facilitate adequate adaptation to climate change;

(c) Promote and cooperate in the development, application and diffusion, including transfer, of technologies, practices and processes that control, reduce or prevent anthropogenic emissions of greenhouse gases not controlled by the Montreal Protocol in all relevant sectors, including the energy, transport, industry, agriculture, forestry and waste management sectors;

(d) Promote sustainable management, and promote and cooperate in the conservation and enhancement, as appropriate, of sinks and reservoirs of all greenhouse gases not controlled by the Montreal Protocol, including biomass, forests and oceans as well as other terrestrial, coastal and marine ecosystems;

(e) Cooperate in preparing for adaptation to the impacts of climate change; develop and elaborate appropriate and integrated plans for coastal zone management, water resources and agriculture, and for the protection and rehabilitation of areas, particularly in Africa, affected by drought and desertification, as well as floods;

(f) Take climate change considerations into account, to the extent feasible, in their relevant social, economic and environmental policies and actions, and employ appropriate methods, for example impact assessments, formulated and determined nationally, with a view to minimizing adverse effects on the economy, on public health and on the quality of the environment, of projects or measures undertaken by them to mitigate or adapt to climate change;

(g) Promote and cooperate in scientific, technological, technical, socio-economic and other research, systematic observation and development of data archives related to the climate system and intended to further the understanding and to reduce or eliminate the remaining uncertainties regarding the causes, effects, magnitude and timing of climate change and the economic and social consequences of various response strategies;

(h) Promote and cooperate in the full, open and prompt exchange of relevant scientific, technological, technical, socio-economic and legal information related to the climate system and climate change, and to the economic and social consequences of various response strategies;

(i) Promote and cooperate in education, training and public awareness related to climate change and encourage the widest participation in this process, including that of non-governmental organizations; and

(j) Communicate to the Conference of the Parties information related to implementation, in accordance with Article 12.

2. The developed country Parties and other Parties included in annex I commit themselves specifically as provided for in the following:

(a) Each of these Parties shall adopt national policies and take corresponding measures on the mitigation of climate change, by limiting its anthropogenic emissions of greenhouse gases and protecting and enhancing its greenhouse gas sinks and reservoirs. These policies and measures will demonstrate that developed countries are taking the lead in modifying longer-term trends in anthropogenic emissions consistent with the objective of the Convention, recognizing that the return by the end of the present decade to earlier levels of anthropogenic emissions of carbon dioxide and other greenhouse gases not controlled by the Montreal Protocol would contribute to such modification, and taking into account the differences in these Parties' starting points and approaches, economic structures and resource bases, the need to maintain strong and sustainable economic growth, available technologies and other individual circumstances, as well as the need for equitable and appropriate contributions by each of these Parties to the global effort regarding that objective. These Parties may implement such policies and measures jointly with other Parties and may assist other Parties in contributing to the achievement of the objective of the Convention and, in particular, that of this subparagraph;

(b) In order to promote progress to this end, each of these Parties shall communicate, within six months of the entry into force of the Convention for it and periodically thereafter, and in accordance with Article 12, detailed information on its policies and measures referred to in subparagraph (a) above, as well as on its resulting projected anthropogenic emissions by sources and removals by sinks of greenhouse gases not controlled by the Montreal Protocol for the period referred to in subparagraph (a), with the aim of returning individually or jointly to their 1990 levels these anthropogenic emissions of carbon dioxide and other greenhouse gases not controlled by the Montreal Protocol. This information will be reviewed by the Conference of the Parties, at its first session and periodically thereafter, in accordance with Article 7;

(c) Calculations of emissions by sources and removals by sinks of greenhouse gases for the purposes of subparagraph (b) above should take into account the best available scientific knowledge, including of the effective capacity of sinks and the respective contributions of such gases to climate change. The Conference of the Parties shall consider and agree on methodologies for these calculations at its first session and review them regularly thereafter;

(d) The Conference of the Parties shall, at its first session, review the adequacy of subparagraphs (a) and (b) above. Such review shall be carried out in the light of the best available scientific information and assessment on climate change and its impacts, as well as relevant technical, social and economic information. Based on this review, the Conference of the Parties shall take appropriate action, which may include the adoption of amendments to the commitments in subparagraphs (a) and (b) above. The Conference of the Parties, at its first session, shall also take decisions regarding criteria for joint implementation as indicated in subparagraph (a) above. A second review of subparagraphs (a) and (b) shall take place not later than 31 December 1998, and thereafter at regular intervals determined by the Conference of the Parties, until the objective of the Convention is met;

(e) Each of these Parties shall:

(i) Coordinate as appropriate with other such Parties, relevant economic and administrative instruments developed to achieve the objective of the Convention; and

(ii) Identify and periodically review its own policies and practices which encourage activities that lead to greater levels of anthropogenic emissions of greenhouse gases not controlled by the Montreal Protocol than would otherwise occur;

(f) The Conference of the Parties shall review, not later than 31 December 1998, available information with a view to taking decisions regarding such amendments to the lists in Annexes I and II as may be appropriate, with the approval of the Party concerned;

(g) Any Party not included in Annex I may, in its instrument of ratification, acceptance, approval or accession, or at any time thereafter, notify the Depositary that it intends to be bound by subparagraphs (a) and (b) above. The Depositary shall inform the other signatories and Parties of any such notification.

3. The developed country Parties and other developed Parties included in Annex II shall provide new and additional financial resources to meet the agreed full costs incurred by developing country Parties in complying with their obligations under Article 12, paragraph 1. They shall also provide such financial resources, including for the transfer of technology, needed by the developing country Parties to meet the agreed full incremental costs of implementing measures that are covered by paragraph 1 of this Article and that are agreed between a developing country Party and the international entity or entities referred to in Article 11, in accordance with that Article. The implementation of these commitments shall take into account the need for adequacy and predictability in the flow of funds and the importance of appropriate burden sharing among the developed country Parties.

4. The developed country Parties and other developed Parties included in Annex II shall also assist the developing country Parties that are particularly vulnerable to the adverse effects of climate change in meeting costs of adaptation to those adverse effects.

5. The developed country Parties and other developed Parties included in Annex II shall take all practicable steps to promote, facilitate and finance, as appropriate, the transfer of, or access to, environmentally sound technologies and know-how to other Parties, particularly developing country Parties, to enable them to implement the provisions of the Convention. In this process, the developed country Parties shall support the development and enhancement of

endogenous capacities and technologies of developing country Parties. Other Parties and organizations in a position to do so may also assist in facilitating the transfer of such technologies.

6. In the implementation of their commitments under paragraph 2 above, a certain degree of flexibility shall be allowed by the Conference of the Parties to the Parties included in Annex I undergoing the process of transition to a market economy, in order to enhance the ability of these Parties to address climate change, including with regard to the historical level of anthropogenic emissions of greenhouse gases not controlled by the Montreal Protocol chosen as a reference.

7. The extent to which developing country Parties will effectively implement their commitments under the Convention will depend on the effective implementation by developed country Parties of their commitments under the Convention related to financial resources and transfer of technology and will take fully into account that economic and social development and poverty eradication are the first and overriding priorities of the developing country Parties.

8. In the implementation of the commitments in this Article, the Parties shall give full consideration to what actions are necessary under the Convention, including actions related to funding, insurance and the transfer of technology, to meet the specific needs and concerns of developing country Parties arising from the adverse effects of climate change and/or the impact of the implementation of response measures, especially on:

(a) Small island countries;
(b) Countries with low-lying coastal areas;
(c) Countries with arid and semi-arid areas, forested areas and areas liable to forest decay;
(d) Countries with areas prone to natural disasters;
(e) Countries with areas liable to drought and desertification;
(f) Countries with areas of high urban atmospheric pollution;
(g) Countries with areas with fragile ecosystems, including mountainous ecosystems;
(h) Countries whose economies are highly dependent on income generated from the production, processing and export, and/or on consumption of fossil fuels and associated energy-intensive products; and
(i) Land-locked and transit countries.

Further, the Conference of the Parties may take actions, as appropriate, with respect to this paragraph.

9. The Parties shall take full account of the specific needs and special situations of the least developed countries in their actions with regard to funding and transfer of technology.

10. The Parties shall, in accordance with Article 10, take into consideration in the implementation of the commitments of the Convention the situation of Parties, particularly developing country Parties, with economies that are vulnerable to the adverse effects of the implementation of measures to respond to climate change. This applies notably to Parties with economies that are highly dependent on income generated from the production, processing and export, and/or consumption of fossil fuels and associated energy-intensive products and/or the use of fossil fuels for which such Parties have serious difficulties in switching to alternatives.

ARTICLE 5	RESEARCH AND SYSTEMATIC OBSERVATION

In carrying out their commitments under Article 4, paragraph 1(g), the Parties shall:

(a) Support and further develop, as appropriate, international and intergovernmental programmes and networks or organizations aimed at defining, conducting, assessing and financing research, data collection and systematic observation, taking into account the need to minimize duplication of effort;

(b) Support international and intergovernmental efforts to strengthen systematic observation and national scientific and technical research capacities and capabilities, particularly in developing countries, and to promote access to, and the exchange of, data and analyses thereof obtained from areas beyond national jurisdiction; and

(c) Take into account the particular concerns and needs of developing countries and cooperate in improving their endogenous capacities and capabilities to participate in the efforts referred to in subparagraphs (a) and (b) above.

ARTICLE 6   EDUCATION, TRAINING AND PUBLIC AWARENESS

In carrying out their commitments under Article 4, paragraph 1(i), the Parties shall:

(a) Promote and facilitate at the national and, as appropriate, subregional and regional levels, and in accordance with national laws and regulations, and within their respective capacities:

(i) The development and implementation of educational and public awareness programmes on climate change and its effects;

(ii) Public access to information on climate change and its effects;

(iii) Public participation in addressing climate change and its effects and developing adequate responses; and

(iv) Training of scientific, technical and managerial personnel.

(b) Cooperate in and promote, at the international level, and, where appropriate, using existing bodies:

(i) The development and exchange of educational and public awareness material on climate change and its effects; and

(ii) The development and implementation of education and training programmes, including the strengthening of national institutions and the exchange or secondment of personnel to train experts in this field, in particular for developing countries.

ARTICLE 7   CONFERENCE OF THE PARTIES

1. A Conference of the Parties is hereby established.

2. The Conference of the Parties, as the supreme body of this Convention, shall keep under regular review the implementation of the Convention and any related legal instruments that the Conference of the Parties may adopt, and shall make, within its mandate, the decisions necessary to promote the effective implementation of the Convention. To this end, it shall:

(a) Periodically examine the obligations of the Parties and the institutional arrangements under the Convention, in the light of the objective of the Convention, the experience gained in its implementation and the evolution of scientific and technological knowledge;

(b) Promote and facilitate the exchange of information on measures adopted by the Parties to address climate change and its effects, taking into account the differing circumstances, responsibilities and capabilities of the Parties and their respective commitments under the Convention;

(c) Facilitate, at the request of two or more Parties, the coordination of measures adopted by them to address climate change and its effects, taking into account the differing circumstances, responsibilities and capabilities of the Parties and their respective commitments under the Convention.

(d) Promote and guide, in accordance with the objective and provisions of the Convention, the development and periodic refinement of comparable methodologies, to be agreed on by the Conference of the Parties, inter alia, for preparing inventories of greenhouse gas emissions by sources and removals by sinks, and for evaluating the effectiveness of measures to limit the emissions and enhance the removals of these gases;

(e) Assess, on the basis of all information made available to it in accordance with the provisions of the Convention, the implementation of the Convention by the Parties, the overall effects of the measures taken pursuant to the Convention, in particular environmental, economic and social effects as well as their cumulative impacts and the extent to which progress towards the objective of the Convention is being achieved;

(f) Consider and adopt regular reports on the implementation of the Convention and ensure their publication;

(g) Make recommendations on any matters necessary for the implementation of the Convention;

(h) Seek to mobilize financial resources in accordance with Article 4, paragraphs 3, 4 and 5, and Article 11;

(i) Establish such subsidiary bodies as are deemed necessary for the implementation of the Convention;

(j) Review reports submitted by its subsidiary bodies and provide guidance to them;

(k) Agree upon and adopt, by consensus, rules of procedure and financial rules for itself and for any subsidiary bodies;

(l) Seek and utilize, where appropriate, the services and cooperation of, and information provided by, competent international organizations and intergovernmental and non-governmental bodies; and

(m) Exercise such other functions as are required for the achievement of the objective of the Convention as well as all other functions assigned to it under the Convention.

3. The Conference of the Parties shall, at its first session, adopt its own rules of procedure as well as those of the subsidiary bodies established by the Convention, which shall include decision-making procedures for matters not already covered by decision-making procedures stipulated in the Convention. Such procedures may include specified majorities required for the adoption of particular decisions.

4. The first session of the Conference of the Parties shall be convened by the interim secretariat referred to in Article 21 and shall take place not later than one year after the date of entry into force of the Convention. Thereafter, ordinary sessions of the Conference of the Parties shall be held every year unless otherwise decided by the Conference of the Parties.

5. Extraordinary sessions of the Conference of the Parties shall be held at such other times as may be deemed necessary by the Conference, or at the written request of any Party, provided that, within six months of the request being communicated to the Parties by the secretariat, it is supported by at least one-third of the Parties.

6. The United Nations, its specialized agencies and the International Atomic Energy Agency, as well as any State member thereof or observers thereto not Party to the Convention, may be represented at sessions of the Conference of the Parties as observers. Any body or agency, whether national or international, governmental or non-governmental, which is qualified in matters covered by the Convention, and which has informed the secretariat of its wish to be represented at a session of the Conference of the Parties as an observer, may be so admitted unless at least one-third of the Parties present object. The admission and participation of observers shall be subject to the rules of procedure adopted by the Conference of the Parties.

ARTICLE 8   SECRETARIAT

1. A secretariat is hereby established.

2. The functions of the secretariat shall be:

(a) To make arrangements for sessions of the Conference of the Parties and its subsidiary bodies established under the Convention and to provide them with services as required;
(b) To compile and transmit reports submitted to it;
(c) To facilitate assistance to the Parties, particularly developing country Parties, on request, in the compilation and communication of information required in accordance with the provisions of the Convention;
(d) To prepare reports on its activities and present them to the Conference of the Parties;
(e) To ensure the necessary coordination with the secretariats of other relevant international bodies;
(f) To enter, under the overall guidance of the Conference of the Parties, into such administrative and contractual arrangements as may be required for the effective discharge of its functions; and
(g) To perform the other secretariat functions specified in the Convention and in any of its protocols and such other functions as may be determined by the Conference of the Parties.

3. The Conference of the Parties, at its first session, shall designate a permanent secretariat and make arrangements for its functioning.

ARTICLE 9   SUBSIDIARY BODY FOR SCIENTIFIC AND TECHNOLOGICAL ADVICE

1. A subsidiary body for scientific and technological advice is hereby established to provide the Conference of the Parties and, as appropriate, its other subsidiary bodies with timely information and advice on scientific and technological matters relating to the Convention. This body shall be open to participation by all Parties and shall be multidisciplinary. It shall comprise government representatives competent in the relevant field of expertise. It shall report regularly to the Conference of the Parties on all aspects of its work.

2. Under the guidance of the Conference of the Parties, and drawing upon existing competent international bodies, this body shall:

(a) Provide assessments of the state of scientific knowledge relating to climate change and its effects;

(b) Prepare scientific assessments on the effects of measures taken in the implementation of the Convention;

(c) Identify innovative, efficient and state-of-the-art technologies and know-how and advise on the ways and means of promoting development and/or transferring such technologies;

(d) Provide advice on scientific programmes, international cooperation in research and development related to climate change, as well as on ways and means of supporting endogenous capacity-building in developing countries; and

(e) Respond to scientific, technological and methodological questions that the Conference of the Parties and its subsidiary bodies may put to the body.

3. The functions and terms of reference of this body may be further elaborated by the Conference of the Parties.

ARTICLE 10   SUBSIDIARY BODY FOR IMPLEMENTATION

1. A subsidiary body for implementation is hereby established to assist the Conference of the Parties in the assessment and review of the effective implementation of the Convention. This body shall be open to participation by all Parties and comprise government representatives who are experts on matters related to climate change. It shall report regularly to the Conference of the Parties on all aspects of its work.

2. Under the guidance of the Conference of the Parties, this body shall:

(a) Consider the information communicated in accordance with Article 12, paragraph 1, to assess the overall aggregated effect of the steps taken by the Parties in the light of the latest scientific assessments concerning climate change;

(b) Consider the information communicated in accordance with Article 12, paragraph 2, in order to assist the Conference of the Parties in carrying out the reviews required by Article 4, paragraph 2(d); and

(c) Assist the Conference of the Parties, as appropriate, in the preparation and implementation of its decisions.

ARTICLE 11   FINANCIAL MECHANISM

1. A mechanism for the provision of financial resources on a grant or concessional basis, including for the transfer of technology, is hereby defined. It shall function under the guidance of and be accountable to the Conference of the Parties, which shall decide on its policies, programme priorities and eligibility criteria related to this Convention. Its operation shall be entrusted to one or more existing international entities.

2. The financial mechanism shall have an equitable and balanced representation of all Parties within a transparent system of governance.

3. The Conference of the Parties and the entity or entities entrusted with the operation of the financial mechanism shall agree upon arrangements to give effect to the above paragraphs, which shall include the following:

(a) Modalities to ensure that the funded projects to address climate change are in conformity with the policies, programme priorities and eligibility criteria established by the Conference of the Parties;

(b) Modalities by which a particular funding decision may be reconsidered in light of these policies, programme priorities and eligibility criteria;

(c) Provision by the entity or entities of regular reports to the Conference of the Parties on its funding operations, which is consistent with the requirement for accountability set out in paragraph 1 above; and

(d) Determination in a predictable and identifiable manner of the amount of funding necessary and available for the implementation of this Convention and the conditions under which that amount shall be periodically reviewed.

4. The Conference of the Parties shall make arrangements to implement the above mentioned provisions at its first session, reviewing and taking into account the interim arrangements referred to in Article 21, paragraph 3, and shall decide whether these interim arrangements shall be maintained. Within four years thereafter, the Conference of the Parties shall review the financial mechanism and take appropriate measures.

5. The developed country Parties may also provide and developing country Parties avail themselves of, financial resources related to the implementation of the Convention through bilateral, regional and other multilateral channels.

ARTICLE 12   COMMUNICATION OF INFORMATION RELATED TO IMPLEMENTATION

1. In accordance with Article 4, paragraph 1, each Party shall communicate to the Conference of the Parties, through the secretariat, the following elements of information:

(a) A national inventory of anthropogenic emissions by sources and removals by sinks of all greenhouse gases not controlled by the Montreal Protocol, to the extent its capacities permit, using comparable methodologies to be promoted and agreed upon by the Conference of the Parties;

(b) A general description of steps taken or envisaged by the Party to implement the Convention; and

(c) Any other information that the Party considers relevant to the achievement of the objective of the Convention and suitable for inclusion in its communication, including, if feasible, material relevant for calculations of global emission trends.

2. Each developed country Party and each other Party included in Annex I shall incorporate in its communication the following elements of information:

(a) A detailed description of the policies and measures that it has adopted to implement its commitment under Article 4, paragraphs 2(a) and 2(b); and

(b) A specific estimate of the effects that the policies and measures referred to in subparagraph (a) immediately above will have on anthropogenic emissions by its sources and removals by its sinks of greenhouse gases during the period referred to in Article 4, paragraph 2(a).

3. In addition, each developed country Party and each other developed Party included in Annex II shall incorporate details of measures taken in accordance with Article 4, paragraphs 3, 4 and 5.

4. Developing country Parties may, on a voluntary basis, propose projects for financing, including specific technologies, materials, equipment, techniques or practices that would be needed to implement such projects, along with, if possible, an estimate of all incremental costs, of the reductions of emissions and increments of removals of greenhouse gases, as well as an estimate of the consequent benefits.

5. Each developed country Party and each other Party included in Annex I shall make its initial communication within six months of the entry into force of the Convention for that Party. Each Party not so listed shall make its initial communication within three years of the entry into force of the Convention for that Party, or of the availability of financial resources in accordance with Article 4, paragraph 3. Parties that are least developed countries may make their initial communication at their discretion. The frequency of subsequent communications by all Parties shall be determined by the Conference of the Parties, taking into account the differentiated timetable set by this paragraph.

6. Information communicated by Parties under this Article shall be transmitted by the secretariat as soon as possible to the Conference of the Parties and to any subsidiary bodies concerned. If necessary, the procedures for the communication of information may be further considered by the Conference of the Parties.

7. From its first session, the Conference of the Parties shall arrange for the provision to developing country Parties of technical and financial support, on request, in compiling and communicating information under this Article, as well as in identifying the technical and financial needs associated with proposed projects and response measures under Article 4. Such support may be provided by other Parties, by competent international organizations and by the secretariat, as appropriate.

8. Any group of Parties may, subject to guidelines adopted by the Conference of the Parties, and to prior notification to the Conference of the Parties, make a joint communication in fulfillment of their obligations under this Article, provided that such a communication includes information on the fulfillment by each of these Parties of its individual obligations under the Convention.

9. Information received by the secretariat that is designated by a Party as confidential, in accordance with criteria to be established by the Conference of the Parties, shall be aggregated by the secretariat to protect its confidentiality before being made available to any of the bodies involved in the communication and review of information.

10. Subject to paragraph 9 above, and without prejudice to the ability of any Party to make public its communication at any time, the secretariat shall make communications by Parties under this Article publicly available at the time they are submitted to the Conference of the Parties.

ARTICLE 13 RESOLUTION OF QUESTIONS REGARDING IMPLEMENTATION

The Conference of the Parties shall, at its first session, consider the establishment of a multilateral consultative process, available to Parties on their request, for the resolution of questions regarding the implementation of the Convention.

ARTICLE 14 SETTLEMENT OF DISPUTES

1. In the event of a dispute between any two or more Parties concerning the interpretation or application of the Convention, the Parties concerned shall seek a settlement of the dispute through negotiation or any other peaceful means of their own choice.

2. When ratifying, accepting, approving or acceding to the Convention, or at any time thereafter, a Party which is not a regional economic integration organization may declare in a written instrument submitted to the Depositary that, in respect of any dispute concerning the interpretation or application of the Convention, it recognizes as compulsory ipso facto and without special agreement, in relation to any Party accepting the same obligation:

    (a) Submission of the dispute to the International Court of Justice, and/or
    (b) Arbitration in accordance with procedures to be adopted by the Conference of the Parties as soon as practicable, in an annex on arbitration.

A Party which is a regional economic integration organization may make a declaration with like effect in relation to arbitration in accordance with the procedures referred to in subparagraph (b) above.

3. A declaration made under paragraph 2 above shall remain in force until it expires in accordance with its terms or until three months after written notice of its revocation has been deposited with the Depositary.

4. A new declaration, a notice of revocation or the expiry of a declaration shall not in any way affect proceedings pending before the International Court of Justice or the arbitral tribunal, unless the parties to the dispute otherwise agree.

5. Subject to the operation of paragraph 2 above, if after twelve months following notification by one Party to another that a dispute exists between them, the Parties concerned have not been able to settle their dispute through the means mentioned in paragraph 1 above, the dispute shall be submitted, at the request of any of the parties to the dispute, to conciliation.

6. A conciliation commission shall be created upon the request of one of the parties to the dispute. The commission shall be composed of an equal number of members appointed by each party concerned and a chairman chosen jointly by the members appointed by each party. The commission shall render a recommendatory award, which the parties shall consider in good faith.

7. Additional procedures relating to conciliation shall be adopted by the Conference of the Parties, as soon as practicable, in an annex on conciliation.

8. The provisions of this Article shall apply to any related legal instrument which the Conference of the Parties may adopt, unless the instrument provides otherwise.

ARTICLE 15   AMENDMENTS TO THE CONVENTION

1. Any Party may propose amendments to the Convention.

2. Amendments to the Convention shall be adopted at an ordinary session of the Conference of the Parties. The text of any proposed amendment to the Convention shall be communicated to the Parties by the secretariat at least six months before the meeting at which it is proposed for adoption. The secretariat shall also communicate proposed amendments to the signatories to the Convention and, for information, to the Depositary.

3. The Parties shall make every effort to reach agreement on any proposed amendment to the Convention by consensus. If all efforts at consensus have been exhausted, and no agreement reached, the amendment shall as a last resort be adopted by a three-fourths majority vote of the Parties present and voting at the meeting. The adopted amendment shall be communicated by the secretariat to the Depositary, who shall circulate it to all Parties for their acceptance.

4. Instruments of acceptance in respect of an amendment shall be deposited with the Depositary. An amendment adopted in accordance with paragraph 3 above shall enter into force for those Parties having accepted it on the ninetieth day after the date of receipt by the Depositary of an instrument of acceptance by at least three-fourths of the Parties to the Convention.

5. The amendment shall enter into force for any other Party on the ninetieth day after the date on which that Party deposits with the Depositary its instrument of acceptance of the said amendment.

6. For the purposes of this Article, "Parties present and voting" means Parties present and casting an affirmative or negative vote.

ARTICLE 16   ADOPTION AND AMENDMENT OF ANNEXES TO THE CONVENTION

1. Annexes to the Convention shall form an integral part thereof and, unless otherwise expressly provided, a reference to the Convention constitutes at the same time a reference to any annexes thereto. Without prejudice to the provisions of Article 14, paragraphs 2(b) and 7, such annexes shall be restricted to lists, forms and any other material of a descriptive nature that is of a scientific, technical, procedural or administrative character.

2. Annexes to the Convention shall be proposed and adopted in accordance with the procedure set forth in Article 15, paragraphs 2, 3, and 4.

3. An annex that has been adopted in accordance with paragraph 2 above shall enter into force for all Parties to the Convention six months after the date of the communication by the Depositary to such Parties of the adoption of the annex, except for those Parties that have notified the Depositary, in writing, within that period of their non-acceptance of the annex. The annex shall enter into force for Parties which withdraw their notification of non-acceptance on the ninetieth day after the date on which withdrawal of such notification has been received by the Depositary.

4. The proposal, adoption and entry into force of amendments to annexes to the Convention shall be subject to the same procedure as that for the proposal, adoption and entry into force of annexes to the Convention in accordance with paragraphs 2 and 3 above.

5. If the adoption of an annex or an amendment to an annex involves an amendment to the Convention, that annex or amendment to an annex shall not enter into force until such time as the amendment to the Convention enters into force.

ARTICLE 17   PROTOCOLS

1. The Conference of the Parties may, at any ordinary session, adopt protocols to the Convention.

2. The text of any proposed protocol shall be communicated to the Parties by the secretariat at least six months before such a session.

3. The requirements for the entry into force of any protocol shall be established by that instrument.

4. Only Parties to the Convention may be Parties to a protocol.

5. Decisions under any protocol shall be taken only by the Parties to the protocol concerned.

ARTICLE 18   RIGHT TO VOTE

1. Each Party to the Convention shall have one vote, except as provided for in paragraph 2 below.

2. Regional economic integration organizations, in matters within their competence, shall exercise their right to vote with a number of votes equal to the number of their member States that are Parties to the Convention. Such an organization shall not exercise its right to vote if any of its member States exercises its right, and vice versa.

ARTICLE 19   DEPOSITARY

The Secretary-General of the United Nations shall be the Depositary of the Convention and of protocols adopted in accordance with Article 17.

ARTICLE 20   SIGNATURE

This Convention shall be open for signature by States Members of the United Nations or of any of its specialized agencies or that are Parties to the Statute of the International Court of Justice and by regional economic integration organizations at Rio de Janeiro, during the United Nations Conference on Environment and Development, and thereafter at United Nations Headquarters in New York from 20 June 1992 to 19 June 1993.

ARTICLE 21   INTERIM ARRANGEMENTS

1. The secretariat functions referred to in Article 8 will be carried out on an interim basis by the secretariat established by the General Assembly of the United Nations in its resolution 45/212 of 21 December 1990, until the completion of the first session of the Conference of the Parties.

2. The head of the interim secretariat referred to in paragraph 1 above will cooperate closely with the Intergovernmental Panel on Climate Change to ensure that the Panel can respond to the need for objective scientific and technical advice. Other relevant scientific bodies could also be consulted.

3. The Global Environment Facility of the United Nations Development Programme, the United Nations Environment Programme and the International Bank for Reconstruction and Development shall be the international entity entrusted with the operation of the financial mechanism referred to in Article 11 on an interim basis. In this connection, the Global Environment Facility should be appropriately restructured and its membership made universal to enable it to fulfil the requirements of Article 11.

ARTICLE 22   RATIFICATION, ACCEPTANCE, APPROVAL OR ACCESSION

1. The Convention shall be subject to ratification, acceptance, approval or accession by States and by regional economic integration organizations. It shall be open for accession from the day after the date on which the Convention is closed for signature. Instruments of ratification, acceptance, approval or accession shall be deposited with the Depositary.

2. Any regional economic integration organization which becomes a Party to the Convention without any of its member States being a Party shall be bound by all the obligations under the Convention. In the case of such organizations, one or more of whose member States is a Party to the Convention, the organization and its member States shall decide on their respective responsibilities for the performance of their obligations under the Convention. In such cases, the organization and the member States shall not be entitled to exercise rights under the Convention concurrently.

3. In their instruments of ratification, acceptance, approval or accession, regional economic integration organizations shall declare the extent of their competence with respect to the matters governed by the Convention. These organizations shall also inform the Depositary, who shall in turn inform the Parties, of any substantial modification in the extent of their competence.

ARTICLE 23   ENTRY INTO FORCE

1. The Convention shall enter into force on the ninetieth day after the date of deposit of the fiftieth instrument of ratification, acceptance, approval or accession.

2. For each State or regional economic integration organization that ratifies, accepts or approves the Convention or accedes thereto after the deposit of the fiftieth instrument of ratification, acceptance, approval or accession, the Convention shall enter into force on the ninetieth day after the date of deposit by such State or regional economic integration organization of its instrument of ratification, acceptance, approval or accession.

3. For the purposes of paragraphs 1 and 2 above, any instrument deposited by a regional economic integration organization shall not be counted as additional to those deposited by States members of the organization.

ARTICLE 24   RESERVATIONS

No reservations may be made to the Convention.

ARTICLE 25   WITHDRAWAL

1. At any time after three years from the date on which the Convention has entered into force for a Party, that Party may withdraw from the Convention by giving written notification to the Depositary.

2. Any such withdrawal shall take effect upon expiry of one year from the date of receipt by the Depositary of the notification of withdrawal, or on such later date as may be specified in the notification of withdrawal.

3. Any Party that withdraws from the Convention shall be considered as also having withdrawn from any protocol to which it is a Party.

ARTICLE 26   AUTHENTIC TEXTS

The original of this Convention, of which the Arabic, Chinese, English, French, Russian and Spanish texts are equally authentic, shall be deposited with the Secretary-General of the United Nations. IN WITNESS WHEREOF the undersigned, being duly authorized to that effect, have signed this Convention. DONE at New York this ninth day of May one thousand nine hundred and ninety-two.

ANNEX I

Australia	Austria	Belarus *a/*	Belgium
Bulgaria *a/*	Canada	Czechoslovakia *a/*	Denmark
European Community	Estonia *a/*	Finland	France
Germany	Greece	Hungary *a/*	Iceland
Ireland	Italy	Japan	Latvia *a/*
Lithuania *a/*	Luxembourg	Netherlands	New Zealand
Norway	Poland *a/*	Portugal	Romania *a/*
Russian Federation *a/*	Spain	Sweden	Switzerland
Turkey	Ukraine *a/*	United Kingdom	United States of America

a/ Countries that are undergoing the process of transition to a market economy.

ANNEX II

Australia	Austria	Belgium	Canada
Denmark	European Community	Finland	France
Germany	Greece	Iceland	Ireland
Italy	Japan	Luxembourg	Netherlands
New Zealand	Norway	Portugal	Spain
Sweden	Switzerland	Turkey	United Kingdom
United States of America			

———————————————

KYOTO PROTOCOL TO THE UNITED NATIONS FRAMEWORK CONVENTION ON CLIMATE CHANGE

FCCC/CP/1997/L.7/Add.1
Signed: December 11, 1997
Entered into Force: February 16, 2005

Secretariat Homepage: http://www.unfccc.de/

The Parties to this Protocol,

Being Parties to the United Nations Framework Convention on Climate Change, hereinafter referred to as "the Convention,"

In pursuit of the ultimate objective of the Convention as stated in its Article 2,

Recalling the provisions of the Convention,

Being guided by Article 3 of the Convention,

Pursuant to the Berlin Mandate adopted by decision 1/CP.1 of the Conference of the Parties to the Convention at its first session,

Have agreed as follows:

Article 1

For the purposes of this Protocol, the definitions contained in Article 1 of the Convention shall apply. In addition:

1. "Conference of the Parties" means the Conference of the Parties to the Convention.

2. "Convention" means the United Nations Framework Convention on Climate Change, adopted in New York on 9 May 1992.

3. "Intergovernmental Panel on Climate Change" means the Intergovernmental Panel on Climate Change established in 1988 jointly by the World Meteorological Organization and the United Nations Environment Programme.

4. "Montreal Protocol" means the Montreal Protocol on Substances that Deplete the Ozone Layer, adopted in Montreal on 16 September 1987 and as subsequently adjusted and amended.

5. "Parties present and voting" means Parties present and casting an affirmative or negative vote.

6. "Party" means, unless the context otherwise indicates, a Party to this Protocol.

7. "Party included in Annex I" means a Party included in Annex I to the Convention, as may be amended, or a Party which has made a notification under Article 4, paragraph 2(g), of the Convention.

Article 2

1. Each Party included in Annex I, in achieving its quantified emission limitation and reduction commitments under Article 3, in order to promote sustainable development, shall:
   (a) Implement and/or further elaborate policies and measures in accordance with its national circumstances, such as:
      (i) Enhancement of energy efficiency in relevant sectors of the national economy;
      (ii) Protection and enhancement of sinks and reservoirs of greenhouse gases not controlled by the Montreal Protocol, taking into account its commitments under relevant international

environmental agreements; promotion of sustainable forest management practices, afforestation and reforestation;

(iii) Promotion of sustainable forms of agriculture in light of climate change considerations;

(iv) Research on, and promotion, development and increased use of, new and renewable forms of energy, of carbon dioxide sequestration technologies and of advanced and innovative environmentally sound technologies;

(v) Progressive reduction or phasing out of market imperfections, fiscal incentives, tax and duty exemptions and subsidies in all greenhouse gas emitting sectors that run counter to the objective of the Convention and application of market instruments;

(vi) Encouragement of appropriate reforms in relevant sectors aimed at promoting policies and measures which limit or reduce emissions of greenhouse gases not controlled by the Montreal Protocol;

(vii) Measures to limit and/or reduce emissions of greenhouse gases not controlled by the Montreal Protocol in the transport sector;

(viii) Limitation and/or reduction of methane emissions through recovery and use in waste management, as well as in the production, transport and distribution of energy;

(b) Cooperate with other such Parties to enhance the individual and combined effectiveness of their policies and measures adopted under this Article, pursuant to Article 4, paragraph 2(e)(i), of the Convention. To this end, these Parties shall take steps to share their experience and exchange information on such policies and measures, including developing ways of improving their comparability, transparency and effectiveness. The Conference of the Parties serving as the meeting of the Parties to this Protocol shall, at its first session or as soon as practicable thereafter, consider ways to facilitate such cooperation, taking into account all relevant information.

2. The Parties included in Annex I shall pursue limitation or reduction of emissions of greenhouse gases not controlled by the Montreal Protocol from aviation and marine bunker fuels, working through the International Civil Aviation Organization and the International Maritime Organization, respectively.

3. The Parties included in Annex I shall strive to implement policies and measures under this Article in such a way as to minimize adverse effects, including the adverse effects of climate change, effects on international trade, and social, environmental and economic impacts on other Parties, especially developing country Parties and in particular those identified in Article 4, paragraphs 8 and 9, of the Convention, taking into account Article 3 of the Convention. The Conference of the Parties serving as the meeting of the Parties to this Protocol may take further action, as appropriate, to promote the implementation of the provisions of this paragraph.

4. The Conference of the Parties serving as the meeting of the Parties to this Protocol, if it decides that it would be beneficial to coordinate any of the policies and measures in paragraph 1(a) above, taking into account different national circumstances and potential effects, shall consider ways and means to elaborate the coordination of such policies and measures.

Article 3

1. The Parties included in Annex I shall, individually or jointly, ensure that their aggregate anthropogenic carbon dioxide equivalent emissions of the greenhouse gases listed in Annex A do not exceed their assigned amounts, calculated pursuant to their quantified emission limitation and reduction commitments inscribed in Annex B and in accordance with the provisions of this Article, with a view to reducing their overall emissions of such gases by at least 5 per cent below 1990 levels in the commitment period 2008 to 2012.

2. Each Party included in Annex I shall, by 2005, have made demonstrable progress in achieving its commitments under this Protocol.

3. The net changes in greenhouse gas emissions by sources and removals by sinks resulting from direct human-induced land-use change and forestry activities, limited to afforestation, reforestation and deforestation since 1990, measured as verifiable changes in carbon stocks in each commitment period, shall be used to meet the commitments under this Article of each Party included in Annex I. The greenhouse gas emissions by sources and removals by sinks associated with those activities shall be reported in a transparent and verifiable manner and reviewed in accordance with Articles 7 and 8.

4. Prior to the first session of the Conference of the Parties serving as the meeting of the Parties to this Protocol, each Party included in Annex I shall provide, for consideration by the Subsidiary Body for Scientific and Technological Advice, data to establish its level of carbon stocks in 1990 and to enable an estimate to be made of its changes in carbon stocks in subsequent years. The Conference of the Parties serving as the meeting of the Parties to this Protocol shall, at its first session or as soon as practicable thereafter, decide upon modalities, rules and guidelines as to how and which, additional human-induced activities related to changes in greenhouse gas emissions by sources and removals by sinks in the agricultural soils and land-use change and forestry categories shall be added to, or subtracted from, the assigned amount for Parties included in Annex I, taking into account uncertainties, transparency in reporting, verifiability, the methodological work of the Intergovernmental Panel on Climate Change, the advice provided by the Subsidiary Body for Scientific and Technological Advice in accordance with Article 5 and the decisions of the Conference of the Parties. Such a decision shall apply in the second and subsequent commitment periods. A Party may choose to apply such a decision on these additional human-induced activities for its first commitment period, provided that these activities have taken place since 1990.

5. The Parties included in Annex I undergoing the process of transition to a market economy whose base year or period was established pursuant to decision 9/CP.2 of the Conference of the Parties at its second session shall use that base year or period for the implementation of their commitments under this Article. Any other Party included in Annex I undergoing the process of transition to a market economy which has not yet submitted its first national communication under Article 12 of the Convention may also notify the Conference of the Parties serving as the meeting of the Parties to this Protocol that it intends to use an historical base year or period other than 1990 for the implementation of its commitments under this Article. The Conference of the Parties serving as the meeting of the Parties to this Protocol shall decide on the acceptance of such notification.

6. Taking into account Article 4, paragraph 6, of the Convention, in the implementation of their commitments under this Protocol other than those under this Article, a certain degree of flexibility shall be allowed by the Conference of the Parties serving as the meeting of the Parties to this Protocol to the Parties included in Annex I undergoing the process of transition to a market economy.

7. In the first quantified emission limitation and reduction commitment period, from 2008 to 2012, the assigned amount for each Party included in Annex I shall be equal to the percentage inscribed for it in Annex B of its aggregate anthropogenic carbon dioxide equivalent emissions of the greenhouse gases listed in Annex A in 1990, or the base year or period determined in accordance with paragraph 5 above, multiplied by five. Those Parties included in Annex I for whom land-use change and forestry constituted a net source of greenhouse gas emissions in 1990 shall include in their 1990 emissions base year or period the aggregate anthropogenic carbon dioxide equivalent emissions by sources minus removals by sinks in 1990 from land-use change for the purposes of calculating their assigned amount.

8. Any Party included in Annex I may use 1995 as its base year for hydrofluorocarbons, perfluorocarbons and sulphur hexafluoride, for the purposes of the calculation referred to in paragraph 7 above.

9. Commitments for subsequent periods for Parties included in Annex I shall be established in amendments to Annex B to this Protocol, which shall be adopted in accordance with the provisions of Article 21, paragraph 7. The Conference of the Parties serving as the meeting of the Parties to this Protocol shall initiate the consideration of such commitments at least seven years before the end of the first commitment period referred to in paragraph 1 above.

10. Any emission reduction units, or any part of an assigned amount, which a Party acquires from another Party in accordance with the provisions of Article 6 or of Article 17 shall be added to the assigned amount for the acquiring Party.

11. Any emission reduction units, or any part of an assigned amount, which a Party transfers to another Party in accordance with the provisions of Article 6 or of Article 17 shall be subtracted from the assigned amount for the transferring Party.

12. Any certified emission reductions which a Party acquires from another Party in accordance with the provisions of Article 12 shall be added to the assigned amount for that Party.

13. If the emissions of a Party included in Annex I in a commitment period are less than its assigned amount under this Article, this difference shall, on request of that Party, be added to the assigned amount for that Party for subsequent commitment periods.

14. Each Party included in Annex I shall strive to implement the commitments mentioned in paragraph 1 above in such a way as to minimize adverse social, environmental and economic impacts on developing country Parties, particularly those identified in Article 4, paragraphs 8 and 9, of the Convention. In line with relevant decisions of the Conference of the Parties on the implementation of those paragraphs, the Conference of the Parties serving as the meeting of the Parties to this Protocol shall, at its first session, consider what actions are necessary to minimize the adverse effects of climate change and/or the impacts of response measures on Parties referred to in those paragraphs. Among the issues to be considered shall be the establishment of funding, insurance and transfer of technology.

Article 4

1. Any Parties included in Annex I that have reached an agreement to jointly fulfil their commitments under Article 3 jointly, shall be deemed to have met those commitments provided that their total combined aggregate anthropogenic carbon dioxide equivalent emissions of the greenhouse gases listed in Annex A do not exceed their assigned amounts calculated pursuant to their quantified emission limitation and reduction commitments inscribed in Annex B and in accordance with the provisions of Article 3. The respective emission level allocated to each of the Parties to the agreement shall be set out in that agreement.

2. The Parties to any such agreement shall notify the secretariat of the terms of the agreement on the date of deposit of their instruments of ratification, acceptance or approval of this Protocol, or accession thereto. The secretariat shall in turn inform the Parties and signatories to the Convention of the terms of the agreement.

3. Any such agreement shall remain in operation for the duration of the commitment period specified in Article 3, paragraph 7.

4. If Parties acting jointly do so in the framework of, and together with, a regional economic integration organization, any alteration in the composition of the organization after adoption of this Protocol shall not affect existing commitments under this Protocol. Any alteration in the composition of the organization shall only apply for the purposes of those commitments under Article 3 that are adopted subsequent to that alteration.

5. In the event of failure by the Parties to such an agreement to achieve their total combined level of emission reductions, each Party that an agreement shall be responsible for its own level of emissions set out in the agreement.

6. If Parties acting jointly do so in the framework of, and together with, a regional economic integration organization which is itself a Party to this Protocol, each member State of that regional economic integration organization individually, and together with the regional economic integration organization acting in accordance with Article 24, shall, in the event of failure to achieve the total combined level of emission reductions, be responsible for its level of emissions as notified in accordance with this Article.

Article 5

1. Each Party included in Annex I shall have in place, no later than one year prior to the start of the first commitment period, a national system for the estimation of anthropogenic emissions by sources and removals by sinks of all greenhouse gases not controlled by the Montreal Protocol. Guidelines for such national systems, which shall incorporate the methodologies specified in paragraph 2 below, shall be decided upon by the Conference of the Parties serving as the meeting of the Parties to this Protocol at its first session.

2. Methodologies for estimating anthropogenic emissions by sources and removals by sinks of all greenhouse gases not controlled by the Montreal Protocol shall be those accepted by the Intergovernmental Panel on Climate Change and agreed upon by the Conference of the Parties at its third session. Where such methodologies are not used, appropriate adjustments shall be applied according to methodologies agreed upon by the Conference of the Parties serving as the meeting of the Parties to this Protocol at its first session. Based on the work of, *inter alia*, the Intergovernmental Panel on Climate Change and advice provided by the Subsidiary Body for Scientific and Technological Advice, the Conference of the Parties serving as the meeting of the Parties to this Protocol shall

regularly review and, as appropriate, revise such methodologies and adjustments, taking fully into account any relevant decisions by the Conference of the Parties. Any revision to methodologies or adjustments shall be used only for the purposes of ascertaining compliance with commitments under Article 3 in respect of any commitment period adopted subsequent to that revision.

3. The global warming potentials used to calculate the carbon dioxide equivalence of anthropogenic emissions by sources and removals by sinks of greenhouse gases listed in Annex A shall be those accepted by the Intergovernmental Panel on Climate Change and agreed upon by the Conference of the Parties at its third session. Based on the work of, *inter alia*, the Intergovernmental Panel on Climate Change and advice provided by the Subsidiary Body for Scientific and Technological Advice, the Conference of the Parties serving as the meeting of the Parties to this Protocol shall regularly review and, as appropriate, revise the global warming potential of each such greenhouse gas, taking fully into account any relevant decisions by the Conference of the Parties. Any revision to a global warming potential shall apply only to commitments under Article 3 in respect of any commitment period adopted subsequent to that revision.

Article 6

1. For the purpose of meeting its commitments under Article 3, any Party included in Annex I may transfer to, or acquire from, any other such Party emission reduction units resulting from projects aimed at reducing anthropogenic emissions by sources or enhancing anthropogenic removals by sinks of greenhouse gases in any sector of the economy, provided that:
    (a) Any such project has the approval of the Parties involved;
    (b) Any such project provides a reduction in emissions by sources, or an enhancement of removals by sinks, that is additional to any that would otherwise occur;
    (c) It does not acquire any emission reduction units if it is not in compliance with its obligations under Articles 5 and 7; and
    (d) The acquisition of emission reduction units shall be supplemental to domestic actions for the purposes of meeting commitments under Article 3.

2. The Conference of the Parties serving as the meeting of the Parties to this Protocol may, at its first session or as soon as practicable thereafter, further elaborate guidelines for the implementation of this Article, including for verification and reporting.

3. A Party included in Annex I may authorize legal entities to participate, under its responsibility, in actions leading to the generation, transfer or acquisition under this Article of emission reduction units.

4. If a question of implementation by a Party included in Annex I of the requirements referred to in this Article is identified in accordance with the relevant provisions of Article 8, transfers and acquisitions of emission reduction units may continue to be made after the question has been identified, provided that any such units may not be used by a Party to meet its commitments under Article 3 until any issue of compliance is resolved.

Article 7

1. Each Party included in Annex I shall incorporate in its annual inventory of anthropogenic emissions by sources and removals by sinks of greenhouse gases not controlled by the Montreal Protocol, submitted in accordance with the relevant decisions of the Conference of the Parties, the necessary supplementary information for the purposes of ensuring compliance with Article 3, to be determined in accordance with paragraph 4 below.

2. Each Party included in Annex I shall incorporate in its national communication, submitted under Article 12 of the Convention, the supplementary information necessary to demonstrate compliance with its commitments under this Protocol, to be determined in accordance with paragraph 4 below.

3. Each Party included in Annex I shall submit the information required under paragraph 1 above annually, beginning with the first inventory due under the Convention for the first year of the commitment period after this Protocol has entered into force for that Party. Each such Party shall submit the information required under paragraph 2 above as part of the first national communication due under the Convention after this Protocol has entered into force for it and after the adoption of guidelines as provided for in paragraph 4 below. The frequency of subsequent

submission of information required under this Article shall be determined by the Conference of the Parties serving as the meeting of the Parties to this Protocol, taking into account any timetable for the submission of national communications decided upon by the Conference of the Parties.

4. The Conference of the Parties serving as the meeting of the Parties to this Protocol shall adopt at its first session, and review periodically thereafter, guidelines for the preparation of the information required under this Article, taking into account guidelines for the preparation of national communications by Parties included in Annex I adopted by the Conference of the Parties. The Conference of the Parties serving as the meeting of the Parties to this Protocol shall also, prior to the first commitment period, decide upon modalities for the accounting of assigned amounts.

Article 8

1. The information submitted under Article 7 by each Party included in Annex I shall be reviewed by expert review teams pursuant to the relevant decisions of the Conference of the Parties and in accordance with guidelines adopted for this purpose by the Conference of the Parties serving as the meeting of the Parties to this Protocol under paragraph 4 below. The information submitted under Article 7, paragraph 1, by each Party included in Annex I shall be reviewed as part of the annual compilation and accounting of emissions inventories and assigned amounts. Additionally, the information submitted under Article 7, paragraph 2, by each Party included in Annex I shall be reviewed as part of the review of communications.

2. Expert review teams shall be coordinated by the secretariat and shall be composed of experts selected from those nominated by Parties to the Convention and, as appropriate, by intergovernmental organizations, in accordance with guidance provided for this purpose by the Conference of the Parties.

3. The review process shall provide a thorough and comprehensive technical assessment of all aspects of the implementation by a Party of this Protocol. The expert review teams shall prepare a report to the Conference of the Parties serving as the meeting of the Parties to this Protocol, assessing the implementation of the commitments of the Party and identifying any potential problems in, and factors influencing, the fulfilment of commitments. Such reports shall be circulated by the secretariat to all Parties to the Convention. The secretariat shall list those questions of implementation indicated in such reports for further consideration by the Conference of the Parties serving as the meeting of the Parties to this Protocol.

4. The Conference of the Parties serving as the meeting of the Parties of this Protocol shall adopt at its first session, and review periodically thereafter, guidelines for the review of implementation by expert review teams taking into account the relevant decisions of the Conference of the Parties.

5. The Conference of the Parties serving as the meeting of the Parties to this Protocol shall, with the assistance of the Subsidiary Body for Implementation and, as appropriate, the Subsidiary Body for Scientific and Technological Advice, consider:

(a) The information submitted by the Parties under Article 7 and the reports of the expert reviews thereon conducted under this Article; and

(b) Those questions of implementation listed by the secretariat under paragraph 3 above, as well as any questions raised by Parties.

6. Pursuant to its consideration of the information referred to in paragraph 5 above, the Conference of the Parties serving as the meeting of the Parties to this Protocol shall take decisions on any matter required for the implementation of this Protocol.

Article 9

1. The Conference of the Parties serving as the meeting of the Parties to this Protocol shall periodically review this Protocol in the light of the best available scientific information and assessments on climate change and its impacts, as well as relevant technical, social and economic information. Such reviews shall be coordinated with pertinent reviews under the Convention, in particular those required by Article 4, paragraph 2(d), and Article 7, paragraph 2(a), of the Convention. Based on these reviews, the Conference of the Parties serving as the meeting of the Parties to this Protocol shall take appropriate action.

2. The first review shall take place at the second session of the Conference of the Parties serving as the meeting of the Parties to this Protocol. Further reviews shall take place at regular intervals and in a timely manner.

Article 10

All Parties, taking into account their common but differentiated responsibilities and their specific national and regional development priorities, objectives and circumstances, without introducing any new commitments for Parties not included in Annex I, but reaffirming existing commitments in Article 4, paragraph 1, of the Convention, and continuing to advance the implementation of these commitments in order to achieve sustainable development, taking into account Article 4, paragraphs 3, 5 and 7, of the Convention, shall:

(a) Formulate, where relevant and to the extent possible, cost-effective national and, where appropriate, regional programmes to improve the quality of local emission factors, activity data and/or models which reflect the socio-economic conditions of each Party for the preparation and periodic updating of national inventories of anthropogenic emissions by sources and removals by sinks of all greenhouse gases not controlled by the Montreal Protocol, using comparable methodologies to be agreed upon by the Conference of the Parties, and consistent with the guidelines for the protection of national communications adopted by the Conference of the Parties;

(b) Formulate, implement, publish and regularly update national and, where appropriate, regional programmes containing measures to mitigate climate change and measures to facilitate adequate adaptation to climate change:

> (i) Such programmes would, *inter alia*, concern the energy, transport and industry sectors as well as agriculture, forestry and waste management. Furthermore, adaptation technologies and methods for improving spatial planning would improve adaptation to climate change; and
> (ii) Parties included in Annex I shall submit information on action under this Protocol, including national programmes, in accordance with Article 7; and other Parties shall seek to include in their national communications, as appropriate, information on programmes which contain measures that the Party believes contribute to addressing climate change and its adverse impacts, including the abatement of increase in greenhouse gas emissions, and enhancement of and removals by sinks, capacity building and adaptation measures.

(c) Cooperate in the promotion of effective modalities for the development, application and diffusion of, and take all practicable steps to promote, facilitate and finance, as appropriate, the transfer of, or access to, environmentally sound technologies, know-how, practices and processes pertinent to climate change, in particular to developing countries, including the formulation of policies and programmes for the effective transfer of environmentally sound technologies that are publicly owned or in the public domain and the creation of an enabling environment for the private sector, to promote and enhance the transfer of, and access to, environmentally sound technologies;

(d) Cooperate in scientific and technical research and promote the maintenance and the development of systematic observation systems and development of data archives to reduce uncertainties related to the climate system, the adverse impacts of climate change and the economic and social consequences of various response strategies, and promote the development and strengthening of endogenous capacities and capabilities to participate in international and intergovernmental efforts, programmes and networks on research and systematic observation, taking into account Article 5 of the Convention;

(e) Cooperate in and promote at the international level, and, where appropriate, using existing bodies, the development and implementation of education and training programmes, including the strengthening of national capacity building, in particular human and institutional capacities and the exchange or secondment of personnel to train experts in this field, in particular for developing countries, and facilitate at the national level public awareness of, and public access to information on, climate change. Suitable modalities should be developed to implement these activities through the relevant bodies of the Convention taking into account Article 6 of the Convention;

(f) Include in their national communications information on programmes and activities undertaken pursuant to this Article in accordance with relevant decisions of the Conference of the Parties; and

(g) Give full consideration, in implementing the commitments under this Article, to Article 4, paragraph 8, of the Convention.

Article 11

1. In the implementation of Article 10, Parties shall take into account the provisions of Article 4, paragraphs 4, 5, 7, 8 and 9 of the Convention.

2. In the context of the implementation of Article 4, paragraph 1, of the Convention, in accordance with the provisions of Article 4, paragraph 3, and Article 11 of the Convention, and through the entity or entities entrusted with the operation of the financial mechanism of the Convention, the developed country Parties and other developed Parties included in Annex II to the Convention shall:

(a) Provide new and additional financial resources to meet the agreed full costs incurred by developing country Parties in advancing the implementation of existing commitments under Article 4, paragraph 1(a), of the Convention that are covered in Article 10, subparagraph (a); and

(b) Also provide such financial resources, including for the transfer of technology, needed by the developing country Parties to meet the agreed full incremental costs of advancing the implementation of existing commitments under Article 4, paragraph 1, of the Convention that are covered by Article 10 and that are agreed between a developing country Party and the international entity or entities referred to in Article 11 of the Convention, in accordance with that Article.

The implementation of these existing commitments shall take into account the need for adequacy and predictability in the flow of funds and the importance of appropriate burden sharing among developed country Parties. The guidance to the entity or entities entrusted with the operation of the financial mechanism of the Convention in relevant decisions of the Conference of the Parties, including those agreed before the adoption of this Protocol, shall apply *mutatis mutandis* to the provisions of this paragraph.

3. The developed country Parties and other developed Parties in Annex II to the Convention may also provide, and developing country Parties avail themselves of, financial resources for the implementation of Article 10, through bilateral, regional and other multilateral channels.

Article 12

1. A clean development mechanism is hereby defined.

2. The purpose of the clean development mechanism shall be to assist Parties not included in Annex I in achieving sustainable development and in contributing to the ultimate objective of the Convention, and to assist Parties included in Annex I in achieving compliance with their quantified emission limitation and reduction commitments under Article 3.

3. Under the clean development mechanism:

(a) Parties not included in Annex I will benefit from project activities resulting in certified emission reductions; and

(b) Parties included in Annex I may use the certified emission reductions accruing from such project activities to contribute to compliance with part of their quantified emission limitation and reduction commitments under Article 3, as determined by the Conference of the Parties serving as the meeting of the Parties to this Protocol.

4. The clean development mechanism shall be subject to the authority and guidance of the Conference of the Parties serving as the meeting of the Parties to this Protocol and be supervised by an executive board of the clean development mechanism.

5. Emission reductions resulting from each project activity shall be certified by operational entities to be designated by the Conference of the Parties serving as the meeting of the Parties to this Protocol, on the basis of:

(a) Voluntary participation approved by each Party involved;

(b) Real, measurable, and long-term benefits related to the mitigation of climate change; and (c) Reductions in emissions that are additional to any that would occur in the absence of the certified project activity.

6. The clean development mechanism shall assist in arranging funding of certified project activities as necessary.

7. The Conference of the Parties serving as the meeting of the Parties to this Protocol shall, at its first session, elaborate modalities and procedures with the objective of ensuring transparency, efficiency and accountability through independent auditing and verification of project activities.

8. The Conference of the Parties serving as the meeting of the Parties to this Protocol shall ensure that a share of the proceeds from certified project activities is used to cover administrative expenses as well as to assist developing country Parties that are particularly vulnerable to the adverse effects of climate change to meet the costs of adaptation.

9. Participation under the clean development mechanism, including in activities mentioned in paragraph 3(a) above and in the acquisition of certified emission reductions, may involve private and/or public entities, and is to be subject to whatever guidance may be provided by the executive board of the clean development mechanism.

10. Certified emission reductions obtained during the period from the year 2000 up to the beginning of the first commitment period can be used to assist in achieving compliance in the first commitment period.

Article 13

1. The Conference of the Parties, the supreme body of the Convention, shall serve as the meeting of the Parties to this Protocol.

2. Parties to the Convention that are not Parties to this Protocol may participate as observers in the proceedings of any session of the Conference of the Parties serving as the meeting of the Parties to this Protocol. When the Conference of the Parties serves as the meeting of the Parties to this Protocol, decisions under this Protocol shall be taken only by those that are Parties to the Protocol.

3. When the Conference of the Parties serves as the meeting of the Parties to this Protocol, any member of the Bureau of the Conference of the Parties representing a Party to the Convention but, at that time, not a Party to this Protocol, shall be replaced by an additional member to be elected by and from amongst the Parties to this Protocol.

4. The Conference of the Parties serving as the meeting of the Parties to this Protocol shall keep under regular review the implementation of this Protocol and shall make, within its mandate, the decisions necessary to promote its effective implementation. It shall perform the functions assigned to it by this Protocol and shall:

(a) Assess, on the basis of all information made available to it in accordance with the provisions of this Protocol, the implementation of this Protocol by the Parties, the overall effects of the measures taken pursuant to this Protocol, in particular environmental, economic and social effects as well as their cumulative impacts and the extent to which progress towards the objective of the Convention is being achieved;

(b) Periodically examine the obligations of the Parties under this Protocol, giving due consideration to any reviews required by Article 4, paragraph 2(d), and Article 7, paragraph 2, of the Convention, in the light of the objective of the Convention, the experience gained in its implementation and the evolution of scientific and technological knowledge, and in this respect consider and adopt regular reports on the implementation of this Protocol;

(c) Promote and facilitate the exchange of information on measures adopted by the Parties to address climate change and its effects, taking into account the differing circumstances, responsibilities and capabilities of the Parties and their respective commitments under this Protocol;

(d) Facilitate, at the request of two or more Parties, the coordination of measures adopted by them to address climate change and its effects, taking into account the differing circumstances, responsibilities and capabilities of the Parties and their respective commitments under this Protocol;

(e) Promote and guide, in accordance with the objective of the Convention and the provisions of this Protocol, and taking fully into account the relevant decisions by the Conference of the Parties, the development and periodic refinement of comparable methodologies for the effective implementation of this Protocol, to be agreed on by the Conference of the Parties serving as the meeting of the Parties to this Protocol;

(f) Make recommendations on any matters necessary for the implementation of this Protocol;

(g) Seek to mobilize additional financial resources in accordance with Article 11, paragraph 2;

(h) Establish such subsidiary bodies as are deemed necessary for the implementation of this Protocol;

(i) Seek and utilize, where appropriate, the services and cooperation of, and information provided by, competent international organizations and intergovernmental and non-governmental bodies; and

(j) Exercise such other functions as may be required for the implementation of this Protocol, and consider any assignment resulting from a decision by the Conference of the Parties.

5. The rules of procedure of the Conference of the Parties and financial procedures applied under the Convention shall be applied *mutatis mutandis* under this Protocol, except as may be otherwise decided by consensus by the Conference of the Parties serving as the meeting of the Parties to this Protocol.

6. The first session of the Conference of the Parties serving as the meeting of the Parties to this Protocol shall be convened by the secretariat in conjunction with the first session of the Conference of the Parties that is scheduled after the date of the entry into force of this Protocol. Subsequent ordinary sessions of the Conference of the Parties serving as the meeting of the Parties to this Protocol shall be held every year and in conjunction with ordinary sessions of the Conference of the Parties, unless otherwise decided by the Conference of the Parties serving as the meeting of the Parties to this Protocol.

7. Extraordinary sessions of the Conference of the Parties serving as the meeting of the Parties to this Protocol shall be held at such other times as may be deemed necessary by the Conference of the Parties serving as the meeting of the Parties to this Protocol, or at the written request of any Party, provided that, within six months of the request being communicated to the Parties by the secretariat, it is supported by at least one third of the Parties.

8. The United Nations, its specialized agencies and the International Atomic Energy Agency, as well as any State member thereof or observers thereto not party to the Convention, may be represented at sessions of the Conference of the Parties serving as the meeting of the Parties to this Protocol as observers. Any body or agency, whether national or international, governmental or non-governmental, which is qualified in matters covered by this Protocol and which has informed the secretariat of its wish to be represented at a session of the Conference of the Parties serving as the meeting of the Parties to this Protocol as an observer, may be so admitted unless at least one third of the Parties present object. The admission and participation of observers shall be subject to the rules of procedure, as referred to in paragraph 5 above.

Article 14

1. The secretariat established by Article 8 of the Convention shall serve as the secretariat of this Protocol.

2. Article 8, paragraph 2, of the Convention on the functions of the secretariat, and Article 8, paragraph 3, of the Convention on arrangements made for the functioning of the secretariat, shall apply *mutatis mutandis* to this Protocol. The secretariat shall, in addition, exercise the functions assigned to it under this Protocol.

Article 15

1. The Subsidiary Body for Scientific and Technological Advice and the Subsidiary Body for Implementation established by Articles 9 and 10 of the Convention shall serve as, respectively, the Subsidiary Body for Scientific and Technological Advice and the Subsidiary Body for Implementation of this Protocol. The provisions relating to the functioning of these two bodies under the Convention shall apply *mutatis mutandis* to this Protocol. Sessions of the meetings of the Subsidiary Body for Scientific and Technological Advice and the Subsidiary Body for Implementation of this Protocol shall be held in conjunction with the meetings of, respectively, the Subsidiary Body for Scientific and Technological Advice and the Subsidiary Body for Implementation of the Convention.

2. Parties to the Convention that are not Parties to this Protocol may participate as observers in the proceedings of any session of the subsidiary bodies. When the subsidiary bodies serve as the subsidiary bodies of this Protocol, decisions under this Protocol shall be taken only by the Parties to this Protocol.

3. When the subsidiary bodies established by Articles 9 and 10 of the Convention exercise their functions with regard to matters concerning this Protocol, any member of the Bureau of those subsidiary bodies representing a Party to the Convention but, at that time, not a party to this Protocol, shall be replaced by an additional member to be elected by and from amongst the Parties to this Protocol.

Article 16

The Conference of the Parties serving as the meeting of the Parties to this Protocol shall, as soon as practicable, consider the application to this Protocol of, and modify as appropriate, the multilateral consultative process referred to in Article 13 of the Convention, in the light of any relevant decisions that may be taken by the Conference of the Parties. Any multilateral consultative process that may be applied to this Protocol shall operate without prejudice to the procedures and mechanisms established in accordance with Article 18.

Article 17

The Conference of the Parties shall define the relevant principles, modalities, rules and guidelines, in particular for verification, reporting and accountability for emissions trading. The Parties included in Annex B may participate in emissions trading for the purposes of fulfilling their commitments under Article 3. Any such trading shall be supplemental to domestic actions for the purpose of meeting quantified emission limitation and reduction commitments under that Article.

Article 18

The Conference of the Parties serving as the meeting of the Parties to this Protocol shall, at its first session, approve appropriate and effective procedures and mechanisms to determine and to address cases of non-compliance with the provisions of this Protocol, including through the development of an indicative list of consequences, taking into account the cause, type, degree and frequency of non-compliance. Any procedures and mechanisms under this Article entailing binding consequences shall be adopted by means of an amendment to this Protocol.

Article 19

The provisions of Article 14 of the Convention on settlement of disputes shall apply *mutatis mutandis* to this Protocol.

Article 20

1. Any Party may propose amendments to this Protocol.

2. Amendments to this Protocol shall be adopted at an ordinary session of the Conference of the Parties serving as the meeting of the Parties to this Protocol. The text of any proposed amendment to this Protocol shall be communicated to the Parties by the secretariat at least six months before the meeting at which it is proposed for adoption. The Secretariat shall also communicate the text of any proposed amendments to the Parties and signatories to the Convention and, for information, to the Depositary.

3. The Parties shall make every effort to reach agreement on any proposed amendment to this Protocol by consensus. If all efforts at consensus have been exhausted, and no agreement reached, the amendment shall as a last resort be adopted by a three-fourths majority vote of the Parties present and voting at the meeting. The adopted amendment shall be communicated by the secretariat to the Depositary, who shall circulate it to all Parties for their acceptance.

4. Instruments of acceptance in respect of an amendment shall be deposited with the Depositary. An amendment adopted in accordance with paragraph 3 above shall enter into force for those Parties having accepted it on the ninetieth day after the date of receipt by the Depositary of an instrument of acceptance by at least three fourths of the Parties to this Protocol.

5. The amendment shall enter into force for any other Party on the ninetieth day after the date on which that Party deposits with the Depositary its instrument of acceptance of the said amendment.

Article 21

1. Annexes to this Protocol shall form an integral part thereof and, unless otherwise expressly provided, a reference to this Protocol constitutes at the same time a reference to any annexes thereto. Any annexes adopted after the entry into force of this Protocol shall be restricted to lists, forms and any other material of a descriptive nature that is of a scientific, technical, procedural or administrative character.

2. Any Party may make proposals for an annex to this Protocol and may propose amendments to annexes to this Protocol.

3. Annexes to this Protocol and amendments to annexes to this Protocol shall be adopted at an ordinary session of the Conference of the Parties serving as the meeting of the Parties to this Protocol. The text of any proposed annex or amendment to an annex shall be communicated to the Parties by the secretariat at least six months before the meeting at which it is proposed for adoption. The secretariat shall also communicate the text of any proposed annex or amendment to an annex to the Parties and signatories to the Convention and, for information, to the Depositary.

4. The Parties shall make every effort to reach agreement on any proposed annex or amendment to an annex by consensus. If all efforts at consensus have been exhausted, and no agreement reached, the annex or amendment to an annex shall as a last resort be adopted by a three-fourths majority vote of the Parties present and voting at the meeting. The adopted annex or amendment to an annex shall be communicated by the secretariat to the Depositary, who shall circulate it to all Parties for their acceptance.

5. An annex, or amendment to an annex other than Annex A or B, that has been adopted in accordance with paragraphs 3 and 4 above shall enter into force for all Parties to this Protocol six months after the date of the communication by the Depositary to such Parties of the adoption of the annex or adoption of the amendment to the annex, except for those Parties that have notified the Depositary, in writing, within that period of their non-acceptance of the annex or amendment to the annex. The annex or amendment to an annex shall enter into force for Parties which withdraw their notification of non-acceptance on the ninetieth day after the date on which withdrawal of such notification has been received by the Depositary.

6. If the adoption of an annex or an amendment to an annex involves an amendment to this Protocol, that annex or amendment to an annex shall not enter into force until such time as the amendment to this Protocol enters into force.

7. Amendments to Annexes A and B to this Protocol shall be adopted and enter into force in accordance with the procedure set out in Article 20, provided that any amendment to Annex B shall be adopted only with the written consent of the Party concerned.

Article 22

1. Each Party shall have one vote, except as provided for in paragraph 2 below.

2. Regional economic integration organizations, in matters within their competence, shall exercise their right to vote with a number of votes equal to the number of their member States that are Parties to this Protocol. Such an organization shall not exercise its right to vote if any of its member States exercises its right, and vice versa.

Article 23

The Secretary-General of the United Nations shall be the Depositary of this Protocol.

Article 24

1. This Protocol shall be open for signature and subject to ratification, acceptance or approval by States and regional economic integration organizations which are Parties to the Convention. It shall be open for signature at United Nations Headquarters in New York from 16 March 1998 to 15 March 1999. This Protocol shall be open for accession from the day after the date on which it is closed for signature. Instruments of ratification, acceptance, approval or accession shall be deposited with the Depositary.

2. Any regional economic integration organization which becomes a Party to this Protocol without any of its member States being a Party shall be bound by all the obligations under this Protocol. In the case of such organizations, one or more of whose member States is a Party to this Protocol, the organization and its member States shall decide on their respective responsibilities for the performance of their obligations under this Protocol. In such cases, the organization and the member States shall not be entitled to exercise rights under this Protocol concurrently.

3. In their instruments of ratification, acceptance, approval or accession, regional economic integration organizations shall declare the extent of their competence with respect to the matters governed by this Protocol. These organizations shall also inform the Depositary, who shall in turn inform the Parties, of any substantial modification in the extent of their competence.

Article 25

1. This Protocol shall enter into force on the ninetieth day after the date on which not less than 55 Parties to the Convention, incorporating Parties included in Annex I which accounted in total for at least 55 per cent of the total carbon dioxide emissions for 1990 of the Parties included in Annex I, have deposited their instruments of ratification, acceptance, approval or accession.

2. For the purposes of this Article, "the total carbon dioxide emissions for 1990 of the Parties included in Annex I" means the amount communicated on or before the date of adoption of this Protocol by the Parties included in Annex I in their first national communications submitted in accordance with Article 12 of the Convention.

3. For each State or regional economic integration organization that ratifies, accepts or approves this Protocol or accedes thereto after the conditions set out in paragraph 1 above for entry into force have been fulfilled, this Protocol shall enter into force on the ninetieth day following the date of deposit of its instrument of ratification, acceptance, approval or accession.

4. For the purposes of this Article, any instrument deposited by a regional economic integration organization shall not be counted as additional to those deposited by States members of the organization.

Article 26

No reservations may be made to this Protocol.

Article 27

1. At any time after three years from the date on which this Protocol has entered into force for a Party, that Party may withdraw from this Protocol by giving written notification to the Depositary.

2. Any such withdrawal shall take effect upon expiry of one year from the date of receipt by the Depositary of the notification of withdrawal, or on such later date as may be specified in the notification of withdrawal.

3. Any Party that withdraws from the Convention shall be considered as also having withdrawn from this Protocol.

Article 28

The original of this Protocol, of which the Arabic, Chinese, English, French, Russian and Spanish texts are equally authentic, shall be deposited with the Secretary-General of the United Nations.

DONE at Kyoto this eleventh day of December one thousand nine hundred and ninety-seven.

IN WITNESS WHEREOF the undersigned, being duly authorized to that effect, have affixed their signatures to this Protocol on the dates indicated.

Annex A

<u>**Greenhouse gases**</u>:
    Carbon dioxide (CO_2)
    Methane (CH_4)
    Nitrous oxide (N_2O)
    Hydrofluorocarbons (HFCs)
    Perfluorocarbons (PFCs)
    Sulphur hexafluoride (SF_6)

<u>**Sectors/source categories**</u>:
Energy:
    Fuel combustion
    Energy industries
    Manufacturing industries and construction
    Transport
    Other sectors
    Other

Fugitive emissions from fuels:
    Solid fuels
    Oil and natural gas
    Other

Industrial processes:
    Mineral products
    Chemical industry
    Metal production
    Other production
    Production of halocarbons and sulphur hexafluoride
    Consumption of halocarbons and sulphur hexafluoride
    Other

<u>**Solvent and other product use**</u>:
Agriculture:
    Enteric fermentation
    Manure management
    Rice cultivation
    Agricultural soils
    Prescribed burning of savannas
    Field burning of agricultural residues
    Other

Waste:
    Solid waste disposal on land
    Wastewater handling
    Waste incineration
    Other

Annex B

<u>Quantified emission limitation or reduction commitment (percentage of base year or period)</u>

<u>Party</u>

Australia 108	Austria 92	Belgium 92	Bulgaria* 92
Canada 94	Croatia* 95	Czech Republic* 92	Denmark 92
Estonia* 92	European Comm. 92	Finland 92	France 92
Germany 92	Greece 92	Hungary* 94	Iceland 110
Ireland 92	Italy 92	Japan 94	Latvia* 92
Liechtenstein 92	Lithuania* 92	Luxembourg 92	Monaco 92
Netherlands 92	New Zealand 100	Norway 101	Poland* 94
Portugal 92	Romania* 92	Russian Federation* 100	Slovakia* 92
Slovenia* 92	Spain 92	Sweden 92	Switzerland 92
Ukraine* 100	United Kingdom 92	United States of America 93	

* Countries that are undergoing the process of transition to a market economy.

———————————————

Copenhagen Accord

UNFCCC, Decision 2/Cp.15
FCCC/CP/2009/11/Add.1, at page5
December 18, 2009
http://unfccc.int/resource/docs/2009/cop15/eng/11a01.pdf

The Heads of State, Heads of Government, Ministers, and other heads of the following delegations present at the United Nations Climate Change Conference 2009 in Copenhagen, (NB: List of delegations is omitted):

In pursuit of the ultimate objective of the Convention as stated in its Article 2,

Being guided by the principles and provisions of the Convention,

Noting the results of work done by the two Ad hoc Working Groups,

Endorsing decision x/CP.15 on the Ad hoc Working Group on Long-term Cooperative Action and decision x/CMP.5 that requests the Ad hoc Working Group on Further Commitments of Annex I Parties under the Kyoto Protocol to continue its work,

Have agreed on this Copenhagen Accord which is operational immediately.

1. We underline that climate change is one of the greatest challenges of our time. We emphasise our strong political will to urgently combat climate change in accordance with the principle of common but differentiated responsibilities and respective capabilities. To achieve the ultimate objective of the Convention to stabilize greenhouse gas concentration in the atmosphere at a level that would prevent dangerous anthropogenic interference with the climate system, we shall, recognizing the scientific view that the increase in global temperature should be below 2 degrees Celsius, on the basis of equity and in the context of sustainable development, enhance our long-term cooperative action to combat climate change. We recognize the critical impacts of climate change and the potential impacts of response measures on countries particularly vulnerable to its adverse effects and stress the need to establish a comprehensive adaptation programme including international support.

2. We agree that deep cuts in global emissions are required according to science, and as documented by the IPCC Fourth Assessment Report with a view to reduce global emissions so as to hold the increase in global temperature below 2 degrees Celsius, and take action to meet this objective consistent with science and on the basis of equity. We should cooperate in achieving the peaking of global and national emissions as soon as possible, recognizing that the time frame for peaking will be longer in developing countries and bearing in mind that social and economic development and poverty eradication are the first and overriding priorities of developing countries and that a low-emission development strategy is indispensable to sustainable development.

3. Adaptation to the adverse effects of climate change and the potential impacts of response measures is a challenge faced by all countries. Enhanced action and international cooperation on adaptation is urgently required to ensure the implementation of the Convention by enabling and supporting the implementation of adaptation actions aimed at reducing vulnerability and building resilience in developing countries, especially in those that are particularly vulnerable, especially least developed countries, small island developing States and Africa. We agree that developed countries shall provide adequate, predictable and sustainable financial resources, technology and capacity-building to support the implementation of adaptation action in developing countries.

4. Annex I Parties commit to implement individually or jointly the quantified economy-wide emissions targets for 2020, to be submitted in the format given in Appendix I by Annex I Parties to the secretariat by 31 January 2010 for compilation in an INF document. Annex I Parties that are Party to the Kyoto Protocol will thereby further strengthen the emissions reductions initiated by the Kyoto Protocol. Delivery of reductions and financing by developed countries will be measured, reported and verified in accordance with existing and any further guidelines adopted by

the Conference of the Parties, and will ensure that accounting of such targets and finance is rigorous, robust and transparent.

5. Non-Annex I Parties to the Convention will implement mitigation actions, including those to be submitted to the secretariat by non-Annex I Parties in the format given in Appendix II by 31 January 2010, for compilation in an INF document, consistent with Article 4.1 and Article 4.7 and in the context of sustainable development. Least developed countries and small island developing States may undertake actions voluntarily and on the basis of support. Mitigation actions subsequently taken and envisaged by Non-Annex I Parties, including national inventory reports, shall be communicated through national communications consistent with Article 12.1(b) every two years on the basis of guidelines to be adopted by the Conference of the Parties. Those mitigation actions in national communications or otherwise communicated to the Secretariat will be added to the list in appendix II. Mitigation actions taken by Non-Annex I Parties will be subject to their domestic measurement, reporting and verification the result of which will be reported through their national communications every two years. Non-Annex I Parties will communicate information on the implementation of their actions through National Communications, with provisions for international consultations and analysis under clearly defined guidelines that will ensure that national sovereignty is respected. Nationally appropriate mitigation actions seeking international support will be recorded in a registry along with relevant technology, finance and capacity building support. Those actions supported will be added to the list in appendix II. These supported nationally appropriate mitigation actions will be subject to international measurement, reporting and verification in accordance with guidelines adopted by the Conference of the Parties.

6. We recognize the crucial role of reducing emission from deforestation and forest degradation and the need to enhance removals of greenhouse gas emission by forests and agree on the need to provide positive incentives to such actions through the immediate establishment of a mechanism including REDD-plus, to enable the mobilization of financial resources from developed countries.

7. We decide to pursue various approaches, including opportunities to use markets, to enhance the cost-effectiveness of, and to promote mitigation actions. Developing countries, especially those with low emitting economies should be provided incentives to continue to develop on a low emission pathway. '

8. Scaled up, new and additional, predictable and adequate funding as well as improved access shall be provided to developing countries, in accordance with the relevant provisions of the Convention, to enable and support enhanced action on mitigation, including substantial finance to reduce emissions from deforestation and forest degradation (REDD-plus), adaptation, technology development and transfer and capacity-building, for enhanced implementation of the Convention. The collective commitment by developed countries is to provide new and additional resources, including forestry and investments through international institutions, approaching USD 30 billion for the period 2010 œ 2012 with balanced allocation between adaptation and mitigation. Funding for adaptation will be prioritized for the most vulnerable developing countries, such as the least developed countries, small island developing States and Africa. In the context of meaningful mitigation actions and transparency on implementation, developed countries commit to a goal of mobilizing jointly USD 100 billion dollars a year by 2020 to address the needs of developing countries. This funding will come from a wide variety of sources, public and private, bilateral and multilateral, including alternative sources of finance. New multilateral funding for adaptation will be delivered through effective and efficient fund arrangements, with a governance structure providing for equal representation of developed and developing countries. A significant portion of such funding should flow through the Copenhagen Green Climate Fund.

9. To this end, a High Level Panel will be established under the guidance of and accountable to the Conference of the Parties to study the contribution of the potential sources of revenue, including alternative sources of finance, towards meeting this goal.

10. We decide that the Copenhagen Green Climate Fund shall be established as an operating entity of the financial mechanism of the Convention to support projects, programme, policies and other activities in developing countries related to mitigation including REDD-plus, adaptation, capacity-building, technology development and transfer.

11. In order to enhance action on development and transfer of technology we decide to establish a Technology Mechanism to accelerate technology development and transfer in support of action on adaptation and mitigation that will be guided by a country-driven approach and be based on national circumstances and priorities.

12. We call for an assessment of the implementation of this Accord to be completed by 2015, including in light of the Convention's ultimate objective. This would include consideration of strengthening the long-term goal referencing various matters presented by the science, including in relation to temperature rises of 1.5 degrees Celsius.

APPENDIX I
Quantified economy-wide emissions targets for 2020

Annex I Parties	Quantified economy-wide emissions targets for 2020	
	Emissions reduction in 2020	Base year

APPENDIX II
Nationally appropriate mitigation actions of developing country Parties

Non-Annex I	Actions

UNITED NATIONS CONVENTION ON THE LAW OF THE SEA
(excerpts)

1833 U.N.T.S. 3
Signed: 10 December 1982
Entry into Force: 16 November 1994
Secretariat Homepage: http://www.un.org/Depts/los/index.htm

The States Parties to this Convention,

Prompted by the desire to settle, in a spirit of mutual understanding and co-operation, all issues relating to the law of the sea and aware of the historic significance of this Convention as an important contribution to the maintenance of peace, justice and progress for all peoples of the world,

Noting that developments since the United Nations Conferences on the Law of the Sea held at Geneva in 1958 and 1960 have accentuated the need for a new and generally acceptable Convention on the law of the sea,

Conscious that the problems of ocean space are closely interrelated and need to be considered as a whole,

Recognizing the desirability of establishing through this Convention, with due regard for the sovereignty of all States, a legal order for the seas and oceans which will facilitate international communication, and will promote the peaceful uses of the seas and oceans, the equitable and efficient utilization of their resources, the conservation of their living resources, and the study, protection and preservation of the marine environment,

Bearing in mind that the achievement of these goals will contribute to the realization of a just and equitable international economic order which takes into account the interests and needs of mankind as a whole and, in particular, the special interests and needs of developing countries, whether coastal or land-locked,

Desiring by this Convention to develop the principles embodied in resolution 2749 (XXV) of 17 December 1970 in which the General Assembly of the United Nations solemnly declared inter alia that the area of the sea-bed and ocean floor and the subsoil thereof, beyond the limits of national jurisdiction, as well as its resources, are the common heritage of mankind, the exploration and exploitation of which shall be carried out for the benefit of mankind as a whole, irrespective of the geographical location of States,

Believing that the codification and progressive development of the law of the sea achieved in this Convention will contribute to the strengthening of peace, security, co-operation and friendly relations among all nations in conformity with the principles of justice and equal rights and will promote the economic and social advancement of all peoples of the world, in accordance with the Purposes and Principles of the United Nations as set forth in the Charter,

Affirming that matters not regulated by this Convention continue to be governed by the rules and principles of general international law,

Have agreed as follows:

PART I   INTRODUCTION

Article 1   Use of terms and scope

1. For the purposes of this Convention:
    (1) "Area" means the sea-bed and ocean floor and subsoil thereof beyond the limits of national jurisdiction;
    (2) "Authority" means the International Sea-Bed Authority;

    (3) "activities in the Area" means all activities of exploration for, and exploitation of, the resources of the Area;

(4) "pollution of the marine environment" means the introduction by man, directly or indirectly, of substances or energy into the marine environment, including estuaries, which results or is likely to result in such deleterious effects as harm to living resources and marine life, hazards to human health, hindrance to marine activities, including fishing and other legitimate uses of the sea, impairment of quality for use of sea water and reduction of amenities;

(5) (a) "dumping" means:

(i) any deliberate disposal of wastes or other matter from vessels, aircraft, platforms or other man-made structures at sea;

(ii) any deliberate disposal of vessels, aircraft, platforms or other man-made structures at sea

(b) "dumping" does not include:

(i) the disposal of wastes or other matter incidental to, or derived from the normal operations of vessels, aircraft, platforms or other man-made structures at sea and their equipment, other than wastes or other matter transported by or to vessels, aircraft, platforms or other man-made structures at sea, operating for the purpose of disposal of such matter or derived from the treatment of such wastes or other matter on such vessels, aircraft, platforms or structures;

(ii) placement of matter for a purpose other than the mere disposal thereof, provided that such placement is not contrary to the aims of this Convention.

2.   (1) "States Parties" means States which have consented to be bound by this Convention and for which this Convention is in force.

(2) This Convention applies mutatis mutandis to the entities referred to in article 305, paragraph 1(b), (c), (d), (e) and (f), which become Parties to this Convention in accordance with the conditions relevant to each, and to that extent "States Parties" refers to those entities.

PART II TERRITORIAL SEA AND CONTIGUOUS ZONE

Section 1   General Provisions

Article 2   Legal status of the territorial sea, of the air space over the territorial sea and of its bed and subsoil

1. The sovereignty of a coastal State extends, beyond its land territory and internal waters and, in the case of an archipelagic State, its archipelagic waters, to an adjacent belt of sea, described as the territorial sea.

2. This sovereignty extends to the air space over the territorial sea as well as to its bed and subsoil.

3. The sovereignty over the territorial sea is exercised subject to this Convention and to other rules of international law.

Section 2   Limits of the Territorial Sea

Article 3   Breadth of the territorial sea

Every State has the right to establish the breadth of its territorial sea up to a limit not exceeding 12 nautical miles, measured from baselines determined in accordance with this Convention.

Article 4   Outer limit of the territorial sea

The outer limit of the territorial sea is the line every point of which is at a distance from the nearest point of the baseline equal to the breadth of the territorial sea.

Article 5   Normal baseline

Except where otherwise provided in this Convention, the normal baseline for measuring the breadth of the territorial sea is the low-water line along the coast as marked on large-scale charts officially recognized by the coastal State.

Article 6   Reefs

In the case of islands situated on atolls or of islands having fringing reefs, the baseline for measuring the breadth of the territorial sea is the seaward low-water line of the reef, as shown by the appropriate symbol on charts officially recognized by the coastal State.

Article 7   Straight baselines

1. In localities where the coastline is deeply indented and cut into, or if there is a fringe of islands along the coast in its immediate vicinity, the method of straight baselines joining appropriate points may be employed in drawing the baseline from which the breadth of the territorial sea is measured.

2. Where because of the presence of a delta and other natural conditions the coastline is highly unstable, the appropriate points may be selected along the furthest seaward extent of the low-water line and, notwithstanding subsequent regression of the low-water line, the straight baselines shall remain effective until changed by the coastal State in accordance with this Convention.

3. The drawing of straight baselines must not depart to any appreciable extent from the general direction of the coast, and the sea areas lying within the lines must be sufficiently closely linked to the land domain to be subject to the regime of internal waters.

4. Straight baselines shall not be drawn to and from low-tide elevations, unless lighthouses or similar installations which are permanently above sea level have been built on them or except in instances where the drawing of baselines to and from such elevations has received general international recognition.

5. Where the method of straight baselines is applicable under paragraph 1, account may be taken, in determining particular baselines, of economic interests peculiar to the region concerned, the reality and the importance of which are clearly evidenced by long usage.

6. The system of straight baselines may not be applied by a State in such a manner as to cut off the territorial sea of another State from the high seas or an exclusive economic zone.

Article 8   Internal waters

1. Except as provided in Part IV, waters on the landward side of the baseline of the territorial sea form part of the internal waters of the State.

2. Where the establishment of a straight baseline in accordance with the method set forth in article 7 has the effect of enclosing as internal waters areas which had not previously been considered as such, a right of innocent passage as provided in this Convention shall exist in those waters.

Article 9   Mouths of rivers

If a river flows directly into the sea, the baseline shall be a straight line across the mouth of the river between points on the low-water line of its banks.

Article 10   Bays

1. This article relates only to bays the coasts of which belong to a single State.

2. For the purposes of this Convention, a bay is a well-marked indentation whose penetration is in such proportion to the width of its mouth as to contain land-locked waters and constitute more than a mere curvature of the coast. An indentation shall not, however, be regarded as a bay unless its area is as large as, or larger than, that of the semi-circle whose diameter is a line drawn across the mouth of that indentation.

3. For the purpose of measurement, the area of an indentation is that lying between the low-water mark around the shore of the indentation and a line joining the low-water mark of its natural entrance points. Where, because of the

presence of islands, an indentation has more than one mouth, the semicircle shall be drawn on a line as long as the sum total of the lengths of the lines across the different mouths. Islands within an indentation shall be included as if they were part of the water area of the indentation.

4. If the distance between the low-water marks of the natural entrance points of a bay does not exceed 24 nautical miles, a closing line may be drawn between these two low-water marks, and the waters enclosed thereby shall be considered as internal waters.

5. Where the distance between the low-water marks of the natural entrance points of a bay exceeds 24 nautical miles, a straight baseline of 24 nautical miles shall be drawn within the bay in such a manner as to enclose the maximum area of water that is possible with a line of that length.

6. The foregoing provisions do not apply to so-called "historic" bays, or in any case where the system of straight baselines provided for in article 7 is applied.

Article 11   Ports

For the purpose of delimiting the territorial sea, the outermost permanent harbour works which form an integral part of the harbour system are regarded as forming part of the coast. Off-shore installations and artificial islands shall not be considered as permanent harbour works.

Article 12   Roadsteads

Roadsteads which are normally used for the loading, unloading and anchoring of ships, and which would otherwise be situated wholly or partly outside the outer limit of the territorial sea, are included in the territorial sea.

Article 13   Low-tide elevations

1. A low-tide elevation is a naturally formed area of land which is surrounded by and above water at low tide but submerged at high tide. Where a low-tide elevation is situated wholly or partly at a distance not exceeding the breadth of the territorial sea from the mainland or an island, the low-water line on that elevation may be used as the baseline for measuring the breadth of the territorial sea.

2. Where a low-tide elevation is wholly situated at a distance exceeding the breadth of the territorial sea from the mainland or an island, it has no territorial sea of its own.

Article 14   Combination of methods for determining baselines

The coastal State may determine baselines in turn by any of the methods provided for in the foregoing articles to suit different conditions.

Article 15   Delimitation of the territorial sea between States with opposite or adjacent coasts

Where the coasts of two States are opposite or adjacent to each other, neither of the two States is entitled, failing agreement between them to the contrary, to extend its territorial sea beyond the median line every point of which is equidistant from the nearest points on the baselines from which the breadth of the territorial seas of each of the two States is measured. The above provision does not apply, however, where it is necessary by reason of historic title or other special circumstances to delimit the territorial seas of the two States in a way which is at variance therewith.

Article 16   Charts and lists of geographical co-ordinates

1. The baselines for measuring the breadth of the territorial sea determined in accordance with articles 7, 9 and 10, or the limits derived therefrom, and the lines of delimitation drawn in accordance with articles 12 and 15 shall be shown on charts of a scale or scales adequate for ascertaining their position. Alternatively, a list of geographical co-ordinates of points, specifying the geodetic datum, may be substituted.

2. The coastal State shall give due publicity to such charts or lists of geographical co-ordinates and shall deposit a copy of each such chart or list with the Secretary-General of the United Nations.

Section 3   Innocent Passage in the Territorial Sea

Subsection A   Rules Applicable to all ships

Article 17   Right of innocent passage

Subject to this Convention, ships of all States, whether coastal or land-locked, enjoy the right of innocent passage through the territorial sea.

Article 18   Meaning of passage

1. Passage means navigation through the territorial sea for the purpose of:
(a) traversing that sea without entering internal waters or calling at a roadstead or port facility outside internal waters; or
(b) proceeding to or from internal waters or a call at such roadstead or port facility.

2. Passage shall be continuous and expeditious. However, passage includes stopping and anchoring, but only in so far as the same are incidental to ordinary navigation or are rendered necessary by force majeure or distress or for the purpose of rendering assistance to persons, ships or aircraft in danger or distress.

Article 19   Meaning of innocent passage

1. Passage is innocent so long as it is not prejudicial to the peace, good order or security of the coastal State. Such passage shall take place in conformity with this Convention and with other rules of international law.

2. Passage of a foreign ship shall be considered to be prejudicial to the peace, good order or security of the coastal State if in the territorial sea it engages in any of the following activities:

(a) any threat or use of force against the sovereignty, territorial integrity or political independence of the coastal State, or in any other manner in violation of the principles of international law embodied in the Charter of the United Nations;
(b) any exercise or practice with weapons of any kind;
(c) any act aimed at collecting information to the prejudice of the defence or security of the coastal State;
(d) any act of propaganda aimed at affecting the defence or security of the coastal State;
(e) the launching, landing or taking on board of any aircraft;
(f) the launching, landing or taking on board of any military device;
(g) the loading or unloading of any commodity, currency or person contrary to the customs, fiscal, immigration or sanitary laws and regulations of the coastal State;
(h) any act of wilful and serious pollution contrary to this Convention;
(i) any fishing activities;
(j) the carrying out of research or survey activities;
(k) any act aimed at interfering with any systems of communication or any other facilities or installations of the coastal State;
(l) any other activity not having a direct bearing on passage.

Article 20   Submarines and other underwater vehicles

In the territorial sea, submarines and other underwater vehicles are required to navigate on the surface and to show their flag.

Article 21 **Laws and regulations of the coastal State relating to innocent passage**

1. The coastal State may adopt laws and regulations, in conformity with the provisions of this Convention and other rules of international law, relating to innocent passage through the territorial sea, in respect of all or any of the following:

(a) the safety of navigation and the regulation of maritime traffic;

(b) the protection of navigational aids and facilities and other facilities or installations;

(c) the protection of cables and pipelines;

(d) the conservation of the living resources of the sea;

(e) the prevention of infringement of the fisheries laws and regulations of the coastal State;

(f) the preservation of the environment of the coastal State and the prevention, reduction and control of pollution thereof;

(g) marine scientific research and hydrographic surveys;

(h) the prevention of infringement of the customs, fiscal, immigration or sanitary laws and regulations of the coastal State.

2. Such laws and regulations shall not apply to the design, construction, manning or equipment of foreign ships unless they are giving effect to generally accepted international rules or standards.

3. The coastal State shall give due publicity to all such laws and regulations.

4. Foreign ships exercising the right of innocent passage through the territorial sea shall comply with all such laws and regulations and all generally accepted international regulations relating to the prevention of collisions at sea.

Article 22 **Sea lanes and traffic separation schemes in the territorial sea**

1. The coastal State may, where necessary having regard to the safety of navigation, require foreign ships exercising the right of innocent passage through its territorial sea to use such sea lanes and traffic separation schemes as it may designate or prescribe for the regulation of the passage of ships.

2. In particular, tankers, nuclear-powered ships and ships carrying nuclear or other inherently dangerous or noxious substances or materials may be required to confine their passage to such sea lanes.

3. In the designation of sea lanes and the prescription of traffic separation schemes under this article, the coastal State shall take into account:

(a) the recommendations of the competent international organization;

(b) any channels customarily used for international navigation;

(c) the special characteristics of particular ships and channels; and

(d) the density of traffic.

4. The coastal State shall clearly indicate such sea lanes and traffic separation schemes on charts to which due publicity shall be given.

Article 23 **Foreign nuclear-powered ships and ships carrying nuclear or other inherently dangerous or noxious substances**

Foreign nuclear-powered ships and ships carrying nuclear or other inherently dangerous or noxious substances shall, when exercising the right of innocent passage through the territorial sea, carry documents and observe special precautionary measures established for such ships by international agreements.

Article 24 **Duties of the coastal State**

1. The coastal State shall not hamper the innocent passage of foreign ships through the territorial sea except in accordance with this Convention. In particular, in the application of this Convention or of any laws or regulations adopted in conformity with this Convention, the coastal State shall not:

(a) impose requirements on foreign ships which have the practical effect of denying or impairing the right of innocent passage; or

(b) discriminate in form or in fact against the ships of any State or against ships carrying cargoes to, from or on behalf of any State.

2. The coastal State shall give appropriate publicity to any danger to navigation, of which it has knowledge, within its territorial sea.

Article 25   Rights of protection of the coastal State

1. The coastal State may take the necessary steps in its territorial sea to prevent passage which is not innocent.

2. In the case of ships proceeding to internal waters or a call at a port facility outside internal waters, the coastal State also has the right to take the necessary steps to prevent any breach of the conditions to which admission of those ships to internal waters or such a call is subject.

3. The coastal State may, without discrimination in form or in fact among foreign ships, suspend temporarily in specified areas of its territorial sea the innocent passage of foreign ships if such suspension is essential for the protection of its security, including weapons exercises. Such suspension shall take effect only after having been duly published.

* * *

Subsection B   Rules Applicable to Merchant Ships Operated for Commercial Purposes

Article 27   Criminal jurisdiction on board a foreign ship

1. The criminal jurisdiction of the coastal State should not be exercised on board a foreign ship passing through the territorial sea to arrest any person or to conduct any investigation in connection with any crime committed on board the ship during its passage, save only in the following cases:

(a) if the consequences of the crime extend to the coastal State;

(b) if the crime is of a kind to disturb the peace of the country or the good order of the territorial sea;

(c) if the assistance of the local authorities has been requested by the master of the ship or by a diplomatic agent or consular officer of the flag State; or

(d) if such measures are necessary for the suppression of illicit traffic in narcotic drugs or psychotropic substances.

2. The above provisions do not affect the right of the coastal State to take any steps authorized by its laws for the purpose of an arrest or investigation on board a foreign ship passing through the territorial sea after leaving internal waters.

3. In the cases provided for in paragraphs 1 and 2, the coastal State shall, if the master so requests, notify a diplomatic agent or consular officer of the flag State before taking any steps, and shall facilitate contact between such agent or officer and the ship's crew. In cases of emergency this notification may be communicated while the measures are being taken.

4. In considering whether or in what manner an arrest should be made, the local authorities shall have due regard to the interests of navigation.

5. Except as provided in Part XII or with respect to violations of laws and regulations adopted in accordance with Part V, the coastal State may not take any steps on board a foreign ship passing through the territorial sea to arrest any person or to conduct any investigation in connection with any crime committed before the ship entered the territorial sea, if the ship, proceeding from a foreign port, is only passing through the territorial sea without entering internal waters.

Article 28	Civil jurisdiction in relation to foreign ships

1. The coastal State should not stop or divert a foreign ship passing through the territorial sea for the purpose of exercising civil jurisdiction in relation to a person on board the ship.

2. The coastal State may not levy execution against or arrest the ship for the purpose of any civil proceedings, save only in respect of obligations or liabilities assumed or incurred by the ship itself in the course or for the purpose of its voyage through the waters of the coastal State.

3. Paragraph 2 is without prejudice to the right of the coastal State, in accordance with its laws, to levy execution against or to arrest, for the purpose of any civil proceedings, a foreign ship lying in the territorial sea, or passing through the territorial sea after leaving internal waters.

* * *

Section 4   Contiguous Zone

Article 33	Contiguous zone

1. In a zone contiguous to its territorial sea, described as the contiguous zone, the coastal State may exercise the control necessary to:

(a) prevent infringement of its customs, fiscal, immigration or sanitary laws and regulations within its territory or territorial sea;

(b) punish infringement of the above laws and regulations committed within its territory or territorial sea.

2. The contiguous zone may not extend beyond 24 nautical miles from the baselines from which the breadth of the territorial sea is measured.

PART III
STRAITS USED FOR INTERNATIONAL NAVIGATION

Section 1   General Provisions

Article 34	Legal status of waters forming straits used for international navigation

1. The regime of passage through straits used for international navigation established in this Part shall not in other respects affect the legal status of the waters forming such straits or the exercise by the States bordering the straits of their sovereignty or jurisdiction over such waters and their air space, bed and subsoil.

2. The sovereignty or jurisdiction of the States bordering the straits is exercised subject to this Part and to other rules of international law.

* * *

Article 42	Laws and regulations of States bordering straits relating to transit passage

1. Subject to the provisions of this section, States bordering straits may adopt laws and regulations relating to transit passage through straits, in respect of all or any of the following:

(a) the safety of navigation and the regulation of maritime traffic, as provided in article 41;

(b) the prevention, reduction and control of pollution, by giving effect to applicable international regulations regarding the discharge of oil, oily wastes and other noxious substances in the strait;

(c) with respect to fishing vessels, the prevention of fishing, including the stowage of fishing gear;

(d) the loading or unloading of any commodity, currency or person in contravention of the customs, fiscal, immigration or sanitary laws and regulations of States bordering straits.

2. Such laws and regulations shall not discriminate in form or in fact among foreign ships or in their application have the practical effect of denying, hampering or impairing the right of transit passage as defined in this section.

3. States bordering straits shall give due publicity to all such laws and regulations.

4. Foreign ships exercising the right of transit passage shall comply with such laws and regulations.

5. The flag State of a ship or the State of registry of an aircraft entitled to sovereign immunity which acts in a manner contrary to such laws and regulations or other provisions of this Part shall bear international responsibility for any loss or damage which results to States bordering straits.

<table>
<tr><td>Article 43</td><td>Navigational and safety aids and other improvements and the prevention, reduction and control of pollution</td></tr>
</table>

User States and States bordering a strait should by agreement co-operate:

(a) in the establishment and maintenance in a strait of necessary navigational and safety aids or other improvements in aid of international navigation; and

(b) for the prevention, reduction and control of pollution from ships.

PART IV
ARCHIPELAGIC STATES * * *

PART V
EXCLUSIVE ECONOMIC ZONE

<table>
<tr><td>Article 55</td><td>Specific legal regime of the exclusive economic zone</td></tr>
</table>

The exclusive economic zone is an area beyond and adjacent to the territorial sea, subject to the specific legal regime established in this Part, under which the rights and jurisdiction of the coastal State and the rights and freedoms of other States are governed by the relevant provisions of this Convention.

<table>
<tr><td>Article 56</td><td>Rights, jurisdiction and duties of the coastal State in the exclusive economic zone</td></tr>
</table>

1. In the exclusive economic zone, the coastal State has:
(a) sovereign rights for the purpose of exploring and exploiting, conserving and managing the natural resources, whether living or non-living, of the waters superjacent to the sea-bed and of the sea-bed and its subsoil, and with regard to other activities for the economic exploitation and exploration of the zone, such as the production of energy from the water, currents and winds;
(b) jurisdiction as provided for in the relevant provisions of this Convention with regard to:
(i) the establishment and use of artificial islands, installations and structures;
(ii) marine scientific research;
(iii) the protection and preservation of the marine environment;
(c) other rights and duties provided for in this Convention.

2. In exercising its rights and performing its duties under this Convention in the exclusive economic zone, the coastal State shall have due regard to the rights and duties of other States and shall act in a manner compatible with the provisions of this Convention.

3. The rights set out in this article with respect to the sea-bed and subsoil shall be exercised in accordance with Part VI.

Article 57	**Breadth of the exclusive economic zone**

The exclusive economic zone shall not extend beyond 200 nautical miles from the baselines from which the breadth of the territorial sea is measured.

Article 58	**Rights and duties of other States in the exclusive economic zone**

1. In the exclusive economic zone all States, whether coastal or land-locked, enjoy, subject to the relevant provisions of this Convention, the freedoms referred to in article 87 of navigation and overflight and of the laying of submarine cables and pipelines, and other internationally lawful uses of the sea related to these freedoms, such as those associated with the operation of ships, aircraft and submarine cables and pipelines, and compatible with the other provisions of this Convention.

2. Articles 88 to 115 and other pertinent rules of international law apply to the exclusive economic zone in so far as they are not incompatible with this Part.

3. In exercising their rights and performing their duties under this Convention in the exclusive economic zone, States shall have due regard to the rights and duties of the coastal State and shall comply with the laws and regulations adopted by the coastal State in accordance with the provisions of this Convention and other rules of international law in so far as they are not incompatible with this Part.

Article 59	**Basis for the resolution of conflicts regarding the attribution of rights and jurisdiction in the exclusive economic zone**

In cases where this Convention does not attribute rights or jurisdiction to the coastal State or to other States within the exclusive economic zone, and a conflict arises between the interests of the coastal State and any other State or States, the conflict should be resolved on the basis of equity and in the light of all the relevant circumstances, taking into account the respective importance of the interests involved to the parties as well as to the international community as a whole.

Article 60	**Artificial islands, installations and structures in the exclusive economic zone**

1. In the exclusive economic zone, the coastal State shall have the exclusive right to construct and to authorize and regulate the construction, operation and use of:
    (a) artificial islands;
    (b) installations and structures for the purposes provided for in article 56 and other economic purposes;
    (c) installations and structures which may interfere with the exercise of the rights of the coastal State in the zone.

2. The coastal State shall have exclusive jurisdiction over such artificial islands installations and structures, including jurisdiction with regard to customs fiscal health, safety and immigration laws and regulations.

3. Due notice must be given of the construction of such artificial islands, installations or structures, and permanent means for giving warning of their presence must be maintained. Any installations or structures which are abandoned or disused shall be removed to ensure safety of navigation, taking into account any generally accepted international standards established in this regard by the competent international organization. Such removal shall also have due regard to fishing, the protection of the marine environment and the rights and duties of other States. Appropriate publicity shall be given to the depth, position and dimensions of any installations or structures not entirely removed.

4. The coastal State may, where necessary, establish reasonable safety zones around such artificial islands, installations and structures in which it may take appropriate measures to ensure the safety both of navigation and of the artificial islands, installations and structures.

5. The breadth of the safety zones shall be determined by the coastal State, taking into account applicable international standards. Such zones shall be designed to ensure that they are reasonably related to the nature and function of the artificial islands, installations or structures, and shall not exceed a distance of 500 metres around

them, measured from each point of their outer edge, except as authorized by generally accepted international standards or as recommended by the competent international organization. Due notice shall be given of the extent of safety zones.

6. All ships must respect these safety zones and shall comply with generally accepted international standards regarding navigation in the vicinity of artificial islands, installations, structures and safety zones.

7. Artificial islands, installations and structures and the safety zones around them may not be established where interference may be caused to the use of recognized sea lanes essential to international navigation.

8. Artificial islands, installations and structures do not possess the status of islands. They have no territorial sea of their own, and their presence does not affect the delimitation of the territorial sea, the exclusive economic zone or the continental shelf.

Article 61   Conservation of the living resources

1. The coastal State shall determine the allowable catch of the living resources in its exclusive economic zone.

2. The coastal State, taking into account the best scientific evidence available to it, shall ensure through proper conservation and management measures that the maintenance of the living resources in the exclusive economic zone is not endangered by over-exploitation. As appropriate, the coastal State and competent international organizations, whether subregional, regional or global, shall co-operate to this end.

3. Such measures shall also be designed to maintain or restore populations of harvested species at levels which can produce the maximum sustainable yield, as qualified by relevant environmental and economic factors, including the economic needs of coastal fishing communities and the special requirements of developing States, and taking into account fishing patterns, the interdependence of stocks and any generally recommended international minimum standards, whether subregional, regional or global.

4. In taking such measures the coastal State shall take into consideration the effects on species associated with or dependent upon harvested species with a view to maintaining or restoring populations of such associated or dependent species above levels at which their reproduction may become seriously threatened.

5. Available scientific information, catch and fishing effort statistics, and other data relevant to the conservation of fish stocks shall be contributed and exchanged on a regular basis through competent international organizations, whether subregional, regional or global, where appropriate and with participation by all States concerned, including States whose nationals are allowed to fish in the exclusive economic zone.

Article 62   Utilization of the living resources

1. The coastal State shall promote the objective of optimum utilization of the living resources in the exclusive economic zone without prejudice to article 61.

2. The coastal State shall determine its capacity to harvest the living resources of the exclusive economic zone. Where the coastal State does not have the capacity to harvest the entire allowable catch, it shall, through agreements or other arrangements and pursuant to the terms, conditions, laws and regulations referred to in paragraph 4, give other States access to the surplus of the allowable catch, having particular regard to the provisions of articles 69 and 70, especially in relation to the developing States mentioned therein.

3. In giving access to other States to its exclusive economic zone under this article the coastal State shall take into account all relevant factors, including, inter alia, the significance of the living resources of the area to the economy of the coastal State concerned and its other national interests, the provisions of articles 69 and 70, the requirements of developing States in the subregion or region in harvesting part of the surplus and the need to minimize economic dislocation in States whose nationals have habitually fished in the zone or which have made substantial efforts in research and identification of stocks.

4. Nationals of other States fishing in the exclusive economic zone shall comply with the conservation measures and with the other terms and conditions established in the laws and regulations of the coastal State. These laws and regulations shall be consistent with this Convention and may relate, inter alia, to the following:

(a) licensing of fishermen, fishing vessels and equipment, including payment of fees and other forms of remuneration, which, in the case of developing coastal States, may consist of adequate compensation in the field of financing, equipment and technology relating to the fishing industry;

(b) determining the species which may be caught, and fixing quotas of catch, whether in relation to particular stocks or groups of stocks or catch per vessel over a period of time or to the catch by nationals of any State during a specified period;

(c) regulating seasons and areas of fishing, the types, sizes and amount of gear, and the types, sizes and number of fishing vessels that may be used;

(d) fixing the age and size of fish and other species that may be caught;

(e) specifying information required of fishing vessels, including catch and effort statistics and vessel position reports;

(f) requiring, under the authorization and control of the coastal State, the conduct of specified fisheries research programmes and regulating the conduct of such research, including the sampling of catches, disposition of samples and reporting of associated scientific data;

(g) the placing of observers or trainees on board such vessels by the coastal State;

(h) the landing of all or any part of the catch by such vessels in the ports of the coastal State;

(i) terms and conditions relating to joint ventures or other co-operative arrangements;

(j) requirements for the training of personnel and the transfer of fisheries technology, including enhancement of the coastal State's capability of undertaking fisheries research;

(k) enforcement procedures.

5. Coastal States shall give due notice of conservation and management laws and regulations.

Article 63	**Stocks occurring within the exclusive economic zones of two or more coastal States or both within the exclusive economic zone and in an area beyond and adjacent to it**

1. Where the same stock or stocks of associated species occur within the exclusive economic zones of two or more coastal States, these States shall seek, either directly or through appropriate subregional or regional organizations, to agree upon the measures necessary to co-ordinate and ensure the conservation and development of such stocks without prejudice to the other provisions of this Part.

2. Where the same stock or stocks of associated species occur both within the exclusive economic zone and in an area beyond and adjacent to the zone, the coastal State and the States fishing for such stocks in the adjacent area shall seek, either directly or through appropriate subregional or regional organizations, to agree upon the measures necessary for the conservation of these stocks in the adjacent area.

Article 64	**Highly migratory species**

1. The coastal State and other States whose nationals fish in the region for the highly migratory species listed in Annex I shall co-operate directly or through appropriate international organizations with a view to ensuring conservation and promoting the objective of optimum utilization of such species throughout the region, both within and beyond the exclusive economic zone. In regions for which no appropriate international organization exists, the coastal State and other States whose nationals harvest these species in the region shall co-operate to establish such an organization and participate in its work.

2. The provisions of paragraph 1 apply in addition to the other provisions of this Part.

Article 65   Marine mammals

Nothing in this Part restricts the right of a coastal State or the competence of an international organization, as appropriate, to prohibit, limit or regulate the exploitation of marine mammals more strictly than provided for in this Part. States shall co-operate with a view to the conservation of marine mammals and in the case of cetaceans shall in particular work through the appropriate international organizations for their conservation, management and study.

Article 66   Anadromous stocks

1. States in whose rivers anadromous stocks originate shall have the primary interest in and responsibility for such stocks.

2. The State of origin of anadromous stocks shall ensure their conservation by the establishment of appropriate regulatory measures for fishing in all waters landward of the outer limits of its exclusive economic zone and for fishing provided for in paragraph 3(b). The State of origin may, after consultations with the other States referred to in paragraphs 3 and 4 fishing these stocks, establish total allowable catches for stocks originating in its rivers.

3.   (a) Fisheries for anadromous stocks shall be conducted only in waters landward of the outer limits of exclusive economic zones, except in cases where this provision would result in economic dislocation for a State other than the State of origin. With respect to such fishing beyond the outer limits of the exclusive economic zone, States concerned shall maintain consultations with a view to achieving agreement on terms and conditions of such fishing giving due regard to the conservation requirements and the needs of the State of origin in respect of these stocks.

     (b) The State of origin shall co-operate in minimizing economic dislocation in such other States fishing these stocks, taking into account the normal catch and the mode of operations of such States, and all the areas in which such fishing has occurred.

     (c) States referred to in subparagraph (b), participating by agreement with the State of origin in measures to renew anadromous stocks, particularly by expenditures for that purpose, shall be given special consideration by the State of origin in the harvesting of stocks originating in its rivers.

     (d) Enforcement of regulations regarding anadromous stocks beyond the exclusive economic zone shall be by agreement between the State of origin and the other States concerned.

4. In cases where anadromous stocks migrate into or through the water is landward of the outer limits of the exclusive economic zone of a State other than the State of origin, such State shall co-operate with the State of origin with regard to the conservation and management of such stocks.

5. The State of origin of anadromous stocks and other States fishing these stocks shall make arrangements for the implementation of the provisions of this article, where appropriate, through regional organizations.

Article 67   Catadromous species

1. A coastal State in whose waters catadromous species spend the greater part of their life cycle shall have responsibility for the management of these species and shall ensure the ingress and egress of migrating fish.

2. Harvesting of catadromous species shall be conducted only in waters landward of the outer limits of exclusive economic zones. When conducted in exclusive economic zones, harvesting shall be subject to this article and the other provisions of this Convention concerning fishing in these zones.

3. In cases where catadromous fish migrate through the exclusive economic zone of another State, whether as juvenile or maturing fish, the management, including harvesting, of such fish shall be regulated by agreement between the State mentioned in paragraph 1 and the other State concerned. Such agreement shall ensure the rational management of the species and take into account the responsibilities of the State mentioned in paragraph I for the maintenance of these species.

Article 68   Sedentary species

This Part does not apply to sedentary species as defined in article 77, paragraph 4.

Article 69   Right of land-locked States

1. Land-locked States shall have the right to participate, on an equitable basis, in the exploitation of an appropriate part of the surplus of the living resources of the exclusive economic zones of coastal States of the same subregion or region, taking into account the relevant economic and geographical circumstances of all the States concerned and in conformity with the provisions of this article and of articles 61 and 62.

2. The terms and modalities of such participation shall be established by the States concerned through bilateral, subregional or regional agreements taking into account, inter alia:

(a) the need to avoid effects detrimental to fishing communities or fishing industries of the coastal State;
(b) the extent to which the land-locked State, in accordance with the provisions of this article, is participating or is entitled to participate under existing bilateral, subregional or regional agreements in the exploitation of living resources of the exclusive economic zones of other coastal States;
(c) the extent to which other land-locked States and geographically disadvantaged States are participating in the exploitation of the living resources of the exclusive economic zone of the coastal State and the consequent need to avoid a particular burden for any single coastal State or a part of it;
(d) the nutritional needs of the populations of the respective States.

3. When the harvesting capacity of a coastal State approaches a point which would enable it to harvest the entire allowable catch of the living resources in its exclusive economic zone, the coastal State and other States concerned shall co-operate in the establishment of equitable arrangements on a bilateral, subregional or regional basis to allow for participation of developing land-locked States of the same subregion or region in the exploitation of the living resources of the exclusive economic zones of coastal States of the subregion or region, as may be appropriate in the circumstances and on terms satisfactory to all parties. In the implementation of this provision the factors mentioned in paragraph 2 shall also be taken into account.

4. Developed land-locked States shall, under the provisions of this article, be entitled to participate in the exploitation of living resources only in the exclusive economic zones of developed coastal States of the same subregion or region having regard to the extent to which the coastal State, in giving access to other States to the living resources of its exclusive economic zone, has taken into account the need to minimize detrimental effects on fishing communities and economic dislocation in States whose nationals have habitually fished in the zone.

5. The above provisions are without prejudice to arrangements agreed upon in subregions or regions where the coastal States may grant to land-locked States of the same subregion or region equal or preferential rights for the exploitation of the living resources in the exclusive economic zones.

Article 70   Right of geographically disadvantaged States

1. Geographically disadvantaged States shall have the right to participate, on an equitable basis, in the exploitation of an appropriate part of the surplus of the living resources of the exclusive economic zones of coastal States of the same subregion or region, taking into account the relevant economic and geographical circumstances of all the States concerned and in conformity with the provisions of this article and of articles 61 and 62.

2. For the purposes of this Part, "geographically disadvantaged States" means coastal States, including States bordering enclosed or semi-enclosed seas, whose geographical situation makes them dependent upon the exploitation of the living resources of the exclusive economic zones of other States in the subregion or region for adequate supplies of fish for the nutritional purposes of their populations or parts thereof, and coastal States which can claim no exclusive economic zones of their own.

3. The terms and modalities of such participation shall be established by the States concerned through bilateral, subregional or regional agreements taking into account, inter alia:
(a) the need to avoid effects detrimental to fishing communities or fishing industries of the coastal State;
(b) the extent to which the geographically disadvantaged State, in accordance with the provisions of this article, is participating or is entitled to participate under existing bilateral, subregional or regional agreements in the exploitation of living resources of the exclusive economic zones of other coastal States;

(c) the extent to which other geographically disadvantaged States and landlocked States are participating in the exploitation of the living resources of the exclusive economic zone of the coastal State and the consequent need to avoid a particular burden for any single coastal State or a part of it;

(d) the nutritional needs of the populations of the respective States.

4. When the harvesting capacity of a coastal State approaches a point which would enable it to harvest the entire allowable catch of the living resources in its exclusive economic zone, the coastal State and other States concerned shall co-operate in the establishment of equitable arrangements on a bilateral, subregional or regional basis to allow for participation of developing geographically disadvantaged States of the same subregion or region in the exploitation of the living resources of the exclusive economic zones of coastal States of the subregion or region, as may be appropriate in the circumstances and on terms satisfactory to all parties. In the implementation of this provision the factors mentioned in paragraph 3 shall also be taken into account.

5. Developed geographically disadvantaged States shall, under the provisions of this article, be entitled to participate in the exploitation of living resources only in the exclusive economic zones of developed coastal States of the same subregion or region having regard to the extent to which the coastal State, in giving access to other States to the living resources of its exclusive economic zone, has taken into account the need to minimize detrimental effects on fishing communities and economic dislocation in States whose nationals have habitually fished in the zone.

6. The above provisions are without prejudice to arrangements agreed upon in subregions or regions where the coastal States may grant to geographically disadvantaged States of the same subregion or region equal or preferential rights for the exploitation of the living resources in the exclusive economic zones.

Article 71   Non-applicability of articles 69 and 70

The provisions of articles 69 and 70 do not apply in the case of a coastal State whose economy is overwhelmingly dependent on the exploitation of the living resources of its exclusive economic zone.

Article 72   Restrictions on transfer of rights

1. Rights provided under articles 69 and 70 to exploit living resources shall not be directly or indirectly transferred to third States or their nationals by lease or licence, by establishing joint ventures or in any other manner which has the effect of such transfer unless otherwise agreed by the States concerned.

2. The foregoing provision does not preclude the States concerned from obtaining technical or financial assistance from third States or international organizations in order to facilitate the exercise of the rights pursuant to articles 69 and 70, provided that it does not have the effect referred to in paragraph 1.

Article 73   Enforcement of laws and regulations of the coastal State

1. The coastal State may, in the exercise of its sovereign rights to explore, exploit, conserve and manage the living resources in the exclusive economic zone, take such measures, including boarding, inspection, arrest and judicial proceedings, as may be necessary to ensure compliance with the laws and regulations adopted by it in conformity with this Convention.

2. Arrested vessels and their crews shall be promptly released upon the posting of reasonable bond or other security.

3. Coastal State penalties for violations of fisheries laws and regulations in the exclusive economic zone may not include imprisonment, in the absence of agreements to the contrary by the States concerned, or any other form of corporal punishment.

4. In cases of arrest or detention of foreign vessels the coastal State shall promptly notify the flag State, through appropriate channels, of the action taken and of any penalties subsequently imposed.

* * *

PART VI

CONTINENTAL SHELF

Article 76   Definition of the continental shelf

1. The continental shelf of a coastal State comprises the sea-bed and subsoil of the submarine areas that extend beyond its territorial sea throughout the natural prolongation of its land territory to the outer edge of the continental margin, or to a distance of 200 nautical miles from the baselines from which the breadth of the territorial sea is measured where the outer edge of the continental margin does not extend up to that distance.

2. The continental shelf of a coastal State shall not extend beyond the limits provided for in paragraphs 4 to 6.

3. The continental margin comprises the submerged prolongation of the land mass of the coastal State, and consists of the sea-bed and subsoil of the shelf the slope and the rise. It does not include the deep ocean floor with its oceanic ridges or the subsoil thereof.

4.   (a) For the purposes of this Convention, the coastal State shall establish the outer edge of the continental margin wherever the margin extends beyond 200 nautical miles from the baselines from which the breadth of the territorial sea is measured, by either:

        (i) a line delineated in accordance with paragraph 7 by reference to the outermost fixed points at each of which the thickness of sedimentary rocks is at least 1 per cent of the shortest distance from such point to the foot of the continental slope; or

        (ii) a line delineated in accordance with paragraph 7 by reference to fixed points not more than 60 nautical miles from the foot of the continental slope.

    (b) In the absence of evidence to the contrary, the foot of the continental slope shall be determined as the point of maximum change in the gradient at its base.

5. The fixed points comprising the line of the outer limits of the continental shelf on the sea-bed, drawn in accordance with paragraph 4 (a)(i) and (ii), either shall not exceed 350 nautical miles from the baselines from which the breadth of the territorial sea is measured or shall not exceed 100 nautical miles from the 2,500 metre isobath, which is a line connecting the depth of 2,500 metres.

6. Notwithstanding the provisions of paragraph 5, on submarine ridges, the outer limit of the continental shelf shall not exceed 350 nautical miles from the baselines from which the breadth of the territorial sea is measured. This paragraph does not apply to submarine elevations that are natural components of the continental margin, such as its plateaux, rises, caps, banks and spurs.

7. The coastal State shall delineate the outer limits of its continental shelf, where that shelf extends beyond 200 nautical miles from the baselines from which the breadth of the territorial sea is measured, by straight lines not exceeding 60 nautical miles in length, connecting fixed points, defined by coordinates of latitude and longitude.

8. Information on the limits of the continental shelf beyond 200 nautical miles from the baselines from which the breadth of the territorial sea is measured shall be submitted by the coastal State to the Commission on the Limits of the Continental Shelf set up under Annex II on the basis of equitable geographical representation. The Commission shall make recommendations to coastal States on matters related to the establishment of the outer limits of their continental shelf. The limits of the shelf established by a coastal State on the basis of these recommendations shall be final and binding.

9. The coastal State shall deposit with the Secretary-General of the United Nations charts and relevant information, including geodetic data, permanently describing the outer limits of its continental shelf. The Secretary-General shall give due publicity thereto.

10. The provisions of this article are without prejudice to the question of delimitation of the continental shelf between States with opposite or adjacent coasts.

Article 77   **Rights of the coastal State over the continental shelf**

1. The coastal State exercises over the continental shelf sovereign rights for the purpose of exploring it and exploiting its natural resources.

2. The rights referred to in paragraph 1 are exclusive in the sense that if the coastal State does not explore the continental shelf or exploit its natural resources, no one may undertake these activities without the express consent of the coastal State.

3. The rights of the coastal State over the continental shelf do not depend on occupation, effective or notional, or on any express proclamation.

4.   The natural resources referred to in this Part consist of the mineral and other non-living resources of the sea-bed and subsoil together with living organisms belonging to sedentary species, that is to say, organisms which, at the harvestable stage, either are immobile on or under the sea-bed or are unable to move except in constant physical contact with the sea-bed or the subsoil.

Article 78   **Legal status of the superjacent waters and air space and the rights and freedoms of other States**

1. The rights of the coastal State over the continental shelf do not affect the legal status of the superjacent waters or of the air space above those waters.

2. The exercise of the rights of the coastal State over the continental shelf must not infringe or result in any unjustifiable interference with navigation and other rights and freedoms of other States as provided for in this Convention.

Article 79   **Submarine cables and pipelines on the continental shelf**

1. All States are entitled to lay submarine cables and pipelines on the continental shelf, in accordance with the provisions of this article.

2. Subject to its right to take reasonable measures for the exploration of the continental shelf, the exploitation of its natural resources and the prevention, reduction and control of pollution from pipelines, the coastal State may not impede the laying or maintenance of such cables or pipelines.

3. The delineation of the course for the laying of such pipelines on the continental shelf is subject to the consent of the coastal State.

4. Nothing in this Part affects the right of the coastal State to establish conditions for cables or pipelines entering its territory or territorial sea, or its jurisdiction over cables and pipelines constructed or used in connection with the exploration of its continental shelf or exploitation of its resources or the operations of artificial islands, installations and structures under its jurisdiction.

5. When laying submarine cables or pipelines, States shall have due regard to cables or pipelines already in position. In particular, possibilities of repairing existing cables or pipelines shall not be prejudiced.

Article 80   **Artificial islands, installations and structures on the continental shelf**

Article 60 applies mutatis mutandis to artificial islands, installations and structures on the continental shelf.

Article 81   **Drilling on the continental shelf**

The coastal State shall have the exclusive right to authorize and regulate drilling on the continental shelf for all purposes.

Article 82   **Payments and contributions with respect to the exploitation of the continental shelf beyond 200 nautical miles**

1. The coastal State shall make payments or contributions in kind in respect of the exploitation of the non-living resources of the continental shelf beyond 200 nautical miles from the baselines from which the breadth of the territorial sea is measured.

2. The payments and contributions shall be made annually with respect to all production at a site after the first five years of production at that site. For the sixth year, the rate of payment or contribution shall be 1 per cent of the value or volume of production at the site. The rate shall increase by 1 per cent for each subsequent year until the twelfth year and shall remain at 7 per cent thereafter. Production does not include resources used in connection with exploitation.

3. A developing State which is a net importer of a mineral resource produced from its continental shelf is exempt from making such payments or contributions in respect of that mineral resource.

4. The payments or contributions shall be made through the Authority, which shall distribute them to States Parties to this Convention, on the basis of equitable sharing criteria, taking into account the interests and needs of developing States, particularly the least developed and the land-locked among them.

* * *

PART VII
HIGH SEAS

Section 1   General Provisions

Article 86   **Application of the provisions of this Part**

The provisions of this Part apply to all parts of the sea that are not included in the exclusive economic zone, in the territorial sea or in the internal waters of a State, or in the archipelagic waters of an archipelagic State. This article does not entail any abridgement of the freedoms enjoyed by all States in the exclusive economic zone in accordance with article 58.

Article 87   **Freedom of the high seas**

1. The high seas are open to all States, whether coastal or land-locked. Freedom of the high seas is exercised under the conditions laid down by this Convention and by other rules of international law. It comprises, inter alia, both for coastal and land-locked States:

    (a) freedom of navigation;
    (b) freedom of overflight;
    (c) freedom to lay submarine cables and pipelines, subject to Part VI;
    (d) freedom to construct artificial islands and other installations permitted under international law, subject to Part VI;
    (e) freedom of fishing, subject to the conditions laid down in section 2;
    (f) freedom of scientific research, subject to Parts VI and XIII.

2. These freedoms shall be exercised by all States with due regard for the interests of other States in their exercise of the freedom of the high seas, and also with due regard for the rights under this Convention with respect to activities in the Area.

| Article 88 | **Reservation of the high seas for peaceful purposes** |

The high seas shall be reserved for peaceful purposes.

| Article 89 | **Invalidity of claims of sovereignty over the high seas** |

No State may validly purport to subject any part of the high seas to its sovereignty.

| Article 90 | **Right of navigation** |

Every State, whether coastal or land-locked, has the right to sail ships flying its flag on the high seas.

| Article 91 | **Nationality of ships** |

1. Every State shall fix the conditions for the grant of its nationality to ships, for the registration of ships in its territory, and for the right tony its flag. Ships have the nationality of the State whose flag they are entitled to fly. There must exist a genuine link between the State and the ship.

2. Every State shall issue to ships to which it has granted the right to fly its flag documents to that effect.

| Article 92 | **Status of ships** |

1. Ships shall sail under the flag of one State only and, save in exceptional cases expressly provided for in international treaties or in this Convention, shall be subject to its exclusive jurisdiction on the high seas. A ship may not change its flag during a voyage or while in a port of call, save in the case of a real transfer of ownership or change of registry.

2. A ship which sails under the flags of two or more States, using them according to convenience, may not claim any of the nationalities in question with respect to any other State, and may be assimilated to a ship without nationality.

| Article 93 | **Ships flying the flag of the United Nations, its specialized agencies and the International Atomic Energy Agency** |

The preceding articles do not prejudice the question of ships employed on the official service of the United Nations, its specialized agencies or the International Atomic Energy Agency, flying the flag of the organization.

| Article 94 | **Duties of the flag State** |

1. Every State shall effectively exercise its jurisdiction and control in administrative, technical and social matters over ships flying its flag.

2. In particular every State shall:

(a) maintain a register of ships containing the names and particulars of ships flying its flag, except those which are excluded from generally accepted international regulations on account of their small size; and

(b) assume jurisdiction under its internal law over each ship flying its flag and its master, officers and crew in respect of administrative, technical and social matters concerning the ship.

3. Every State shall take such measures for ships flying its flag as are necessary to ensure safety at sea with regard, inter alia, to:

(a) the construction, equipment and seaworthiness of ships;

(b) the manning of ships, labour conditions and the training of crews, taking into account the applicable international instruments;

(c) the use of signals, the maintenance of communications and the prevention of collisions.

4. Such measures shall include those necessary to ensure:

(a) that each ship, before registration and thereafter at appropriate intervals, is surveyed by a qualified surveyor of ships, and has on board such charts, nautical publications and navigational equipment and instruments as are appropriate for the safe navigation of the ship;

(b) that each ship is in the charge of a master and officers who possess appropriate qualifications, in particular in seamanship, navigation, communications and marine engineering, and that the crew is appropriate in qualification and numbers for the type, size, machinery and equipment of the ship;

(c) that the master, officers and, to the extent appropriate, the crew are fully conversant with and required to observe the applicable international regulations concerning the safety of life at sea, the prevention of collisions, the prevention, reduction and control of marine pollution, and the maintenance of communications by radio.

5. In taking the measures called for in paragraphs 3 and 4 each State is required to conform to generally accepted international regulations, procedures and practices and to take any steps which may be necessary to secure their observance.

6. A State which has clear grounds to believe that proper jurisdiction and control with respect to a ship have not been exercised may report the facts to the flag State. Upon receiving such a report, the flag State shall investigate the matter and, if appropriate, take any action necessary to remedy the situation.

7. Each State shall cause an inquiry to be held by or before a suitably qualified person or persons into every marine casualty or incident of navigation on the high seas involving a ship flying its flag and causing loss of life or serious injury to nationals of another State or serious damage to ships or installations of another State or to the marine environment. The flag State and the other State shall co-operate in the conduct of any inquiry held by that other State into any such marine casualty or incident of navigation.

Article 95   Immunity of warships on the high seas

Warships on the high seas have complete immunity from the jurisdiction of any State other than the flag State.

* * *

Article 101   Definition of piracy

Piracy consists of any of the following acts:

(a) any illegal acts of violence or detention, or any act of depredation, committed for private ends by the crew or the passengers of a private ship or a private aircraft, and directed:

(i) on the high seas, against another ship or aircraft, or against persons or property on board such ship or aircraft;

(ii) against a ship, aircraft, persons or property in a place outside the jurisdiction of any State;

(b) any act of voluntary participation in the operation of a ship or of an aircraft with knowledge of facts making it a pirate ship or aircraft;

(c) any act of inciting or of intentionally facilitating an act described in subparagraph (a) or (b).

* * *

Article 106   **Liability for seizure without adequate grounds**

Where the seizure of a ship or aircraft on suspicion of piracy has been effected without adequate grounds, the State making the seizure shall be liable to the State the nationality of which is possessed by the ship or aircraft for any loss or damage caused by the seizure.

* * *

Section 2   Conservation and Management of the Living Resources of the High Seas

Article 116   **Right to fish on the high seas**

All States have the right for their nationals to engage in fishing on the high seas subject to:

(a) their treaty obligations;
(b) the rights and duties as well as the interests of coastal States provided for, inter alia, in article 63, paragraph 2, and articles 64 to 67; and
(c) the provisions of this section.

Article 117   **Duty of States to adopt with respect to their nationals measures for the conservation of the living resources of the high seas**

All States have the duty to take, or to co-operate with other States in taking, such measures for their respective nationals as may be necessary for the conservation of the living resources of the high seas.

Article 118   **Co-operation of States in the conservation and management of living resources**

States shall co-operate with each other in the conservation and management of living resources in the areas of the high seas. States whose nationals exploit identical living resources, or different living resources in the same area, shall enter into negotiations with a view to taking the measures necessary for the conservation of the living resources concerned. They shall, as appropriate, cooperate to establish subregional or regional fisheries organizations to this end.

Article 119   **Conservation of the living resources of the high seas**

1. In determining the allowable catch and establishing other conservation measures for the living resources in the high seas, States shall:

(a) take measures which are designed, on the best scientific evidence available to the States concerned, to maintain or restore populations of harvested species at levels which can produce the maximum sustainable yield, as qualified by relevant environmental and economic factors, including the special requirements of developing States, and taking into account fishing patterns, the interdependence of stocks and any generally recommended international minimum standards, whether subregional, regional or global;
(b) take into consideration the effects on species associated with or dependent upon harvested species with a view to maintaining or restoring populations of such associated or dependent species above levels at which their reproduction may become seriously threatened.

2. Available scientific information, catch and fishing effort statistics, and other data relevant to the conservation of fish stocks shall be contributed and exchanged on a regular basis through competent international organizations, whether subregional, regional or global, where appropriate and with participation by all States concerned.

3. States concerned shall ensure that conservation measures and their implementation do not discriminate in form or in fact against the fishermen of any State.

Article 120	**Marine mammals**

Article 65 also applies to the conservation and management of marine mammals in the high seas.

* * *

PART XI   THE AREA
Section 1   General Provisions

Article 133	**Use of terms**

For the purposes of this Part:

(a) "resources" means all solid, liquid or gaseous mineral resources in situ in the Area at or beneath the sea-bed, including polymetallic nodules;

(b) resources, when recovered from the Area, are referred to as "minerals".

Article 134	**Scope of this Part**

1. This Part applies to the Area.

2. Activities in the Area shall be governed by the provisions of this Part.

3. The requirements concerning deposit of, and publicity to be given to, the charts or lists of geographical co-ordinates showing the limits referred to in article 1, paragraph 1(1), are set forth in Part VI.

4. Nothing in this article affects the establishment of the outer limits of the continental shelf in accordance with Part VI or the validity of agreements relating to delimitation between States with opposite or adjacent coasts.

Article 135	**Legal status of the superjacent waters and air space**

Neither this Part nor any rights granted or exercised pursuant thereto shall affect the legal status of the waters superjacent to the Area or that of the air space above those waters.

Section 2   Principles Governing the Area

Article 136	**Common heritage of mankind**

The Area and its resources are the common heritage of mankind.

Article 137	**Legal status of the Area and its resources**

1. No State shall claim or exercise sovereignty or sovereign rights over any part of the Area or its resources, nor shall any State or natural or juridical person appropriate any part thereof. No such claim or exercise of sovereignty or sovereign rights nor such appropriation shall be recognized.

2. All rights in the resources of the Area are vested in mankind as a whole on whose behalf the Authority shall act. These resources are not subject to alienation. The minerals recovered from the Area, however, may only be alienated in accordance with this Part and the rules, regulations and procedures of the Authority.

3. No State or natural or juridical person shall claim, acquire or exercise rights with respect to the minerals recovered from the Area except in accordance with this Part. Otherwise, no such claim, acquisition or exercise of such rights shall be recognized.

Article 138   **General conduct of States in relation to the Area**

The general conduct of States in relation to the Area shall be in accordance with the provisions of this Part, the principles embodied in the Charter of the United Nations and other rules of international law in the interests of maintaining peace and security and promoting international co-operation and mutual understanding.

Article 139   **Responsibility to ensure compliance and liability for damage**

1. States Parties shall have the responsibility to ensure that activities in the Area, whether carried out by States Parties, or state enterprises or natural or juridical persons which possess the nationality of States Parties or are effectively controlled by them or their nationals, shall be carried out in conformity with this Part. The same responsibility applies to international organizations for activities in the Area carried out by such organizations.

2. Without prejudice to the rules of international law and Annex III, article 22, damage caused by the failure of a State Party or international organization to carry out its responsibilities under this Part shall entail liability, States Parties or international organizations acting together shall bear joint and several liability. A State Party shall not however be liable for damage caused by any failure to comply with this Part by a person whom it has sponsored under article 153, paragraph 2(b), if the State Party has taken all necessary and appropriate measures to secure effective compliance under article 153, paragraph 4, and Annex III, article 4, paragraph 4.

3. States Parties that are members of international organizations shall take appropriate measures to ensure the implementation of this article with respect to such organizations.

Article 140   **Benefit of mankind**

1. Activities in the Area shall, as specifically provided for in this Part, be carried out for the benefit of mankind as a whole, irrespective of the geographical location of States, whether coastal or land-locked, and taking into particular consideration the interests and needs of developing States and of peoples who have not attained full independence or other self-governing status recognized by the United Nations in accordance with General Assembly resolution 1514 (XV) and other relevant General Assembly resolutions.

2. The Authority shall provide for the equitable sharing of financial and other economic benefits derived from activities in the Area through any appropriate mechanism on a non-discriminatory basis, in accordance with article 160, paragraph 2(f)(i).

Article 141   **Use of the Area exclusively for peaceful purposes**

The Area shall be open to use exclusively for peaceful purposes by all States, whether coastal or land-locked, without discrimination and without prejudice to the other provisions of this Part.

Article 142   **Rights and legitimate interests of coastal States**

1. Activities in the Area, with respect to resource deposits in the Area which lie across limits of national jurisdiction, shall be conducted with due regard to the rights and legitimate interests of any coastal State across whose jurisdiction such deposits lie.

2. Consultations, including a system of prior notification, shall be maintained with the State concerned, with a view to avoiding infringement of such rights and interests. In cases where activities in the Area may result in the exploitation of resources lying within national jurisdiction, the prior consent of the coastal State concerned shall be required.

3. Neither this Part nor any rights granted or exercised pursuant thereto shall affect the rights of coastal States to take such measures consistent with the relevant provisions of Part XII as may be necessary to prevent, mitigate or

eliminate grave and imminent danger to their coastline, or related interests from pollution or threat thereof or from other hazardous occurrences resulting from or caused by any activities in the Area.

Article 143   **Marine scientific research**

1. Marine scientific research in the Area shall be carried out exclusively for peaceful purposes and for the benefit of mankind as a whole in accordance with Part XIII.2. The Authority may carry out marine scientific research concerning the Area and its resources, and may enter into contracts for that purpose. The Authority shall promote

and encourage the conduct of marine scientific research in the Area, and shall co-ordinate and disseminate the results of such research and analysis when available.

3. States Parties may carry out marine scientific research in the Area. States Parties shall promote international co-operation in marine scientific research in the Area by:

    (a) participating in international programmes and encouraging co-operation in marine scientific research by personnel of different countries and of the Authority;
    (b) ensuring that programmes are developed through the Authority or other international organizations as appropriate for the benefit of developing States and technologically less developed States with a view to:
        (i) strengthening their research capabilities;
        (ii) training their personnel and the personnel of the Authority in the techniques and applications of research;
        (iii) fostering the employment of their qualified personnel in research in the Area;
    (c) effectively disseminating the results of research and analysis when available, through the Authority or other international channels when appropriate.

Article 144   **Transfer of technology**

1. The Authority shall take measures in accordance with this Convention:

    (a) to acquire technology and scientific knowledge relating to activities in the Area; and
    (b) to promote and encourage the transfer to developing States of such technology and scientific knowledge so that all States Parties benefit therefrom.

2. To this end the Authority and States Parties shall co.operate in promoting the transfer of technology and scientific knowledge relating to activities in the Area so that the Enterprise and all States Parties may benefit therefrom. In particular they shall initiate and promote:

    (a) programmes for the transfer of technology to the Enterprise and to developing States with regard to activities in the Area, including, inter alia, facilitating the access of the Enterprise and of developing States to the relevant technology, under fair and reasonable terms and conditions;
    (b) measures directed towards the advancement of the technology of the Enterprise and the domestic technology of developing States, particularly by providing opportunities to personnel from the Enterprise and from developing States for training in marine science and technology and for their full participation in activities in the Area.

Article 145   **Protection of the marine environment**

Necessary measures shall be taken in accordance with this Convention with respect to activities in the Area to ensure effective protection for the marine environment from harmful effects which may arise from such activities. To this end the Authority shall adopt appropriate rules, regulations and procedures for inter alia:

    (a) the prevention, reduction and control of pollution and other hazards to the marine environment, including the coastline, and of interference with the ecological balance of the marine environment, particular attention being paid to the need for protection from harmful effects of such activities as drilling, dredging, excavation, disposal of waste, construction and operation or maintenance of installations, pipelines and other devices related to such activities;
    (b) the protection and conservation of the natural resources of the Area and the prevention of damage to the flora and fauna of the marine environment.

Article 146   Protection of human life

With respect to activities in the Area, necessary measures shall be taken to ensure effective protection of human life. To this end the Authority shall adopt appropriate rules, regulations and procedures to supplement existing international law as embodied in relevant treaties.

Article 147   Accommodation of activities in the Area and in the marine environment

1. Activities in the Area shall be carried out with reasonable regard for other activities in the marine environment.

2. Installations used for carrying out activities in the Area shall be subject to the following conditions:

(a) such installations shall be erected, emplaced and removed solely in accordance with this Part and subject to the rules, regulations and procedures of the Authority. Due notice must be given of the erection, emplacement and removal of such installations, and permanent means for giving warning of their presence must be maintained;

(b) such installations may not be established where interference may be caused to the use of recognized sea lanes essential to international navigation or in areas of intense fishing activity;

(c) safety zones shall be established around such installations with appropriate markings to ensure the safety of both navigation and the installations. The configuration and location of such safety zones shall not be such as to form a belt impeding the lawful access of shipping to particular maritime zones or navigation along international sea lanes;

(d) such installations shall be used exclusively for peaceful purposes;

(e) such installations do not possess the status of islands. They have no territorial sea of their own, and their presence does not affect the delimitation of the territorial sea, the exclusive economic zone or the continental shelf.

3. Other activities in the marine environment shall be conducted with reasonable regard for activities in the Area.

Article 148   Participation of developing States in activities in the Area

The effective participation of developing States in activities in the Area shall be promoted as specifically provided for in this Part, having due regard to their special interests and needs, and in particular to the special need of the landlocked and geographically disadvantaged among them to overcome obstacles arising from their disadvantaged location, including remoteness from the Area and difficulty of access to and from it.

Article 149   Archaeological and historical objects

All objects of an archaeological and historical nature found in the Area shall be preserved or disposed of for the benefit of mankind as a whole, particular regard being paid to the preferential rights of the State or country of origin, or the State of cultural origin, or the State of historical and archaeological origin.

[Note: See also, the Agreement Relating to the Implementation of Part XI of the United Nations Convention on the Law of the Sea of 10 December 1982, 33 I.L.M. 1309]

***

PART XII   PROTECTION AND PRESERVATION OF THE MARINE ENVIRONMENT

Section 1   General Provisions

Article 192   General obligation

States have the obligation to protect and preserve the marine environment.

Article 193   **Sovereign right of States to exploit their natural resources**

States have the sovereign right to exploit their natural resources pursuant to their environmental policies and in accordance with their duty to protect and preserve the marine environment.

Article 194   **Measures to prevent, reduce and control pollution of the marine environment**

1. States shall take, individually or jointly as appropriate, all measures consistent with this Convention that are necessary to prevent, reduce and control pollution of the marine environment from any source, using for this purpose the best practicable means at their disposal and in accordance with their capabilities, and they shall endeavour to harmonize their policies in this connection.

2. States shall take all measures necessary to ensure that activities under their jurisdiction or control are so conducted as not to cause damage by pollution to other States and their environment, and that pollution arising from incidents or activities under their jurisdiction or control does not spread beyond the areas where they exercise sovereign rights in accordance with this Convention.

3. The measures taken pursuant to this Part shall deal with all sources of pollution of the marine environment. These measures shall include, inter alia, those designed to minimize to the fullest possible extent:

    (a) the release of toxic, harmful or noxious substances, especially those which are persistent, from land-based sources, from or through the atmosphere or by dumping;
    (b) pollution from vessels, in particular measures for preventing accidents and dealing with emergencies, ensuring the safety of operations at sea, preventing intentional and unintentional discharges, and regulating the design, construction, equipment, operation and manning of vessels;
    (c) pollution from installations and devices used in exploration or exploitation of the natural resources of the sea-bed and subsoil, in particular measures for preventing accidents and dealing with emergencies, ensuring the safety of operations at sea, and regulating the design, construction, equipment, operation and manning of such installations or devices;
    (d) pollution from other installations and devices operating in the marine environment, in particular measures for preventing accidents and dealing with emergencies, ensuring the safety of operations at sea, and regulating the design, construction, equipment, operation and manning of such installations or devices.

4. In taking measures to prevent, reduce or control pollution of the marine environment, States shall refrain from unjustifiable interference with activities carried out by other States in the exercise of their rights and in pursuance of their duties in conformity with this Convention.

5. The measures taken in accordance with this Part shall include those necessary to protect and preserve rare or fragile ecosystems as well as the habitat of depleted, threatened or endangered species and other forms of marine life.

Article 195   **Duty not to transfer damage or hazards or transform one type of pollution into another**

In taking measures to prevent, reduce and control pollution of the marine environment, States shall act so as not to transfer, directly or indirectly, damage or hazards from one area to another or transform one type of pollution into another.

Article 196   **Use of technologies or introduction of alien or new species**

1. States shall take all measures necessary to prevent, reduce and control pollution of the marine environment resulting from the use of technologies under their jurisdiction or control, or the intentional or accidental introduction

of species, alien or new, to a particular part of the marine environment, which may cause significant and harmful changes thereto.

2. This article does not affect the application of this Convention regarding the prevention, reduction and control of pollution of the marine environment.

Section 2   Global and Regional Cooperation

Article 197   Co-operation on a global or regional basis

States shall co-operate on a global basis and, as appropriate, on a regional basis, directly or through competent international organizations, in formulating and elaborating international rules, standards and recommended practices and procedures consistent with this Convention, for the protection and preservation of the marine environment, taking into account characteristic regional features.

Article 198   Notification of imminent or actual damage

When a State becomes aware of cases in which the marine environment is in imminent danger of being damaged or has been damaged by pollution, it shall immediately notify other States it deems likely to be affected by such damage, as well as the competent international organizations.

Article 199   Contingency plans against pollution

In the cases referred to in article 198, States in the area affected, in accordance with their capabilities, and the competent international organizations shall co-operate, to the extent possible, in eliminating the effects of pollution and preventing or minimizing the damage. To this end, States shall jointly develop and promote contingency plans for responding to pollution incidents in the marine environment.

Article 200   Studies, research programmes and exchange of information and data

States shall co-operate, directly or through competent international organizations, for the purpose of promoting studies, undertaking programmes of scientific research and encouraging the exchange of information and data acquired about pollution of the marine environment. They shall endeavour to participate actively in regional and global programmes to acquire knowledge for the assessment of the nature and extent of pollution, exposure to it, and its pathways, risks and remedies.

Article 201   Scientific criteria for regulations

In the light of the information and data acquired pursuant to article 200, States shall co-operate, directly or through competent international organizations, in establishing appropriate scientific criteria for the formulation and elaboration of rules, standards and recommended practices and procedures for the prevention, reduction and control of pollution of the marine environment.

Section 3   Technical Assistance

Article 202   Scientific and technical assistance to developing States

States shall, directly or through competent international organizations:

(a) promote programmes of scientific, educational, technical and other assistance to developing States for the protection and preservation of the marine environment and the prevention, reduction and control of marine pollution. Such assistance shall include, inter alia:
 (i) training of their scientific and technical personnel;
 (ii) facilitating their participation in relevant international programmes;
 (iii) supplying them with necessary equipment and facilities;

(iv) enhancing their capacity to manufacture such equipment;

(v) advice on and developing facilities for research, monitoring, educational and other programmes;

(b) provide appropriate assistance, especially to developing States, for the minimization of the effects of major incidents which may cause serious pollution of the marine environment;

(c) provide appropriate assistance, especially to developing States, concerning the preparation of environmental assessments.

Article 203   Preferential treatment for developing States

Developing States shall, for the purposes of prevention, reduction and control of pollution of the marine environment or minimization of its effects, be granted preference by international organizations in:

(a) the allocation of appropriate funds and technical assistance; and
(b) the utilization of their specialized services.

Section 4   Monitoring and Environmental Assessment

Article 204   Monitoring of the risks or effects of pollution

1. States shall, consistent with the rights of other States, endeavour, as far as practicable, directly or through the competent international organizations, to observe, measure, evaluate and analyse, by recognized scientific methods, the risks or effects of pollution of the marine environment.

2. In particular, States shall keep under surveillance the effects of any activities which they permit or in which they engage in order to determine whether these activities are likely to pollute the marine environment.

Article 205   Publication of reports

States shall publish reports of the results obtained pursuant to article204 or provide such reports at appropriate intervals to the competent international organizations, which should make them available to all States.

Article 206   Assessment of potential effects of activities

When States have reasonable grounds for believing that planned activities under their jurisdiction or control may cause substantial pollution of or significant and harmful changes to the marine environment, they shall, as far as practicable, assess the potential effects of such activities on the marine environment and shall communicate reports of the results of such assessments in the manner provided in article 205.

Section 5   International Rules and National Legislation to Prevent, Reduce and Control Pollution of the Marine Environment

Article 207   Pollution from land-based sources

1. States shall adopt laws and regulations to prevent, reduce and control pollution of the marine environment from land-based sources, including rivers, estuaries, pipelines and outfall structures, taking into account internationally agreed rules, standards and recommended practices and procedures.

2. States shall take other measures as may be necessary to prevent, reduce and control such pollution.

3. States shall endeavour to harmonize their policies in this connection at the appropriate regional level.

4. States, acting especially through competent international organizations or diplomatic conference, shall endeavour to establish global and regional rules, standards and recommended practices and procedures to prevent, reduce and control pollution of the marine environment from land-based sources, taking into account characteristic regional features, the economic capacity of developing States and their need for economic development. Such rules, standards and recommended practices and procedures shall be reexamined from time to time as necessary.

5. Laws, regulations, measures, rules, standards and recommended practices and procedures referred to in paragraphs 1, 2 and 4 shall include those designed to minimize, to the fullest extent possible, the release of toxic, harmful or noxious substances, especially those which are persistent, into the marine environment.

Article 208   Pollution from sea-bed activities subject to national jurisdiction

1. Coastal States shall adopt laws and regulations to prevent, reduce and control pollution of the marine environment arising from or in connection with seabed activities subject to their jurisdiction and from artificial islands, installations and structures under their jurisdiction, pursuant to articles 60 and 80.

2. States shall take other measures as may be necessary to prevent, reduce and control such pollution.

3. Such laws, regulations and measures shall be no less effective than international rules, standards and recommended practices and procedures.

4. States shall endeavour to harmonize their policies in this connection at the appropriate regional level.

5. States, acting especially through competent international organizations or diplomatic conference, shall establish global and regional rules, standards and recommended practices and procedures to prevent, reduce and control pollution of the marine environment referred to in paragraph 1. Such rules, standards and recommended practices and procedures shall be re-examined from time to time as necessary.

Article 209   Pollution from activities in the Area

1. International rules, regulations and procedures shall be established in accordance with Part XI to prevent, reduce and control pollution of the marine environment from activities in the Area. Such rules, regulations and procedures shall be re-examined from time to time as necessary.

2. Subject to the relevant provisions of this section, States shall adopt laws and regulations to prevent, reduce and control pollution of the marine environment from activities in the Area undertaken by vessels, installations, structures and other devices flying their flag or of their registry or operating under their authority, as the case may be. The requirements of such laws and regulations shall be no less effective than the international rules, regulations and procedures referred to in paragraph 1.

Article 210   Pollution by dumping

1. States shall adopt laws and regulations to prevent, reduce and control pollution of the marine environment by dumping.

2. States shall take other measures as may be necessary to prevent, reduce and control such pollution.

3. Such laws, regulations and measures shall ensure that dumping is not carried out without the permission of the competent authorities of States.

4. States, acting especially through competent international organizations or diplomatic conference, shall endeavour to establish global and regional rules, standards and recommended practices and procedures to prevent, reduce and control such pollution. Such rules, standards and recommended practices and procedures shall be re-examined from time to time as necessary.

5. Dumping within the territorial sea and the exclusive economic zone or onto the continental shelf shall not be carried out without the express prior approval of the coastal State, which has the right to permit, regulate and control

such dumping after due consideration of the matter with other States which by reason of their geographical situation may be adversely affected thereby.

6. National laws, regulations and measures shall be no less effective in preventing, reducing and controlling such pollution than the global rules and standards.

Article 211   Pollution from vessels

1. States, acting through the competent international organization or general diplomatic conference, shall establish international rules and standards to prevent, reduce and control pollution of the marine environment from vessels and promote the adoption, in the same manner, wherever appropriate, of routing systems designed to minimize the threat of accidents which might cause pollution of the marine environment, including the coastline, and pollution damage to the related interests of coastal States. Such rules and standards shall, in the same manner, be re-examined from time to time as necessary.

2. States shall adopt laws and regulations for the prevention, reduction and control of pollution of the marine environment from vessels flying their flag or of their registry. Such laws and regulations shall at least have the same effect as that of generally accepted international rules and standards established through the competent international organization or general diplomatic conference.

3. States which establish particular requirements for the prevention, reduction and control of pollution of the marine environment as a condition for the entry of foreign vessels into their ports or internal waters or for a call at their off-shore terminals shall give due publicity to such requirements and shall communicate them to the competent international organization. Whenever such requirements are established in identical form by two or more coastal States in an endeavour to harmonize policy, the communication shall indicate which States are participating in such co-operative arrangements. Every State shall require the master of a vessel flying its flag or of its registry, when navigating within the territorial sea of a State participating in such co-operative arrangements, to furnish, upon the request of that State, information as to whether it is proceeding to a State of the same region participating in such co-operative arrangements and, if so, to indicate whether it complies with the port entry requirements of that State. This article is without prejudice to the continued exercise by a vessel of its right of innocent passage or to the application of article 25, paragraph 2.

4. Coastal States may, in the exercise of their sovereignty within their territorial sea, adopt laws and regulations for the prevention, reduction and control of marine pollution from foreign vessels, including vessels exercising the right of innocent passage. Such laws and regulations shall, in accordance with Part II, section 3, not hamper innocent passage of foreign vessels.

5. Coastal States, for the purpose of enforcement as provided for in section 6, may in respect of their exclusive economic zones adopt laws and regulations for the prevention, reduction and control of pollution from vessels conforming to and giving effect to generally accepted international rules and standards established through the competent international organization or general diplomatic conference.

6.   (a) Where the international rules and standards referred to in paragraph 1 are inadequate to meet special circumstances and coastal States have reasonable grounds for believing that a particular, clearly defined area of their respective exclusive economic zones is an area where the adoption of special mandatory measures for the prevention of pollution from vessels is required for recognized technical reasons in relation to its oceanographical and ecological conditions, as well as its utilization or the protection of its resources and the particular character of its traffic, the coastal States, after appropriate consultations through the competent international organization with any other States concerned, may, for that area, direct a communication to that organization, submitting scientific and technical evidence in support and information on necessary reception facilities. Within 12 months after receiving such a communication, the organization shall determine whether the conditions in that area correspond to the requirements set out above. If the organization so determines, the coastal States may, for that area, adopt laws and regulations for the prevention, reduction and control of pollution from vessels implementing such international rules and standards or navigational practices as are made applicable, through the organization, for special areas. These laws and regulations shall not become applicable to foreign vessels until 15 months after the submission of the communication to the organization.

          (b) The coastal States shall publish the limits of any such particular, clearly defined area.

          (c) If the coastal States intend to adopt additional laws and regulations for the same area for the prevention, reduction and control of pollution from vessels, they shall, when submitting the aforesaid communication, at the same time notify the organization thereof. Such additional laws and regulations may relate to discharges or navigational practices but shall not require foreign vessels to observe design, construction, manning or equipment standards other than generally accepted international rules and standards; they shall become applicable to foreign vessels 15 months after the submission of the communication to the organization, provided that the organization agrees within 12 months after the submission of the communication.

7. The international rules and standards referred to in this article should include inter alia those relating to prompt notification to coastal States, whose coastline or related interests may be affected by incidents, including maritime casualties, which involve discharges or probability of discharges.

| Article 212 | Pollution from or through the atmosphere |

1. States shall adopt laws and regulations to prevent, reduce and control pollution of the marine environment from or through the atmosphere, applicable to the air space under their sovereignty and to vessels flying their flag or vessels or aircraft of their registry, taking into account internationally agreed rules standards and recommended practices and procedures and the safety of air navigation.

2. States shall take other measures as may be necessary to prevent, reduce and control such pollution.

3. States, acting especially through competent international organizations or diplomatic conference, shall endeavour to establish global and regional rules, standards and recommended practices and procedures to prevent, reduce and control such pollution.

Section 6   Enforcement

| Article 213 | Enforcement with respect to pollution from land-based sources |

States shall enforce their laws and regulations adopted in accordance with article 207 and shall adopt laws and regulations and take other measures necessary to implement applicable international rules and standards established through competent international organizations or diplomatic conference to prevent, reduce and control pollution of the marine environment from land-based sources.

| Article 214 | Enforcement with respect to pollution from sea-bed activities |

States shall enforce their laws and regulations adopted in accordance with article 208 and shall adopt laws and regulations and take other measures necessary to implement applicable international rules and standards established through competent international organizations or diplomatic conference to prevent, reduce and control pollution of the marine environment arising from or in connection with sea-bed activities subject to their jurisdiction and from artificial islands, installations and structures under their jurisdiction, pursuant to articles 60 and 80.

| Article 215 | Enforcement with respect to pollution from activities in the Area |

Enforcement of international rules, regulations and procedures established in accordance with Part XI to prevent, reduce and control pollution of the marine environment from activities in the Area shall be governed by that Part.

| Article 216 | Enforcement with respect to pollution by dumping |

1. Laws and regulations adopted in accordance with this Convention and applicable international rules and standards established through competent international organizations or diplomatic conference for the prevention, reduction and control of pollution of the marine environment by dumping shall be enforced:

(a) by the coastal State with regard to dumping within its territorial sea or its exclusive economic zone or onto its continental shelf;
(b) by the flag State with regard to vessels flying its flag or vessels or aircraft of its registry;

(c) by any State with regard to acts of loading of wastes or other matter occurring within its territory or at its off-shore terminals.

2. No State shall be obliged by virtue of this article to institute proceedings when another State has already instituted proceedings in accordance with this article.

Article 217   Enforcement by flag States

1. States shall ensure compliance by vessels flying their flag or of their registry with applicable international rules and standards, established through the competent international organization or general diplomatic conference, and with their laws and regulations adopted in accordance with this Convention for the prevention, reduction and control of pollution of the marine environment from vessels and shall accordingly adopt laws and regulations and take other measures necessary for their implementation. Flag States shall provide for the effective enforcement of such rules, standards, laws and regulations, irrespective of where a violation occurs.

2. States shall, in particular, take appropriate measures in order to ensure that vessels flying their flag or of their registry are prohibited from sailing, until they can proceed to sea in compliance with the requirements of the international rules and standards referred to in paragraph I, including requirements in respect of design, construction, equipment and manning of vessels.

3. States shall ensure that vessels flying their flag or of their registry carry on board certificates required by and issued pursuant to international rules and standards referred to in paragraph 1. States shall ensure that vessels flying their flag are periodically inspected in order to verify that such certificates are in conformity with the actual condition of the vessels. These certificates shall be accepted by other States as evidence of the condition of the vessels and shall be regarded as having the same force as certificates issued by them, unless there are clear grounds for believing that the condition of the vessel does not correspond substantially with the particulars of the certificates.

4. If a vessel commits a violation of rules and standards established through the competent international organization or general diplomatic conference, the flag State, without prejudice to articles 218, 220 and 228, shall provide for immediate investigation and where appropriate institute proceedings in respect of the alleged violation irrespective of where the violation occurred or where the pollution caused by such violation has occurred or has been spotted.

5. Flag States conducting an investigation of the violation may request the assistance of any other State whose co-operation could be useful in clarifying the circumstances of the case. States shall endeavour to meet appropriate requests of flag States.

6. States shall, at the written request of any State, investigate any violation alleged to have been committed by vessels flying their flag. If satisfied that sufficient evidence is available to enable proceedings to be brought in respect of the alleged violation, flag States shall without delay institute such proceedings in accordance with their laws.

7. Flag States shall promptly inform the requesting State and the competent international organization of the action taken and its outcome. Such information shall be available to all States.

8. Penalties provided for by the laws and regulations of States for vessels flying their flag shall be adequate in severity to discourage violations wherever they occur.

Article 218   Enforcement by port States

1. When a vessel is voluntarily within a port or at an off-shore terminal of a State, that State may undertake investigations and, where the evidence so warrants, institute proceedings in respect of any discharge from that vessel outside the internal waters, territorial sea or exclusive economic zone of that State in violation of applicable international rules and standards established through the competent international organization or general diplomatic conference.

2. No proceedings pursuant to paragraph 1 shall be instituted in respect of a discharge violation in the internal waters, territorial sea or exclusive economic zone of another State unless requested by that State, the flag State, or a

State damaged or threatened by the discharge violation, or unless the violation has caused or is likely to cause pollution in the internal waters, territorial sea or exclusive economic zone of the State instituting the proceedings.

3. When a vessel is voluntarily within a port or at an off-shore terminal of a State, that State shall, as far as practicable, comply with requests from any State for investigation of a discharge violation referred to in paragraph 1, believed to have occurred in, caused, or threatened damage to the internal waters, territorial sea or exclusive economic zone of the requesting State. It shall likewise, as far as practicable, comply with requests from the flag State for investigation of such a violation, irrespective of where the violation occurred.

4. The records of the investigation carried out by a port State pursuant to this article shall be transmitted upon request to the flag State or to the coastal State. Any proceedings instituted by the port State on the basis of such an investigation may, subject to section 7, be suspended at the request of the coastal State when the violation has occurred within its internal waters, territorial sea or exclusive economic zone. The evidence and records of the case, together with any bond or other financial security posted with the authorities of the port State, shall in that event be transmitted to the coastal State. Such transmittal shall preclude the continuation of proceedings in the port State.

Article 219	**Measures relating to seaworthiness of vessels to avoid pollution**

Subject to section 7, States which, upon request or on their own initiative, have ascertained that a vessel within one of their ports or at one of their offshore terminals is in violation of applicable international rules and standards relating to seaworthiness of vessels and thereby threatens damage to the marine environment shall, as far as practicable, take administrative measures to prevent the vessel from sailing. Such States may permit the vessel to proceed only to the nearest appropriate repair yard and, upon removal of the causes of the violation, shall permit the vessel to continue immediately.

Article 220	**Enforcement by coastal States**

1. When a vessel is voluntarily within a port or at an off-shore terminal of a State, that State may, subject to section 7, institute proceedings in respect of any violation of its laws and regulations adopted in accordance with this Convention or applicable international rules and standards for the prevention, reduction and control of pollution from vessels when the violation has occurred within the territorial sea or the exclusive economic zone of that State.

2. Where there are clear grounds for believing that a vessel navigating in the territorial sea of a State has, during its passage therein, violated laws and regulations of that State adopted in accordance with this Convention or applicable international rules and standards for the prevention, reduction and control of pollution from vessels, that State, without prejudice to the application of the relevant provisions of Part II, section 3, may undertake physical inspection of the vessel relating to the violation and may, where the evidence so warrants institute proceedings, including detention of the vessel, in accordance with its laws, subject to the provisions of section 7.

3. Where there are clear grounds for believing that a vessel navigating in the exclusive economic zone or the territorial sea of a State has, in the exclusive economic zone, committed a violation of applicable international rules and standards for the prevention, reduction and control of pollution from vessels or laws and regulations of that State conforming and giving effect to such rules and standards, that State may require the vessel to give information regarding its identity and port of registry, its last and its next port of call and other relevant information required to establish whether a violation has occurred.

4. States shall adopt laws and regulations and take other measures so that vessels flying their flag comply with requests for information pursuant to paragraph 3.

5. Where there are clear grounds for believing that a vessel navigating in the exclusive economic zone or the territorial sea of a State has, in the exclusive economic zone, committed a violation referred to in paragraph 3 resulting in a substantial discharge causing or threatening significant pollution of the marine environment, that State may undertake physical inspection of the vessel for matters relating to the violation if the vessel has refused to give information or if the information supplied by the vessel is manifestly at variance with the evident factual situation and if the circumstances of the case justify such inspection.

6. Where there is clear objective evidence that a vessel navigating in the exclusive economic zone or the territorial sea of a State has, in the exclusive economic zone, committed a violation referred to in paragraph 3 resulting in a discharge causing major damage or threat of major damage to the coastline or related interests of the coastal State, or to any resources of its territorial sea or exclusive economic zone, that State may, subject to section 7, provided that the evidence so warrants, institute proceedings, including detention of the vessel, in accordance with its laws.

7. Notwithstanding the provisions of paragraph 6, whenever appropriate procedures have been established, either through the competent international organization or as otherwise agreed, whereby compliance with requirements for bonding or other appropriate financial security has been assured, the coastal State if bound by such procedures shall allow the vessel to proceed.

8. The provisions of paragraphs 3, 4, 5, 6 and 7 also apply in respect of national laws and regulations adopted pursuant to article 211, paragraph 6.

Article 221   Measures to avoid pollution arising from Maritime casualties

1. Nothing in this Part shall prejudice the right of States, pursuant to international law, both customary and conventional, to take and enforce measures beyond the territorial sea proportionate to the actual or threatened damage to protect their coastline or related interests, including fishing, from pollution or threat of pollution following upon a maritime casualty or acts relating to such a casualty, which may reasonably be expected to result in major harmful consequences.

2. For the purposes of this article, "maritime casualty" means a collision of vessels, stranding or other incident of navigation, or other occurrence on board a vessel or external to it resulting in material damage or imminent threat of material damage to a vessel or cargo.

Article 222   Enforcement with respect to pollution from or through the atmosphere

States shall enforce, within the air space under their sovereignty or with regard to vessels flying their flag or vessels or aircraft of their registry, their laws and regulations adopted in accordance with article 212, paragraph 1, and with other provisions of this Convention and shall adopt laws and regulations and take other measures necessary to implement applicable international rules and standards established through competent international organizations or diplomatic conference to prevent, reduce and control pollution of the marine environment from or through the atmosphere, in conformity with all relevant international rules and standards concerning the safety of air navigation.

Section 7   Safeguards

Article 223   Measures to facilitate proceedings

In proceedings instituted pursuant to this Part, States shall take measures to facilitate the hearing of witnesses and the admission of evidence submitted by authorities of another State, or by the competent international organization, and shall facilitate the attendance at such proceedings of official representatives of the competent international organization, the flag State and any State affected by pollution arising out of any violation. The official representatives attending such proceedings shall have such rights and duties as may be provided under national laws and regulations or international law.

Article 224   Exercise of powers of enforcement

The powers of enforcement against foreign vessels under this Part may only be exercised by officials or by warships, military aircraft, or other ships or aircraft clearly marked and identifiable as being on government service and authorized to that effect.

Article 225   Duty to avoid adverse consequences in the exercise of the powers of enforcement

In the exercise under this Convention of their powers of enforcement against foreign vessels, States shall not endanger the safety of navigation or otherwise create any hazard to a vessel, or bring it to an unsafe port or anchorage, or expose the marine environment to an unreasonable risk.

Article 226   Investigation of foreign vessels

1.   (a) States shall not delay a foreign vessel longer than is essential for purposes of the investigations provided for in articles 216, 218 and 220. Any physical inspection of a foreign vessel shall be limited to an examination of

such certificates, records or other documents as the vessel is required to carry by generally accepted international rules and standards or of any similar documents which it is carrying; further physical inspection of the vessel may be undertaken only after such an examination and only when:

      (i) there are clear grounds for believing that the condition of the vessel or its equipment does not correspond substantially with the particulars of those documents;

      (ii) the contents of such documents are not sufficient to confirm or verify a suspected violation; or

      (iii) the vessel is not carrying valid certificates and records.

   (b) If the investigation indicates a violation of applicable laws and regulations or international rules and standards for the protection and preservation of the marine environment, release shall be made promptly subject to reasonable procedures such as bonding or other appropriate financial security.

   (c) Without prejudice to applicable international rules and standards relating to the seaworthiness of vessels, the release of a vessel may, whenever it would present an unreasonable threat of damage to the marine environment, be refused or made conditional upon proceeding to the nearest appropriate repair yard. Where release has been refused or made conditional, the flag State of the vessel must be promptly notified, and may seek release of the vessel in accordance with Part XV.

2. States shall co-operate to develop procedures for the avoidance of un necessary physical inspection of vessels at sea.

Article 227   Non-discrimination with respect to foreign vessels

In exercising their rights and performing their duties under this Part, States shall not discriminate in form or in fact against vessels of any other State.

Article 228   Suspension and restrictions on institution of proceedings

1. Proceedings to impose penalties in respect of any violation of applicable laws and regulations or international rules and standards relating to the prevention, reduction and control of pollution from vessels committed by a foreign vessel beyond the territorial sea of the State instituting proceedings shall be suspended upon the taking of proceedings to impose penalties in respect of corresponding charges by the flag State within six months of the date on which proceedings were first instituted, unless those proceedings relate to a case of major damage to the coastal State or the flag State in question has repeatedly disregarded its obligation to enforce effectively the applicable international rules and standards in respect of violations committed by its vessels. The flag State shall in due course make available to the State previously instituting proceedings a full dossier of the case and the records of the proceedings, whenever the flag State has requested the suspension of proceedings in accordance with this article. When proceedings instituted by the flag State have been brought to a conclusion, the suspended proceedings shall be terminated. Upon payment of costs incurred in respect of such proceedings, any bond posted or other financial security provided in connection with the suspended proceedings shall be released by the coastal State.

2. Proceedings to impose penalties on foreign vessels shall not be instituted after the expiry of three years from the date on which the violation was committed, and shall not be taken by any State in the event of proceedings having been instituted by another State subject to the provisions set out in paragraph 1.

3. The provisions of this article are without prejudice to the right of the flag State to take any measures, including proceedings to impose penalties, according to its laws irrespective of prior proceedings by another State.

| Article 229 | Institution of civil proceedings |

Nothing in this Convention affects the institution of civil proceedings in respect of any claim for loss or damage resulting from pollution of the marine environment.

| Article 230 | Monetary penalties and the observance of recognized rights of the accused |

1. Monetary penalties only may be imposed with respect to violations of national laws and regulations or applicable international rules and standards for the prevention, reduction and control of pollution of the marine environment, committed by foreign vessels beyond the territorial sea.

2. Monetary penalties only may be imposed with respect to violations of national laws and regulations or applicable international rules and standards for the prevention, reduction and control of pollution of the marine environment, committed by foreign vessels in the territorial sea, except in the case of a wilful and serious act of pollution in the territorial sea.

3. In the conduct of proceedings in respect of such violations committed by a foreign vessel which may result in the imposition of penalties, recognized rights of the accused shall be observed.

| Article 231 | Notification to the flag State and other States concerned |

States shall promptly notify the flag State and any other State concerned of any measures taken pursuant to section 6 against foreign vessels, and shall submit to the flag State all official reports concerning such measures. However, with respect to violations committed in the territorial sea, the foregoing obligations of the coastal State apply only to such measures as are taken in proceedings. The diplomatic agents or consular officers and where possible the maritime authority of the flag State, shall be immediately informed of any such measures taken pursuant to section 6 against foreign vessels.

| Article 232 | Liability of States arising from enforcement measures |

States shall be liable for damage or loss attributable to them arising from measures taken pursuant to section 6 when such measures are unlawful or exceed those reasonably required in the light of available information. States shall provide for recourse in their courts for actions in respect of such damage or loss.

| Article 233 | Safeguards with respect to straits used for international navigation |

Nothing in sections 5, 6 and 7 affects the legal regime of straits used for international navigation. However, if a foreign ship other than those referred to in section 10 has committed a violation of the laws and regulations referred to in article 42, paragraph 1 (a) and (b), causing or threatening major damage to the marine environment of the straits, the States bordering the straits may take appropriate enforcement measures and if so shall respect mutatis mutandis the provisions of this section.

Section 8 Ice-Covered Areas

| Article 234 | Ice-covered areas |

Coastal States have the right to adopt and enforce non-discriminatory laws and regulations for the prevention, reduction and control of marine pollution from vessels in ice-covered areas within the limits of the exclusive economic zone, where particularly severe climatic conditions and the presence of ice covering such areas for most of the year create obstructions or exceptional hazards to navigation, and pollution of the marine environment could cause major harm to or irreversible disturbance of the ecological balance. Such laws and regulations shall have due regard to navigation and the protection and preservation of the marine environment based on the best available scientific evidence.

Section 9   Responsibility and Liability

Article 235   Responsibility and liability

1. States are responsible for the fulfilment of their international obligations concerning the protection and preservation of the marine environment. They shall be liable in accordance with international law.

2. States shall ensure that recourse is available in accordance with their legal systems for prompt and adequate compensation or other relief in respect of damage caused by pollution of the marine environment by natural or juridical persons under their jurisdiction.

3. With the objective of assuring prompt and adequate compensation in respect of all damage caused by pollution of the marine environment, States shall co-operate in the implementation of existing international law and the further development of international law relating to responsibility and liability for the assessment of and compensation for damage and the settlement of related disputes, as well as, where appropriate, development of criteria and procedures for payment of adequate compensation, such as compulsory insurance or compensation funds.

Section 10   Sovereign Immunity

Article 236   Sovereign immunity

The provisions of this Convention regarding the protection and preservation of the marine environment do not apply to any warship, naval auxiliary, other vessels or aircraft owned or operated by a State and used, for the time being only on government non-commercial service. However, each State shall ensure, by the adoption of appropriate measures not impairing operations or operational capabilities of such vessels or aircraft owned or operated by it, that such vessels or aircraft act in a manner consistent, so far as is reasonable and practicable, with this Convention.

Section 11   Obligations under Other Conventions on the Protection and Preservation of the Marine Environment

Article 237   Obligations under other conventions on the protection and preservation of the marine environment

1. The provisions of this Part are without prejudice to the specific obligations assumed by States under special conventions and agreements concluded previously which relate to the protection and preservation of the marine environment and to agreements which may be concluded in furtherance of the general principles set forth in this Convention.

2. Specific obligations assumed by States under special conventions, with respect to the protection and preservation of the marine environment, should be carried out in a manner consistent with the general principles and objectives of this Convention.

PART XIII   MARINE SCIENTIFIC RESEARCH

Section 1   General Provisions

Article 238   Right to conduct marine scientific research

All States, irrespective of their geographical location, and competent international organizations have the right to conduct marine scientific research subject to the rights and duties of other States as provided for in this Convention.

Article 239   Promotion of marine scientific research

States and competent international organizations shall promote and facilitate the development and conduct of marine scientific research in accordance with this Convention.

Article 240   General principles for the conduct of marine scientific research

In the conduct of marine scientific research the following principles shall apply:

(a) marine scientific research shall be conducted exclusively for peaceful purposes;

(b) marine scientific research shall be conducted with appropriate scientific methods and means compatible with this Convention;

(c) marine scientific research shall not unjustifiably interfere with other legitimate uses of the sea compatible with this Convention and shall be duly respected in the course of such uses;

(d) marine scientific research shall be conducted in compliance with all relevant regulations adopted in conformity with this Convention including those for the protection and preservation of the marine environment.

Article 241   Non-recognition of marine scientific research activities as the legal basis for claims

Marine scientific research activities shall not constitute the legal basis for any claim to any part of the marine environment or its resources.

* * *

Article 245   Marine scientific research in the territorial sea

Coastal States, in the exercise of their sovereignty, have the exclusive right to regulate, authorize and conduct marine scientific research in their territorial sea. Marine scientific research therein shall be conducted only with the express consent of and under the conditions set forth by the coastal State.

Article 246   Marine scientific research in the exclusive economic zone and on the continental shelf

1. Coastal States, in the exercise of their jurisdiction, have the right to regulate, authorize and conduct marine scientific research in their exclusive economic zone and on their continental shelf in accordance with the relevant provisions of this Convention.

2. Marine scientific research in the exclusive economic zone and on the continental shelf shall be conducted with the consent of the coastal State.

3. Coastal States shall, in normal circumstances, grant their consent for marine scientific research projects by other States or competent international organizations in their exclusive economic zone or on their continental shelf to be carried out in accordance with this Convention exclusively for peaceful purposes and in order to increase scientific knowledge of the marine environment for the benefit of all mankind. To this end, coastal States shall establish rules and procedures ensuring that such consent will not be delayed or denied unreasonably.

4. For the purposes of applying paragraph 3, normal circumstances may exist in spite of the absence of diplomatic relations between the coastal State and the researching State.

5. Coastal States may however in their discretion withhold their consent to the conduct of a marine scientific research project of another State or competent international organization in the exclusive economic zone or on the continental shelf of the coastal State if that project:

(a) is of direct significance for the exploration and exploitation of natural resources, whether living or non-living;

(b) involves drilling into the continental shelf, the use of explosives or the introduction of harmful substances into the marine environment;

(c) involves the construction, operation or use of artificial islands, installations and structures referred to in articles 60 and 80;

(d) contains information communicated pursuant to article 248 regarding the nature and objectives of the project which is inaccurate or if the researching State or competent international organization has outstanding obligations to the coastal State from a prior research project.

6. Notwithstanding the provisions of paragraph 5, coastal States may not exercise their discretion to withhold consent under subparagraph (a) of that paragraph in respect of marine scientific research projects to be undertaken in accordance with the provisions of this Part on the continental shelf, beyond 200 nautical miles from the baselines from which the breadth of the territorial sea is measured, outside those specific areas which coastal States may at any time publicly designate as areas in which exploitation or detailed exploratory operations focused on those areas are occurring or will occur within a reasonable period of time. Coastal States shall give reasonable notice of the designation of such areas, as well as any modifications thereto, but shall not be obliged to give details of the operations therein.

7. The provisions of paragraph 6 are without prejudice to the rights of coastal States over the continental shelf as established in article 77.

8. Marine scientific research activities referred to in this article shall not unjustifiably interfere with activities undertaken by coastal States in the exercise of their sovereign rights and jurisdiction provided for in this Convention.

Article 247	**Marine scientific research projects undertaken by or under the auspices of international organizations**

A coastal State which is a member of or has a bilateral agreement with an international organization, and in whose exclusive economic zone or on whose continental shelf that organization wants to carry out a marine scientific research project, directly or under its auspices, shall be deemed to have authorized the project to be carried out in conformity with the agreed specifications if that State approved the detailed project when the decision was made by the organization for the undertaking of the project, or is willing to participate in it, and has not expressed any objection within four months of notification of the project by the organization to the coastal State.

Article 248	**Duty to provide information to the coastal State**

States and competent international organizations which intend to undertake marine scientific research in the exclusive economic zone or on the continental shelf of a coastal State shall, not less than six months in advance of the expected starting date of the marine scientific research project, provide that State with a full description of:

(a) the nature and objectives of the project;

(b) the method and means to be used, including name, tonnage, type and class of vessels and a description of scientific equipment;

(c) the precise geographical areas in which the project is to be conducted;

(d) the expected date of first appearance and final departure of the research vessels, or deployment of the equipment and its removal, as appropriate;

(e) the name of the sponsoring institution, its director, and the person in charge of the project; and

(f) the extent to which it is considered that the coastal State should be able to participate or to be represented in the project.

* * *

PART XV   SETTLEMENT OF DISPUTES
(omitted)

PART XVI   GENERAL PROVISIONS

Article 300   Good faith and abuse of rights

States Parties shall fulfil in good faith the obligations assumed under this Convention and shall exercise the rights, jurisdiction and freedoms recognized in this Convention in a manner which would not constitute an abuse of right.

Article 301   Peaceful uses of the seas

In exercising their rights and performing their duties under this Convention, States Parties shall refrain from any threat or use of force against the territorial integrity or political independence of any State, or in any other manner inconsistent with the principles of international law embodied in the Charter of the United Nations.

Article 302   Disclosure of information

Without prejudice to the right of a State Party to resort to the procedures for the settlement of disputes provided for in this Convention, nothing in this Convention shall be deemed to require a State Party, in the fulfilment of its obligations under this Convention, to supply information the disclosure of which is contrary to the essential interests of its security.

Article 303   Archaeological and historical objects found at sea

1. States have the duty to protect objects of an archaeological and historical nature found at sea and shall co-operate for this purpose.

2. In order to control traffic in such objects, the coastal State may, in applying article 33, presume that their removal from the sea-bed in the zone referred to in that article without its approval would result in an infringement within its territory or territorial sea of the laws and regulations referred to in that article.

3. Nothing in this article affects the rights of identifiable owners, the law of salvage or other rules of admiralty, or laws and practices with respect to cultural exchanges.
4. This article is without prejudice to other international agreements and rules of international law regarding the

protection of objects of an archaeological and historical nature.

Article 304   Responsibility and liability for damage

The provisions of this Convention regarding responsibility and liability for damage are without prejudice to the application of existing rules and the development of further rules regarding responsibility and liability under international law.

* * *

PART XVII   FINAL PROVISIONS

* * *

Article 309   Reservations and exceptions

No reservations or exceptions may be made to this Convention unless expressly permitted by other articles of this Convention.

Article 310   Declarations and statements

Article 309 does not preclude a State, when signing, ratifying or acceding to this Convention, from making declarations or statements, however phrased or named, with a view, inter alia, to the harmonization of its laws and regulations with the provisions of this Convention, provided that such declarations or statements do not purport to exclude or to modify the legal effect of the provisions of this Convention in their application to that State.

Article 311   **Relation to other conventions and international agreements**

1. This Convention shall prevail, as between States Parties, over the Geneva Conventions on the Law of the Sea of 29 April 1958.

2. This Convention shall not alter the rights and obligations of States Parties which arise from other agreements compatible with this Convention and which do not affect the enjoyment by other States Parties of their rights or the performance of their obligations under this Convention.

3. Two or more States Parties may conclude agreements modifying or suspending the operation of provisions of this Convention, applicable solely to the relations between them, provided that such agreements do not relate to a provision derogation from which is incompatible with the effective execution of the object and purpose of this Convention, and provided further that such agreements shall not affect the application of the basic principles embodied herein, and that the provisions of such agreements do not affect the enjoyment by other States Parties of their rights or the performance of their obligations under this Convention.

4. States Parties intending to conclude an agreement referred to in paragraph 3 shall notify the other States Parties through the depositary of this Convention of their intention to conclude the agreement and of the modification or suspension for which it provides.

5. This article does not affect international agreements expressly permitted or preserved by other articles of this Convention.

6. States Parties agree that there shall be no amendments to the basic principle relating to the common heritage of mankind set forth in article 136 and that they shall not be party to any agreement in derogation thereof.

Article 312   **Amendment**

1. After the expiry of a period of 10 years from the date of entry into force of this Convention, a State Party may, by written communication addressed to the Secretary-General of the United Nations, propose specific amendments to this Convention, other than those relating to activities in the Area, and request the convening of a conference to

consider such proposed amendments. The Secretary-General shall circulate such communication to all States Parties. If, within 12 months from the date of the circulation of the communication, not less than one half of the States Parties reply favourably to the request, the Secretary-General shall convene the conference.

2. The decision making procedure applicable at the amendment conference shall be the same as that applicable at the Third United Nations Conference on the Law of the Sea unless otherwise decided by the conference. The conference should make every effort to reach agreement on any amendments by way of consensus and there should be no voting on them until all efforts at consensus have been exhausted.

* * *

Article 317   **Denunciation**

1. A State Party may, by written notification addressed to the Secretary-General of the United Nations, denounce this Convention and may indicate its reasons. Failure to indicate reasons shall not affect the validity of the denunciation. The denunciation shall take effect one year after the date of receipt of the notification, unless the notification specifies a later date.

2. A State shall not be discharged by reason of the denunciation from the financial and contractual obligations which accrued while it was a Party to this Convention, nor shall the denunciation affect any right, obligation or legal situation of that State created through the execution of this Convention prior to its termination for that State.

3. The denunciation shall not in any way affect the duty of any State Party to fulfil any obligation embodied in this Convention to which it would be subject under international law independently of this Convention.

AGREEMENT FOR THE IMPLEMENTATION OF THE PROVISIONS OF THE UNITED NATIONS CONVENTION OF THE LAW OF THE SEA OF 10 DECEMBER 1982, RELATING TO THE CONSERVATION AND MANAGEMENT OF STRADDLING FISH STOCKS AND HIGHLY MIGRATORY FISH STOCKS

UNDOC A/ Conf.164/37
Signed: August 4, 1995
Entered into Force: December 11, 2001

The States Parties to this Agreement,

Recalling the relevant provisions of the United Nations Convention on the Law of the Sea of 10 December 1982,

Determined to ensure the long-term conservation and sustainable use of straddling fish stocks and highly migratory fish stocks,

Resolved to improve cooperation between States to that end,

Calling for more effective enforcement by flag States, port States and coastal States of the conservation and management measures adopted for such stocks,

Seeking to address in particular the problems identified in Agenda 21, chapter 17, Programme Area C, adopted by the United Nations Conference on Environment and Development, namely, that the management of high seas fisheries is inadequate in many areas and that some resources are overutilized; noting that there are problems of unregulated fishing, over-capitalization, excessive fleet size, vessel reflagging to escape controls, insufficiently selective gear, unreliable databases and lack of sufficient cooperation between States,

Committing themselves to responsible fisheries,

Conscious of the need to avoid adverse impacts on the marine environment, preserve biodiversity, maintain the integrity of marine ecosystems and minimize the risk of long-term or irreversible effects of fishing operations,

Recognizing the need for specific assistance, including financial, scientific and technological assistance, in order that developing States can participate effectively in the conservation, management and sustainable use of straddling fish stocks and highly migratory fish stocks,

Convinced that an agreement relating to the implementation of the relevant provisions of the Convention would best serve these purposes and contribute to the maintenance of international peace and security,

Affirming that matters not regulated by the Convention or by this Agreement continue to be governed by the rules and principles of general international law,

Have agreed as follows:

PART I : GENERAL PROVISIONS

Article 1   Use of terms and scope

1. For the purposes of this Agreement:

    (a) "Convention" means the United Nations Convention on the Law of the Sea of 10 December 1982;

    (b) "conservation and management measures" means measures to conserve or manage one or more species of living marine resources that are adopted and applied consistent with the relevant rules of international law as reflected in the Convention and this Agreement;

    (c) "fish" includes molluscs and crustaceans except those belonging to sedentary species as defined in article 77 of the Convention; and

    (d) "arrangement" means a cooperative mechanism established in accordance with the Convention and this

Agreement by two or more States for the purpose, inter alia, of establishing conservation and management measures in a subregion or region for one or more straddling fish stocks or highly migratory fish stocks.

2.　　　　(a) "States Parties" means States which have consented to be bound by this Agreement and for which the Agreement is in force.

　　　　(b) This Agreement applies mutatis mutandis:

　　　　　　(i) to any entity referred to in article 305, paragraph 1 (c), (d) and (e), of the Convention and

　　　　　　(ii) subject to article 47, to any entity referred to as an "international organization" in article 1 of Annex IX, to the Convention which becomes a Party to this Agreement, and to that extent "State Parties" refers to those entities.

3. This Agreement applies mutatis mutandis to other fishing entities whose vessels fish on the high seas.

Article 2　　　　Objective

The objective of this Agreement is to ensure the long-term conservation and sustainable use of straddling fish stocks and highly migratory fish stocks through effective implementation of the relevant provisions of the Convention.

Article 3　　　　Application

1. Unless otherwise provided, this Agreement applies to the conservation and management of straddling fish stocks and highly migratory fish stocks beyond areas under national jurisdiction, except that articles 6 and 7 apply also to the conservation and management of such stocks within areas under national jurisdiction, subject to the different legal regimes that apply within areas under national jurisdiction and in areas beyond national jurisdiction as provided for in the Convention.

2. In the exercise of its sovereign rights for the purpose of exploring and exploiting, conserving and managing straddling fish stocks and highly migratory fish stocks within areas under national jurisdiction, the coastal State shall apply mutatis mutandis the general principles enumerated in article 5.

3. States shall give due consideration to the respective capacities of developing States to apply articles 5, 6 and 7 within areas under national jurisdiction and their need for assistance as provided for in this Agreement. To this end, Part VII applies mutatis mutandis in respect of areas under national jurisdiction.

Article 4　　　　Relationship between this Agreement and the Convention

Nothing in this Agreement shall prejudice the rights, jurisdiction and duties of States under the Convention. This Agreement shall be interpreted and applied in the context of and in a manner consistent with the Convention.

PART II: CONSERVATION AND MANAGEMENT OF STRADDLING FISH STOCKS AND HIGHLY MIGRATORY FISH STOCKS

Article 5　　　　General principles

In order to conserve and manage straddling fish stocks and highly migratory fish stocks, coastal States and States fishing on the high seas shall, in giving effect to their duty to cooperate in accordance with the Convention:

　　　　(a) adopt measures to ensure long-term sustainability of straddling fish stocks and highly migratory fish stocks and promote the objective of their optimum utilization;

　　　　(b) ensure that such measures are based on the best scientific evidence available and are designed to maintain or restore stocks at levels capable of producing maximum sustainable yield, as qualified by relevant environmental and economic factors, including the special requirements of developing States, and taking into account fishing patterns, the interdependence of stocks and any generally recommended international minimum standards, whether subregional, regional or global;

　　　　(c) apply the precautionary approach in accordance with article 6;

　　　　(d) assess the impacts of fishing, other human activities and environmental factors on target stocks and species belonging to the same ecosystem or dependent upon or associated with the target stocks;

(e) adopt, where necessary, conservation and management measures for species belonging to the same ecosystem dependent upon or associated with the target stocks, with a view to maintaining or restoring populations of such species above levels at which their reproduction may become seriously threatened;

(f) minimize pollution, waste, discards, catch by lost or abandoned gear, catch of non-target species, both fish and non-fish species (hereinafter referred to as non-target species) and impacts on associated or dependent species, in particular endangered species, through measures including, to the extent practicable, the development and use of selective, environmentally safe and cost-effective fishing gear and techniques;

(g) protect biodiversity in the marine environment;

(h) take measures to prevent or eliminate overfishing and excess fishing capacity and to ensure that levels of fishing effort do not exceed those commensurate with the sustainable use of fishery resources;

(i) take into account the interests of artisanal and subsistence fishers;

(j) collect and share, in a timely manner, complete and accurate data concerning fishing activities on, inter alia, vessel position, catch of target and non-target species and fishing effort, as set out in Annex I, as well as information from national and international research programmes;

(k) promote and conduct scientific research and develop appropriate technologies in support of fishery conservation and management; and

(1) implement and enforce conservation and management measures through effective monitoring, control and surveillance.

Article 6	Application of the precautionary approach

1. States shall apply the precautionary approach widely to conservation, management and exploitation of straddling fish stocks and highly migratory fish stocks in order to protect the living marine resources and preserve the marine environment.

2. States shall be more cautious when information is uncertain, unreliable or inadequate. The absence of adequate scientific information shall not be used as a reason for postponing or failing to take conservation and management measures.

3. In implementing the precautionary approach, States shall:

(a) improve decision-making for fishery resource conservation and management by obtaining and sharing the best scientific information available and implementing improved techniques for dealing with risk and uncertainty;

(b) apply the guidelines set out in Annex II and determine, on the basis of the best scientific information available, stock-specific reference points and the action to be taken if they are exceeded;

(c) take into account, inter alia, uncertainties relating to the size and productivity of the stocks, reference points, stock condition in relation to such reference points, levels and distribution of fishing mortality and the impact of fishing activities on non-target and associated or dependent species, as well as existing and predicted oceanic, environmental and socio-economic conditions; and

(d) develop data collection and research programmes to assess the impact of fishing on non-target and associated or dependent species and their environment, and adopt plans which are necessary to ensure the conservation of such species and to protect habitats of special concern.

4. States shall take measures to ensure that, when reference points are approached, they will not be exceeded. In the event that they are exceeded, States shall, without delay, take the action determined under paragraph 3 (b) to restore the stocks.

5. Where the status of target stocks or non-target or associated or dependent species is of concern, States shall subject such stocks and species to enhanced monitoring in order to review their status and the efficacy of conservation and management measures. They shall revise those measures regularly in the light of new information.

6. For new or exploratory fisheries, States shall adopt as soon as possible cautious conservation and management measures, including, inter alia, catch limits and effort limits. Such measures shall remain in force until there are sufficient data to allow assessment of the impact of the fisheries on the long-term sustainability of the stocks, whereupon conservation and management measures based on that assessment shall be implemented. The latter measures shall, if appropriate, allow for the gradual development of the fisheries.

7. If a natural phenomenon has a significant adverse impact on the status of straddling fish stocks or highly migratory fish stocks, States shall adopt conservation and management measures on an emergency basis to ensure that fishing activity does not exacerbate such adverse impact. States shall also adopt such measures on an emergency basis where fishing activity presents a serious threat to the sustainability of such stocks. Measures taken on an emergency basis shall be temporary and shall be based on the best scientific evidence available.

Article 7   **Compatibility of conservation and management measures**

1. Without prejudice to the sovereign rights of coastal States for the purpose of exploring and exploiting, conserving and managing the living marine resources within areas under national jurisdiction as provided for in the Convention, and the right of all States for their nationals to engage in fishing on the high seas in accordance with the Convention:

(a) with respect to straddling fish stocks, the relevant coastal States and the States whose nationals fish for such stocks in the adjacent high seas area shall seek, either directly or through the appropriate mechanisms for cooperation provided for in Part III, to agree upon the measures necessary for the conservation of these stocks in the adjacent high seas area;

(b) with respect to highly migratory fish stocks, the relevant coastal States and other States whose nationals fish for such stocks in the region shall cooperate, either directly or through the appropriate mechanisms for cooperation provided for in Part III, with a view to ensuring conservation and promoting the objective of optimum utilization of such stocks throughout the region, both within and beyond the areas under national jurisdiction.

2. Conservation and management measures established for the high seas and those adopted for areas under national jurisdiction shall be compatible in order to ensure conservation and management of the straddling fish stocks and highly migratory fish stocks in their entirety. To this end, coastal States and States fishing on the high seas have a duty to cooperate for the purpose of achieving compatible measures in respect of such stocks. In determining compatible conservation and management measures, States shall:

(a) take into account the conservation and management measures adopted and applied in accordance with article 61 of the Convention in respect of the same stocks by coastal States within areas under national jurisdiction and ensure that measures established in respect of such stocks for the high seas do not undermine the effectiveness of such measures;

(b) take into account previously agreed measures established and applied for the high seas in accordance with the Convention in respect of the same stocks by relevant coastal States and States fishing on the high seas;

(c) take into account previously agreed measures established and applied in accordance with the Convention in respect of the same stocks by a subregional or regional fisheries management organization or arrangement;

(d) take into account the biological unity and other biological characteristics of the stocks and the relationships between the distribution of the stocks, the fisheries and the geographical particularities of the region concerned, including the extent to which the stocks occur and are fished in areas under national jurisdiction;

(e) take into account the respective dependence of the coastal States and the States fishing on the high seas on the stocks concerned; and

(f) ensure that such measures do not result in harmful impact on the living marine resources as a whole.

3. In giving effect to their duty to cooperate, States shall make every effort to agree on compatible conservation and management measures within a reasonable period of time.

4. If no agreement can be reached within a reasonable period of time, any of the States concerned may invoke the procedures for the settlement of disputes provided for in Part VIII.

5. Pending agreement on compatible conservation and management measures, the States concerned, in a spirit of understanding and cooperation, shall make every effort to enter into provisional arrangements of a practical nature. In the event that they are unable to agree on such arrangements, any of the States concerned may, for the purpose of obtaining provisional measures, submit the dispute to a court or tribunal in accordance with the procedures for the settlement of disputes provided for in Part VIII.

6. Provisional arrangements or measures entered into or prescribed pursuant to paragraph 5 shall take into account the provisions of this Part, shall have due regard to the rights and obligations of all States concerned, shall not

jeopardize or hamper the reaching of final agreement on compatible conservation and management measures and shall be without prejudice to the final outcome of any dispute settlement procedure.

7. Coastal States shall regularly inform States fishing on the high seas in the subregion or region, either directly or through appropriate subregional or regional fisheries management organizations or arrangements, or through other appropriate means, of the measures they have adopted for straddling fish stocks and highly migratory fish stocks within areas under their national jurisdiction.

8. States fishing on the high seas shall regularly inform other interested States, either directly or through appropriate subregional or regional fisheries management organizations or arrangements, or through other appropriate means, of the measures they have adopted for regulating the activities of vessels flying their flag which fish for such stocks on the high seas.

PART III: MECHANISMS FOR INTERNATIONAL COOPERATION CONCERNING STRADDLING FISH STOCKS AND HIGHLY MIGRATORY FISH STOCKS

Article 8   **Cooperation for conservation and management**

1. Coastal States and States fishing on the high seas shall, in accordance with the Convention, pursue cooperation in relation to straddling fish stocks and highly migratory-fish stocks either directly or through appropriate subregional or regional fisheries management organizations or arrangements, taking into account the specific characteristics of the subregion or region, to ensure effective conservation and management of such stocks.

2. States shall enter into consultations in good faith and without delay, particularly where there is evidence that the straddling fish stocks and highly migratory fish stocks concerned may be under threat of over-exploitation or where a new fishery is being developed for such stocks. To this end, consultations may be initiated at the request of any interested State with a view to establishing appropriate arrangements to ensure conservation and management of the stocks. Pending agreement on such arrangements, States shall observe the provisions of this Agreement and shall act in good faith and with due regard to the rights, interests and duties of other States.

3. Where a subregional or regional fisheries management organization or arrangement has the competence to establish conservation and management measures for particular straddling fish stocks or highly migratory fish stocks, States fishing for the stocks on the high seas and relevant coastal States shall give effect to their duty to cooperate by becoming members of such organization or participants in such arrangement, or by agreeing to apply the conservation and management measures established by such organization or arrangement. States having a real interest in the fisheries concerned may become members of such organizations or participants in such arrangement. The terms of participation in such organizations or arrangements shall not preclude such States from membership or participation; nor shall they be applied in a manner which discriminates against any State or group of States having a real interest in the fisheries concerned.

4. Only those States which are members of such an organization or participants in such an arrangement, or which agree to apply the conservation and management measures established by such organization or arrangement, shall have access to the fishery resources to which those measures apply.

5. Where there is no subregional or regional fisheries management organization or arrangement to establish conservation and management measures for a particular straddling fish stock or highly migratory fish stock, relevant coastal States and States fishing on the high seas for such stocks in the subregion or region shall cooperate to establish such an organization or enter into other appropriate arrangements to ensure conservation and management of such stock and shall participate in the work of the organization or arrangement.

6. Any State intending to propose that action be taken by an intergovernmental organization having competence with respect to living resources should, where such action would have a significant effect on conservation and management measures already established by a competent subregional or regional fisheries management organization or arrangement, consult through that organization or arrangement with its member States or participants. To the extent practicable, such consultation should take place prior to the submission of the proposal to the intergovernmental organization.

	Article 9	**Subregional and regional fisheries management organizations and arrangements**

1. In establishing subregional or regional fisheries management organizations or in entering into subregional or regional fisheries management arrangements for straddling fish stocks and highly migratory fish stocks, States shall agree, inter alia, on:

(a) the stocks to which conservation and management measures apply, taking into account the biological characteristics of the stocks concerned and the nature of the fisheries involved;

(b) the area of application, taking into account article 7, paragraph 1, and the characteristics of the subregion or region, including socio-economic, geographical and environmental factors;

(c) the relationship between the work of the new organization or arrangement and the role, objectives and operations of any relevant existing fisheries management organizations or arrangements; and

(d) the mechanisms by which the organization or arrangement will obtain scientific advice and review the status of the stocks, including, where appropriate, the establishment of a scientific advisory body.

2. States cooperating in the formation of a subregional or regional fisheries management organization or arrangement shall inform other States which they are aware have a real interest in the work of the proposed organization or arrangement of such cooperation.

	Article 10	**Functions of subregional and regional fisheries management organizations and arrangements**

In fulfilling their obligation to cooperate through subregional or regional fisheries management organizations or arrangements, States shall:

(a) agree on and comply with conservation and management measures to ensure the long-term sustainability of straddling fish stocks and highly migratory fish stocks;

(b) agree, as appropriate, on participatory rights such as allocations of allowable catch or levels of fishing effort;

(c) adopt and apply any generally recommended international minimum standards for the responsible conduct of fishing operations;

(d) obtain and evaluate scientific advice, review the status of the stocks and assess the impact of fishing on non-target and associated or dependent species;

(e) agree on standards for collection, reporting, verification and exchange of data on fisheries for the stocks;

(f) compile and disseminate accurate and complete statistical data, as described in Annex I, to ensure that the best scientific evidence is available, while maintaining confidentiality where appropriate;

(g) promote and conduct scientific assessments of the stocks and relevant research and disseminate the results thereof;

(h) establish appropriate cooperative mechanisms for effective monitoring, control, surveillance and enforcement;

(i) agree on means by which the fishing interests of new members of new participants in the organization or arrangement will be accommodated;

(j) agree on decision-making procedures which facilitate the adoption of conservation and management measures in a timely and effective manner;

(k) promote the peaceful settlement of disputes in accordance with Part VIII;

(l) ensure the full cooperation of their relevant national agencies and industries in implementing the recommendations and decisions of the subregional or regional fisheries management organization or arrangement; and

(m) give due publicity to the conservation and management measures established by the organization or arrangement.

Article 11   New members or Participants

In determining the nature and extent of participatory rights for new members of a subregional or regional fisheries management organization, or for new participants in a subregional or regional fisheries management arrangement, States shall take into account, inter alia:

(a) the state of the straddling fish stocks and highly migratory fish stocks and the existing level of fishing effort in the fishery;

(b) the respective interests, fishing patterns and fishing practices of new and existing members or participants;

(c) the respective contributions of new and existing members or participants to conservation and management of the stocks, to the collection and provision of accurate data and to the conduct of scientific research on the stocks;

(d) the needs of coastal fishing communities which are dependent mainly on fishing for the stocks;

(e) the needs of coastal States whose economies are overwhelmingly dependent on the exploitation of living marine resources; and

(f) the interests of developing States from the subregion or region in whose areas of national jurisdiction the stocks also occur.

Article 12   Transparency in activities of subregional and regional fisheries management organizations and arrangements

1. States shall provide for transparency in the decision-making process and other activities of subregional and regional fisheries management organizations and arrangements.

2. Representatives from other intergovernmental organizations and representatives from non-governmental organizations concerned with straddling fish stocks and highly migratory fish stocks shall be afforded the opportunity to take part in meetings of subregional and regional fisheries management organizations and arrangements as observers or otherwise, as appropriate, in accordance with the procedures of the organization or arrangement concerned. Such procedures shall not be unduly restrictive in this respect. Such intergovernmental organizations and non-governmental organizations shall have timely access to the records and reports of such organizations and arrangements, subject to the procedural rules on access to them.

Article 13   Strengthening of existing organizations and arrangements

States shall cooperate to strengthen existing subregional and regional fisheries management organizations and arrangements in order to improve their effectiveness in establishing and implementing conservation and management measures for straddling fish stocks and highly migratory fish stocks.

Article 14   Collection and provision of information and cooperation in scientific research

1. States shall ensure that fishing vessels flying their flag provide such information as may be necessary in order to fulfil their obligations under this Agreement. To this end, States shall in accordance with Annex I:

(a) collect and exchange scientific, technical and statistical data with respect to fisheries for straddling fish stocks and highly migratory fish stocks;

(b) ensure that data are collected in sufficient detail to facilitate effective stock assessment and are provided in a timely manner to fulfil the requirements of subregional or regional fisheries management organizations or arrangements; and

(c) take appropriate measures to verify the accuracy of such data.

2. States shall cooperate, either directly or through subregional or regional fisheries management organizations or arrangements, to:

(a) agree on the specification of data and the format in which they are to be provided to such organizations or arrangements, taking into account the nature of the stocks and the fisheries for those stocks; and

(b) develop and share analytical techniques and stock assessment methodologies to improve measures for the conservation and management of straddling fish stocks and highly migratory fish stocks.

3. Consistent with Part XIII of the Convention, States shall cooperate, either directly or through competent international organizations, to strengthen scientific research capacity in the field of fisheries and promote scientific research related to the conservation and management of straddling fish stocks and highly migratory fish stocks for the benefit of all. To this end, a State or the competent international organization conducting such research beyond areas under national jurisdiction shall actively promote the publication and dissemination to any interested States of the results of that research and information relating to its objectives and methods and, to the extent practicable, shall facilitate the participation of scientists from those States in such research.

Article 15	Enclosed and semi-enclosed seas

In implementing this Agreement in an enclosed or semi-enclosed sea, States shall take into account the natural characteristics of that sea and shall also act in a manner consistent with Part IX of the Convention and other relevant provisions thereof.

Article 16	Areas of high seas surrounded entirely by an area under the national jurisdiction of a single State

1. States fishing for straddling fish stocks and highly migratory fish stocks in an area of the high seas surrounded entirely by an area under the national jurisdiction of a single State and the latter State shall cooperate to establish conservation and management measures in respect of those stocks in the high seas area. Having regard to the natural characteristics of the area, States shall pay special attention to the establishment of compatible conservation and management measures for such stocks pursuant to article 7. Measures taken in respect of the high seas shall take into account the rights, duties and interests of the coastal State under the Convention, shall be based on the best scientific evidence available and shall also take into account any conservation and management measures adopted and applied in respect of the same stocks in accordance with article 61 of the Convention by the coastal State in the area under national jurisdiction. States shall also agree on measures for monitoring, control, surveillance and enforcement to ensure compliance with the conservation and management measures in respect of the high seas.

2. Pursuant to article 8, States shall act in good faith and make every effort to agree without delay on conservation and management measures to be applied in the carrying out of fishing operations in the area referred to in paragraph 1. If, within a reasonable period of time, the fishing States concerned and the coastal State are unable to agree on such measures, they shall, having regard to paragraph 1 of this article, apply article 7, paragraphs 4, 5 and 6, relating to provisional arrangements or measures. Pending the establishment of such provisional arrangements or measures, the States concerned shall take measures in respect of vessels flying their flag in order that they do not engage in fisheries which could undermine the stocks concerned.

PART IV: NON-MEMBERS AND NON-PARTICIPANTS

Article 17	Non-members of organizations and non-participants in arrangements

1. A State which is not a member of a subregional or regional fisheries management organization or is not a participant in a subregional or regional fisheries management arrangement, and which does not otherwise agree to apply the conservation and management measures established by such organization or arrangement, is not discharged from the obligation to cooperate, in accordance with the Convention and this Agreement, in the conservation and management of the relevant straddling fish stocks and highly migratory fish stocks.

2. Such State shall not authorize vessels flying its flag to engage in fishing operations for the straddling fish stocks or highly migratory fish stocks which are subject to the conservation and management measures established by such organization or arrangement.

3. States which are members of a subregional or regional fisheries management organization or participants in a subregional or regional fisheries management arrangement shall, individually or jointly, request the fishing entities referred to in article 1, paragraph 3, which have fishing vessels in the relevant area to cooperate fully with such organization or arrangement in implementing the conservation and management measures it has established, with a view to having such measures applied de facto as extensively as possible to fishing activities in the relevant area. Such fishing entities shall enjoy benefits from participation in the fishery commensurate with their commitment to comply with conservation and management measures in respect of the stocks.

4. States which are members of such organizations or participants in such arrangements shall exchange information with respect to the activities of fishing vessels flying the flags of States which are neither members of the organization nor participants in the arrangement and which are engaged in fishing operations for the relevant stocks. They shall take measures consistent with this Agreement and international law to deter activities of such vessels which undermine the effectiveness of subregional or regional conservation and management measures.

PART V   DUTIES OF THE FLAG STATE

Article 18   Duties of the flag State

1. A State whose vessels fish on the high seas shall take such measures as may be necessary to ensure that vessels flying its flag comply with subregional and regional conservation and management measures and that such vessels do not engage in any activity which undermines the effectiveness of such measures.

2. A State shall authorize the use of vessels flying its flag for fishing on the high seas only where it is able to exercise effectively its responsibilities in respect of such vessels under the Convention and this Agreement.

3. Measures to be taken by a State in respect of vessels flying its flag shall include:

(a) control of such vessels on the high seas by means of fishing licences, authorizations or permits, in accordance with any applicable procedures agreed at the subregional, regional or global level;

(b) establishment of regulations to:

(i) apply terms and conditions to the licence, authorization or permit sufficient to fulfil any subregional, regional or global obligations of the flag State;

(ii) prohibit fishing on the high seas by vessels which are not duly licensed or authorized to fish, or fishing on the high seas by vessels otherwise than in accordance with the terms and conditions of a licence, authorization or permit;

(iii) require vessels fishing on the high seas to carry the licence, authorization or permit on board at all times and to produce it on demand for inspection by a duly authorized person; and

(iv) ensure that vessels flying its flag do not conduct unauthorized fishing within areas under the national jurisdiction of other States;

(c) establishment of a national record of fishing vessels authorized to fish on the high seas and provision of access to the information contained in that record on request by directly interested States, taking into account any national laws of the flag State regarding the release of such information;

(d) requirements for marking of fishing vessels and fishing gear for identification in accordance with uniform and internationally recognizable vessel and gear marking systems, such as the Food and Agriculture Organization of the United Nations Standard Specifications for the Marking and Identification of Fishing Vessels;

(e) requirements for recording and timely reporting of vessel position, catch of target and non-target species, fishing effort and other relevant fisheries data in accordance with subregional, regional and global standards for collection of such data;

(f) requirements for verifying the catch of target and non-target species through such means as observer programmes, inspection schemes, unloading reports, supervision of transshipment and monitoring of landed catches and market statistics;

(g) monitoring, control and surveillance of such vessels, their fishing operations and related activities by, *inter alia*:

(i) the implementation of national inspection schemes and subregional and regional schemes for cooperation in enforcement pursuant to articles 21 and 22, including requirements for such vessels to permit access by duly authorized inspectors from other States;

(ii) the implementation of national observer programmes and subregional and regional observer programmes in which the flag State is a participant, including requirements for such vessels to permit access by observers from other States to carry out the functions agreed under the programmes; and

(iii) the development and implementation of vessel monitoring systems, including, as appropriate, satellite transmitter systems, in accordance with any national programmes and those which have been subregionally, regionally or globally agreed among the States concerned;

(h) regulation of transshipment on the high seas to ensure that the effectiveness of conservation and management measures is not undermined; and

(i) regulation of fishing activities to ensure compliance with subregional, regional or global measures, including those aimed at minimizing catches of non-target species.

4. Where there is a subregionally, regionally or globally agreed system of monitoring, control and surveillance in effect, States shall ensure that the measures they impose on vessels flying their flag are compatible with that system.

PART VI: COMPLIANCE AND ENFORCEMENT

Article 19   Compliance and enforcement by the flag State

1. A State shall ensure compliance by vessels flying its flag with subregional and regional conservation and management measures for straddling fish stocks and highly migratory fish stocks. To this end, that State shall:

(a) enforce such measures irrespective of where violations occur;

(b) investigate immediately and fully any alleged violation of subregional or regional conservation and management measures, which may include the physical inspection of the vessels concerned, and report promptly to the State alleging the violation and the relevant subregional or regional organization or arrangement on the progress and outcome of the investigation;

(c) require any vessel flying its flag to give information to the investigating authority regarding vessel position, catches, fishing gear, fishing operations and related activities in the area of an alleged violation;

(d) if satisfied that sufficient evidence is available in respect of an alleged violation, refer the case to its authorities with a view to instituting proceedings, without delay, in accordance with its laws and, where appropriate, detain the vessel concerned; and

(e) ensure that, where it has been established, in accordance with its laws, that a vessel has been involved in the commission of a serious violation of such measures, the vessel does not engage in fishing operations on the high seas until such time as all outstanding sanctions imposed by the flag State in respect of the violation have been complied with.

2. All investigations and judicial proceedings shall be carried out expeditiously. Sanctions applicable in respect of violations shall be adequate in severity to be effective in securing compliance and to discourage violations wherever they occur and shall deprive offenders of the benefits accruing from their illegal activities. Measures applicable in respect of masters and other officers of fishing vessels shall include provisions which may permit, inter alia, refusal, withdrawal or suspension of authorizations to serve as masters or officers on such vessels.

Article 20   International cooperation in enforcement

1. States shall cooperate, either directly or through subregional or regional fisheries management organizations or arrangements, to ensure compliance with and enforcement of subregional and regional conservation and management measures for straddling fish stocks and highly migratory fish stocks.

2. A flag State conducting an investigation of an alleged violation of conservation and management measures for straddling fish stocks or highly migratory fish stocks may request the assistance of any other State whose cooperation may be useful in the conduct of that investigation. All States shall endeavor to meet reasonable requests made by a flag State in connection with such investigations.

3. A flag State may undertake such investigations directly, in cooperation with other interested States or through the relevant subregional or regional fisheries management organization or arrangement. Information on the progress and

outcome of the investigations shall be provided to all States having an interest in, or affected by, the alleged violation.

4. States shall assist each other in identifying vessels reported to have engaged in activities undermining the effectiveness of subregional, regional or global conservation and management measures.

5. States shall, to the extent permitted by national laws and regulations, establish arrangements for making available to prosecuting authorities in other States evidence relating to alleged violations of such measures.

6. Where there are reasonable grounds for believing that a vessel on the high seas has been engaged in unauthorized fishing within an area under the jurisdiction of a coastal State, the flag State of that vessel, at the request of the coastal State concerned, shall immediately and fully investigate the matter. The flag State shall cooperate with the coastal State in taking appropriate enforcement action in such cases and may authorize the relevant authorities of the coastal State to board and inspect the vessel on the high seas. This paragraph is without prejudice to article III of the Convention.

7. States Parties which are members of a subregional or regional fisheries management organization or participants in a subregional or regional fisheries management arrangement may take action in accordance with international law, including through recourse to subregional or regional procedures established for this purpose, to deter vessels which have engaged in activities that undermine the effectiveness of or otherwise violate the conservation and management measures established by that organization or arrangement from fishing on the high seas in the subregion or region until such time as appropriate action is taken by the flag State.

Article 21   **Subregional and regional cooperation in enforcement**

1. In any high seas area covered by a subregional or regional fisheries management organization or arrangement, a State Party which is a member of, or a participant in, such organization or arrangement may, through its duly authorized inspectors, board and inspect, in accordance with paragraph 2, fishing vessels flying the flag of another State Party to this Agreement, whether or not such State Party is also a member of, or a participant in, the organization or arrangement, for the purpose of ensuring compliance with conservation and management measures for straddling fish stocks and highly migratory fish stocks established by that organization or arrangement.

2. States shall establish, through subregional or regional fisheries management organizations or arrangements, procedures for boarding and inspection pursuant to paragraph 1, as well as procedures to implement other provisions of this article. Such procedures shall be consistent with this article and the basic procedures set out in article 22 and shall not discriminate against non-members of the organization or non-participants in the arrangement. Boarding and inspection as well as any subsequent enforcement action shall be conducted in accordance with such procedures. States shall give due publicity to procedures established pursuant to this paragraph.

3. If, within two years of the adoption of this Agreement, any organization or arrangement has not established such procedures, boarding and inspection pursuant to paragraph 1, as well as any subsequent enforcement action, shall, pending the establishment of such procedures, be conducted in accordance with this article and the basic procedures set out in article 22.

4. Prior to taking action under this article, inspecting States shall, either directly or through the relevant subregional or regional fisheries management organization or arrangement, inform all States whose vessels fish on the high seas in the subregion or region of the form of identification issued to their duly authorized inspectors. The vessels used for boarding and inspection shall be clearly marked and identifiable as being on government service. At the time of becoming a Party to this Agreement, States shall designate an appropriate authority to receive notifications pursuant to this article and shall give due publicity of such designation through the relevant subregional or regional fisheries management organization or arrangement.

5. Where, following boarding and inspection, there are clear grounds for believing that a vessel has engaged in any activity contrary to the conservation and management measures referred to in paragraph 1, the inspecting State shall, where appropriate, secure evidence and shall promptly notify the flag State of the alleged violation.

6. The flag State shall respond to the notification referred to in paragraph 5 within three working days of its receipt, or such other period as may be prescribed in procedures established in accordance with paragraph 2, and shall either:

(a) fulfil, without delay, its obligations under article 19 to investigate and, if evidence so warrants, take enforcement action with respect to the vessel, in which case it shall promptly inform the inspecting State of the results of the investigation and of any enforcement action taken; or

(b) authorize the inspecting State to investigate.

7. Where the flag State authorizes the inspecting State to investigate an alleged violation, the inspecting State shall, without delay, communicate the results of that investigation to the flag State. The flag State shall, if evidence so warrants, fulfil its obligations to take enforcement action with respect to the vessel. Alternatively, the flag State may authorize the inspecting State to take such enforcement action as the flag State may specify with respect to the vessel, consistent with the rights and obligations of the flag State under this Agreement.

8. Where, following boarding and inspection, there are clear grounds for believing that a vessel has committed a serious violation, and the flag State has either failed to respond or failed to take action as required under paragraphs 6 or 7, the inspectors may remain on board and secure evidence and may require the master to assist in further investigation including, where appropriate, by bringing the vessel without delay to the nearest appropriate port, or to such other port as may be specified in procedures established in accordance with paragraph 2. The inspecting State shall immediately inform the flag State of the name of the port to which the vessel is to proceed. The inspecting State and the flag State and, as appropriate, the port State shall take all necessary steps to ensure the well-being of the crew regardless of their nationality.

9. The inspecting State shall inform the flag State and the relevant organization or the participants in the relevant arrangement of the results of any further investigation.

10. The inspecting State shall require its inspectors to observe International rules and generally accepted practices and procedures relating to the safety of the vessel and the crew, minimize interference with fishing operations and, to the extent practicable, avoid action which would adversely affect the quality of the catch on board. The inspecting State shall ensure that boarding and inspection is not conducted in a manner that would constitute harassment of any fishing vessel.

11. For the purposes of this article, a serious violation means:

(a) fishing without a valid licence, authorization or permit issued by the flag State in accordance with article 18, paragraph 3 (a);

(b) failing to maintain accurate records of catch and catch-related data, as required by the relevant subregional or regional fisheries management organization or arrangement, or serious misreporting of catch, contrary to the catch reporting requirements of such organization or arrangement;

(c) fishing in a closed area, fishing during a closed season or fishing without, or after attainment of, a quota established by the relevant subregional or regional fisheries management organization or arrangement;

(d) directed fishing for a stock which is subject to a moratorium or for which fishing is prohibited;

(e) using prohibited fishing gear;

(f) falsifying or concealing the markings, identity or registration of a fishing vessel;

(g) concealing, tampering with or disposing of evidence relating to an investigation;

(h) multiple violations which together constitute a serious disregard of conservation and management measures; or

(i) such other violations as may be specified in procedures established by the relevant subregional or regional fisheries management organization or arrangement.

12. Notwithstanding the other provisions of this article, the flag State may, at any time, take action to fulfil its obligations under article 19 with respect to an alleged violation. Where the vessel is under the direction of the inspecting State, the inspecting State shall, at the request of the flag State, release the vessel to the flag State along with full information on the progress and outcome of its investigation.

13. This article is without prejudice to the right of the flag State to take any measures, including proceedings to impose penalties, according to its laws.

14. This article applies mutatis mutandis to boarding and inspection by a State Party which is a member of a subregional or regional fisheries management organization or a participant in a subregional or regional fisheries management arrangement and which has clear grounds for believing that a fishing vessel flying the flag of another State Party has engaged in any activity contrary to relevant conservation and management measures referred to in paragraph 1 in the high seas area covered by such organization or arrangement, and such vessel has subsequently, during the same fishing trip, entered into an area under the national jurisdiction of the inspecting State.

15. Where a subregional or regional fisheries management organization or arrangement has established an alternative mechanism which effectively discharges the obligation under this Agreement of the members of such organizations or the participants in such arrangements to ensure compliance with the conservation and management measures established by the organization or arrangement, members of such organization or participants in such arrangement may agree to limit the application of paragraph 1 as between themselves in respect of the conservation and management measures which have been established in the relevant high seas area.

16. Action taken by States other than the flag State in respect of vessels having engaged in activities contrary to subregional or regional conservation and management measures shall be proportional to the seriousness of the violation.

17. Where there are reasonable grounds for suspecting that a fishing vessel on the high seas is without nationality, a State may board and inspect the vessel. Where evidence so warrants, the State may take such action as may be appropriate in accordance with international law.

18. States shall be liable for damage or loss attributable to them arising from action taken pursuant to this article when such action is unlawful or exceeds that reasonably required in the light of available information to implement the provisions of this article.

Article 22	Basic procedures for boarding and inspection pursuant to article 21

1. The inspecting State shall ensure that its duly authorized inspectors:

   (a) present credentials to the master of the vessel and produce a copy of the text of the relevant conservation and management measures or rules and regulations in force in the high seas area in question pursuant to those measures;
   (b) initiate notice to the flag State at the time of the boarding and inspection;
   (c) do not interfere with the master's ability to communicate with the authorities of the flag State during the boarding and inspection;
   (d) provide a copy of a report on the boarding and inspection to the master and to the authorities of the flag State, noting therein any objection or statement which the master wishes to have included in the report;
   (e) promptly leave the vessel following completion of the inspection if they find no evidence of a serious violation; and
   (f) avoid the use of force except when and to the degree necessary to ensure the safety of the inspectors and where the inspectors are obstructed in the execution of their duties. The degree of force used shall not exceed that reasonably required in the circumstances.

2. The duly authorized inspectors of an inspecting State shall have the authority to inspect the vessel, its licence, gear, equipment, records, facilities, fish and fish products and any relevant documents necessary to verify compliance with the relevant conservation and management measures.

3. The flag State shall ensure that vessel masters:

   (a) accept and facilitate prompt and safe boarding by the inspectors;
   (b) cooperate with and assist in the inspection of the vessel conducted pursuant to these procedures;
   (c) do not obstruct, intimidate or interfere with the inspectors in the performance of their duties;
   (d) allow the inspectors to communicate with the authorities of the flag State and the inspecting State during the boarding and inspection;
   (e) provide reasonable facilities, including, where appropriate, food and accommodation, to the inspectors; and

(f) facilitate safe disembarkation by the inspectors.

4. In the event that the master of a vessel refuses to accept boarding and inspection in accordance with this article and article 21, the flag State shall, except in circumstances where, in accordance with generally accepted international regulations, procedures and practices relating to safety at sea, it is necessary to delay the boarding and inspection, direct the master of the vessel to submit immediately to boarding and inspection and, if the master does not comply with such direction, shall suspend the vessel's authorization to fish and order the vessel to return immediately to port. The flag State shall advise the inspecting State of the action it has taken when the circumstances referred to in this paragraph arise.

Article 23   Measures taken by a port State

1. A port State has the right and the duty to take measures, in accordance with international law, to promote the effectiveness of subregional, regional and global conservation and management measures. When taking such measures a port State shall not discriminate in form or in fact against the vessels of any State.

2. A port State may, inter alia, inspect documents, fishing gear and catch on board fishing vessels, when such vessels are voluntarily in its ports or at its offshore terminals.

3. States may adopt regulations empowering the relevant national authorities to prohibit landings and transshipments where it has been established that the catch has been taken in a manner which undermines the effectiveness of the subregional, regional or global conservation and management measures on the high seas.

4. Nothing in this article affects the exercise by States of their sovereignty over ports in their territory in accordance with international law.

PART VII   REQUIREMENTS OF DEVELOPING STATES

Article 24   Recognition of the special requirements of developing States

1. States shall give full recognition to the special requirements of developing States in relation to conservation and management of straddling fish stocks and highly migratory fish stocks and development of fisheries for such stocks. To this end, States shall, either directly or through the United Nations Development Programme, the Food and Agriculture Organization of the United Nations and other specialized agencies, the Global Environment Facility, the Commission on Sustainable Development and other appropriate international and regional organizations and bodies, provide assistance to developing States.

2. In giving effect to the duty to cooperate in the establishment of conservation and management measures for straddling fish stocks and highly migratory fish stocks, States shall take into account the special requirements of developing States, in particular:

(a) the vulnerability of developing States which are dependent on the exploitation of living marine resources, including for meeting the nutritional requirements of their populations or parts thereof;

(b) the need to avoid adverse impacts on, and ensure access to fisheries by, subsistence, small-scale and artisanal fishers and women fishworkers, as well as indigenous people in developing States, particularly small island developing States; and

(c) the need to ensure that such measures do not result in transferring, directly or indirectly, a disproportionate burden of conservation action onto developing States.

Article 25   Forms of cooperation with developing States

1. States shall cooperate, either directly or through subregional, regional or global organizations to:

(a) enhance the ability of developing States, in particular the least developed among them and small island developing States, to conserve and manage straddling fish stocks and highly migratory fish stocks and to develop their own fisheries for such stocks;

(b) assist developing States, in particular the least developed among them and small island developing States, to enable them to participate in high seas fisheries for such stocks, including facilitating access to such fisheries subject to articles 5 and 11; and

(c) facilitate the participation of developing States in subregional and regional fisheries management organizations and arrangements.

2. Cooperation with developing States for the purposes set out in this article shall include the provision of financial assistance, assistance relating to human resources development, technical assistance, transfer of technology, including through joint venture arrangements, and advisory and consultative services.

3. Such assistance shall, inter alia, be directed specifically towards:

(a) improved conservation and management of straddling fish stocks and highly migratory fish stocks through collection, reporting, verification, exchange and analysis of fisheries data and related information;

(b) stock assessment and scientific research; and

(c) monitoring, control, surveillance, compliance and enforcement, including training and capacity-building at the local level, development and funding of national and regional observer programmes and access to technology and equipment.

Article 26	Special assistance in the implementation of this Agreement

1. States shall cooperate to establish special funds to assist developing States in the implementation of this Agreement, including assisting developing States to meet the costs involved in any proceedings for the settlement of disputes to which they may be parties.

2. States and international organizations should assist developing States in establishing new subregional or regional fisheries management organizations or arrangements, or in strengthening existing organizations or arrangements, for the conservation and management of straddling fish stocks and highly migratory fish stocks.

PART VIII   PEACEFUL SETTLEMENT OF DISPUTES

Article 27	Obligation to settle disputes by peaceful means

States have the obligation to settle their disputes by negotiation, inquiry, mediation, conciliation, arbitration, judicial settlement, resort to regional agencies or arrangements, or other peaceful means of their own choice.

Article 28	Prevention of disputes

States shall cooperate in order to prevent disputes. To this end, States shall agree on efficient and expeditious decision-making procedures within subregional and regional fisheries management organizations and arrangements and shall strengthen existing decision-making procedures as necessary.

Article 29	Disputes of a technical nature

Where a dispute concerns a matter of a technical nature, the States concerned may refer the dispute to an ad hoc expert panel established by them. The panel shall confer with the States concerned and shall endeavour to resolve the dispute expeditiously, without recourse to binding procedures for the settlement of disputes.

Article 30	Procedures for the settlement of disputes

1. The provisions relating to the settlement of disputes set out in Part XV of the Convention apply mutatis mutandis to any dispute between States Parties to this Agreement concerning the interpretation or application of this Agreement, whether or not they are also Parties to the Convention.

2. The provisions relating to the settlement of disputes set out in Part XV of the Convention apply mutatis mutandis to any dispute between States Parties to this Agreement concerning the interpretation or application of a subregional, regional or global fisheries agreement relating to straddling fish stocks or highly migratory fish stocks to which they are parties, including any dispute concerning the conservation and management of such stocks, whether or not they are also Parties to the Convention.

3. Any procedure accepted by a State Party to this Agreement and the Convention pursuant to article 287 of the Convention shall apply to the settlement of disputes under this Part, unless that State Party, when signing, ratifying or acceding to this Agreement, or at any time thereafter, has accepted another procedure pursuant to article 287 for the settlement of disputes under this Part.

4. A State Party to this Agreement which is not a Party to the Convention, when signing, ratifying or acceding to this Agreement, or at any time thereafter, shall be free to choose, by means of a written declaration, one or more of the means set out in article 287, paragraph 1, of the Convention for the settlement of disputes under this Part. Article 287 shall apply to such a declaration, as well as to any dispute to which such State is a party which is not covered by a declaration in force. For the purposes of conciliation and arbitration in accordance with Annexes V, VII and VIII to the Convention, such State shall be entitled to nominate conciliators, arbitrators and experts to be included in the lists referred to in Annex V, article 2, Annex VII, article 2, and Annex VIII, article 2, for the settlement of disputes under this Part.

5. Any court or tribunal to which a dispute has been submitted under this Part shall apply the relevant provisions of the Convention, of this Agreement and of any relevant subregional, regional or global fisheries agreement, as well as generally accepted standards for the conservation and management of living marine resources and other rules of international law not incompatible with the Convention, with a view to ensuring the conservation of the straddling fish stocks and highly migratory fish stocks concerned.

Article 31   Provisional measures

1. Pending the settlement of a dispute in accordance with this Part, the parties to the dispute shall make every effort to enter into provisional arrangements of a practical nature.

2. Without prejudice to article 290 of the Convention, the court or tribunal to which the dispute has been submitted under this Part may prescribe any provisional measures which it considers appropriate under the circumstances to preserve the respective rights of the parties to the dispute or to prevent damage to the stocks in question, as well as in the circumstances referred to in article 7, paragraph 5, and article 16, paragraph 2.

3. A State Party to this Agreement which is not a Party to the Convention may declare that, notwithstanding article 290, paragraph 5, of the Convention, the International Tribunal for the Law of the Sea shall not be entitled to prescribe, modify or revoke provisional measures without the agreement of such State.

Article 32   Limitations on applicability of procedures for the settlement of disputes

Article 297, paragraph 3, of the Convention applies also to this Agreement.

PART IX   NON-PARTIES TO THIS AGREEMENT

Article 33   Non-parties to this Agreement

1. States Parties shall encourage non-parties to this Agreement to become parties thereto and to adopt laws and regulations consistent with its provisions.

2. States Parties shall take measures consistent with this Agreement and international law to deter the activities of vessels flying the flag of non-parties which undermine the effective implementation of this Agreement.

PART X   GOOD FAITH AND ABUSE OF RIGHTS

Article 34   Good faith and abuse of rights

States Parties shall fulfill in good faith the obligations assumed under this Agreement and shall exercise the rights recognized in this Agreement in a manner which would not constitute an abuse of right.

PART XI   RESPONSIBILITY AND LIABILITY

Article 35   Responsibility and liability

States Parties are liable in accordance with international law for damage or loss attributable to them in regard to this Agreement.

PART XII   REVIEW CONFERENCE

Article 36   Review conference

1. Four years after the date of entry into force of this Agreement, the Secretary-General of the United Nations shall convene a conference with a view to assessing the effectiveness of this Agreement in securing the conservation and management of straddling fish stocks and highly migratory fish stocks. The Secretary-General shall invite to the conference all States Parties and those States and entities which are entitled to become parties to this Agreement as well as those intergovernmental and non-governmental organizations entitled to participate as observers.

2. The conference shall review and assess the adequacy of the provisions of this Agreement and, if necessary, propose means of strengthening the substance and methods of implementation of those provisions in order better to address any continuing problems in the conservation and management of straddling fish stocks and highly migratory fish stocks.

PART XIII   FINAL PROVISIONS

Article 37   Signature

This Agreement shall be open for signature by all States and the other entities referred to in article 1, paragraph 2(b), and shall remain open for signature at United Nations Headquarters for twelve months from the fourth of December 1995.

Article 38   Ratification

This Agreement is subject to ratification by States and the other entities referred to in article 1, paragraph 2(b). The instruments of ratification shall be deposited with the Secretary-General of the United Nations.

Article 39   Accession

This Agreement shall remain open for accession by States and the other entities referred to in article 1, paragraph 2(b). The instruments of accession shall be deposited with the Secretary-General of the United Nations.

Article 40   Entry into force

1. This Agreement shall enter into force 30 days after the date of deposit of the thirtieth instrument of ratification or accession.

2. For each State or entity which ratifies the Agreement or accedes thereto after the deposit of the thirtieth instrument of ratification or accession, this Agreement shall enter into force on the thirtieth day following the deposit of its instrument of ratification or accession.

Article 41   Provisional application

1. This Agreement shall be applied provisionally by a State or entity which consents to its provisional application by so notifying the depositary in writing. Such provisional application shall become effective from the date of receipt of the notification.

2. Provisional application by a State or entity shall terminate upon the entry into force of this Agreement for that State or entity or upon notification by that State or entity to the depositary in writing of its intention to terminate provisional application.

Article 42   Reservations and exceptions

No reservations or exceptions may be made to this Agreement.

Article 43   Declarations and statements

Article 42 does not preclude a State or entity, when signing, ratifying or acceding to this Agreement, from making declarations or statements, however phrased or named, with a view, inter alia, to the harmonization of its laws and regulations with the provisions of this Agreement, provided that such declarations or statements do not purport to exclude or to modify the legal effect of the provisions of this Agreement in their application to that State or entity.

Article 44   Relation to other agreements

1. This Agreement shall not alter the rights and obligations of States Parties which arise from other agreements compatible with this Agreement and which do not affect the enjoyment by other States Parties of their rights or the performance of their obligations under this Agreement.

2. Two or more States Parties may conclude agreements modifying or suspending the operation of provisions of this Agreement, applicable solely to the relations between them, provided that such agreements do not relate to a provision derogation from which is incompatible with the effective execution of the object and purpose of this Agreement, and provided further that such agreements shall not affect the application of the basic principles embodied herein, and that the provisions of such agreements do not affect the enjoyment by other States Parties of their rights or the performance of their obligations under this Agreement.

3. States Parties intending to conclude an agreement referred to in paragraph 2 shall notify the other States Parties through the depositary of this Agreement of their intention to conclude the agreement and of the modification or suspension for which it provides.

Article 45   Amendment

1. A State Party may, by written communication addressed to the Secretary-General of the United Nations, propose amendments to this Agreement and request the convening of a conference to consider such proposed amendments. The Secretary-General shall circulate such communication to all States Parties. If, within six months from the date of the circulation of the communication, not less than one half of the States Parties reply favorably to the request, the Secretary-General shall convene the conference.

2. The decision-making procedure applicable at the amendment conference convened pursuant to paragraph 1 shall be the same as that applicable at the United Nations Conference on Straddling Fish Stocks and Highly Migratory Fish Stocks, unless otherwise decided by the conference. The conference should make every effort to reach agreement on any amendments by way of consensus and there should be no voting on them until all efforts at consensus have been exhausted.

3. Once adopted, amendments to this Agreement shall be open for signature by States Parties for twelve months from the date of adoption at United Nations Headquarters, unless otherwise provided in the amendment itself.

4. Articles 38, 39, 47 and 50 apply to all amendments to this Agreement.

5. Amendments to this Agreement shall enter into force for the States Parties which establish their consent to be bound by it on the thirtieth day following the deposit of instruments of ratification or accession by two thirds of the

States Parties. Thereafter, for each State Party ratifying or acceding to an amendment after the deposit of the required number of such instruments, the amendment shall enter into force on the thirtieth day following the deposit of its instrument of ratification or accession.

6. An amendment may provide that a smaller or a larger number of ratifications or accessions shall be required for its entry into force than are required by this article.

7. A State which becomes a Party to this Agreement after the entry into force of amendments in accordance with paragraph 5 shall, failing an expression of a different intention by that State:

    (a) be considered as a Party to this Agreement as so amended; and
    (b) be considered as a Party to the unamended Agreement in relation to any State Party not bound by the amendment.

Article 46   Denunciation

1. A State Party may, by written notification addressed to the Secretary-General of the United Nations, denounce this Agreement and may indicate its reasons. Failure to indicate reasons shall not affect the validity of the denunciation. The denunciation shall take effect one year after the date of receipt of the notification, unless the notification specifies a later date.

2. The denunciation shall not in any way affect the duty of any State Party to fulfil any obligation embodied in this Agreement to which it would be subject under international law independently of this Agreement.

Article 47   Participation by international organizations

1. In cases where an international organization referred to in Annex IX, article 1, of the Convention does not have competence over all the matters governed by this Agreement, Annex IX to the Convention shall apply mutatis mutandis to participation by such international organization in this Agreement, except that the following provisions of that Annex shall not apply:

    (a) article 2, first sentence; and
    (b) article 3, paragraph 1.

2. In cases where an international organization referred to in Annex IX, article 1, of the Convention has competence over all the matters governed by this Agreement, the following provisions shall apply to participation by such international organization in this Agreement:

    (a) at the time of signature or accession, such international organization shall make a declaration stating: that it has competence over all the matters governed by this Agreement;
        (i) that, for this reason, its member States shall not become States Parties, except in respect of their territories for which the international organization has no responsibility; and
        (ii) that it accepts the rights and obligations of States under this Agreement;
    (b) participation of such an international organization shall in no case confer any rights under this Agreement on member states of the international organization;
    (c) in the event of a conflict between the obligations of an international organization under this Agreement and its obligations under the agreement establishing the international organization or any acts relating to it, the obligations under this Agreement shall prevail.

Article 48   Annexes

1. The Annexes form an integral part of this Agreement and, unless expressly provided otherwise, a reference to this Agreement or to one of its Parts includes a reference to the Annexes relating thereto.

2. The Annexes may be revised from time to time by States Parties. Such revisions shall be based on scientific and technical considerations. Notwithstanding the provisions of article 45, if a revision to an Annex is adopted by consensus at a meeting of States Parties, it shall be incorporated in this Agreement and shall take effect from the

date of its adoption or from such other date as may be specified in the revision. If a revision to an Annex is not adopted by consensus at such a meeting, the amendment procedures set out in article 45 shall apply.

Article 49   **Depositary**

The Secretary-General of the United Nations shall be the depositary of this Agreement and any amendments or revisions thereto.

Article 50   **Authentic texts**

The Arabic, Chinese, English, French, Russian and Spanish texts of this Agreement are equally authentic. IN WITNESS WHEREOF, the undersigned Plenipotentiaries, being duly authorized thereto, have signed this Agreement. OPENED FOR SIGNATURE at New York, this fourth day of December, one thousand nine hundred and ninety-five, in a single original, in the Arabic, Chinese, English, French, Russian and Spanish languages.

ANNEX I   **STANDARD REQUIREMENTS FOR THE COLLECTION AND SHARING OF DATA**

Article 1   **General principles**

1. The timely collection, compilation and analysis of data are fundamental to the effective conservation and management of straddling fish stocks and highly migratory fish stocks. To this end, data from fisheries for these stocks on the high seas and those in areas under national jurisdiction are required and should be collected and compiled in such a way as to enable statistically meaningful analysis for the purposes of fishery resource conservation and management. These data include catch and fishing effort statistics and other fishery-related information, such as vessel-related and other data for standardizing the fishing effort. Data collected should also include information on non-target and associated or dependent species. All data should be verified to ensure accuracy. Confidentiality of non-aggregated data shall be maintained. The dissemination of such data shall be subject to the terms on which they have been provided.

2. Assistance, including training as well as financial and technical assistance, shall be provided to developing States in order to build capacity in the field of conservation and management of living marine resources. Assistance should focus on enhancing capacity to implement data collection and verification, observer programmes, data analysis and research projects supporting stock assessments. The fullest possible involvement of developing State scientists and managers in conservation and management of straddling fish stocks and highly migratory fish stocks should be promoted.

Article 2   **Principles of data collection, compilation and exchange**

The following general principles should be considered in defining the parameters for collection, compilation and exchange of data from fishing operations for straddling fish stocks and highly migratory fish stocks:

    (a) States should ensure that data are collected from vessels flying their flag on fishing activities according to the operational characteristics of each fishing method (e.g., each individual tow for trawl, each set for long-line and purse-seine, each school fished for pole-and-line and each day fished for troll) and in sufficient detail to facilitate effective stock assessment;

    (b) States should ensure that fishery data are verified through an appropriate system;

    (c) States should compile fishery-related and other supporting scientific data and provide them in an agreed format and in a timely manner to the relevant subregional or regional fisheries management organization or arrangement where one exists. Otherwise, States should cooperate to exchange data directly or through such other cooperative mechanisms as may be agreed among them;

    (d) States should agree, within the framework of subregional or regional fisheries management organizations or arrangements, or otherwise, on the specification of data and the format in which they are to be provided, in accordance with this Annex and taking into account the nature of the stocks and the fisheries for those stocks in the region. Such organizations or arrangements should request non-members or non-participants to provide data concerning relevant fishing activities by vessels flying their flag;

(e) such organizations or arrangements shall compile data and make them available in a timely manner and in an agreed format to all interested States under the terms and conditions established by the organizations or arrangements; and

(f) scientists of the flag State and from the relevant subregional or regional fisheries management organization or arrangement should analyse the data separately or jointly, as appropriate.

Article 3   Basic Fishery Data

1. States shall collect and make available to the relevant subregional or regional fisheries management organization or arrangement the following types of data in sufficient detail to facilitate effective stock assessment in accordance with agreed procedures:

(a) time series of catch and effort statistics by fishery and fleet;

(b) total catch in number, nominal weight or both by species (both target and non-target) as is appropriate to each fishery. [Nominal weight is defined by the Food and Agriculture Organization of the United Nations as the live-weight equivalent of the landings];

(c) discard statistics, including estimates where necessary, reported as number or nominal weight by species, as is appropriate to each fishery;

(d) effort statistics appropriate to each fishing method; and

(e) fishing location, date and time fished and other statistics on fishing operations as appropriate.

2. States shall also collect where appropriate and provide to the relevant subregional or regional fisheries management organization or arrangement information to support stock assessment, including:

(a) composition of the catch according to length, weight and sex;

(b) other biological information supporting stock assessments, such as information on age, growth, recruitment, distribution and stock identity; and

(c) other relevant research, including surveys of abundance, biomass surveys, hydro-acoustic surveys, research on environmental factors affecting stock abundance, and oceanographic and ecological studies.

Article 4   Vessel data and information

1. States should collect the following types of vessel-related data for standardizing fleet composition and vessel fishing power and for converting between different measures of effort in the analysis of catch and effort data:

(a) vessel identification, flag and port of registry;

(b) vessel type;

(c) vessel specifications (e.g., material of construction, date built, registered length, gross registered tonnage, power of main engines, hold capacity and catch storage methods); and

(d) fishing gear description (e.g., types, gear specifications and quantity).

2. The flag State will collect the following information:

(a) navigation and position fixing aids;

(b) communication equipment and international radio call sign; and

(c) crew size.

Article 5   Reporting

A State shall ensure that vessels flying its flag send to its national fisheries administration and, where agreed, to the relevant subregional or regional fisheries management organization or arrangement, logbook data on catch and effort, including data on fishing operations on the high seas, at sufficiently frequent intervals to meet national requirements and regional and international obligations. Such data shall be transmitted, where necessary, by radio, telex, facsimile or satellite transmission or by other means.

Article 6   Data verification

States or, as appropriate, subregional or regional fisheries management organizations or arrangements should establish mechanisms for verifying fishery data, such as:

(a) position verification through vessel monitoring systems;

(b) scientific observer programmes to monitor catch, effort, catch composition (target and non-target) and other details of fishing operations;

(c) vessel trip, landing and transshipment reports; and

(d) port sampling.

Article 7   Data exchange

1. Data collected by flag States must be shared with other flag States and relevant coastal States through appropriate subregional or regional fisheries management organizations or arrangements. Such organizations or arrangements shall compile data and make them available in a timely manner and in an agreed format to all interested States under the terms and conditions established by the organizations or arrangements, while maintaining confidentiality of non-aggregated data, and should, to the extent feasible, develop database systems which provide efficient access to data.

2. At the global level, collection and dissemination of data should be effected through the Food and Agriculture Organization of the United Nations. Where a subregional or regional fisheries management organization or arrangement does not exist, that organization may also do the same at the subregional or regional level by arrangement with the States concerned.

ANNEX II   GUIDELINES FOR APPLICATION OF PRECAUTIONARY REFERENCE POINTS IN CONSERVATION AND MANAGEMENT OF STRADDLING FISH STOCKS AND HIGHLY MIGRATORY FISH STOCKS

1. A precautionary reference point is an estimated value derived through an agreed scientific procedure, which corresponds to the state of the resource and of the fishery, and which can be used as a guide for fisheries management.

2. Two types of precautionary reference points should be used: conservation, or limit, reference points and management, or target, reference points. Limit reference points set boundaries which are intended to constrain harvesting within safe biological limits within which the stocks can produce maximum sustainable yield. Target reference points are intended to meet management objectives.

3. Precautionary reference points should be stock-specific to account, inter alia, for the reproductive capacity, the resilience of each stock and the characteristics of fisheries exploiting the stock, as well as other sources of mortality and major sources of uncertainty.

4. Management strategies shall seek to maintain or restore populations of harvested stocks, and where necessary associated or dependent species, at levels consistent with previously agreed precautionary reference points. Such reference points shall be used to trigger pre-agreed conservation and management action. Management strategies shall include measures which can be implemented when precautionary reference points are approached.

5. Fishery management strategies shall ensure that the risk of exceeding limit reference points is very low. If a stock falls below a limit reference point or is at risk of falling below such a reference point, conservation and management action should be initiated to facilitate stock recovery. Fishery management strategies shall ensure that target reference points are not exceeded on average.

6. When information for determining reference points for a fishery is poor or absent, provisional reference points shall be set. Provisional reference points may be established by analogy to similar and better-known stocks. In such situations, the fishery shall be subject to enhanced monitoring so as to enable revision of provisional reference points as improved information becomes available.

7. The fishing mortality rate which generates maximum sustainable yield should be regarded as a minimum standard for limit reference points. For stocks which are not overfished, fishery management strategies shall ensure that fishing mortality does not exceed that which corresponds to maximum sustainable yield, and that the biomass does not fall below a predefined threshold. For overfished stocks, the biomass which would produce maximum sustainable yield can serve as a rebuilding target.

INTERNATIONAL CONVENTION FOR THE PREVENTION OF POLLUTION FROM SHIPS, 1973
(including excerpts of Annex I)

2 I.L.M. 1319 (1973)
Signed: November 2, 1973
Entered Into Force: *MARPOL 73/78, October 2, 1983*
                     Protocol I, October 2, 1983
                     Protocol II, October 2, 1983
                     Annex I, October 2, 1983
                     Annex II, April 6, 1987
                     Annex III, July 1, 1992
                     Annex IV, Not Yet in Force
                     Annex V, December 31, 1988
                     Annex VI, Not Yet in Force
Secretariat Homepage: http://www.imo.org/

The Parties to the Convention,

Being conscious of the need to preserve the human environment in general and the marine environment in particular,

Recognizing that deliberate, negligent or accidental release of oil and other harmful substances from ships constitutes a serious source of pollution,

Recognizing also the importance of the International Convention for the Prevention of Pollution of the Sea by Oil, 1954, as being the first multilateral instrument to be concluded with the prime objective of protecting the environment, and appreciating the significant contribution which that Convention has made in preserving the seas and coastal environment from pollution,

Desiring to achieve the complete elimination of intentional pollution of the marine environment by oil and other harmful substances and the minimization of accidental discharge of such substances,

Considering that this object may best be achieved by establishing rules not limited to oil pollution having a universal purport,

Have agreed as follows:

Article 1	General Obligations under the Convention

1 The Parties to the Convention undertake to give effect to the provisions of the present Convention and those Annexes thereto by which they are bound, in order to prevent the pollution of the marine environment by the discharge of harmful substances or effluents containing such substances in contravention of the Convention.

2. Unless expressly provided otherwise, a reference to the present Convention constitutes at the same time a reference to its Protocol and to the Annexes.

Article 2	Definitions

For the purposes of the present Convention, unless expressly provided otherwise:

1. "Regulations" means the Regulations contained in the Annexes to the present Convention.

2. "Harmful substance" means any substance which, if introduced into the sea, is liable to create hazards to human health, to harm living resources and marine life, to damage amenities or to interfere with other legitimate uses of the sea, and includes any substance subject to control by the present Convention.

3.   a) "Discharge", in relation to harmful substances or effluents containing such substances, means any release howsoever caused from a ship and includes any escape, disposal, spilling, leaking, pumping, emitting or emptying;

    b) "Discharge" does not include:
>   (i) dumping within the meaning of the Convention on the Prevention of Marine Pollution by Dumping of Wastes and Other Matter, done at London on 13 November 1972; or
>   (ii) release of harmful substances directly arising from the exploration, exploitation and associated off-shore processing of sea-bed mineral resources; or
>   (iii) release of harmful substances for purpose of legitimate scientific research into pollution abatement or control.

4. "Ship" means a vessel of any type whatsoever operating in the marine environment and includes hydrofoil boats, air-cushion vehicles, submersibles, floating craft and fixed or floating platforms.

5. "Administration" means the Government of the State under whose authority the ship is operating. With respect to a ship entitled to fly a flag of any State, the Administration is the Government of that State. With respect to fixed or floating platforms engaged in exploration and exploitation of the sea-bed and subsoil thereof adjacent to the coast over which the coastal State exercises sovereign rights for the purposes of exploration and exploitation of their natural resources, the Administration is the Government of the coastal State concerned.

6. "Incident" means an event involving the actual or probable discharge into the sea of a harmful substance, or effluents containing such a substance.

7. "Organization" means the Inter-Governmental Maritime Consultative Organization.

Article 3   Application

1. The present Convention shall apply to:
    a) ships entitled to fly the flag of a Party to the Convention; and
    b) ships not entitled to fly the flag of a Party but which operate under the authority of a Party.

2. Nothing in the present Article shall be construed as derogating from or extending the sovereign rights of the Parties under international law over the sea-bed and subsoil thereof adjacent to their coasts for the purposes of exploration and exploitation of their natural resources.

3. The present Convention shall not apply to any warship, naval auxiliary or other ship owned or operated by a State and used, for the time being only on government non-commercial service. However, each Party shall ensure by the adoption of appropriate measures not impairing the operations or operational capabilities of such ships owned or operated by it, that such ships act in a manner consistent, so far as is reasonable and practiable, with the present Convention.

Article 4   Violation

1. Any violation of the requirements of the present Convention shall be prohibited and sanctions shall be established therefor under the law of the Administration of the ship concerned wherever the violation occurs. If the Administration is informed of such a violation and is satisfied that sufficient evidence is available to enable proceedings to be brought in respect of the alleged violation, it shall cause such proceedings to be taken as soon as possible, in accordance with its law.

2. Any violation of the requirements of the present Convention within the jurisdiction of any Party to the Convention shall be prohibited and sanctions shall be established therefore under the law of that Party. Whenever and violation occurs, the Party shall either:
    a) cause proceedings to be taken in accordance with its law; or
    b) furnish to the Administration of the ship such information and evidence as may be in its possession that a violation has occurred.

3. Where information or evidence with respect to any violation of the present Convention by a ship is furnished to the Administration of that ship, the Administration shall promptly inform the Party which has furnished the information or evidence and the Organization, of the action taken.

4. The penalties specified under the law of a Party pursuant to the present Article shall be adequate in severity to discharge violations of the present Convention and shall be equally severe irrespective of where the violations occur.

Article 5　　　**Certificates and Special Rules on Inspection of Ships**

1. Subject to the provisions of paragraph (2) of the present Article a certificate issued under the authority of a Party to the Convention in accordance with the provisions of the Regulations shall be accepted by the other Parties and regarded for all purposes covered by the present Convention as having the same validity as a certificate issued by them.

2. A ship required to hold a certificate in accordance with the provisions of the Regulations is subject, while in the ports or off-shore terminals under the jurisdiction of a Party, to inspection by officers duly authorized by that Party. Any such inspection shall be limited to verifying that there is on board a valid certificate, unless there are clear grounds for believing that the condition of the ship or its equipment does not correspond substantially with the particulars of that certificate. In that case, or if the ship does not carry a valid certificate the Party carrying out the inspection shall take such steps as will ensure that the ship shall not sail until it can proceed to sea without presenting an unreasonable threat of harm to the marine environment. That Party may, however, grant such a ship permission to leave the port or off-shore terminal for the purpose of proceedings to the nearest appropriate repair yard available.

3. If a Party denies a foreign ship entry to the ports or off-shore terminals under its jurisdiction or takes any action against such a ship for the reason that the ship does not comply with the provisions of the present Convention, the Party shall immediately inform the consul or diplomatic representative of the Party whose flag the ship is entitled to fly, or if this is not possible, the Administration of the ship concerned. Before denying entry or taking such action the Party may request consultation with the Administration of the ship concerned. Information shall also be given to the Administration when a ship does not carry a valid certificate in accordance with the provisions of the Regulations.

4. With respect to the ships of non-Parties to the Convention, Parties shall apply the requirements of the present Convention as may be necessary to ensure that no more favourable treatment is given to such ships.

Article 6　　　**Detection of Violations and Enforcement of the Convention**

1. Parties to the Convention shall co-operate in the detection of violations and the enforcement of the provisions of the present Convention, using all appropriate and practicable measures of detection and environmental monitoring, adequate procedures for reporting and accumulation of evidence.

2. A ship to which the present Convention applies may, in any port or off-shore terminal of a Party, be subject to inspection by officers appointed or authorized by that Party for the purpose of verifying whether the ship has discharged any harmful substances in violation of the provisions of the Regulations. If an inspection indicates a violation of the Convention, a report shall be forwarded to the Administration for any appropriate action.

3. Any Party shall furnish to the Administration evidence, if any, that the ship had discharged harmful substances in violation of the provisions of the Regulations. If it is practicable to do so, the competent authority of the former Party shall notify the Master of the ship of the alleged violation.

4. Upon receiving such evidence, the Administration so informed shall investigate the matter, and may request the other Party to furnish further or better evidence of the alleged contravention. If the Administration is satisfied that sufficient evidence is available to enable proceedings to be brought in respect of the alleged violation, it shall cause such proceedings to be taken in accordance with its law as soon as possible. The Administration shall promptly inform the Party which has reported the alleged violation, as well as the Organization, of the action taken.

5. A Party may also inspect a ship to which the present Convention applies when it enters the ports or off-shore terminals under its jurisdiction, if a request for an investigation is received from any Party together with sufficient evidence that the ship has discharged harmful substances or effluents containing such substances in any place. The report of such investigation shall be sent to the Party requesting it and to the Administration so that the appropriate action may be taken under the present Convention.

Article 7   **Undue Delay to Ships**

1. All possible efforts shall be made to avoid a ship being unduly detained or delayed under Article 4, 5, or 6 of the present Convention.

2. When a ship is unduly detained or delayed under Article 4, 5, 6 of the present Convention, it shall be entitled to compensation for any loss or damage suffered.

Article 8   **Reports on Incidents Involving Harmful Substances**

1. A report of an incident shall be made without delay to the fullest extent possible in accordance with the provisions of Protocol I to the present Convention.

2. Each Party to the Convention shall:
  a) make all arrangements necessary for an appropriate officer or agency to receive and process all reports on incidents; and
  b) notify the Organization with complete details of such arrangements for circulation to other Parties and Member States of the Organization.

3. Whenever a Party receives a report under the provisions of the present Article, the Party shall relay the report without delay to:
  a) the Administration of the ship involved; and
  b) any other State which may be affected.

4. Each Party to the Convention undertakes to issue instructions to its maritime inspection vessels and aircraft and to other appropriate services to report to its authorities any incident referred to in Protocol I to the present Convention. That Party shall, if it considers it appropriate, report accordingly to the Organization and to any other party concerned.

Article 9   **Other Treaties and Interpretation**

1. Upon its entry into force, the present Convention supersedes the International Convention for the Prevention of Pollution of the Sea by Oil, 1954, as amended, as between Parties to that Convention.

2. Nothing in the present Convention shall prejudice the codification and development of the law of the sea by the United Nations Conference on the Law of the Sea convened pursuant to Resolution 2750 C (XXV) of the General Assembly of the United Nations nor the present or future claims and legal views of any State concerning the law of the sea and the nature and extent of coastal and flag State jurisdiction.

3. The term "jurisdiction" in the present Convention shall be construed in the light of international law in force at the time of application or interpretation of the present Convention.

Article 10   **Settlement of Disputes**

Any dispute between two or more Parties to the Convention concerning the interpretation or application of the present Convention shall, if settlement by negotiation between the Parties involved has not been possible, and if these Parties do not otherwise agree, be submitted upon request of any of them to arbitration as set out in Protocol II to the present Convention.

Article 11   **Communication of Information**

1. The Parties to the Convention undertake to communicate to the Organization:

    a) the text of laws, orders, decrees and regulations and other instruments which have been promulgated on the various matters within the scope of the present Convention;

    b) a list of non-governmental agencies which are authorized to act on their behalf in matters relating to the design, construction and equipment of ships carrying harmful substances in accordance with the provisions of the Regulations;

    c) a sufficient number of specimens of their certificates issued under the provisions of the Regulations;

    d) a list of reception facilities including their location, capacity and available facilities and other characteristics;

    e) official reports or summaries of official reports in so far as they show the results of the application of the present Convention; and

    f) an annual statistical report, in a form standardized by the Organization, of penalties actually imposed for infringement of the present Convention.

2. The Organization shall notify Parties of the receipt of any communications under the present Article and circulate to all Parties any information communicated to it under sub-paragraphs (1) (b) to (f) of the present Article.

Article 12   Casualties to Ships

1. Each Administration undertakes to conduct an investigation of any casualty occurring to any of its ships subject to the provisions of the Regulations if such casualty has produced a major deleterious effect upon the marine environment.

2. Each Party to the Convention undertakes to supply the Organization with information concerning the findings of such investigation, when it judges that such information may assist in determining what changes in the present Convention might be desirable.

Article 13   Signatures, Ratification, Acceptance, Approval, and Accession

1. The present Convention shall remain open for signature at the Headquarters of the Organization from 15 January 1974 until 31 December 1974 and shall thereafter remain open for accession. States may become Parties to the present Convention by:

    a) signature without reservation as to ratification, acceptance or approval; or

    b) signature subject to ratification, acceptance or approval, followed by ratification, acceptance or approval; or

    c) accession.

2. Ratification, acceptance, approval or accession shall be effected by the deposit of an instrument to that effect with the Secretary-General of the Organization.

3. The Secretary-General of the Organization shall inform all States which have signed the present Convention or acceded to it of any signature or of the deposit of any new instrument of ratification, acceptance, approval or accession and the date of its deposit.

Article 14   Optional Annexes

1. A State may at the time of signing, ratifying, accepting, approving or acceding to the present Convention declare that it does not accept any one or all of Annexes III, IV, and V (hereinafter referred to as "Optional Annexes") of the present Convention. Subject to the above, Parties to the Convention shall be bound by any Annex in its entirety.

2. A State which has declared that it is not bound by an Optional Annex may at any time accept such Annex by depositing with the Organization an instrument of the kind referred to in Article 13 (2).

3. A State which makes a declaration under paragraph (1) of the present Article in respect of an Optional Annex and which has not subsequently accepted that Annex in accordance with paragraph (2) of the present Article shall not be

under any obligation nor entitled to claim any privileges under the present Convention in respect of matters related to such Annex and all reference to Parties in the present Convention shall include that State in so far as matters related to such Annex are concerned.

4. The Organization shall inform the States which have signed or acceded to the present Convention of any declaration under the present Article as well as the receipt of any instrument deposited in accordance with the provisions of paragraph (2) of the present Article.

Article 15   Entry into Force

1. The Convention shall enter into force twelve months after the date on which not less than 15 States, the combined merchant fleets of which constitute not less than fifty per cent of the gross tonnage of the world's merchant shipping, have become parties to it in accordance with Article 13.

2. An Optional Annex shall enter into force twelve months after the date on which the conditions stipulated in paragraph (1) of the present Article have been satisfied in relation to that Annex.

3. The Organization shall inform the States which have signed the present Convention or acceded to it of the date on which it enters into force and of the date on which the Optional Annex enters into force in accordance with paragraph (2) of the present Article.

4. For States which have deposited an instrument of ratification, acceptance, approval or accession in respect of the present Convention or any Optional Annex after the requirements for entry into force thereof have been met but prior to the date of entry into force, the ratification, acceptance, approval or accession shall take effect on the date of entry into force of the Convention or such Annex or three months after the date of deposit of the instrument whichever is the later date.

5. For States which have deposited an instrument of ratification, acceptance, approval or accession after the date on which the Convention or an Optional Annex entered into force, the Convention or the Optional Annex shall become effective three months after the date of deposit of the instrument.

6. After the date on which all the conditions required under Article 16 to bring an amendment to the present Convention or an Optional Annex into force have been fulfilled, any instrument of ratification, acceptance, approval or accession deposited shall apply to the Convention or Annex as amended.

Article 16   Amendments

1. The present Convention may be amended by any of the procedures specified in the following paragraphs.

2. Amendments after consideration by the Organization:
     a) any amendment proposed by a Party to the Convention shall be submitted to the Organization and circulated by its Secretary-General to all Members of the Organization and all Parties at least six months prior to its consideration;
     b) any amendment proposed and circulated as above shall be submitted to an appropriate body by the Organization for consideration;
     c) Parties to the Convention, whether or not Members of the Organization, shall be entitled to participate in the proceedings of the appropriate body;
     d) amendments shall be adopted by a two-thirds majority of only the Parties to the Convention present and voting;
     e) if adopted in accordance with sub-paragraph c) above, amendments shall be communicated by the Secretary-General of the Organization to all the Parties to the Convention for acceptance;
     f) an amendment shall be deemed to have been accepted in the following circumstances:
          (i) an amendment to an Article of the Convention shall be deemed to have been accepted on the date on which it is accepted by two-thirds of the Parties, the combined merchant fleets of which constitute not less than fifty per cent of the gross tonnage of the world's merchant fleet;
          (ii) an amendment to an Annex to the Convention shall be deemed to have been accepted in accordance with the procedure specified in subparagraph (f) (iii) unless the appropriate body, at the

time of its adoption, determines that the amendment shall be deemed to have been accepted on the date on which it is accepted by two-thirds of the Parties, the combined merchant fleets of which constitute not less than fifty per cent of the gross tonnage of the world's merchant fleet. Nevertheless, at any time before the entry into force of an amendment to an Annex to the Convention, a Party may notify the Secretary-General of the Organization that its express approval will be necessary before the amendment enters into force for it. The latter shall bring such notification and the date of its receipt to the notice of Parties.

(iii) an amendment to an Appendix to an Annex to the Convention shall be deemed to have been accepted at the end Article 16 of a period to be determined by the appropriate body at the time of its adoption, which period shall be not less than ten months, unless within that period an objection is communicated to the Organization by not less than one-third of the Parties or by the Parties the combined merchant fleets of which constitute not less than fifty per cent of the gross tonnage of the world's merchant fleet whichever condition is fulfilled;

(iv) an amendment to Protocol I to the Convention shall be subject to the same procedures as for the amendments to the Annexes to the Convention, as provided for in sub-paragraphs (f) (ii) or (f) (iii), above;

(v) an amendment to Protocol II to the Convention shall be subject to the same procedures as for the amendments to an Article of the Convention, as provided for in sub-paragraph (f) (i) above;

g) the amendment shall enter into force under the following conditions:

(i) in the case of an amendment to an Article of the Convention, to Protocol II, or to Protocol I or to an Annex to the Convention not under the procedure specified in sub-paragraph (f) (iii), the amendment accepted in conformity with the foregoing provisions shall enter into force six months after the date of its acceptance with respect to the Parties which have declared that they have accepted it;

(ii) in the case of an amendment to Protocol I, to an Appendix to an Annex or to an Annex to the Convention under the procedure specified in subparagraph (f) (iii), the amendment deemed to have been accepted in accordance with the foregoing conditions shall enter into force six months after its acceptance for all the Parties with the exception of those which, before that date, have made a declaration that they do not accept it or a declaration under sub-paragraph (f) (ii), that their express approval is necessary.

3. Amendment by a Conference.

a) Upon the request of a Party, concurred in by at least one-third of the Parties, the Organization shall convene a Conference of Parties to the Convention to consider amendments to the present Convention.

b) Every amendment by such a Conference by a two-thirds majority of those present and voting of the Parties shall be communicated by the Secretary-General of the Organization to all Contracting Parties for their acceptance.

c) Unless the Conference decides otherwise, the amendment shall be deemed to have been accepted and to have entered into force in accordance with the procedures specified for that purpose in paragraph (2) (f) and (g) above.

4.   a) In the case of an amendment to an Optional Annex, a reference in the present Article to a "Party to the Convention" shall be deemed to mean a reference to a Party bound by that Annex.

b) Any Party which has declined to accept an amendment to an Annex shall be treated as a non-Party only for the purpose of application of that Amendment.

5. The adoption and entry into force of a new Annex shall be subject to the same procedures as for the adoption and entry into force of an Article of the Convention.

6. Unless expressly provided otherwise, any amendment to the present Convention made under this Article, which relates to the structure of a ship, shall apply only to ships for which the building contract is placed, or in the absence of a building contract, the keel of which is laid, on or after the date on which the amendment comes into force.

7. Any amendment to a Protocol or to an Annex shall relate to the substance of that Protocol or Annex and shall be consistent with the Articles of the present Convention.

8. The Secretary-General of the Organization shall inform all Parties of any amendments which enter into force under the present Article, together with the date on which each such amendment enters into force.

9. Any declaration of acceptance or of objection to an amendment under the present Article shall be notified in writing to the Secretary-General of the Organization. The latter shall bring such notification and the date of its receipt to the notice of the Parties to the Convention.

Article 17   Promotion of Technical Cooperation

The Parties to the Convention shall promote in consultation with the Organization and other international bodies, with assistance and coordination by the Executive Director of the United Nations Environment Programme, support for those Parties which request technical assistance for:

     a) the training of scientific and technical personnel;

     b) the supply of necessary equipment and facilities for reception and monitoring;

     c) the facilitation of other measures and arrangements to prevent or mitigate pollution of the marine environment by ships; and

     d) the encouragement of research; preferably within the countries concerned, so furthering the aims and purposes of the present Convention.

Article 18   Denunciation

1. The present Convention or any Optional Annex may be denounced by any Party to the Convention at any time after the expiry of five years from the date on which the Convention or such Annex enters into force for that Party.

2. Denunciation shall be effected by notification in writing to the Secretary-General of the Organization who shall inform all the other Parties of any such notification received and of the date of its receipt as well as the date on which such denunciation takes effect.

3. A denunciation shall take effect twelve months after receipt of the notification of denunciation by the Secretary-General of the Organization or after the expiry of any other longer period which may be indicated in the notification.

Article 19   Deposit and Registration

1. The present Convention shall be deposited with the Secretary-General of the Organization who shall transmit certified true copies thereof to all States which have signed the present Convention or acceded to it.

2. As soon as the present Convention enters into force, the text shall be transmitted by the Secretary-General of the Organization to the Secretary-General of the United Nations for registration and publication, in accordance with Article 102 of the Charter of the United Nations.

Article 20   Languages

The present Convention is established in a single copy in the English, French, Russian and Spanish languages, each text being equally authentic. Official translations in the Arabic, German, Italian and Japanese languages shall be prepared and deposited with the signed original.

In Witness Whereof the undersigned being duly authorized by their respective Governments for that purpose have signed the present Convention.

Done at London this second day of November, one thousand nine hundred and seventy-three.

---

* * *

(Protocols not included)

ANNEX I	**REGULATIONS FOR THE PREVENTION OF POLLUTION BY OIL**
Chapter I	**General**
Regulation 1	**Definitions**

For the purposes of this Annex:

1. "Oil" means petroleum in any form including crude oil, fuel oil, sludge, oil refuse and refined products (other than petrochemicals which are subject to the provisions of Annex II of the present Convention) and, without limiting the generality of the foregoing, includes the substances listed in Appendix I to this Annex.

2. "Oily mixture" means a mixture with any oil content.

3. "Oil fuel" means any oil used as fuel in connexion with the propulsion and auxiliary machinery of the ship in which such oil is carried.

4. "Oil tanker" means a ship constructed or adapted primarily to carry oil in bulk in its cargo spaces and includes combination carriers and any "chemical tanker" as defined in Annex II of the present Convention when it is carrying a cargo or part cargo of oil in bulk.

5. "Combination carrier" means a ship designed to carry either oil or solid cargoes in bulk.

6. "New ship" means a ship:
        a) for which the building contract is placed after 31 December 1975; or
        b) in the absence of a building contract, the keel of which is laid or which is at a similar stage of construction after 30 June 1976; or
        c) the delivery of which is after 31 December 1979; or
        d) which has undergone a major conversion:
            (i) for which the contract is placed after 31 December 1975; or
            (ii) in the absence of a contract, the construction work of which is begun after 30 June 1976; or
            (iii) which is completed after 31 December 1979.

7. "Existing ship" means a ship which is not a new ship.

8.   a) "Major conversion" means a conversion of an existing ship:
            i) which substantially alters the dimensions or carrying capacity of the ship; or
            ii) which changes the type of the ship; or
            iii) the intent of which in the opinion of the Administration is substantially to prolong its life; or
            iv) which otherwise so alters the ship that if it were a new ship, it would become subject to relevant provisions of the present Convention not applicable to it as an existing ship.
       b) Notwithstanding the provisions of sub-paragraph (a) of this paragraph, conversion of an existing oil tanker of 20,000 tons deadweight and above to meet the requirements of Regulation 13 of this annex shall not be deemed to constitute a major conversion for the purposes of this Annex.

9. "Nearest land". The term "from the nearest land" means from the baseline from which the territorial sea of the territory in question is established in accordance with international law, except that for the purposes of the present Convention "from the nearest land" off the north eastern coast of Australia shall mean from a line drawn from a point on the coast of Australia in

    latitude 11 deg 00 deg South, longitude 142 deg 08 min East to a point in latitude 10 deg 35 min South, longitude 141 deg 55 min East thence to a point latitude 10 deg 00 min South, longitude 142 deg 00 min East, thence to a point latitude 9 deg 10 min South, longitude 143 deg 52 min East, thence to a point latitude 9 deg 00 min South, longitude 144 deg 00 min East, thence to a point latitude 15 deg min South, longitude 147 deg 00 min East, thence to a point latitude 21 deg 00 min South, longitude 153 deg 00 min East, thence to a point on the coast of Australia in latitude 24 deg 42 deg South, longitude 153 deg 15 min East.

10. "Special area" means a sea where for recognized technical reasons in relation to its oceanographical and ecological condition and to the particular character of its traffic the adoption of special mandatory methods for the prevention of sea pollution by oil is required. Special areas shall include those listed in Regulation 10 of this Annex.

11. "Instantaneous rate of discharge of oil content" means the rate of discharge of oil litres per hour at any instant divided by the speed of the ship in knots at the same instant.

12. "Tank" means an enclosed space which is formed by the permanent structure of a ship and which is designed for the carriage of liquid in bulk.

13. "Wing tank" means any tank adjacent to the side shell plating.

14. "Centre tank" means any tank inboard of a longitudinal bulkhead.

15. "Slop tank" means a tank specifically designated for the collection of tank drainings, tank washings and other oily mixtures.

16. "Clean ballast" means the ballast in a tank which since oil was last carried therein, has been so cleaned that effluent therefrom if it were discharged from a ship which is stationary into clean calm water on a clear day would not produce visible traces of oil on the surface of the water or upon adjoining shorelines or cause a sludge or emulsion to be deposited beneath the surface of the water or upon adjoining shorelines. If the ballast is discharged through an oil discharge monitoring and control system approved by the Administration, evidence based on such a system to the effect that the oil content of the effluent did not exceed 15 parts per million shall be determinative that the ballast was clean, notwithstanding the presence of visible traces.

17. "Segregated ballast" means the ballast water introduced into a tank which is completely separated from the cargo oil and oil fuel system and which is permanently allocated to the carriage of ballast or to the carriage of ballast or cargoes other than oil or noxious substances as variously defined in the Annexes of the present Convention.

18. "Length" (L) means 96 per cent of the total length on a waterline at 85 per cent of the least moulded depth measured from the top of the keel, or the length from the foreside of the stem to the axis of the rudder stock on that waterline, if that be greater. In ships designed with a rake of keel the waterline on which this length is measured shall be parallel to the designed waterline. The length (L) shall be measured in meters.

* * *

Regulation 2   Application

1. Unless expressly provided otherwise, the provisions of this Annex shall apply to all ships.

2. In ships other than oil tankers fitted with cargo spaces which are constructed and utilized to carry oil in bulk of an aggregate capacity of 200 cubic meters or more, the requirements of Regulations 9, 10, 14, 15 (1), (2) and (3), 18, 20 and 24 (4) of this Annex for oil tankers shall apply to the construction and operation of those spaces, except that where such aggregate capacity is less than 1,000 cubic metres the requirements of Regulation 15(4) of this Annex may apply in lieu of Regulation 15(1), (2) and (3).

3. Where a cargo subject to the provisions of Annex II of the present Convention is carried in a cargo space of an oil tanker, the appropriate requirements of Annex II of the present Convention shall also apply.

4.   a) Any hydrofoil, air-cushion vehicle and other new type of vessel (near-surface craft, submarine craft, etc) whose constructional features are such as to render the application of any of the provisions of Chapters II and III of this Annex relating to construction and equipment unreasonable or impracticable may be exempted by the Administration from such provisions, provided that the construction and equipment of that ship provides equivalent protection against pollution by oil, having regard to the service for which it is intended.

b) Particulars of any such exemption granted by the Administration shall be indicated in the Certificate referred to in Regulation 5 of this Annex.

c) The Administration which allows any such exemption shall, as soon as possible, but not more than ninety days thereafter, communicate to the Organization particulars of same and the reasons therefor, which the Organization shall circulate to the Parties to the Convention for their information and appropriate action, if any.

Regulation 3   Equivalents

1. The Administration may allow any fitting, material, appliance or apparatus to be fitted in a ship as an alternative to that required by this Annex if such fitting, material, appliance or apparatus is at least as effective as that required by this Annex. This authority of the Administration shall not extend to substitution of operational methods to effect the control of discharge of oil as equivalent to those design and construction features which are prescribed by Regulations in this Annex.

2. The Administration which allows a fitting, material, appliance or apparatus, as an alternative to that required by this Annex shall communicate to the Organization for circulation to the Parties to the Convention particulars thereof, for their information and appropriate action, if any.

Regulation 4   Surveys

1. Every oil tanker of 150 tons gross tonnage and above, and every other ship of 400 tons gross tonnage and above shall be subject to the surveys specified below:

a) An initial survey before the ship is put in service or before the Certificate required under Regulation 5 of this Annex is issued for the first time, which shall include a complete survey of its structure, equipment, fittings, arrangements and material in so far as the ship is covered by this Annex. This survey shall be such as to ensure that the structure, equipment, fittings, arrangements and material fully comply with the applicable requirements of this Annex.

b) Periodical surveys at intervals specified by the Administration, but not exceeding five years, which shall be such as to ensure that the structure, equipment, fittings, arrangements and material fully comply with the applicable requirements of this Annex. However, where the duration of the International Oil Pollution Certificate (1973) is extended as specified in Regulation 8 (3) or (4) of this Annex, the interval of the periodical survey may be extended correspondingly.

c) Intermediate surveys at intervals specified by the Administration but not exceeding thirty months, which shall be such as to ensure that the equipment and associated pump and piping systems, including oil discharge monitoring and control systems, oily-water separating equipment and oil filtering systems, fully comply with the applicable requirements of this Annex and are in good working order. Such intermediate surveys shall be endorsed on the International Oil Pollution Prevention Certificate (1973) issued under Regulation 5 of this Annex.

2. The Administration shall establish appropriate measures for ships which are not subject to the provisions of paragraph (1) of this Regulation in order to ensure that the applicable provisions of this Annex are complied with.

3. Surveys of the ship as regards enforcement of the provisions of this Annex shall be carried out by officers of the Administration. The Administration may, however, entrust the surveys either to surveyors nominated for the purpose or to organizations recognized by it. In every case the Administration concerned fully guarantees the completeness and efficiency of the surveys.

* * *

Regulation 5   Issue of Certificate

1. An International Oil Pollution Certificate (1973) shall be issued, after survey in accordance with the provisions of Regulation 4 of this Annex, to any oil tanker of 150 tons gross tonnage and above and any other ships of 400 tons gross tonnage and above which are engaged in voyages to ports or off-shore terminals under the jurisdiction of other Parties to the Convention. In the case of existing ships this requirement shall apply twelve months after the date of entry into force of the present Convention.

2. Such Certificate shall be issued either by the Administration or by any persons or organization duly authorized by it. In every case the Administration assumes full responsibility for the Certificate.

Regulation 6   Issue of a Certificate by Another Government

1. The Government of a Party to the Convention may, at the request of the Administration, cause a ship to be surveyed and, if satisfied that the provisions of this Annex are complied with, shall issue or authorize the issue of an International Oil Pollution Prevention Certificate to the ship in accordance with this Annex.

2. A copy of the Certificate and a copy of the survey report shall be transmitted as soon as possible to the requesting Administration.

3. A Certificate so issued shall contain a statement to the effect that it has been issued at the request of the Administration and it shall have the same force and receive the same force and receive the same recognition as the Certificate issued under Regulation 5 of this Annex.

4. No International Oil Pollution Prevention Certificate shall be issued to a ship which is entitled to fly the flag of a State which is not a Party.

* * *

Regulation 7   Form of Certification

* * *

Regulation 8   Duration of Certificate

* * *

Chapter II   Requirements for Control of Operational Pollution

Regulation 9   Control of Discharge of Oil

1. Subject to the provisions of Regulations 10 and 11 of this Annex and paragraph (2) of this Regulation, any discharge into the sea of oil or oily mixtures from ships to which this Annex applies shall be prohibited except when all the following conditions are satisfied:

    a) for an oil tanker, except as provided for in subparagraph (b) of this paragraph:

        (i) the tanker is not within a special area;

        (ii) the tanker is more than 50 nautical miles from the nearest land;

        (iii) the tanker is proceeding en route;

        (iv) the instantaneous rate of discharge of oil content does not exceed 60 litres per nautical mile;

        (v) the total quantity of oil discharged into the sea does not exceed for existing tankers 1/15,000 of the total quantity of the particular cargo of which the residue formed a part, and for new tankers 1/30,000 of the total quantity of the particular cargo of which the residue formed a part; and

        (vi) the tanker has in operation, except as provided for in Regulation 15(3) of this Annex, an oil discharge monitoring and control system and a slop tank arrangements as required by Regulation 15 of this Annex;

    b) from a ship of 400 tons gross tonnage and above other than an oil tanker and from machinery space bilges excluding cargo pump room bilges of an oil tanker unless mixed with oil cargo residue:

        (i) the ship is not within a special area;

        (ii) the ship is more than 12 nautical miles from the nearest land;

        (iii) the ship is proceeding en route;

        (iv) the oil content of the effluent is less than 100 parts per million; and

        (v) the ship has in operation an oil discharge monitoring and control system, oily-water separating equipment, oil filtering system or other installation as required by Regulation 16 of this Annex.

2. In the case of a ship of less than 400 tons gross tonnage other than oil tanker whilst outside the special area, the Administration shall ensure that it is equipped as far as practicable and reasonable with installations to ensure the storage of oil residues on board and their discharge to reception facilities or into the sea in compliance with the requirements of paragraph (1) (b) of this Regulation.

3. Whenever visible traces of oil are observed on or below the surface of the water in the immediate vicinity of a ship or its wake, Governments of Parties to the Convention should, to the extent they are reasonably able to do so, promptly investigate the facts bearing on the issue of whether there has been a violation of the provisions of this Regulation or Regulation 10 of this Annex. The investigation should include, in particular, the wind and sea conditions, the track and speed of the ship, other possible sources of visible traces in the vicinity, and any relevant oil discharge records.

4. The provisions of paragraph (1) of this Regulation shall not apply to the discharge of clean or segregated ballast. The provisions of subparagraph (1)(b) of this Regulation shall not apply to the discharge of oily mixture which without dilution has an oil content not exceeding 15 parts per million.

5. No discharge into the sea shall contain chemicals or other substances in quantities or concentrations which are hazardous to the marine environment or chemicals or other substances introduced for the purpose of circumventing the conditions of discharge specified in this Regulation.

6. The oil residues which cannot be discharged into the sea in compliance with paragraphs (1), (2) and (4) of this Regulation shall be retained on board or discharged to reception facilities.

Regulation 10　　　　　　**Methods for the Prevention of Oil Pollution from Ships While Operating in Special Areas**

1. For the purposes of this Annex the special areas are the Mediterranean Sea area, the Baltic Sea area, the Black Sea area and the "Gulfs area" which are defined as follows:

　　a) The Mediterranean Sea area means the Mediterranean Sea proper including the gulfs and seas therein with the boundary between the Mediterranean and the Black Sea constituted by the 41 deg N parallel and bounded to the west by the Straits of Gibraltar at the meridian of 5 deg 36 min W.

　　b) The Baltic Sea area means the Baltic Sea proper with the Gulf of Bothnia, the Gulf of Finland and the entrance to the Baltic Sea bounded by the parallel of the Skaw in the Skagerrak at 57 deg 44.8 min N.

　　c) The Black Sea area means the Black Sea proper with the boundary between the Mediterranean and the Black Sea constituted by the parallel 41 deg N.

　　d) The Red Sea area means the Red Sea proper including the Gulfs of Suez and Aqaba bounded at the South by the rhumb line between Ras si Ane (12 deg 8.5 min N, 43 deg 19.6 min E) and Husn Murad (12 deg 40.4 min N, 43 deg 30.2 min E).

　　e) The Gulfs area means the sea area located north west of the rhumb line between Ras al Hadd (22 deg 30 min N, 59 deg 48 min E) and RAs Al Fasteh (25 deg 04 min N, 61 deg 25 min E).

2.　　　a) Subject to the provisions of Regulation 11 of this Annex, any discharge into the sea of oil or oily mixture from any oil tanker and any ship or 400 tons gross tonnage and above other than an oil tanker shall be prohibited, while in a special area.

　　b) Such ships while in a special area shall retain on board all oil drainage and sludge, dirty ballast and tank washing waters and discharge them only to reception facilities.

3.　　　a) Subject to the provisions of Regulation 11 of this Annex, any discharge into the sea of oil or mixture from a ship of less than 400 tons gross tonnage, other than oil tanker, shall be prohibited while in a special area, except when the oil content of the effluent without dilution does not exceed 15 parts per million or alternatively when all of the following conditions are satisfied:

　　　　　(i) the ship is proceeding en route;
　　　　　(ii) the oil content of the effluent is less than 100 parts per million; and
　　　　　(iii) the discharge is made as far as practicable from the land, but in no case less than 12 nautical miles from the nearest land.

　　b) No discharge into the sea shall contain chemicals or other substances in quantities or concentrations which are hazardous to the marine environment or chemicals or other substances introduced for the purpose of circumventing the conditions of discharge specified in this Regulation.

　　c) The oil residues which cannot be discharged into the sea in compliance with sub-paragraph (a) of this paragraph shall be retained on board or discharged to reception facilities.

4. The provisions of this Regulation shall not apply to the discharge of clean or segregated ballast.

5. Nothing in this Regulation shall prohibit a ship on a voyage only part of which is in a special area from discharging outside the special area in accordance with Regulation 9 of this Annex.

6. Whenever visible traces of oil are observed on or below the surface of the water in the immediate vicinity of a ship or its wake, the Governments of Parties to the Convention should, to the extent they are reasonably able to do so, promptly investigate the facts bearing on the issue of whether there has been a violation of the provisions of this Regulation or Regulation 9 of this Annex. The investigation should include, in particular, the wind and sea conditions, the track and speed of the ship, other possible sources of the visible traces in the vicinity, and any relevant oil discharge records.

* * *

Regulation 11   Exceptions

Regulations 9 and 10 of this Annex shall not apply to:
a) the discharge into the sea of oil or oily mixture necessary for the purpose of securing the safety of a ship or saving life at sea; or
b) the discharge into the sea of oil or oily mixture resulting from damage to a ship or its equipment:
(i) provided that all reasonable precautions have been taken after the occurrence of the damage or discovery of the discharge for the purpose of preventing or minimizing the discharge; and
(ii) except if the owner or the Master acted either with intent to cause damage, or recklessly and with knowledge that damage would probably result; or
c) the discharge into the sea of substances containing oil, approved by the Administration, when being used for the purpose of combating specific pollution incidents in order to minimize the damage from pollution. Any such discharge shall be subject to the approval of any Government in whose jurisdiction it is contemplated the discharge will occur.

Regulation 12   Reception Facilities

1. Subject to the provisions of Regulation 10 of this Annex, the Government of each Party undertakes to ensure the provision at oil loading terminals, repair ports, and in other ports in which ships have oily residues to discharge, of facilities for the reception of such residues and oily mixtures as remain from oil tankers and other ships adequate to meet the needs of the ships using them without causing undue delay to ships.

2. Reception facilities in accordance with paragraph (1) of this Regulation shall be provided in:
a) all ports and terminals in which crude oil is loaded into oil tankers where such tankers have immediately prior to arrival completed a ballast voyage of not more than 72 hours or not more than 1,200 nautical miles;
b) all ports and terminals in which oil other than crude oil in bulk is loaded at an average quantity of more than 1,000 metric tons per day;
c) all ports having ship repair yards or tank cleaning facilities;
d) all ports and terminals which handle ships provided with the sludge tank(s) required by Regulation 17 of this Annex:
e) all ports in respect of oily bilge waters and other residues, which cannot be discharged in accordance with Regulation 9 of this Annex; and
f) all loading ports for bulk cargoes in respect of oil residues from combination carriers which cannot be discharged in accordance with Regulation 9 of this Annex.

3. The capacity for the reception facilities shall be as follows:
a) Crude oil loading terminals shall have sufficient reception facilities to receive oil and oily mixtures which cannot be discharged in accordance with the provisions of Regulation 9(1)(a) of this Annex from all oil tankers on voyages as described in paragraph (2) (a) of this Regulation.
b) Loading ports and terminals referred to in paragraph (2)(b) of this Regulation shall have sufficient reception facilities to receive oil and oily mixtures which cannot be discharged in accordance with the provisions of Regulation 9(1) (a) of this Annex from oil tankers which load oil other than crude oil in bulk.
c) All ports having ship repair yards or tank cleaning facilities shall have sufficient reception facilities to receive all residues and oily mixtures which remain on board for disposal from ships prior to entering such yards or facilities.

d) All facilities provided in ports and terminals under paragraph (2)(d) of this Regulation shall be sufficient to receive all residues retained according to Regulation 17 of this Annex from all ships that may reasonably be expected to call at such ports and terminals.

e) All facilities provided in ports and terminals under this Regulation shall be sufficient to receive oily bilge waters and other residues which cannot be discharged in accordance with Regulation 9 of this Annex.

f) The facilities provided in loading ports for bulk cargoes shall take into account the special problems of combination carriers as appropriate.

4. The reception facilities prescribed in paragraphs (2) and (3) of this Regulation shall be made available no later than one year from the date of entry into force of the present Convention or by 1 January 1977, whichever occurs later.

5. Each Party shall notify the Organization for transmission to the Parties concerned of all cases where the facilities provided under this Regulation are alleged to be inadequate.

Regulation 13 Segregated Ballast Oil Tankers

1. Every new oil tanker of 70,000 tons deadweight and above shall be provided with segregated ballast tanks and shall comply with the requirements of this Regulation.

2. The capacity of the segregated ballast tanks shall be so determined that the ship may operate safely on ballast voyages without recourse to the use of oil tanks for water ballast except as provided for in paragraph (3) of this Regulation. In all cases, however, the capacity of segregated ballast tanks shall be at least such that in any ballast condition at any part of the voyage, including the conditions consisting of lightweight plus segregated ballast only, the ship's draughts and trim can meet each of the following requirements:

a) the moulded draught amidships (dm) in metres (without taking into account any ship's deformation) shall not be les than: $dm = 2.0 + 0.02L$;

b) the draughts at the forward and after perpendiculars shall correspond to those determined by the draught amidships (dm), as specified in sub-paragraph (a) of this paragraph, in association with the trim by the stern of not greater than 0.015L; and

c) in any case the draught at the after perpendicular shall not be less than that which is necessary to obtain full immersion of the propeller(s).

3. In no case shall ballast water be carried in oil tanks except in weather conditions so severe that, in the opinion of the Master, it is necessary to carry additional ballast water in oil tanks for the safety of the ship. Such additional ballast water shall be processed and discharged in compliance with Regulation 9 and in accordance with the requirements of Regulation 15 of this Annex, and entry shall be made in the Oil Record Book referred to in Regulation 20 of this Annex.

4. Any oil tanker which is not required to be provided with segregated ballast tanks in accordance with paragraph (1) of this Regulation may, however, be qualified as a segregated ballast tanker, provided that in the case of an oil tanker of 150 metres in length and above it fully complies with the requirements of paragraphs (2) and (3) of this Regulation and in the case of an oil tanker of less than 150 metres in length the segregated ballast conditions shall be to the satisfaction of the Administration.

Regulation 14 **Segregation of Oil and Water Ballast**
* * *

Regulation 15 **Retention of Oil on Board**
* * *

Regulation 16 **Oil Discharge Monitoring and Control System and Oil-Water Separating Equipment**
* * *

Regulation 17 **Tanks for Oil Residues (Sludge)**

* * *

Regulation 18 **Pumping, Piping and Discharge Arrangements of Oil Tankers**
* * *

Regulation 19   Standard Discharge Connection
* * *

Regulation 20   Oil Record Book

1. Every oil tanker of 150 tons gross tonnage and above and every ship of 400 tons gross tonnage and above other than oil tanker shall be provided with an Oil Record Book, whether as part of the ship's official log book or otherwise, in the form specified in Appendix III to this Annex.

2. The Oil Record Book shall be completed on each occasion, on a tank-to-tank basis, whenever any of the following operations take place in the ship:
   a) For oil tankers
       (i) loading of oil cargo;
       (ii) internal transfer of oil cargo during voyage;
       (iii) opening or closing before and after loading and unloading operations of valves or similar devices which inter-connect cargo tanks;
       (iv) opening or closing of means of communication between cargo piping and seawater ballast piping;
       (v) opening or closing of ship's side valves before, during and after loading and unloading operations;
       (vi) unloading of oil cargo;
       (vii) ballasting of cargo tanks;
       (viii) cleaning of cargo tanks;
       (ix) discharge of ballast except from segregated ballast tanks;
       (x) discharge of water from slop tanks;
       (xi) disposal of residues;
       (xii) discharge overboard of bilge water which has accumulated in machinery spaces whilst in port and the routine discharge at sea of bilge water which has accumulated in machinery spaces.
   b) For ships other than oil tankers
       (i) ballasting or cleaning of fuel oil tanks or oil cargo spaces;
       (ii) discharge of ballast or cleaning water from tanks referred to under (i) of this sub-paragraph;
       (iii) disposal of residues;
       (iv) discharge overboard of bilge water which has accumulated in machinery spaces whilst in port, and the routine discharge at sea of bilge water which has accumulated in machinery spaces.

3. In the event of such discharge of oil or oily mixture as is referred to in Regulation 11 of this Annex or in the event of accidental or other exceptional discharge of oil not expected by that Regulation, a statement shall be made in the Oil Record Book of the circumstances of, and the reasons for the discharge.

4. Each operation described in paragraph (2) of this Regulation shall be fully recorded without delay in the Oil Record Book so that all the entries in the book appropriate to that operation are completed. Each section of the book shall be signed by the officer or officers in charge of the operations concerned and shall be countersigned by the Master of the ship. The entries in the Oil Record Book shall be in an official language of the State whose flag the ship is entitled to fly, and, for ships holding an International Oil Pollution Prevention Certificate (1973), in English or French. The entries in an official national language of the State whose flag the ship is entitled to fly shall prevail in case of a dispute or discrepancy.

5. The Oil Record Book shall be kept in such a place as to be readily available for inspection at all reasonable times and, except in the case of unmanned ships under tow, shall be kept on board the ship. It shall be preserved for a period of three years after the last entry has been made.

6. The competent authority of the Government of a party to the Convention may inspect the Oil Record Book on board any ship to which this Annex applies while the ship is in its port or offshore terminals and may take a copy of any entry in that book and may require the Master of the ship to certify that the copy is a true copy of such entry. Any copy so made which has been certified by the Master of the ship as a true copy of an entry in the ship's Oil Record Book shall be made admissible in any judicial proceedings as evidence of the facts stated in the entry. The inspection of an Oil Record Book and the taking of a certified copy of the competent authority under this paragraph shall be performed as expeditiously as possible without causing the ship to be unduly delayed.

* * *

Regulation 21   **Special Requirements for Drilling Rigs and other Platforms**

* * *

Regulation 22   **Damage Assumptions**

* * *

Regulation 23   **Hypothetical Outflow of Oil**

* * *

Regulation 24   **Limitation of Size and Arrangement of Cargo Tanks**

* * *

Regulation 25   **Subdivision and Stability**

* * *

APPENDIX I   **LIST OF OILS**

* * *

APPENDIX II   FORM OF CERTIFICATE

INTERNATIONAL OIL PREVENTION CERTIFICATE (1973)

Issued under the Provisions of the International Convention for the Prevention of Pollution from Ships, 1973, under the Authority of the Government of .... (full designation of the country)

by ....
(full designation of the competent person or organization authorized under the provisions of the International Convention for the Prevention of Pollution from Ships, 1973)

Name of Ship   Number or Distinctive Letter
Port of Registry
Gross Tonnage

Type of ship:

   Oil tanker, including combination carrier
   Asphalt carrier
   Ship other than oil tanker with cargo tanks coming under Regulation 2(2) of Annex I of the Convention
   Ship other than any of the above
   New/existing ship

Date of building or major conversion contract..

Date on which keel was laid or ship was at a similar stage of construction or on which major conversion was commenced...

Date of delivery or completion of major conversion..

PART A   All Ships

The ship is equipped with:
for ships of 400 tons gross tonnage and above:
   a) oily-water separating equipment* (capable of producing the effluent with an oil content not exceeding 100 parts per million) or
   b) an oil filtering system* (capable of producing the effluent with an oil content not exceeding 100 parts per million) for ships of 10,000 tons gross tonnage and above:
   c) an oil discharge monitoring and control system* (additional to (a) or (b) above) or
   d) oil-water separating equipment and an oil filtering system* (capable of producing the effluent with an oil content not exceeding 15 pars per million) in lieu of (a) or (b) above.

Particulars of requirement from which exemption is granted under Regulation 2(2) and 2(4)(a) of Annex I of the Convention:

....

....

Remarks:

PART B   Oil Tanker

Deadweight ....metric tons.
 Length of ship............... metres.

It is certified that this ship is:
        a) required to be constructed according to and complies with
        b) not required to be constructed according to
        c) nor required to be constructed according to, but complies with the requirements of Regulation 24 of
Annex I of the Convention.

The capacity of segregated ballast tanks is...................................cubic metres and complies with the requirements of Regulation 24 of Annex I of the Convention

The segregated ballast is distributed as follows:
Tank   Quantity   Tank   Quantity

This Part should be completed for oil tankers including combination carriers and asphalt carriers, and those entries which are applicable should be completed for ships other than oil tankers which are constructed and utilized to carry oil in bulk of an aggregate capacity of 200 cubic metres or above.

THIS IS TO CERTIFY:

That the ship has been surveyed in accordance with Regulation 4 of Annex I of the International Convention for the Prevention of Pollution from Ships, 1973, concerning the prevention of pollution of oil; and

That the survey shows that the structure, equipment, fittings, arrangements and material of the ship and the condition thereof are in all respects, satisfactory and that the ship complies with the applicable requirements of Annex I of the Convention.

This Certificate is valid until............................
subject to intermediate survey(s) at intervals of ....
Issued at...
             (place of issue of Certificate)

.......................19.... ....
(Signature of duly authorized official issuing the Certificate)
(Seal or stamp of the issuing Authority, as appropriate)

Endorsement for existing ships

This is to certify that this ship has been so equipped as to comply with the requirements of the International Convention for the Prevention of Pollution from Ships, 1973 as relating to existing ships three years from the date of entry into force of the Convention.

signed......................
(Signature of duly authorized official)

Place of endorsement ....

Date of endorsement ....

(Seal or stamp of the Authority, as appropriate)

Intermediate survey

This is to certify that at an intermediate survey required by Regulation 4(1)(c) of Annex I of the Convention, this ship and the condition thereof are found to comply with the relevant provisions of the Convention.

Signed ....
(Signature of duly authorized official)

Place................ Date................
(Seal or stamp of the Authority, as appropriate)

 Signed....................
(Signature of duly authorized official)

Place................
Date................
(Seal or stamp of the Authority, as appropriate)

Under the provisions of Regulation 8(2) and (4) of Annex I of the Convention the validity of this Certificate is extended until..

Signed....................
(Signature of duly authorized official)

Place................
Date................
(Seal or stamp of the Authority, as appropriate)

APPENDIX III OIL RECORD BOOK

This Part should be completed for oil tankers including combination carriers and asphalt carriers, and those entries which are applicable shall be completed for ships other than oil tankers which are constructed and utilized to carry oil in bulk of an aggregate capacity of 200 cubic metres or above. This Part need not be reproduced on an Oil Record Book issued to any ship other than those referred to above.

Name of ship ....

Total cargo carrying capacity of ship in cubic metres
....Voyage
..........(date).....to .... (date)

a) Loading of oil cargo
    1. Date and place of loading
    2. Types of oil loaded
    3. Identity of tank(s)loaded
    4. Closing of applicable cargo tank valves and applicable line cut-off valves on completion of loading

The undersigned certifies that in addition to the above, all sea valves, overboard discharges valves, cargo tank and pipeline connections and inter-connections, were secured on completion of loading oil cargo.

Date of entry.......... Officer in charge.............. Master ....

b) Internal transfer of oil cargo during voyage
    5. Date of internal transfer

6. Identity of tank(s)
       (i) From
       (ii) To
7. Was(were) tank(s) in 6(i) emptied?

The undersigned certifies that in addition to the above, all sea valves overboard discharge valves, cargo tank and pipeline connections and inter-connections, were secured on completion of internal transfer of oil cargo.

Date of entry............. Officer in charge........... Master.................

c) Unloading of oil cargo
       8. Date and place of unloading
       9. Identity of tank(s) unloaded
       10. Was(were) tank(s) emptied?
       11. Opening of applicable cargo tank valves and applicable line cut-off valves on completion of unloading2
       12. Closing of applicable cargo tank valves and applicable line cut off valves on completion of unloading

The tank certifies that in addition to the above, all sea valves, overboard discharge valves, cargo tank and pipeline connections and inter-connections, were secured on completion of unloading of oil cargo.

Date of entry...........Officer in charge.............. Master ....

d) Ballasting of cargo tanks
       13. Identity of tank(s) ballasted
       14. Date and position of ship at start of ballasting
       15. If valves connecting cargo lines and segregated ballast lines were used give time, date and position of ship when valves were (a) opened, and (b) closed

The undersigned certifies that in addition to the above, all sea valves, overboard discharge valves, cargo tank and pipeline connections and inter-connections, were secured on completion of unloading of oil cargo.

Date of entry.............. Officer in charge................ Master ....

e) Cleaning of cargo tanks
       16. Identity of tank(s) cleaned
       17. Date and duration of cleaning
       18. Methods of cleaning

Date of entry..............Officer in charge .... Master ....

f) Discharge of dirty ballast
       19. Identity of tank(s)
       20. Date and position of ship at start of discharge to sea
       21. Date and position of ship at finish of discharge to sea
       22. Ship's speed(s) during discharge
       23. Quantity discharged to sea
       24. Quantity of polluted water transferred to slop tank(s) (identify slop tank(s)
       25. Date and port of discharge into shore reception facilities (if applicable)
       26. Was any part of the discharge conducted during darkness, if so, for how long?
       27. Was a regular check kept on the effluent and the surface of the water in the locality of the discharge?
       28. Was any oil observed on the surface of the water in the locality of the discharge?

Date of entry............. Officer in charge .... Master.........................

g) Discharge of water from slop tanks
       29. Identity of slop tank(s)
       30. Time of settling from last entry of residues, or
       31. Time of settling from last discharge

32. Date, time and position of ship at start of discharge
33. Sounding of total contents at start of discharge
34. Sounding of oil/water interface at start of discharge
35. Bulk quantity discharged and rate of discharge
36. Final quantity discharged and rate of discharge
37. Date, time and position of ship at end of discharge
38. Ship's speed(s) during discharge
39. Sounding of oil/water interface at end of discharge
40. Was any part of the discharge conducted during darkness, if so, for how long?
41. Was a regular check kept on the effluent and surface of the water in the locality of the discharge?
42. Was any oil observed on the surface of the water in the locality of the discharge?

Date of entry............. Officer in charge .... Master........................

h) Disposal of residues
43. Identity of tank(s)
44. Quantity disposed from each tank
45. Method of disposal of residue:
    (a) Reception of facilities
    (b) Mixed with cargo
    (c) Transferred to another (other) tank(s) (identify tank(s)
    (d) Other method (state which)
46. Date and port of disposal of residue

Date of entry............. Officer in charge .... Master........................

i) Discharge of clean ballast contained in cargo tanks
47. Date and position of ship at commencement of discharge of clean ballast
48. Identity of tank(s) discharged
49. Was(were) the tank(s) empty on completion?
50. Position of vessel on completion if different from 47
51. Was any part of the discharge conducted during darkness, if so, for how long?
52. Was a regular check kept on the effluent and the surface of the water in the locality of the discharge?
53. Was any oil observed on the surface of the water in the locality of the discharge?

Date of entry............. Officer in charge .... Master........................

j) Discharge overboard of bilge water containing oil which has accumulated in machinery spaces whilst in port
54. Port
55. Duration of stay
56. Quantity disposed
57. Date and place of disposal
58. Method of disposal (state whether a separator was used)

Date of entry............. Officer in charge .... Master........................

k) Accidental or other exceptional discharges of oil
59. Date and time of occurrence
60. Place or position of ship at time of occurrence
61. Approximate quantity and type of oil
62. Circumstances of discharge or escape, the reasons therefor and general remarks

Date of entry............. Officer in charge .... Master........................

1) Has the oil monitoring and control system been out of operation at any time when discharging overboard? If so, give time and date of failure and time and date of restoration and confirm that this was due to equipment failure and state reason if
known..

Date of entry............. Officer in charge .... Master........................

m) Additional operational procedures and general remarks ....

 For oil tankers of less than 150 tons gross tonnage operating in accordance with Regulation 15(4) of Annex I of the Convention, an appropriate oil record book should be developed by the Administration.
 For asphalt carriers, a separate oil record book may be developed by the Administration utilizing sections (a), (b), (c), (e), (h), (j), (k) and (m) of this form of oil record book.

* * *

ANNEX II	**REGULATIONS FOR THE CONTROL OF POLLUTION BY NOXIOUS LIQUID IN BULK**

* * *

ANNEX III	**REGULATIONS FOR THE PREVENTION OF POLLUTION BY HARMFUL SUBSTANCES CARRIED BY SEA IN PACKAGED FORMS OR IN FREIGHT CONTAINERS, PORTABLE TANKS OR ROAD AND RAIL TANK WAGONS**

* * *

ANNEX IV	**REGULATIONS FOR THE PREVENTION OF POLLUTION BY SEWAGE FROM SHIPS**

* * *

ANNEX V	**REGULATIONS FOR THE PREVENTION OF POLLUTION BY GARBAGE FROM SHIPS**

* * *

ANNEX VI	**PREVENTION OF AIR POLLUTION FROM SHIPS**

Protocol of 1978 relating to the International Convention
for the Prevention of Pollution from Ships, 1973
(annexes not included)

17 I.L.M. 546 (1978)
Signed: February 17, 1978
Entered into Force: October 2, 1983
Secretariat Homepage: http://www.imo.org/

Preamble

The Parties to the present Protocol,

Recognizing the significant contribution which can be made by the International Convention for the Prevention of Pollution from Ships, 1973, to the protection of the marine environment from pollution from ships,

Recognizing also the need to improve further the prevention and control of marine pollution from ships, particularly oil tankers,

Recognizing further the need for implementing the Regulations for the Prevention of Pollution by Oil contained in Annex 1 of that Convention as early and as widely as possible,

Acknowledging however the need to defer the application of Annex 11 of that Convention until certain technical problems have been satisfactorily resolved,

Considering that these objectives may best be achieved by the conclusion of a Protocol relating to the International Convention for the Prevention of Pollution from Ships, 1973,

Have agreed as follows:

Article I   General obligations

1. The Parties to the present Protocol undertake to give effect to the provisions of :

    (a) the present Protocol and the Annex hereto which shall constitute an integral part of the present Protocol; and

    (b) the International Convention for the Prevention of Pollution from Ships, 1973 (hereinafter referred to as "the Convention"), subject to the modifications and additions set out in the present Protocol.

2. The provisions of the Convention and the present Protocol shall be read and interpreted together as one single instrument.

3. Every reference to the present Protocol constitutes at the same time a reference to the Annex hereto.

Article II   Implementation of Annex II of the Convention

1. Notwithstanding the provisions of article 14(1) of the Convention, the Parties to the present Protocol agree that they shall not be bound by the provisions of Annex 11 of the Convention for a period of three years from the date of entry into force of the present Protocol or for such longer period as may be decided by a two-thirds majority of the Parties to the present Protocol in the Marine Environment Protection Committee (hereinafter referred to as "the Committee") of the Inter-Governmental Maritime Consultative Organization (hereinafter referred to as "the Organization") [now known as the IMO].

2. During the period specified in paragraph 1 of this article, the Parties to the present Protocol shall not be under any obligations nor entitled to claim any privileges under the Convention in respect of matters relating to Annex 11 of the Convention and all reference to Parties in the Convention shall not include the Parties to the present Protocol in so far as matters relating to that Annex are concerned.

Article III   Communication of information

The text of article 11 (1)(b) of the Convention is replaced by the following: "a list of nominated surveyors or recognized organizations which are authorized to act on their behalf in the administration of matters relating to the design, construction, equipment and operation of ships carrying harmful substances in accordance with the provisions of the regulations for circulation to the Parties for information of their officers. The Administration shall therefore notify the Organization of the specific responsibilities and conditions of the authority delegated to nominated surveyors or recognized organizations."

Article IV   Signature, ratification, acceptance, approval and accession

1. The present Protocol shall be open for signature at the Headquarters of the Organization from 1 June 1978 to 31 May 1979 and shall thereafter remain open for accession. States may become Parties to the present Protocol by :

(a) signature without reservation as to ratification, acceptance or approval; or
(b) signature, subject to ratification, acceptance or approval, followed by ratification, acceptance or approval; or
(c) accession.

2. Ratification, acceptance, approval or accession shall be effected by the deposit of an instrument to that effect with the Secretary-General of the Organization.

Article V   Entry into force

1. The present Protocol shall enter into force 12 months after the date on which not less than 15 States, the combined merchant fleets of which constitute not less than 50 per cent of the gross tonnage of the world's merchant shipping, have become Parties to it in accordance with article IV of the present Protocol.

2. Any instrument of ratification, acceptance, approval or accession deposited after the date on which the present Protocol enters into force shall take effect three months after the date of deposit.

3. After the date on which an amendment to the present Protocol is deemed to have been accepted in accordance with article 16 of the Convention, any instrument of ratification, acceptance, approval or accession deposited shall apply to the present Protocol as amended.

Article VI   Amendments

The procedures set out in article 16 of the Convention in respect of amendments to the articles, an Annex and an appendix to an Annex of the Convention shall apply respectively to amendments to the articles, the Annex and an appendix to the Annex of the present Protocol.

Article VII   Denunciation

1. The present Protocol may be denounced by, any Party to the present Protocol at any time after the expiry of five years from the date on which the Protocol enters into force for that Party.

2. Denunciation shall be effected by the deposited of an instrument of denunciation with the Secretary-General of the Organization.

3.   A denunciation shall take effect 12 months after receipt of the notification by the Secretary-General of the Organization or after the expiry of any other longer period which may be indicated in the notification.

Article VIII   Depository

1.   The present Protocol shall be deposited with the Secretary-General of the Organization (hereinafter referred to as "the Depository").

2.   The Depository shall:

> (a) inform all States which have signed the present Protocol or acceded thereto of:
> > (i) each new signature or deposit of an instrument of ratification, acceptance, approval or accession, together with the date thereof;
> > (ii) the date of entry into force of the present Protocol;
> > (iii) the deposit of any instrument of denunciation of the present Protocol together with the date on which it was received and the date on which the denunciation takes effect;
> > (iv) any decision made in accordance with article 11(1) of the present Protocol.
>
> (b) transmit certified true copies of the present Protocol to all States which have signed the present Protocol or acceded thereto.

3.   As soon as the present Protocol enters into force, a certified true copy thereof shall be transmitted by the Depository to the Secretariat of the United Nations for registration and publication in accordance with Article 102 of the Charter of the United Nations.

Article IX   Languages

The present Protocol is established in a single original in the English, French, Russian and Spanish languages, each text being equally authentic. Official translations in the Arabic, German, Italian and Japanese languages shall be prepared and deposited with the signed original.

IN WITNESS WHEREOF the undersigned being duly authorized by their respective Governments for that purpose have signed the present Protocol.

DONE AT LONDON this seventeenth day of February one thousand nine hundred and seventy-eight.

* * *

Amendments to Annexes not included

UNITED NATIONS CONVENTION ON THE LAW
OF THE NON-NAVIGATIONAL USES OF INTERNATIONAL WATERCOURSES

UNDOC A/51/869
Signed: May 21, 1997
Not Yet Entered Into Force

The Parties to the present Convention,

Conscious of the importance of international watercourses and the non-navigational uses thereof in many regions of the world,

Having in mind Article 13, paragraph 1 (a), of the Charter of the United Nations, which provides that the General Assembly shall initiate studies and make recommendations for the purpose of encouraging the progressive development of international law and its codification,

Considering that successful codification and progressive development of rules of international law regarding non-navigational uses of international watercourses would assist in promoting and implementing the purposes and principles set forth in Articles 1 and 2 of the Charter of the United Nations,

Taking into account the problems affecting many international watercourses resulting from, among other things, increasing demands and pollution,

Expressing the conviction that a framework convention will ensure the utilization, development, conservation, management and protection of international watercourses and the promotion of the optimal and sustainable utilization thereof for present and future generations,

Affirming the importance of international cooperation and good-neighbourliness in this field,

Aware of the special situation and needs of developing countries,

Recalling the principles and recommendations adopted by the United Nations Conference on Environment and Development of 1992 in the Rio Declaration and Agenda 21,

Recalling also the existing bilateral and multilateral agreements regarding the non-navigational uses of international watercourses,

Mindful of the valuable contribution of international organizations, both governmental and non-governmental, to the codification and progressive development of international law in this field,

Appreciative of the work carried out by the International Law Commission on the law of the non-navigational uses of international watercourses,

Bearing in mind United Nations General Assembly resolution 49/52 of 9 December 1994,

Have agreed as follows:

PART I	**INTRODUCTION**
Article 1	**Scope of the present Convention**

1. The present Convention applies to uses of international watercourses and of their waters for purposes other than navigation and to measures of protection, preservation and management related to the uses of those watercourses and their waters.

2. The uses of international watercourses for navigation is not within the scope of the present Convention except insofar as other uses affect navigation or are affected by navigation.

Article 2   Use of Terms

For the purposes of the present Convention:

(a) "Watercourse" means a system of surface waters and groundwaters constituting by virtue of their physical relationship a unitary whole and normally flowing into a common terminus;
(b) "International watercourse" means a watercourse, parts of which are situated in different States;
(c) "Watercourse State" means a State Party to the present Convention in whose territory part of an international watercourse is situated, or a Party that is a regional economic integration organization, in the territory of one or more of whose Member States part of an international watercourse is situated;
(d) "Regional economic integration organization" means an organization constituted by sovereign States of a given region, to which its member States have transferred competence in respect of matters governed by this Convention and which has been duly authorized in accordance with its internal procedures, to sign, ratify, accept, approve or accede to it.

Article 3   Watercourse Agreements

1. In the absence of an agreement to the contrary, nothing in the present Convention shall affect the rights or obligations of a watercourse State arising from agreements in force for it on the date on which it became a party to the present Convention.

2. Notwithstanding the provisions of paragraph 1, parties to agreements referred to in paragraph 1 may, where necessary, consider harmonizing such agreements with the basic principles of the present Convention.

3. Watercourse States may enter into one or more agreements, hereinafter referred to as "watercourse agreements", which apply and adjust the provisions of the present Convention to the characteristics and uses of a particular international watercourse or part thereof.

4. Where a watercourse agreement is concluded between two or more watercourse States, it shall define the waters to which it applies. Such an agreement may be entered into with respect to an entire international watercourse or any part thereof or a particular project, programme or use except insofar as the agreement adversely affects, to a significant extent, the use by one or more other watercourse States of the waters of the watercourse, without their express consent.

5. Where a watercourse State considers that adjustment and application of the provisions of the present Convention is required because of the characteristics and uses of a particular international watercourse, watercourse States shall consult with a view to negotiating in good faith for the purpose of concluding a watercourse agreement or agreements.

6. Where some but not all watercourse States to a particular international watercourse are parties to an agreement, nothing in such agreement shall affect the rights or obligations under the present Convention of watercourse States that are not parties to such an agreement.

Article 4   Parties to watercourse agreements

1. Every watercourse State is entitled to participate in the negotiation of and to become a party to any watercourse agreement that applies to the entire international watercourse, as well as to participate in any relevant consultations.

2. A watercourse State whose use of an international watercourse may be affected to a significant extent by the implementation of a proposed watercourse agreement that applies only to a part of the watercourse or to a particular project, programme or use is entitled to participate in consultations on such an agreement and, where appropriate, in the negotiation thereof in good faith with a view to becoming a party thereto, to the extent that its use is thereby affected.

PART II   GENERAL PRINCIPLES

Article 5   Equitable and reasonable utilization and participation

1. Watercourse States shall in their respective territories utilize an international watercourse in an equitable and reasonable manner. In particular, an international watercourse shall be used and developed by watercourse States with a view to attaining optimal and sustainable utilization thereof and benefits therefrom, taking into account the interests of the watercourse States concerned, consistent with adequate protection of the watercourse.

2. Watercourse States shall participate in the use, development and protection of an international watercourse in an equitable and reasonable manner. Such participation includes both the right to utilize the watercourse and the duty to cooperate in the protection and development thereof, as provided in the present Convention.

Article 6   Factors relevant to equitable and reasonable utilization

1. Utilization of an international watercourse in an equitable and reasonable manner within the meaning of article 5 requires taking into account all relevant factors and circumstances, including:

    (a) Geographic, hydrographic, hydrological, climatic, ecological and other factors of a natural character;
    (b) The social and economic needs of the watercourse States concerned;
    (c) The population dependent on the watercourse in each watercourse State;
    (d) The effects of the use or uses of the watercourses in one watercourse State on other watercourse States;
    (e) Existing and potential uses of the watercourse;
    (f) Conservation, protection, development and economy of use of the water resources of the watercourse and the costs of measures taken to that effect;
    (g) The availability of alternatives, of comparable value, to a particular planned or existing use.

2. In the application of article 5 or paragraph 1 of this article, watercourse States concerned shall, when the need arises, enter into consultations in a spirit of cooperation.

3. The weight to be given to each factor is to be determined by its importance in comparison with that of other relevant factors. In determining what is a reasonable and equitable use, all relevant factors are to be considered together and a conclusion reached on the basis of the whole.

Article 7   Obligation not to cause significant harm

1. Watercourse States shall, in utilizing an international watercourse in their territories, take all appropriate measures to prevent the causing of significant harm to other watercourse States.

2. Where significant harm nevertheless is caused to another watercourse State, the States whose use causes such harm shall, in the absence of agreement to such use, take all appropriate measures, having due regard for the provisions of articles 5 and 6, in consultation with the affected State, to eliminate or mitigate such harm and, where appropriate, to discuss the question of compensation.

Article 8   General obligation to cooperate

1. Watercourse States shall cooperate on the basis of sovereign equality, territorial integrity, mutual benefit and good faith in order to attain optimal utilization and adequate protection of an international watercourse.

2. In determining the manner of such cooperation, watercourse States may consider the establishment of joint mechanisms or commissions, as deemed necessary by them, to facilitate cooperation on relevant measures and procedures in the light of experience gained through cooperation in existing joint mechanisms and commissions in various regions.

Article 9	**Regular exchange of data and information**

1. Pursuant to article 8, watercourse States shall on a regular basis exchange readily available data and information on the condition of the watercourse, in particular that of a hydrological, meteorological, hydrogeological and ecological nature and related to the water quality as well as related forecasts.

2. If a watercourse State is requested by another watercourse State to provide data or information that is not readily available, it shall employ its best efforts to comply with the request but may condition its compliance upon payment by the requesting State of the reasonable costs of collecting and, where appropriate, processing such data or information.

3. Watercourse States shall employ their best efforts to collect and, where appropriate, to process data and information in a manner which facilitates its utilization by the other watercourse States to which it is communicated.

Article 10	**Relationship between different kinds of uses**

1. In the absence of agreement or custom to the contrary, no use of an international watercourse enjoys inherent priority over other uses.

2. In the event of a conflict between uses of an international watercourse, it shall be resolved with reference to articles 5 to 7, with special regard being given to the requirements of vital human needs.

Article 11	**Information concerning planned measures**

Watercourse States shall exchange information and consult each other and, if necessary, negotiate on the possible effects of planned measures on the condition of an international watercourse.

Article 12	**Notification concerning planned measures with possible adverse effects**

Before a watercourse State implements or permits the implementation of planned measures which may have a significant adverse effect upon other watercourse States, it shall provide those States with timely notification thereof. Such notification shall be accompanied by available technical data and information, including the results of any environmental impact assessment, in order to enable the notified States to evaluate the possible effects of the planned measures.

Article 13	**Period for reply to notification**

Unless otherwise agreed:

(a) A watercourse State providing a notification under article 12 shall allow the notified States a period of six months within which to study and evaluate the possible effects of the planned measures and to communicate the findings to it;

(b) This period shall, at the request of a notified State for which the evaluation of the planned measures poses special difficulty, be extended for a period of six months.

Article 14	**Obligations of the notifying State during the period for reply**

During the period referred to in article 13, the notifying State:

(a) Shall cooperate with the notified States by providing them, on request, with any additional data and information that is available and necessary for an accurate evaluation; and

(b) Shall not implement or permit the implementation of the planned measures without the consent of the notified States.

Article 15	Reply to notification

The notified States shall communicate their findings to the notifying State as early as possible within the period applicable pursuant to article 13. If a notified State finds that implementation of the planned measures would be inconsistent with the provisions of articles 5 or 7, it shall attach to its finding a documented explanation setting forth the reasons for the finding.

Article 16	Absence of reply to notification

1. If, within the period applicable pursuant to article 13, the notifying State receives no communication under article 15, it may, subject to its obligations under articles 5 and 7, proceed with the implementation of the planned measures, in accordance with the notification and any other data and information provided to the notified States.

2. Any claim to compensation by a notified State which has failed to reply within the period applicable pursuant to article 13 may be offset by the costs incurred by the notifying State for action undertaken after the expiration of the time for a reply which would not have been undertaken if the notified State had objected within that period.

Article 17	Consultations and negotiations concerning planned measures

1. If a communication is made under article 15 that implementation of the planned measures would be inconsistent with the provisions of articles 5 or 7, the notifying State and the State making the communication shall enter into consultations and, if necessary, negotiations with a view to arriving at an equitable resolution of the situation.

2. The consultations and negotiations shall be conducted on the basis that each State must in good faith pay reasonable regard to the rights and legitimate interests of the other State.

3. During the course of the consultations and negotiations, the notifying State shall, if so requested by the notified State at the time it makes the communication, refrain from implementing or permitting the implementation of the planned measures for a period of six months unless otherwise agreed.

Article 18	Procedures in the absence of notification

1. If a watercourse State has reasonable grounds to believe that another watercourse State is planning measures that may have a significant adverse effect upon it, the former State may request the latter to apply the provisions of article 12. The request shall be accompanied by a documented explanation setting forth its grounds.

2. In the event that the State planning the measures nevertheless finds that it is not under an obligation to provide a notification under article 12, it shall so inform the other State, providing a documented explanation setting forth the reasons for such finding. If this finding does not satisfy the other State, the two States shall, at the request of that other State, promptly enter into consultations and negotiations in the manner indicated in paragraphs 1 and 2 of article 17.

3. During the course of the consultations and negotiations, the State planning the measures shall, if so requested by the other State at the time it requests the initiation of consultations and negotiations, refrain from implementing or permitting the implementation of those measures for a period of six months unless otherwise agreed.

Article 19	Urgent implementation of planned measures

1. In the event that the implementation of planned measures is of the utmost urgency in order to protect public health, public safety or other equally important interests, the State planning the measures may, subject to articles 5 and 7, immediately proceed to implementation, notwithstanding the provisions of article 14 and paragraph 3 of article 17.

2. In such case, a formal declaration of the urgency of the measures shall be communicated without delay to the other watercourse States referred to in article 12 together with the relevant data and information.

3. The State planning the measures shall, at the request of any of the States referred to in paragraph 2, promptly enter into consultations and negotiations with it in the manner indicated in paragraphs 1 and 2 of article 17.

Article 20 Protection and preservation of ecosystems

Watercourse States shall, individually and, where appropriate, jointly, protect and preserve the ecosystems of international watercourses.

Article 21 Prevention, reduction and control of pollution

1. For the purpose of this article, "pollution of an international watercourse" means any detrimental alteration in the composition or quality of the waters of an international watercourse which results directly or indirectly from human conduct.

2. Watercourse States shall, individually and, where appropriate, jointly, prevent, reduce and control the pollution of an international watercourse that may cause significant harm to other watercourse States or to their environment, including harm to human health or safety, to the use of the waters for any beneficial purpose or to the living resources of the watercourse. Watercourse States shall take steps to harmonize their policies in this connection.

3. Watercourse States shall, at the request of any of them, consult with a view to arriving at mutually agreeable measures and methods to prevent, reduce and control pollution of an international watercourse, such as:

(a) Setting joint water quality objectives and criteria;
(b) Establishing techniques and practices to address pollution from point and non-point sources;
(c) Establishing lists of substances the introduction of which into the waters of an international watercourse is to be prohibited, limited, investigated or monitored.

Article 22 Introduction of alien or new species

Watercourse States shall take all measures necessary to prevent the introduction of species, alien or new, into an international watercourse which may have effects detrimental to the ecosystem of the watercourse resulting in significant harm to other watercourse States.

Article 23 Protection and preservation of the marine environment

Watercourse States shall, individually and, where appropriate, in cooperation with other States, take all measures with respect to an international watercourse that are necessary to protect and preserve the marine environment, including estuaries, taking into account generally accepted international rules and standards.

Article 24 Management

1. Watercourse States shall, at the request of any of them, enter into consultations concerning the management of an international watercourse, which may include the establishment of a joint management mechanism.

2. For the purposes of this article, "management" refers, in particular, to:
(a) Planning the sustainable development of an international watercourse and providing for the implementation of any plans adopted; and
(b) Otherwise promoting the rational and optimal utilization, protection and control of the watercourse.

Article 25 Regulation

1. Watercourse States shall cooperate, where appropriate, to respond to needs or opportunities for regulation of the flow of the waters of an international watercourse.

2. Unless otherwise agreed, watercourse States shall participate on an equitable basis in the construction and maintenance or defrayal of the costs of such regulation works as they may have agreed to undertake.

3. For the purposes of this article, "regulation" means the use of hydraulic works or any other continuing measure to alter, vary or otherwise control the flow of the waters of an international watercourse.

Article 26   Installations

1. Watercourse States shall, within their respective territories, employ their best efforts to maintain and protect installations, facilities and other works related to an international watercourse.

2. Watercourse States shall, at the request of any of them which has reasonable grounds to believe that it may suffer significant adverse effects, enter into consultations with regard to:

> (a) The safe operation and maintenance of installations, facilities or other works related to an international watercourse; and
> (b) The protection of installations, facilities or other works from willful or negligent acts or the forces of nature.

Article 27   Prevention and mitigation of harmful conditions

Watercourse States shall, individually and, where appropriate, jointly, take all appropriate measures to prevent or mitigate conditions related to an international watercourse that may be harmful to other watercourse States, whether resulting from natural causes or human conduct, such as flood or ice conditions, water-borne diseases, siltation, erosion, salt-water intrusion, drought or desertification.

Article 28   Emergency situations

1. For the purposes of this article, "emergency" means a situation that causes, or poses an imminent threat of causing, serious harm to watercourse States or other States and that results suddenly from natural causes, such as floods, the breaking up of ice, landslides or earthquakes, or from human conduct, such as industrial accidents.

2. A watercourse State shall, without delay and by the most expeditious means available, notify other potentially affected States and competent international organizations of any emergency originating within its territory.

3. A watercourse State within whose territory an emergency originates shall, in cooperation with potentially affected States and, where appropriate, competent international organizations, immediately take all practicable measures necessitated by the circumstances to prevent, mitigate and eliminate harmful effects of the emergency.

4. When necessary, watercourse States shall jointly develop contingency plans for responding to emergencies, in cooperation, where appropriate, with other potentially affected States and competent international organizations.

BASEL CONVENTION ON THE CONTROL OF TRANSBOUNDARY MOVEMENTS OF HAZARDOUS WASTES AND THEIR DISPOSAL

1673 U.N.T.S. 57
Signed: March 22, 1989
Entered into Force: May 5, 1992
Secretariat Homepage: http://www.basel.int/

PREAMBLE

The Parties to this Convention,

Aware of the risk of damage to human health and the environment caused by hazardous wastes and other wastes and the transboundary movement thereof,

Mindful of the growing threat to human health and the environment posed by the increased generation and complexity, and transboundary movement of hazardous wastes and other wastes,

Mindful also that the most effective way of protecting human health and the environment from the dangers posed by such wastes is the reduction of their generation to a minimum in terms of quantity and/or hazard potential,

Convinced that States should take necessary measures to ensure that the management of hazardous wastes and other wastes including their transboundary movement and disposal is consistent with the protection of human health and the environment whatever the place of their disposal,

Noting that States should ensure that the generator should carry out duties with regard to the transport and disposal of hazardous wastes and other wastes in a manner that is consistent with the protection of the environment, whatever the place of disposal,

Fully recognizing that any State has the sovereign right to ban the entry or disposal of foreign hazardous wastes and other wastes in its territory,

Recognizing also the increasing desire for the prohibition of transboundary movements of hazardous wastes and their disposal in other States, especially developing countries,

Convinced that hazardous wastes and other wastes should, as far as is compatible with environmentally sound and efficient management, be disposed of in the State where they were generated,

Aware also that transboundary movements of such wastes from the State of their generation to any other State should be permitted only when conducted under conditions which do not endanger human health and the environment, and under conditions in conformity with the provisions of this Convention,

Considering that enhanced control of transboundary movement of hazardous wastes and other wastes will act as an incentive for their environmentally sound management and for the reduction of the volume of such transboundary movement,

Convinced that States should take measures for the proper exchange of information on and control of the transboundary movement of hazardous wastes and other wastes from and to those States,

Noting that a number of international and regional agreements have addressed the issue of protection and preservation of the environment with regard to the transit of dangerous goods,

Taking into account the Declaration of the United Nations Conference on the Human Environment (Stockholm, 1972), the Cairo Guidelines and Principles for the Environmentally Sound Management of Hazardous Wastes adopted by the Governing Council of the United Nations Environment Programme (UNEP) by decision 14/30 of 17 June 1987, the Recommendations of the United Nations Committee of Experts on the Transport of Dangerous Goods (formulated in 1957 and updated biennially), relevant recommendations, declarations, instruments and regulations adopted within the United Nations system and the work and studies done within other international and regional organizations,

Mindful of the spirit, principles, aims and functions of the World Charter for Nature adopted by the General Assembly of the United Nations at its thirty-seventh session (1982) as the rule of ethics in respect of the protection of the human environment and the conservation of natural resources,

Affirming that States are responsible for the fulfilment of their international obligations concerning the protection of human health and protection and preservation of the environment, and are liable in accordance with international law,

Recognizing that in the case of a material breach of the provisions of this Convention or any protocol thereto the relevant international law of treaties shall apply,

Aware of the need to continue the development and implementation of environmentally sound low-waste technologies, recycling options, good house-keeping and management systems with a view to reducing to a minimum the generation of hazardous wastes and other wastes,

Aware also of the growing international concern about the need for stringent control of transboundary movement of hazardous wastes and other wastes, and of the need as far as possible to reduce such movement to a minimum,

Concerned about the problem of illegal transboundary traffic in hazardous wastes and other wastes,

Taking into account also the limited capabilities of the developing countries to manage hazardous wastes and other wastes,

Recognizing the need to promote the transfer of technology for the sound management of hazardous wastes and other wastes produced locally, particularly to the developing countries in accordance with the spirit of the Cairo guidelines and decision 14/16 of the Governing Council of UNEP on Promotion of the transfer of environmental protection technology,

Recognizing also that hazardous wastes and other wastes should be transported in accordance with relevant international conventions and recommendations

Convinced also that the transboundary movement of hazardous wastes and other wastes should be permitted only when the transport and the ultimate disposal of such wastes is environmentally sound, and

Determined to protect, by strict control, human health and the environment against the adverse effects which may result from the generation and management of hazardous wastes and other wastes,

HAVE AGREED AS FOLLOWS:

Article 1   Scope of the Convention

1. The following wastes that are subject to transboundary movement shall be "hazardous wastes" for the purposes of this Convention:
    (a) Wastes that belong to any category contained in Annex I, unless they do not possess any of the characteristics contained in Annex III; and
    (b) Wastes that are not covered under paragraph (a) but are defined as, or are considered to be, hazardous wastes by the domestic legislation of the Party of export, import or transit.

2. Wastes that belong to any category contained in Annex II that are subject to transboundary movement shall be "other wastes" for the purposes of this Convention.

3. Wastes which, as a result of being radioactive, are subject to other international control systems, including international instruments, applying specifically to radioactive materials, are excluded from the scope of this Convention.

4. Wastes which derive from the normal operations of a ship, the discharge of which is covered by another international instrument, are excluded from the scope of this Convention.

Article 2   Definitions

For the purposes of this Convention:

1. "Wastes" are substances or objects which are disposed of or are intended to be disposed of or are required to be disposed of by the provisions of national law;

2. "Management" means the collection, transport and disposal of hazardous wastes or other wastes, including after-care of disposal sites;

3. "Transboundary movement" means any movement of hazardous wastes or other wastes from an area under the national jurisdiction of one State to or through an area under the national jurisdiction of another State or to or through an area not under the national jurisdiction of any State, provided at least two States are involved in the movement;

4. "Disposal" means any operation specified in Annex IV to this Convention;

5. "Approved site or facility" means a site or facility for the disposal of hazardous wastes or other wastes which is authorized or permitted to operate for this purpose by a relevant authority of the State where the site or facility is located;

6. "Competent authority" means one governmental authority designated by a Party to be responsible, within such geographical areas as the Party may think tit, for receiving the notification of a transboundary movement of hazardous wastes or other wastes, and any information related to it, and for responding to such a notification, as provided in Article 6;

7. "Focal point" means the entity of a Party referred to in Article 5 responsible for receiving and submitting information as provided for in Articles 13 and 16;

8. "Environmentally sound management of hazardous wastes or other wastes" means taking all practicable steps to ensure that hazardous wastes or other wastes are managed in a manner which will protect human health and the environment against the adverse effects which may result from such wastes;

9. "Area under the national jurisdiction of a State" means any land, marine area or airspace within which a State exercises administrative and regulatory responsibility in accordance with international law in regard to the protection of human health or the environment;

10. "State of export" means a Party from which a transboundary movement of hazardous wastes or other wastes is planned to be initiated or is initiated;

11. "State of import" means a Party to which a transboundary movement of hazardous wastes or other wastes is planned or takes place for the purpose of disposal therein or for the purpose of loading prior to disposal in an area not under the national jurisdiction of any State;

12. "State of transit" means any State, other than the State of export or import, through which a movement of hazardous wastes or other wastes is planned or takes place;

13. "States concerned" means Parties which are States of export or import, or transit States, whether or not Parties;

14. "Person" means any natural or legal person;

15. "Exporter" means any person under the jurisdiction of the State of export who arranges for hazardous wastes or other wastes to be exported;

16. "Importer" means any person under the jurisdiction of the State of import who arranges for hazardous wastes or other wastes to be imported;

17. "Carrier" means any person who carries out the transport of hazardous wastes or other wastes;

18. "Generator" means any person whose activity produces hazardous wastes or other wastes or, if that person is not known, the person who is in possession and/or control of those wastes;

19. "Disposer" means any person to whom hazardous wastes or other wastes are shipped and who carries out the disposal of such wastes;

20. "Political and/or economic integration organization" means an organization constituted by sovereign States to which its member States have transferred competence in respect of matters governed by this Convention and which has been duly authorized, in accordance with its internal procedures, to sign, ratify, accept, approve, formally confirm or accede to it;

21. "Illegal traffic" means any transboundary movement of hazardous wastes or other wastes as specified in Article 9.

Article 3   National Definitions of Hazardous Wastes

1. Each Party shall, within six months of becoming a Party to this Convention, inform the Secretariat of the convention of the wastes, other than those listed in Annexes I and II, considered or defined as hazardous under its national legislation and of any requirements concerning transboundary movement procedures applicable to such wastes.

2. Each Party shall subsequently inform the Secretariat of any significant changes to the information it has provided pursuant to paragraph 1.

3. The Secretariat shall forthwith inform all Parties of the information it has received pursuant to paragraphs 1 and 2.

4. Parties shall be responsible for making the information transmitted to them by the Secretariat under paragraph 3 available to their exporters.

Article 4   General Obligations

1.   (a) Parties exercising their right to prohibit the import of hazardous wastes or other wastes for disposal shall inform the other Parties of their decision pursuant to Article 13.
          (b) Parties shall prohibit or shall not permit the export of hazardous wastes and other wastes to the Parties which have prohibited the import of such wastes, when notified pursuant to subparagraph (a) above.
          (c) Parties shall prohibit or shall not permit the export of hazardous wastes and other wastes if the State of import does not consent in writing to the specific import, in the case where that State of import has not prohibited the import of such wastes.

2. Each Party shall take the appropriate measures to:

          (a) Ensure that the generation of hazardous wastes and other wastes within it is reduced to a minimum, taking into account social, technological and economic aspects;
          (b) Ensure the availability of adequate disposal facilities, for the environmentally sound management of hazardous wastes and other wastes, that shall be located, to the extent possible, within it, whatever the place of their disposal;

(c) Ensure that persons involved in the management of hazardous wastes or other wastes within it take such steps as are necessary to prevent pollution due to hazardous wastes and other wastes arising from such management and, if such pollution occurs, to minimize the consequences thereof for human health and the environment;

(d) Ensure that the transboundary movement of hazardous wastes and other wastes is reduced to the minimum consistent with the environmentally sound and efficient management of such wastes, and is conducted in a manner which will protect human health and the environment against the adverse effects which may result from such movement;

(e) Not allow the export of hazardous wastes or other wastes to a State or group of States belonging to an economic and/or political integration organization that are Parties, particularly developing countries, which have prohibited by their legislation all imports, or if it has reason to believe that the wastes in question will not be managed in an environmentally sound manner, according to criteria to be decided on by the Parties at their first meeting.

(f) Require that information about a proposed transboundary movement of hazardous wastes and other wastes be provided to the States concerned, according to Annex V(A), to state clearly the effects of the proposed movement on human health and the environment;

(g) Prevent the import of hazardous wastes and other wastes if it has reason to believe that the wastes in question will not be managed in an environmentally sound manner;

(h) Co-operate in activities with other Parties and interested organizations, directly and through the Secretariat, including the dissemination of information on the transboundary movement of hazardous wastes and other wastes, in order to improve the environmentally sound management of such wastes and to achieve the prevention of illegal traffic;

3. The Parties consider that illegal traffic in hazardous wastes or other wastes is criminal.

4. Each Party shall take appropriate legal, administrative and other measures to implement and enforce the provisions of this Convention, including measures to prevent and punish conduct in contravention of the Convention.

5. A Party shall not permit hazardous wastes or other wastes to be exported to a non-Party or to be imported from a non-Party.

6. The Parties agree not to allow the export of hazardous wastes or other wastes for disposal within the area south of 60 degrees South latitude, whether or not such wastes are subject to transboundary movement.

7. Furthermore, each Party shall:

(a) Prohibit all persons under its national jurisdiction from transporting or disposing of hazardous wastes or other wastes unless such persons are authorized or allowed to perform such types of operations;

(b) Require that hazardous wastes and other wastes that are to be the subject of a transboundary movement be packaged, labeled, and transported in conformity with generally accepted and recognized international rules and standards in the field of packaging, labeling, and transport, and that due account is taken of relevant internationally recognized practices;

(c) Require that hazardous wastes and other wastes be accompanied by a movement document from the point at which a transboundary movement commences to the point of disposal.

8. Each Party shall require that hazardous wastes or other wastes, to be exported, are managed in an environmentally sound manner in the State of import or elsewhere. Technical guidelines for the environmentally sound management of wastes subject to this Convention shall be decided by the Parties at their first meeting.

9. Parties shall take the appropriate measures to ensure that the transboundary movement of hazardous wastes and other wastes only be allowed if:

(a) The State of export does not have the technical capacity and the necessary facilities, capacity or suitable disposal sites in order to dispose of the wastes in question in an environmentally sound and efficient manner; or

(b) The wastes in question are required as a raw material for recycling or recovery industries in the State of import; or

(c) The transboundary movement in question is in accordance with other criteria to be decided by the Parties, provided those criteria do not differ from the objectives of this Convention.

10. The obligation under this Convention of States in which hazardous wastes and other wastes are generated to require that those wastes are managed in an environmentally sound manner may not under any circumstances be transferred to the States of import or transit.

11. Nothing in this Convention shall prevent a Party from imposing additional requirements that are consistent with the provisions of this Convention, and are in accordance with the rules of international law, in order better to protect human health and the environment.

12. Nothing in this Convention shall affect in any way the sovereignty of States over their territorial sea established in accordance with international law, and the sovereign rights and the jurisdiction which States have in their exclusive economic zones and their continental shelves in accordance with international law, and the exercise by ships and aircraft of all States of navigational rights and freedoms as provided for in international law and as reflected in relevant international instruments.

13. Parties shall undertake to review periodically the possibilities for the reduction of the amount and/or the pollution potential of hazardous wastes and other wastes which are exported to other States, in particular to developing countries.

Article 5   Designation of Competent Authorities and Focal Point

To facilitate the implementation of this Convention, the Parties shall:

1. Designate or establish one or more competent authorities and one focal point. One competent authority shall be designated to receive the notification in case of a State of transit.

2. Inform the Secretariat, within three months of the date of the entry into force of this Convention for them, which agencies they have designated as their focal point and their competent authorities.

3. Inform the Secretariat, within one month of the date of decision, of any changes regarding the designation made by them under paragraph 2 above.

Article 6   Transboundary Movement between Parties

1. The State of export shall notify, or shall require the generator or exporter to notify, in writing, through the channel of the competent authority of the State of export, the competent authority of the States concerned of any proposed transboundary movement of hazardous wastes or other wastes. Such notification shall contain the declarations and information specified in Annex V(A), written in a language acceptable to the State of import. Only one notification needs to be sent to each State concerned.

2. The State of import shall respond to the notifier in writing, consenting to the movement with or without conditions, denying permission for the movement, or requesting additional information. A copy of the final response of the State of import shall be sent to the competent authorities of the States concerned which are Parties.

3. The State of export shall not allow the generator or exporter to commence the transboundary movement until it has received written confirmation that:
      (a) The notifier has received the written consent of the State of import; and
      (b) The notifier has received from the State of import confirmation of the existence of a contract between the exporter and the disposer specifying environmentally sound management of the wastes in question.

4. Each State of transit which is a Party shall promptly acknowledge to the notifier receipt of the notification. It may subsequently respond to the notifier in writing, within 60 days, consenting to the movement with or without conditions, denying permission for the movement, or requesting additional information. The State of export shall not allow the transboundary movement to commence until it has received the written consent of the State of transit. However, if at any time a Party decides not to require prior written consent, either generally or under specific conditions, for transit transboundary movements of hazardous wastes or other wastes, or modifies its requirements in

this respect, it shall forthwith inform the other Parties of its decision pursuant to Article 13. In this latter case, if no response is received by the State of export within 60 days of the receipt of a given notification by the State of transit, the State of export may allow the export to proceed through the State of transit.

5. In the case of a transboundary movement of wastes where the wastes are legally defined as or considered to be hazardous wastes only:
> (a) By the State of export, the requirements of paragraph 9 of this Article that apply to the importer or disposer and the State of import shall apply mutatis mutandis to the exporter and State of export, respectively;
> (b) By the State of import, or by the States of import and transit which are Parties, the requirements of paragraphs 1, 3, 4 and 6 of this Article that apply to the exporter and State of export shall apply mutatis mutandis to the importer or disposer and State of import, respectively; or
> (c) By any State of transit which is a Party, the provisions of paragraph 4 shall apply to such State.

6. The State of export may, subject to the written consent of the States concerned, allow the generator or the exporter to use a general notification where hazardous wastes or other wastes having the same physical and chemical characteristics are shipped regularly to the same disposer via the same customs office of exit of the State of export via the same customs office of entry of the State of import, and, in the case of transit, via the same customs office of entry and exit of the State or States of transit.

7. The States concerned may make their written consent to the use of the general notification referred to in paragraph 6 subject to the supply of certain information, such as the exact quantities or periodical lists of hazardous wastes or other wastes to be shipped.

8. The general notification and written consent referred to in paragraphs 6 and 7 may cover multiple shipments of hazardous wastes or other wastes during a maximum period of 12 months.

9. The Parties shall require that each person who takes charge of a transboundary movement of hazardous wastes or other wastes sign the movement document either upon delivery or receipt of the wastes in question. They shall also require that the disposer inform both the exporter and the competent authority of the State of export of receipt by the disposer of the wastes in question and, in due course, of the completion of disposal as specified in the notification. If no such information is received within the State of export, the competent authority of the State of export or the exporter shall so notify the State of import.

10. The notification and response required by this Article shall be transmitted to the competent authority of the Parties concerned or to such governmental authority as may be appropriate in the case of non-Parties.

11. Any transboundary movement of hazardous wastes or other wastes shall be covered by insurance, bond or other guarantee as may be required by the State of import or any State of transit which is a Party.

Article 7   Transboundary Movement from a Party through States which are not Parties

Paragraph 2 of Article 6 of the Convention shall apply mutatis mutandis to transboundary movement of hazardous wastes or other wastes from a Party through a State or States which are not Parties.

Article 8   Duty to Re-import

When a transboundary movement of hazardous wastes or other wastes to which the consent of the States concerned has been given, subject to the provisions of this Convention, cannot be completed in accordance with the terms of the contract, the State of export shall ensure that the wastes in question are taken back into the State of export, by the exporter, if alternative arrangements cannot be made for their disposal in an environmentally sound manner, within 90 days from the time that the importing State informed the State of export and the Secretariat, or such other period of time as the States concerned agree. To this end, the State of export and any Party of transit shall not oppose, hinder or prevent the return of those wastes to the State of export.

Article 9　　　　Illegal Traffic

1. For the purpose of this Convention, any transboundary movement of hazardous wastes or other wastes:
    (a) without notification pursuant to the provisions of this Convention to all States concerned; or
    (b) without the consent pursuant to the provisions of this Convention of a State concerned; or
    (c) with consent obtained from States concerned through falsification, misrepresentation or fraud; or
    (d) that does not conform in a material way with the documents; or
    (e) that results in deliberate disposal (e.g. dumping) of hazardous wastes or other wastes in contravention of this Convention and of general principles of international law, shall be deemed to be illegal traffic.

2. In case of a transboundary movement of hazardous wastes or other wastes deemed to be illegal traffic as the result of conduct on the part of the exporter or generator, the State of export shall ensure that the wastes in question are:
    (a) taken back by the exporter or the generator or, if necessary, by itself into the State of export, or, if impracticable,
    (b) are otherwise disposed of in accordance with the provisions of this Convention, within 30 days from the time the State of export has been informed about the illegal traffic or such other period of time as States concerned may agree. To this end the Parties concerned shall not oppose, hinder or prevent the return of those wastes to the State of export.

3. In the case of a transboundary movement of hazardous wastes or other wastes deemed to be illegal traffic as the result of conduct on the part of the importer or disposer, the State of import shall ensure that the wastes in question are disposed of in an environmentally sound manner by the importer or disposer or, if necessary, by itself within 30 days from the time the illegal traffic has come to the attention of the State of import or such other period of time as the States concerned may agree. To this end, the Parties concerned shall co-operate, as necessary, in the disposal of the wastes in an environmentally sound manner.

4. In cases where the responsibility for the illegal traffic cannot be assigned either to the exporter or generator or to the importer or disposer, the Parties concerned or other Parties, as appropriate, shall ensure, through co-operation, that the wastes in question are disposed of as soon as possible in an environmentally sound manner either in the State of export or the State of import or elsewhere as appropriate.

5. Each Party shall introduce appropriate national/domestic legislation to prevent and punish illegal traffic. The Parties shall co-operate with a view to achieving the objects of this Article.

Article 10　　　　International Co-operation

1. The Parties shall co-operate with each other in order to improve and achieve environmentally sound management of hazardous wastes and other wastes.

2. To this end, the Parties shall:
    (a) Upon request, make available information, whether on a bilateral or multilateral basis, with a view to promoting the environmentally sound management of hazardous wastes and other wastes, including harmonization of technical standards and practices for the adequate management of hazardous wastes and other wastes;
    (b) Co-operate in monitoring the effects of the management of hazardous wastes on human health and the environment;
    (c) Co-operate, subject to their national laws, regulations and policies, in the development and implementation of new environmentally sound low-waste technologies and the improvement of existing technologies with a view to eliminating, as far as practicable, the generation of hazardous wastes and other wastes and achieving more effective and efficient methods of ensuring their management in an environmentally sound manner, including the study of the economic, social and environmental effects of the adoption of such new or improved technologies;
    (d) Co-operate actively, subject to their national laws, regulations and policies, in the transfer of technology and management systems related to the environmentally sound management of hazardous wastes and other wastes. They shall also co-operate in developing the technical capacity among Parties, especially those which may need and request technical assistance in this field;
    (e) Co-operate in developing appropriate technical guidelines and/or codes of practice.

3. The Parties shall employ appropriate means to cooperate in order to assist developing countries in the implementation of subparagraphs a, b, c, and d of paragraph 2 of Article 4.

4. Taking into account the needs of developing countries, co-operation between Parties and the competent international organizations is encouraged to promote, inter alia, public awareness, the development of sound management of hazardous wastes and other wastes and the adoption of new low-waste technologies.

| **Article 11** | **Bilateral, Multilateral and Regional Agreements** |

1. Notwithstanding the provisions of Article 4 paragraph 5, Parties may enter into bilateral, multilateral, or regional agreements or arrangements regarding transboundary movement of hazardous wastes or other wastes with Parties or non-Parties provided that such agreements or arrangements do not derogate from the environmentally sound management of hazardous wastes and other wastes as required by this Convention. These agreements or arrangements shall stipulate provisions which are not less environmentally sound than those provided for by this Convention in particular taking into account the interests of developing countries.

2. Parties shall notify the Secretariat of any bilateral, multilateral or regional agreements or arrangements referred to in paragraph 1 and those which they have entered into prior to the entry into force of this Convention for them, for the purpose of controlling transboundary movements of hazardous wastes and other wastes which take place entirely among the Parties to such agreements. The provisions of this Convention shall not affect transboundary movements which take place pursuant to such agreements provided that such agreements are compatible with the environmentally sound management of hazardous wastes and other wastes as required by this Convention.

| **Article 12** | **Consultations on Liability** |

The Parties shall co-operate with a view to adopting, as soon as practicable, a protocol setting out appropriate rules and procedures in the field of liability and compensation for damage resulting from the transboundary movement and disposal of hazardous wastes and other wastes.

| **Article 13** | **Transmission of Information** |

1. The Parties shall, whenever it comes to their knowledge, ensure that, in the case of an accident occurring during the transboundary movement of hazardous wastes or other wastes or their disposal, which are likely to present risks to human health and the environment in other States, those states are immediately informed.

2. The Parties shall inform each other, through the Secretariat, of:
  (a) Changes regarding the designation of competent authorities and/or focal points, pursuant to Article 5;
  (b) Changes in their national definition of hazardous wastes, pursuant to Article 3; and, as soon as possible,
  (c) Decisions made by them not to consent totally or partially to the import of hazardous wastes or other wastes for disposal within the area under their national jurisdiction;
  (d) Decisions taken by them to limit or ban the export of hazardous wastes or other wastes;
  (e) Any other information required pursuant to paragraph 4 of this Article.

3. The Parties, consistent with national laws and regulations, shall transmit, through the Secretariat, to the Conference of the Parties established under Article 15, before the end of each calendar year, a report on the previous calendar year, containing the following information:
  (a) Competent authorities and focal points that have been designated by them pursuant to Article 5;
  (b) Information regarding transboundary movements of hazardous wastes or other wastes in which they have been involved, including:
    (i) The amount of hazardous wastes and other wastes exported, their category, characteristics, destination, any transit country and disposal method as stated on the response to notification;
    (ii) The amount of hazardous wastes and other wastes imported, their category, characteristics, origin, and disposal methods;
    (iii) Disposals which did not proceed as intended;
    (iv) Efforts to achieve a reduction of the amount of hazardous wastes or other wastes subject to transboundary movement;

(c) Information on the measures adopted by them in implementation of this Convention;

(d) Information on available qualified statistics which have been compiled by them on the effects on human health and the environment of the generation, transportation and disposal of hazardous wastes or other wastes;

(e) Information concerning bilateral, multilateral and regional agreements and arrangements entered into pursuant to Article 11 of this Convention;

(f) Information on accidents occurring during the transboundary movement and disposal of hazardous wastes and other wastes and on the measures undertaken to deal with them;

(g) Information on disposal options operated within the area of their national jurisdiction;

(h) Information on measures undertaken for development of technologies for the reduction and/or elimination of production of hazardous wastes and other wastes; and

(i) Such other matters as the Conference of the Parties shall deem relevant.

4. The Parties, consistent with national laws and regulations, shall ensure that copies of each notification concerning any given transboundary movement of hazardous wastes or other wastes, and the response to it, are sent to the Secretariat when a Party considers that its environment may be affected by that transboundary movement has requested that this should be done.

Article 14   Financial Aspects

1. The Parties agree that, according to the specific needs of different regions and subregions, regional or sub-regional centres for training and technology transfers regarding the management of hazardous wastes and other wastes and the minimization of their generation should be established. The Parties shall decide on the establishment of appropriate funding mechanisms of a voluntary nature.

2. The Parties shall consider the establishment of an evolving fund to assist on an interim basis in case of emergency situations to minimize damage from accidents arising from transboundary movements of hazardous wastes and other wastes or during the disposal of those wastes.

Article 15   Conference of the Parties

1. A Conference of the Parties is hereby established. The first meeting of the Conference of the Parties shall be convened by the Executive Director of UNEP not later than one year after the entry into force of this Convention. Thereafter, ordinary meetings of the Conference of the Parties shall be held at regular intervals to be determined by the Conference at its first meeting.

2. Extraordinary meetings of the Conference of the Parties shall be held at such other times as may be deemed necessary by the Conference, or at the written request of any Party, provided that, within six months of the request being communicated to them by the Secretariat, it is supported by at least one third of the Parties.

3. The Conference of the Parties shall by consensus agree upon and adopt rules of procedure for itself and for any subsidiary body it may establish, as well as financial rules to determine in particular the financial participation of the Parties under this Convention.

4. The Parties at their first meeting shall consider any additional measures needed to assist them in fulfilling their responsibilities with respect to the protection and the preservation of the marine environment in the context of this Convention.

5. The Conference of the Parties shall keep under continuous review an devaluation the effective implementation of this Convention, and, in addition, shall:

(a) Promote the harmonization of appropriate policies, strategies and measures for minimizing harm to human health and the environment by hazardous wastes and other wastes;

(b) Consider and adopt, as required, amendments to this Convention and its annexes, taking into consideration, inter alia, available scientific, technical, economic and environmental information;

(c) Consider and undertake any additional action that may be required for the achievement of the purposes of this Convention in the light of experience gained in its operation and in the operation of the agreements and arrangements envisaged in Article 11;

(d) Consider and adopt protocols as required; and

(e) Establish such subsidiary bodies as are deemed necessary for the implementation of this Convention.

6. The United Nations, its specialized agencies, as well as any State not party to this Convention, may be represented as observers at meetings of the Conference of the Parties. Any other body or agency, whether national or international, governmental or non-governmental, qualified in fields relating to hazardous wastes or other wastes which has informed the Secretariat of its wish to be represented as an observer at a meeting of the Conference of the Parties, may be admitted unless at least one third of the Parties present object. The admission and participation of observers shall be subject to the rules of procedure adopted by the conference of the Parties.

7. The Conference of the Parties shall undertake three years after the entry into force of this Convention, and at least every six years thereafter, an evaluation of its effectiveness and, if deemed necessary, to consider the adoption of a complete or partial ban of transboundary movements of hazardous wastes and other wastes in light of the latest scientific, environmental, technical and economic information.

Article 16   Secretariat

1. The functions of the Secretariat shall be:
    (a) To arrange for and service meetings provided for in Articles 15 and 17;
    (b) To prepare and transmit reports based upon information received in accordance with Articles 3, 4, 6, 11 and 13 as well as upon information derived from meetings of subsidiary bodies established under Article 15 as well as upon, as appropriate, information provided by relevant intergovernmental and non-governmental entities;
    (c) To prepare reports on its activities carried out in implementation of its functions under this Convention and present them to the Conference of the Parties;
    (d) To ensure the necessary coordination with relevant international bodies, and in particular to enter into such administrative and contractual arrangements as may be required for the effective discharge of its functions;
    (e) To communicate with focal points and competent authorities established by the Parties in accordance with Article 5 of this Convention;
    (f) To compile information concerning authorized national sites and facilities of Parties available for the disposal of their hazardous wastes and other wastes and to circulate this information among Parties;
    (g) To receive and convey information from and to Parties on;
        -- sources of technical assistance and training;
        -- available technical and scientific know-how;
        -- sources of advice and expertise; and
        -- availability of resources with a view to assisting them, upon request, in such areas as:
        -- the handling of the notification system of this Convention;
        -- the management of hazardous wastes and other wastes;
        -- environmentally sound technologies relating to hazardous wastes and
           other wastes, such as low- and non-waste technology;
        -- the assessment of disposal capabilities and sites;
        -- the monitoring of hazardous wastes and other wastes; and
        -- emergency responses;
    (h) To provide Parties, upon request, with information on consultants or consulting firms having the necessary technical competence in the field, which can assist them to examine a notification for a transboundary movement, the concurrence of a shipment of hazardous wastes or other wastes with the relevant notification, and/or the fact that the proposed disposal facilities for hazardous wastes or other wastes are environmentally sound, when they have reason to believe that the wastes in question will not be managed in an environmentally sound manner. Any such examination would not be at the expense of the Secretariat;
    (i) To assist Parties upon request in their identification of cases of illegal traffic and to circulate immediately to the Parties concerned any information it has received regarding illegal traffic;
    (j) To co-operate with Parties and with relevant and competent international organizations and agencies in the provision of experts and equipment for the purpose of rapid assistance to States in the event of an emergency situation; and
    (k) To perform such other functions relevant to the purposes of this Convention as may be determined by the Conference of the Parties.

2. The secretariat functions will be carried out on an interim basis by UNEP until the completion of the first meeting of the Conference of the Parties held pursuant to Article 15.

3. At its first meeting, the Conference of the Parties shall designate the Secretariat from among those existing competent intergovernmental organizations which have signified their willingness to carry out the secretariat functions under this Convention. At this meeting, the Conference of the Parties shall also evaluate the implementation by the interim Secretariat of the functions assigned to it, in particular under paragraph 1 above, and decide upon the structures appropriate for those functions.

Article 17   Amendment of the Convention

1. Any Party may propose amendments to this Convention and any Party to a protocol may propose amendments to that protocol. Such amendments shall take due account, inter alia, of relevant scientific and technical considerations.

2. Amendments to this Convention shall be adopted at a meeting of the Conference of the Parties. Amendments to any protocol shall be adopted at a meeting of the Parties to the protocol in question. The text of any proposed amendment to this Convention or to any protocol, except as may otherwise be provided in such protocol, shall be communicated to the Parties by the Secretariat at least six months before the meeting at which it is proposed for adoption. The Secretariat shall also communicate proposed amendments to the Signatories to this Convention for information.

3. The Parties shall make every effort to reach agreement on any proposed amendment to this Convention by consensus. If all efforts at consensus have been exhausted, and no agreement reached, the amendment shall as a last resort be adopted by a three-fourths majority vote of the Parties present and voting at the meeting, and shall be submitted by the Depositary to all Parties for ratification, approval, formal confirmation or acceptance.

4. The procedure mentioned in paragraph 3 above shall apply to amendments to any protocol, except that a two-thirds majority of the Parties to that protocol present and voting at the meeting shall suffice for their adoption.

5. Instruments of ratification, approval, formal confirmation or acceptance of amendments shall be deposited with the Depositary. Amendments adopted in accordance with paragraphs 3 or 4 above shall enter into force between Parties having accepted them on the ninetieth day after the receipt by the Depositary of their instrument of ratification, approval, formal confirmation or acceptance by at least three-fourths of the Parties who accepted the amendments to the protocol concerned, except as may otherwise be provided in such protocol. The amendments shall enter into force for any other Party on the ninetieth day after that Party deposits its instrument of ratification, approval, formal confirmation or acceptance of the amendments.

6. For the purpose of this Article, "Parties present and voting" means Parties present and casting an affirmative or negative vote.

Article 18   Adoption and Amendment of Annexes

1. The annexes to this Convention or to any protocol shall form an integral part of this Convention or of such protocol, as the case may be and, unless expressly provided otherwise, a reference to this Convention or its protocols constitutes at the same time a reference to any annexes thereto. Such annexes shall be restricted to scientific, technical and administrative matters.

2. Except as may be otherwise provided in any protocol with respect to its annexes, the following procedure shall apply to the proposal, adoption and entry into force of additional annexes to this Convention or of annexes to a protocol:
          (a) Annexes to this Convention and its protocols shall be proposed and adopted according to the procedure laid down in Article 17, paragraphs 2, 3 and 4;
          (b) Any Party that is unable to accept an additional annex to this Convention or an annex to any protocol to which it is party shall so notify the Depositary, in writing, within six months from the date of the communication of the adoption by the Depositary. The Depositary shall without delay notify all Parties of any such notification received. A Party may at any time substitute an acceptance for a previous declaration of objection and the annexes shall thereupon enter into force for that Party;

(c) On the expiry of six months from the date of the circulation of the communication by the Depositary, the annex shall become effective for all Parties to this Convention or to any protocol concerned, which have not submitted a notification in accordance with the provision of subparagraph(b) above.

3. The proposal, adoption and entry into force of amendments to annexes to this Convention or to any protocol shall be subject to the same procedures for the proposal, adoption and entry into force of annexes to the Convention or annexes to a protocol. Annexes and amendments thereto shall take due account, inter alia, of relevant scientific and technical considerations.

4. If an additional annex or an amendment to an annex involves an amendment to this Convention or to any protocol, the additional annex or amended annex shall not enter into force until such time as the amendment to this Convention or to the protocol enters into force.

Article 19   Verification

Any Party which has reason to believe that another Party is acting or has acted in breach of its obligations under this Convention may inform the Secretariat thereof, and in such an event, shall simultaneously and immediately inform, directly or through the Secretariat, the Party against whom the allegations are made. All relevant information should be submitted by the Secretariat to the Parties.

Article 20   Settlement of Disputes

1. In case of a dispute between Parties as to the interpretation or application of, or compliance with, this Convention or any protocol thereto, they shall seek a settlement of the dispute through negotiation or any other peaceful means of their own choice.

2. If the Parties concerned cannot settle their dispute through the means mentioned in the preceding paragraph, the dispute, if the parties to the dispute agree, shall be submitted to the International Court of Justice or to arbitration under the conditions set out in Annex VI on Arbitration. However, failure to reach common agreement on submission of the dispute to the International Court of Justice or to arbitration shall not absolve the Parties from the responsibility of continuing to seek to resolve it by the means referred to in paragraph 1.

3. When ratifying, accepting, approving, formally confirming or acceding to this Convention, or at any time thereafter, a State or political and/or economic integration organization may declare that it recognizes as compulsory ipso facto and without special agreement, in relation to any Party accepting the same obligation:
    (a) submission of the dispute to the International Court of Justice; and/or
    (b) arbitration in accordance with the procedures set out in Annex VI.

Such declaration shall be notified in writing to the Secretariat which shall communicate it to the Parties.

Article 21   Signature

This Convention shall be open for signature by States, by Namibia represented by the United Nations Council for Namibia and by political and/or economic integration organizations, in Basel on 22 March 1989, at the Federal Department of Foreign Affairs of Switzerland in Berne from 23 March 1989 to 30 June 1989, and at United Nations Headquarters in New York from 1 July 1989 to 22 March 1990.

Article 22   Ratification, Acceptance, Formal Confirmation or Approval

1. This Convention shall be subject to ratification, acceptance or approval by States and by Namibia, represented by the United Nations Council for Namibia and to formal confirmation or approval by political and/or economic integration organizations. Instruments of ratification, acceptance, formal confirmation, or approval shall be deposited with the Depositary.

2. Any organization referred to in paragraph 1 above which becomes a Party to this Convention without any of its member States being a Party shall be bound by all the obligations under the Convention. In the case of such

organizations, one or more of whose member States is a Party to the Convention, the organization and its member States shall decide on the irrespective responsibilities for the performance of their obligations under the Convention. In such cases, the organization and the member States shall not be entitled to exercise rights under the Convention concurrently.

3. In their instruments of formal confirmation or approval, the organizations referred to in paragraph 1 above shall declare the extent of their competence with respect to the matters governed by the Convention. These organizations shall also inform the Depositary, who will inform the Parties of any substantial modification in the extent of their competence.

Article 23   Accession

1. This Convention shall be open for accession by States, by Namibia, represented by the United Nations Council for Namibia, and by political and/or economic integration organizations from the day after the date on which the Convention is closed for signature. The instruments of accession shall be deposited with the Depositary.

2. In their instruments of accession, the organizations referred to in paragraph 1 above shall declare the extent of their competence with respect to the matters governed by the Convention. These organizations shall also inform the Depositary of any substantial modification in the extent of their competence.

3. The provisions of Article 22 paragraph 2, shall apply to political and/or economic integration organizations which accede to this Convention.

Article 24   Right to Vote

1. Except as provided for in paragraph 2 below, each Contracting Party to this Convention shall have one vote.

2. Political and/or economic integration organizations, in matters within their competence, in accordance with Article 22, paragraph 3, and Article 23, paragraph 2, shall exercise their right to vote with a number of votes equal to the number of their member States which are Parties to the Convention or the relevant protocol. Such organizations shall not exercise their right to vote if their member States exercise theirs, and vice versa.

Article 25   Entry into Force

1. This Convention shall enter into force on the ninetieth day after the date of deposit of the twentieth instrument of ratification, acceptance, formal confirmation, approval or accession.

2. For each State or political and/or economic integration organization which ratifies, accepts, approves or formally confirms this Convention or accedes thereto after the date of the deposit of the twentieth instrument of ratification, acceptance, approval, formal confirmation or accession, it shall enter into force on the ninetieth day after the date of deposit by such State or political and/or economic integration organization of its instrument of ratification, acceptance, approval, formal confirmation or accession.

3. For the purposes of paragraphs 1 and 2 above, any instrument deposited by a political and/or economic integration organization shall not be counted as additional to those deposited by member States of such organization.

Article 26   Reservations and Declarations

1. No reservation or exception may be made to this Convention.

2. Paragraph 1 of this Article does not preclude a State or political and/or economic integration organizations, when signing, ratifying, accepting, approving, formally confirming or acceding to this Convention, from making declarations or statements, however phrased or named, with a view, inter alia, to the harmonization of its laws and regulations with the provisions of this Convention, provided that such declarations or statements do not purport to exclude or to modify the legal effects of the provisions of the Convention in their application to that State.

Article 27   Withdrawal

1. At any time after three years from the date on which this Convention has entered into force for a Party, that Party may withdraw from the Convention by giving written notification to the Depositary.

2. Withdrawal shall be effective one year from receipt of notification by the Depositary, or on such later date as may be specified in the notification.

Article 28   Depository

The Secretary-General of the United Nations shall be the Depository of this Convention and of any protocol thereto.

Article 29   Authentic texts

The original Arabic, Chinese, English, French, Russian and Spanish texts of this Convention are equally authentic. IN WITNESS WHEREOF the undersigned, being duly authorized to that effect, have signed this Convention.

Done at on the day of 1989

ANNEX I
CATEGORIES OF WASTES TO BE CONTROLLED

Waste Streams

Y1 Clinical wastes from medical care in hospitals, medical centers and clinics
Y2 Wastes from the production and preparation of pharmaceutical products
Y3 Waste pharmaceuticals, drugs and medicines
Y4 Wastes from the production, formulation and use of biocides and phytopharmaceuticals
Y5 Wastes from the manufacture, formulation and use of wood preserving chemicals
Y6 Wastes from the production, formulation and use of organic solvents
Y7 Wastes from heat treatment and tempering operations containing cyanides
Y8 Waste mineral oils unfit for their originally intended use
Y9 Waste oils/water, hydrocarbons/water mixtures, emulsions
Y10 Waste substances and articles containing or contaminated with polychlorinated biphenyls (PCBs) and/or polychlorinated terphenyls (PCTs) and/or polybrominated biphenyls (PBBs)
Y11 Waste tarry residues arising from refining, distillation and any pyrolytic treatment
Y12 Wastes from production, formulation and use of inks, dyes, pigments, paints, lacquers, varnish
Y13 Wastes from production, formulation and use of resins, latex, plasticizers, glues/adhesives
Y14 Waste chemical substances arising from research and development or teaching activities which are not identified and/or are new and whose effects on man and/or the environment are not known
Y15 Wastes of an explosive nature not subject to other legislation
Y16 Wastes from production, formulation and use of photographic chemicals and processing materials
Y17 Wastes resulting from surface treatment of metals and plastics
Y18 Residues arising from industrial waste disposal operations

Wastes having as constituents:

Y19 Metal carbonyls
Y20 Beryllium; beryllium compounds
Y21 Hexavalent chromium compounds
Y22 Copper compounds
Y23 Zinc compounds
Y24 Arsenic; arsenic compounds
Y25 Selenium, selenium compounds
Y26 Cadmium; cadmium compounds
Y27 Antimony; antimony compounds
Y28 Tellurium; tellurium compounds
Y29 Mercury; mercury compounds

Y30 Thallium; thallium compounds
Y31 Lead, lead compounds
Y32 Inorganic fluorine compounds excluding calcium fluoride
Y33 Inorganic cyanides
Y34 Acidic solutions or acids in solid form
Y35 Basic solutions or bases in solid form
Y36 Asbestos (dust and fibres)
Y37 Organic phosphorous compounds
Y38 Organic cyanides
Y39 Phenols; phenol compounds including chlorophenols
Y40 Ethers
Y41 Halogenated organic solvents
Y42 Organic solvents excluding halogenated solvents
Y43 Any congenor of polychlorinated dibenzo-furan
Y44 Any congenor of polychlorinated dibenzo-p-dioxin
Y45 Organohalogen compounds other than substances referred to in this Annex (e.g. Y39, Y41, Y42, Y43, Y44).

ANNEX II
CATEGORIES OF WASTES REQUIRING SPECIAL CONSIDERATION

Y46 Wastes collected from households
Y47 Residues arising from the incineration of household

ANNEX III
LIST OF HAZARDOUS CHARACTERISTICS

UN Class*	Code	Characteristics

- 1   H1   Explosive
An explosive substance or waste is a solid or liquid substance or waste (or mixture of substances or wastes) which is in itself capable by chemical reaction of producing gas at such a temperature and pressure and at such a speed as to cause damage to the surroundings.

- 3   H3   Flammable liquids
The word "flammable" has the same meaning as "inflammable". Flammable liquids are liquids, or mixtures of liquids, or liquids containing solids in solution or suspension (for example, paints, varnishes, lacquers, etc., but not including substances or wastes otherwise classified on account of their dangerous characteristics) which give off a flammable vapour at temperatures of not more than 60.5 deg. C, closed-cup test, or not more than 65.6 deg C, open-cup test. (Since the results of open-cup tests and of closed-cup tests are not strictly comparable and even individual results by the same test are often variable, regulations varying from the above figures to make allowance for such differences would be within the spirit of this definition.)

- 4.1   H4.1   Flammable solids
Solids, or waste solids, other than those classed as explosives, which under conditions encountered in transport are readily combustible, or may cause or contribute to fire through friction.

- 4.2   H4.2   Substances or wastes liable to spontaneous combustion
Substances or wastes which are liable to spontaneous heating under normal conditions encountered in transport, or to heating up on contact with air, and being then liable to catch fire.

-4.3	H4.2	Substances or wastes which, in contact with water emit flammable gases
		Substances or wastes which, by interaction with water, are liable to become spontaneously flammable or to give off flammable gases in dangerous quantities.
- 5.1	H5.1	Oxidizing
		Substances or wastes which, while in themselves not necessarily combustible, may, generally by yielding oxygen cause, or contribute to, the combustion of other materials.
- 5.2	H5.2	Organic Peroxides
		Organic substances or wastes which contain the bivalent-o-o-structure are thermally unstable substances which may undergo exothermic self-accelerating decomposition.
- 6.1	H6.1	Poisonous (Acute)
		Substances or wastes liable either to cause death or serious injury or to harm human health if swallowed or inhaled or by skin contact.
- 6.2	H6.2	Infectious substances
		Substances or wastes containing viable micro organisms or their toxins which are known or suspected to cause disease in animals or humans.
- 8	H8	Corrosives
		Substances or wastes which, by chemical action, will cause severe damage when in contact with living tissue, or, in the case of leakage, will materially damage, or even destroy, other goods or the means of transport; they may also cause other hazards.
- 9	H10	Liberation of toxic gases in contact with air or water
		Substances or wastes which, by interaction with air or water, are liable to give off toxic gases in dangerous quantities.
- 9	H11	Toxic (Delayed or chronic)
		Substances or wastes which, if they are inhaled or ingested or if they penetrate the skin, may involve delayed or chronic effects, including carcinogenicity.
- 9	H12	Ecotoxic
		Substances or wastes which if released present or may present immediate or delayed adverse impacts to the environment by means of bioaccumulation and/or toxic effects upon biotic systems.
- 9	H13	Capable, by any means, after disposal, of yielding another material, e.g., leachate, which possesses any of the characteristics listed above.

Tests

The potential hazards posed by certain types of wastes are not yet fully documented; tests to define quantitatively these hazards do not exist. Further research is necessary in order to develop means to characterize potential hazards posed to man and/or the environment by these wastes. Standardized tests have been derived with respect to pure substances and materials. Many countries have developed national tests which can be applied to materials listed in Annex 1, in order to decide if these materials exhibit any of the characteristics listed in this Annex.

*Corresponds to the hazard classification system included in the United Nations Recommendations on the Transport of Dangerous Goods (ST/SG/AC.10/1/Rev.5, United Nations, New York, 1988).

ANNEX IV   DISPOSAL OPERATIONS

A.   OPERATIONS WHICH DO NOT LEAD TO THE POSSIBILITY OF RESOURCE RECOVERY, RECYCLING, RECLAMATION, DIRECT RE-USE OR ALTERNATIVE USES

Section A encompasses all such disposal operations which occur in practice.

D1   Deposit into or onto land, (e.g., landfill, etc.)
D2   Land treatment, (e.g., biodegradation of liquid or sludgy discards in soils, etc.)
D3   Deep injection, (e.g., injection of pumpable discards into wells, salt domes or naturally occurring repositories, etc.)
D4   Surface impoundment, (e.g., placement of liquid or sludge discards into pits, ponds or lagoons, etc.)
D5   Specially engineered landfill, (e.g., placement into lined discrete cells which are capped and isolated from one another and the environment, etc.)
D6   Release into a water body except seas/oceans
D7   Release into seas/oceans including sea-bed insertion
D8   Biological treatment not specified elsewhere in this Annex which results in final compounds or mixtures which are discarded by means of any of the operations in Section A
D9   Physico chemical treatment not specified elsewhere in this Annex which results in final compounds or mixtures which are discarded by means of any of the operations in Section A, (e.g., evaporation, drying, calcination, neutralisation, precipitation, etc.)
D10 Incineration on land
D11 Incineration at sea
D12 Permanent storage (e.g., emplacement of containers in a mine, etc.)
D13 Blending or mixing prior to submission to any of the operations in Section A
D14 Repackaging prior to submission to any of the operations in Section A
D15 Storage pending any of the operations in Section A

B.   OPERATIONS WHICH MAY LEAD TO RESOURCE RECOVERY, RECYCLING, RECLAMATION, DIRECT RE-USE OR ALTERNATIVE USES

Section B encompasses all such operations with respect to materials legally defined as or considered to be hazardous wastes and which otherwise would have been destined for operations included in Section A

R1   Use as a fuel (other than in direct incineration) or other means to generate energy
R2   Solvent reclamation/regeneration
R3   Recycling/reclamation of organic substances which are not used as solvents
R4   Recycling/reclamation of metals and metal compounds
R5   Recycling/reclamation of other inorganic materials
R6   Regeneration of acids or bases
R7   Recovery of components used for pollution abatement
R8   Recovery of components from catalysts
R9   Used oil re-refining or other reuses of previously used oil
R10 Land treatment resulting in benefit to agriculture or ecological improvement
R11 Uses of residual materials obtained from any of the operations numbered R1-R10
R12 Exchange of wastes for submission to any of the operations numbered R1-R11
R13 Accumulation of material intended for any operation in Section B

ANNEX V (A)
INFORMATION TO BE PROVIDED ON NOTIFICATION

ANNEX V (B)
INFORMATION TO BE PROVIDED ON THE MOVEMENT DOCUMENT

ANNEX VI
ARBITRATION

ROTTERDAM CONVENTION ON PRIOR INFORMED CONSENT PROCEDURE FOR CERTAIN HAZARDOUS CHEMICALS AND PESTICIDES IN INTERNATIONAL TRADE

38 I.L.M. 1 (1999)
Signed: September 11, 1998
Entered into force: February 24, 2004

The Parties to this Convention,

Aware of the harmful impact on human health and the environment from certain hazardous chemicals and pesticides in international trade,

Recalling the pertinent provisions of the Rio Declaration on Environment and Development and chapter 19 of Agenda 21 on "Environmentally sound management of toxic chemicals, including prevention of illegal international traffic in toxic and dangerous products",

Mindful of the work undertaken by the United Nations Environment Programme (UNEP) and the Food and Agriculture Organization of the United Nations (FAO) in the operation of the voluntary Prior Informed Consent procedure, as set out in the UNEP Amended London Guidelines for the Exchange of Information on Chemicals in International Trade (hereinafter referred to as the "Amended London Guidelines") and the FAO International Code of Conduct on the Distribution and Use of Pesticides (hereinafter referred to as the "International Code of Conduct"),

Taking into account the circumstances and particular requirements of developing countries and countries with economies in transition, in particular the need to strengthen national capabilities and capacities for the management of chemicals, including transfer of technology, providing financial and technical assistance and promoting cooperation among the Parties,

Noting the specific needs of some countries for information on transit movements,

Recognizing that good management practices for chemicals should be promoted in all countries, taking into account, *inter alia,* the voluntary standards laid down in the International Code of Conduct and the UNEP Code of Ethics on the International Trade in Chemicals,

Desiring to ensure that hazardous chemicals that are exported from their territory are packaged and labelled in a manner that is adequately protective of human health and the environment, consistent with the principles of the Amended London Guidelines and the International Code of Conduct,

Recognizing that trade and environmental policies should be mutually supportive with a view to achieving sustainable development,

Emphasizing that nothing in this Convention shall be interpreted as implying in any way a change in the rights and obligations of a Party under any existing international agreement applying to chemicals in international trade or to environmental protection,

Understanding that the above recital is not intended to create a hierarchy between this Convention and other international agreements,

Determined to protect human health, including the health of consumers and workers, and the environment against potentially harmful impacts from certain hazardous chemicals and pesticides in international trade,

Have agreed as follows:

Article 1   Objective

The objective of this Convention is to promote shared responsibility and cooperative efforts among Parties in the international trade of certain hazardous chemicals in order to protect human health and the environment from potential harm and to contribute to their environmentally sound use, by facilitating information exchange about their characteristics, by providing for a national decision-making process on their import and export and by disseminating these decisions to Parties.

Article 2   Definitions

For the purposes of this Convention:

(a) "Chemical" means a substance whether by itself or in a mixture or preparation and whether manufactured or obtained from nature, but does not include any living organism. It consists of the following categories: pesticide (including severely hazardous pesticide formulations) and industrial;

(b) "Banned chemical" means a chemical all uses of which within one or more categories have been prohibited by final regulatory action, in order to protect human health or the environment. It includes a chemical that has been refused approval for first-time use or has been withdrawn by industry either from the domestic market or from further consideration in the domestic approval process and where there is clear evidence that such action has been taken in order to protect human health or the environment;

(c) "Severely restricted chemical" means a chemical virtually all use of which within one or more categories has been prohibited by final regulatory action in order to protect human health or the environment, but for which certain specific uses remain allowed. It includes a chemical that has, for virtually all use, been refused for approval or been withdrawn by industry either from the domestic market or from further consideration in the domestic approval process, and where there is clear evidence that such action has been taken in order to protect human health or the environment;

(d) "Severely hazardous pesticide formulation" means a chemical formulated for pesticidal use that produces severe health or environmental effects observable within a short period of time after single or multiple exposure, under conditions of use;

(e) "Final regulatory action" means an action taken by a Party, that does not require subsequent regulatory action by that Party, the purpose of which is to ban or severely restrict a chemical;

(f) "Export" and "import" mean, in their respective connotations, the movement of a chemical from one Party to another Party, but exclude mere transit operations;

(g) "Party" means a State or regional economic integration organization that has consented to be bound by this Convention and for which the Convention is in force;

(h) "Regional economic integration organization" means an organization constituted by sovereign States of a given region to which its member States have transferred competence in respect of matters governed by this Convention and which has been duly authorized, in accordance with its internal procedures, to sign, ratify, accept, approve or accede to this Convention;

(i) "Chemical Review Committee" means the subsidiary body referred to in paragraph 6 of Article 18.

Article 3   Scope of the Convention

1. This Convention applies to:

    (a) Banned or severely restricted chemicals; and
    (b) Severely hazardous pesticide formulations.

2. This Convention does not apply to:

 (a) Narcotic drugs and psychotropic substances;
 (b) Radioactive materials;
 (c) Wastes;
 (d) Chemical weapons;
 (e) Pharmaceuticals, including human and veterinary drugs;
 (f) Chemicals used as food additives;
 (g) Food;
 (h) Chemicals in quantities not likely to affect human health or the environment provided they are imported:
 (i) For the purpose of research or analysis; or
 (ii) By an individual for his or her own personal use in quantities reasonable for such use.

Article 4   Designated national authorities

1. Each Party shall designate one or more national authorities that shall be authorized to act on its behalf in the performance of the administrative functions required by this Convention.

2. Each Party shall seek to ensure that such authority or authorities have sufficient resources to perform their tasks effectively.

3. Each Party shall, no later than the date of the entry into force of this Convention for it, notify the name and address of such authority or authorities to the Secretariat. It shall forthwith notify the Secretariat of any changes in the name and address of such authority or authorities.

4. The Secretariat shall forthwith inform the Parties of the notifications it receives under paragraph 3.

Article 5   Procedures for banned or severely restricted chemicals

1. Each Party that has adopted a final regulatory action shall notify the Secretariat in writing of such action. Such notification shall be made as soon as possible, and in any event no later than ninety days after the date on which the final regulatory action has taken effect, and shall contain the information required by Annex I, where available.

2. Each Party shall, at the date of entry into force of this Convention for it, notify the Secretariat in writing of its final regulatory actions in effect at that time, except that each Party that has submitted notifications of final regulatory actions under the Amended London Guidelines or the International Code of Conduct need not resubmit those notifications.

3. The Secretariat shall, as soon as possible, and in any event no later than six months after receipt of a notification under paragraphs 1 and 2, verify whether the notification contains the information required by Annex I. If the notification contains the information required, the Secretariat shall forthwith forward to all Parties a summary of the information received. If the notification does not contain the information required, it shall inform the notifying Party accordingly.

4. The Secretariat shall every six months communicate to the Parties a synopsis of the information received pursuant to paragraphs 1 and 2, including information regarding those notifications which do not contain all the information required by Annex I.

5. When the Secretariat has received at least one notification from each of two Prior Informed Consent regions regarding a particular chemical that it has verified meet the requirements of Annex I, it shall forward them to the Chemical Review Committee. The composition of the Prior Informed Consent regions shall be defined in a decision to be adopted by consensus at the first meeting of the Conference of the Parties.

6. The Chemical Review Committee shall review the information provided in such notifications and, in accordance with the criteria set out in Annex II, recommend to the Conference of the Parties whether the chemical in question should be made subject to the Prior Informed Consent procedure and, accordingly, be listed in Annex III.

Article 6   **Procedures for severely hazardous pesticide formulations**

1. Any Party that is a developing country or a country with an economy in transition and that is experiencing problems caused by a severely hazardous pesticide formulation under conditions of use in its territory, may propose to the Secretariat the listing of the severely hazardous pesticide formulation in Annex III. In developing a proposal, the Party may draw upon technical expertise from any relevant source. The proposal shall contain the information required by part 1 of Annex IV.

2. The Secretariat shall, as soon as possible, and in any event no later than six months after receipt of a proposal under paragraph 1, verify whether the proposal contains the information required by part 1 of Annex IV. If the proposal contains the information required, the Secretariat shall forthwith forward to all Parties a summary of the information received. If the proposal does not contain the information required, it shall inform the proposing Party accordingly.

3. The Secretariat shall collect the additional information set out in part 2 of Annex IV regarding the proposal forwarded under paragraph 2.

4. When the requirements of paragraphs 2 and 3 above have been fulfilled with regard to a particular severely hazardous pesticide formulation, the Secretariat shall forward the proposal and the related information to the Chemical Review Committee.

5. The Chemical Review Committee shall review the information provided in the proposal and the additional information collected and, in accordance with the criteria set out in part 3 of Annex IV, recommend to the Conference of the Parties whether the severely hazardous pesticide formulation in question should be made subject to the Prior Informed Consent procedure and, accordingly, be listed in Annex III.

Article 7   **Listing of chemicals in Annex III**

1. For each chemical that the Chemical Review Committee has decided to recommend for listing in Annex III, it shall prepare a draft decision guidance document. The decision guidance document should, at a minimum, be based on the information specified in Annex I, or, as the case may be, Annex IV, and include information on uses of the chemical in a category other than the category for which the final regulatory action applies.

2. The recommendation referred to in paragraph 1 together with the draft decision guidance document shall be forwarded to the Conference of the Parties. The Conference of the Parties shall decide whether the chemical should be made subject to the Prior Informed Consent procedure and, accordingly, list the chemical in Annex III and approve the draft decision guidance document.

3. When a decision to list a chemical in Annex III has been taken and the related decision guidance document has been approved by the Conference of the Parties, the Secretariat shall forthwith communicate this information to all Parties.

Article 8   **Chemicals in the voluntary prior consent procedure**

For any chemical, other than a chemical listed in Annex III, that has been included in the voluntary Prior Informed Consent procedure before the date of the first meeting of the Conference of the Parties, the Conference of the Parties shall decide at that meeting to list the chemical in Annex III, provided that it is satisfied that all the requirements for listing in that Annex have been fulfilled.

| | **Article 9** | **Removal of chemicals from Annex III** |

1. If a Party submits to the Secretariat information that was not available at the time of the decision to list a chemical in Annex III and that information indicates that its listing may no longer be justified in accordance with the relevant criteria in Annex II or, as the case may be, Annex IV, the Secretariat shall forward the information to the Chemical Review Committee.

2. The Chemical Review Committee shall review the information it receives under paragraph 1. For each chemical that the Chemical Review Committee decides, in accordance with the relevant criteria in Annex II or, as the case may be, Annex IV, to recommend for removal from Annex III, it shall prepare a revised draft decision guidance document.

3. A recommendation referred to in paragraph 2 shall be forwarded to the Conference of the Parties and be accompanied by a revised draft decision guidance document. The Conference of the Parties shall decide whether the chemical should be removed from Annex III and whether to approve the revised draft decision guidance document.

| | **Article 10** | **Obligations in relation to imports of chemicals listed in Annex III** |

1. Each Party shall implement appropriate legislative or administrative measures to ensure timely decision with respect to the import of chemicals listed in Annex III.

2. Each Party shall transmit to the Secretariat, as soon as possible, and in any event no later than nine months after the date of dispatch of the decision guidance document referred to in paragraph 3 of Article 7, a response concerning the future import of the chemical concerned. If a Party modifies this response, it shall forthwith submit the revised response to the Secretariat.

3. The Secretariat shall, at the expiration of the time period in paragraph 2, forthwith address to a Party that has not provided such a response, a written request to do so. Should the Party be unable to provide a response, the Secretariat shall, where appropriate, help it to provide a response within the time period specified in the last sentence of paragraph 2 of Article 11.

4. A response under paragraph 2 shall consist of either:

(a) A final decision, pursuant to legislative or administrative measures:

> (i) To consent to import;
> (ii) Not to consent to import; or
> (iii) To consent to import only subject to specified conditions; or

(b) An interim response, which may include:

> (i) An interim decision consenting to import with or without specified conditions, or not consenting to import during the interim period;
> (ii) A statement that a final decision is under active consideration;
> (iii) A request to the Secretariat, or to the Party that notified the final regulatory action, for further information;
> (iv) A request to the Secretariat for assistance in evaluating the chemical.

5. A response under subparagraphs (a) or (b) of paragraph 4 shall relate to the category or categories specified for the chemical in Annex III.

6. A final decision should be accompanied by a description of any legislative or administrative measures upon which it is based.

7. Each Party shall, no later than the date of entry into force of this Convention for it, transmit to the Secretariat responses with respect to each chemical listed in Annex III. A Party that has provided such responses under the Amended London Guidelines or the International Code of Conduct need not resubmit those responses.

8. Each Party shall make its responses under this Article available to those concerned within its jurisdiction, in accordance with its legislative or administrative measures.

9. A Party that, pursuant to paragraphs 2 and 4 above and paragraph 2 of Article 11, takes a decision not to consent to import of a chemical or to consent to its import only under specified conditions shall, if it has not already done so, simultaneously prohibit or make subject to the same conditions:

    (a) Import of the chemical from any source; and
    (b) Domestic production of the chemical for domestic use.

10. Every six months the Secretariat shall inform all Parties of the responses it has received. Such information shall include a description of the legislative or administrative measures on which the decisions have been based, where available. The Secretariat shall, in addition, inform the Parties of any cases of failure to transmit a response.

Article 11   Obligations in relation to exports of chemicals listed in Annex III

1. Each exporting Party shall:

    (a) Implement appropriate legislative or administrative measures to communicate the responses forwarded by the Secretariat in accordance with paragraph 10 of Article 10 to those concerned within its jurisdiction;

    (b) Take appropriate legislative or administrative measures to ensure that exporters within its jurisdiction comply with decisions in each response no later than six months after the date on which the Secretariat first informs the Parties of such response in accordance with paragraph 10 of Article 10;

    (c) Advise and assist importing Parties, upon request and as appropriate:

        (i) To obtain further information to help them to take action in accordance with paragraph 4 of Article 10 and paragraph 2 (c) below; and
        (ii) To strengthen their capacities and capabilities to manage chemicals safely during their life-cycle.

2. Each Party shall ensure that a chemical listed in Annex III is not exported from its territory to any importing Party that, in exceptional circumstances, has failed to transmit a response or has transmitted an interim response that does not contain an interim decision, unless:

    (a) It is a chemical that, at the time of import, is registered as a chemical in the importing Party; or

    (b) It is a chemical for which evidence exists that it has previously been used in, or imported into, the importing Party and in relation to which no regulatory action to prohibit its use has been taken; or

    (c) Explicit consent to the import has been sought and received by the exporter through a designated national authority of the importing Party. The importing Party shall respond to such a request within sixty days and shall promptly notify the Secretariat of its decision.

The obligations of exporting Parties under this paragraph shall apply with effect from the expiration of a period of six months from the date on which the Secretariat first informs the Parties, in accordance with paragraph 10 of Article 10, that a Party has failed to transmit a response or has transmitted an interim response that does not contain an interim decision, and shall apply for one year.

Article 12   **Export notification**

1. Where a chemical that is banned or severely restricted by a Party is exported from its territory, that Party shall provide an export notification to the importing Party. The export notification shall include the information set out in Annex V.

2. The export notification shall be provided for that chemical prior to the first export following adoption of the corresponding final regulatory action. Thereafter, the export notification shall be provided before the first export in any calendar year. The requirement to notify before export may be waived by the designated national authority of the importing Party.

3. An exporting Party shall provide an updated export notification after it has adopted a final regulatory action that results in a major change concerning the ban or severe restriction of that chemical.

4. The importing Party shall acknowledge receipt of the first export notification received after the adoption of the final regulatory action. If the exporting Party does not receive the acknowledgement within thirty days of the dispatch of the export notification, it shall submit a second notification. The exporting Party shall make reasonable efforts to ensure that the importing Party receives the second notification.

5. The obligations of a Party set out in paragraph 1 shall cease when:

> (a) The chemical has been listed in Annex III;
> (b) The importing Party has provided a response for the chemical to the Secretariat in accordance with paragraph 2 of Article 10; and
> (c) The Secretariat has distributed the response to the Parties in accordance with paragraph 10 of Article 10.

Article 13   **Information to accompany exported chemicals**

1. The Conference of the Parties shall encourage the World Customs Organization to assign specific Harmonized System customs codes to the individual chemicals or groups of chemicals listed in Annex III, as appropriate. Each Party shall require that, whenever a code has been assigned to such a chemical, the shipping document for that chemical bears the code when exported.

2. Without prejudice to any requirements of the importing Party, each Party shall require that both chemicals listed in Annex III and chemicals banned or severely restricted in its territory are, when exported, subject to labeling requirements that ensure adequate availability of information with regard to risks and/or hazards to human health or the environment, taking into account relevant international standards.

3. Without prejudice to any requirements of the importing Party, each Party may require that chemicals subject to environmental or health labelling requirements in its territory are, when exported, subject to labelling requirements that ensure adequate availability of information with regard to risks and/or hazards to human health or the environment, taking into account relevant international standards.

4. With respect to the chemicals referred to in paragraph 2 that are to be used for occupational purposes, each exporting Party shall require that a safety data sheet that follows an internationally recognized format, setting out the most up-to-date information available, is sent to each importer.

5. The information on the label and on the safety data sheet should, as far as practicable, be given in one or more of the official languages of the importing Party.

Article 14   Information exchange

1. Each Party shall, as appropriate and in accordance with the objective of this Convention, facilitate:

> (a) The exchange of scientific, technical, economic and legal information concerning the chemicals within the scope of this Convention, including toxicological, ecotoxicological and safety information;
> (b) The provision of publicly available information on domestic regulatory actions relevant to the objectives of this Convention; and
> (c) The provision of information to other Parties, directly or through the Secretariat, on domestic regulatory actions that substantially restrict one or more uses of the chemical, as appropriate.

2. Parties that exchange information pursuant to this Convention shall protect any confidential information as mutually agreed.

3. The following information shall not be regarded as confidential for the purposes of this Convention:

> (a) The information referred to in Annexes I and IV, submitted pursuant to Articles 5 and 6 respectively;
> (b) The information contained in the safety data sheet referred to in paragraph 4 of Article 13;
> (c) The expiry date of the chemical;
> (d) Information on precautionary measures, including hazard classification, the nature of the risk and the relevant safety advice; and
> (e) The summary results of the toxicological and ecotoxicological tests.

4. The production date of the chemical shall generally not be considered confidential for the purposes of this Convention.

5. Any Party requiring information on transit movements through its territory of chemicals listed in Annex III may report its need to the Secretariat, which shall inform all Parties accordingly.

Article 15   Implementation of the Convention

1. Each Party shall take such measures as may be necessary to establish and strengthen its national infrastructures and institutions for the effective implementation of this Convention. These measures may include, as required, the adoption or amendment of national legislative or administrative measures and may also include:

> (a) The establishment of national registers and databases including safety information for chemicals;
> (b) The encouragement of initiatives by industry to promote chemical safety; and
> (c) The promotion of voluntary agreements, taking into consideration the provisions of Article 16.

2. Each Party shall ensure, to the extent practicable, that the public has appropriate access to information on chemical handling and accident management and on alternatives that are safer for human health or the environment than the chemicals listed in Annex III.

3. The Parties agree to cooperate, directly or, where appropriate, through competent international organizations, in the implementation of this Convention at the subregional, regional and global levels.

4. Nothing in this Convention shall be interpreted as restricting the right of the Parties to take action that is more stringently protective of human health and the environment than that called for in this Convention, provided that such action is consistent with the provisions of this Convention and is in accordance with international law.

Article 16   Technical assistance

The Parties shall, taking into account in particular the needs of developing countries and countries with economies in transition, cooperate in promoting technical assistance for the development of the infrastructure and the capacity necessary to manage chemicals to enable implementation of this Convention. Parties with more advanced programmes for regulating chemicals should provide technical assistance, including training, to other Parties in developing their infrastructure and capacity to manage chemicals throughout their life-cycle.

Article 17   **Non-Compliance**

The Conference of the Parties shall, as soon as practicable, develop and approve procedures and institutional mechanisms for determining non-compliance with the provisions of this Convention and for treatment of Parties found to be in non-compliance.

Article 18   **Conference of the Parties**

1. A Conference of the Parties is hereby established.

2. The first meeting of the Conference of the Parties shall be convened by the Executive Director of UNEP and the Director-General of FAO, acting jointly, no later than one year after the entry into force of this Convention. Thereafter, ordinary meetings of the Conference of the Parties shall be held at regular intervals to be determined by the Conference.

3. Extraordinary meetings of the Conference of the Parties shall be held at such other times as may be deemed necessary by the Conference, or at the written request of any Party provided that it is supported by at least one third of the Parties.

4. The Conference of the Parties shall by consensus agree upon and adopt at its first meeting rules of procedure and financial rules for itself and any subsidiary bodies, as well as financial provisions governing the functioning of the Secretariat.

5. The Conference of the Parties shall keep under continuous review and evaluation the implementation of this Convention. It shall perform the functions assigned to it by the Convention and, to this end, shall:

(a) Establish, further to the requirements of paragraph 6 below, such subsidiary bodies as it considers necessary for the implementation of the Convention;

(b) Cooperate, where appropriate, with competent international organizations and intergovernmental and non-governmental bodies; and

(c) Consider and undertake any additional action that may be required for the achievement of the objectives of the Convention.

6. The Conference of the Parties shall, at its first meeting, establish a subsidiary body, to be called the Chemical Review Committee, for the purposes of performing the functions assigned to that Committee by this Convention. In this regard:

(a) The members of the Chemical Review Committee shall be appointed by the Conference of the Parties. Membership of the Committee shall consist of a limited number of government-designated experts in chemicals management. The members of the Committee shall be appointed on the basis of equitable geographical distribution, including ensuring a balance between developed and developing Parties;

(b) The Conference of the Parties shall decide on the terms of reference, organization and operation of the Committee;

(c) The Committee shall make every effort to make its recommendations by consensus. If all efforts at consensus have been exhausted, and no consensus reached, such recommendation shall as a last resort be adopted by a two-thirds majority vote of the members present and voting.

7. The United Nations, its specialized agencies and the International Atomic Energy Agency, as well as any State not Party to this Convention, may be represented at meetings of the Conference of the Parties as observers. Any body or agency, whether national or international, governmental or non-governmental, qualified in matters covered by the Convention, and which has informed the Secretariat of its wish to be represented at a meeting of the Conference of the Parties as an observer may be admitted unless at least one third of the Parties present object. The admission and participation of observers shall be subject to the rules of procedure adopted by the Conference of the Parties.

Article 19   Secretariat

1. A Secretariat is hereby established.

2. The functions of the Secretariat shall be:

(a) To make arrangements for meetings of the Conference of the Parties and its subsidiary bodies and to provide them with services as required;

(b) To facilitate assistance to the Parties, particularly developing Parties and Parties with economies in transition, on request, in the implementation of this Convention;

(c) To ensure the necessary coordination with the secretariats of other relevant international bodies;

(d) To enter, under the overall guidance of the Conference of the Parties, into such administrative and contractual arrangements as may be required for the effective discharge of its functions; and

(e) To perform the other secretariat functions specified in this Convention and such other functions as may be determined by the Conference of the Parties.

3. The secretariat functions for this Convention shall be performed jointly by the Executive Director of UNEP and the Director-General of FAO, subject to such arrangements as shall be agreed between them and approved by the Conference of the Parties.

4. The Conference of the Parties may decide, by a three-fourths majority of the Parties present and voting, to entrust the secretariat functions to one or more other competent international organizations, should it find that the Secretariat is not functioning as intended.

Article 20   Settlement of disputes

1. Parties shall settle any dispute between them concerning the interpretation or application of this Convention through negotiation or other peaceful means of their own choice.

2. When ratifying, accepting, approving or acceding to this Convention, or at any time thereafter, a Party that is not a regional economic integration organization may declare in a written instrument submitted to the Depositary that, with respect to any dispute concerning the interpretation or application of the Convention, it recognizes one or both of the following means of dispute settlement as compulsory in relation to any Party accepting the same obligation:

(a) Arbitration in accordance with procedures to be adopted by the Conference of the Parties in an annex as soon as practicable; and

(b) Submission of the dispute to the International Court of Justice.

3. A Party that is a regional economic integration organization may make a declaration with like effect in relation to arbitration in accordance with the procedure referred to in paragraph 2 (a).

4. A declaration made pursuant to paragraph 2 shall remain in force until it expires in accordance with its terms or until three months after written notice of its revocation has been deposited with the Depositary.

5. The expiry of a declaration, a notice of revocation or a new declaration shall not in any way affect proceedings pending before an arbitral tribunal or the International Court of Justice unless the parties to the dispute otherwise agree.

6. If the parties to a dispute have not accepted the same or any procedure pursuant to paragraph 2, and if they have not been able to settle their dispute within twelve months following notification by one party to another that a dispute exists between them, the dispute shall be submitted to a conciliation commission at the request of any party to the dispute. The conciliation commission shall render a report with recommendations. Additional procedures relating to the conciliation commission shall be included in an annex to be adopted by the Conference of the Parties no later than the second meeting of the Conference.

Article 21   Amendments to the Convention

1. Amendments to this Convention may be proposed by any Party.

2. Amendments to this Convention shall be adopted at a meeting of the Conference of the Parties. The text of any proposed amendment shall be communicated to the Parties by the Secretariat at least six months before the meeting at which it is proposed for adoption. The Secretariat shall also communicate the proposed amendment to the signatories to this Convention and, for information, to the Depositary.

3. The Parties shall make every effort to reach agreement on any proposed amendment to this Convention by consensus. If all efforts at consensus have been exhausted, and no agreement reached, the amendment shall as a last resort be adopted by a three-fourths majority vote of the Parties present and voting at the meeting.

4. The amendment shall be communicated by the Depositary to all Parties for ratification, acceptance or approval.

5. Ratification, acceptance or approval of an amendment shall be notified to the Depositary in writing. An amendment adopted in accordance with paragraph 3 shall enter into force for the Parties having accepted it on the ninetieth day after the date of deposit of instruments of ratification, acceptance or approval by at least three fourths of the Parties. Thereafter, the amendment shall enter into force for any other Party on the ninetieth day after the date on which that Party deposits its instrument of ratification, acceptance or approval of the amendment.

Article 22   Adoption and amendment of annexes

1. Annexes to this Convention shall form an integral part thereof and, unless expressly provided otherwise, a reference to this Convention constitutes at the same time a reference to any annexes thereto.

2. Annexes shall be restricted to procedural, scientific, technical or administrative matters.

3. The following procedure shall apply to the proposal, adoption and entry into force of additional annexes to this Convention:

      (a) Additional annexes shall be proposed and adopted according to the procedure laid down in paragraphs 1, 2 and 3 of Article 21;

      (b) Any Party that is unable to accept an additional annex shall so notify the Depositary, in writing, within one year from the date of communication of the adoption of the additional annex by the Depositary. The Depositary shall without delay notify all Parties of any such notification received. A Party may at any time withdraw a previous notification of non-acceptance in respect of an additional annex and the annex shall thereupon enter into force for that Party subject to subparagraph (c) below; and

      (c) On the expiry of one year from the date of the communication by the Depositary of the adoption of an additional annex, the annex shall enter into force for all Parties that have not submitted a notification in accordance with the provisions of subparagraph (b) above.

4. Except in the case of Annex III, the proposal, adoption and entry into force of amendments to annexes to this Convention shall be subject to the same procedures as for the proposal, adoption and entry into force of additional annexes to the Convention.

5. The following procedure shall apply to the proposal, adoption and entry into force of amendments to Annex III:

      (a) Amendments to Annex III shall be proposed and adopted according to the procedure laid down in Articles 5 to 9 and paragraph 2 of Article 21;

      (b) The Conference of the Parties shall take its decisions on adoption by consensus;

      (c) A decision to amend Annex III shall forthwith be communicated to the Parties by the Depositary. The amendment shall enter into force for all Parties on a date to be specified in the decision.

6. If an additional annex or an amendment to an annex is related to an amendment to this Convention, the additional annex or amendment shall not enter into force until such time as the amendment to the Convention enters into force.

Article 23   Voting

1. Each Party to this Convention shall have one vote, except as provided for in paragraph 2 below.

2. A regional economic integration organization, on matters within its competence, shall exercise its right to vote with a number of votes equal to the number of its member States that are Parties to this Convention. Such an organization shall not exercise its right to vote if any of its member States exercises its right to vote, and vice versa.

3. For the purposes of this Convention, "Parties present and voting" means Parties present and casting an affirmative or negative vote.

Article 24   Signature

This Convention shall be open for signature at Rotterdam by all States and regional economic integration organizations on 11 September 1998, and at United Nations Headquarters in New York from 12 September 1998 to 10 September 1999.

Article 25   Ratification, acceptance, approval or accession

1. This Convention shall be subject to ratification, acceptance or approval by States and by regional economic integration organizations. It shall be open for accession by States and by regional economic integration organizations from the day after the date on which the Convention is closed for signature. Instruments of ratification, acceptance, approval or accession shall be deposited with the Depositary.

2. Any regional economic integration organization that becomes a Party to this Convention without any of its member States being a Party shall be bound by all the obligations under the Convention. In the case of such organizations, one or more of whose member States is a Party to this Convention, the organization and its member States shall decide on their respective responsibilities for the performance of their obligations under the Convention. In such cases, the organization and the member States shall not be entitled to exercise rights under the Convention concurrently.

3. In its instrument of ratification, acceptance, approval or accession, a regional economic integration organization shall declare the extent of its competence in respect of the matters governed by this Convention. Any such organization shall also inform the Depositary, who shall in turn inform the Parties, of any relevant modification in the extent of its competence.

Article 26   Entry into force

1. This Convention shall enter into force on the ninetieth day after the date of deposit of the fiftieth instrument of ratification, acceptance, approval or accession.

2. For each State or regional economic integration organization that ratifies, accepts or approves this Convention or accedes thereto after the deposit of the fiftieth instrument of ratification, acceptance, approval or accession, the Convention shall enter into force on the ninetieth day after the date of deposit by such State or regional economic integration organization of its instrument of ratification, acceptance, approval or accession.

3. For the purpose of paragraphs 1 and 2, any instrument deposited by a regional economic integration organization shall not be counted as additional to those deposited by member States of that organization.

Article 27   Reservations

No reservations may be made to this Convention.

Article 28   Withdrawal

1. At any time after three years from the date on which this Convention has entered into force for a Party, that Party may withdraw from the Convention by giving written notification to the Depositary.

2. Any such withdrawal shall take effect upon expiry of one year from the date of receipt by the Depositary of the notification of withdrawal, or on such later date as may be specified in the notification of withdrawal.

Article 29   Depositary

The Secretary-General of the United Nations shall be the Depositary of this Convention.

Article 30   Authentic texts

The original of this Convention, of which the Arabic, Chinese, English, French, Russian and Spanish texts are equally authentic, shall be deposited with the Secretary-General of the United Nations.

IN WITNESS WHEREOF the undersigned, being duly authorized to that effect, have signed this Convention.

Done at Rotterdam on this tenth day of September, one thousand nine.

***

Annex I
Information requirements for notifications made pursuant to Article 5

Notifications shall include:

1. Properties, identification and uses

    (a) Common name;
    (b) Chemical name according to an internationally recognized nomenclature (for example, International Union of Pure and Applied Chemistry (IUPAC)), where such nomenclature exists;
    (c) Trade names and names of preparations;
    (d) Code numbers: Chemicals Abstract Service (CAS) number, Harmonized System customs code and other numbers;
    (e) Information on hazard classification, where the chemical is subject to classification requirements;
    (f) Use or uses of the chemical;
    (g) Physico-chemical, toxicological and ecotoxicological properties.

2. Final regulatory action

    (a) Information specific to the final regulatory action:
        (i) Summary of the final regulatory action;
        (ii) Reference to the regulatory document;
        (iii) Date of entry into force of the final regulatory action;
        (iv) Indication of whether the final regulatory action was taken on the basis of a risk or hazard evaluation and, if so, information on such evaluation, covering a reference to the relevant documentation;
        (v) Reasons for the final regulatory action relevant to human health, including the health of consumers and workers, or the environment;
        (vi) Summary of the hazards and risks presented by the chemical to human health, including the health of consumers and workers, or the environment and the expected effect of the final regulatory action;

    (b) Category or categories where the final regulatory action has been taken, and for each category:
        (i) Use or uses prohibited by the final regulatory action;
        (ii) Use or uses that remain allowed;
        (iii) Estimation, where available, of quantities of the chemical produced, imported, exported and used;

(c) An indication, to the extent possible, of the likely relevance of the final regulatory action to other States and regions;

(d) Other relevant information that may cover:
  (i) Assessment of socio-economic effects of the final regulatory action;
  (ii) Information on alternatives and their relative risks, where available, such as:
  - Integrated pest management strategies;
  - Industrial practices and processes, including cleaner technology.

Annex II
Criteria for listing banned or severely restricted chemicals in Annex III

In reviewing the notifications forwarded by the Secretariat pursuant to paragraph 5 of Article 5, the Chemical Review Committee shall:

(a) Confirm that the final regulatory action has been taken in order to protect human health or the environment;

(b) Establish that the final regulatory action has been taken as a consequence of a risk evaluation. This evaluation shall be based on a review of scientific data in the context of the conditions prevailing in the Party in question. For this purpose, the documentation provided shall demonstrate that:
  (i) Data have been generated according to scientifically recognized methods;
  (ii) Data reviews have been performed and documented according to generally recognized scientific principles and procedures;
  (iii) The final regulatory action was based on a risk evaluation involving prevailing conditions within the Party taking the action;

(c) Consider whether the final regulatory action provides a sufficiently broad basis to merit listing of the chemical in Annex III, by taking into account:

  (i) Whether the final regulatory action led, or would be expected to lead, to a significant decrease in the quantity of the chemical used or the number of its uses;
  (ii) Whether the final regulatory action led to an actual reduction of risk or would be expected to result in a significant reduction of risk for human health or the environment of the Party that submitted the notification;
  (iii) Whether the considerations that led to the final regulatory action being taken are applicable only in a limited geographical area or in other limited circumstances;
  (iv) Whether there is evidence of ongoing international trade in the chemical;

(d) Take into account that intentional misuse is not in itself an adequate reason to list a chemical in Annex III.

Annex III
Chemicals subject to the prior informed consent procedure

Chemical	Relevant CAS number(s)	Category
2,4,5-T	93-76-5	Pesticide
Aldrin	309-00-2	Pesticide
Captafol	2425-06-1	Pesticide
Binapacryl	485-31-4	Pesticide
Chlordane	57-74-9	Pesticide
Chlordimeform	6164-98-3	Pesticide
Chlorobenzilate	510-15-6	Pesticide
DDT	50-29-3	Pesticide
Dieldrin	60-57-1	Pesticide
Dinitro-ortho-cresol (DNOC) and its salts (such as ammonium salt, potassium salt and sodium salt)	534-52-1; 2980-64-5; 5787-96-2; 2312-76-7	Pesticide
Dinoseb and dinoseb salts	88-85-7	Pesticide
1,2-dibromoethane (EDB)	106-93-4	Pesticide
Fluoroacetamide	640-19-7	Pesticide
Ethylene dichloride	107-06-2	Pesticide
Ethylene oxide	75-21-8	Pesticide
HCH (mixed isomers)	608-73-1	Pesticide
Heptachlor	76-44-8	Pesticide
Hexachlorobenzene	118-74-1	Pesticide
Lindane	58-89-9	Pesticide

Chemical	Relevant CAS number(s)	Category
Mercury compounds, including inorganic mercury compounds, alkyl mercury compounds and alkyloxyalkyl and aryl mercury compounds		Pesticide
Pentachlorophenol	87-86-5	Pesticide
Monocrotophos (Soluble liquid formulations of the substance that exceed 600 g active ingredient/l)	6923-22-4	Severely hazardous pesticide formulation
Toxaphene	8001-35-2	Pesticide
Methamidophos (Soluble liquid formulations of the substance that exceed 600 g active ingredient/l)	10265-92-6	Severely hazardous pesticide formulation
Phosphamidon (Soluble liquid formulations of the substance that exceed 1000 g active ingredient/l)	13171-21-6 (mixture, (E)&(Z) isomers); 23783-98-4 ((Z)-isomer); 297-99-4 ((E)-isomer)	Severely hazardous pesticide formulation
Methyl-parathion (emulsifiable concentrates (EC) with 19.5%, 40%, 50%, 60% active ingredient and dusts containing 1.5%, 2% and 3% active ingredient)	298-00-0	Severely hazardous pesticide formulation
Parathion (all formulations - aerosols, dustable powder(DP), emulsifiable concentrate (EC), granules (GR) and wettable powders (WP) - of this substance are included, except capsule suspensions (CS))	56-38-2	Severely hazardous pesticide formulation
Dustable powder formulations containing a combination of: benomyl at or above 7 per cent, carbofuran at above 10 per cent, thiram at or above 15 per cent (17804-35-2; 1563-66-2; 137-26-8)		Severely hazardous pesticide formulation

Asbestos
  Crocidolite
  Actinolite
  Anthophyllite
  Amosite
  Tremolite
	12001-28-4
	77536-66-4
	77536-67-5
	12172-73-5
	77536-68-6
		Industrial

Chemical	Relevant CAS number(s)	Category
Polybrominated biphenyls (PBB)	36355-01-8(hexa-) 27858-07-7 (octa-) 13654-09-6 (deca-)	Industrial
Polychlorinated biphenyls (PCB)	1336-36-3	Industrial
Polychlorinated terphenyls (PCT)	61788-33-8	Industrial
Tetraethyl lead	78-00-2	Industrial
Tetramethyl lead	75-74-1	Industrial
Tris (2,3-dibromopropyl) phosphate	126-72-7	Industrial

Annex IV

Information and criteria for listing severely hazardous pesticide formulations in Annex III

Part 1. Documentation required from a proposing Party

Proposals submitted pursuant to paragraph 1 of Article 6 shall include adequate documentation containing the following information:

(a) Name of the hazardous pesticide formulation;

(b) Name of the active ingredient or ingredients in the formulation;

(c) Relative amount of each active ingredient in the formulation;

(d) Type of formulation;

(e) Trade names and names of the producers, if available;

(f) Common and recognized patterns of use of the formulation within the proposing Party;

(g) A clear description of incidents related to the problem, including the adverse effects and the way in which the formulation was used;

(h) Any regulatory, administrative or other measure taken, or intended to be taken, by the proposing Party in response to such incidents.

Part 2. Information to be collected by the Secretariat

Pursuant to paragraph 3 of Article 6, the Secretariat shall collect relevant information relating to the formulation, including:

(a) The physico-chemical, toxicological and ecotoxicological properties of the formulation;

(b) The existence of handling or applicator restrictions in other States;

(c) Information on incidents related to the formulation in other States;

(d) Information submitted by other Parties, international organizations, non-governmental organizations or other relevant sources, whether national or international;

(e) Risk and/or hazard evaluations, where available;

(f) Indications, if available, of the extent of use of the formulation, such as the number of registrations or production or sales quantity;

(g) Other formulations of the pesticide in question, and incidents, if any, relating to these formulations;

(h) Alternative pest-control practices;

(i) Other information which the Chemical Review Committee may identify as relevant.

Part 3. Criteria for listing severely hazardous pesticide formulations in Annex III

In reviewing the proposals forwarded by the Secretariat pursuant to paragraph 5 of Article 6, the Chemical Review Committee shall take into account:

(a) The reliability of the evidence indicating that use of the formulation, in accordance with common or recognized practices within the proposing Party, resulted in the reported incidents;

(b) The relevance of such incidents to other States with similar climate, conditions and patterns of use of the formulation;

(c) The existence of handling or applicator restrictions involving technology or techniques that may not be reasonably or widely applied in States lacking the necessary infrastructure;

(d) The significance of reported effects in relation to the quantity of the formulation used;

(e) That intentional misuse is not in itself an adequate reason to list a formulation in Annex III.

Annex V
Information requirements for export notification

1. Export notifications shall contain the following information:
   (a) Name and address of the relevant designated national authorities of the exporting Party and the importing Party;
   (b) Expected date of export to the importing Party;
   I Name of the banned or severely restricted chemical and a summary of the information specified in Annex I that is to be provided to the Secretariat in accordance with Article 5. Where more than one such chemical is included in a mixture or preparation, such information shall be provided for each chemical;
   (d) A statement indicating, if known, the foreseen category of the chemical and its foreseen use within that category in the importing Party;
   (e) Information on precautionary measures to reduce exposure to, and emission of, the chemical;
   (f) In the case of a mixture or a preparation, the concentration of the banned or severely restricted chemical or chemicals in question;
   (g) Name and address of the importer;
   (h) Any additional information that is readily available to the relevant designated national authority of the exporting Party that would be of assistance to the designated national authority of the importing Party.

2. In addition to the information referred to in paragraph 1, the exporting Party shall provide such further information specified in Annex I as may be requested by the importing Party.

STOCKHOLM CONVENTION ON PERSISTENT ORGANIC POLLUTANTS

U.N. Doc. UNEP/POPS/CONF/4
Signed: May 22, 2001
Entered into Force: May 17, 2004
Secretariat Homepage: www.pops.int/

The Parties to this Convention,

Recognizing that persistent organic pollutants possess toxic properties, resist degradation, bioaccumulate and are transported, through air, water and migratory species, across international boundaries and deposited far from their place of release, where they accumulate in terrestrial and aquatic ecosystems,

Aware of the health concerns, especially in developing countries, resulting from local exposure to persistent organic pollutants, in particular impacts upon women and, through them, upon future generations,

Acknowledging that the Arctic ecosystems and indigenous communities are particularly at risk because of the biomagnification of persistent organic pollutants and that contamination of their traditional foods is a public health issue,

Conscious of the need for global action on persistent organic pollutants,

Mindful of decision 19/13 C of 7 February 1997 of the Governing Council of the United Nations Environment Programme to initiate international action to protect human health and the environment through measures which will reduce and/or eliminate emissions and discharges of persistent organic pollutants,

Recalling the pertinent provisions of the relevant international environmental conventions, especially the Rotterdam Convention on the Prior Informed Consent Procedure for Certain Hazardous Chemicals and Pesticides in International Trade, and the Basel Convention on the Control of Transboundary Movements of Hazardous Wastes and their Disposal including the regional agreements developed within the framework of its Article 11,

Recalling also the pertinent provisions of the Rio Declaration on Environment and Development and Agenda 21,

Acknowledging that precaution underlies the concerns of all the Parties and is embedded within this Convention,

Recognizing that this Convention and other international agreements in the field of trade and the environment are mutually supportive,

Reaffirming that States have, in accordance with the Charter of the United Nations and the principles of international law, the sovereign right to exploit their own resources pursuant to their own environmental and developmental policies, and the responsibility to ensure that activities within their jurisdiction or control do not cause damage to the environment of other States or of areas beyond the limits of national jurisdiction,

Taking into account the circumstances and particular requirements of developing countries, in particular the least developed among them, and countries with economies in transition, especially the need to strengthen their national capabilities for the management of chemicals, including through the transfer of technology, the provision of financial and technical assistance and the promotion of cooperation among the Parties,

Taking full account of the Programme of Action for the Sustainable Development of Small Island Developing States, adopted in Barbados on 6 May 1994,

Noting the respective capabilities of developed and developing countries, as well as the common but differentiated responsibilities of States as set forth in Principle 7 of the Rio Declaration on Environment and Development,

Recognizing the important contribution that the private sector and non-governmental organizations can make to achieving the reduction and/or elimination of emissions and discharges of persistent organic pollutants,

Underlining the importance of manufacturers of persistent organic pollutants taking responsibility for reducing adverse effects caused by their products and for providing information to users, Governments and the public on the hazardous properties of those chemicals,

Conscious of the need to take measures to prevent adverse effects caused by persistent organic pollutants at all stages of their life cycle,

Reaffirming Principle 16 of the Rio Declaration on Environment and Development which states that national authorities should endeavour to promote the internalization of environmental costs and the use of economic instruments, taking into account the approach that the polluter should, in principle, bear the cost of pollution, with due regard to the public interest and without distorting international trade and investment,

Encouraging Parties not having regulatory and assessment schemes for pesticides and industrial chemicals to develop such schemes,

Recognizing the importance of developing and using environmentally sound alternative processes and chemicals,

Determined to protect human health and the environment from the harmful impacts of persistent organic pollutants,

Have agreed as follows:

Article 1 Objective

Mindful of the precautionary approach as set forth in Principle 15 of the Rio Declaration on Environment and Development, the objective of this Convention is to protect human health and the environment from persistent organic pollutants.

Article 2 Definitions

For the purposes of this Convention:

(a) "Party" means a State or regional economic integration organization that has consented to be bound by this Convention and for which the Convention is in force;

(b) "Regional economic integration organization" means an organization constituted by sovereign States of a given region to which its member States have transferred competence in respect of matters governed by this Convention and which has been duly authorized, in accordance with its internal procedures, to sign, ratify, accept, approve or accede to this Convention;

(c) "Parties present and voting" means Parties present and casting an affirmative or negative vote.

Article 3 Measures to reduce or eliminate releases from intentional production and use

1. Each Party shall:

(a) Prohibit and/or take the legal and administrative measures necessary to eliminate:

(i)   Its production and use of the chemicals listed in Annex A subject to the provisions of that Annex; and its import and export of the chemicals listed in Annex A in accordance with the provisions of paragraph 2; and

(b) Restrict its production and use of the chemicals listed in Annex B in accordance with the provisions of that Annex.

2. Each Party shall take measures to ensure:

(a) That a chemical listed in Annex A or Annex B is imported only:

(i)   For the purpose of environmentally sound disposal as set forth in paragraph 1 (d) of Article 6; or

(ii)   For a use or purpose which is permitted for that Party under Annex A or Annex B;

(b) That a chemical listed in Annex A for which any production or use specific exemption is in effect or a chemical listed in Annex B for which any production or use specific exemption or acceptable purpose is in effect, taking into account any relevant provisions in existing international prior informed consent instruments, is exported only:

(i)   For the purpose of environmentally sound disposal as set forth in paragraph 1 (d) of Article 6;

(ii)   To a Party which is permitted to use that chemical under Annex A or Annex B; or

(iii)   To a State not Party to this Convention which has provided an annual certification to the exporting Party. Such certification shall specify the intended use of the chemical and include a statement that, with respect to that chemical, the importing State is committed to:

           a.   Protect human health and the environment by taking the necessary measures to minimize or prevent releases;

           b.   Comply with the provisions of paragraph 1 of Article 6; and

           c.   Comply, where appropriate, with the provisions of paragraph 2 of Part II of Annex B.

The certification shall also include any appropriate supporting documentation, such as legislation, regulatory instruments, or administrative or policy guidelines. The exporting Party shall transmit the certification to the Secretariat within sixty days of receipt.

(c) That a chemical listed in Annex A, for which production and use specific exemptions are no longer in effect for any Party, is not exported from it except for the purpose of environmentally sound disposal as set forth in paragraph 1 (d) of Article 6;

(d) For the purposes of this paragraph, the term "State not Party to this Convention" shall include, with respect to a particular chemical, a State or regional economic integration organization that has not agreed to be bound by the Convention with respect to that chemical.

3. Each Party that has one or more regulatory and assessment schemes for new pesticides or new industrial chemicals shall take measures to regulate with the aim of preventing the production and use of new pesticides or new industrial chemicals which, taking into consideration the criteria in paragraph 1 of Annex D, exhibit the characteristics of persistent organic pollutants.

4. Each Party that has one or more regulatory and assessment schemes for pesticides or industrial chemicals shall, where appropriate, take into consideration within these schemes the criteria in paragraph 1 of Annex D when conducting assessments of pesticides or industrial chemicals currently in use.

5. Except as otherwise provided in this Convention, paragraphs 1 and 2 shall not apply to quantities of a chemical to be used for laboratory-scale research or as a reference standard.

6. Any Party that has a specific exemption in accordance with Annex A or a specific exemption or an acceptable purpose in accordance with Annex B shall take appropriate measures to ensure that any production or use under such exemption or purpose is carried out in a manner that prevents or minimizes human exposure and release into the environment. For exempted uses or acceptable purposes that involve intentional release into the environment under conditions of normal use, such release shall be to the minimum extent necessary, taking into account any applicable standards and guidelines.

Article 4   Register of specific exemptions

1. A Register is hereby established for the purpose of identifying the Parties that have specific exemptions listed in Annex A or Annex B. It shall not identify Parties that make use of the provisions in Annex A or Annex B that may be exercised by all Parties. The Register shall be maintained by the Secretariat and shall be available to the public.

2. The Register shall include:

(a) A list of the types of specific exemptions reproduced from Annex A and Annex B;

(b) A list of the Parties that have a specific exemption listed under Annex A or Annex B; and

(c) A list of the expiry dates for each registered specific exemption.

3. Any State may, on becoming a Party, by means of a notification in writing to the Secretariat, register for one or more types of specific exemptions listed in Annex A or Annex B.

4. Unless an earlier date is indicated in the Register by a Party, or an extension is granted pursuant to paragraph 7, all registrations of specific exemptions shall expire five years after the date of entry into force of this Convention with respect to a particular chemical.

5. At its first meeting, the Conference of the Parties shall decide upon its review process for the entries in the Register.

6. Prior to a review of an entry in the Register, the Party concerned shall submit a report to the Secretariat justifying its continuing need for registration of that exemption. The report shall be circulated by the Secretariat to all Parties. The review of a registration shall be carried out on the basis of all available information. Thereupon, the Conference of the Parties may make such recommendations to the Party concerned as it deems appropriate.

7. The Conference of the Parties may, upon request from the Party concerned, decide to extend the expiry date of a specific exemption for a period of up to five years. In making its decision, the Conference of the Parties shall take due account of the special circumstances of the developing country Parties and Parties with economies in transition.

8. A Party may, at any time, withdraw an entry from the Register for a specific exemption upon written notification to the Secretariat. The withdrawal shall take effect on the date specified in the notification.

9. When there are no longer any Parties registered for a particular type of specific exemption, no new registrations may be made with respect to it.

Article 5   Measures to reduce or eliminate releases from unintentional production

Each Party shall at a minimum take the following measures to reduce the total releases derived from anthropogenic sources of each of the chemicals listed in Annex C, with the goal of their continuing minimization and, where feasible, ultimate elimination:

(a) Develop an action plan or, where appropriate, a regional or subregional action plan within two years of the date of entry into force of this Convention for it, and subsequently implement it as part of its implementation plan specified in Article 7, designed to identify, characterize and address the release of the chemicals listed in Annex C and to facilitate implementation of subparagraphs (b) to (e). The action plan shall include the following elements:

(i)   An evaluation of current and projected releases, including the development and maintenance of source inventories and release estimates, taking into consideration the source categories identified in Annex C;

(ii)   An evaluation of the efficacy of the laws and policies of the Party relating to the management of such releases;

(iii)   Strategies to meet the obligations of this paragraph, taking into account the evaluations in (i) and (ii);

(iv)   Steps to promote education and training with regard to, and awareness of, those strategies;

(v)   A review every five years of those strategies and of their success in meeting the obligations of this paragraph; such reviews shall be included in reports submitted pursuant to Article 15;

(vi)   A schedule for implementation of the action plan, including for the strategies and measures I identified therein;

(b) Promote the application of available, feasible and practical measures that can expeditiously achieve a realistic and meaningful level of release reduction or source elimination;

(c) Promote the development and, where it deems appropriate, require the use of substitute or modified materials, products and processes to prevent the formation and release of the chemicals listed in Annex C, taking into consideration the general guidance on prevention and release reduction measures in Annex C and guidelines to be adopted by decision of the Conference of the Parties;

(d) Promote and, in accordance with the implementation schedule of its action plan, require the use of best available techniques for new sources within source categories which a Party has identified as warranting such action in its action plan, with a particular initial focus on source categories identified in Part II of Annex C. In any case, the requirement to use best available techniques for new sources in the categories listed in Part II of that Annex shall be phased in as soon as practicable but no later than four years after the entry into force of the Convention for that Party. For the identified categories, Parties shall promote the use of best environmental practices. When applying best available techniques and best environmental practices, Parties should take into consideration the general guidance on prevention and release reduction measures in that Annex and guidelines on best available techniques and best environmental practices to be adopted by decision of the Conference of the Parties;

(e) Promote, in accordance with its action plan, the use of best available techniques and best environmental practices:

(i)   For existing sources, within the source categories listed in Part II of Annex C and within source categories such as those in Part III of that Annex; and

(ii)   For new sources, within source categories such as those listed in Part III of Annex C which a Party has not addressed under subparagraph (d).

When applying best available techniques and best environmental practices, Parties should take into consideration the general guidance on prevention and release reduction measures in Annex C and guidelines on best available techniques and best environmental practices to be adopted by decision of the Conference of the Parties;

(f) For the purposes of this paragraph and Annex C:

(i)   "Best available techniques" means the most effective and advanced stage in the development of activities and their methods of operation which indicate the practical suitability of particular techniques for providing in principle the basis for release limitations designed to prevent and, where that is not practicable, generally to reduce releases of chemicals listed in Part I of Annex C and their impact on the environment as a whole. In this regard:

(ii)   "Techniques" includes both the technology used and the way in which the installation is designed, built, maintained, operated and decommissioned;

(iii)	"Available" techniques means those techniques that are accessible to the operator and that are developed on a scale that allows implementation in the relevant industrial sector, under economically and technically viable conditions, taking into consideration the costs and advantages; and
(iv)	"Best" means most effective in achieving a high general level of protection of the environment as a whole;
(v)	"Best environmental practices" means the application of the most appropriate combination of environmental control measures and strategies;
(vi)	"New source" means any source of which the construction or substantial modification is commenced at least one year after the date of:

      a.   Entry into force of this Convention for the Party concerned; or

      b.   Entry into force for the Party concerned of an amendment to Annex C where the source becomes subject to the provisions of this Convention only by virtue of that amendment.

(g) Release limit values or performance standards may be used by a Party to fulfill its commitments for best available techniques under this paragraph.

Article 6	**Measures to reduce or eliminate releases from stockpiles and wastes**

1. In order to ensure that stockpiles consisting of or containing chemicals listed either in Annex A or Annex B and wastes, including products and articles upon becoming wastes, consisting of, containing or contaminated with a chemical listed in Annex A, B or C, are managed in a manner protective of human health and the environment, each Party shall:

(a) Develop appropriate strategies for identifying:

(i) Stockpiles consisting of or containing chemicals listed either in Annex A or Annex B; and

(ii) Products and articles in use and wastes consisting of, containing or contaminated with a chemical listed in Annex A, B or C;

(b) Identify, to the extent practicable, stockpiles consisting of or containing chemicals listed either in Annex A or Annex B on the basis of the strategies referred to in subparagraph (a);

(c) Manage stockpiles, as appropriate, in a safe, efficient and environmentally sound manner. Stockpiles of chemicals listed either in Annex A or Annex B, after they are no longer allowed to be used according to any specific exemption specified in Annex A or any specific exemption or acceptable purpose specified in Annex B, except stockpiles which are allowed to be exported according to paragraph 2 of Article 3, shall be deemed to be waste and shall be managed in accordance with subparagraph (d);

(d) Take appropriate measures so that such wastes, including products and articles upon becoming wastes, are:

(i) Handled, collected, transported and stored in an environmentally sound manner;

(ii) Disposed of in such a way that the persistent organic pollutant content is destroyed or irreversibly transformed so that they do not exhibit the characteristics of persistent organic pollutants or otherwise disposed of in an environmentally sound manner when destruction or irreversible transformation does not represent the environmentally preferable option or the persistent organic pollutant content is low, taking into account international rules, standards, and guidelines, including those that may be developed pursuant to paragraph 2, and relevant global and regional regimes governing the management of hazardous wastes;

(iii) Not permitted to be subjected to disposal operations that may lead to recovery, recycling, reclamation, direct reuse or alternative uses of persistent organic pollutants; and

(iv) Not transported across international boundaries without taking into account relevant international rules, standards and guidelines;

(e) Endeavour to develop appropriate strategies for identifying sites contaminated by chemicals listed in Annex A, B or C; if remediation of those sites is undertaken it shall be performed in an environmentally sound manner.

2. The Conference of the Parties shall cooperate closely with the appropriate bodies of the Basel Convention on the Control of Transboundary Movements of Hazardous Wastes and their Disposal to, inter alia:

(a) Establish levels of destruction and irreversible transformation necessary to ensure that the characteristics of persistent organic pollutants as specified in paragraph 1 of Annex D are not exhibited;

(b) Determine what they consider to be the methods that constitute environmentally sound disposal referred to above; and

(c) Work to establish, as appropriate, the concentration levels of the chemicals listed in Annexes A, B and C in order to define the low persistent organic pollutant content referred to in paragraph 1(d)(ii).

Article 7   Implementation plans

1. Each Party shall:

(a) Develop and endeavour to implement a plan for the implementation of its obligations under this Convention;

(b) Transmit its implementation plan to the Conference of the Parties within two years of the date on which this Convention enters into force for it; and

(c) Review and update, as appropriate, its implementation plan on a periodic basis and in a manner to be specified by a decision of the Conference of the Parties.

2. The Parties shall, where appropriate, cooperate directly or through global, regional and subregional organizations, and consult their national stakeholders, including women's groups and groups involved in the health of children, in order to facilitate the development, implementation and updating of their implementation plans.

3. The Parties shall endeavour to utilize and, where necessary, establish the means to integrate national implementation plans for persistent organic pollutants in their sustainable development strategies where appropriate.

Article 8   Listing of chemicals in Annexes A, B and C

1. A Party may submit a proposal to the Secretariat for listing a chemical in Annexes A, B and/or C. The proposal shall contain the information specified in Annex D. In developing a proposal, a Party may be assisted by other Parties and/or by the Secretariat.

2. The Secretariat shall verify whether the proposal contains the information specified in Annex D. If the Secretariat is satisfied that the proposal contains the information so specified, it shall forward the proposal to the Persistent Organic Pollutants Review Committee.

3. The Committee shall examine the proposal and apply the screening criteria specified in Annex D in a flexible and transparent way, taking all information provided into account in an integrative and balanced manner.

4. If the Committee decides that:

>   (a) It is satisfied that the screening criteria have been fulfilled, it shall, through the Secretariat, make the proposal and the evaluation of the Committee available to all Parties and observers and invite them to submit the information specified in Annex E; or

>   (b) It is not satisfied that the screening criteria have been fulfilled, it shall, through the Secretariat, inform all Parties and observers and make the proposal and the evaluation of the Committee available to all Parties and the proposal shall be set aside.

5. Any Party may resubmit a proposal to the Committee that has been set aside by the Committee pursuant to paragraph 4. The resubmission may include any concerns of the Party as well as a justification for additional consideration by the Committee. If, following this procedure, the Committee again sets the proposal aside, the Party may challenge the decision of the Committee and the Conference of the Parties shall consider the matter at its next session. The Conference of the Parties may decide, based on the screening criteria in Annex D and taking into account the evaluation of the Committee and any additional information provided by any Party or observer, that the proposal should proceed.

6. Where the Committee has decided that the screening criteria have been fulfilled, or the Conference of the Parties has decided that the proposal should proceed, the Committee shall further review the proposal, taking into account any relevant additional information received, and shall prepare a draft risk profile in accordance with Annex E. It shall, through the Secretariat, make that draft available to all Parties and observers, collect technical comments from them and, taking those comments into account, complete the risk profile.

7. If, on the basis of the risk profile conducted in accordance with Annex E, the Committee decides:

>   (a) That the chemical is likely as a result of its long-range environmental transport to lead to significant adverse human health and/or environmental effects such that global action is warranted, the proposal shall proceed. Lack of full scientific certainty shall not prevent the proposal from proceeding. The Committee shall, through the Secretariat, invite information from all Parties and observers relating to the considerations specified in Annex F. It shall then prepare a risk management evaluation that includes an analysis of possible control measures for the chemical in accordance with that Annex; or

>   (b) That the proposal should not proceed, it shall, through the Secretariat, make the risk profile available to all Parties and observers and set the proposal aside.

8. For any proposal set aside pursuant to paragraph 7(b), a Party may request the Conference of the Parties to consider instructing the Committee to invite additional information from the proposing Party and other Parties during a period not to exceed one year. After that period and on the basis of any information received, the Committee shall reconsider the proposal pursuant to paragraph 6 with a priority to be decided by the Conference of the Parties. If, following this procedure, the Committee again sets the proposal aside, the Party may challenge the decision of the Committee and the Conference of the Parties shall consider the matter at its next session. The Conference of the Parties may decide, based on the risk profile prepared in accordance with Annex E and taking into account the evaluation of the Committee and any additional information provided by any Party or observer, that the proposal should proceed. If the Conference of the Parties decides that the proposal shall proceed, the Committee shall then prepare the risk management evaluation.

9. The Committee shall, based on the risk profile referred to in paragraph 6 and the risk management evaluation referred to in paragraph 7(a) or paragraph 8, recommend whether the chemical should be considered by the Conference of the Parties for listing in Annexes A, B and/or C. The Conference of the Parties, taking due account of the recommendations of the Committee, including any scientific uncertainty, shall decide, in a precautionary manner, whether to list the chemical, and specify its related control measures, in Annexes A, B and/or C.

Article 9   Information exchange

1. Each Party shall facilitate or undertake the exchange of information relevant to:

(a) The reduction or elimination of the production, use and release of persistent organic pollutants; and

(b) Alternatives to persistent organic pollutants, including information relating to their risks as well as to their economic and social costs.

2. The Parties shall exchange the information referred to in paragraph 1 directly or through the Secretariat.

3. Each Party shall designate a national focal point for the exchange of such information.

4. The Secretariat shall serve as a clearing-house mechanism for information on persistent organic pollutants, including information provided by Parties, intergovernmental organizations and non-governmental organizations.

5. For the purposes of this Convention, information on health and safety of humans and the environment shall not be regarded as confidential. Parties that exchange other information pursuant to this Convention shall protect any confidential information as mutually agreed.

Article 10   Public information, awareness and education

Each Party shall, within its capabilities, promote and facilitate:

(a) Awareness among its policy and decision makers with regard to persistent organic pollutants;

(b) Provision to the public of all available information on persistent organic pollutants, taking into account paragraph 5 of Article 9;

(c) Development and implementation, especially for women, children and the least educated, of educational and public awareness programmes on persistent organic pollutants, as well as on their health and environmental effects and on their alternatives;

(d) Public participation in addressing persistent organic pollutants and their health and environmental effects and in developing adequate responses, including opportunities for providing input at the national level regarding implementation of this Convention;

(e) Training of workers, scientists, educators and technical and managerial personnel;

(f) Development and exchange of educational and public awareness materials at the national and international levels; and

(g) Development and implementation of education and training programmes at the national and international levels.

2. Each Party shall, within its capabilities, ensure that the public has access to the public information referred to in paragraph 1 and that the information is kept up-to-date.

3. Each Party shall, within its capabilities, encourage industry and professional users to promote and facilitate the provision of the information referred to in paragraph 1 at the national level and, as appropriate, subregional, regional and global levels.

4. In providing information on persistent organic pollutants and their alternatives, Parties may use safety data sheets, reports, mass media and other means of communication, and may establish information centres at national and regional levels.

5. Each Party shall give sympathetic consideration to developing mechanisms, such as pollutant release and transfer registers, for the collection and dissemination of information on estimates of the annual quantities of the chemicals listed in Annex A, B or C that are released or disposed of.

Article 11   Research, development and monitoring

1. The Parties shall, within their capabilities, at the national and international levels, encourage and/or undertake appropriate research, development, monitoring and cooperation pertaining to persistent organic pollutants and, where relevant, to their alternatives and to candidate persistent organic pollutants, including on their:

(a) Sources and releases into the environment;

(b) Presence, levels and trends in humans and the environment;

(c) Environmental transport, fate and transformation;

(d) Effects on human health and the environment;

(e) Socio-economic and cultural impacts;

(f) Release reduction and/or elimination; and

(g) Harmonized methodologies for making inventories of generating sources and analytical techniques for the measurement of releases.

2. In undertaking action under paragraph 1, the Parties shall, within their capabilities:

(a) Support and further develop, as appropriate, international programmes, networks and organizations aimed at defining, conducting, assessing and financing research, data collection and monitoring, taking into account the need to minimize duplication of effort;

(b) Support national and international efforts to strengthen national scientific and technical research capabilities, particularly in developing countries and countries with economies in transition, and to promote access to, and the exchange of, data and analyses;

(c) Take into account the concerns and needs, particularly in the field of financial and technical resources, of developing countries and countries with economies in transition and cooperate in improving their capability to participate in the efforts referred to in subparagraphs (a) and (b);

(d) Undertake research work geared towards alleviating the effects of persistent organic pollutants on reproductive health;

(e) Make the results of their research, development and monitoring activities referred to in this paragraph accessible to the public on a timely and regular basis; and

(f) Encourage and/or undertake cooperation with regard to storage and maintenance of information generated from research, development and monitoring.

Article 12   Technical assistance

1. The Parties recognize that rendering of timely and appropriate technical assistance in response to requests from developing country Parties and Parties with economies in transition is essential to the successful implementation of this Convention.

2. The Parties shall cooperate to provide timely and appropriate technical assistance to developing country Parties and Parties with economies in transition, to assist them, taking into account their particular needs, to develop and strengthen their capacity to implement their obligations under this Convention.

3. In this regard, technical assistance to be provided by developed country Parties, and other Parties in accordance with their capabilities, shall include, as appropriate and as mutually agreed, technical assistance for capacity-building relating to implementation of the obligations under this Convention. Further guidance in this regard shall be provided by the Conference of the Parties.

4. The Parties shall establish, as appropriate, arrangements for the purpose of providing technical assistance and promoting the transfer of technology to developing country Parties and Parties with economies in transition relating to the implementation of this Convention. These arrangements shall include regional and subregional centres for capacity-building and transfer of technology to assist developing country Parties and Parties with economies in transition to fulfil their obligations under this Convention. Further guidance in this regard shall be provided by the Conference of the Parties.

5. The Parties shall, in the context of this Article, take full account of the specific needs and special situation of least developed countries and small island developing states in their actions with regard to technical assistance.

Article 13   Financial resources and mechanisms

1. Each Party undertakes to provide, within its capabilities, financial support and incentives in respect of those national activities that are intended to achieve the objective of this Convention in accordance with its national plans, priorities and programmes.

2. The developed country Parties shall provide new and additional financial resources to enable developing country Parties and Parties with economies in transition to meet the agreed full incremental costs of implementing measures which fulfill their obligations under this Convention as agreed between a recipient Party and an entity participating in the mechanism described in paragraph 6. Other Parties may also on a voluntary basis and in accordance with their capabilities provide such financial resources. Contributions from other sources should also be encouraged. The implementation of these commitments shall take into account the need for adequacy, predictability, the timely flow of funds and the importance of burden sharing among the contributing Parties.

3. Developed country Parties, and other Parties in accordance with their capabilities and in accordance with their national plans, priorities and programmes, may also provide and developing country Parties and Parties with economies in transition avail themselves of financial resources to assist in their implementation of this Convention through other bilateral, regional and multilateral sources or channels.

4. The extent to which the developing country Parties will effectively implement their commitments under this Convention will depend on the effective implementation by developed country Parties of their commitments under this Convention relating to financial resources, technical assistance and technology transfer. The fact that sustainable economic and social development and eradication of poverty are the first and overriding priorities of the developing country Parties will be taken fully into account, giving due consideration to the need for the protection of human health and the environment.

5. The Parties shall take full account of the specific needs and special situation of the least developed countries and the small island developing states in their actions with regard to funding.

6. A mechanism for the provision of adequate and sustainable financial resources to developing country Parties and Parties with economies in transition on a grant or concessional basis to assist in their implementation of the Convention is hereby defined. The mechanism shall function under the authority, as appropriate, and guidance of, and be accountable to the Conference of the Parties for the purposes of this Convention. Its operation shall be entrusted to one or more entities, including existing international entities, as may be decided upon by the Conference of the Parties. The mechanism may also include other entities providing multilateral, regional and bilateral financial and technical assistance. Contributions to the mechanism shall be additional to other financial transfers to developing country Parties and Parties with economies in transition as reflected in, and in accordance with, paragraph 2.

7. Pursuant to the objectives of this Convention and paragraph 6, the Conference of the Parties shall at its first meeting adopt appropriate guidance to be provided to the mechanism and shall agree with the entity or entities participating in the financial mechanism upon arrangements to give effect thereto. The guidance shall address, *inter alia*:

> (a) The determination of the policy, strategy and programme priorities, as well as clear and detailed criteria and guidelines regarding eligibility for access to and utilization of financial resources including monitoring and evaluation on a regular basis of such utilization;

(b) The provision by the entity or entities of regular reports to the Conference of the Parties on adequacy and sustainability of funding for activities relevant to the implementation of this Convention;

(c) The promotion of multiple-source funding approaches, mechanisms and arrangements;

(d) The modalities for the determination in a predictable and identifiable manner of the amount of funding necessary and available for the implementation of this Convention, keeping in mind that the phasing out of persistent organic pollutants might require sustained funding, and the conditions under which that amount shall be periodically reviewed; and

(e) The modalities for the provision to interested Parties of assistance with needs assessment, information on available sources of funds and on funding patterns in order to facilitate coordination among them.

8. The Conference of the Parties shall review, not later than its second meeting and thereafter on a regular basis, the effectiveness of the mechanism established under this Article, its ability to address the changing needs of the developing country Parties and Parties with economies in transition, the criteria and guidance referred to in paragraph 7, the level of funding as well as the effectiveness of the performance of the institutional entities entrusted to operate the financial mechanism. It shall, based on such review, take appropriate action, if necessary, to improve the effectiveness of the mechanism, including by means of recommendations and guidance on measures to ensure adequate and sustainable funding to meet the needs of the Parties.

Article 14   Interim financial arrangements

The institutional structure of the Global Environment Facility, operated in accordance with the Instrument for the Establishment of the Restructured Global Environment Facility, shall, on an interim basis, be the principal entity entrusted with the operations of the financial mechanism referred to in Article 13, for the period between the date of entry into force of this Convention and the first meeting of the Conference of the Parties, or until such time as the Conference of the Parties decides which institutional structure will be designated in accordance with Article 13. The institutional structure of the Global Environment Facility should fulfill this function through operational measures related specifically to persistent organic pollutants taking into account that new arrangements for this area may be needed.

Article 15   Reporting

1. Each Party shall report to the Conference of the Parties on the measures it has taken to implement the provisions of this Convention and on the effectiveness of such measures in meeting the objectives of the Convention.

2. Each Party shall provide to the Secretariat:

(a) Statistical data on its total quantities of production, import and export of each of the chemicals listed in Annex A and Annex B or a reasonable estimate of such data; and

(b) To the extent practicable, a list of the States from which it has imported each such substance and the States to which it has exported each such substance.

3. Such reporting shall be at periodic intervals and in a format to be decided by the Conference of the Parties at its first meeting.

Article 16   Effectiveness evaluation

1. Commencing four years after the date of entry into force of this Convention, and periodically thereafter at intervals to be decided by the Conference of the Parties, the Conference shall evaluate the effectiveness of this Convention.

2. In order to facilitate such evaluation, the Conference of the Parties shall, at its first meeting, initiate the establishment of arrangements to provide itself with comparable monitoring data on the presence of the chemicals listed in Annexes A, B and C as well as their regional and global environmental transport. These arrangements:

(a) Should be implemented by the Parties on a regional basis when appropriate, in accordance with their technical and financial capabilities, using existing monitoring programmes and mechanisms to the extent possible and promoting harmonization of approaches;

(b) May be supplemented where necessary, taking into account the differences between regions and their capabilities to implement monitoring activities; and

(c) Shall include reports to the Conference of the Parties on the results of the monitoring activities on a regional and global basis at intervals to be specified by the Conference of the Parties.

3. The evaluation described in paragraph 1 shall be conducted on the basis of available scientific, environmental, technical and economic information, including:

(a) Reports and other monitoring information provided pursuant to paragraph 2;

(b) National reports submitted pursuant to Article 15; and

(c) Non-compliance information provided pursuant to the procedures established under Article 17.

Article 17   Non-compliance

The Conference of the Parties shall, as soon as practicable, develop and approve procedures and institutional mechanisms for determining non-compliance with the provisions of this Convention and for the treatment of Parties found to be in non-compliance.

Article 18   Settlement of disputes

1. Parties shall settle any dispute between them concerning the interpretation or application of this Convention through negotiation or other peaceful means of their own choice.

2. When ratifying, accepting, approving or acceding to the Convention, or at any time thereafter, a Party that is not a regional economic integration organization may declare in a written instrument submitted to the depositary that, with respect to any dispute concerning the interpretation or application of the Convention, it recognizes one or both of the following means of dispute settlement as compulsory in relation to any Party accepting the same obligation:

(a) Arbitration in accordance with procedures to be adopted by the Conference of the Parties in an annex as soon as practicable;

(b) Submission of the dispute to the International Court of Justice.

3. A Party that is a regional economic integration organization may make a declaration with like effect in relation to arbitration in accordance with the procedure referred to in paragraph 2 (a).

4. A declaration made pursuant to paragraph 2 or paragraph 3 shall remain in force until it expires in accordance with its terms or until three months after written notice of its revocation has been deposited with the depositary.

5. The expiry of a declaration, a notice of revocation or a new declaration shall not in any way affect proceedings pending before an arbitral tribunal or the International Court of Justice unless the parties to the dispute otherwise agree.

6. If the parties to a dispute have not accepted the same or any procedure pursuant to paragraph 2, and if they have not been able to settle their dispute within twelve months following notification by one party to another that a dispute exists between them, the dispute shall be submitted to a conciliation commission at the request of any party to the dispute. The conciliation commission shall render a report with recommendations. Additional procedures relating to the conciliation commission shall be included in an annex to be adopted by the Conference of the Parties no later than at its second meeting.

Article 19   Conference of the Parties

1. A Conference of the Parties is hereby established.

2. The first meeting of the Conference of the Parties shall be convened by the Executive Director of the United Nations Environment Programme no later than one year after the entry into force of this Convention. Thereafter, ordinary meetings of the Conference of the Parties shall be held at regular intervals to be decided by the Conference.

3. Extraordinary meetings of the Conference of the Parties shall be held at such other times as may be deemed necessary by the Conference, or at the written request of any Party provided that it is supported by at least one third of the Parties.

4. The Conference of the Parties shall by consensus agree upon and adopt at its first meeting rules of procedure and financial rules for itself and any subsidiary bodies, as well as financial provisions governing the functioning of the Secretariat.

5. The Conference of the Parties shall keep under continuous review and evaluation the implementation of this Convention. It shall perform the functions assigned to it by the Convention and, to this end, shall:

   (a) Establish, further to the requirements of paragraph 6, such subsidiary bodies as it considers necessary for the implementation of the Convention;

   (b) Cooperate, where appropriate, with competent international organizations and intergovernmental and non-governmental bodies; and

   (c) Regularly review all information made available to the Parties pursuant to Article 15, including consideration of the effectiveness of paragraph 2 (b) (iii) of Article 3;

   (d) Consider and undertake any additional action that may be required for the achievement of the objectives of the Convention.

6. The Conference of the Parties shall, at its first meeting, establish a subsidiary body to be called the Persistent Organic Pollutants Review Committee for the purposes of performing the functions assigned to that Committee by this Convention. In this regard:

   (a) The members of the Persistent Organic Pollutants Review Committee shall be appointed by the Conference of the Parties. Membership of the Committee shall consist of government-designated experts in chemical assessment or management. The members of the Committee shall be appointed on the basis of equitable geographical distribution;

   (b) The Conference of the Parties shall decide on the terms of reference, organization and operation of the Committee; and

   (c) The Committee shall make every effort to adopt its recommendations by consensus. If all efforts at consensus have been exhausted, and no consensus reached, such recommendation shall as a last resort be adopted by a two-thirds majority vote of the members present and voting.

7. The Conference of the Parties shall, at its third meeting, evaluate the continued need for the procedure contained in paragraph 2 (b) of Article 3, including consideration of its effectiveness.

8. The United Nations, its specialized agencies and the International Atomic Energy Agency, as well as any State not Party to this Convention, may be represented at meetings of the Conference of the Parties as observers. Any body or agency, whether national or international, governmental or non-governmental, qualified in matters covered by the Convention, and which has informed the Secretariat of its wish to be represented at a meeting of the Conference of the Parties as an observer may be admitted unless at least one third of the Parties present object. The admission and participation of observers shall be subject to the rules of procedure adopted by the Conference of the Parties.

Article 20   Secretariat

1. A Secretariat is hereby established.

2. The functions of the Secretariat shall be:

(a) To make arrangements for meetings of the Conference of the Parties and its subsidiary bodies and to provide them with services as required;

(b) To facilitate assistance to the Parties, particularly developing country Parties and Parties with economies in transition, on request, in the implementation of this Convention;

(c) To ensure the necessary coordination with the secretariats of other relevant international bodies;

(d) To prepare and make available to the Parties periodic reports based on information received pursuant to Article 15 and other available information;

(e) To enter, under the overall guidance of the Conference of the Parties, into such administrative and contractual arrangements as may be required for the effective discharge of its functions; and

(f) To perform the other secretariat functions specified in this Convention and such other functions as may be determined by the Conference of the Parties.

3. The secretariat functions for this Convention shall be performed by the Executive Director of the United Nations Environment Programme, unless the Conference of the Parties decides, by a three-fourths majority of the Parties present and voting, to entrust the secretariat functions to one or more other international organizations.

Article 21   Amendments to the Convention

1. Amendments to this Convention may be proposed by any Party.

2. Amendments to this Convention shall be adopted at a meeting of the Conference of the Parties. The text of any proposed amendment shall be communicated to the Parties by the Secretariat at least six months before the meeting at which it is proposed for adoption. The Secretariat shall also communicate proposed amendments to the signatories to this Convention and, for information, to the depositary.

3. The Parties shall make every effort to reach agreement on any proposed amendment to this Convention by consensus. If all efforts at consensus have been exhausted, and no agreement reached, the amendment shall as a last resort be adopted by a three-fourths majority vote of the Parties present and voting.

4. The amendment shall be communicated by the depositary to all Parties for ratification, acceptance or approval.

5. Ratification, acceptance or approval of an amendment shall be notified to the depositary in writing. An amendment adopted in accordance with paragraph 3 shall enter into force for the Parties having accepted it on the ninetieth day after the date of deposit of instruments of ratification, acceptance or approval by at least three-fourths of the Parties. Thereafter, the amendment shall enter into force for any other Party on the ninetieth day after the date on which that Party deposits its instrument of ratification, acceptance or approval of the amendment.

Article 22   Adoption and amendment of annexes

1. Annexes to this Convention shall form an integral part thereof and, unless expressly provided otherwise, a reference to this Convention constitutes at the same time a reference to any annexes thereto.

2. Any additional annexes shall be restricted to procedural, scientific, technical or administrative matters.

3. The following procedure shall apply to the proposal, adoption and entry into force of additional annexes to this Convention:

(a) Additional annexes shall be proposed and adopted according to the procedure laid down in paragraphs 1, 2 and 3 of Article 21;

(b) Any Party that is unable to accept an additional annex shall so notify the depositary, in writing, within one year from the date of communication by the depositary of the adoption of the additional annex. The depositary shall without delay notify all Parties of any such notification received. A Party may at any time withdraw a previous notification of non-acceptance in respect of any additional annex, and the annex shall thereupon enter into force for that Party subject to subparagraph (c); and

(c) On the expiry of one year from the date of the communication by the depositary of the adoption of an additional annex, the annex shall enter into force for all Parties that have not submitted a notification in accordance with the provisions of subparagraph (b).

4. The proposal, adoption and entry into force of amendments to Annex A, B or C shall be subject to the same procedures as for the proposal, adoption and entry into force of additional annexes to this Convention, except that an amendment to Annex A, B or C shall not enter into force with respect to any Party that has made a declaration with respect to amendment to those Annexes in accordance with paragraph 4 of Article 25, in which case any such amendment shall enter into force for such a Party on the ninetieth day after the date of deposit with the depositary of its instrument of ratification, acceptance, approval or accession with respect to such amendment.

5. The following procedure shall apply to the proposal, adoption and entry into force of an amendment to Annex D, E or F:

(a) Amendments shall be proposed according to the procedure in paragraphs 1 and 2 of Article 21;

(b) The Parties shall take decisions on an amendment to Annex D, E or F by consensus; and

(c) A decision to amend Annex D, E or F shall forthwith be communicated to the Parties by the depositary. The amendment shall enter into force for all Parties on a date to be specified in the decision.

6. If an additional annex or an amendment to an annex is related to an amendment to this Convention, the additional annex or amendment shall not enter into force until such time as the amendment to the Convention enters into force.

Article 23   Right to vote

1. Each Party to this Convention shall have one vote, except as provided for in paragraph 2.

2. A regional economic integration organization, on matters within its competence, shall exercise its right to vote with a number of votes equal to the number of its member States that are Parties to this Convention. Such an organization shall not exercise its right to vote if any of its member States exercises its right to vote, and vice versa.

Article 24   Signature

This Convention shall be open for signature at Stockholm by all States and regional economic integration organizations on 23 May 2001, and at the United Nations Headquarters in New York from 24 May 2001 to 22 May 2002.

Article 25   Ratification, acceptance, approval or accession

1. This Convention shall be subject to ratification, acceptance or approval by States and by regional economic integration organizations. It shall be open for accession by States and by regional economic integration organizations from the day after the date on which the Convention is closed for signature. Instruments of ratification, acceptance, approval or accession shall be deposited with the depositary.

2. Any regional economic integration organization that becomes a Party to this Convention without any of its member States being a Party shall be bound by all the obligations under the Convention. In the case of such

organizations, one or more of whose member States is a Party to this Convention, the organization and its member States shall decide on their respective responsibilities for the performance of their obligations under the Convention. In such cases, the organization and the member States shall not be entitled to exercise rights under the Convention concurrently.

3. In its instrument of ratification, acceptance, approval or accession, a regional economic integration organization shall declare the extent of its competence in respect of the matters governed by this Convention. Any such organization shall also inform the depositary, who shall in turn inform the Parties, of any relevant modification in the extent of its competence.

4. In its instrument of ratification, acceptance, approval or accession, any Party may declare that, with respect to it, any amendment to Annex A, B or C shall enter into force only upon the deposit of its instrument of ratification, acceptance, approval or accession with respect thereto.

Article 26   Entry into force

1. This Convention shall enter into force on the ninetieth day after the date of deposit of the fiftieth instrument of ratification, acceptance, approval or accession.

2. For each State or regional economic integration organization that ratifies, accepts or approves this Convention or accedes thereto after the deposit of the fiftieth instrument of ratification, acceptance, approval or accession, the Convention shall enter into force on the ninetieth day after the date of deposit by such State or regional economic integration organization of its instrument of ratification, acceptance, approval or accession.

3. For the purpose of paragraphs 1 and 2, any instrument deposited by a regional economic integration organization shall not be counted as additional to those deposited by member States of that organization.

Article 27   Reservations

No reservations may be made to this Convention.

Article 28   Withdrawal

1. At any time after three years from the date on which this Convention has entered into force for a Party, that Party may withdraw from the Convention by giving written notification to the depositary.

2. Any such withdrawal shall take effect upon the expiry of one year from the date of receipt by the depositary of the notification of withdrawal, or on such later date as may be specified in the notification of withdrawal.

Article 29   Depositary

The Secretary-General of the United Nations shall be the depositary of this Convention.

Article 30   Authentic texts

The original of this Convention, of which the Arabic, Chinese, English, French, Russian and Spanish texts are equally authentic, shall be deposited with the Secretary-General of the United Nations.

IN WITNESS WHEREOF the undersigned, being duly authorized to that effect, have signed this Convention.

Done at Stockholm on this twenty-second day of May, two thousand and one.

Annex A

ELIMINATION

Part I

Chemical	Activity	Specific exemption
Aldrin* CAS No: 309-00-2	Production	None
	Use	Local ectoparasiticide Insecticide
Chlordane* CAS No: 57-74-9	Production	As allowed for the Parties listed in the Register
	Use	Local ectoparasiticide Insecticide Termiticide Termiticide in buildings and dams Termiticide in roads Additive in plywood adhesives
Dieldrin* CAS No: 60-57-1	Production	None
	Use	In agricultural operations
Endrin* CAS No: 72-20-8	Production	None
	Use	None
Heptachlor* CAS No: 76-44-8	Production	None
	Use	Termiticide Termiticide in structures of houses Termiticide (subterranean) Wood treatment In use in underground cable boxes
Hexachlorobenzene CAS No: 118-74-1	Production	As allowed for the Parties listed in the Register
	Use	Intermediate Solvent in pesticide Closed system site limited intermediate
Mirex* CAS No: 2385-85-5	Production	As allowed for the Parties listed in the Register
	Use	Termiticide
Toxaphene* CAS No: 8001-35-2	Production	None
	Use	None
Polychlorinated Biphenyls (PCB)*	Production	None
	Use	Articles in use in accordance with the provisions of Part II of this Annex

Notes:

(i)   Except as otherwise specified in this Convention, quantities of a chemical occurring as unintentional trace contaminants in products and articles shall not be considered to be listed in this Annex;

(ii)   This note shall not be considered as a production and use specific exemption for purposes of paragraph 2 of Article 3. Quantities of a chemical occurring as constituents of articles manufactured or already in use before or on the date of entry into force of the relevant obligation with respect to that chemical, shall not be considered as listed in this Annex, provided that a Party has notified the Secretariat that a particular type of article remains in use within that Party. The Secretariat shall make such notifications publicly available;

(iii)   This note, which does not apply to a chemical that has an asterisk following its name in the Chemical column in Part I of this Annex, shall not be considered as a production and use specific exemption for purposes of paragraph 2 of Article 3. Given that no significant quantities of the chemical are expected to reach humans and the environment during the production and use of a closed-system site-limited intermediate, a Party, upon notification to the Secretariat, may allow the production and use of quantities of a chemical listed in this Annex as a closed-system site-limited intermediate that is chemically transformed in the manufacture of other chemicals that, taking into consideration the criteria in paragraph 1 of Annex D, do not exhibit the characteristics of persistent organic pollutants. This notification shall include information on total production and use of such chemical or a reasonable estimate of such information and information regarding the nature of the closed-system site-limited process including the amount of any non-transformed and unintentional trace contamination of the persistent organic pollutant-starting material in the final product. This procedure applies except as otherwise specified in this Annex. The Secretariat shall make such notifications available to the Conference of the Parties and to the public. Such production or use shall not be considered a production or use specific exemption. Such production and use shall cease after a ten-year period, unless the Party concerned submits a new notification to the Secretariat, in which case the period will be extended for an additional ten years unless the Conference of the Parties, after a review of the production and use decides otherwise. The notification procedure can be repeated;

(iv)   All the specific exemptions in this Annex may be exercised by Parties that have registered exemptions in respect of them in accordance with Article 4 with the exception of the use of polychlorinated biphenyls in articles in use in accordance with the provisions of Part II of this Annex, which may be exercised by all Parties.

Part II

Polychlorinated biphenyls

Each Party shall:

(a) With regard to the elimination of the use of polychlorinated biphenyls in equipment (e.g. transformers, capacitors or other receptacles containing liquid stocks) by 2025, subject to review by the Conference of the Parties, take action in accordance with the following priorities:

(i) Make determined efforts to identify, label and remove from use equipment containing greater than 10 per cent polychlorinated biphenyls and volumes greater than 5 litres;

(ii) Make determined efforts to identify, label and remove from use equipment containing greater than 0.05 per cent polychlorinated biphenyls and volumes greater than 5 litres;

(iii) Endeavour to identify and remove from use equipment containing greater than 0.005 percent polychlorinated biphenyls and volumes greater than 0.05 litres;

(b) Consistent with the priorities in subparagraph (a), promote the following measures to reduce exposures and risk to control the use of polychlorinated biphenyls:

(i) Use only in intact and non-leaking equipment and only in areas where the risk from environmental release can be minimised and quickly remedied;

(ii) Not use in equipment in areas associated with the production or processing of food or feed;

(iii) When used in populated areas, including schools and hospitals, all reasonable measures to protect from electrical failure which could result in a fire, and regular inspection of equipment for leaks;

(c) Notwithstanding paragraph 2 of Article 3, ensure that equipment containing polychlorinated biphenyls, as described in subparagraph (a), shall not be exported or imported except for the purpose of environmentally sound waste management;

(d) Except for maintenance and servicing operations, not allow recovery for the purpose of reuse in other equipment of liquids with polychlorinated biphenyls content above 0.005 per cent;

(e) Make determined efforts designed to lead to environmentally sound waste management of liquids containing polychlorinated biphenyls and equipment contaminated with polychlorinated biphenyls having a polychlorinated biphenyls content above 0.005 per cent, in accordance with paragraph 1 of Article 6, as soon as possible but no later than 2028, subject to review by the Conference of the Parties;

(f) In lieu of note (ii) in Part I of this Annex, endeavour to identify other articles containing more than 0.005 per cent polychlorinated biphenyls (e.g. cable-sheaths, cured caulk and painted objects) and manage them in accordance with paragraph 1 of Article 6;

(g) Provide a report every five years on progress in eliminating polychlorinated biphenyls and submit it to the Conference of the Parties pursuant to Article 15;

(h) The reports described in subparagraph (g) shall, as appropriate, be considered by the Conference of the Parties in its reviews relating to polychlorinated biphenyls. The Conference of the Parties shall review progress towards elimination of polychlorinated biphenyls at five year intervals or other period, as appropriate, taking into account such reports.

Annex B

RESTRICTION

Part I

Chemical	Activity	Acceptable purpose or specific exemption
DDT (1,1,1-trichloro-2,2-bis(4-chlorophenyl)ethane) CAS No: 50-29-3	Production	Acceptable purpose: Disease vector control use in accordance with Part II of this Annex Specific exemption: Intermediate in production of dicofol Intermediate
	Use	Acceptable purpose: Disease vector control in accordance with Part II of this Annex Specific exemption: Production of dicofol Intermediate

Notes:

(i)   Except as otherwise specified in this Convention, quantities of a chemical occurring as unintentional trace contaminants in products and articles shall not be considered to be listed in this Annex;

(ii)   This note shall not be considered as a production and use acceptable purpose or specific exemption for purposes of paragraph 2 of Article 3. Quantities of a chemical occurring as constituents of articles manufactured or already in use before or on the date of entry into force of the relevant obligation with respect to that chemical, shall not be considered as listed in this Annex, provided that a Party has notified the Secretariat that a particular type of article remains in use within that Party. The Secretariat shall make such notifications publicly available;

(iii)   This note shall not be considered as a production and use specific exemption for purposes of paragraph 2 of Article 3. Given that no significant quantities of the chemical are expected to reach humans and the environment during the production and use of a closed-system site-limited intermediate, a Party, upon notification to the Secretariat, may allow the production and use of quantities of a chemical listed in this Annex as a closed-system site-limited intermediate that is chemically transformed in the manufacture of other chemicals that, taking into consideration the criteria in paragraph 1 of Annex D, do not exhibit the characteristics of persistent organic pollutants. This notification shall include information on total production and use of such chemical or a reasonable estimate of such information and information regarding the nature of the closed-system site-limited process including the amount of any non-transformed and unintentional trace contamination of the persistent organic pollutant-starting material in the final product. This procedure applies except as otherwise specified in this Annex. The Secretariat shall make such notifications available to the Conference of the Parties and to the public. Such production or use shall not be considered a production or use specific exemption.

Such production and use shall cease after a ten-year period, unless the Party concerned submits a new notification to the Secretariat, in which case the period will be extended for an additional ten years unless the Conference of the Parties, after a review of the production and use decides otherwise. The notification procedure can be repeated;

(iv)   All the specific exemptions in this Annex may be exercised by Parties that have registered in respect of them in accordance with Article 4.

Part II

DDT (1,1,1-trichloro-2,2-bis(4-chlorophenyl)ethane)

1. The production and use of DDT shall be eliminated except for Parties that have notified the Secretariat of their intention to produce and/or use it. A DDT Register is hereby established and shall be available to the public. The Secretariat shall maintain the DDT Register.

2. Each Party that produces and/or uses DDT shall restrict such production and/or use for disease vector control in accordance with the World Health Organization recommendations and guidelines on the use of DDT and when locally safe, effective and affordable alternatives are not available to the Party in question.

3. In the event that a Party not listed in the DDT Register determines that it requires DDT for disease vector control, it shall notify the Secretariat as soon as possible in order to have its name added forthwith to the DDT Register. It shall at the same time notify the World Health Organization.

4. Every three years, each Party that uses DDT shall provide to the Secretariat and the World Health Organization information on the amount used, the conditions of such use and its relevance to that Party's disease management strategy, in a format to be decided by the Conference of the Parties in consultation with the World Health Organization.

5. With the goal of reducing and ultimately eliminating the use of DDT, the Conference of the Parties shall encourage:

    (a) Each Party using DDT to develop and implement an action plan as part of the implementation plan specified in Article 7. That action plan shall include:

        (i)   Development of regulatory and other mechanisms to ensure that DDT use is restricted to disease vector control;

        (ii)   Implementation of suitable alternative products, methods and strategies, including resistance management strategies to ensure the continuing effectiveness of these alternatives;

        (iii)   Measures to strengthen health care and to reduce the incidence of the disease.

    (b) The Parties, within their capabilities, to promote research and development of safe alternative chemical and non-chemical products, methods and strategies for Parties using DDT, relevant to the conditions of those countries and with the goal of decreasing the human and economic burden of disease. Factors to be promoted when considering alternatives or combinations of alternatives shall include the human health risks and environmental implications of such alternatives. Viable alternatives to DDT shall pose less risk to human health and the environment, be suitable for disease control based on conditions in the Parties in question and be supported with monitoring data.

6. Commencing at its first meeting, and at least every three years thereafter, the Conference of the Parties shall, in consultation with the World Health Organization, evaluate the continued need for DDT for disease vector control on the basis of available scientific, technical, environmental and economic information, including:

    (a) The production and use of DDT and the conditions set out in paragraph 2;

    (b) The availability, suitability and implementation of the alternatives to DDT; and

    (c) Progress in strengthening the capacity of countries to transfer safely to reliance on such alternatives.

7. A Party may, at any time, withdraw its name from the DDT Registry upon written notification to the Secretariat. The withdrawal shall take effect on the date specified in the notification.

Annex C

UNINTENTIONAL PRODUCTION

Part I: Persistent organic pollutants subject to the requirements of Article 5

This Annex applies to the following persistent organic pollutants when formed and released unintentionally from anthropogenic sources:

Chemical
Polychlorinated dibenzo-p-dioxins and dibenzofurans (PCDD/PCDF) Hexachlorobenzene (HCB) (CAS No: 118-74-1) Polychlorinated biphenyls (PCB)

Part II: Source categories

Polychlorinated dibenzo-p-dioxins and dibenzofurans, hexachlorobenzene and polychlorinated biphenyls are unintentionally formed and released from thermal processes involving organic matter and chlorine as a result of incomplete combustion or chemical reactions. The following industrial source categories have the potential for comparatively high formation and release of these chemicals to the environment:

(a) Waste incinerators, including co-incinerators of municipal, hazardous or medical waste or of sewage sludge;

(b) Cement kilns firing hazardous waste;

(c) Production of pulp using elemental chlorine or chemicals generating elemental chlorine for bleaching;

(d) The following thermal processes in the metallurgical industry:

      (i)   Secondary copper production;
      (ii)   Sinter plants in the iron and steel industry;
      (iii)   Secondary aluminium production;
      (iv)   Secondary zinc production.

Part III: Source categories

Polychlorinated dibenzo-p-dioxins and dibenzofurans, hexachlorobenzene and polychlorinated biphenyls may also be unintentionally formed and released from the following source categories, including:

(a) Open burning of waste, including burning of landfill sites;

(b) Thermal processes in the metallurgical industry not mentioned in Part II;

(c) Residential combustion sources;

(d) Fossil fuel-fired utility and industrial boilers;

(e) Firing installations for wood and other biomass fuels;

(f) Specific chemical production processes releasing unintentionally formed persistent organic pollutants, especially production of chlorophenols and chloranil;

(g) Crematoria;

(h) Motor vehicles, particularly those burning leaded gasoline;

(i) Destruction of animal carcasses;

(j) Textile and leather dyeing (with chloranil) and finishing (with alkaline extraction);

(k) Shredder plants for the treatment of end of life vehicles;

(l) Smouldering of copper cables;

(m) Waste oil refineries.

Part IV: Definitions

1. For the purposes of this Annex:

(a) "Polychlorinated biphenyls" means aromatic compounds formed in such a manner that the hydrogen atoms on the biphenyl molecule (two benzene rings bonded together by a single carbon-carbon bond) may be replaced by up to ten chlorine atoms; and

(b) "Polychlorinated dibenzo-p-dioxins" and "polychlorinated dibenzofurans" are tricyclic, aromatic compounds formed by two benzene rings connected by two oxygen atoms in polychlorinated dibenzo-p-dioxins and by one oxygen atom and one carbon-carbon bond in polychlorinated dibenzofurans and the hydrogen atoms of which may be replaced by up to eight chlorine atoms.

2.   In this Annex, the toxicity of polychlorinated dibenzo-p-dioxins and dibenzofurans is expressed using the concept of toxic equivalency which measures the relative dioxin-like toxic activity of different congeners of polychlorinated dibenzo-p-dioxins and dibenzofurans and coplanar polychlorinated biphenyls in comparison to 2,3,7,8-tetrachlorodibenzo-p-dioxin.   The toxic equivalent factor values to be used for the purposes of this Convention shall be consistent with accepted international standards, commencing with the World Health Organization 1998 mammalian toxic equivalent factor values for polychlorinated dibenzo-p-dioxins and dibenzofurans and coplanar polychlorinated biphenyls. Concentrations are expressed in toxic equivalents.

Part V: General guidance on best available techniques and best environmental practices

This Part provides general guidance to Parties on preventing or reducing releases of the chemicals listed in Part I.

A. General prevention measures relating to both best available techniques and best environmental practices

Priority should be given to the consideration of approaches to prevent the formation and release of the chemicals listed in Part I. Useful measures could include:

(a) The use of low-waste technology;
(b) The use of less hazardous substances;
(c) The promotion of the recovery and recycling of waste and of substances generated and used in a process;
(d) Replacement of feed materials which are persistent organic pollutants or where there is a direct link between the materials and releases of persistent organic pollutants from the source;
(e) Good housekeeping and preventive maintenance programmes;
(f) Improvements in waste management with the aim of the cessation of open and other uncontrolled burning of wastes, including the burning of landfill sites. When considering proposals to construct new waste disposal facilities, consideration should be given to alternatives such as activities to minimize the generation of municipal and medical waste, including resource recovery, reuse, recycling, waste separation and promoting products that generate less waste.   Under this approach, public health concerns should be carefully considered;
(g) Minimization of these chemicals as contaminants in products;
(h) Avoiding elemental chlorine or chemicals generating elemental chlorine for bleaching.

B. Best available techniques

The concept of best available techniques is not aimed at the prescription of any specific technique or technology, but at taking into account the technical characteristics of the installation concerned, its geographical location and the local environmental conditions. Appropriate control techniques to reduce releases of the chemicals listed in Part I are in general the same. In determining best available techniques, special consideration should be given, generally or in specific cases, to the following factors, bearing in mind the likely costs and benefits of a measure and consideration of precaution and prevention:

(a) General considerations:

(i) The nature, effects and mass of the releases concerned: techniques may vary depending on source size;

(ii) The commissioning dates for new or existing installations;

(iii) The time needed to introduce the best available technique;

(iv) The consumption and nature of raw materials used in the process and its energy efficiency;

(v) The need to prevent or reduce to a minimum the overall impact of the releases to the environment and the risks to it;

(vi) The need to prevent accidents and to minimize their consequences for the environment;

(vii) The need to ensure occupational health and safety at workplaces;

(viii) Comparable processes, facilities or methods of operation which have been tried with success on an industrial scale;

(ix) Technological advances and changes in scientific knowledge and understanding.

(b) General release reduction measures: When considering proposals to construct new facilities or significantly modify existing facilities using processes that release chemicals listed in this Annex, priority consideration should be given to alternative processes, techniques or practices that have similar usefulness but which avoid the formation and release of such chemicals. In cases where such facilities will be constructed or significantly modified, in addition to the prevention measures outlined in section A of Part V the following reduction measures could also be considered in determining best available techniques:

(i) Use of improved methods for flue-gas cleaning such as thermal or catalytic oxidation, dust precipitation, or adsorption;

(ii) Treatment of residuals, wastewater, wastes and sewage sludge by, for example, thermal treatment or rendering them inert or chemical processes that detoxify them;

(iii) Process changes that lead to the reduction or elimination of releases, such as moving to closed systems;

(iv) Modification of process designs to improve combustion and prevent formation of the chemicals listed in this Annex, through the control of parameters such as incineration temperature or residence time.

C. Best environmental practices

The Conference of the Parties may develop guidance with regard to best environmental practices.

Annex D

INFORMATION REQUIREMENTS AND SCREENING CRITERIA

1. A Party submitting a proposal to list a chemical in Annexes A, B and/or C shall identify the chemical in the manner described in subparagraph (a) and provide the information on the chemical, and its transformation products where relevant, relating to the screening criteria set out in subparagraphs (b) to (e):

    (a) Chemical identity:
        (i)   Names, including trade name or names, commercial name or names and synonyms, Chemical Abstracts Service (CAS) Registry number, International Union of Pure and Applied Chemistry (IUPAC) name; and
        (ii)   Structure, including specification of isomers, where applicable, and the structure of the chemical class;

    (b) Persistence:
        (i)   Evidence that the half-life of the chemical in water is greater than two months, or that its half-life in soil is greater than six months, or that its half-life in sediment is greater than six months; or
        (ii)   Evidence that the chemical is otherwise sufficiently persistent to justify its consideration within the scope of this Convention;

    (c) Bio-accumulation:
        (i)   Evidence that the bio-concentration factor or bio-accumulation factor in aquatic species for the chemical is greater than 5,000 or, in the absence of such data, that the log Kow is greater than 5;
        (ii)   Evidence that a chemical presents other reasons for concern, such as high bio-accumulation in other species, high toxicity or ecotoxicity; or
        (iii)   Monitoring data in biota indicating that the bio-accumulation potential of the chemical is sufficient to justify its consideration within the scope of this Convention;

    (d) Potential for long-range environmental transport:
        (i)   Measured levels of the chemical in locations distant from the sources of its release that are of potential concern;
        (ii)   Monitoring data showing that long-range environmental transport of the chemical, with the potential for transfer to a receiving environment, may have occurred via air, water or migratory species; or
        (iii)   Environmental fate properties and/or model results that demonstrate that the chemical has a potential for long-range environmental transport through air, water or migratory species, with the potential for transfer to a receiving environment in locations distant from the sources of its release. For a chemical that migrates significantly through the air, its half-life in air should be greater than two days; and

    (e) Adverse effects:
        (i)   Evidence of adverse effects to human health or to the environment that justifies consideration of the chemical within the scope of this Convention; or
        (ii)   Toxicity or ecotoxicity data that indicate the potential for damage to human health or to the environment.

2. The proposing Party shall provide a statement of the reasons for concern including, where possible, a comparison of toxicity or ecotoxicity data with detected or predicted levels of a chemical resulting or anticipated from its long-range environmental transport, and a short statement indicating the need for global control.

3. The proposing Party shall, to the extent possible and taking into account its capabilities, provide additional information to support the review of the proposal referred to in paragraph 6 of Article 8. In developing such a proposal, a Party may draw on technical expertise from any source.

Annex E

INFORMATION REQUIREMENTS FOR THE RISK PROFILE

The purpose of the review is to evaluate whether the chemical is likely, as a result of its long-range environmental transport, to lead to significant adverse human health and/or environmental effects, such that global action is warranted. For this purpose, a risk profile shall be developed that further elaborates on, and evaluates, the information referred to in Annex D and includes, as far as possible, the following types of information:

(a) Sources, including as appropriate:

   (i)   Production data, including quantity and location;
   (ii)   Uses; and
   (iii) Releases, such as discharges, losses and emissions;

(b) Hazard assessment for the endpoint or endpoints of concern, including a consideration of toxicological interactions involving multiple chemicals;

(c) Environmental fate, including data and information on the chemical and physical properties of a chemical as well as its persistence and how they are linked to its environmental transport, transfer within and between environmental compartments, degradation and transformation to other chemicals. A determination of the bio-concentration factor or bio-accumulation factor, based on measured values, shall be available, except when monitoring data are judged to meet this need;

(d) Monitoring data;

(e) Exposure in local areas and, in particular, as a result of long-range environmental transport, and including information regarding bio-availability;

(f) National and international risk evaluations, assessments or profiles and labelling information and hazard classifications, as available; and

(g) Status of the chemical under international conventions.

<u>Annex F</u>

INFORMATION ON SOCIO-ECONOMIC CONSIDERATIONS

An evaluation should be undertaken regarding possible control measures for chemicals under consideration for inclusion in this Convention, encompassing the full range of options, including management and elimination. For this purpose, relevant information should be provided relating to socio-economic considerations associated with possible control measures to enable a decision to be taken by the Conference of the Parties. Such information should reflect due regard for the differing capabilities and conditions among the Parties and should include consideration of the following indicative list of items:

(a) Efficacy and efficiency of possible control measures in meeting risk reduction goals:

      (i)   Technical feasibility; and
      (ii)   Costs, including environmental and health costs;

(b) Alternatives (products and processes):

      (i)   Technical feasibility;
      (ii)   Costs, including environmental and health costs;
      (iii)   Efficacy;
      (iv)   Risk;
      (v)   Availability; and
      (vi)   Accessibility;

(c) Positive and/or negative impacts on society of implementing possible control measures:

      (i)   Health, including public, environmental and occupational health;
      (ii)   Agriculture, including aquaculture and forestry;
      (iii)   Biota (biodiversity);
      (iv)   Economic aspects;
      (v)   Movement towards sustainable development; and
      (vi)   Social costs;

(d) Waste and disposal implications (in particular, obsolete stocks of pesticides and clean-up of contaminated sites):
      (i)   Technical feasibility; and
      (ii)   Cost;

(e) Access to information and public education;

(f) Status of control and monitoring capacity; and

(g) Any national or regional control actions taken, including information on alternatives, and other relevant risk management information.

CONVENTION ON NATURE PROTECTION AND WILD LIFE PRESERVATION IN THE WESTERN HEMISPHERE (1940)

Entered into force: 1 May 1942

Preamble

The Governments of the American Republics, wishing to protect and preserve in their natural habitat representatives of all species and genera of their native flora and fauna, including migratory birds, in sufficient numbers and over areas extensive enough to assure them from becoming extinct through any agency within man's control; and

Wishing to protect and preserve scenery of extraordinary beauty, unusual and striking geologic formations, regions and natural objects of aesthetic, historic or scientific value, and areas characterized by primitive conditions in those cases covered by this Convention; and

Wishing to conclude a convention on the protection of nature and the preservation of flora and fauna to effectuate the foregoing purposes have agreed upon the following Articles:

Article I

DESCRIPTION OF TERMS USED IN THE WORDING OF THIS CONVENTION

1. The expression national parks shall denote:

Areas established for the protection and preservation of superlative scenery, flora and fauna of national significance which the general public may enjoy and from which it may benefit when placed under public control.

2. The expression national reserves shall denote:

Regions established for conservation and utilization of natural resources under government control, on which protection of animal and plant life will be afforded in so far as this may be consistent with the primary purpose of such reserves.

3. The expression nature monuments shall denote:

Regions, objects, or living species of flora and fauna of aesthetic, historic or scientific interest to which strict protection is given. The purpose of nature monuments is the protection of a specific object, or a species of flora or fauna, by setting aside an area, an object, or a single species, as an inviolate nature monument, except for duly authorized scientific investigations or government Inspection.

4. The expression strict wilderness reserves shall denote:

A region under public control characterized by primitive conditions of flora, fauna, transportation and habitation wherein there is no provision for the passage of motorized transportation and all commercial developments are excluded.

5. The expression migratory birds shall denote:

Birds of those species, all or some of whose individual members, may at any season cross any of the boundaries between the American countries. Some of the species of the following families are examples of birds characterized as migratory: Charadriidae, Scolopacidae, Caprimulgidae, Hirundinidae.

Article II

1. The Contracting Governments will explore at once the possibility of establishing in their territories national parks, national reserves, nature monuments, and strict wilderness reserves as defined in the preceding article. In all cases

where such establishment is feasible, the creation thereof shall be begun as soon as possible after the effective date of the present Convention.

2. If in any country the establishment of national parks, national reserves, nature monuments, or strict wilderness reserves is found to be impractical at present, suitable areas, objects or living species of fauna or flora, as the case may be, shall be selected as early as possible to be transformed into national parks, national reserves, nature monuments or strict wilderness reserves as soon as, in the opinion of the authorities concerned, circumstances will permit.

3. The Contracting Governments shall notify the Pan American Union of the establishment of any national parks, national reserves, nature monuments, or strict wilderness reserves, and of the legislation, including the methods of administrative control, adopted in connection therewith.

Article III

The Contracting Governments agree that the boundaries of national parks shall not be altered, or any portion thereof be capable of alienation except by the competent legislative authority. The resources of these reserves shall not be subject to exploitation for commercial profit.

The Contracting Governments agree to prohibit hunting, killing and capturing of members of the fauna and destruction or collection of representatives of the flora in national parks except by or under the direction or, control of the park authorities, or for duly authorized scientific investigations.

The Contracting Governments further agree to provide facilities for public recreation and education in national parks consistent with the purposes of this Convention.

Article IV

The Contracting Governments agree to maintain the strict wilderness reserves inviolate, as far as practicable, except for duly authorized scientific investigations or government inspection, or such uses as are consistent with the purposes for which the area was established.

Article V

1. The Contracting Governments agree to adopt, or to propose such adoption to their respective appropriate law-making bodies, suitable laws and regulations for the protection and preservation of flora and fauna within their national boundaries but not included in the national parks, national reserves, nature monuments, or strict wilderness reserves referred to in Article II hereof. Such regulations shall contain proper provisions for the taking of the specimens of flora and fauna for scientific study and investigation by properly accredited individuals and agencies.

2. The Contracting Governments agree to adopt or to recommend that their respective legislatures adopt, laws which will assure the protection and preservation of the natural scenery, striking geological formations, and regions and natural objects of aesthetic interest or historic or scientific value.

Article VI

The Contracting Governments agree to cooperate among themselves in promoting the objectives of the present Convention. To this end they will lend proper assistance, consistent with national laws, to scientists of the American Republics engaged in research and field study; they may, when circumstances warrant, enter into agreements with one another or with scientific institutions of the Americas in order to increase the effectiveness of this collaboration; and they shall make available to all the American Republics equally through publication or otherwise the scientific knowledge resulting from such cooperative effort.

Article VII

The Contracting Governments shall adopt appropriate measures for the protection of migratory birds of economic or aesthetic value or to prevent the threatened extinction of any given species. Adequate measures shall be adopted which will permit, in so far as the respective governments may see fit, a rational utilization of migratory birds for the purpose of sports as well as for food, commerce, and industry, and for scientific study and investigation.

Article VIII

The protection of the species mentioned in the Annex to the present Convention is declared to be of special urgency and importance. Species included therein shall be protected as completely as possible, and their hunting, killing, capturing, or taking, shall be allowed only with the permission of the appropriate government authorities in the country. Such permission shall be granted only under special circumstances, in order to further scientific purposes, or when essential for the administration of the area in which the animal or plant is found.

Article IX

Each Contracting Government shall take the necessary measures to control and regulate the importation, exportation and transit of protected fauna and flora or any part thereof by the following means:

1. The issuing of certificates authorizing the exportation or transit of protected species of flora or fauna, or parts thereof.

2. The prohibition of the importation of any species of fauna or flora or any part thereof protected by the country of origin unless accompanied by a certificate of lawful exportation as provided for in Paragraph 1 of this Article.

Article X

1. The terms of this convention shall in no way be interpreted as replacing international agreements previously entered into by one or more of the High Contracting Powers.

2. The Pan American Union shall notify the Contracting Parties of any information relevant to the purposes of the present Convention communicated to it by any national museums or by any organizations, national or international established within their jurisdiction and interested in the purposes of the Convention.

Article XI

1. The original of the present Convention in Spanish, English, Portuguese and French shall be deposited with the Pan American Union and opened for signature by the American Governments on 12 October 1940.

2. The present Convention shall remain open for signature by the American Governments. The instruments of ratification shall be deposited with the Pan American Union, which shall notify their receipt and the dates thereof, and the terms of any accompanying declarations or reservations, to all participating Governments.

3. The present Convention shall come into force three months after the deposit of not less than five ratifications with the Pan American Union.

4. Any ratification received after the date of the entry into force of the Convention, shall take effect three months after the date of its deposit with the Pan American Union.

Article XII

1. Any Contracting Government may at any time denounce the present Convention by a notification in writing addressed to the Pan American Union. Such denunciation shall take effect one year after the date of the receipt of the notification by the Pan American Union, provided, however, that no denunciation shall take effect until the expiration of five years from the date of the entry into force of this Convention.

2. If, as the result of simultaneous or successive denunciations, the number of Contracting Governments is reduced to less than three, the Convention shall cease to be in force from the date on which the last of such denunciations takes effect in accordance with the provisions of the preceding Paragraph.

3. The Pan American Union shall notify all of the American Governments of any denunciations and the date on which they take effect.

4. Should the Convention cease to be in force under the provisions of Paragraph 2 of this article, the Pan American Union shall notify all of the American Governments, indicating the date on which this will become effective.

In witness whereof, the undersigned Plenipotentiaries, having deposited their full powers found to be in due and proper form, sign this Convention at the Pan American Union, Washington, D.C., on behalf of their respective Governments and affix thereto their seals on the dates appearing opposite their signatures.

———————————

CONVENTION ON BIOLOGICAL DIVERSITY

1760 U.N.T.S. 79
Signed: June 5, 1992
Entered into Force: December 29, 1993
Secretariat Homepage: http://www.biodiv.org/

Preamble

The Contracting Parties,

Conscious of the intrinsic value of biological diversity and of the ecological, genetic, social, economic, scientific, educational, cultural, recreational and aesthetic values of biological diversity and its components,

Conscious also of the importance of biological diversity for evolution and for maintaining life sustaining systems of the biosphere,

Affirming that the conservation of biological diversity is a common concern of humankind,

Reaffirming that States have sovereign rights over their own biological resources,

Reaffirming also that States are responsible for conserving their biological diversity and for using their biological resources in a sustainable manner,

Concerned that biological diversity is being significantly reduced by certain human activities,

Aware of the general lack of information and knowledge regarding biological diversity and of the urgent need to develop scientific, technical and institutional capacities to provide the basic understanding upon which to plan and implement appropriate measures,

Noting that it is vital to anticipate, prevent and attack the causes of significant reduction or loss of biological diversity at source,

Noting also that where there is a threat of significant reduction or loss of biological diversity, lack of full scientific certainty should not be used as a reason for postponing measures to avoid or minimize such a threat,

Noting further that the fundamental requirement for the conservation of biological diversity is the *in-situ* conservation of ecosystems and natural habitats and the maintenance and recovery of viable populations of species in their natural surroundings,

Noting further that *ex-situ* measures, preferably in the country of origin, also have an important role to play,

Recognizing the close and traditional dependence of many indigenous and local communities embodying traditional lifestyles on biological resources, and the desirability of sharing equitably benefits arising from the use of traditional knowledge, innovations and practices relevant to the conservation of biological diversity and the sustainable use of its components,

Recognizing also the vital role that women play in the conservation and sustainable use of biological diversity and affirming the need for the full participation of women at all levels of policy-making and implementation for biological diversity conservation,

Stressing the importance of, and the need to promote, international, regional and global cooperation among States and intergovernmental organizations and the non-governmental sector for the conservation of biological diversity and the sustainable use of its components,

Acknowledging that the provision of new and additional financial resources and appropriate access to relevant technologies can be expected to make a substantial difference in the world's ability to address the loss of biological diversity,

Acknowledging further that special provision is required to meet the needs of developing countries, including the provision of new and additional financial resources and appropriate access to relevant technologies,

Noting in this regard the special conditions of the least developed countries and small island States,

Acknowledging that substantial investments are required to conserve biological diversity and that there is the expectation of a broad range of environmental, economic and social benefits from those investments,

Recognizing that economic and social development and poverty eradication are the first and overriding priorities of developing countries,

Aware that conservation and sustainable use of biological diversity is of critical importance for meeting the food, health and other needs of the growing world population, for which purpose access to and sharing of both genetic resources and technologies are essential,

Noting that, ultimately, the conservation and sustainable use of biological diversity will strengthen friendly relations among States and contribute to peace for humankind,

Desiring to enhance and complement existing international arrangements for the conservation of biological diversity and sustainable use of its components, and

Determined to conserve and sustainably use biological diversity for the benefit of present and future generations,

Have agreed as follows:

Article 1　　　Objectives

The objectives of this Convention, to be pursued in accordance with its relevant provisions, are the conservation of biological diversity, the sustainable use of its components and the fair and equitable sharing of the benefits arising out of the utilization of genetic resources, including by appropriate access to genetic resources and by appropriate transfer of relevant technologies, taking into account all rights over those resources and to technologies, and by appropriate funding.

Article 2　　　Use of Terms

For the purposes of this Convention:

"Biological diversity" means the variability among living organisms from all sources including, *inter alia*, terrestrial, marine and other aquatic ecosystems and the ecological complexes of which they are part; this includes diversity within species, between species and of ecosystems.

"Biological resources" includes genetic resources, organisms or parts thereof, populations, or any other biotic component of ecosystems with actual or potential use or value for humanity.

"Biotechnology" means any technological application that uses biological systems, living organisms, or derivatives thereof, to make or modify products or processes for specific use.

"Country of origin of genetic resources" means the country which possesses those genetic resources in *in-situ* conditions.

"Country providing genetic resources" means the country supplying genetic resources collected from *in-situ* sources, including populations of both wild and domesticated species, or taken from *ex-situ* sources, which may or may not have originated in that country.

"Domesticated or cultivated species" means species in which the evolutionary process has been influenced by humans to meet their needs.

"Ecosystem" means a dynamic complex of plant, animal and micro-organism communities and their non-living environment interacting as a functional unit.

"Ex-situ conservation" means the conservation of components of biological diversity outside their natural habitats.

"Genetic material" means any material of plant, animal, microbial or other origin containing functional units of heredity.

"Genetic resources" means genetic material of actual or potential value.

"Habitat" means the place or type of site where an organism or population naturally occurs.

"In-situ conditions" means conditions where genetic resources exist within ecosystems and natural habitats, and, in the case of domesticated or cultivated species, in the surroundings where they have developed their distinctive properties.

"In-situ conservation" means the conservation of ecosystems and natural habitats and the maintenance and recovery of viable populations of species in their natural surroundings and, in the case of domesticated or cultivated species, in the surroundings where they have developed their distinctive properties.

"Protected area" means a geographically defined area which is designated or regulated and managed to achieve specific conservation objectives.

"Regional economic integration organization" means an organization constituted by sovereign States of a given region, to which its member States have transferred competence in respect of matters governed by this Convention and which has been duly authorized, in accordance with its internal procedures, to sign, ratify, accept, approve or accede to it.

"Sustainable use" means the use of components of biological diversity in a way and at a rate that does not lead to the long-term decline of biological diversity, thereby maintaining its potential to meet the needs and aspirations of present and future generations.

"Technology" includes biotechnology.

Article 3   Principle

States have, in accordance with the Charter of the United Nations and the principles of international law, the sovereign right to exploit their own resources pursuant to their own environmental policies, and the responsibility to ensure that activities within their jurisdiction or control do not cause damage to the environment of other States or of areas beyond the limits of national jurisdiction.

Article 4   Jurisdictional Scope

Subject to the rights of other States, and except as otherwise expressly provided in this Convention, the provisions of this Convention apply, in relation to each Contracting Party:

    (a) In the case of components of biological diversity, in areas within the limits of its national jurisdiction; and

    (b) In the case of processes and activities, regardless of where their effects occur, carried out under its jurisdiction or control, within the area of its national jurisdiction or beyond the limits of national jurisdiction.

Article 5   Cooperation

Each Contracting Party shall, as far as possible and as appropriate, cooperate with other Contracting Parties, directly or, where appropriate, through competent international organizations, in respect of areas beyond national jurisdiction and on other matters of mutual interest, for the conservation and sustainable use of biological diversity.

Article 6   **General Measures for Conservation and Sustainable Use**

Each Contracting Party shall, in accordance with its particular conditions and capabilities:

(a) Develop national strategies, plans or programmes for the conservation and sustainable use of biological diversity or adapt for this purpose existing strategies, plans or programmes which shall reflect, *inter alia*, the measures set out in this Convention relevant to the Contracting Party concerned; and

(b) Integrate, as far as possible and as appropriate, the conservation and sustainable use of biological diversity into relevant sectoral or cross-sectoral plans, programmes and policies.

Article 7   **Identification and Monitoring**

Each Contracting Party shall, as far as possible and as appropriate, in particular for the purposes of Articles 8 to 10:

(a) Identify components of biological diversity important for its conservation and sustainable use having regard to the indicative list of categories set down in Annex I;

(b) Monitor, through sampling and other techniques, the components of biological diversity identified pursuant to subparagraph (a) above, paying particular attention to those requiring urgent conservation measures and those which offer the greatest potential for sustainable use;

(c) Identify processes and categories of activities which have or are likely to have significant adverse impacts on the conservation and sustainable use of biological diversity, and monitor their effects through sampling and other techniques; and

(d) Maintain and organize, by any mechanism, data derived from identification and monitoring activities pursuant to subparagraphs (a), (b) and (c) above.

Article 8   **In-situ Conservation**

Each Contracting Party shall, as far as possible and as appropriate:

(a) Establish a system of protected areas or areas where special measures need to be taken to conserve biological diversity;

(b) Develop, where necessary, guidelines for the selection, establishment and management of protected areas or areas where special measures need to be taken to conserve biological diversity;

(c) Regulate or manage biological resources important for the conservation of biological diversity whether within or outside protected areas, with a view to ensuring their conservation and sustainable use;

(d) Promote the protection of ecosystems, natural habitats and the maintenance of viable populations of species in natural surroundings;

(e) Promote environmentally sound and sustainable development in areas adjacent to protected areas with a view to furthering protection of these areas;

(f) Rehabilitate and restore degraded ecosystems and promote the recovery of threatened species, *inter alia*, through the development and implementation of plans or other management strategies;

(g) Establish or maintain means to regulate, manage or control the risks associated with the use and release of living modified organisms resulting from biotechnology which are likely to have adverse environmental impacts that could affect the conservation and sustainable use of biological diversity, taking also into account the risks to human health;

(h) Prevent the introduction of, control or eradicate those alien species which threaten ecosystems, habitats or species;

(i) Endeavour to provide the conditions needed for compatibility between present uses and the conservation of biological diversity and the sustainable use of its components;

(j) Subject to its national legislation, respect, preserve and maintain knowledge, innovations and practices of indigenous and local communities embodying traditional lifestyles relevant for the conservation and sustainable use of biological diversity and promote their wider application with the approval and involvement of the holders of such knowledge, innovations and practices and encourage the equitable sharing of the benefits arising from the utilization of such knowledge, innovations and practices;

(k) Develop or maintain necessary legislation and/or other regulatory provisions for the protection of threatened species and populations;

(l) Where a significant adverse effect on biological diversity has been determined pursuant to Article 7, regulate or manage the relevant processes and categories of activities; and

(m) Cooperate in providing financial and other support for *in-situ* conservation outlined in subparagraphs (a) to (l) above, particularly to developing countries.

Article 9   Ex-situ Conservation

Each contracting Party shall, as far as possible and as appropriate, and predominantly for the purpose of complementing *in-situ* measures:

(a) Adopt measures for the *ex-situ* conservation of components of biological diversity, preferably in the country of origin of such components;

(b) Establish and maintain facilities for *ex-situ* conservation of and research on plants, animals and micro-organisms, preferably in the country of origin of genetic resources;

(c) Adopt measures for the recovery and rehabilitation of threatened species and for their reintroduction into their natural habitats under appropriate conditions;

(d) Regulate and manage collection of biological resources from natural habitats for ex-situ conservation purposes so as not to threaten ecosystems and in-situ populations of species, except where special temporary ex-situ measures are required under subparagraph (c) above; and

(e) Cooperate in providing financial and other support for *ex-situ* conservation outlined in subparagraphs (a) to (d) above and in the establishment and maintenance of *ex-situ* conservation facilities in developing countries.

Article 10   Sustainable Use of Components of Biological Diversity

Each Contracting Party shall, as far as possible and as appropriate:

(a) Integrate consideration of the conservation and sustainable use of biological resources into national decision-making;

(b) Adopt measures relating to the use of biological resources to avoid or minimize adverse impacts on biological diversity;

(c) Protect and encourage customary use of biological resources in accordance with traditional cultural practices that are compatible with conservation or sustainable use requirements;

(d) Support local populations to develop and implement remedial action in degraded areas where biological diversity has been reduced; and

(e) Encourage cooperation between its governmental authorities and its private sector in developing methods for sustainable use of biological resources.

Article 11   Incentive Measures

Each Contracting Party shall, as far as possible and as appropriate, adopt economically and socially sound measures that act as incentives for the conservation and sustainable use of components of biological diversity.

Article 12   Research and Training

The contracting Parties, taking into account the special needs of developing countries, shall:

(a) Establish and maintain programmes for scientific and technical education and training in measures for the identification, conservation and sustainable use of biological diversity and its components and provide support for such education and training for the specific needs of developing countries;

(b) promote and encourage research which contributes to the conservation and sustainable use of biological diversity, particularly in developing countries, *inter alia*, in accordance with decisions of the Conference of the Parties taken in consequence of recommendations of the Subsidiary Body on Scientific, Technical and Technological Advice; and

(c) In keeping with the provisions of Articles 16, 18 and 20, promote and cooperate in the use of scientific advances in biological diversity research in developing methods for conservation and sustainable use of biological resources.

Article 13   Public Education and Awareness

The Contracting Parties shall:

(a) Promote and encourage understanding of the importance of, and the measures required for, the conservation of biological diversity, as well as its propagation through media, and the inclusion of these topics in educational programmes; and

(b) Cooperate, as appropriate, with other States and international organizations in developing educational and public awareness programmes, with respect to conservation and sustainable use of biological diversity.

Article 14   Impact Assessment and Minimizing Adverse Impacts

1. Each Contracting Party, as far as possible and as appropriate, shall:

(a) Introduce appropriate procedures requiring environmental impact assessment of its proposed projects that are likely to have significant adverse effects on biological diversity with a view to avoiding or minimizing such effects and, where appropriate, allow for public participation in such procedures;

(b) Introduce appropriate arrangements to ensure that the environmental consequences of its programmes and policies that are likely to have significant adverse impacts on biological diversity are duly taken into account;

(c) Promote, on the basis of reciprocity, notification, exchange of information and consultation on activities under their jurisdiction or control which are likely to significantly affect adversely the biological diversity of other States or areas beyond the limits of national jurisdiction, by encouraging the conclusion of bilateral, regional or multilateral arrangements, as appropriate;

(d) In the case of imminent or grave danger or damage, originating under its jurisdiction or control, to biological diversity within the area under jurisdiction of other States or in areas beyond the limits of national jurisdiction, notify immediately the potentially affected States of such danger or damage, as well as initiate action to prevent or minimize such danger or damage; and

(e) Promote national arrangements for emergency responses' to activities or events, whether caused naturally or otherwise, which present a grave and imminent danger to biological diversity and encourage international cooperation to supplement such national efforts and, where appropriate and agreed by the States or regional economic integration organizations concerned, to establish joint contingency plans.

2. The Conference of the Parties shall examine, on the basis of studies to be carried out, the issue of liability and redress, including restoration and compensation, for damage to biological diversity, except where such liability is a purely internal matter.

Article 15   Access to Genetic Resources

1. Recognizing the sovereign rights of States over their natural resources, the authority to determine access to genetic resources rests with the national governments and is subject to national legislation.

2. Each Contracting Party shall endeavour to create conditions to facilitate access to genetic resources for environmentally sound uses by other Contracting Parties and not to impose restrictions that run counter to the objectives of this Convention.

3. For the purpose of this Convention, the genetic resources being provided by a Contracting Party, as referred to in this Article and Articles 16 and 19, are only those that are provided by Contracting Parties that are countries of origin of such resources or by the Parties that have acquired the genetic resources in accordance with this Convention.

4. Access, where granted, shall be on mutually agreed terms and subject to the provisions of this Article.

5. Access to genetic resources shall be subject to prior informed consent of the Contracting Party providing such resources, unless otherwise determined by that Party.

6. Each Contracting Party shall endeavour to develop and carry out scientific research based on genetic resources provided by other Contracting Parties with the full participation of, and where possible in, such Contracting Parties.

7. Each Contracting Party shall take legislative, administrative or policy measures, as appropriate, and in accordance with Articles 16 and 19 and, where necessary, through the financial mechanism established by Articles 20 and 21 with the aim of sharing in a fair and equitable way the results of research and development and the benefits arising from the commercial and other utilization of genetic resources with the Contracting Party providing such resources. Such sharing shall be upon mutually agreed terms.

Article 16   Access to and Transfer of Technology

1. Each Contracting Party, recognizing that technology includes biotechnology, and that both access to and transfer of technology among Contracting Parties are essential elements for the attainment of the objectives of this Convention, undertakes subject to the provisions of this article to provide and/or facilitate access for and transfer to other Contracting Parties of technologies that are relevant to the conservation and sustainable use of biological diversity or make use of genetic resources and do not cause significant damage to the environment.

2. Access to and transfer of technology referred to in paragraph 1 above to developing countries shall be provided and/or facilitated under fair and most favorable terms, including on concessional and preferential terms where mutually agreed, and, where necessary, in accordance with the financial mechanism established by Articles 20 and 21. In the case of technology subject to patents and other intellectual property rights, such access and transfer shall be provided on terms which recognize and are consistent with the adequate and effective protection of intellectual property rights. The application of this paragraph shall be consistent with paragraphs 3, 4 and 5 below.

3. Each Contracting Party shall take legislative, administrative or policy measures, as appropriate, with the aim that Contracting Parties, in particular those that are developing countries, which provide genetic resources are provided access to and transfer of technology which makes use of those resources, on mutually agreed terms, including technology protected by patents and other intellectual property rights, where necessary, through the provisions of Articles 20 and 21 and in accordance with international law and consistent with paragraphs 4 and 5 below.

4. Each Contracting Party shall take legislative, administrative or policy measures, as appropriate, with the aim that the private sector facilitates access to, joint development and transfer of technology referred to in paragraph 1 above for the benefit of both governmental institutions and the private sector of developing countries and in this regard shall abide by the obligations included in paragraphs 1, 2 and 3 above.

5. The Contracting Parties, recognizing that patents and other intellectual property rights may have an influence on the implementation of this Convention, shall cooperate in this regard subject to national legislation and international law in order to ensure that such rights are supportive of and do not run counter to its objectives.

Article 17   Exchange of Information

1. The Contracting Parties shall facilitate the exchange of information, from all publicly available sources, relevant to the conservation and sustainable use of biological diversity, taking into account the special needs of developing countries.

2. Such exchange of information shall include exchange of results of technical, scientific and socio-economic research, as well as information on training and surveying programmes, specialized knowledge, indigenous and traditional knowledge as such and in combination with the technologies referred to in Article 16, paragraph 1. It shall also, where feasible, include repatriation of information.

Article 18   Technical and Scientific Cooperation

1. The Contracting Parties shall promote international technical and scientific cooperation in the field of conservation and sustainable use of biological diversity, where necessary, through the appropriate international and national institutions.

2. Each Contracting Party shall promote technical and scientific cooperation with other Contracting Parties, in particular developing countries, in implementing this Convention, *inter alia*, through the development and

implementation of national policies. In promoting such cooperation, special attention should be given to the development and strengthening of national capabilities, by means of human resources development and institution building.

3. The Conference of the Parties, at its first meeting, shall determine how to establish a clearing-house mechanism to promote and facilitate technical and scientific cooperation.

4. The Contracting Parties shall, in accordance with national legislation and policies, encourage and develop methods of cooperation for the development and use of technologies, including indigenous and traditional technologies, in pursuance of the objectives of this Convention. For this purpose, the Contracting Parties shall also promote cooperation in the training of personnel and exchange of experts.

5. The Contracting Parties shall, subject to mutual agreement, promote the establishment of joint research programmes and joint ventures for the development of technologies relevant to the objectives of this Convention.

Article 19   Handling of Biotechnology and Distribution of its Benefits

1. Each Contracting Party shall take legislative, administrative or policy measures, as appropriate, to provide for the effective participation in biotechnological research activities by those Contracting Parties, especially developing countries, which provide the genetic resources for such research, and where feasible in such Contracting Parties.

2. Each Contracting Party shall take all practicable measures to promote and advance priority access on a fair and equitable basis by Contracting Parties, especially developing countries, to the results and benefits arising from biotechnologies based upon genetic resources provided by those Contracting Parties. Such access shall be on mutually agreed terms.

3. The Parties shall consider the need for and modalities of a protocol setting out appropriate procedures, including, in particular, advance informed agreement, in the field of the safe transfer, handling and use of any living modified organism resulting from biotechnology that may have adverse effect on the conservation and sustainable use of biological diversity.

4. Each Contracting Party shall, directly or by requiring any natural or legal person under its jurisdiction providing the organisms referred to in paragraph 3 above, provide any available information about the use and safety regulations required by that Contracting Party in handling such organisms, as well as any available information on the potential adverse impact of the specific organisms concerned to the Contracting Party into which those organisms are to be introduced.

Article 20   Financial Resources

1. Each Contracting Party undertakes to provide, in accordance with its capabilities, financial support and incentives in respect of those national activities which are intended to achieve the objectives of this Convention, in accordance with its national plans, priorities and programmes.

2. The developed country Parties shall provide new and additional financial resources to enable developing country Parties to meet the agreed full incremental costs to them of implementing measures which fulfil the obligations of this Convention and to benefit from its provisions and which costs are agreed between a developing country Party and the institutional structure referred to in Article 21, in accordance with policy, strategy, programme priorities and eligibility criteria and an indicative list of incremental costs established by the Conference of the Parties. Other Parties, including countries undergoing the process of transition to a market economy, may voluntarily assume the obligations of the developed country Parties. For the purpose of this Article, the Conference of the Parties, shall at its first meeting establish a list of developed country Parties and other Parties which voluntarily assume the obligations of the developed country Parties. The Conference of the Parties shall periodically review and if necessary amend the list. Contributions from other countries and sources on a voluntary basis would also be encouraged. The implementation of these commitments shall take into account the need for adequacy, predictability and timely flow of funds and the importance of burden-sharing among the contributing Parties included in the list.

3. The developed country Parties may also provide, and developing country Parties avail themselves of, financial resources related to the implementation of this Convention through bilateral, regional and other multilateral channels.

4. The extent to which developing country Parties will effectively implement their commitments under this Convention will depend on the effective implementation by developed country Parties of their commitments under this Convention related to financial resources and transfer of technology and will take fully into account the fact that economic and social development and eradication of poverty are the first and overriding priorities of the developing country Parties.

5. The Parties shall take full account of the specific needs and special situation of least developed countries in their actions with regard to funding and transfer of technology.

6. The Contracting Parties shall also take into consideration the special conditions resulting from the dependence on, distribution and location of, biological diversity within developing country Parties, in particular small island States.

7. Consideration shall also be given to the special situation of developing countries, including those that are most environmentally vulnerable, such as those with arid and semi-arid zones, coastal and mountainous areas.

Article 21 Financial Mechanism

1. There shall be a mechanism for the provision of financial resources to developing country Parties for purposes of this Convention on a grant or concessional basis the essential elements of which are described in this Article. The mechanism shall function under the authority and guidance of, and be accountable to, the Conference of the Parties for purposes of this Convention. The operations of the mechanism shall be carried out by such institutional structure as may be decided upon by the Conference of the Parties at its first meeting. For purposes of this Convention, the Conference of the Parties shall determine the policy, strategy, programme priorities and eligibility criteria relating to the access to and utilization of such resources. The contributions shall be such as to take into account the need for predictability, adequacy and timely flow of funds referred to in Article 20 in accordance with the amount of resources needed to be decided periodically by the Conference of the Parties and the importance of burden-sharing among the contributing Parties included in the list referred to in Article 20, paragraph 2. Voluntary contributions may also be made by the developed country Parties and by other countries and sources. The mechanism shall operate within a democratic and transparent system of governance.

2. Pursuant to the objectives of this Convention, the Conference of the Parties shall at its first meeting determine the policy, strategy and programme priorities, as well as detailed criteria and guideline for eligibility for access to and utilization of the financial resources including monitoring and evaluation on a regular basis of such utilization. The Conference of the Parties shall decide on the arrangements to give effect to paragraph 1 above after consultation with the institutional structure entrusted with the operation of the financial mechanism.

3. The Conference of the Parties shall review the effectiveness of the mechanism established under this Article, including the criteria and guidelines referred to in paragraph 2 above, not less than two years after the entry into force of this Convention and thereafter on a regular basis. Based on such review, it shall take appropriate action to improve the effectiveness of the mechanism if necessary.

4. The Contracting Parties shall consider strengthening existing financial institutions to provide financial resources for the conservation and sustainable use of biological diversity.

Article 22 Relationship with Other International Conventions

1. The provisions of this Convention shall not affect the rights and obligations of any Contracting Party deriving from any existing international agreement, except where the exercise of those rights and obligations would cause a serious damage or threat to biological diversity.

2. Contracting Parties shall implement this Convention with respect to the marine environment consistently with the rights and obligations of States under the law of the sea.

Article 23　　　Conference of the Parties

1. A Conference of the Parties is hereby established. The first meeting of the Conference of the Parties shall be convened by the Executive Director of the United Nations Environment Programme not later than one year after the entry into force of this Convention. Thereafter, ordinary meetings of the Conference of the Parties shall be held at regular intervals to be determined by the Conference at its first meeting.

2. Extraordinary meetings of the Conference of the Parties shall be held at such other times as may be deemed necessary by the Conference, or at the written request of any Party, provided that, within six months of the request being communicated to them by the Secretariat, it is supported by at least one third of the Parties.

3. The Conference of the Parties shall by consensus agree upon and adopt rules of procedure for itself and for any subsidiary body it may establish as well as financial rules governing the funding of the Secretariat. At each ordinary meeting, it shall adopt a budget for the financial period until the next ordinary meeting.

4. The Conference of the Parties shall keep under review the implementation of this Convention, and, for this purpose, shall:
(a) Establish the form and the intervals for transmitting the information to be submitted in accordance with Article 26 and consider such information as well as reports submitted by any subsidiary body;
(b) Review scientific, technical and technological advice on biological diversity provided in accordance with Article 25;
(c) Consider and adopt, as required, protocols in accordance with Article 28;
(d) Consider and adopt, as required, in accordance with Articles 29 and 30, amendments to this Convention and its annexes;
(e) Consider amendments to any protocol, as well as to any annexes thereto, and, if so decided, recommend their adoption to the parties to the protocol concerned;
(f) Consider and adopt, as required, in accordance with Article 30, additional annexes to this Convention;
(g) Establish such subsidiary bodies, particularly to provide scientific and technical advice, as are deemed necessary for the implementation of this Convention;
(h) Contact, through the Secretariat, the executive bodies of conventions dealing with matters covered by this Convention with a view to establishing appropriate forms of cooperation with them; and
(i) Consider and undertake any additional action that may be required for the achievement of the purposes of this Convention in the light of experience gained in its operation.

5. The United Nations, its specialized agencies and the International Atomic Energy Agency, as well as any State not Party to this Convention, may be represented as observers at meetings of the Conference of the Parties. Any other body or agency, whether governmental or nongovernmental, qualified in fields relating to conservation and sustainable use of biological diversity, which has informed the Secretariat of its wish to be represented as an observer at a meeting of the Conference of the Parties, may be admitted unless at least one third of the Parties present object. The admission and participation of observers shall be subject to the rules of procedure adopted by the Conference of the Parties.

Article 24　　　Secretariat

1. A secretariat is hereby established. Its functions shall be:
(a) To arrange for and service meetings of the Conference of the Parties provided for in Article 23;
(b) To perform the functions assigned to it by any protocol;
(c) To prepare reports on the execution of its functions under this Convention and present them to the Conference of the Parties;
(d) To coordinate with other relevant international bodies and, in particular to enter into such administrative and contractual arrangements as may be required for the effective discharge of its functions; and
(e) To perform such other functions as may be determined by the Conference of the parties.

2. At its first ordinary meeting, the Conference of the Parties shall designate the secretariat from amongst those existing competent international organizations which have signified their willingness to carry out the secretariat functions under this Convention.

Article 25   Subsidiary Body on Scientific, Technical and Technological Advice

1. A subsidiary body for the provision of scientific, technical and technological advice is hereby established to provide the Conference of the Paris and, as appropriate, its other subsidiary bodies with timely advice relating to the implementation of this Convention. This body shall be open to participation by all Parties and shall be multidisciplinary. It shall comprise government representatives competent in the relevant field of expertise. It shall report regularly to the Conference of the Paris on all aspects of its work.

2. Under the authority of and in accordance with guidelines laid down by the Conference of the Parties, and upon its request, this body shall:
    (a) Provide scientific and technical assessments of the status of biological diversity;
    (b) Prepare scientific and technical assessments of the effects of types of measures taken in accordance with the provisions of this Convention;
    (c) Identify innovative, efficient and state-of-the-art technologies and know-how relating to the conservation and sustainable use of biological diversity and advise on the ways and means of promoting development and/or transferring such technologies;
    (d) Provide advice on scientific programmes and international cooperation in research and development related to conservation and sustainable use of biological diversity; and
    (e) Respond to scientific, technical, technological and methodological questions that the Conference of the Parties and its subsidiary bodies may put to the body.

3. The functions, terms of reference, organization and operation of this body may be further elaborated by the Conference of the Parties.

Article 26   Reports

Each Contracting Party shall, at intervals to be determined by the Conference of the Parties, present to the Conference of the Parties, reports on measures which it has taken for the implementation of the provisions of this Convention and their effectiveness in meeting the objectives of this Convention.

Article 27   Settlement of Disputes

1. In the event of a dispute between Contracting Parties concerning the interpretation or application of this Convention, the parties concerned shall seek solution by negotiation.

2. If the parties concerned cannot reach agreement by negotiation, they may jointly seek the good offices of, or request mediation by, a third party.

3. When ratifying, accepting, approving or acceding to this Convention, or at any time thereafter, a State or regional economic integration organization may declare in writing to the Depositary that for a dispute not resolved in accordance with paragraph 1 or paragraph 2 above, it accepts one or both of the following means of dispute settlement as compulsory:

    (a) Arbitration in accordance with the procedure laid down in Part 1 of Annex II;
    (b) Submission of the dispute to the International Court of Justice.

4. If the parties to the dispute have not, in accordance with paragraph 3 above, accepted the same or any procedure, the dispute shall be submitted to conciliation in accordance with Part 2 of Annex II unless the parties otherwise agree.

5. The provisions of this Article shall apply with respect to any protocol except as otherwise provided in the protocol concerned.

Article 28   Adoption of Protocols

1. The Contracting Parties shall cooperate in the formulation and adoption of protocols to this Convention.

2. Protocols shall be adopted at a meeting of the Conference of the Parties.

3. The text of any proposed protocol shall be communicated to the Contracting Parties by the Secretariat at least six months before such a meeting.

**Article 29   Amendment of the Convention or
                             Protocols**

1. Amendments to this Convention may be proposed by any Contracting Party. Amendments to any protocol may be proposed by any Party to that protocol.

2. Amendments to this Convention shall be adopted at a meeting of the conference of the Parties. Amendments to any protocol shall be adopted at meeting of the Parties to the Protocol in question. The text of any proposed amendment to this Convention or to any protocol, except as may otherwise be provided in such protocol, shall be communicated to the Parties to the instrument in question by the secretariat at least six months before the meeting at which it is proposed for adoption. The secretariat shall also communicate proposed amendments to the signatories of this Convention for information.

3. The Parties shall make every effort to reach agreement on any proposed amendment to this Convention or to any protocol by consensus. If all efforts at consensus have been exhausted, and no agreement reached, the amendment shall as a last resort be adopted by a two-third majority vote of the Parties to the instrument in question present and voting at the meeting, and shall be submitted by the Depositary to all Parties for ratification, acceptance or approval.

4. Ratification, acceptance or approval of amendments shall be notified to the Depositary in writing. Amendments adopted in accordance with paragraph 3 above shall enter into force among Parties having accepted them on the ninetieth day after the deposit of instruments of ratification, acceptance or approval by at least two thirds of the Contracting Parties to his Convention or of the Parties to the protocol concerned, except as may otherwise be provided in such protocol. Thereafter the amendments shall enter into force for any other Party on the ninetieth day after that Party deposits its instrument of ratification, acceptance or approval of the amendments.

5. For the purposes of this Article, "Parties present and voting" means parties present and casting an affirmative or negative vote.

Article 30   Adoption and Amendment of Annexes

1. The annexes to this Convention or to any protocol shall an integral part of the Convention or of such protocol, as the case may be, and, unless expressly provided otherwise, a reference to this Convention or its protocols constitutes at the same time a reference to any annexes thereto. Such annexes shall be restricted to procedural, scientific, technical and administrative matters.

2. Except as may be otherwise provided in any protocol with respect to its annexes, the following procedure shall apply to the proposal, adoption and entry into force of additional annexes to this Convention or of annexes to any protocol:

          (a) Annexes to this Convention or to any protocol shall be proposed and adopted according to the procedure laid down in Article 29;
          (b) Any Party that is unable to approve an additional annex to this Convention or an annex to any protocol to which it is Party shall so notify the Depositary, in writing, within one year from the date of the communication of the adoption by the Depositary. The Depositary shall without delay notify all Parties of any such notification received. A Party may at any time withdraw a previous declaration of objection and the annexes shall thereupon enter into force for that Party subject to subparagraph (c) below;

    (c) On the expiry of one year from the date of the communication of the adoption by the Depositary, the annex shall enter into force for all Parties to this Convention or to any protocol concerned which have not submitted a notification in accordance with the provisions of subparagraph (b) above.

3. The proposal, adoption and entry into force of amendments to annexes to this Convention or to any protocol shall be subject to the same procedure as for the proposal, adoption and entry into force of annexes to the Convention or annexes to any protocol.

4. If an additional annex or an amendment to an annex is related to an amendment to this Convention or to any protocol, the additional annex or amendment shall not enter into force until such time as the amendment to the Convention or to the protocol concerned enters into force.

Article 31   Right to Vote

1. Except as provided for in paragraph 2 below, each Contracting Party to this Convention or to any protocol shall have one vote.

2. Regional economic integration organizations, in matters within their competence, shall exercise their right to vote with a number of votes equal to the number of their member States which are Contracting Parties to this Convention or the relevant protocol. Such organizations shall not exercise their right to vote' if their member States exercise theirs, and vice versa.

**Article 32   Relationship between this Convention
and Its Protocols**

1. A State or a regional economic integration organization may not become a Party to a protocol unless it is, or becomes at the same time, a Contracting Party to this Convention.

2. Decisions under any protocol shall be taken only by the Parties to the protocol concerned. Any Contracting Party that has not ratified, accepted or approved a protocol may participate as an observer in any meeting of the parties to that protocol.

Article 33   Signature

This Convention shall be open for signature at Rio de Janeiro by all States and any regional economic' integration organization from 5 June 1992 until 14 June 1992, and at the United Nations Headquarters in New York from 15 June 1992 to 4 June 1993.

Article 34   Ratification, Acceptance or Approval

1. This Convention and any protocol shall be subject to ratification, acceptance or approval by States and by regional economic integration organizations. Instruments of ratification, acceptance or approval shall be deposited with the Depositary.

2. Any organization referred to in paragraph 1 above which becomes a Contracting Party to this Convention or any protocol without any of its member States being a Contracting Party shall be bound by all the obligations under the Convention or the protocol, as the case may be. In the case of such organizations, one or more of whose member States is a Contracting Party to this Convention or relevant protocol, the organization and its member States shall decide on their respective responsibilities for the performance of their obligations under the Convention or protocol, as he case may be. In such cases, the organization and the member States shall not be entitled to exercise rights under the Convention or relevant protocol concurrently.

3. In their instruments of ratification, acceptance or approval, the organizations referred to in paragraph 1 above shall declare the extent of their competence with respect to the matters governed by the Convention or the relevant protocol. These organizations shall also inform the depositary of any relevant modification in the extent of their competence.

Article 35   Accession

1. This Convention and any protocol shall be open for accession by States and by regional economic integration organizations from the date on which he Convention or the protocol concerned is closed for signature. The instruments of accession shall be deposited with the Depositary.

2. In their instruments of accession, the organizations referred to in paragraph 1 above shall declare the extent of their competence with respect to the matters governed by the Convention or the relevant protocol. These organizations shall also inform the Depositary of any relevant modification in the extent of their competence.

3. The provisions of Article 34, paragraph 2, shall apply to regional economic integration organizations which accede to this Convention or any protocol.

Article 36   Entry Into Force

1. This Convention shall enter into force on the ninetieth day after the date of deposit of the thirtieth instrument of ratification, acceptance, approval or accession.

2. Any protocol shall enter into force on the ninetieth day after the date of deposit of the number of instruments of ratification, acceptance, approval or accession, specified in that protocol, has been deposited.

3. For each Contracting Party which ratifies, accepts or approves this invention or accedes thereto after the deposit of the thirtieth instrument of ratification, acceptance, approval or accession, it shall enter into force on the ninetieth day after the date of deposit by such Contracting Party of its instrument of ratification, acceptance, approval or accession.

4. Any protocol, except as otherwise provided in such protocol, shall enter into force for a Contracting Party that ratifies, accepts or approves that protocol or accedes thereto after its entry into force pursuant to paragraph 2 above, on the ninetieth day after the date on which that Contracting Party deposits its instrument of ratification, acceptance, approval or accession, or on the date on which this Convention enters into force for that Contracting Party, whichever shall be the later.

5. For the purposes of paragraphs 1 and 2 above, any instrument deposited by a regional economic integration organization shall not be counted as additional to those deposited by member States of such organization.

Article 37   Reservations

No reservations may be made to this Convention.

Article 38   Withdrawals

1. At any time after two years from the date on which this Convention has entered into force for a Contracting Party, that Contracting Party may withdraw from the Convention by giving written notification to the Depositary.

2. Any such withdrawal shall take place upon expiry of one year after the date of its receipt by the Depositary, or on such later date as may be specified in the notification of the withdrawal.

3. Any Contracting Party which withdraws from this Convention shall be considered as also having withdrawn from any protocol to which it is party.

Article 39   Financial Interim Arrangements

Provided that it has been fully restructured in accordance with the requirements of Article 21, the Global Environment Facility of the United Nations Development Programme, the United Nations Environment Programme and the International Bank for Reconstruction and Development shall be the institutional structure referred to in Article 21 on an interim basis, for the period between the entry into force of this Convention and the first meeting of the Conference of the Parties or until the Conference of the Parties decides which institutional structure will be designated in accordance with Article 21.

Article 40   Secretariat Interim Arrangements

The secretariat to be provided by the Executive Director of the United Nations Environment Programme shall be the secretariat referred to in Article 24, paragraph 2, on an interim basis for the period between the entry into force of this Convention and the first meeting of the Conference of the Parties.

Article 41   Depositary

The Secretary-General of the United Nations shall assume the functions of Depositary of this Convention and any protocols.

Article 42   Authentic Texts

The original of this Convention, of which the Arabic, Chinese, English, French, Russian and Spanish texts are equally authentic, shall be deposited with the Secretary-General of the United Nations.

IN WITNESS WHEREOF the undersigned, being duly authorized to that effect, haven signed this Convention.

Done at Rio de Janeiro on this fifth day of June, one thousand nine hundred and ninety-two.

Annex I   Identification and Monitoring

1.   Ecosystems and habitats: containing high diversity, large numbers of endemic or threatened species, or wilderness; required by migratory species; of social, economic, cultural or scientific importance; or, which are representative, unique or associated with key evolutionary or other biological processes;

2.   Species and communities which are: threatened; wild relatives of domesticated or cultivated species; of medicinal, agricultural or other economic value; or social, scientific or cultural importance; or importance for research into the conservation and sustainable use of biological diversity, such as indicator species; and

3. Described genomes and genes of social, scientific or economic importance.

Annex II   Arbitration and Conciliation
(omitted)

CARTAGENA PROTOCOL ON BIOSAFETY TO THE CONVENTION ON BIOLOGICAL DIVERSITY

39 I.L.M. 1027 (2000)
Signed: January 29, 2000
Entered into Force

Preamble

The Parties to this Protocol,

Being Parties to the Convention on Biological Diversity, hereinafter referred to as "the Convention",

Recalling Article 19, paragraphs 3 and 4, and Articles 8 (g) and 17 of the Convention,

Recalling also decision II/5 of 17 November 1995 of the Conference of the Parties to the Convention to develop a Protocol on biosafety, specifically focusing on transboundary movement of any living modified organism resulting from modern biotechnology that may have adverse effect on the conservation and sustainable use of biological diversity, setting out for consideration, in particular, appropriate procedures for advance informed agreement,

Reaffirming the precautionary approach contained in Principle 15 of the Rio Declaration on Environment and Development,

Aware of the rapid expansion of modern biotechnology and the growing public concern over its potential adverse effects on biological diversity, taking also into account risks to human health,

Recognizing that modern biotechnology has great potential for human well-being if developed and used with adequate safety measures for the environment and human health,

Recognizing also the crucial importance to humankind of centres of origin and centres of genetic diversity,

Taking into account the limited capabilities of many countries, particularly developing countries, to cope with the nature and scale of known and potential risks associated with living modified organisms,

Recognizing that trade and environment agreements should be mutually supportive with a view to achieving sustainable development,

Emphasizing that this Protocol shall not be interpreted as implying a change in the rights and obligations of a Party under any existing international agreements,

Understanding that the above recital is not intended to subordinate this Protocol to other international agreements,

Have agreed as follows:

Article 1   Objective

In accordance with the precautionary approach contained in Principle 15 of the Rio Declaration on Environment and Development, the objective of this Protocol is to contribute to ensuring an adequate level of protection in the field of the safe transfer, handling and use of living modified organisms resulting from modern biotechnology that may have adverse effects on the conservation and sustainable use of biological diversity, taking also into account risks to human health, and specifically focusing on transboundary movements.

Article 2   General Provisions

1. Each Party shall take necessary and appropriate legal, administrative and other measures to implement its obligations under this Protocol.

2. The Parties shall ensure that the development, handling, transport, use, transfer and release of any living modified organisms are undertaken in a manner that prevents or reduces the risks to biological diversity, taking also into account risks to human health.

3. Nothing in this Protocol shall affect in any way the sovereignty of States over their territorial sea established in accordance with international law, and the sovereign rights and the jurisdiction which States have in their exclusive economic zones and their continental shelves in accordance with international law, and the exercise by ships and aircraft of all States of navigational rights and freedoms as provided for in international law and as reflected in relevant international instruments.

4. Nothing in this Protocol shall be interpreted as restricting the right of a Party to take action that is more protective of the conservation and sustainable use of biological diversity than that called for in this Protocol, provided that such action is consistent with the objective and the provisions of this Protocol and is in accordance with its other obligations under international law.

5. The Parties are encouraged to take into account, as appropriate, available expertise, instruments and work undertaken in international fora with competence in the area of risks to human health.

Article 3   Use of Terms

(a) "Conference of the Parties" means the Conference of the Parties to the Convention.

(b) "Contained use" means any operation, undertaken within a facility, installation or other physical structure, which involves living modified organisms that are controlled by specific measures that effectively limit their contact with, and their impact on, the external environment.

(c) "Export" means intentional transboundary movement from one Party to another Party.

(d) "Exporter" means any legal or natural person, under the jurisdiction of the Party of export, who arranges for a living modified organism to be exported.

(e) "Import" means intentional transboundary movement into one Party from another Party.

(f) "Importer" means any legal or natural person, under the jurisdiction of the Party of import, who arranges for a living modified organism to be imported.

(g) "Living modified organism" means any living organism that possesses a novel combination of genetic material obtained through the use of modern biotechnology.

(h) "Living organism" means any biological entity capable of transferring or replicating genetic material, including sterile organisms, viruses and viroids.

(i) "Modern biotechnology" means the application of:

(i) In vitro nucleic acid techniques, including recombinant deoxyribonucleic acid (DNA) and direct injection of nucleic acid into cells or organelles, or
(ii) Fusion of cells beyond the taxonomic family that overcome natural physiological reproductive or recombination barriers and that are not techniques used in traditional breeding and selection.

(j) "Regional economic integration organization" means an organization constituted by sovereign States of a given region, to which its member States have transferred competence in respect of matters governed by this Protocol and which has been duly authorized, in accordance with its internal procedures, to sign, ratify, accept, approve or accede to it.

(k) "Transboundary movement" means the movement of a living modified organism from one Party to another Party, save that for the purposes of Articles 17 and 24 transboundary movement extends to movement between Parties and non-Parties.

Article 4   Scope

This Protocol shall apply to the transboundary movement, transit, handling and use of all living modified organisms that may have adverse effects on the conservation and sustainable use of biological diversity, taking also into account risks to human health.

Article 5   Pharmaceuticals

Notwithstanding Article 4 and without prejudice to any right of a Party to subject all living modified organisms to risk assessment prior to the making of decisions on import, this Protocol shall not apply to the transboundary movement of living modified organisms which are pharmaceuticals for humans that are addressed by other relevant international agreements or organisations.

Article 6   Transit and contained use

1. Notwithstanding Article 4 and without prejudice to any right of a Party of transit to regulate the transport of living modified organisms through its territory and make available to the Biosafety Clearing-House, any decision of that Party, subject to Article 2, paragraph 3 of this Protocol, regarding the transit through its territory of a specific living modified organism, the provisions of this Protocol with respect to the advance informed agreement procedure shall not apply to living modified organisms in transit.

2. Notwithstanding Article 4 and without prejudice to any right of a Party to subject all living modified organisms to risk assessment prior to decisions on import and to set standards for contained use within its jurisdiction, the provisions of this Protocol with respect to the advance informed agreement procedure shall not apply to the transboundary movement of living modified organisms destined for contained use undertaken in accordance with the standards of the Party of import.

Article 7   Application of the advance informed agreement procedure

1. Subject to Articles 5 and 6, the advance informed agreement procedure in Articles 8-10 and 12 shall apply prior to the first intentional transboundary movement of living modified organisms for intentional introduction into the environment of the Party of import.

2. "Intentional introduction into the environment" in paragraph 1 above does not refer to living modified organisms intended for direct use as food or feed, or for processing.

3. Article 11 shall apply prior to the first transboundary movement of living modified organisms intended for direct use as food or feed, or for processing.

4. The advance informed agreement procedure shall not apply to the intentional transboundary movement of living modified organisms identified in a decision of the Conference of the Parties serving as the meeting of the Parties to this Protocol as being not likely to have adverse effects on the conservation and sustainable use of biological diversity, taking also into account risks to human health.

Article 8   Notification

1. The Party of export shall notify, or require the exporter to ensure notification in writing to, the competent national authority of the Party of import prior to the intentional transboundary movement of a living modified organism that falls within the scope of Article 7, paragraph 1. The notification shall contain, at a minimum, the information specified in Annex I.

2. The Party of export shall ensure that there is a legal requirement for the accuracy of information provided by the exporter.

Article 9   Acknowledgement of receipt of
                                notification

1. The Party of import shall acknowledge receipt of the notification, in writing, to the notifier within ninety days of its receipt.

2. The acknowledgement shall state:

(a) The date of receipt of the notification;
(b) Whether the notification, prima facie, contains the information referred to in Article 8;
(c) Whether to proceed according to the domestic regulatory framework of the Party of import or according to the procedure specified in Article 10.

3. The domestic regulatory framework referred to in paragraph 2 (c) above, shall be consistent with this Protocol.

4. A failure by the Party of import to acknowledge receipt of a notification shall not imply its consent to an intentional transboundary movement.

Article 10   Decision Procedure

1. Decisions taken by the Party of import shall be in accordance with Article 15.

2. The Party of import shall, within the period of time referred to in Article 9, inform the notifier, in writing, whether the intentional transboundary movement may proceed:

(a) Only after the Party of import has given its written consent;
(b) After no less than ninety days without a subsequent written consent.

3. Within two hundred and seventy days of the date of receipt of notification, the Party of import shall communicate, in writing, to the notifier and to the Biosafety Clearing-House the decision referred to in paragraph 2 (a) above:

(a) Approving the import, with or without conditions, including how the decision will apply to subsequent imports of the same living modified organism;
(b) Prohibiting the import;
(c) Requesting additional relevant information in accordance with its domestic regulatory framework or Annex I; in calculating the time within which the Party of import is to respond, the number of days it has to wait for additional relevant information shall not be taken into account; or
(d) Informing the notifier that the period specified in this paragraph is extended by a defined period of time.

4. Except in a case in which consent is unconditional, a decision under paragraph 3 above shall set out the reasons on which it is based.

5. A failure by the Party of import to communicate its decision within two hundred and seventy days of the date of receipt of the notification shall not imply its consent to an intentional transboundary movement.

6. Lack of scientific certainty due to insufficient relevant scientific information and knowledge regarding the extent of the potential adverse effects of a living modified organism on the conservation and sustainable use of biological diversity in the Party of import, taking also into account risks to human health, shall not prevent that Party from taking a decision, as appropriate, with regard to the import of the living modified organism in question as referred to in paragraph 3 above, in order to avoid or minimize such potential adverse effects.

7. The Conference of the Parties serving as the meeting of the Parties shall, at its first meeting, decide upon appropriate procedures and mechanisms to facilitate decision-making by Parties of import.

Article 11	Procedure for living modified organisms intended for direct use as food or feed, or for processing

1. A Party that makes a final decision regarding domestic use, including placing on the market, of a living modified organism that may be subject to transboundary movement for direct use as food or feed, or for processing shall, within fifteen days of making that decision, inform the Parties through the Biosafety Clearing-House. This information shall contain, at a minimum, the information specified in Annex II. The Party shall provide a written copy of the information to the national focal point of each Party that informs the Secretariat in advance that it does not have access to the Biosafety Clearing-House. This provision shall not apply to decisions regarding field trials.

2. The Party making a decision under paragraph 1 above shall ensure that there is a legal requirement for the accuracy of information provided by the applicant.

3. Any Party may request additional information from the authority identified in paragraph (b) of Annex II.

4. A Party may take a decision on the import of living modified organisms intended for direct use as food or feed, or for processing, under its domestic regulatory framework that is consistent with the objective of this Protocol.

5. Each Party shall make available to the Biosafety Clearing-House copies of any national laws, regulations and guidelines applicable to the import of living modified organisms intended for direct use as food or feed, or for processing, if available.

6. A developing country Party or a Party with an economy in transition may, in the absence of the domestic regulatory framework referred to in paragraph 4 above, and in exercise of its domestic jurisdiction, declare through the Biosafety Clearing-House that its decision prior to the first import of a living modified organism intended for direct use as food or feed, or for processing, on which information has been provided under paragraph 1 above, will be taken according to the following:

(a) A risk assessment undertaken in accordance with Annex III; and

(b) A decision made within a predictable timeframe, not exceeding two hundred and seventy days.

7. Failure by a Party to communicate its decision according to paragraph 6 above, shall not imply its consent or refusal to the import of a living modified organism intended for direct use as food or feed, or for processing, unless otherwise specified by the Party.

8. Lack of scientific certainty due to insufficient relevant scientific information and knowledge regarding the extent of the potential adverse effects of a living modified organism on the conservation and sustainable use of biological diversity in the Party of import, taking also into account risks to human health, shall not prevent that Party from taking a decision, as appropriate, with regard to the import of that living modified organism intended for direct use as food or feed, or for processing in order to avoid or minimize such potential adverse effects.

9. A Party may indicate its needs for financial and technical assistance and capacity-building with respect to living modified organisms for direct use as food or feed, or for processing. Parties shall cooperate to meet these needs in accordance with Articles 22 and 28.

Article 12	Review of Decisions

1. A Party of import may, at any time, in light of new scientific information on potential adverse effects on the conservation and sustainable use of biological diversity, taking also into account the risks to human health, review and change a decision regarding an intentional transboundary movement. In such case, the Party shall, within thirty days, inform any notifier that has previously notified movements of the living modified organism referred to in such decision, as well as the Biosafety Clearing-House, and shall set out the reasons for its decision.

2. A Party of export or a notifier may request the Party of import to review a decision it has made in respect of it under Article 10 where the Party of export or the notifier considers that:

(a) A change in circumstances has occurred that may influence the outcome of the risk assessment upon which the decision was based; or

(b) Additional relevant scientific or technical information has become available.

3. The Party of import shall respond to such a request in writing within ninety days and set out the reasons for its decision.

4. The Party of import may, at its discretion, require a risk assessment for subsequent imports.

Article 13   Simplified Procedure

1. A Party of import may, provided that adequate measures are applied to ensure the safe intentional transboundary movement of living modified organisms in accordance with the objective of this Protocol, specify in advance to the Biosafety Clearing-House:

    (a) Cases in which intentional transboundary movement to it may take place at the same time as the movement is notified to the Party of import: such notifications may apply to subsequent similar movements to the same Party; and

    (b) Imports of living modified organisms to it to be exempted from the advance informed agreement procedure.

2. The information relating to an intentional transboundary movement that is to be provided in the notifications referred to in paragraph 1 (a) above shall be the information specified in Annex I.

Article 14   Bilateral, regional and multilateral agreements and arrangements

1. Parties may enter into bilateral, regional and multilateral agreements and arrangements regarding intentional transboundary movements of living modified organisms, consistent with the objective of this Protocol and provided that such agreements and arrangements do not result in a lower level of protection than that provided for by the Protocol.

2. The Parties shall inform each other, through the Biosafety Clearing-House, of any such bilateral, regional and multilateral agreements and arrangements that they have entered into before or after entry into force of this Protocol.

3. The provisions of this Protocol shall not affect intentional transboundary movements that take place pursuant to such agreements and arrangements as between the parties to those agreements or arrangements.

4. Any Party may determine that its domestic regulations shall apply with respect to specific imports to it and shall notify the Biosafety Clearing-House of its decision.

Article 15   Risk assessment

1. Risk assessments undertaken pursuant to this Protocol shall be carried out in a scientifically sound manner, in accordance with Annex III and taking into account recognized risk assessment techniques. Such risk assessments shall be based at a minimum on information provided in accordance with Article 8 and other available scientific evidence in order to identify and evaluate the possible adverse effects of living modified organisms on the conservation and sustainable use of biological diversity, taking also into account risks to human health.

2. The Party of import shall ensure that risk assessments are carried out for decisions taken under Article 10. It may require the exporter to carry out the risk assessments.

3. The cost of risk assessment shall be borne by the notifier if the Party of import so requires.

Article 16   Risk management

1. The Parties shall, taking into account Article 8 (g) of the Convention, establish and maintain appropriate mechanisms, measures and strategies to regulate, manage and control risks identified in the risk assessment

provisions of this Protocol associated with the use, handling and transboundary movement of living modified organisms.

2. Measures based on risk assessment shall be imposed to the extent necessary to prevent adverse effects of the living modified organism on the conservation and sustainable use of biological diversity, taking also into account risks to human health, within the territory of the Party of import.

3. Each Party shall take appropriate measures to prevent unintentional transboundary movements of living modified organisms, including such measures as requiring risk assessments to be carried out prior to the first release of a living modified organism.

4. Without prejudice to paragraph 2 above, each Party shall endeavor to ensure that any living modified organism, whether imported or locally developed, has undergone an appropriate period of observation that is commensurate with its life-cycle or generation time before it is put to its intended use.

5. Parties shall cooperate with a view to:

(a) Identifying living modified organisms or specific traits of living modified organisms that may have adverse effects on the conservation and sustainable use of biological diversity, taking also into account risks to human health; and
(b) Taking appropriate measures regarding the treatment of such living modified organisms or specific traits.

Article 17   Unintentional transboundary movements and emergency measures

1. Each Party shall take appropriate measures to notify affected or potentially affected States, the Biosafety Clearing-House and, where appropriate, relevant international organizations, when it knows of an occurrence under its jurisdiction resulting in a release that lead or may lead to an unintentional transboundary movement of a living modified organism that is likely to have significant adverse effects on the conservation and sustainable use of biological diversity, taking also into account risks to human health in such States. The notification shall be provided as soon as the Party knows of the above situation.

2. Each Party shall, no later than the date of entry into force of the Protocol for it, make available to the Biosafety Clearing-House the relevant details setting out its point of contact for the purposes of receiving notifications under this Article.

3. Any notification arising from paragraph 1 above should include:

(a) Available relevant information on the estimated quantities and relevant characteristics and/or traits of the living modified organism;
(b) Information on the circumstances and estimated date of the release, and on the use of the living modified organism in the originating Party;
(c) Any available information about the possible adverse effects on the conservation and sustainable use of biological diversity, taking also into account risks to human health, as well as available information about possible risk management measures;
(d) Any other relevant information; and
(e) A point of contact for further information.

4. In order to minimize any significant adverse effects on the conservation and sustainable use of biological diversity, taking also into account risks to human health, each Party, under whose jurisdiction the release of the living modified organism referred to in paragraph 1 above occurs, shall immediately consult the affected or potentially affected States to enable them to determine appropriate responses and initiate necessary action, including emergency measures.

Article 18	Handling, transport, packaging and identification

1. In order to avoid adverse effects on the conservation and sustainable use of biological diversity, taking also into account risks to human health, each Party shall take necessary measures to require that living modified organisms that are subject to intentional transboundary movement within the scope of the Protocol are handled, packaged and transported under conditions of safety, taking into consideration relevant international rules and standards.

2. Each Party shall take measures to require that at a minimum documentation accompanying:

    (a) Living modified organisms that are intended for direct use as food or feed, or for processing, clearly identifies them as "may contain" living modified organisms and as not intended for intentional introduction into the environment, as well as a contact point for further information. The Conference of the Parties serving as the meeting of the Parties to this Protocol shall take a decision on the detailed requirements for this purpose, including specification of their identity and any unique identification, no later than two years after the entry into force of this Protocol;

    (b) Living modified organisms that are destined for contained use clearly identifies them as living modified organisms; and specifies any requirements for the safe handling, storage, transport and use, the contact point for further information, including the name and address of the individual and institution to whom the living modified organisms are consigned; and

    (c) Living modified organisms that are intended for intentional introduction into the environment of the Party of import and any other living modified organisms within the scope of the Protocol, clearly identifies them as living modified organisms; specifies the identity and relevant traits and/or characteristics, any requirements for the safe handling, storage, transport and use, the contact point for further information and, as appropriate, the name and address of the importer and exporter; and contains a declaration that the movement is in conformity with the requirements of this Protocol applicable to the exporter.

3. The Conference of the Parties serving as the meeting of the Parties to this Protocol shall consider the need for and modalities of developing standards with regard to identification, handling, packaging and transport practices, in consultation with other relevant international bodies.

Article 19	Competent national authorities and national focal points

1. Each Party shall designate one national focal point to be responsible on its behalf for liaison with the Secretariat. Each Party shall also designate one or more competent national authorities, which shall be responsible for performing the administrative functions required by this Protocol and which shall be authorized to act on its behalf with respect to those functions. A Party may designate a single entity to fulfill the functions of both focal point and competent national authority.

2. Each Party shall, no later than the date of entry into force of this Protocol for it, notify the Secretariat of the names and addresses of its focal point and its competent national authority or authorities. Where a Party designates more than one competent national authority, it shall convey to the Secretariat, with its notification thereof, relevant information on the respective responsibilities of those authorities. Where applicable, such information shall, at a minimum, specify which competent authority is responsible for which type of living modified organism. Each Party shall forthwith notify the Secretariat of any changes in the designation of its national focal point or in the name and address or responsibilities of its competent national authority or authorities.

3. The Secretariat shall forthwith inform the Parties of the notifications it receives under paragraph 2 above, and shall also make such information available through the Biosafety Clearing-House.

Article 20	Information –sharing and the biosafety clearing-house

1. A Biosafety Clearing-House is hereby established as part of the clearing-house mechanism under Article 18, paragraph 3, of the Convention, in order to:

(a) Facilitate the exchange of scientific, technical, environmental and legal information on, and experience with, living modified organisms; and

(b) Assist Parties to implement the Protocol, taking into account the special needs of developing country Parties, in particular the least developed and small island developing States among them, and countries with economies in transition as well as countries that are centres of origin and centres of genetic diversity.

2. The Biosafety Clearing-House shall serve as a means through which information is made available for the purposes of paragraph 1 above. It shall provide access to information made available by the Parties relevant to the implementation of the Protocol. It shall also provide access, where possible, to other international biosafety information exchange mechanisms.

3. Without prejudice to the protection of confidential information, each Party shall make available to the Biosafety Clearing-House any information required to be made available to the Biosafety Clearing-House under this Protocol, and:

(a) Any existing laws, regulations and guidelines for implementation of the Protocol, as well as information required by the Parties for the advance informed agreement procedure;

(b) Any bilateral, regional and multilateral agreements and arrangements;

(c) Summaries of its risk assessments or environmental reviews of living modified organisms generated by its regulatory process, and carried out in accordance with Article 15, including, where appropriate, relevant information regarding products thereof, namely, processed materials that are of living modified organism origin, containing detectable novel combinations of replicable genetic material obtained through the use of modern biotechnology;

(d) Its final decisions regarding the importation or release of living modified organisms; and

(e) Reports submitted by it pursuant to Article 33, including those on implementation of the advance informed agreement procedure.

4. The modalities of the operation of the Biosafety Clearing-House, including reports on its activities, shall be considered and decided upon by the Conference of the Parties serving as the meeting of the Parties at its first meeting, and kept under review thereafter.

Article 21   Confidential information

1. The Party of import shall permit the notifier to identify information submitted under the procedures of this Protocol or required by the Party of import as part of the advance informed agreement procedure of the Protocol that is to be treated as confidential. Justification shall be given in such cases upon request.

2. The Party of import shall consult the notifier if it decides that information identified by the notifier as confidential does not qualify for such treatment and shall, prior to any disclosure, inform the notifier of its decision providing reasons on request as well as an opportunity for consultation and for an internal review of the decision prior to disclosure.

3. Each Party shall protect confidential information received under this Protocol, including any confidential information received in the context of the advance informed agreement procedure of the Protocol. Each Party shall ensure that it has procedures to protect such information and shall protect the confidentiality of such information in a manner no less favourable than its treatment of confidential information in connection with domestically produced living modified organisms.

4. The Party of import shall not use such information for a commercial purpose, except with the written consent of the notifier.

5. If a notifier withdraws or has withdrawn a notification, the Party of import shall respect the confidentiality of commercial and industrial information, including research and development information as well as information on which the Party and the notifier disagree as to its confidentiality.

6. Without prejudice to paragraph 5 above, the following information shall not be considered confidential:

(a) The name and address of the notifier;

(b) A general description of the living modified organism or organisms;

(c) A summary of the risk assessment of the effects on the conservation and sustainable use of biological diversity, taking also into account risks to human health; and

(d) Any methods and plans for emergency response.

Article 22   Capacity-building

1. Strengthening of human resources and institutional capacities in biosafety, including biotechnology to the extent that it is required for biosafety, for the purpose of the effective implementation of this Protocol, in developing country Parties, in particular the least developed and small island developing States among them, and in Parties with economies in transition, including through existing global, regional, subregional and national institutions and organizations and, as appropriate, through facilitating private sector involvement.

2. For the purposes of implementing paragraph 1 above, in relation to cooperation, the needs of developing country Parties, in particular the least developed and small island developing States among them, for financial resources and access to and transfer of technology and know-how in accordance with the relevant provisions of the Convention, shall be taken fully into account for capacity-building in biosafety. Cooperation in capacity-building shall, subject to the different situation, capabilities and requirements of each Party, include scientific and technical training in the proper and safe management of biotechnology, and in the use of risk assessment and risk management for biosafety, and the enhancement of technological and institutional capacities in biosafety. The needs of Parties with economies in transition shall also be taken fully into account for such capacity-building in biosafety.

Article 23   Public Awareness and Participation

1. The Parties shall:

(a) Promote and facilitate public awareness, education and participation concerning the safe transfer, handling and use of living modified organisms in relation to the conservation and sustainable use of biological diversity, taking also into account risks to human health. In doing so, the Parties shall cooperate, as appropriate, with other States and international bodies;

(b) Endeavour to ensure that public awareness and education encompass access to information on living modified organisms identified in accordance with this Protocol that may be imported.

2. The Parties shall, in accordance with their respective laws and regulations, consult the public in the decision-making process regarding living modified organisms and shall make the results of such decisions available to the public, while respecting confidential information in accordance with Article 21.

3. Each Party shall endeavour to inform its public about the means of public access to the Biosafety Clearing-House.

Article 24   Non-parties

1. Transboundary movements of living modified organisms between Parties and non-Parties shall be consistent with the objective of this Protocol. The Parties may enter into bilateral, regional and multilateral agreements and arrangements with non-Parties regarding such transboundary movements.

2. The Parties shall encourage non-Parties to adhere to this Protocol and to contribute appropriate information to the Biosafety Clearing-House on living modified organisms released in, or moved into or out of, areas within their national jurisdictions.

Article 25   Illegal transboundary movements

1. Each Party shall adopt appropriate domestic measures aimed at preventing and, if appropriate, penalizing transboundary movements of living modified organisms carried out in contravention of its domestic measures to implement this Protocol. Such movements shall be deemed illegal transboundary movements.

2. In the case of an illegal transboundary movement, the affected Party may request the Party of origin to dispose, at its own expense, of the living modified organism in question by repatriation or destruction, as appropriate.

3. Each Party shall make available to the Biosafety Clearing-House information concerning cases of illegal transboundary movements pertaining to it.

Article 26   **Socio-economic considerations**

1. The Parties, in reaching a decision on import under this Protocol or under its domestic measures implementing the Protocol, may take into account, consistent with their international obligations, socio-economic considerations arising from the impact of living modified organisms on the conservation and sustainable use of biological diversity, especially with regard to the value of biological diversity to indigenous and local communities.

2. The Parties are encouraged to cooperate on research and information exchange on any socio-economic impacts of living modified organisms, especially on indigenous and local communities.

Article 27   **Liability and redress**

The Conference of the Parties serving as the meeting of the Parties to this Protocol shall, at its first meeting, adopt a process with respect to the appropriate elaboration of international rules and procedures in the field of liability and redress for damage resulting from transboundary movements of living modified organisms, analysing and taking due account of the ongoing processes in international law on these matters, and shall endeavour to complete this process within four years.

Article 28   **Financial mechanism and resources**

1. In considering financial resources for the implementation of this Protocol, the Parties shall take into account the provisions of Article 20 of the Convention.

2. The financial mechanism established in Article 21 of the Convention shall, through the institutional structure entrusted with its operation, be the financial mechanism for this Protocol.

3. Regarding the capacity-building referred to in Article 22 of this Protocol, the Conference of the Parties serving as the meeting of the Parties to this Protocol, in providing guidance with respect to the financial mechanism referred to in paragraph 2 above, for consideration by the Conference of the Parties, shall take into account the need for financial resources by developing country parties, in particular the least developed and the small island developing States among them.

4. In the context of paragraph 1 above, the Parties shall also take into account the needs of the developing country Parties, in particular the least developed and the small island developing States among them, and of the Parties with economies in transition, in their efforts to identify and implement their capacity-building requirements for the purposes of the implementation of this Protocol.

5. The guidance to the financial mechanism of the Convention in relevant decisions of the Conference of the Parties, including those agreed before the adoption of this Protocol, shall apply, mutatis mutandis, to the provisions of this Article.

6. The developed country Parties may also provide, and the developing country Parties and the Parties with economies in transition avail themselves of, financial and technological resources for the implementation of the provisions of this Protocol through multilateral, bilateral and regional channels.

Article 29   **Conference of the parties serving as the meeting of the parties**

1. The Conference of the Parties shall serve as the meeting of the Parties to this Protocol.

2. Parties to the Convention that are not Parties to this Protocol may participate as observers in the proceedings of any meeting of the Conference of the Parties serving as the meeting of the Parties to this Protocol. When the Conference of the Parties serves as the meeting of the Parties to this Protocol, decisions under this Protocol shall be taken only by those that are Parties to it.

3. When the Conference of the Parties serves as the meeting of the Parties to this Protocol, any member of the bureau of the Conference of the Parties representing a Party to the Convention but, at that time, not a Party to this Protocol, shall be substituted by a member to be elected by and from among the Parties to this Protocol.

4. The Conference of the Parties serving as the meeting of the Parties to this Protocol shall keep under regular review the implementation of this Protocol and shall make, within its mandate, the decisions necessary to promote its effective implementation. It shall perform the functions assigned to it by this Protocol and shall:

(a) Make recommendations on any matters necessary for the implementation of this Protocol;

(b) Establish such subsidiary bodies as are deemed necessary for the implementation of this Protocol;

(c) Seek and utilize, where appropriate, the services and cooperation of, and information provided by, competent international organizations and intergovernmental and non-governmental bodies;

(d) Establish the form and the intervals for transmitting the information to be submitted in accordance with Article 33 of this Protocol and consider such information as well as reports submitted by any subsidiary body;

(e) Consider and adopt, as required, amendments to this Protocol and its annexes, as well as any additional annexes to this Protocol, that are deemed necessary for the implementation of this Protocol; and

(f) Exercise such other functions as may be required for the implementation of this Protocol.

5. The rules of procedure of the Conference of the Parties and financial rules of the Convention shall be applied, mutatis mutandis, under this Protocol, except as may be otherwise decided by consensus by the Conference of the Parties serving as the meeting of the Parties to this Protocol.

6. The first meeting of the Conference of the Parties serving as the meeting of the Parties to this Protocol shall be convened by the Secretariat in conjunction with the first meeting of the Conference of the Parties that is scheduled after the date of the entry into force of this Protocol. Subsequent ordinary meetings of the Conference of the Parties serving as the meeting of the Parties to this Protocol shall be held in conjunction with ordinary meetings of the Conference of the Parties, unless otherwise decided by the Conference of the Parties serving as the meeting of the Parties to this Protocol.

7. Extraordinary meetings of the Conference of the Parties serving as the meeting of the Parties to this Protocol shall be held at such other times as may be deemed necessary by the Conference of the Parties serving as the meeting of the Parties to this Protocol, or at the written request of any Party, provided that, within six months of the request being communicated to the Parties by the Secretariat, it is supported by at least one third of the Parties.

8. The United Nations, its specialized agencies and the International Atomic Energy Agency, as well as any State member thereof or observers thereto not party to the Convention, may be represented as observers at meetings of the Conference of the Parties serving as the meeting of the Parties to this Protocol. Any body or agency, whether national or international, governmental or non-governmental, that is qualified in matters covered by this Protocol and that has informed the Secretariat of its wish to be represented at a meeting of the Conference of the Parties serving as a meeting of the Parties to this Protocol as an observer, may be so admitted, unless at least one third of the Parties present object. Except as otherwise provided in this Article, the admission and participation of observers shall be subject to the rules of procedure, as referred to in paragraph 5 above.

Article 30   Subsidiary bodies

1. Any subsidiary body established by or under the Convention may, upon a decision by the Conference of the Parties serving as the meeting of the Parties, serve the Protocol, in which case the meeting of the Parties shall specify which functions that body shall exercise.

2. Parties to the Convention that are not Parties to this Protocol may participate as observers in the proceedings of any meeting of any such subsidiary bodies. When a subsidiary body of the Convention serves as a subsidiary body to this Protocol, decisions under the Protocol shall be taken only by the Parties to the Protocol.

3. When a subsidiary body of the Convention exercises its functions with regard to matters concerning this Protocol, any member of the bureau of that subsidiary body representing a Party to the Convention but, at that time, not a Party to the Protocol, shall be substituted by a member to be elected by and from among the Parties to the Protocol.

Article 31   Secretariat

1. The Secretariat established by Article 24 of the Convention shall serve as the secretariat to this Protocol.

2. Article 24, paragraph 1, of the Convention on the functions of the Secretariat shall apply, mutatis mutandis, to this Protocol.

3. To the extent that they are distinct, the costs of the secretariat services for this Protocol shall be met by the Parties hereto. The Conference of the Parties serving as the meeting of the Parties to this Protocol shall, at its first meeting, decide on the necessary budgetary arrangements to this end.

Article 32   Relationship with the convention

Except as otherwise provided in this Protocol, the provisions of the Convention relating to its Protocols shall apply to this Protocol.

Article 33   Monitoring and reporting

Each Party shall monitor the implementation of its obligations under this Protocol, and shall, at intervals to be determined by the Conference of the Parties serving as the meeting of the Parties to this Protocol, report to the Conference of the Parties serving as the meeting of the Parties to this Protocol on measures that it has taken to implement the Protocol.

Article 34   Compliance

The Conference of the Parties serving as the meeting of the Parties to this Protocol shall, at its first meeting, consider and approve cooperative procedures and institutional mechanisms to promote compliance with the provisions of this Protocol and to address cases of non-compliance. These procedures and mechanisms shall include provisions to offer advice or assistance, where appropriate. They shall be separate from, and without prejudice to, the dispute settlement procedures and mechanisms established by Article 27 of the Convention.

Article 35   Assessment and review

The Conference of the Parties serving as the meeting of the Parties to this Protocol shall undertake, five years after the entry into force of this Protocol and at least every five years thereafter, an evaluation of the effectiveness of the Protocol, including an assessment of its procedures and annexes.

Article 36   Signature

This Protocol shall be open for signature at Nairobi by States and regional economic integration organizations from 15 to 26 May 2000, and at United Nations Headquarters in New York from 5 June 2000 to 4 June 2001.

Article 37   Entry into force

1. This Protocol shall enter into force on the ninetieth day after the date of deposit of the fiftieth instrument of ratification, acceptance, approval or accession by States or regional economic integration organizations that are Parties to the Convention.

2. This Protocol shall enter into force for a State or regional economic integration organization that ratifies, accepts or approves this Protocol or accedes thereto after its entry into force pursuant to paragraph 1 above, on the ninetieth day after the date on which that State or regional economic integration organization deposits its instrument of ratification, acceptance, approval or accession, or on the date on which the Protocol enters into force for that State or regional economic integration organization, whichever shall be the later.

3. For the purposes of paragraphs 1 and 2 above, any instrument deposited by a regional economic integration organization shall not be counted as additional to those deposited by member States of such organization.

Article 38   Reservations

No reservations may be made to this Protocol.

Article 39   Withdrawal

1. At any time after two years from the date on which this Protocol has entered into force for a Party, that Party may withdraw from the Protocol by giving written notification to the Depositary.

2. Any such withdrawal shall take place upon expiry of one year after the date of its receipt by the Depositary, or on such later date as may be specified in the notification of the withdrawal.

Article 40   Authentic texts

The original of this Protocol, of which the Arabic, Chinese, English, French, Russian and Spanish texts are equally authentic, shall be deposited with the Secretary-General of the United Nations.

Annex I   Information required in notifications under articles 8, 10 and 13

(a)   Name, address and contact details of the exporter.

(b)   Name, address and contact details of the importer.

(c)   Name and identity of the living modified organism, as well as the domestic classification, if any, of the biosafety level of the living modified organism in the State of export.

(d)   Intended date or dates of the transboundary movement, if known.

(e)   Taxonomic status, common name, point of collection or acquisition, and characteristics of recipient organism or parental organisms related to biosafety.

(f)   Centres of origin and centres of genetic diversity, if known, of the recipient organism and/or the parental organisms and a description of the habitats where the organisms may persist or proliferate.

(g)   Taxonomic status, common name, point of collection or acquisition, and characteristics of the donor organism or organisms related to biosafety.

(h)   Description of the nucleic acid or the modification introduced, the technique used, and the resulting characteristics of the living modified organism.

(i)   Intended use of the living modified organism or products thereof, namely, processed materials that are of living modified organism origin, containing detectable novel combinations of replicable genetic material obtained through the use of modern biotechnology.

(j)   Quantity or volume of the living modified organism to be transferred.

(k)   A previous and existing risk assessment report consistent with Annex III.

(l)   Suggested methods for safe handling, storage, transport and use, including packaging, labelling, documentation, disposal and contingency procedures, where appropriate.

(m)   Regulatory status of the living modified organism within the State of export (for example, whether it is prohibited in the State of export, whether there are other restrictions, or whether it has been approved for general release) and, if the living modified organism is banned in the State of export, the reason or reasons for the ban.

(n)   Result and purpose of any notification by the exporter to other States regarding the living modified organism to be transferred.

(o)   A declaration that the above-mentioned information is factually correct.

Annex II   **Information required for living modified organisms intended for direct use as food or feed, or for processing under Article II**

(a) The name and contact details of the applicant for a decision for domestic use.

(b) The name and contact details of the authority responsible for the decision.

(c) Name and identity of the living modified organism.

(d) Description of the gene modification, the technique used, and the resulting characteristics of the living modified organism.

(e) Any unique identification of the living modified organism.

(f) Taxonomic status, common name, point of collection or acquisition, and characteristics of recipient organism or parental organisms related to biosafety.

(g) Centres of origin and centres of genetic diversity, if known, of the recipient organism and /or the parental organisms and a description of the habitats where the organisms may persist or proliferate.

(h) Taxonomic status, common name, point of collection or acquisition, and characteristics of the donor organism or organisms related to biosafety.

(i) Approved uses of the living modified organism.

(j) A risk assessment report consistent with Annex III of this Protocol.

(k) Suggested methods for safe handling, storage, transport and use, including packaging, labelling, documentation, disposal and contingency procedures, where appropriate.

Annex III   **Risk assessment under Article 15**

Objective

1.   The objective of risk assessment, under this Protocol, is to identify and evaluate the potential adverse effects of living modified organisms on the conservation and sustainable use of biological diversity in the likely potential receiving environment, taking also into account risks to human health.

Use of risk assessment

2.   Risk assessment is, inter alia, used by competent authorities to make informed decisions regarding living modified organisms.

General principles

3.   Risk assessment should be carried out in a scientifically sound and transparent manner, and can take into account expert advice of, and guidelines developed by, relevant international organizations.

4.   Lack of scientific knowledge or scientific consensus should not necessarily be interpreted as indicating a particular level of risk, an absence of risk, or an acceptable risk.

5.   Risks associated with living modified organisms or products thereof, namely, processed materials that are of living modified organism origin, containing detectable novel combinations of replicable genetic material obtained through the use of modern biotechnology, should be considered in the context of the risks posed by the non-modified recipients or parental organisms in the likely potential receiving environment.

6.   Risk assessment should be carried out on a case-by-case basis. The required information may vary in nature and level of detail from case to case, depending on the living modified organism concerned, its intended use and the likely potential receiving environment.

Methodology

7.   The process of risk assessment may on the one hand give rise to a need for further information about specific subjects, which may be identified and requested during the assessment process, while on the other hand information on other subjects may not be relevant in some instances.

8.   To fulfil its objective, risk assessment entails, as appropriate, the following steps:

(a)   An identification of any novel genotypic and phenotypic characteristics associated with the living modified organism that may have adverse effects on biological diversity in the likely potential receiving environment, taking also into account risks to human health;

(b)   An evaluation of the likelihood of these adverse effects being realized, taking into account the level and kind of exposure of the likely potential receiving environment to the living modified organism;

(c)   An evaluation of the consequences should these adverse effects be realized;

(d)   An estimation of the overall risk posed by the living modified organism based on the evaluation of the likelihood and consequences of the identified adverse effects being realized;

(e)   A recommendation as to whether or not the risks are acceptable or manageable, including, where necessary, identification of strategies to manage these risks; and

(f)   Where there is uncertainty regarding the level of risk, it may be addressed by requesting further information on the specific issues of concern or by implementing appropriate risk management strategies and/or monitoring the living modified organism in the receiving environment.

Points to consider

9.   Depending on the case, risk assessment takes into account the relevant technical and scientific details regarding the characteristics of the following subjects:

(a)   Recipient organism or parental organisms. The biological characteristics of the recipient organism or parental organisms, including information on taxonomic status, common name, origin, centres of origin and centres of genetic diversity, if known, and a description of the habitat where the organisms may persist or proliferate;

(b)   Donor organism or organisms. Taxonomic status and common name, source, and the relevant biological characteristics of the donor organisms;

(c)   Vector. Characteristics of the vector, including its identity, if any, and its source or origin, and its host range;

(d)   Insert or inserts and/or characteristics of modification. Genetic characteristics of the inserted nucleic acid and the function it specifies, and/or characteristics of the modification introduced;

(e)   Living modified organism. Identity of the living modified organism, and the differences between the biological characteristics of the living modified organism and those of the recipient organism or parental organisms;

(f)   Detection and identification of the living modified organism. Suggested detection and identification methods and their specificity, sensitivity and reliability;

(g)   Information relating to the intended use. Information relating to the intended use of the living modified organism, including new or changed use compared to the recipient organism or parental organisms; and

(h)   Receiving environment. Information on the location, geographical, climatic and ecological characteristics, including relevant information on biological diversity and centres of origin of the likely potential receiving environment.

———————————

NAGOYA PROTOCOL ON ACCESS TO GENETIC RESOURCES AND THE FAIR AND EQUITABLE SHARING OF BENEFITS ARISING FROM THEIR UTILIZATION TO THE CONVENTION ON BIOLOGICAL DIVERSITY

Adopted: October 29, 2010

The Parties to this Protocol,

1.   *Being* Parties to the Convention on Biological Diversity, hereinafter referred to as "the Convention",

2.   *Recalling* that the fair and equitable sharing of benefits arising from the utilization of genetic resources is one of three core objectives of the Convention, and *recognizing* that the Protocol pursues the implementation of this objective within the Convention,

3.   *Reaffirming* the sovereign rights of States over their natural resources and according to the provisions of the Convention,

4.   *Recalling further* Article 15 of the Convention,

5.   *Recognizing* the important contribution to sustainable development made by technology transfer and cooperation to build research and innovation capacities for adding value to genetic resources in developing countries, in accordance with Articles 16 and 19 of the Convention,

6.   *Recognizing* that public awareness of the economic value of ecosystems and biodiversity and the fair and equitable sharing of this economic value with the custodians of biodiversity are key incentives for the conservation of biological diversity and the sustainable use of its components,

7.   *Acknowledging* the potential role of access and benefit-sharing to contribute to the conservation and sustainable use of biological diversity, poverty eradication and environmental sustainability and, thereby contributing to achieving the Millennium Development Goals,

8.   *Acknowledging* the linkage between access to genetic resources and the fair and equitable sharing of benefits arising from the utilization of such resources,

9.   *Recognizing* the importance of providing legal certainty with respect to access to genetic resources and the fair and equitable sharing of benefits arising from their utilization,

10.   *Further recognizing* the importance of promoting equity and fairness in negotiation of mutually agreed terms between providers and users of genetic resources,

11.   *Recognizing also* the vital role that women play in access and benefit sharing and affirming the need for the full participation of women at all levels of policy making and implementation for biodiversity conservation,

12.   *Determined* to further support the effective implementation of the access and benefit-sharing provisions of the Convention,

12*bis.*   *Recognizing* that an innovative solution is required to address the fair and equitable sharing of benefits derived from the utilisation of genetic resources and traditional knowledge associated with genetic resources that occur in transboundary situations or for which it is not possible to grant or obtain prior informed consent,

13.   *Recognizing* the importance of genetic resources to food security, public health, biodiversity conservation, and the mitigation and adaptation to climate change,

14.   *Recognizing* the special nature of agricultural biodiversity, its distinctive features and problems needing distinctive solutions,

15.   *Recognizing* the interdependence of all countries with regard to genetic resources for food and agriculture as well as their special nature and importance for achieving food security worldwide and for sustainable development of agriculture in the context of poverty alleviation and climate change and acknowledging the fundamental role of the International Treaty on Plant Genetic Resources for Food and Agriculture and the FAO Commission on Genetic Resources for Food and Agriculture in this regard,

16. *Mindful* of the International Health Regulations (2005) of the World Health Organization and the importance of ensuring access to human pathogens for public health preparedness and response purposes,

17. *Acknowledging* ongoing work in other international fora relating to access and benefit-sharing,

18. *Recalling* the Multilateral System of Access and Benefit-sharing established under the International Treaty on Plant Genetic Resources for Food and Agriculture developed in harmony with the Convention,

19. *Recognizing* that international instruments related to access and benefit-sharing should be mutually supportive with a view to achieving the objectives of the Convention,

20. *Recalling* the relevance of Article 8(j) of the Convention as it relates to traditional knowledge associated with genetic resources and the fair and equitable sharing of benefits arising from the utilization of such knowledge,

21. *Noting* the interrelationship between genetic resources and traditional knowledge, their inseparable nature for indigenous and local communities, the importance of the traditional knowledge for the conservation of biological diversity and the sustainable use of its components, and for the sustainable livelihoods of these communities,

22. *Recognizing* the diversity of circumstances in which traditional knowledge associated with genetic resources is held or owned by indigenous and local communities,

23. *Mindful* that it is the right of indigenous and local communities to identify the rightful holders of their traditional knowledge associated with genetic resources, within their communities,

24. *Further recognizing* the unique circumstances where traditional knowledge associated with genetic resources is held in countries, which may be oral, documented or in other forms, reflecting a rich cultural heritage relevant for conservation and sustainable use of biological diversity,

25. *Noting* the United Nations Declaration on the Rights of Indigenous Peoples, and

26. *Affirming* that nothing in this Protocol shall be construed as diminishing or extinguishing the existing rights of indigenous and local communities,

Have agreed as follows:

ARTICLE 1
OBJECTIVE

The objective of this Protocol is the fair and equitable sharing of the benefits arising from the utilization of genetic resources, including by appropriate access to genetic resources and by appropriate transfer of relevant technologies, taking into account all rights over those resources and to technologies, and by appropriate funding, thereby contributing to the conservation of biological diversity and the sustainable use of its components.

ARTICLE 2
USE OF TERMS

The terms defined in Article 2 of the Convention shall apply to this Protocol. In addition, for the purposes of this Protocol:

(a) "Conference of the Parties" means the Conference of the Parties to the Convention;

(b) "Convention" means the Convention on Biological Diversity;

(c) "Utilization of genetic resources" means to conduct research and development on the genetic and/or biochemical composition of genetic resources, including through the application of biotechnology as defined in Article 2 of the Convention.

(d) "Biotechnology" as defined in Article 2 of the Convention means any technological application that uses biological systems, living organisms, or derivatives thereof, to make or modify products or processes for specific use.

(e)   "Derivative" means a naturally occurring biochemical compound resulting from the genetic expression or metabolism of biological or genetic resources, even if it does not contain functional units of heredity.

ARTICLE 3
SCOPE

1. This Protocol shall apply to genetic resources within the scope of Article 15 of the Convention and to the benefits arising from the utilization of such resources. This Protocol shall also apply to traditional knowledge associated with genetic resources within the scope of the Convention and to the benefits arising from the utilization of such knowledge.

ARTICLE 3 *bis*
RELATIONSHIP WITH INTERNATIONAL AGREEMENTS AND INSTRUMENTS

1. The provisions of this Protocol shall not affect the rights and obligations of any Party deriving from any existing international agreement, except where the exercise of those rights and obligations would cause a serious damage or threat to biological diversity. This paragraph is not intended to create a hierarchy between this Protocol and other international instruments.

2. Nothing in this Protocol shall prevent the Parties from developing and implementing other relevant international agreements, including other specialised access and benefit-sharing agreements, provided that they are supportive of and do not run counter to the objectives of the Convention and this Protocol.

3. This Protocol shall be implemented in a mutually supportive manner with other international instruments relevant to this Protocol. Due regard should be paid to useful and relevant ongoing work or practices under such international instruments and relevant international organizations, provided that they are supportive of and do not run counter to the objectives of the Convention and this Protocol.

4. This Protocol is the instrument for the implementation of the access and benefit-sharing provisions of the Convention. Where a specialised international access and benefit-sharing instrument applies that is consistent with, and does not run counter to the objectives of the Convention and this Protocol, this Protocol does not apply for the Party or Parties to the specialised instrument in respect of the specific genetic resource covered by and for the purpose of the specialised instrument.

ARTICLE 4
FAIR AND EQUITABLE BENEFIT-SHARING

1. In accordance with Article 15, paragraphs 3 and 7 of the Convention, benefits arising from the utilization of genetic resources as well as subsequent applications and commercialization shall be shared in a fair and equitable way with the Party providing such resources that is the country of origin of such resources or a Party that has acquired the genetic resources in accordance with the Convention. Such sharing shall be upon mutually agreed terms.

1 *bis*. Each Party shall take legislative, administrative or policy measures, as appropriate, with the aim of ensuring that benefits arising from the utilization of genetic resources that are held by indigenous and local communities, in accordance with domestic legislation regarding the established rights of these indigenous and local communities over these genetic resources, are shared in a fair and equitable way with the communities concerned, based on mutually agreed terms.

2. To implement paragraph 1, each Party shall take legislative, administrative or policy measures, as appropriate.

3. Benefits may include monetary and non-monetary benefits, including but not limited to those listed in the Annex.

4. Each Party shall take legislative, administrative or policy measures as appropriate, in order that the benefits arising from the utilization of traditional knowledge associated with genetic resources are shared in a fair and

equitable way with indigenous and local communities holding such knowledge. Such sharing shall be upon mutually agreed terms.

ARTICLE 5
ACCESS TO GENETIC RESOURCES

1. In the exercise of sovereign rights over natural resources, and subject to its domestic access and benefit-sharing legislation or regulatory requirements, access to genetic resources for their utilization, shall be subject to the prior informed consent of the Party providing such resources that is the country of origin of such resources or a Party that has acquired the genetic resources in accordance with the Convention, unless otherwise determined by that Party.

1 *bis.* In accordance with domestic law, each Party shall take measures, as appropriate, with the aim of ensuring that the prior informed consent or approval and involvement of indigenous and local communities is obtained for access to genetic resources where they have the established right to grant access to such resources.

2. Pursuant to paragraph 1 above, each Party requiring prior informed consent, shall take the necessary legislative, administrative or policy measures, as appropriate, to:

    (a)   Provide for legal certainty, clarity and transparency of their domestic access and benefit-sharing legislation or regulatory requirements;

    (a *bis*) Provide for fair and non-arbitrary rules and procedures on accessing genetic resources;

    (b)   Provide information on how to apply for prior informed consent;

    (c)   Provide for a clear and transparent written decision by a competent national authority, in a cost-effective manner and within a reasonable period of time;

    (d)   Provide for the issuance at the time of access of a permit or its equivalent as evidence of the decision to grant prior informed consent and of the establishment of mutually agreed terms, and notify the Access and Benefit-sharing Clearing-House accordingly;

    (e)   Where applicable, and subject to domestic legislation, set out criteria and/or processes for obtaining prior informed consent or approval and involvement of indigenous and local communities for access to genetic resources; and

    (f)   Establish clear rules and procedures for requiring and establishing mutually agreed terms. Such terms shall be set out in writing and may include, *inter alia*:

        (i)   A dispute settlement clause;
        (ii)   Terms on benefit-sharing, including in relation to intellectual property rights;
        (iii)   Terms on subsequent third-party use, if any; and
        (iv)   Terms on changes of intent, where applicable.

ARTICLE 5 *bis*
ACCESS TO TRADITIONAL KNOWLEDGE ASSOCIATED WITH GENETIC RESOURCES

    In accordance with domestic law, each Party shall take measures, as appropriate, with the aim of ensuring that traditional knowledge associated with genetic resources that is held by indigenous and local communities is accessed with the prior and informed consent or approval and involvement of these indigenous and local communities, and that mutually agreed terms have been established.

ARTICLE 6
SPECIAL CONSIDERATIONS

    In the development and implementation of its access and benefit-sharing legislation or regulatory requirements, each Party shall:

    (a)   Create conditions to promote and encourage research which contributes to the conservation and sustainable use of biological diversity, particularly in developing countries, including through simplified measures on access for non-commercial research purposes, taking into account the need to address a change of intent for such research.

(b)   Pay due regard to cases of present or imminent emergencies that threaten or damage human, animal or plant health, as determined nationally or internationally. Parties may take into consideration the need for expeditious access to genetic resources and expeditious fair and equitable sharing of benefits arising out of the use of such genetic resources, including access to affordable treatments by those in need, especially in developing countries.

(c)   Consider the importance of genetic resources for food and agriculture and their special role for food security.

ARTICLE 7
CONTRIBUTION TO CONSERVATION AND SUSTAINABLE USE

The Parties shall encourage users and providers to direct benefits arising from the utilization of genetic resources towards the conservation of biological diversity and the sustainable use of its components.

ARTICLE 7 *bis*
GLOBAL MULTILATERAL BENEFIT-SHARING MECHANISM

Parties shall consider the need for and modalities of a global multilateral benefit-sharing mechanism to address the fair and equitable sharing of benefits derived from the utilisation of genetic resources and traditional knowledge associated with genetic resources that occur in transboundary situations or for which it is not possible to grant or obtain prior informed consent. The benefits shared by users of genetic resources and traditional knowledge associated with genetic resources through this mechanism shall be used to support the conservation of biological diversity and the sustainable use of its components globally.

ARTICLE 8

TRANSBOUNDARY COOPERATION

1. In instances where the same genetic resources are found *in-situ* within the territory of more than one Party, those Parties shall endeavour to cooperate, as appropriate, with the involvement of indigenous and local communities concerned, where applicable, with a view to implementing this Protocol.

2. Where the same traditional knowledge associated with genetic resources is shared by one or more indigenous and local communities in several Parties, those Parties shall endeavour to cooperate, as appropriate, with the involvement of the indigenous and local communities concerned, with a view to implementing the objective of this Protocol.

ARTICLE 9
TRADITIONAL KNOWLEDGE ASSOCIATED WITH GENETIC RESOURCES

1. In implementing their obligations under this Protocol, Parties shall in accordance with domestic law take into consideration indigenous and local communities' customary laws, community protocols and procedures, as applicable, with respect to traditional knowledge associated with genetic resources.

2. Parties, with the effective participation of the indigenous and local communities concerned, shall establish mechanisms to inform potential users of traditional knowledge associated with genetic resources about their obligations, including measures as made available through the Access and Benefit-sharing Clearing-House for access to and fair and equitable sharing of benefits arising from the utilization of such knowledge.

3. Parties shall endeavour to support, as appropriate, the development by indigenous and local communities, including women within these communities, of:

(a)   Community protocols in relation to access to traditional knowledge associated with genetic resources and the fair and equitable sharing of benefits arising out of the utilization of such knowledge;

(b)   Minimum requirements for mutually agreed terms to secure the fair and equitable sharing of benefits arising from the utilization of traditional knowledge associated with genetic resources; and

(c)   Model contractual clauses for benefit-sharing arising from the utilization of traditional knowledge associated with genetic resources.

4. Parties, in their implementation of this Protocol, shall, as far as possible, not restrict the customary use and exchange of genetic resources and associated traditional knowledge within and amongst indigenous and local communities in accordance with the objectives of the Convention.

ARTICLE 10
NATIONAL FOCAL POINTS AND COMPETENT NATIONAL AUTHORITIES

1. Each Party shall designate a national focal point on access and benefit-sharing. The national focal point shall make information available as follows:

      (a)   For applicants seeking access to genetic resources, information on procedures for obtaining prior informed consent and establishing mutually agreed terms, including benefit-sharing;

      (b)   For applicants seeking access to traditional knowledge associated with genetic resources, where possible, information on procedures for obtaining prior informed consent or approval and involvement, as appropriate, of indigenous and local communities and establishing mutually agreed terms including benefit-sharing; and

      (c)   Information on competent national authorities, relevant indigenous and local communities and relevant stakeholders.

The national focal point shall be responsible for liaison with the Secretariat.

2. Each Party shall designate one or more competent national authorities on access and benefit-sharing. Competent national authorities shall, in accordance with applicable national legislative, administrative or policy measures, be responsible for granting access or, as applicable, issuing written evidence that access requirements have been met and be responsible for advising on applicable procedures and requirements for obtaining prior informed consent and entering into mutually agreed terms.

3. A Party may designate a single entity to fulfil the functions of both focal point and competent national authority.

4. Each Party shall, no later than the date of entry into force of this Protocol for it, notify the Secretariat of the contact information of its national focal point and its competent national authority or authorities. Where a Party designates more than one competent national authority, it shall convey to the Secretariat, with its notification thereof, relevant information on the respective responsibilities of those authorities. Where applicable, such information shall, at a minimum, specify which competent authority is responsible for the genetic resources sought. Each Party shall forthwith notify the Secretariat of any changes in the designation of its national focal point or in the contact information or responsibilities of its competent national authority or authorities.

5. The Secretariat shall make information received pursuant to paragraph 4 available through the Access and Benefit-sharing Clearing-House.

ARTICLE 11
THE ACCESS AND BENEFIT-SHARING CLEARING-HOUSE AND INFORMATION-SHARING

1. An Access and Benefit-sharing Clearing-House is hereby established as part of the clearing-house mechanism under Article 18, paragraph 3, of the Convention. It shall serve as a means for sharing of information related to access and benefit-sharing. In particular, it shall provide access to information made available by each Party relevant to the implementation of this Protocol.

2. Without prejudice to the protection of confidential information, each Party shall make available to the Access and Benefit-sharing Clearing-House any information required by this Protocol, as well as information required pursuant to the decisions taken by the Conference of the Parties serving as the meeting of the Parties to this Protocol. The information shall include:

      (a)   Legislative, administrative and policy measures on access and benefit-sharing;
      (b)   Information on the national focal point and competent national authority(ies); and
      (c)   Permits or their equivalent issued at the time of access as evidence of the decision to grant prior informed consent and of the establishment of mutually agreed terms.

3. Additional information, if available and as appropriate, may include:

    (a)   Relevant competent authorities of indigenous and local communities, and information as so decided;

    (b)   Model contractual clauses;

    (c)   Methods and tools developed to monitor genetic resources; and

    (d)   Codes of conduct and best practices.

4. The modalities of the operation of the Access and Benefit-sharing Clearing-House, including reports on its activities, shall be considered and decided upon by the Conference of the Parties serving as the meeting of the Parties to this Protocol at its first meeting, and kept under review thereafter.

ARTICLE 12
COMPLIANCE WITH DOMESTIC LEGISLATION OR REGULATORY REQUIREMENTS ON ACCESS AND BENEFIT-SHARING

1. Each Party shall take appropriate, effective and proportionate legislative, administrative or policy measures to provide that genetic resources utilized within its jurisdiction have been accessed in accordance with prior informed consent and that mutually agreed terms have been established, as required by the domestic access and benefit-sharing legislation or regulatory requirements of the other Party.

2. Parties shall take appropriate, effective and proportionate measures to address situations of non-compliance with measures adopted in accordance with paragraph 1.

3. Parties shall, as far as possible and as appropriate, cooperate in cases of alleged violation of domestic access and benefit-sharing legislation or regulatory requirements referred to in paragraph 1.

ARTICLE 12 *bis*
COMPLIANCE WITH DOMESTIC LEGISLATION OR REGULATORY REQUIREMENTS ON ACCESS AND BENEFIT-SHARING FOR TRADITIONAL KNOWLEDGE ASSOCIATED WITH GENETIC RESOURCES

1. Each Party shall take appropriate, effective and proportionate legislative, administrative or policy measures, as appropriate, to provide that traditional knowledge associated with genetic resources utilized within their jurisdiction has been accessed in accordance with prior informed consent or approval and involvement of indigenous and local communities and that mutually agreed terms have been established, as required by domestic access and benefit sharing legislation or regulatory requirements of the other Party where such indigenous and local communities are located.

2. Each Party shall take appropriate, effective and proportionate measures to address situations of non-compliance with measures adopted in accordance with paragraph 1.

3. Parties shall, as far as possible and as appropriate cooperate in cases of alleged violation of domestic access and benefit-sharing legislation or regulatory requirements referred to in paragraph 1.

ARTICLE 13
MONITORING THE UTILIZATION OF GENETIC RESOURCES

1. To support compliance, each Party shall take measures, as appropriate, to monitor and to enhance transparency about the utilization of genetic resources. Such measures shall include:

    (a)   The designation of one or more checkpoints, as follows:

        (i)   Designated checkpoints would collect or receive, as appropriate, relevant information related to prior informed consent, to the source of the genetic resource, to the establishment of mutually agreed terms, and/or to the utilization of genetic resources, as appropriate.

(ii)   Each Party shall, as appropriate and depending on the particular characteristics of a designated checkpoint, require users of genetic resources to provide the information specified in the above paragraph at a designated checkpoint. Each Party shall take appropriate, effective and proportionate measures to address situations of non-compliance.

(iii) Such information, including from internationally recognized certificates of compliance where they are available, will, without prejudice to the protection of confidential information, be provided to relevant national authorities, to the Party providing prior informed consent and to the Access and Benefit-sharing Clearing-House, as appropriate.

(iv)   Check points must be effective and should have functions relevant to implementation of this sub-paragraph (a). They should be relevant to the utilization of genetic resources, or to the collection of relevant information at, *inter alia*, any stage of research, development, innovation, pre-commercialization or commercialization.

(b)   Encouraging users and providers of genetic resources to include provisions in mutually agreed terms to share information on the implementation of such terms, including through reporting requirements; and

(c)   Encouraging the use of cost-effective communication tools and systems.

2. A permit or its equivalent issued in accordance with Article 5, paragraph 2 (d) and made available to the Access and Benefit-sharing Clearing-House, shall constitute an internationally recognized certificate of compliance.

3. An internationally recognized certificate of compliance shall serve as evidence that the genetic resource which it covers has been accessed in accordance with prior informed consent and that mutually agreed terms have been established, as required by the domestic access and benefit-sharing legislation or regulatory requirements of the Party providing prior informed consent.

4. The internationally recognized certificate of compliance shall contain the following minimum information when it is not confidential:

(a)   Issuing authority;

(b)   Date of issuance;

(c)   The provider;

(d)   Unique identifier of the certificate;

(e)   The person or entity to whom prior informed consent was granted;

(f)   Subject-matter or genetic resources covered by the certificate;

(g)   Confirmation that mutually agreed terms were established;

(h *bis*) Confirmation that prior informed consent was obtained; and

(h)   Commercial and/or non-commercial use.

(i)

ARTICLE 14
COMPLIANCE WITH MUTUALLY AGREED TERMS

1. In the implementation of Article 5, paragraph 2 (f) (i) and Article 5*bis*, each Party shall encourage providers and users of genetic resources and/or traditional knowledge associated with genetic resources to include provisions in mutually agreed terms to cover, where appropriate, dispute resolution including:

(a)   The jurisdiction to which they will subject any dispute resolution processes;
(b)   The applicable law; and/or
(c)   Options for alternative dispute resolution, such as mediation or arbitration.

2. Each Party shall ensure that an opportunity to seek recourse is available under their legal systems, consistent with applicable jurisdictional requirements, in cases of disputes arising from mutually agreed terms.

3. Each Party shall take effective measures, as appropriate, regarding:
(a)   Access to justice; and

(b)   The utilization of mechanisms regarding mutual recognition and enforcement of foreign judgments and arbitral awards.

4.   The effectiveness of this article shall be reviewed by the Conference of the Parties serving as the meeting of the Parties to this Protocol in accordance with Article 25 of this Protocol.

ARTICLE 15
MODEL CONTRACTUAL CLAUSES

1.   Each Party shall encourage, as appropriate, the development, update and use of sectoral and cross-sectoral model contractual clauses for mutually agreed terms.

2.   The Conference of the Parties serving as the meeting of the Parties to this Protocol shall periodically take stock of the use of sectoral and cross-sectoral model contractual clauses.

ARTICLE 16
CODES OF CONDUCT, GUIDELINES AND BEST PRACTICES AND/OR STANDARDS

1.   Each Party shall encourage, as appropriate, the development, update and use of voluntary codes of conduct, guidelines and best practices and/or standards in relation to access and benefit-sharing.

2.   The Conference of the Parties serving as the meeting of the Parties to this Protocol shall periodically take stock of the use of voluntary codes of conduct, guidelines and best practices and/or standards and consider the adoption of specific codes of conduct, guidelines and best practices and/or standards.

ARTICLE 17
AWARENESS-RAISING

Each Party shall take measures to raise awareness of the importance of genetic resources and traditional knowledge associated with genetic resources, and related access and benefit-sharing issues. Such measures may include, *inter alia*:

(a)   Promotion of this Protocol, including its objective;
(b)   Organization of meetings of indigenous and local communities and relevant stakeholders;
(c)   Establishment and maintenance of a help desk for indigenous and local communities and relevant stakeholders;
(d)   Information dissemination through a national clearing-house;
(e)   Promotion of voluntary codes of conduct, guidelines and best practices and/or standards in consultation with indigenous and local communities and relevant stakeholders;
(f)   Promotion of, as appropriate, domestic, regional and international exchanges of experience;
(g)   Education and training of users and providers of genetic resources and traditional knowledge associated with genetic resources about their access and benefit-sharing obligations;
(h)   Involvement of indigenous and local communities and relevant stakeholders in the implementation of this Protocol; and
(i)   Awareness-raising of community protocols and procedures of indigenous and local communities.

ARTICLE 18
CAPACITY

1.   The Parties shall cooperate in the capacity-building, capacity development and strengthening of human resources and institutional capacities to effectively implement this Protocol in developing country Parties, in particular the least developed countries and small islands developing States among them, and Parties with economies in transition, including through existing global, regional, subregional and national institutions and organizations. In this context, Parties should facilitate the involvement of indigenous and local communities and relevant stakeholders, including non-governmental organizations and the private sector.

2. The need of developing country Parties, in particular the least developed countries and small island developing States among them, and Parties with economies in transition for financial resources in accordance with the relevant provisions of the Convention shall be taken fully into account for capacity-building and development to implement this Protocol.

3. As a basis for appropriate measures in relation to the implementation of this Protocol, developing country Parties, in particular the least developed countries and small island developing States among them, and Parties with economies in transition should identify their national capacity needs and priorities through national capacity self-assessments. In doing so, such Parties should support the capacity needs and priorities of indigenous and local communities and relevant stakeholders, as identified by them, emphasizing the capacity needs and priorities of women.

4. In support of the implementation of this Protocol, capacity-building and development may address, *inter alia*, the following key areas:

    (a)   Capacity to implement, and to comply with the obligations of, this Protocol;

    (b)   Capacity to negotiate mutually agreed terms;

    (c)   Capacity to develop, implement and enforce domestic legislative, administrative or policy measures on access and benefit-sharing; and

    (d)   Capacity of countries to develop their endogenous research capabilities to add value to their own genetic resources.

5. Measures in accordance with paragraphs 1 to 4 above may include, *inter alia*:

    (a)   Legal and institutional development;

    (b)   Promotion of equity and fairness in negotiations, such as training to negotiate mutually agreed terms;

    (c)   The monitoring and enforcement of compliance;

    (d)   Employment of best available communication tools and Internet-based systems for access and benefit-sharing activities;

    (e)   Development and use of valuation methods;

    (f)   Bioprospecting, associated research and taxonomic studies;

    (g)   Technology transfer, and infrastructure and technical capacity to make such technology transfer sustainable;

    (h)   Enhancement of the contribution of access and benefit-sharing activities to the conservation of biological diversity and the sustainable use of its components;

    (i)   Special measures to increase the capacity of relevant stakeholders in relation to access and benefit-sharing; and

    (j)   Special measures to increase the capacity of indigenous and local communities with emphasis on enhancing the capacity of women within those communities in relation to access to genetic resources and/or traditional knowledge associated with genetic resources.

6. Information on capacity-building and development initiatives at national, regional and international levels, undertaken in accordance with paragraphs 1 to 5 above, should be provided to the Access and Benefit-sharing Clearing-House with a view to promoting synergy and coordination on capacity-building and development for access and benefit-sharing.

ARTICLE 18 *bis*
TECHNOLOGY TRANSFER, COLLABORATION AND COOPERATION

In accordance with Articles 15, 16, 18 and 19 of the Convention, the Parties shall collaborate and cooperate in technical and scientific research and development programmes, including biotechnological research activities, as a means to achieve the objective of this Protocol. The Parties undertake to promote and encourage access to technology by, and transfer of technology to, developing country Parties, including the least developed and small island developing States among them, and Parties with economies in transition, in order to enable the development and strengthening of a sound and viable technological and scientific base for the attainment of the objectives of the Convention and this Protocol. Where possible and appropriate such collaborative activities shall take place in and with a Party or the Parties providing genetic resources that is the country or are the countries of origin of such resources or a Party or Parties that have acquired the genetic resources in accordance with the Convention.

ARTICLE 18 *ter*
NON-PARTIES

The Parties shall encourage non-Parties to adhere to this Protocol and to contribute appropriate information to the Access and Benefit-sharing Clearing-House.

ARTICLE 19
FINANCIAL MECHANISM AND RESOURCES

1. In considering financial resources for the implementation of this Protocol, the Parties shall take into account the provisions of Article 20 of the Convention.

2. The financial mechanism of the Convention shall be the financial mechanism for this Protocol.

3. Regarding the capacity-building and development referred to in Article 18 of this Protocol, the Conference of the Parties serving as the meeting of the Parties to this Protocol, in providing guidance with respect to the financial mechanism referred to in paragraph 2 above, for consideration by the Conference of the Parties, shall take into account the need of developing country Parties, in particular the least developed and the small island developing States among them, and of Parties with economies in transition, for financial resources, as well as the capacity needs and priorities of indigenous and local communities, including women within these communities.

4. In the context of paragraph 1 above, the Parties shall also take into account the needs of the developing country Parties, in particular the least developed and the small island developing States among them, and of the Parties with economies in transition, in their efforts to identify and implement their capacity-building and development requirements for the purposes of the implementation of this Protocol.

5. The guidance to the financial mechanism of the Convention in relevant decisions of the Conference of the Parties, including those agreed before the adoption of this Protocol, shall apply, *mutatis mutandis*, to the provisions of this Article.

6. The developed country Parties may also provide, and the developing country Parties and the Parties with economies in transition avail themselves of, financial and other resources for the implementation of the provisions of this Protocol through bilateral, regional and multilateral channels.

ARTICLE 20
CONFERENCE OF THE PARTIES SERVING AS THE MEETING OF THE PARTIES TO THIS PROTOCOL

1. The Conference of the Parties shall serve as the meeting of the Parties to this Protocol.

2. Parties to the Convention that are not Parties to this Protocol may participate as observers in the proceedings of any meeting of the Conference of the Parties serving as the meeting of the Parties to this Protocol. When the Conference of the Parties serves as the meeting of the Parties to this Protocol, decisions under this Protocol shall be taken only by those that are Parties to it.

3. When the Conference of the Parties serves as the meeting of the Parties to this Protocol, any member of the Bureau of the Conference of the Parties representing a Party to the Convention but, at that time, not a Party to this Protocol, shall be substituted by a member to be elected by and from among the Parties to this Protocol.

4. The Conference of the Parties serving as the meeting of the Parties to this Protocol shall keep under regular review the implementation of this Protocol and shall make, within its mandate, the decisions necessary to promote its effective implementation. It shall perform the functions assigned to it by this Protocol and shall:

(a)   Make recommendations on any matters necessary for the implementation of this Protocol;

(b)   Establish such subsidiary bodies as are deemed necessary for the implementation of this Protocol;

(c)   Seek and utilize, where appropriate, the services and cooperation of, and information provided by, competent international organizations and intergovernmental and non-governmental bodies;

(d)   Establish the form and the intervals for transmitting the information to be submitted in accordance with Article 23 of this Protocol and consider such information as well as reports submitted by any subsidiary body;

(e)   Consider and adopt, as required, amendments to this Protocol and its annex, as well as any additional annexes to this Protocol, that are deemed necessary for the implementation of this Protocol; and

(f)   Exercise such other functions as may be required for the implementation of this Protocol.

5. The rules of procedure of the Conference of the Parties and financial rules of the Convention shall be applied, *mutatis mutandis*, under this Protocol, except as may be otherwise decided by consensus by the Conference of the Parties serving as the meeting of the Parties to this Protocol.

6. The first meeting of the Conference of the Parties serving as the meeting of the Parties to this Protocol shall be convened by the Secretariat and held concurrently with the first meeting of the Conference of the Parties that is scheduled after the date of the entry into force of this Protocol. Subsequent ordinary meetings of the Conference of the Parties serving as the meeting of the Parties to this Protocol shall be held concurrently with ordinary meetings of the Conference of the Parties, unless otherwise decided by the Conference of the Parties serving as the meeting of the Parties to this Protocol.

7. Extraordinary meetings of the Conference of the Parties serving as the meeting of the Parties to this Protocol shall be held at such other times as may be deemed necessary by the Conference of the Parties serving as the meeting of the Parties to this Protocol, or at the written request of any Party, provided that, within six months of the request being communicated to the Parties by the Secretariat, it is supported by at least one third of the Parties.

8. The United Nations, its specialized agencies and the International Atomic Energy Agency, as well as any State member thereof or observers thereto not party to the Convention, may be represented as observers at meetings of the Conference of the Parties serving as the meeting of the Parties to this Protocol. Any body or agency, whether national or international, governmental or non-governmental, that is qualified in matters covered by this Protocol and that has informed the Secretariat of its wish to be represented at a meeting of the Conference of the Parties serving as a meeting of the Parties to this Protocol as an observer, may be so admitted, unless at least one third of the Parties present object. Except as otherwise provided in this Article, the admission and participation of observers shall be subject to the rules of procedure, as referred to in paragraph 5 above.

ARTICLE 21
SUBSIDIARY BODIES

1. Any subsidiary body established by or under the Convention may serve this Protocol, including upon a decision of the Conference of the Parties serving as the meeting of the Parties to this Protocol. Any such decision shall specify the tasks to be undertaken.

2. Parties to the Convention that are not Parties to this Protocol may participate as observers in the proceedings of any meeting of any such subsidiary bodies. When a subsidiary body of the Convention serves as a subsidiary body to this Protocol, decisions under this Protocol shall be taken only by Parties to this Protocol.

3. When a subsidiary body of the Convention exercises its functions with regard to matters concerning this Protocol, any member of the bureau of that subsidiary body representing a Party to the Convention but, at that time,

not a Party to this Protocol, shall be substituted by a member to be elected by and from among the Parties to this Protocol.

ARTICLE 22
SECRETARIAT

1. The Secretariat established by Article 24 of the Convention shall serve as the secretariat to this Protocol.

2. Article 24, paragraph 1, of the Convention on the functions of the Secretariat shall apply, *mutatis mutandis*, to this Protocol.

3. To the extent that they are distinct, the costs of the secretariat services for this Protocol shall be met by the Parties hereto. The Conference of the Parties serving as the meeting of the Parties to this Protocol shall, at its first meeting, decide on the necessary budgetary arrangements to this end.

ARTICLE 23
MONITORING AND REPORTING

Each Party shall monitor the implementation of its obligations under this Protocol, and shall, at intervals and in the format to be determined by the Conference of the Parties serving as the meeting of the Parties to this Protocol, report to the Conference of the Parties serving as the meeting of the Parties to this Protocol on measures that it has taken to implement this Protocol.

ARTICLE 24
PROCEDURES AND MECHANISMS TO PROMOTE COMPLIANCE WITH THIS PROTOCOL

The Conference of the Parties serving as the meeting of the Parties to this Protocol shall, at its first meeting, consider and approve cooperative procedures and institutional mechanisms to promote compliance with the provisions of this Protocol and to address cases of non-compliance. These procedures and mechanisms shall include provisions to offer advice or assistance, where appropriate. They shall be separate from, and without prejudice to, the dispute settlement procedures and mechanisms under Article 27 of the Convention.

ARTICLE 25
ASSESSMENT AND REVIEW

The Conference of the Parties serving as the meeting of the Parties to this Protocol shall undertake, four years after the entry into force of this Protocol and thereafter at intervals determined by the Conference of the Parties serving as the meeting of the Parties to this Protocol, an evaluation of the effectiveness of this Protocol.

ARTICLE 26
SIGNATURE

This Protocol shall be open for signature by Parties to the Convention at the United Nations Headquarters in New York from 2 February 2011 to 1 February 2012.

ARTICLE 27
ENTRY INTO FORCE

1. This Protocol shall enter into force on the ninetieth day after the date of deposit of the fiftieth instrument of ratification, acceptance, approval or accession by States or regional economic integration organizations that are Parties to the Convention.

2. This Protocol shall enter into force for a State or regional economic integration organization that ratifies, accepts or approves this Protocol or accedes thereto after the deposit of the fiftieth instrument as referred to in paragraph 1 above, on the ninetieth day after the date on which that State or regional economic integration organization deposits its instrument of ratification, acceptance, approval or accession, or on the date on which the Convention enters into force for that State or regional economic integration organization, whichever shall be the later.

3. For the purposes of paragraphs 1 and 2 above, any instrument deposited by a regional economic integration organization shall not be counted as additional to those deposited by member States of such organization.

ARTICLE 28
RESERVATIONS

No reservations may be made to this Protocol.

ARTICLE 29
WITHDRAWAL

1. At any time after two years from the date on which this Protocol has entered into force for a Party, that Party may withdraw from this Protocol by giving written notification to the Depositary.

2. Any such withdrawal shall take place upon expiry of one year after the date of its receipt by the Depositary, or on such later date as may be specified in the notification of the withdrawal.

ARTICLE 30
AUTHENTIC TEXTS

The original of this Protocol, of which the Arabic, Chinese, English, French, Russian and Spanish texts are equally authentic, shall be deposited with the Secretary-General of the United Nations.

IN WITNESS WHEREOF the undersigned, being duly authorized to that effect, have signed this Protocol on the dates indicated.

DONE at Nagoya on this twenty-ninth day of October, two thousand and ten.

Annex I

MONETARY AND NON-MONETARY BENEFITS

1.   Monetary benefits may include, but not be limited to:

    (a)   Access fees/fee per sample collected or otherwise acquired;

    (b)   Up-front payments;

    (c)   Milestone payments;

    (d)   Payment of royalties;

    (e)   Licence fees in case of commercialization;

    (f)   Special fees to be paid to trust funds supporting conservation and sustainable use of biodiversity;

    (g)   Salaries and preferential terms where mutually agreed;

    (h)   Research funding;

    (i)   Joint ventures;

    (j)   Joint ownership of relevant intellectual property rights.

2.   Non-monetary benefits may include, but not be limited to:

    (a)   Sharing of research and development results;

    (b)   Collaboration, cooperation and contribution in scientific research and development programmes, particularly biotechnological research activities, where possible in the Party providing genetic resources;

    (c)   Participation in product development;

    (d)   Collaboration, cooperation and contribution in education and training;

    (e)   Admittance to *ex situ* facilities of genetic resources and to databases;

    (f)   Transfer to the provider of the genetic resources of knowledge and technology under fair and most favourable terms, including on concessional and preferential terms where agreed, in particular, knowledge and technology that make use of genetic resources, including biotechnology, or that are relevant to the conservation and sustainable utilization of biological diversity;

    (g)   Strengthening capacities for technology transfer;

    (h)   Institutional capacity-building;

    (i)   Human and material resources to strengthen the capacities for the administration and enforcement of access regulations;

    (j)   Training related to genetic resources with the full participation of countries providing genetic resources, and where possible, in such countries;

    (k)   Access to scientific information relevant to conservation and sustainable use of biological diversity, including biological inventories and taxonomic studies;

    (l)   Contributions to the local economy;

    (m)   Research directed towards priority needs, such as health and food security, taking into account domestic uses of genetic resources in the Party providing genetic resources;

    (n)   Institutional and professional relationships that can arise from an access and benefit-sharing agreement and subsequent collaborative activities;

    (o)   Food and livelihood security benefits;

    (p)   Social recognition;

    (q)   Joint ownership of relevant intellectual property rights

CONVENTION TO REGULATE INTERNATIONAL TRADE IN ENDANGERED SPECIES OF FLORA AND FAUNA (CITES)
(appendices not included)

12 I.L.M. 1085(1973); 993 U.N.T.S. 243
Signed: March 3, 1973
Entered into Force: July 1, 1975
Secretariat Homepage: http://www.cites.org/

The Contracting States,

Recognizing that wild fauna and flora in their many beautiful and varied forms are an irreplaceable part of the natural systems of the earth which must be protected for this and the generations to come;

Conscious of the ever-growing value of wild fauna and flora from aesthetic, scientific, cultural, recreations and economic points of view;

Recognizing that peoples and States are and should be the best protectors of their own wild fauna and flora;

Recognizing, in addition, that international cooperation is essential for the protection of certain species of wild fauna and flora against over-exploitation through international trade;

Convinced of the urgency of taking appropriate measures to this end;

Having Agreed as follows:

Article I: Definitions

For the purpose of the present Convention, unless the context otherwise requires:

(a)   "Species" means any species, subspecies, or geographically separate population thereof;

(b)   "Specimen" means:
(i) any animal or plant, whether alive or dead;
(ii) in the case of an animal: for species included in Appendices I and II, any readily recognizable part or derivative thereof; and for species included in Appendix III, any readily recognizable part or derivative thereof specified in Appendix III in relation to the species; and
(iii) in the case of a plant: for species included in Appendix I, any readily recognizable part or derivative thereof; and for species included in Appendices II and III, any readily recognizable part or derivative thereof specified in Appendices II and III in relation to the species;

(c)   "Trade" means export, re-export, import and introduction from the sea;

(d)   "Re-export" means export of any specimen that has previously been imported;

(e)   "Introduction from the sea" means transportation into a State of specimens of any species which were taken in the marine environment not under the jurisdiction of any State;

(f)   "Scientific Authority" means a national scientific authority designated in accordance with Article IX;

(g)   "Management Authority" means a national management authority designated in accordance with Article IX;

(h)   "Party" means a State for which the present Convention has entered into force.

Article II: Fundamental Principles

1.   Appendix I shall include all species threatened with extinction which are or may be affected by trade. Trade in specimens of these species must be subject to particularly strict regulation in order not to endanger further their survival and must only be authorized in exceptional circumstances.

2.	Appendix II shall include:
	(a)	all species which although not necessarily now threatened with extinction may become so unless trade in specimens of such species is subject to strict regulation in order to avoid utilization incompatible with their survival; and
	(b)	other species which must be subject to regulation in order that trade in specimens of certain species referred to in sub-paragraph (a) of this paragraph may be brought under effective control.

3.	Appendix III shall include all species which any Party identifies as being subject to regulation within its jurisdiction for the purpose of preventing or restricting exploitation, and as needing the cooperation of other parties in the control of trade.

4.	The Parties shall not allow trade in specimens of species included in Appendices I, II and III except in accordance with the provisions of the present Convention.

Article III: Regulation of trade in specimens of species included in Appendix I

1.	All trade in specimens of species included in Appendix I shall be in accordance with the provisions of this Article.

2.	The export of any specimen of a species included in Appendix I shall require the prior grant and presentation of an export permit. An export permit shall only be granted when the following conditions have been met:
	(a)	a Scientific Authority of the State of export has advised that such export will not be detrimental to the survival of that species;
	(b)	a Management Authority of the State of export is satisfied that the specimen was not obtained in contravention of the laws of that State for the protection of fauna and flora;
	(c)	a Management Authority of the State of export is satisfied that any living specimen will be so prepared and shipped as to minimize the risk of injury, damage to health or cruel treatment; and
	(d)	a Management Authority of the State of export is satisfied that an import permit has been granted for the specimen.

3.	The import of any specimen of a species included in Appendix I shall require the prior grant and presentation of an import permit and either an export permit or a re-export certificate. An import permit shall only be granted when the following conditions have been met:
	(a)	a Scientific Authority of the State of import has advised that the import will be for purposes which are not detrimental to the survival of the species involved;
	(b)	a Scientific Authority of the State of import is satisfied that the proposed recipient of a living specimen is suitably equipped to house and care for it; and
	(c)	a Management Authority of the State of import is satisfied that the specimen is not to be used for primarily commercial purposes.

4.	The re-export of any specimen of a species included in Appendix I shall require the prior grant and presentation of a re-export certificate. A re-export certificate shall only be granted when the following conditions have been met:
	(a)	a Management Authority of the State of re-export is satisfied that the specimen was imported into that State in accordance with the provisions of the present Convention;
	(b)	a Management Authority of the State of re-export is satisfied that any living specimen will be so prepared and shipped as to minimize the risk of injury, damage to health or cruel treatment; and
	(c)	a Management Authority of the State of re-export is satisfied that an import permit has been granted for any living specimen.

5.	The introduction from the sea of any specimen of a species included in Appendix I shall require the prior grant of a certificate from a Management Authority of the State of introduction. A certificate shall only be granted when the following conditions have been met:
	(a)	a Scientific Authority of the State of introduction advise that the introduction will not be detrimental to the survival of the species involved;

(b)   a Management Authority of the State of introduction is satisfied that the proposed recipient of a living specimen is suitably equipped to house and care for it; and

(c)   a Management Authority of the State of introduction is satisfied that the specimen is not to be used for primarily commercial purposes.

Article IV: Regulation of Trade in Specimens of Species Included in Appendix II

1.   All trade in specimens of species included in Appendix II shall be in accordance with the provisions of this Article.

2.   The export of any specimen of a species included in Appendix II shall require the prior grant and presentation of an export permit. An export permit shall only be granted when the following conditions have been met:

(a)   a Scientific Authority of the State of export has advised that such export will not be detrimental to the survival of that species;

(b)   a Management Authority of the State of export is satisfied that the specimen was not obtained in contravention of the laws of that State for the protection of fauna and flora; and

(c)   a Management Authority of the State of export is satisfied that any living specimen will be so prepared and shipped as to minimize the risk of injury, damage to health or cruel treatment.

3.   A Scientific Authority in each Party shall monitor both the export permits granted by that State for specimens of species included in Appendix II and the actual exports of such specimens. Whenever a Scientific Authority determines that the export of specimens of any such species should be limited in order to maintain that species throughout its range at a level consistent with its role in the ecosystems in which it occurs and well above the level at which that species might become eligible for inclusion in Appendix I, the Scientific Authority shall advise the appropriate Management Authority of suitable measures to be taken to limit the grant of export permits for specimens of that species.

4.   The import of any specimen of a species included in Appendix II shall require the prior presentation of either an export permit or a re-export certificate.

5.   The re-export of any specimen of a species included in Appendix II shall require the prior grant and presentation of a re-export certificate. A re-export certificate shall only be granted when the following conditions have been met:

(a)   a Management Authority of the State of re-export is satisfied that the specimen was imported into that State in accordance with the provisions of the present Convention; and

(b)   a Management Authority of the State of re-export is satisfied that any living specimen will be so prepared and shipped as to minimize the risk of injury, damage to health or cruel treatment.

6.   The introduction from the sea of any specimen of a species included in Appendix II shall require the prior grant of a certificate from a Management Authority of the State of introduction. A certificate shall only be granted when the following conditions have been met:

(a)   a Scientific Authority of the State of introduction advises that the introduction will not be detrimental to the survival of the species involved; and

(b)   a Management Authority of the State of introduction is satisfied that any living specimen will be so handled as to minimize the risk of injury, damage to health or cruel treatment.

7.   Certificates referred to in paragraph 6 of this Article may be granted on the advice of a Scientific Authority, in consultation with other national scientific authorities or, when appropriate, international scientific authorities, in respect of periods not exceeding one year for total numbers of specimens to be introduced in such periods.

Article V: Regulation of Trade in Specimens of Species Included in Appendix III

1.   All trade in specimens of species included in Appendix III shall be in accordance with the provisions of this Article.

2.   The export of any specimens of a species included in Appendix III from any State which has included that species in Appendix III shall require the prior grant and presentation of an export permit. An export permit shall only be granted when the following conditions have been met:

(a)   a Management Authority of the State of export is satisfied that the specimen was not obtained in contravention of the laws of that State for the protection of fauna and flora; and

(b)   a Management Authority of the State of export is satisfied that any living specimen will be so prepared and shipped as to minimize the risk of injury, damage to health or cruel treatment.

3.   The import of any specimen of a species included in Appendix III shall require, except in circumstances to which paragraph 4 of this Article applies, the prior presentation of a certificate of origin and, where the import is from a State which has included that species in Appendix III, an export permit.

4.   In the case of re-export, a certificate granted by the Management Authority of the State of re-export that the specimen was processed in that State or is being re-exported shall be accepted by the State of import as evidence that the provisions of the present Convention have been complied with in respect of the specimen concerned.

Article VI: Permits and Certificates

1.   Permits and certificates granted under the provisions of Articles III, IV and V shall be in accordance with the provisions of this Article.

2.   An export permit shall contain the information specified in the model set forth in Appendix IV, and may only be used for export within a period of six months from the date on which it was granted.

3.   Each permit or certificate shall contain the title of the present Convention, the name and any identifying stamp of the Management Authority granting it and a control number assigned by the Management Authority.

4.   Any copies of a permit or certificate issued by a Management Authority shall be clearly marked as copies only and no such copy may be used in place of the original, except to the extent endorsed thereon.

5.   A separate permit or certificate shall be required for each consignment of specimens.

6.   A Management Authority of the State of import of any specimen shall cancel and retain the export permit or re-export certificate and any corresponding import permit presented in respect of the import of that specimen.

7.   Where appropriate and feasible a Management Authority may affix a mark upon any specimen to assist in identifying the specimen. For these purposes "mark" means any indelible imprint, lead seal or other suitable means of identifying a specimen, designed in such a way as to render its imitation by unauthorized persons as difficult as possible.

Article VII: Exemptions and Other Special Provisions Relating to Trade

1.   The provisions of Articles III, IV and V shall not apply to the transit or transshipment of specimens through or in the territory of a Party while the specimens remain in Customs control.

2.   Where a Management Authority of the State of export or re-export is satisfied that a specimen was acquired before the provisions of the present Convention applied to that specimen, the provisions of Articles III, IV and V shall not apply to that specimen where the Management Authority issues a certificate to that effect.

3.   The provisions of Articles III, IV and V shall not apply to specimens that are personal or household effects. This exemption shall not apply where:

(a)   in the case of specimens of a species included in Appendix I, they were acquired by the owner outside his State of usual residence, and are being imported into the State; or

(b)   in the case of specimens of species included in Appendix II:

(i)   they were acquired by the owner outside his State of usual residence and in a State where removal from the wild occurred;

(ii)   they are being imported into the owner's State of usual residence; and

(iii)   the State where removal from the wild occurred requires the prior grant of export permits before any export of such specimens; unless a Management Authority is satisfied that the specimens were acquired before the provisions of the present Convention applied to such specimens.

4.   Specimens of an animal species included in Appendix I bred in captivity for commercial purposes, or of a plant species included in Appendix I artificially propagated for commercial purposes, shall be deemed to be specimens of species included in Appendix II.

5.   Where a Management Authority of the State of export is satisfied that any specimen of an animal species was bred in captivity or any specimen of a plant species was artificially propagated, or is a part of such an animal or plant or was derived therefrom, a certificate by that Management Authority to that effect shall be accepted in lieu of any of the permits or certificates required under the provisions of Articles III, IV or V.

6.   The provisions of Articles III, IV and V shall not apply to the noncommercial loan, donation or exchange between scientists or scientific institutions registered by a Management Authority of their State, of herbarium specimens, other preserved, dried or embedded museum specimens, and live plant material which carry a label issued or approved by a Management Authority.

7.   A Management Authority of any State may waive the requirements of Articles III, IV and V and allow the movement without permits or certificates of specimens which form part of a travelling zoo, circus, menagerie, plant exhibition or other travelling exhibition provided that:
    (a)   the exporter or importer registers full details of such specimens with that Management Authority;
    (b)   the specimens are in either of the categories specified in paragraphs 2 or 5 of this Article; and
    (c)   the Management Authority is satisfied that any living specimen will be so transported and cared for as to minimize the risk of injury, damage to health or cruel treatment.

Article VIII: Measures to Be Taken by the Parties

1.   The Parties shall take appropriate measures to enforce the provisions of the present Convention and to prohibit trade in specimens in violation thereof. These shall include measures:
    (a)   to penalize trade in, or possession of, such specimens, or both; and
    (b)   to provide for the confiscation or return to the State of export of such specimens.

2.   In addition to the measures taken under paragraph 1 of this Article, a Party may, when it deems it necessary, provide for any method of internal reimbursement for expenses incurred as a result of the confiscation of a specimen traded in violation of the measures taken in the application of the provisions of the present Convention.

3.   As far as possible, the Parties shall ensure that specimens shall pass through any formalities required for trade with a minimum of delay. To facilitate such passage, a Party may designate ports of exit and ports of entry at which specimens must be presented for clearance. The Parties shall ensure further that all living specimens, during any period of transit, holding or shipment, are properly cared for so as to minimize the risk of injury, damage to health or cruel treatment.

4.   Where a living specimen is confiscated as a result of measures referred to in paragraph 1 of this Article:
    (a)   the specimen shall be entrusted to a Management Authority of the State of confiscation;
    (b)   the Management Authority shall, after consultation with the State of export, return the specimen to that State at the expense of that State, or to a rescue centre of such other place as the Management Authority deems appropriate and consistent with the purposes of the present Convention; and
    (c)   the Management Authority may obtain the advice of a Scientific Authority, or may, whenever it considers it desirable, consult with the Secretariat in order to facilitate the decision under subparagraph (b) of this paragraph, including the choice of a rescue centre or other place.

5.   A rescue centre as referred to in paragraph 4 of this Article means an institution designated by a Management Authority to look after the welfare of living specimens, particularly those that have been confiscated.

6.   Each party shall maintain records of trade in specimens of species included in Appendices I, II and III which shall cover:
    (a)   the names and addresses of exporters and importers; and

(b)   the number and type of permits and certificates granted; the States with which such trade occurred; the numbers or quantities and types of specimens, names of species as included in Appendices I, II and III and, where applicable, the size and sex of the specimens in question.

7.   Each Party shall prepare periodic reports on its implementation of the present Convention and shall transmit to the Secretariat:

      (a)   an annual report containing a summary of the information specified in sub-paragraph (b) of paragraph 6 of this Article; and

      (b)   a biennial report on legislative, regulatory and administrative measures taken to enforce the provisions of the present Convention.

8.   The information referred to in paragraph 7 of this Article shall be available to the public where this is not inconsistent with the law of the Party concerned.

Article IX: Management and Scientific Authorities

1.   Each Party shall designate for the purposes of the present Convention

      (a)   one or more Management Authorities competent to grant permits or certificates on behalf of that Party; and

      (b)   one or more Scientific Authorities.

2.   A State depositing an instrument of ratification, acceptance, approval or accession shall at that time inform the Depository Government of the name and address of the Management Authority authorized to communicate with other Parties and with the Secretariat.

3.   Any changes in the designations or authorizations under the provisions of this Article shall be communicated by the Party concerned to the Secretariat for transmission to all other Parties.

4.   Any Management Authority referred to in paragraph 2 of this Article shall, if so requested by the Secretariat or the Management Authority of another Party, communicate to it impression of stamps, seals or other devices used to authenticate permits or certificates.

Article X: Trade with States not Party to the Convention

Where export or re-export is to, or import is from, a State not a party to the present Convention, comparable documentation issued by the competent authorities in that State which substantially conforms with the requirements of the present Convention for permits and certificates may be accepted in lieu thereof by any Party.

Article XI: Conference of the Parties

1.   The Secretariat shall call a meeting of the Conference of the Parties not later than two years after the entry into force of the present Convention.

2.   Thereafter the Secretariat shall convene regular meetings at least once every two years, unless the Conference decides otherwise, and extraordinary meetings at any time on the written request of at least one-third of the Parties.

3.   At meetings, whether regular or extraordinary, the Parties shall review the implementation of the present Convention and may:

      (a)   make such provision as may be necessary to enable the Secretariat to carry out its duties, and adopt financial provisions;

      (b)   consider and adopt amendments to Appendices I and II in accordance with Article XV;

      (c)   review the progress made towards the restoration and conservation of the species included in Appendices I, II and III;

      (d)   receive and consider any reports presented by the Secretariat or by any Party; and

      (e)   where appropriate, make recommendations for improving the effectiveness of the present Convention.

4.   At each regular meeting, the Parties may determine the time and venue of the next regular meeting to be held in accordance with the provisions of paragraph 2 of this Article.

5.   At any meeting, the Parties may determine and adopt rules of procedure for the meeting.

6.   The United Nations, its Specialized Agencies and the International Atomic Energy Agency, as well as any State not a Party to the present Convention, may be represented at meetings of the Conference by observers, who shall have the right to participate but not to vote.

7.   Any body or agency technically qualified in protection, conservation or management of wild fauna and flora, in the following categories, which has informed the Secretariat of its desire to be represented at meetings of the Conference by observers, shall be admitted unless at least one-third of the Parties present object:

(a)   international agencies or bodies, either governmental or non-governmental, and national governmental agencies and bodies; and

(b)   national non-governmental agencies or bodies which have been approved for this purpose by the State in which they are located. Once admitted, these observers shall have the right to participate but not to vote.

Article XII: The Secretariat

1.   Upon entry into force of the present Convention, a Secretariat shall be provided by the Executive Director of the United Nations Environment Programme. To the extent and in the manner he considers appropriate, he may be assisted by suitable inter-governmental or non-governmental international or national agencies and bodies technically qualified in protection, conservation and management of wild fauna and flora.

2.   The functions of the Secretariat shall be:

(a)   to arrange for and service meetings of the Parties;

(b)   to perform the functions entrusted to it under the provisions of Articles XV and XVI of the present Convention;

(c)   to undertake scientific and technical studies in accordance with programmes authorized by the Conference of the Parties as will contribute to the implementation of the present Convention, including studies concerning standards for appropriate preparation and shipment of living specimens and the means of identifying specimens;

(d)   to study the reports of Parties and to request from Parties such further information with respect thereto as it deems necessary to ensure implementation of the present Convention;

(e)   to invite the attention of the Parties to any matter pertaining to the aims of the present Convention;

(f)   to publish periodically and distribute to the Parties current editions of Appendices I, II and III together with any information which will facilitate identification of specimens of species included in those Appendices;

(g)   to prepare annual reports to the Parties on its work and on the implementation of the present Convention and such other reports as meetings of the Parties may request;

(h)   to make recommendations for the implementation of the aims and provisions of the present Convention, including the exchange of information of a scientific or technical nature;

(i)   to perform any other function as may be entrusted to it by the Parties.

Article XIII: International Measures

1.   When the Secretariat in the light of information received is satisfied that any species included in Appendices I or II is being affected adversely by trade in specimens of that species or that the provisions of the present Convention are not being effectively implemented, it shall communicate such information to the authorized Management Authority of the Party or Parties concerned.

2.   When any Party receives a communication as indicated in paragraph 1 of this Article, it shall, as soon as possible, inform the Secretariat of any relevant facts insofar as its laws permit and, where appropriate, propose remedial action. Where the Party considers that an inquiry is desirable, such inquiry may be carried out by one or more persons expressly authorized by the Party.

3.   The information provided by the Party or resulting from any inquiry as specified in paragraph 2 of this Article shall be reviewed by the next Conference of the Parties which may make whatever recommendations it deems appropriate.

Article XIV: Effect on Domestic legislation and International Conventions

1.   The provisions of the present Convention shall in no way affect the right of Parties to adopt:
        (a)   stricter domestic measures regarding the conditions for trade, taking possession or transport of specimens of species included in Appendices I, II and III, or the complete prohibition thereof; or
        (b)   domestic measures restricting or prohibiting trade, taking possession, or transport of species not included in Appendices I, II or III.

2.   The provisions of the present Convention shall in no way affect the provisions of any domestic measures or the obligations deriving from any treaty, convention, or international agreement relating to other aspects of trade, taking possession, or transport of specimens which is in force or subsequently may enter into force for any Party including any measures pertaining to Customs, public health, veterinary or plan quarantine fields.

3.   The provisions of the present Convention shall in no way affect the provisions of, or the obligations deriving from, any treaty, convention or international agreement concluded or which may be concluded between States creating a union or regional trade agreement establishing or maintaining a common external Customs control and removing Customs control between the parties thereto insofar as they relate to trade among the States members of the union or agreement.

4.   A State party to the present Convention, which is also a party to any other treaty, convention or international agreement which is in force at the time of the coming into force of the present Convention and under the provisions of which protection is afforded to marine species included in Appendix II, shall be relieved of the obligations imposed on it under the provisions of the present Convention with respect to trade in specimens of species included in Appendix II that are taken by ships registered in that State and in accordance with the provisions of such other treaty, convention or international agreement.

5.   Notwithstanding the provisions of Articles III, IV and V, any export of a specimen taken in accordance with paragraph 4 of this Article shall only require a certificate from a Management Authority of the State of introduction to the effect that the specimen was taken in accordance with the provisions of the other treaty, convention or international agreement in question.

6.   Nothing in the present Convention shall prejudice the codification and development of the law of the sea by the United Nations Conference on the Law of the Sea convened pursuant to Resolution 2750 C (XXV) of the General Assembly of the United Nations nor the present of future claims and legal views of any State concerning the law of the sea and the nature and extent of coastal and flag State jurisdiction.

Article XV: Amendments to Appendices I and II

1.   The following provisions shall apply in relation to amendments to Appendices I and II at meetings of the Conference of the Parties:
        (a)   Any Party may propose an amendment to Appendix I or II for consideration at the next meeting. The text of the proposed amendment shall be communicated to the Secretariat at least 150 days before the meetings. The Secretariat shall consult the other Parties and interested bodies on the amendment in accordance with the provisions of subparagraphs (b) and (c) of paragraph 2 of this Article and shall communicate the response to all Parties not later than 30 days before the meeting.
        (b)   Amendments shall be adopted by a two-thirds majority of Parties present and voting. For these purposes "Parties present and voting" means Parties present and casting an affirmative or negative vote. Parties abstaining from voting shall not be counted among the two-thirds required for adopting an amendment.
        (c)   Amendments adopted at a meeting shall enter into force 90 days after that meeting for all Parties except those which make a reservation in accordance with paragraph 3 of this Article.

2.   The following provisions shall apply in relation to amendments to Appendices I and II between meetings of the Conference of the Parties:
        (a)   Any Party may propose an amendment to Appendix I or II for consideration between meetings by the postal procedures set forth in this paragraph.
        (b)   For marine species, the Secretariat shall, upon receiving the text of the proposed amendment immediately communicate it to the Parties. It shall also consult inter-governmental bodies having a function in

relation to those species especially with a view to obtaining scientific data these bodies may be able to provide and to ensuring co-ordination with any conservation measures enforced by such bodies. The Secretariat shall communicate the views expressed and data provided by these bodies and its own findings and recommendations to the Parties as soon as possible.

(c)   For species other than marine species, the Secretariat shall, upon receiving the text of the proposed amendment, immediately communicate it to the Parties, and, as soon as possible thereafter, its own recommendations.

(d)   Any Party may, within 60 days of the date on which the Secretariat communicated its recommendations to the Parties under subparagraphs (b) or (c) of this paragraph, transmit to the Secretariat any comments on the proposed amendment together with any relevant scientific data and information.

(e)   The Secretariat shall communicate the replies received together with its own recommendations to the Parties as soon as possible. If no objection to the proposed amendment is received by the Secretariat within 30 days of the date the replies and recommendations were communicated under the provisions of sub-paragraph (e) of this paragraph, the amendment shall enter into force 90 days later for all Parties except those which make a reservation in accordance with paragraph 3 of this Article.

(f)   If an objection by any Party is received by the Secretariat, the proposed amendment shall be submitted to a postal vote in accordance with the provisions of sub-paragraphs (h), (i) and (j) of this paragraph.

(g)   The Secretariat shall notify the Parties that notification of objection has been received.

(h)   Unless the Secretariat receives the votes for, against or in abstention from at least one-half of the Parties within 60 days of the date of notification under sub-paragraph (h) of this paragraph, the proposed amendment shall be referred to the next meeting of the Conference for further consideration.

(i)   Provided that votes are received from one-half of the Parties, the amendment shall be adopted by a two-thirds majority of Parties casting an affirmative or negative vote.

(j)   The Secretariat shall notify all Parties of the result of the vote.

(k)   If the proposed amendment is adopted it shall enter into force 90 days after the date of the notification by the Secretariat of its acceptance for all Parties except those which make a reservation in accordance with paragraph 3 of this Article.

3.   During the period of 90 days provided for by sub-paragraph (c) of paragraph 1 or sub-paragraph (l) of paragraph 2 of this Article any Party may by notification in writing to the Depositary Government make a reservation with respect to the amendment. Until such reservation is withdrawn the Party shall be treated as a State not a party to the present Convention with respect to trade in the species concerned.

Article XVI: Appendix III and Amendments thereto

1.   Any party may at any time submit to the Secretariat a list of species which it identifies as being subject to regulation within its jurisdiction for the purpose mentioned in paragraph 3 of Article II. Appendix III shall include the names of the Parties submitting the species for inclusion therein, the scientific names of the species so submitted, and any parts or derivatives of the animals or plants concerned that are specified in relation to the species for the purposes of subparagraph (b) of Article I.

2.   Each list submitted under the provisions of paragraph 1 of this Article shall be communicated to the Parties by the Secretariat as soon as possible after receiving it. The list shall take effect as part of Appendix III 90 days after the date of such communication. At any time after the communication of such list, any Party may by notification in writing to the Depositary Government enter a reservation with respect to any species or any parts or derivatives, and until such reservation is withdrawn, the State shall be treated as a State not a Party to the present Convention with respect to trade in the species or part or derivative concerned.

3.   A Party which has submitted a species for inclusion in Appendix III may withdraw it at any time by notification to the Secretariat which shall communicate the withdrawal to all Parties. The withdrawal shall take effect 30 days after the date of such communication.

4.   Any Party submitting a list under the provisions of paragraph 1 of this Article shall submit to the Secretariat a copy of all domestic laws and regulations applicable to the protection of such species, together with any interpretations which the Party may deem appropriate or the Secretariat may request. The Party shall, for as long as the species in question is included in Appendix III, submit any amendments of such laws and regulations or interpretations as they are adopted.

Article XVII: Amendment of the Convention

1.   An extraordinary meeting of the Conference of the Parties shall be convened by the Secretariat on the written request of at least one-third of the Parties to consider and adopt amendments to the present Convention. Such amendments shall be adopted by a two-thirds majority of Parties present and voting. For these purposes "Parties present and voting" means Parties present and casting an affirmative or negative vote. Parties abstaining from voting shall not be counted among the two-thirds required for adopting an amendment.

2.   The text of any proposed amendment shall be communicated by the Secretariat to all Parties at least 90 days before the meeting.

3.   An amendment shall enter into force for the Parties which have accepted it 60 days after two-thirds of the Parties have deposited an instrument of acceptance of the amendment with the Depositary Government. Thereafter, the amendment shall enter into force for any other Party 60 days after the Party deposits its instrument of the amendment.

Article XVIII: Resolution of disputes

1.   Any dispute which may arise between two or more Parties with respect to the interpretation or application of the provisions of the present Convention shall be subject to negotiation between the Parties involved in the dispute.

2.   If the dispute can not be resolved in accordance with paragraph 1 of this Article, the Parties may, by mutual consent, submit the dispute to arbitration, in particular that of the Permanent Court of Arbitration at The Hague, and the Parties submitting the dispute shall be bound by the arbitral decision.

Article XIX: Signature

The present Convention shall be open for signature at Washington until 30th April 1973 and thereafter at Berne until 31st December 1974.

Article XX: Ratification, Acceptance, Approval

The present Convention shall be subject to ratification, acceptance or approval. Instruments of ratification, acceptance or approval shall be deposited with the Government of the Swiss Confederation which shall be the Depositary Government.

Article XXI: Accession

The present Convention shall be open indefinitely for accession. Instruments of accession shall be deposited with the Depositary Government.

Article XXII: Entry into force

1.   The present Convention shall enter into force 90 days after the date of deposit of the tenth instrument of ratification, acceptance, approval or accession, with the Depositary Government.

2.   For each State which ratifies, accepts or approves the present Convention or accedes thereto after the deposit of the tenth instrument of ratification, acceptance, approval or accession, the present Convention shall enter into force 90 days after the deposit by such State of its instrument of ratification, acceptance, approval or accession.

Article XXIII: Reservations

1.   The provisions of the present Convention shall not be subject to general reservations. Specific reservations may be entered in accordance with the provisions of this Article and Articles XV and XVI.

2.   Any State may, on depositing its instrument of ratification, acceptance, approval or accession, enter a specific reservation with regard to:
    (a)   any species included in Appendix I, II or III; or
    (b)   any parts or derivatives specified in relation to a species included in Appendix III.

3.   Until a Party withdraws its reservation entered under the provisions of this Article, it shall be treated as a State not a party to the present Convention with respect to trade in the particular species or parts or derivatives specified in such reservation.

Article XXIV: Denunciation

Any Party may denounce the present Convention by written notification to the Depositary Government at any time. The denunciation shall take effect twelve months after the Depositary Government has received the notification.

Article XXV: Depositary

1.   The original of the present Convention, in the Chinese, English, French, Russian and Spanish languages, each version being equally authentic, shall be deposited with the Depositary Government, which shall transmit certified copies thereof to all States that have signed it or deposited instruments of accession to it.

2.   The Depositary Government shall inform all signatory and acceding States and the Secretariat of signatures, deposit of instruments of ratification, acceptance, approval or accession, entry into force of the present Convention, amendments thereto, entry and withdrawal of reservations and notifications of denunciation.

3.   As soon as the present Convention enters into force, a certified copy thereof shall be transmitted by the Depositary Government to the Secretariat of the United Nations for registration and publication in accordance with Article 102 of the Charter of the United Nations.

IN WITNESS WHEREOF the undersigned Plenipotentiaries, being duly authorized to that effect, have signed the present Convention.

DONE at Washington this third day of March, One Thousand Nine Hundred and Seventy-three.

CONVENTION ON THE CONSERVATION OF MIGRATORY SPECIES OF WILD ANIMALS

Signed: June 23, 1979
Entered into Force: November 1, 1983

The Contracting Parties,

Recognizing that wild animals in their innumerable forms are an irreplaceable part of the earth's natural system which must be conserved for the good of mankind;

Aware that each generation of man holds the resources of the earth for future generations and has an obligation to ensure that this legacy is conserved and, where utilized, is used wisely;

Conscious of the ever-growing value of wild animals from environmental, ecological, genetic, scientific, aesthetic, recreational, cultural, educational, social and economic points of view;

Concerned particularly with those species of wild animals that migrate across or outside national jurisdictional boundaries;

Recognizing that the States are and must be the protectors of the migratory species of wild animals that live within or pass through their national jurisdictional boundaries;

Convinced that conservation and effective management of migratory species of wild animals require the concerted action of all States within the national jurisdictional boundaries of which such species spend any part of their life cycle;

Recalling Recommendation 32 of the Action Plan adopted by the United Nations Conference on the Human Environment (Stockholm, 1972) and noted with satisfaction at the Twenty-seventh Session of the General Assembly of the United Nations,

Have agreed as follows:

Article I   Interpretation

1. For the purpose of this Convention:

    a) "Migratory species" means the entire population or any geographically separate part of the population of any species or lower taxon of wild animals, a significant proportion of whose members cyclically and predictably cross one or more national jurisdictional boundaries;

    b) "Conservation status of a migratory species" means the sum of the influences acting on the migratory species that may affect its long-term distribution and abundance;

    c) "Conservation status" will be taken as "favourable" when:

> (1) population dynamics data indicate that the migratory species is maintaining itself on a long-term basis as a viable component of its ecosystems;
> (2) the range of the migratory species is neither currently being reduced, nor is likely to be reduced, on a long-term basis;
> (3) there is, and will be in the foreseeable future sufficient habitat to maintain the population of the migratory species on a long-term basis; and
> (4) the distribution and abundance of the migratory species approach historic coverage and levels to the extent that potentially suitable ecosystems exist and to the extent consistent with wise wildlife management;

    d) "Conservation status" will be taken as "unfavourable" if any of the conditions set out in sub-paragraph (c) of this paragraph is not met;

    e) "Endangered" in relation to a particular migratory species means that the migratory species is in danger of extinction throughout all or a significant portion of its range;

    f) "Range" means all the areas of land or water that a migratory species inhabits, stays in temporarily, crosses or overflies at any time on its normal migration route;

g) "Habitat" means any area in the range of a migratory species which contains suitable living conditions for that species;

h) "Range State" in relation to a particular migratory species means any State (and where appropriate any other Party referred to under subparagraph (k) of this paragraph) that exercises jurisdiction over any part of the range of that migratory species, or a State, flag vessels of which are engaged outside national jurisdictional limits in taking that migratory species;

i) "Taking" means taking, hunting, fishing capturing, harassing, deliberate killing, or attempting to engage in any such conduct;

j) "Agreement" means an international agreement relating to the conservation of one or more migratory species as provided for in Articles IV and V of this Convention; and

k) "Party" means a State or any regional economic integration organization constituted by sovereign States which has competence in respect of the negotiation, conclusion and application of international Agreements in matters covered by this Convention for which this Convention is in force.

2. In matters within their competence, the regional economic integration organizations which are Parties to this Convention shall in their own name exercise the rights and fulfill the responsibilities which this Convention attributes to their member States. In such cases the member States of these organizations shall not be entitled to exercise such rights individually.

3. Where this Convention provides for a decision to be taken by either a two-thirds majority or a unanimous decision of "the Parties present and voting" this shall mean "the Parties present and casting an affirmative or negative vote". Those abstaining from voting shall not be counted amongst "the Parties present and voting" in determining the majority.

Article II   Fundamental Principles

1. The Parties acknowledge the importance of migratory species being conserved and of Range States agreeing to take action to this end whenever possible and appropriate, paying special attention to migratory species the conservation status of which is unfavourable, and taking individually or in co-operation appropriate and necessary steps to conserve such species and their habitat.

2. The Parties acknowledge the need to take action to avoid any migratory species becoming endangered.

3. In particular, the Parties:

a) should promote, co-operate in and support research relating to migratory species;

b) shall endeavour to provide immediate protection for migratory species included in Appendix I; and

c) shall endeavour to conclude Agreements covering the conservation and management of migratory species included in Appendix II.

Article III   Endangered Migratory Species: Appendix I

1. Appendix I shall list migratory species which are endangered.

2. A migratory species may be listed in Appendix I provided that reliable evidence, including the best scientific evidence available, indicates that the species is endangered.

3. A migratory species may be removed from Appendix I when the Conference of the Parties determines that:

a) reliable evidence, including the best scientific evidence available, indicates that the species is no longer endangered, and

b) the species is not likely to become endangered again because of loss of protection due to its removal from Appendix I.

4. Parties that are Range States of a migratory species listed in Appendix I shall endeavour:

a) to conserve and, where feasible and appropriate, restore those habitats of the species which are of importance in removing the species from danger of extinction;

b) to prevent, remove, compensate for or minimize, as appropriate, the adverse effects of activities or obstacles that seriously impede or prevent the migration of the species; and

c) to the extent feasible and appropriate, to prevent, reduce or control factors that are endangering or are likely to further endanger the species, including strictly controlling the introduction of, or controlling or eliminating, already introduced exotic species.

5. Parties that are Range States of a migratory species listed in Appendix I shall prohibit the taking of animals belonging to such species. Exceptions may be made to this prohibition only if:

a) the taking is for scientific purposes;
b) the taking is for the purpose of enhancing the propagation or survival of the affected species;
c) the taking is to accommodate the needs of traditional subsistence users of such species; or
d) extraordinary circumstances so require; provided that such exceptions are precise as to content and limited in space and time. Such taking should not operate to the disadvantage of the species.

6. The Conferences of the Parties may recommend to the Parties that are Range States of a migratory species listed in Appendix I that they take further measures considered appropriate to benefit the species.

7. The Parties shall as soon as possible inform the Secretariat of any exceptions made pursuant to paragraph 5 of this Article.

Article IV   **Migratory Species to be the Subject of Agreements: Appendix II**

1. Appendix II shall list migratory species which have an unfavourable conservation status and which require international agreements for their conservation and management, as well as those which have a conservation status which would significantly benefit from the international cooperation that could be achieved by an international agreement.

2. If the circumstances so warrant, a migratory species may be listed both in Appendix I and Appendix II.

3. Parties that are Range States of migratory species listed in Appendix II shall endeavour to conclude Agreements where these should benefit the species and should give priority to those species in an unfavourable conservation status.

4. Parties are encouraged to take action with a view to concluding agreements for any population or any geographically separate part of the population of any species or lower tax on of wild animals, members of which periodically cross one or more national jurisdiction boundaries.

5. The Secretariat shall be provided with a copy of each Agreement concluded pursuant to the provisions of this Article.

Article V   **Guidelines for Agreements**

1. The object of each Agreement shall be to restore the migratory species concerned to a favourable conservation status or to maintain it in such a status. Each Agreement should deal with those aspects of the conservation and management of the migratory species concerned which serve to achieve that object.

2. Each Agreement should cover the whole of the range of the migratory species concerned and should be open to accession by all Range States of that species, whether or not they are Parties to this Convention.

3. An Agreement should, wherever possible, deal with more than one migratory species.

4. Each Agreement should:

a) identify the migratory species covered;
b) describe the range and migration route of the migratory species;
c) provide for each Party to designate its national authority concerned with the implementation of the Agreement.

d) establish, if necessary, appropriate machinery to assist in carrying out the aims of the Agreement, to monitor its effectiveness, and to prepare reports for the Conference of the Parties;

e) provide for procedures for the settlement of disputes between Parties to the Agreement; and at a minimum, prohibit, in relation to a migratory species of the Order Cetacea, any taking that is not permitted for that migratory species under any other multilateral Agreement and provide for accession to the Agreement by States that are not Range States of that migratory species.

5. Where appropriate and feasible, each Agreement should provide for but not be limited to:

a) periodic review of the conservation status of the migratory species concerned and the identification of the factors which may be harmful to that status;

b) co-ordinated conservation and management plans;

c) research into the ecology and population dynamics of the migratory species concerned, with special regard to migration;

d) the exchange of information on the migratory species concerned, special regard being paid to the exchange of the results of research and of relevant statistics;

e) conservation and, where required and feasible, restoration of the habitats of importance in maintaining a favourable conservation status, and protection of such habitats from disturbances, including strict control of the introduction of, or control of already introduced, exotic species detrimental to the migratory species;

f) maintenance of a network of suitable habitats appropriately disposed in relation to the migration routes;

g) where it appears desirable, the provision of new habitats favourable to the migratory species or reintroduction of the migratory species into favourable habitats;

h) elimination of, to the maximum extent possible, or compensation for activities and obstacles which hinder or impede migration;

i) prevention, reduction or control of the release into the habitat of the migratory species of substances harmful to that migratory species;

j) measures based on sound ecological principles to control and manage the taking of the migratory species;

k) procedures for co-ordinating action to suppress illegal taking;

l) exchange of information on substantial threats to the migratory species;

m) emergency procedures whereby conservation action would be considerably and rapidly strengthened when the conservation status of the migratory species is seriously affected; and

n) making the general public aware of the contents and aims of the Agreement.

Article VI   Range States

1. A list of the Range States of migratory species listed in Appendices I and II shall be kept up to date by the Secretariat using information it has received from the Parties.

2. The Parties shall keep the Secretariat informed in regard to which of the migratory species listed in Appendices I and II they consider themselves to be Range States, including provision of information on their flag vessels engaged outside national jurisdictional limits in taking the migratory species concerned and, where possible, future plans in respect of such taking.

3. The Parties which are Range States for migratory species listed in Appendix I or Appendix II should inform the Conference of the Parties through the Secretariat, at least six months prior to each ordinary meeting of the Conference, on measures that they are taking to implement the provisions of this Convention for these species.

Article VII   The Conference of the Parties

1. The Conference of the Parties shall be the decision-making organ of this Convention.

2. The Secretariat shall call a meeting of the Conference of the Parties not later than two years after the entry into force of this Convention.

3. Thereafter the Secretariat shall convene ordinary meetings of the Conference of the Parties at intervals of not more than three years, unless the Conference decides otherwise, and extraordinary meetings at any time on the written request of at least one-third of the Parties.

4. The Conference of the Parties shall establish and keep under review the financial regulations of this Convention. The Conference of the Parties shall, at each of its ordinary meetings, adopt the budget for the next financial period. Each Party shall contribute to this budget according to a scale to be agreed upon by the Conference. Financial regulations, including the provisions on the budget and the scale of contributions as well as their modifications, shall be adopted by unanimous vote of the Parties present and voting.

5. At each of its meetings the Conference of the Parties shall review the implementation of this Convention and may in particular:

a) review and assess the conservation status of migratory species;

b) review the progress made towards the conservation of migratory species, especially those listed in Appendices I and II;

c) make such provision and provide such guidance as may be necessary to enable the Scientific Council and the Secretariat to carry out their duties;

d) receive and consider any reports presented by the Scientific Council, the Secretariat, any Party or any standing body established pursuant to an Agreement;

e) make recommendations to the Parties for improving the conservation status of migratory species and review the progress being made under Agreements;

f) in those cases where an Agreement has not been concluded, make recommendations for the convening of meetings of the Parties that are Range States of a migratory species or group of migratory species to discuss measures to improve the conservation status of the species;

g) make recommendations to the Parties for improving the effectiveness of this Convention; and

h) decide on any additional measure that should be taken to implement the objectives of this Convention.

6. Each meeting of the Conference of the Parties should determine the time and venue of the next meeting.

7. Any meeting of the Conference of the Parties shall determine and adopt rules of procedure for that meeting. Decisions at a meeting of the Conference of the Parties shall require a two-thirds majority of the Parties present and voting, except where otherwise provided for by this Convention.

8. The United Nations, its Specialized Agencies, the International Atomic Energy Agency, as well as any State not a party to this Convention and, for each Agreement, the body designated by the parties to that Agreement, may be represented by observers at meetings of the Conference of the Parties.

9. Any agency or body technically qualified in protection, conservation and management of migratory species, in the following categories, which has informed the Secretariat of its desire to be represented at meetings of the Conference of the Parties by observers, shall be admitted unless at least one-third of the Parties present object:

a) international agencies or bodies, either governmental or non-governmental, and national governmental agencies and bodies; and

b) national non-governmental agencies or bodies which have been approved for this purpose by the State in which they are located. Once admitted, these observers shall have the right to participate but not to vote.

Article VIII   The Scientific Council

1. At its first meeting, the Conference of the Parties shall establish a Scientific Council to provide advice on scientific matters.

2. Any Party may appoint a qualified expert as a member of the Scientific Council. In addition, the Scientific Council shall include as members qualified experts selected and appointed by the Conference of the Parties; the number of these experts, the criteria for their selection and the terms of their appointments shall be as determined by the Conference of the Parties.

3. The Scientific Council shall meet at the request of the Secretariat as required by the Conference of the Parties.

4. Subject to the approval of the Conference of the Parties, the Scientific Council shall establish its own rules of procedure.

5. The Conference of the Parties shall determine the functions of the Scientific Council, which may include:

a) providing scientific advice to the Conference of the Parties, to the Secretariat, and, if approved by the Conference of the Parties, to any body set up under this Convention or an Agreement or to any Party;

b) recommending research and the co-ordination of research on migratory species, evaluating the results of such research in order to ascertain the conservation status of migratory species and reporting to the Conference of the Parties on such status and measures for its improvement;

c) making recommendations to the Conference of the Parties as to the migratory species to be included in Appendices I and II, together with an indication of the range of such migratory species;

d) making recommendations to the Conference of the Parties as to specific conservation and management measures to be included in Agreements on migratory species; and

e) recommending to the Conference of the Parties solutions to problems relating to the scientific aspects of the implementation of this Convention, in particular with regard to the habitats of migratory species.

Article IX   The Secretariat

1. For the purposes of this Convention a Secretariat shall be established.

2. Upon entry into force of this Convention, the Secretariat is provided by the Executive Director of the United Nations Environment Programme. To the extent and in the manner he considers appropriate, he may be assisted by suitable intergovernmental or non-governmental, international or national agencies and bodies technically qualified in protection, conservation and management of wild animals.

3. If the United Nations Environment Programme is no longer able to provide the Secretariat, the Conference of the Parties shall make alternative arrangements for the Secretariat.

4. The functions of the Secretariat shall be:

a) to arrange for and service meetings: (i) of the Conference of the Parties, and (ii) of the Scientific Council;

b) to maintain liaison with and promote liaison between the Parties, the standing bodies set up under Agreements and other international organizations concerned with migratory species;

c) to obtain from any appropriate source reports and other information which will further the objectives and implementation of this Convention and to arrange for the appropriate dissemination of such information;

d) to invite the attention of the Conference of the Parties to any matter pertaining to the objectives of this Convention;

e) to prepare for the Conference of the Parties reports on the work of the Secretariat and on the implementation of this Convention;

f) to maintain and publish a list of Range States of all migratory species included in Appendices I and II;

g) to promote, under the direction of the Conference of the Parties, the conclusion of Agreements,

h) to maintain and make available to the Parties a list of Agreements and, if so required by the Conference of the Parties, to provide any information on such Agreements;

i) to maintain and publish a list of the recommendations made by the Conference of the Parties pursuant to sub-paragraphs (e), (f) and (g) of paragraph 5 of Article VII or of decisions made pursuant to sub-paragraph (h) of that paragraph;

j) to provide for the general public information concerning this Convention and its objectives; and

k) to perform any other function entrusted to it under this Convention or by the Conference of the Parties.

Article X   Amendment of the Convention

1. This Convention may be amended at any ordinary or extraordinary meeting of the Conference of the Parties.

2. Proposals for amendment may be made by any Party.

3. The text of any proposed amendment and the reasons for it shall be communicated to the Secretary at least one hundred and fifty days before the meeting at which it is to be considered and shall promptly be communicated by the Secretary to all Parties. Any comments on the text by the Parties shall be communicated to the Secretariat not less than sixty days before the meeting begins. The Secretariat shall, immediately after the last day for submission of comments, communicate to the Parties all comments submitted by that day.

4. Amendments shall be adopted by a two-thirds majority of Parties present and voting.

5. An amendment adopted shall enter into force for all Parties which have accepted it on the first day of the third month following the date on which two-thirds of the Parties have deposited an instrument of acceptance with the Depositary. For each Party which deposits an instrument of acceptance after the date on which two-thirds of the Parties have deposited an instrument of acceptance, the amendment shall enter into force for that Party on the first day of the third month following the deposit of its instrument of acceptance.

Article XI   Amendment of the Appendices

1. Appendices I and II may be amended at any ordinary or extraordinary meeting of the Conference of the Parties.

2. Proposals for amendment may be made by any Party.

3. The text of any proposed amendment and the reasons for it, based on the best scientific evidence available, shall be communicated to the Secretariat at least one hundred and fifty days before the meeting and shall promptly be communicated by the Secretariat to all Parties. Any comments on the text by the Parties shall be communicated to the Secretariat not less than sixty days before the meeting begins. The Secretariat shall, immediately after the last day for submission of comments, communicate to the Parties all comments submitted by that day.

4. Amendments shall be adopted by a two-thirds majority of Parties present and voting.

5. An amendment to the Appendices shall enter into force for all Parties ninety days after the meeting of the Conference of the Parties at which it was adopted, except for those Parties which make a reservation in accordance with paragraph 6 of this Article.

6. During the period of ninety days provided for in paragraph 5 of this Article, any Party may by notification in writing to the Depositary make a reservation with respect to the amendment. A reservation to an amendment may be withdrawn by written notification to the Depositary and thereupon the amendment shall enter into force for that Party ninety days after the reservation is withdrawn.

Article XII   Effect on International Conventions and Other Legislation

1. Nothing in this Convention shall prejudice the codification and development of the law of the sea by the United Nations Conference on the Law of the Sea convened pursuant to Resolution 2750 C (XXV) of the General Assembly of the United Nations nor the present or future claims and legal views of any State concerning the law of the sea and the nature and extent of coastal and flag State jurisdiction.

2. The provisions of this Convention shall in no way affect the rights or obligations of any Party deriving from any existing treaty, convention or Agreement.

3. The provisions of this Convention shall in no way affect the right of Parties to adopt stricter domestic measures concerning the conservation of migratory species listed in Appendices I and II or to adopt domestic measures concerning the conservation of species not listed in Appendices I and II.

Article XIII   Settlement of Disputes

1. Any dispute which may arise between two or more Parties with respect to the interpretation or application of the provisions of this Convention shall be subject to negotiation between the Parties involved in the dispute.

2. If the dispute cannot be resolved in accordance with paragraph 1 of this Article, the Parties may, by mutual consent, submit the dispute to arbitration, in particular that of the Permanent Court of Arbitration at The Hague, and the Parties submitting the dispute shall be bound by the arbitral decision.

Article XIV   Reservations

1. The provisions of this Convention shall not be subject to general reservations. Specific reservations may be entered in accordance with the provisions of this Article and Article XI.

2. Any State or regional economic integration organization may, on depositing its instrument of ratification, acceptance, approval or accession, enter a specific reservation with regard to the presence on either Appendix I or Appendix II or both, of any migratory species and shall then not be regarded as a Party in regard to the subject of that reservation until ninety days after the Depositary has transmitted to the Parties notification that such reservation has been withdrawn.

Article XV   Signature

This Convention shall be open for signature at Bonn for all States and any regional economic integration organization until the twenty-second day of June, 1980.

Article XVI   Ratification, Acceptance, Approval

This Convention shall be subject to ratification, acceptance or approval. Instruments of ratification, acceptance or approval shall be deposited with the Government of the Federal Republic of Germany, which shall be the Depositary.

Article XVII   Accession

After the twenty-second day of June 1980 this Convention shall be open for accession by all non-signatory States and any regional economic integration organization. Instruments of accession shall be deposited with the Depositary.

Article XVIII   Entry into Force

1. This Convention shall enter into force on the first day of the third month following the date of deposit of the fifteenth instrument of ratification, acceptance, approval or accession with the Depositary.

2. For each State or each regional economic integration organization which ratifies, accepts or approves this Convention or accedes thereto after the deposit of the fifteenth instrument of ratification, acceptance, approval or accession, this Convention shall enter into force on the first day of the third month following the deposit by such State or such organization of its instrument of ratification, acceptance, approval or accession.

Article XIX   Denunciation

Any Party may denounce this Convention by written notification to the Depositary at any time. The denunciation shall take effect twelve months after the Depositary has received the notification.

Article XX   Depositary

1. The original of this Convention, in the English, French, German, Russian and Spanish languages, each version being equally authentic, shall be deposited with the Depositary. The Depositary shall transmit certified copies of each of these versions to all States and all regional economic integration organizations that have signed the Convention or deposited instruments of accession to it.

2. The Depositary shall, after consultation with the Governments concerned, prepare official versions of the text of this Convention in the Arabic and Chinese languages.

3. The Depositary shall inform all signatory and acceding States and all signatory and acceding regional economic integration organizations and the Secretariat of signatures, deposit of instruments of ratification, acceptance, approval or accession, entry into force of this Convention, amendments thereto, specific reservations and notifications of denunciation.

4. As soon as this Convention enters into force, a certified copy thereof shall be transmitted by the Depositary to the Secretariat of the United Nations for registration and publication in accordance with Article 102 of the Charter of the United Nations. In witness whereof the undersigned, being duly authorized to that effect, have signed this Convention.

INTERNATIONAL CONVENTION FOR THE REGULATION OF WHALING

161 U.N.T.S. 72, 10 U.S.T. 952
Signed: December 2, 1946
Entered Into Effect: November 10, 1948
Secretariat Homepage: http://www.unep.ch/seas/main/legal/liwc.html

The Governments whose duly authorized representatives have subscribed hereto,

Recognizing the interest of the nations of the world in safeguarding for future generations the great natural resources represented by the whale stocks;

Considering that the history of whaling has seen over-fishing of one area after another and of one species of whale after another to such a degree that it is essential to protect all species of whales from further over-fishing;

Recognizing that the whale stocks are susceptible of natural increases if whaling is properly regulated, and that increases in the size of whale stocks will permit increases in the numbers of whales which may be captured without endangering these natural resources;

Recognizing that it is in the common interest to achieve the optimum level of whale stocks as rapidly as possible without causing widespread economic and nutritional distress;

Recognizing that in the course of achieving these objectives, whaling operations should be confined to those species best able to sustain exploitation in order to give an interval for recovery to certain species of whales now depleted in numbers;

Desiring to establish a system of international regulation for the whale fisheries to ensure proper and effective conservation and development of whale stocks on the basis of the principles embodied in the provisions of the International Agreement for the Regulation of Whaling signed in London on 8 June 1937, and the protocols to that Agreement signed in London on 24 June 1938, and 26 November 1945; and

Having decided to conclude a convention to provide for the proper conservation of whale stocks and thus make possible the orderly development of the whaling industry;

Have Agreed as follows:

Article I

1. This Convention includes the Schedule attached thereto which forms an integral part thereof. All references to "Convention" shall be understood as including the said Schedule either in its present terms or as amended in accordance with the provisions of Article V.

2. This Convention applies to factory ships, land stations, and whale catchers under the jurisdiction of the Contracting Governments, and to all waters in which whaling is prosecuted by such factory ships, land stations, and whale catchers.

Article II

As used in this Convention:

1. "factory ship" means a ship in which or on which whales are treated whether wholly or in part;

2. "land station" means a factory on the land at which whales are treated whether wholly or in part;

3. "whale catcher" means a ship used for the purpose of hunting, taking, towing, holding on to, or scouting for whales;

4. "Contracting Government" means any Government which has deposited an instrument of ratification or has given notice of adherence to this Convention.

Article III

1. The Contracting Governments agree to establish an International Whaling Commission, hereinafter referred to as the Commission, to be composed of one member from each Contracting Government. Each member shall have one vote and may be accompanied by one or more experts and advisers.

2. The Commission shall elect from its own members a Chairman and Vice-Chairman and shall determine its own Rules of Procedure. Decisions of the Commission shall be taken by a simple majority of those members voting except that a three-fourths majority of those members voting shall be required for action in pursuance of Article V. The Rules of Procedure may provide for decisions otherwise than at meetings of the Commission.

3. The Commission may appoint its own Secretary and staff.

4. The Commission may set up, from among its own members and experts or advisers, such committees as it considers desirable to perform such functions as it may authorize.

5. The expenses of each member of the Commission and of his experts and advisers shall be determined and paid by his own Government.

6. Recognizing that specialized agencies related to the United Nations will be concerned with the conservation and development of whale fisheries and the products arising therefrom and desiring to avoid duplication of functions, the Contracting Governments will consult among themselves within two years after the coming into force of this Convention to decide whether the Commission shall be brought within the framework of a specialized agency related to the United Nations.

7. In the meantime the Government of the United Kingdom of Great Britain and Northern Ireland shall arrange, in consultation with the other Contracting Governments, to convene the first meeting of the Commission, and shall initiate the consultation referred to in paragraph 6 above.

8. Subsequent meetings of the Commission shall be convened as the Commission may determine.

Article IV

1. The Commission may either in collaboration with or through independent agencies of the Contracting Governments or other public or private agencies, establishments, or organizations, or independently

    a) encourage, recommend, or if necessary, organize studies and investigations relating to whales and whaling;

    b) collect and analyze statistical information concerning the current condition and trend of the whale stocks and the effects of whaling activities thereon;

    c) study, appraise, and disseminate information concerning methods of maintaining and increasing the populations of whale stocks.

2. The Commission shall arrange for the publication of reports of its activities, and it may publish independently or in collaboration with the International Bureau for Whaling Statistics at Sandefjord in Norway and other organizations and agencies such reports as it deems appropriate, as well as statistical, scientific, and other pertinent information relating to whales and whaling.

Article V

1. The Commission may amend from time to time the provisions of the Schedule by adopting regulations with respect to the conservation and utilization of whale resources, fixing

    (a) protected and unprotected species;

    (b) open and closed seasons;

(c) open and closed waters, including the designation of sanctuary areas;

(d) size limits for each species;

(e) time, methods, and intensity of whaling (including the maximum catch of whales to be taken in any one season);

(f) types and specifications of gear and apparatus and appliances which may be used;

(g) methods of measurement;

(h) catch returns and other statistical and biological records; and

(i) methods of inspection.

2. These amendments of the Schedule

(a) shall be such as are necessary to carry out the objectives and purposes of this Convention and to provide for the conservation, development, and optimum utilization of the whale resources;

(b) shall be based on scientific findings;

(c) shall not involve restrictions on the number or nationality of factory ships or land stations, nor allocate specific quotas to any factory ship or land station or to any group of factory ships or land stations; and

(d) shall take into consideration the interests of the consumers of whale products and the whaling industry.

3. Each of such amendments shall become effective with respect to the Contracting Governments ninety days following notification of the amendment by the Commission to each of the Contracting Governments, except that

(a) if any Government presents to the Commission objection to any amendment prior to the expiration of this ninety-day period, the amendment shall not become effective with respect to any of the Governments for an additional ninety days;

(b) thereupon, any other Contracting Government may present objection to the amendment at any time prior to the expiration of the additional ninety-day period, or before the expiration of thirty days from the date of receipt of the last objection received during such additional ninety-day period, whichever date shall be the later; and

(c) thereafter, the amendment shall become effective with respect to all Contracting Governments which have not presented objection but shall not become effective with respect to any Government which has so objected until such date as the objection is withdrawn. The Commission shall notify each Contracting Government immediately upon receipt of each objection and withdrawal and each Contracting Government shall acknowledge receipt of all notifications of amendments, objections, and withdrawals.

4. No amendments shall become effective before 1 July 1949.

Article VI

The Commission may from time to time make recommendations to any or all Contracting Governments on any matters which relate to whales or whaling and to the objectives and purposes of this Convention.

Article VII

The Contracting Governments shall ensure prompt transmission to the International Bureau of Whaling Statistics at Sandefjord in Norway, or to such other body as the Commission may designate, of notifications and statistical and other information required by this Convention in such form and manner as may be prescribed by the Commission.

Article VIII

1. Notwithstanding anything contained in this Convention, any Contracting Government may grant to any of its nationals a special permit authorizing that national to kill, take, and treat whales for purposes of scientific research subject to such restrictions as to number and subject to such other conditions as the Contracting Government thinks fit, and the killing, taking, and treating of whales in accordance with the provisions of this Article shall be exempt from the operation of this Convention. Each Contracting Government shall report at once to the Commission all such authorizations which it has granted. Each Contracting Government may at any time revoke any such special permit which it has granted.

2. Any whales taken under these special permits shall so far as practicable be processed and the proceeds shall be dealt with in accordance with directions issued by the Government by which the permit was granted.

3. Each Contracting Government shall transmit to such body as may be designated by the Commission, in so far as practicable, and at intervals of not more than one year, scientific information available to that Government with

respect to whales and whaling, including the results of research conducted pursuant to paragraph 1 of this Article and to Article IV.

4. Recognizing that continuous collection and analysis of biological data in connection with the operations of factory ships and land stations are indispensable to sound and constructive management of the whale fisheries, the Contracting Governments will take all practicable measures to obtain such data.

Article IX

1. Each Contracting Government shall take appropriate measures to ensure the application of the provisions of this Convention and the punishment of infractions against the said provisions in operations carried out by persons or by vessels under its jurisdiction.

2. No bonus or other remuneration calculated with relation to the results of their work shall be paid to the gunners and crews of whale catchers in respect of any whales the taking of which is forbidden by this Convention.

3. Prosecution for infractions against or contraventions of this Convention shall be instituted by the Government having jurisdiction over the offence.

4. Each Contracting Government shall transmit to the Commission full details of each infraction of the provisions of this Convention by persons or vessels under the jurisdiction of that Government as reported by its inspectors. This information shall include a statement of measures taken for dealing with the infraction and of penalties imposed.

Article X

1. This Convention shall be ratified and the instruments of ratification shall be deposited with the Government of the United States of America.

2. Any Government which has not signed this Convention may adhere thereto after it enters into force by a notification in writing to the Government of the United States of America.

3. The Government of the United States of America shall inform all other signatory Governments and all adhering Governments of all ratifications deposited and adherences received.

4. This Convention shall, when instruments of ratification have been deposited by at least six signatory Governments, which shall include the Governments of the Netherlands, Norway, the Union of Soviet Socialist Republics, the United Kingdom of Great Britain and Northern Ireland, and the United States of America, enter into force with respect to those Governments and shall enter into force with respect to each Government which subsequently ratifies or adheres on the date of the deposit of its instrument of ratification or the receipt of its notification of adherence.

5. The provisions of the Schedule shall not apply prior to 1 July 1948. Amendments to the Schedule adopted pursuant to Article V shall not apply prior to 1 July 1949.

Article XI

Any Contracting Government may withdraw from this Convention on June thirtieth of any year by giving notice on or before January first of the same year to the depositary Government, which upon receipt of such a notice shall at once communicate it to the other Contracting Governments. Any other Contracting Government may, in like manner, within one month of the receipt of a copy of such a notice from the depositary Government, give notice of withdrawal, so that the Convention shall cease to be in force on June thirtieth of the same year with respect to the Government giving such notice of withdrawal.

This Convention shall bear the date on which it is opened for signature and shall remain open for signature for a period of fourteen days thereafter.

IN WITNESS WHEREOF the undersigned, being duly authorized, have signed this Convention.

DONE in Washington this second day of December 1946, in the English language, the original of which shall be deposited in the archives of the Government of the United States of America. The Government of the United States of America shall transmit certified copies thereof to all the other signatory and adhering Governments.

———————————

CONVENTION ON WETLANDS OF INTERNATIONAL IMPORTANCE ESPECIALLY AS WATERFOWL HABITAT

11 I.L.M. 963
Signed: February 2, 1971
as amended by the Protocol of December 3, 1982
and the Amendments of May 28, 1987
Entered into Force: December 21, 1975
Secretariat Homepage: http://ramsar.org/

The Contracting Parties,

Recognizing the interdependence of man and his environment;

Considering the fundamental ecological functions of wetlands as regulators of water regimes and as habitats supporting a characteristic flora and fauna, especially waterfowl;

Being convinced that wetlands constitute a resource of great economic, cultural, scientific and recreational value, the loss of which would be irreparable;

Desiring to stem the progressive encroachment on and loss of wetlands now and in the future;

Recognizing that waterfowl in their seasonal migrations may transcend frontiers and so should be regarded as an international resource;

Being confident that the conservation of wetlands and their flora and fauna can be ensured by combining far-sighted national policies with coordinated international action;

Have agreed as follows:

Article 1

1. For the purpose of this Convention wetlands are areas of marsh, fen, peatland or water, whether natural or artificial, permanent or temporary, with water that is static or flowing, fresh, brackish or salt, including areas of marine water the depth of which at low tide does not exceed six metres.

2. For the purpose of this Convention waterfowl are birds ecologically dependent on wetlands.

Article 2

1. Each Contracting Party shall designate suitable wetlands within its territory for inclusion in a List of Wetlands of International Importance, hereinafter referred to as "the List" which is maintained by the bureau established under Article 8. The boundaries of each wetland shall be precisely described and also delimited on a map and they may incorporate riparian and coastal zones adjacent to the wetlands, and islands or bodies of marine water deeper than six metres at low tide lying within the wetlands, especially where these have importance as waterfowl habitat.

2. Wetlands should be selected for the List on account of their international significance in terms of ecology, botany, zoology, limnology or hydrology. In the first instance wetlands of international importance to waterfowl at any season should be included.

3. The inclusion of a wetland in the List does not prejudice the exclusive sovereign rights of the Contracting Party in whose territory the wetland is situated.

4. Each Contracting Party shall designate at least one wetland to be included in the List when signing this Convention or when depositing its instrument of ratification or accession, as provided in Article 9.

5. Any Contracting Party shall have the right to add to the List further wetlands situated within its territory, to extend the boundaries of those wetlands already included by it in the List, or, because of its urgent national interests,

to delete or restrict the boundaries of wetlands already included by it in the List and shall, at the earliest possible time, inform the organization or government responsible for the continuing bureau duties specified in Article 8 of any such changes.

6. Each Contracting Party shall consider its international responsibilities for the conservation, management and wise use of migratory stocks of waterfowl, both when designating entries for the List and when exercising its right to change entries in the List relating to wetlands within its territory.

Article 3

1. The Contracting Parties shall formulate and implement their planning so as to promote the conservation of the wetlands included in the List, and as far as possible the wise use of wetlands in their territory.

2. Each Contracting Party shall arrange to be informed at the earliest possible time if the ecological character of any wetland in its territory and included in the List has changed, is changing or is likely to change as the result of technological developments, pollution or other human interference. Information on such changes shall be passed without delay to the organization or government responsible for the continuing bureau duties specified in Article 8.

Article 4

1. Each Contracting Party shall promote the conservation of wetlands and waterfowl by establishing nature reserves on wetlands, whether they are included in the List or not, and provide adequately for their wardening.

2. Where a Contracting Party in its urgent national interest, deletes or restricts the boundaries of a wetland included in the List, it should as far as possible compensate for any loss of wetland resources, and in particular it should create additional nature reserves for waterfowl and for the protection, either in the same area or elsewhere, of an adequate portion of the original habitat.

3. The Contracting Parties shall encourage research and the exchange of data and publications regarding wetlands and their flora and fauna.

4. The Contracting Parties shall endeavour through management to increase waterfowl populations on appropriate wetlands.

5. The Contracting Parties shall promote the training of personnel competent in the fields of wetland research, management and wardening.

Article 5

The Contracting Parties shall consult with each other about implementing obligations arising from the Convention especially in the case of a wetland extending over the territories of more than one Contracting Party or where a water system is shared by Contracting Parties. They shall at the same time endeavour to coordinate and support present and future policies and regulations concerning the conservation of wetlands and their flora and fauna.

Article 6

1. There shall be established a Conference of the Contracting Parties to review and promote the implementation of this Convention. The Bureau referred to in Article 8, paragraph 1, shall convene ordinary meetings of the Conference of the Contracting Parties at intervals of not more than three years, unless the Conference decides otherwise, and extraordinary meetings at the written requests of at least one third of the Contracting Parties. Each ordinary meeting of the Conference of the Contracting Parties shall determine the time and venue of the next ordinary meeting.

2. The Conference of the Contracting Parties shall be competent:
    a. to discuss the implementation of this Convention;
    b. to discuss additions to and changes in the List;
    c. to consider information regarding changes in the ecological character of wetlands included in the List provided in accordance with paragraph 2 of Article 3;

    d. to make general or specific recommendations to the Contracting Parties regarding the conservation, management and wise use of wetlands and their flora and fauna;

    e. to request relevant international bodies to prepare reports and statistics on matters which are essentially international in character affecting wetlands;

    f. to adopt other recommendations, or resolutions, to promote the functioning of this Convention.

3. The Contracting Parties shall ensure that those responsible at all levels for wetlands management shall be informed of, and take into consideration, recommendations of such Conferences concerning the conservation, management and wise use of wetlands and their flora and fauna.

4. The Conference of the Contracting Parties shall adopt rules of procedure for each of its meetings.

5. The Conference of the Contracting Parties shall establish and keep under review the financial regulations of this Convention. At each of its ordinary meetings, it shall adopt the budget for the next financial period by a two-third majority of Contracting Parties present and voting.

6. Each Contracting Party shall contribute to the budget according to a scale of contributions adopted by unanimity of the Contracting Parties present and voting at a meeting of the ordinary Conference of the Contracting Parties.

Article 7

1. The representatives of the Contracting Parties at such Conferences should include persons who are experts on wetlands or waterfowl by reason of knowledge and experience gained in scientific, administrative or other appropriate capacities.

2. Each of the Contracting Parties represented at a Conference shall have one vote, recommendations, resolutions and decisions being adopted by a simple majority of the Contracting Parties present and voting, unless otherwise provided for in this Convention.

Article 8

1. The International Union for the Conservation of Nature and Natural Resources shall perform the continuing bureau duties under this Convention until such time as another organization or government is appointed by a majority of two-thirds of all Contracting Parties.

2. The continuing bureau duties shall be, inter alia:

    a) to assist in the convening and organizing of Conferences specified in Article 6;

    b) to maintain the List of Wetlands of International Importance and to be informed by the Contracting Parties of any additions, extensions, deletions or restrictions concerning wetlands included in the List provided in accordance with paragraph 5 of Article 2;

    c) to be informed by the Contracting Parties of any changes in the ecological character of wetlands included in the List provided in accordance with paragraph 2 of Article 3;

    d) to forward notification of any alterations to the List, or changes in character of wetlands included therein, to all Contracting Parties and to arrange for these matters to be discussed at the next Conference;

    e) to make known to the Contracting Party concerned, the recommendations of the Conferences in respect of such alterations to the List or of changes in the character of wetlands included therein.

Article 9

1. This Convention shall remain open for signature indefinitely.

2. Any member of the United Nations or of one of the Specialized Agencies or of the International Atomic Energy Agency or Party to the Statute of the International Court of Justice may become a Party to this Convention by:

    a) signature without reservation as to ratification;

    b) signature subject to ratification followed by ratification;

    c) accession.

3. Ratification or accession shall be effected by the deposit of an instrument of ratification or accession with the Director-General of the United Nations Educational, Scientific and Cultural Organization (hereinafter referred to as "the Depository").

Article 10

1. This Convention shall enter into force four months after seven States have become Parties to this Convention in accordance with paragraph 2 of Article 9.

2. Thereafter this Convention shall enter into force for each Contracting Party four months after the day of its signature without reservation as to ratification, or its deposit of an instrument of ratification or accession.

Article 10 bis

1. This Convention may be amended at a meeting of the Contracting Parties convened for that purpose in accordance with this article.

2. Proposals for amendment may be made by any Contracting Party.

3. The text of any proposed amendment and the reasons for it shall be communicated to the organization or government performing the continuing bureau duties under the Convention (hereinafter referred to as "the Bureau") and shall promptly be communicated by the Bureau to all Contracting Parties. Any comments on the text by the Contracting Parties shall be communicated to the Bureau within three months of the date on which the amendments were communicated to the Contracting Parties by the Bureau. The Bureau shall, immediately after the last day for submission of comments, communicate to the Contracting Parties all comments submitted by that day.

4. A meeting of Contracting Parties to consider an amendment communicated in accordance with paragraph 3 shall be convened by the Bureau upon the written request of one third of the Contracting Parties. The Bureau shall consult the Parties concerning the time and venue of the meeting.

5. Amendments shall be adopted by a two-thirds majority of the Contracting Parties present and voting.

6. An amendment adopted shall enter into force for the Contracting Parties which have accepted it on the first day of the fourth month following the date on which two thirds of the Contracting Parties have deposited an instrument of acceptance with the Depositary. For each Contracting Party which deposits an instrument of acceptance after the date on which two thirds of the Contracting Parties have deposited an instrument of acceptance, the amendment shall enter into force on the first day of the fourth month following the date of the deposit of its instrument of acceptance.

Article 11

1. This Convention shall continue in force for an indefinite period.

2. Any Contracting Party may denounce this Convention after a period of five years from the date on which it entered into force for that Party by giving written notice thereof to the Depository. Denunciation shall take effect four months after the day on which notice thereof is received by the Depository.

Article 12

1. The Depository shall inform all States that have signed and acceded to this Convention as soon as possible of:
   a) signatures to the Convention;
   b) deposits of instruments of ratification of this Convention;
   c) deposits of instruments of accession to this Convention;
   d) the date of entry into force of this Convention;
   e) notifications of denunciation of this Convention.

2. When this Convention has entered into force, the Depository shall have it registered with the Secretariat of the United Nations in accordance with Article 102 of the Charter.

IN WITNESS WHEREOF, the undersigned, being duly authorized to that effect, have signed this Convention.

DONE at Ramsar this 2nd day of February 1971, in a single original in the English, French, German and Russian languages, all texts being equally authentic, which shall be deposited with the Depository which shall send true copies thereof to all Contracting Parties.

CONVENTION CONCERNING THE PROTECTION OF THE
WORLD CULTURAL AND NATURAL HERITAGE

11 I.L.M. 1358; 1037 U.N.T.S. 151
Signed: November 16, 1972
Entered into Force: December 17, 1975

The General Conference of the United Nations Education, Scientific and Cultural Organization meeting in Paris from 17 October to 21 November 1972, at its seventeenth session,

Noting that the cultural heritage and the natural heritage are increasingly threatened with destruction not only by the traditional causes of decay, but also by changing social and economic conditions which aggravate the situation with even more formidable phenomena of damage or destruction,

Considering that deterioration or disappearance of any item of the cultural or natural heritage constitutes a harmful impoverishment of the heritage of all the nations of the world,

Considering that protection of this heritage at the national level often remains incomplete because of the scale of the resources which it requires and of the insufficient economic, scientific, and technological resources of the country where the property to be protected is situated,

Recalling that the Constitution of the Organization provides that it will maintain, increase, and diffuse knowledge by assuring the conservation and protection of the world's heritage, and recommending to the nations concerned the necessary international conventions,

Considering that the existing international conventions, recommendations and resolutions concerning cultural and natural property demonstrate the importance, for all the peoples of the world, of safeguarding this unique and irreplaceable property, to whatever people it may belong,

Considering that parts of the cultural or natural heritage are of outstanding interest and therefore need to be preserved as part of the world heritage of mankind as a whole,

Considering that in view of the magnitude and gravity of the new dangers threatening them, it is incumbent on the international community as a whole to participate in the protection of the cultural and natural heritage of outstanding universal value, by the granting of collective assistance which, although not taking the place of action by the State concerned, will serve as an efficient complement thereto,

Considering that it is essential for this purpose to adopt new provisions in the form of a convention establishing an effective system of collective protection of the cultural and natural heritage of outstanding universal value, organized on a permanent basis and in accordance with modern scientific methods,

Having decided, at its sixteenth session, that this question should be made the subject of an international convention, Adopts this sixteenth day of November 1972 this Convention.

I.   DEFINITION OF THE CULTURAL AND NATURAL HERITAGE

Article 1

For the purpose of this Convention, the following shall be considered as "cultural heritage":

> monuments: architectural works, works of monumental sculpture and painting, elements or structures of an archeological nature, inscriptions, cave dwellings and combinations of features, which are of outstanding universal value from the point of view of history, art or science;

groups of buildings: groups of separate or connected buildings which, because of their architecture, their homogeneity or their place in the landscape, are of outstanding universal value from the point of view of history, art or science;

sites: works of man or the combined works of nature and man, and areas including archaeological sites which are of outstanding universal value from the historical, aesthetic, ethnological or anthropological point of view.

Article 2

For the purposes of this Convention, the following shall be considered as "natural heritage":

natural features consisting of physical and biological formations or groups of such formations, which are of outstanding universal value from the aesthetic or scientific point of view;

geological and physiographical formations and precisely delineated areas which constitute the habitat of threatened species of animals and plants of outstanding universal value from the point of view of science or conservation;

natural sites or precisely delineated natural areas of outstanding universal value from the point of view of science, conservation or natural beauty.

Article 3

It is for each State Party to this Convention to identify and delineate the different properties situated on its territory mentioned in Articles 1 and 2 above.

II.   NATIONAL PROTECTION AND INTERNATIONAL PROTECTION OF THE CULTURAL AND NATURAL HERITAGE

Article 4

Each State Party to this Convention recognizes that the duty of ensuring the identification, protection, conservation, presentation and transmission to future generations of the cultural and natural heritage referred to in Articles 1 and 2 and situated on its territory, belongs primarily to that State. It will do all it can to this end, to the utmost of its own resources and, where appropriate, with any international assistance and co-operation, in particular, financial, artistic, scientific and technical, which it may be able to obtain.

Article 5

To ensure that effective and active measures are taken for the protection, conservation and presentation of the cultural and natural heritage situated on its territory, each State Party to this Convention shall endeavor, in so far as possible, and as appropriate for each country:

(a)   to adopt a general policy which aims to give the cultural and natural heritage a function in the life of the community and to integrate the protection of that heritage into comprehensive planning programmes;

(b)   to set up within its territories, where such services do not exist, one or more services for the protection, conservation and presentation of the cultural and natural heritage with an appropriate staff and possessing the means to discharge their functions;

(c)   to develop scientific and technical studies and research and to work out such operating methods as will make the State capable of counteracting the dangers that threaten its cultural or natural heritage;

(d)   to take the appropriate legal, scientific, technical, administrative and financial measures necessary for the identification, protection, conservation, presentation and rehabilitation of this heritage; and

(e)   to foster the establishment or development of national or regional centres for training in the protection, conservation and presentation of the cultural and natural heritage and to encourage scientific research in this field.

Article 6

1.   Whilst fully respecting the sovereignty of the States on whose territory the cultural and natural heritage mentioned in Articles 1 and 2 is situated, and without prejudice to property right provided by national legislation, the States Parties to this Convention recognize that such heritage constitutes a world heritage for whose protection it is the duty of the international community as a whole to co-operate.

2.   The States Parties undertake, in accordance with the provisions of this Convention, to give their help in the identification, protection, conservation and presentation of the cultural and natural heritage referred to in paragraphs 2 and 4 of Article 11 if the States on whose territory it is situated so request.

3.   Each State Party to this Convention undertakes not to take any deliberate measures which might damage directly or indirectly the cultural and natural heritage referred to in Articles 1 and 2 situated on the territory of other States Parties to this Convention.

Article 7

For the purpose of this Convention, international protection of the world cultural and natural heritage shall be understood to mean the establishment of a system of international co-operation and assistance designed to support States Parties to the Convention in their efforts to conserve and identify that heritage.

III. INTERGOVERNMENTAL COMMITTEE FOR THE PROTECTION OF THE WORLD CULTURAL AND NATURAL HERITAGE

Article 8

1.   An Intergovernmental Committee for the Protection of the Cultural and Natural Heritage of Outstanding Universal Value, called "the World Heritage Committee", is hereby established within the United Nations Education, Scientific and Cultural Organization. It shall be composed of 15 States Parties to the Convention, elected by States Parties to the Convention meeting in general assembly during the ordinary session of the General Conference of the United Nations Educational, Scientific and Cultural Organization. The number of States members of the Committee shall be increased to 21 as from the date of the ordinary session of the General Conference following the entry into force of this Convention for at least 40 States.

2.   Election of members of the Committee shall ensure an equitable representation of the different regions and cultures of the world.

3.   A representative of the International Centre for the Study of the Preservation and Restoration of Cultural Property (Rome Centre), a representative of the International Council of Monuments and Sites (ICOMOS) and a representative of the International Union for Conservation of Nature and Natural Resources (IUCN), to whom may be added, at the request of States Parties to the Convention meeting in general assembly during the ordinary sessions of the General Conference of the United Nations Educational, Scientific and Cultural Organization, representatives of other intergovernmental or non-governmental organizations, with similar objectives, may attend the meetings of the Committee in an advisory capacity.

Article 9

1.   The term of office of States members of the World Heritage Committee shall extend from the end of the ordinary session of the General Conference during which they are elected until the end of its third subsequent ordinary session.

2.   The term of office of one-third of the members designated at the time of the first election shall, however, cease at the end of the first ordinary session of the General Conference following that at which they were elected; and the term of office of a further third of the members designated at the same time shall cease at the end of the second ordinary session of the General Conference following that at which they were elected. The names of these members shall be chosen by lot by the President of the General Conference of the United Nations Education, Scientific and Cultural Organization after the first election.

3.   States members of the Committee shall choose as their representatives persons qualified in the field of the cultural or natural heritage.

Article 10

1. The World Heritage Committee shall adopt its Rules of Procedure.

2. The Committee may at any time invite public or private organizations or individuals to participate in its meetings for consultation on particular problems.

3. The Committee may create such consultative bodies as it deems necessary for the performance of its functions.

Article 11

1.   Every State Party to this Convention shall, in so far as possible, submit to the World Heritage Committee an inventory of property forming part of the cultural and natural heritage, situated in its territory and suitable for inclusion in the list provided for in paragraph 2 of this Article. This inventory, which shall not be considered exhaustive, shall include documentation about the location of the property in question and its significance.

2.   On the basis of the inventories submitted by States in accordance with paragraph 1, the Committee shall establish, keep up to date and publish, under the title of "World Heritage List," a list of properties forming part of the cultural heritage and natural heritage, as defined in Articles 1 and 2 of this Convention, which it considers as having outstanding universal value in terms of such criteria as it shall have established. An updated list shall be distributed at least every two years.

3.   The inclusion of a property in the World Heritage List requires the consent of the State concerned. The inclusion of a property situated in a territory, sovereignty or jurisdiction over which is claimed by more than one State shall in no way prejudice the rights of the parties to the dispute.

4.   The Committee shall establish, keep up to date and publish, whenever circumstances shall so require, under the title of "list of World Heritage in Danger", a list of the property appearing in the World Heritage List for the conservation of which major operations are necessary and for which assistance has been requested under this Convention. This list shall contain an estimate of the cost of such operations. The list may include only such property forming part of the cultural and natural heritage as is threatened by serious and specific dangers, such as the threat of disappearance caused by accelerated deterioration, large-scale public or private projects or rapid urban or tourist development projects; destruction caused by changes in the use or ownership of the land; major alterations due to unknown causes; abandonment for any reason whatsoever; the outbreak or the threat of an armed conflict; calamities and cataclysms; serious fires, earthquakes, landslides; volcanic eruptions; changes in water level, floods and tidal waves. The Committee may at any time, in case of urgent need, make a new entry in the List of World Heritage in Danger and publicize such entry immediately.

5.   The Committee shall define the criteria on the basis of which a property belonging to the cultural or natural heritage may be included in either of the lists mentioned in paragraphs 2 and 4 of this article.

6.   Before refusing a request for inclusion in one of the two lists mentioned in paragraphs 2 and 4 of this article, the Committee shall consult the State Party in whose territory the cultural or natural property in question is situated.

7.   The Committee shall, with the agreement of the States concerned, co-ordinate and encourage the studies and research needed for the drawing up of the lists referred to in paragraphs 2 and 4 of this article.

Article 12

The fact that a property belonging to the cultural or natural heritage has not been included in either of the two lists mentioned in paragraphs 2 and 4 of Article 11 shall in no way be construed to mean that it does not have an outstanding universal value for purposes other than those resulting from inclusion in these lists.

Article 13

1. The World Heritage Committee shall receive and study requests for international assistance formulated by States Parties to this Convention with respect to property forming part of the cultural or natural heritage, situated in their territories, and included or potentially suitable for inclusion in the lists mentioned referred to in paragraphs 2 and 4 of Article 11. The purpose of such requests may be to secure the protection, conservation, presentation or rehabilitation of such property.

2. Requests for international assistance under paragraph 1 of this article may also be concerned with identification of cultural or natural property defined in Articles 1 and 2, when preliminary investigations have shown that further inquiries would be justified.

3. The Committee shall decide on the action to be taken with regard to these requests, determine where appropriate, the nature and extent of its assistance, and authorize the conclusion, on its behalf, of the necessary arrangements with the government concerned.

4. The Committee shall determine an order of priorities for its operations. It shall in so doing bear in mind the respective importance for the world cultural and natural heritage of the property requiring protection, the need to give international assistance to the property most representative of a natural environment or of the genius and the history of the peoples of the world, the urgency of the work to be done, the resources available to the States on whose territory the threatened property is situated and in particular the extent to which they are able to safeguard such property by their own means.

5. The Committee shall draw up, keep up to date and publicize a list of property for which international assistance has been granted.

6. The Committee shall decide on the use of the resources of the Fund established under Article 15 of this Convention. It shall seek ways of increasing these resources and shall take all useful steps to this end.

7. The Committee shall co-operate with international and national governmental and non-governmental organizations having objectives similar to those of this Convention. For the implementation of its programmes and projects, the Committee may call on such organizations, particularly the International Centre for the Study of the Preservation and Restoration of Cultural Property (the Rome Centre), the International Council of Monuments and Sites (ICOMOS) and the International Union for Conservation of Nature and Natural Resources (IUCN), as well as on public and private bodies and individuals.

8. Decisions of the Committee shall be taken by a majority of two-thirds of its members present and voting. A majority of the members of the Committee shall constitute a quorum.

Article 14

1. The World Heritage Committee shall be assisted by a Secretariat appointed by the Director-General of the United Nations Educational, Scientific and Cultural Organization.

2. The Director-General of the United Nations Educational, Scientific and Cultural Organization, utilizing to the fullest extent possible the services of the International Centre for the Study of the Preservation and the Restoration of Cultural Property (the Rome Centre), the International Council of Monuments and Sites (ICOMOS) and the International Union for Conservation of Nature and Natural Resources (IUCN) in their respective areas of competence and capability, shall prepare the Committee's documentation and the agenda of its meetings and shall have the responsibility for the implementation of its decisions.

IV. FUND FOR THE PROTECTION OF THE WORLD CULTURAL AND NATURAL HERITAGE

Article 15

1. A Fund for the Protection of the World Cultural and Natural Heritage of Outstanding Universal Value, called "the World Heritage Fund", is hereby established.

2. The Fund shall constitute a trust fund, in conformity with the provisions of the Financial Regulations of the United Nations Educational, Scientific and Cultural Organization.

3. The resources of the Fund shall consist of:
    (a) compulsory and voluntary contributions made by States Parties to this Convention,
    (b) Contributions, gifts or bequests which may be made by:
        (i) other States;
        (ii) the United Nations Educational, Scientific and Cultural Organization, other organizations of the United Nations system, particularly the United Nations Development Programme or other intergovernmental organizations;
        (iii) public or private bodies or individuals;
    (c) any interest due on the resources of the Fund;
    (d) funds raised by collections and receipts from events organized for the benefit of the fund; and
    (e) all other resources authorized by the Fund's regulations, as drawn up by the World Heritage Committee.

4. Contributions to the Fund and other forms of assistance made available to the Committee may be used only for such purposes as the Committee shall define. The Committee may accept contributions to be used only for a certain programme or project, provided that the Committee shall have decided on the implementation of such programme or project. No political conditions may be attached to contributions made to the Fund.

Article 16

1. Without prejudice to any supplementary voluntary contribution, the States Parties to this Convention undertake to pay regularly, every two years, to the World Heritage Fund, contributions, the amount of which, in the form of a uniform percentage applicable to all States, shall be determined by the General Assembly of States Parties to the Convention, meeting during the sessions of the General Conference of the United Nations Educational, Scientific and Cultural Organization. This decision of the General Assembly requires the majority of the States Parties present and voting, which have not made the declaration referred to in paragraph 2 of this Article. In no case shall the compulsory contribution of States Parties to the Convention exceed 1% of the contribution to the regular budget of the United Nations Educational, Scientific and Cultural Organization.

2. However, each State referred to in Article 31 or in Article 32 of this Convention may declare, at the time of the deposit of its instrument of ratification, acceptance or accession, that it shall not be bound by the provisions of paragraph 1 of this Article.

3. A State Party to the Convention which has made the declaration referred to in paragraph 2 of this Article may at any time withdraw the said declaration by notifying the Director-General of the United Nations Educational, Scientific and Cultural Organization. However, the withdrawal of the declaration shall not take effect in regard to the compulsory contribution due by the State until the date of the subsequent General Assembly of States parties to the Convention.

4. In order that the Committee may be able to plan its operations effectively, the contributions of States Parties to this Convention which have made the declaration referred to in paragraph 2 of this Article, shall be paid on a regular basis, at least every two years, and should not be less than the contributions which they should have paid if they had been bound by the provisions of paragraph 1 of this Article.

5. Any State Party to the Convention which is in arrears with the payment of its compulsory or voluntary contribution or the current year and the calendar year immediately preceding it shall not be eligible as a Member of the World Heritage Committee, although this provision shall not apply to the first election. The terms of office of any such State which is already a member of the Committee shall terminate at the time of the elections provided for in Article 8, paragraph 1 of this Convention.

Article 17

The States Parties to this Convention shall consider or encourage the establishment of national public and private foundations or associations whose purpose is to invite donations for the protection of the cultural and natural heritage as defined in Articles 1 and 2 of this Convention.

Article 18

The States Parties to this Convention shall give their assistance to international fund-raising campaigns organized for the World Heritage Fund under the auspices of the United Nations Educational, Scientific and Cultural Organization. They shall facilitate collections made by the bodies mentioned in paragraph 3 of Article 15 for this purpose.

V.   CONDITIONS AND ARRANGEMENTS FOR INTERNATIONAL ASSISTANCE

Article 19

Any State Party to this Convention may request international assistance for property forming part of the cultural or natural heritage of outstanding universal value situated within its territory. It shall submit with its request such information and documentation provided for in Article 21 as it has in its possession and as will enable the Committee to come to a decision.

Article 20

Subject to the provisions of paragraph 2 of Article 13, sub- paragraph (c) of Article 22 and Article 23, international assistance provided for by this Convention may be granted only to property forming part of the cultural and natural heritage which the World Heritage Committee has decided, or may decide, to enter in one of the lists mentioned in paragraphs 2 and 4 of Article 11.

Article 21

1.   The World Heritage Committee shall define the procedure by which requests to it for international assistance shall be considered and shall specify the content of the request, which should define the operation contemplated, the work that is necessary, the expected cost thereof, the degree of urgency and the reasons why the resources of the State requesting assistance do not allow it to meet all the expenses. Such requests must be supported by experts' reports whenever possible.

2.   Requests based upon disasters or natural calamities should, by reasons of the urgent work which they may involve, be given immediate, priority consideration by the Committee, which should have a reserve fund at its disposal against such contingencies.

3.   Before coming to a decision, the Committee shall carry out such studies and consultations as it deems necessary.

Article 22

Assistance granted by the World Heritage Fund may take the following forms:

(a) studies concerning the artistic, scientific and technical problems raised by the protection, conservation, presentation and rehabilitation of the cultural and natural heritage, as defined in paragraphs 2 and 4 of Article 11 of this Convention;

(b) provisions of experts, technicians and skilled labour to ensure that the approved work is correctly carried out;

(c) training of staff and specialists at all levels in the field of identification, protection, conservation, presentation and rehabilitation of the cultural and natural heritage;

(d) supply of equipment which the State concerned does not possess or is not in a position to acquire;

(e) low-interest or interest-free loans which might be repayable on a long-term basis;

(f) the granting, in exceptional cases and for special reasons, of non-repayable subsidies.

Article 23

The World Heritage Committee may also provide international assistance to national or regional centres for the training of staff and specialists at all levels in the field of identification, protection, conservation, presentation and rehabilitation of the cultural and natural heritage.

Article 24

International assistance on a large scale shall be preceded by detailed scientific, economic and technical studies. These studies shall draw upon the most advanced techniques for the protection, conservation, presentation and rehabilitation of the natural and cultural heritage and shall be consistent with the objectives of this Convention. The studies shall also seek means of making rational use of the resources available in the State concerned.

Article 25

As a general rule, only part of the cost of work necessary shall be borne by the international community. The contribution of the State benefiting from international assistance shall constitute a substantial share of the resources devoted to each programme or project, unless its resources do not permit this.

Article 26

The World Heritage Committee and the recipient State shall define in the agreement they conclude the conditions in which a programme or project for which international assistance under the terms of this Convention is provided, shall be carried out. It shall be the responsibility of the State receiving such international assistance to continue to protect, conserve and present the property so safeguarded, in observance of the conditions laid down by the agreement.

VI. EDUCATIONAL PROGRAMMES

Article 27

1.   The States Parties to this Convention shall endeavor by all appropriate means, and in particular by educational and information programmes, to strengthen appreciation and respect by their peoples of the cultural and natural heritage defined in Articles 1 and 2 of the Convention.

2.   They shall undertake to keep the public broadly informed of the dangers threatening this heritage and of the activities carried on in pursuance of this Convention.

Article 28

States Parties to this Convention which receive international assistance under the Convention shall take appropriate measures to make known the importance of the property for which assistance has been received and the role played by such assistance.

VII. REPORTS

Article 29

1.   The States Parties to this Convention shall, in the reports which they submit to the General Conference of the United Nations Educational, Scientific and Cultural Organization on dates and in a manner to be determined by it, give information on the legislative and administrative provisions which they have adopted and other action which they have taken for the application of this Convention, together with details of the experience acquired in this field.

2.   These reports shall be brought to the attention of the World Heritage Committee.

3.   The Committee shall submit a report on its activities at each of the ordinary sessions of the General Conference of the United Nations Educational, Scientific and Cultural Organization.

VIII. FINAL CLAUSES

Article 30

This Convention is drawn up in Arabic, English, French, Russian and Spanish, the five texts being equally authoritative.

Article 31

1.   This Convention shall be subject to ratification or acceptance by States members of the United Nations Educational, Scientific and Cultural Organization in accordance with their respective constitutional procedures.

2.   The instruments of ratification or acceptance shall be deposited with the Director-General of the United Nations Educational, Scientific and Cultural Organization.

Article 32

1.   This Convention shall be open to accession by all States not members of the United Nations Educational, Scientific and Cultural Organization which are invited by the General Conference of the Organization to accede to it.

2.   Accession shall be effected by the deposit of an instrument of accession with the Director-General of the United Nations Educational, Scientific and Cultural Organization.

Article 33

This Convention shall enter into force three months after the date of the deposit of the twentieth instrument of ratification, acceptance or accession, but only with respect to those States which have deposited their respective instruments of ratification, acceptance or accession on or before that date. It shall enter into force with respect to any other State three months after the deposit of its instrument of ratification, acceptance or accession.

Article 34

The following provisions shall apply to those States Parties to this Convention which have a federal or non-unitary constitutional system:
     (a)   with regard to the provisions of this Convention, the implementation of which comes under the legal jurisdiction of the federal or central legislative power, the obligations of the federal or central government shall be the same as for those States parties which are not federal States;
     (b)   with regard to the provisions of this Convention, the implementation of which comes under the legal jurisdiction of individual constituent States, countries, provinces or cantons that are not obliged by the constitutional system of the federation to take legislative measures, the federal government shall inform the competent authorities of such States, countries, provinces or cantons of the said provisions, with its recommendation for their adoption.

Article 35

1.   Each State Party to this Convention may denounce the Convention.

2.   The denunciation shall be notified by an instrument in writing, deposited with the Director-General of the United Nations Educational, Scientific and Cultural Organization.

3.   The denunciation shall take effect twelve months after the receipt of the instrument of denunciation. It shall not affect the financial obligations of the denouncing State until the date on which the withdrawal takes effect.

Article 36

The Director-General of the United Nations Educational, Scientific and Cultural Organization shall inform the States members of the Organization, the States not members of the Organization which are referred to in Article 32, as well as the United Nations, of the deposit of all the instruments of ratification, acceptance, or accession provided for in Articles 31 and 32, and of the denunciations provided for in Article 35.

Article 37

1. This Convention may be revised by the General Conference of the United Nations Educational, Scientific and Cultural Organization. Any such revision shall, however, bind only the States which shall become Parties to the revising convention.

2. If the General Conference should adopt a new convention revising this Convention in whole or in part, then, unless the new convention otherwise provides, this Convention shall cease to be open to ratification, acceptance or accession, as from the date on which the new revising convention enters into force.

Article 38

In conformity with Article 102 of the Charter of the United Nations, this Convention shall be registered with the Secretariat of the United Nations at the request of the Director-General of the United Nations Educational, Scientific and Cultural Organization.

Done in Paris, this twenty-third day of November 1972, in two authentic copies bearing the signature of the President of the seventeenth session of the General Conference and of the Director-General of the United Nations Educational, Scientific and Cultural Organization, which shall be deposited in the archives of the United Nations Educational, Scientific and Cultural Organization, and certified true copies of which shall be delivered to all the States referred to in Articles 31 and 32 as well as to the United Nations.

Protocol on Environmental Protection to the Antarctic Treaty
(schedule included, annexes not included)

30 I.L.M. 1461
Signed: October 4, 1991
Entered into Force: January 14, 1998

PREAMBLE

The States Parties to this Protocol to the Antarctic Treaty, hereinafter referred to as the Parties,

Convinced of the need to enhance the protection of the Antarctic environment and dependent and associated ecosystems;

Convinced of the need to strengthen the Antarctic Treaty system so as to ensure that Antarctic shall continue forever to be used exclusively for peaceful purposes and shall not become the scene or object of international discord;

Bearing in mind the special legal and political status of Antarctic and the special responsibility of the Antarctic Treaty Consultative Parties to ensure that all activities in Antarctic are consistent with the purposes and principles of the Antarctic Treaty;

Recalling the designation of Antarctic as a Special Conservation Area and other measures adopted under the Antarctic Treaty system to protect the Antarctic environment and dependent and associated ecosystems;

Acknowledging further the unique opportunities Antarctic offers for scientific monitoring of and research on processes of global as well as regional importance;

Reaffirming the conservation principles of the Convention on the Conservation of Antarctic Marine Living Resources;

Convinced that the development of a comprehensive regime for the protection of the Antarctic environment and dependent and associated ecosystems is in the interest of mankind as a whole;

Desiring to supplement the Antarctic Treaty to this end;

Have agreed as follows:

Article 1   Definitions

For the purposes of this Protocol:

(a) "The Antarctic Treaty" means the Antarctic Treaty done at Washington on 1 December 1959;
(b) "Antarctic Treaty area" means the area to which the provisions of the Antarctic Treaty apply in accordance with Article VI of that Treaty;
(c) "Antarctic Treaty Consultative Meetings" means the meetings referred to in Article IX of the Antarctic Treaty;
(d) "Antarctic Treaty Consultative Parties" means the Contracting Parties to the Antarctic Treaty entitled to appoint representatives to participate in the meetings referred to in Article IX of that Treaty;
(e) "Antarctic Treaty system" means the Antarctic Treaty, the measures in effect under that Treaty, its associated separate international instruments in force and the measures in effect under those instruments;
(f) "Arbitral Tribunal" means the Arbitral Tribunal established in accordance with the Schedule to this Protocol, which forms an integral part thereof;
(g) "Committee" means the Committee for Environmental Protection established in accordance with Article 11.

Article 2   Objective and Designation

The Parties commit themselves to the comprehensive protection of the Antarctic environment and dependent and associated ecosystems and hereby designate Antarctica as a natural reserve, devoted to peace and science.

Article 3   Environmental Principles

1. The protection of the Antarctic environment and dependent and associated ecosystems and the intrinsic value of Antarctica, including its wilderness and aesthetic values and its value as an area for the conduct of scientific research, in particular research essential to understanding the global environment, shall be fundamental considerations in the planning and conduct of all activities in the Antarctic Treaty area.

2. To this end:

(a) activities in the Antarctic Treaty area shall be planned and conducted so as to limit adverse impacts on the Antarctic environment and dependent and associated ecosystems;

(b) activities in the Antarctic Treaty area shall be planned and conducted so as to avoid:

(i) adverse effects on climate or weather patterns;

(ii) significant adverse effects on air or water quality;

(iii) significant changes in the atmospheric, terrestrial (including aquatic), glacial or marine environments;

(iv) detrimental changes in the distribution, abundance or productivity of species or populations of species of fauna and flora;

(v) further jeopardy to endangered or threatened species or populations of such species; or

(vi) degradation of, or substantial risk to, areas of biological, scientific, historic, aesthetic or wilderness significance;

(c) activities in the Antarctic Treaty area shall be planned and conducted on the basis of information sufficient to allow prior assessments of, and informed judgments about, their possible impacts on the Antarctic environment and dependent and associated ecosystems and on the value of Antarctic for the conduct of scientific research; such judgments shall take full account of:

(i) the scope of the activity, including its area, duration and intensity;

(ii) the cumulative impacts of the activity, both by itself and in combination with other activities in the Antarctic Treaty area;

(iii) whether the activity will detrimentally affect any other activity in the Antarctic Treaty area;

(iv) whether technology and procedures are available to provide for environmentally safe operations;

(v) whether there exists the capacity to monitor key environmental parameters and ecosystem components so as to identify and provide early warning of any adverse effects of the activity and to provide for such modification of operating procedures as may be necessary in the light of the results of monitoring or increased knowledge of the Antarctic environment and dependent and associated ecosystems; and

(vi) whether there exists the capacity to respond promptly and effectively to accidents, particularly those with potential environmental effects;

(d) regular and effective monitoring shall take place to allow assessment of the impacts of ongoing activities, including the verification of predicted impacts;

(e) regular and effective monitoring shall take place to facilitate early detection of the possible unforeseen effects of activities carried on both within and outside the Antarctic Treaty area on the Antarctic environment and dependent and associated ecosystems.

3. Activities shall be planned and conducted in the Antarctic Treaty area so as to accord priority to scientific research and to preserve the value of Antarctica as an area for the conduct of such research, including research essential to understanding the global environment.

4. Activities undertaken in the Antarctic Treaty area pursuant to scientific research programmes, tourism and all other governmental and non-governmental activities in the Antarctic Treaty area for which advance notice is required in accordance with Article VII (5) of the Antarctic Treaty, including associated logistic support activities, shall:

(a) take place in a manner consistent with the principles in this Article; and

(b) be modified, suspended or cancelled if they result in or threaten to result in impacts upon the Antarctic environment or dependent or associated ecosystems inconsistent with those principles.

Article 4   Relationship with the Other Components of the Antarctic Treaty System

1. This Protocol shall supplement the Antarctic Treaty and shall neither modify nor amend that Treaty.

2. Nothing in this Protocol shall derogate from the rights and obligations of the Parties to this Protocol under the other international instruments in force within the Antarctic Treaty system.

Article 5   Consistency with the Other Components of the Antarctic Treaty System

The Parties shall consult and co-operate with the Contracting Parties to the other international instruments in force within the Antarctic Treaty system and their respective institutions with a view to ensuring the achievement of the objectives and principles of this Protocol and avoiding any interference with the achievement of the objectives and principles of those instruments or any inconsistency between the implementation of those instruments and of this Protocol.

Article 6   Cooperation

1. The Parties shall co-operate in the planning and conduct of activities in the Antarctic Treaty area. To this end, each Party shall endeavour to:

(a) promote co-operative programmes of scientific, technical and educational value, concerning the protection of the Antarctic environment and dependent and associated ecosystems;

(b) provide appropriate assistance to other Parties in the preparation of environmental impact assessments;

(c) provide to other Parties upon request information relevant to any potential environmental risk and assistance to minimize the effects of accidents which may damage the Antarctic environment or dependent and associated ecosystems;

(d) consult with other Parties with regard to the choice of sites for prospective stations and other facilities so as to avoid the cumulative impacts caused by their excessive concentration in any location;

(e) where appropriate, undertake joint expeditions and share the use of stations and other facilities; and

(f) carry out such steps as may be agreed upon at Antarctic Treaty Consultative Meetings.

2. Each Party undertakes, to the extent possible, to share information that may be helpful to other Parties in planning and conducting their activities in the Antarctic Treaty area, with a view to the protection of the Antarctic environment and dependent and associated ecosystems.

3. The Parties shall co-operate with those Parties which may exercise jurisdiction in areas adjacent to the Antarctic Treaty area with a view to ensuring that activities in the Antarctic Treaty area do not have adverse environmental impacts on those areas.

Article 7   Prohibition of Mineral Resource Activities

Any activity relating to mineral resources, other than scientific research, shall be prohibited.

Article 8   Environmental Impact Assessment

1. Proposed activities referred to in paragraph 2 below shall be subject to the procedures set out in Annex I for prior assessment of the impacts of those activities on the Antarctic environment or on dependent or associated ecosystems according to whether those activities are identified as having:

    (a) less than a minor or transitory impact;
    (b) a minor or transitory impact; or
    (c) more than a minor or transitory impact.

2. Each Party shall ensure that the assessment procedures set out in Annex I are applied in the planning processes leading to decisions about any activities undertaken in the Antarctic Treaty area pursuant to scientific research programmes, tourism and all other governmental and non-governmental activities in the Antarctic Treaty area for which advance notice is required under Article VII (5) of the Antarctic Treaty, including associated logistic support activities.

3. The assessment procedures set out in Annex I shall apply to any change in an activity whether the change arises from an increase or decrease in the intensity of an existing activity, from the addition of an activity, the decommissioning of a facility, or otherwise.

4. Where activities are planned jointly by more than one Party, the Parties involved shall nominate one of their number to coordinate the implementation of the environmental impact assessment procedures set out in Annex I.

Article 9   Annexes

1. The Annexes to this Protocol shall form an integral part thereof.

2. Annexes, additional to Annexes I-IV, may be adopted and become effective in accordance with Article IX of the Antarctic Treaty.

3. Amendments and modifications to Annexes may be adopted and become effective in accordance with Article IX of the Antarctic Treaty, provided that any Annex may itself make provision for amendments and modifications to become effective on an accelerated basis.

4. Annexes and any amendments and modifications thereto which have become effective in accordance with paragraphs 2 and 3 above shall, unless an Annex itself provides otherwise in respect of the entry into effect of any amendment or modification thereto, become effective for a Contracting Party to the Antarctic Treaty which is not an Antarctic Treaty Consultative Party, or which was not an Antarctic Treaty Consultative Party at the time of the adoption, when notice of approval of that Contracting Party has been received by the Depositary.

5. Annexes shall, except to the extent that an Annex provides otherwise, be subject to the procedures for dispute settlement set out in Articles 18 to 20.

Article 10   Antarctic Treaty Consultative Meetings

1. Antarctic Treaty Consultative Meetings shall, drawing upon the best scientific and technical advice available:

    (a) define, in accordance with the provisions of this Protocol, the general policy for the comprehensive protection of the Antarctic environment and dependent and associated ecosystems; and
    (b) adopt measures under Article IX of the Antarctic Treaty for the implementation of this Protocol.

2. Antarctic Treaty Consultative Meetings shall review the work of the Committee and shall draw fully upon its advice and recommendations in carrying out the tasks referred to in paragraph 1 above, as well as upon the advice of the Scientific Committee on Antarctic Research.

Article 11	Committee for Environmental Protection

1. There is hereby established the Committee for Environmental Protection.

2. Each Party shall be entitled to be a member of the Committee and to appoint a representative who may be accompanied by experts and advisers.

3. Observer status in the Committee shall be open to any Contracting Party to the Antarctic Treaty which is not a Party to this Protocol.

4. The Committee shall invite the President of the Scientific Committee on Antarctic Research and the Chairman of the Scientific Committee for the Conservation of Antarctic Marine Living Resources to participate as observers at its sessions. The Committee may also, with the approval of the Antarctic Treaty Consultative Meeting, invite such other relevant scientific, environmental and technical organisations which can contribute to its work to participate as observers at its sessions.

5. The Committee shall present a report on each of its sessions to the Antarctic Treaty Consultative Meeting. The report shall cover all matters considered at the session and shall reflect the views expressed. The report shall be circulated to the Parties and to observers attending the session, and shall thereupon be made publicly available.

6. The Committee shall adopt its rules of procedure which shall be subject to approval by the Antarctic Treaty Consultative Meeting.

Article 12	Functions of the Committee

1. The functions of the Committee shall be to provide advice and formulate recommendations to the Parties in connection with the implementation of this Protocol, including the operation of its Annexes, for consideration at Antarctic Treaty Consultative Meetings, and to perform such other functions as may be referred to it by the Antarctic Treaty Consultative Meetings. In particular, it shall provide advice on:

(a) the effectiveness of measures taken pursuant to this Protocol;
(b) the need to update, strengthen or otherwise improve such measures;
(c) the need for additional measures, including the need for additional Annexes, where appropriate;
(d) the application and implementation of the environmental impact assessment procedures set out in Article 8 and Annex I;
(e) means of minimising or mitigating environmental impacts of activities in the Antarctic Treaty area;
(f) procedures for situations requiring urgent action, including response action in environmental emergencies;
(g) the operation and further elaboration of the Antarctic Protected Area system;
(h) inspection procedures, including formats for inspection reports and checklists for the conduct of inspections;
(i) the collection, archiving, exchange and evaluation of information related to environmental protection;
(j) the state of the Antarctic environment; and
(k) the need for scientific research, including environmental monitoring, related to the implementation of this Protocol.

2. In carrying out its functions, the Committee shall, as appropriate, consult with the Scientific Committee on Antarctic Research, the Scientific Committee for the Conservation of Antarctic Marine Living Resources and other relevant scientific, environmental and technical organizations.

Article 13	Compliance with this Protocol

1. Each Party shall take appropriate measures within its competence, including the adoption of laws and regulations, administrative actions and enforcement measures, to ensure compliance with this Protocol.

2. Each Party shall exert appropriate efforts, consistent with the Charter of the United Nations, to the end that no one engages in any activity contrary to this Protocol.

3. Each Party shall notify all other Parties of the measures it takes pursuant to paragraphs 1 and 2 above.

4. Each Party shall draw the attention of all other Parties to any activity which in its opinion affects the implementation of the objectives and principles of this Protocol.

5. The Antarctic Treaty Consultative Meetings shall draw the attention of any State which is not a Party to this Protocol to any activity undertaken by that State, its agencies, instrumentalities, natural or juridical persons, ships, aircraft or other means of transport which affects the implementation of the objectives and principles of this Protocol.

Article 14   Inspection

1. In order to promote the protection of the Antarctic environment and dependent and associated ecosystems, and to ensure compliance with this Protocol, the Antarctic Treaty Consultative Parties shall arrange, individually or collectively, for inspections by observers to be made in accordance with Article VII of the Antarctic Treaty.

2. Observers are:

(a) observers designated by any Antarctic Treaty Consultative Party who shall be nationals of that Party; and
(b) any observers designated at Antarctic Treaty Consultative Meetings to carry out inspections under procedures to be established by an Antarctic Treaty Consultative Meeting.

3. Parties shall co-operate fully with observers undertaking inspections, and shall ensure that during inspections, observers are given access to all parts of stations, installations, equipment, ships and aircraft open to inspection under Article VII (3) of the Antarctic Treaty, as well as to all records maintained thereon which are called for pursuant to this Protocol.

4. Reports of inspections shall be sent to the Parties whose stations, installations, equipment, ships or aircraft are covered by the reports. After those Parties have been given the opportunity to comment, the reports and any comments thereon shall be circulated to all the Parties and to the Committee, considered at the next Antarctic Treaty Consultative Meeting, and thereafter made publicly available.

Article 15   Emergency Response Action

1. In order to respond to environmental emergencies in the Antarctic Treaty area, each Party agrees to:

(a) provide for prompt and effective response action to such emergencies which might arise in the performance of scientific research programmes, tourism and all other governmental and nongovernmental activities in the Antarctic Treaty area for which advance notice is required under Article VII (5) of the Antarctic Treaty, including associated logistic support activities; and
(b) establish contingency plans for response to incidents with potential adverse effects on the Antarctic environment or dependent and associated ecosystems.

2. To this end, the Parties shall:

(a) co-operate in the formulation and implementation of such contingency plans; and
(b) establish procedures for immediate notification of, and co-operative response to, environmental emergencies.

3. In the implementation of this Article, the Parties shall draw upon the advice of the appropriate international organisations.

Article 16   Liability

Consistent with the objectives of this Protocol for the comprehensive protection of the Antarctic environment and dependent and associated ecosystems, the Parties undertake to elaborate rules and procedures relating to liability for damage arising from activities taking place in the Antarctic Treaty area and covered by this Protocol. Those rules and procedures shall be included in one or more Annexes to be adopted in accordance with Article 9 (2).

Article 17   Annual Report by Parties

1. Each Party shall report annually on the steps taken to implement this Protocol. Such reports shall include notifications made in accordance with Article 13 (3), contingency plans established in accordance with Article 15 and any other notifications and information called for pursuant to this Protocol for which there is no other provision concerning the circulation and exchange of information.

2. Reports made in accordance with paragraph 1 above shall be circulated to all Parties and to the Committee, considered at the next Antarctic Treaty Consultative Meeting, and made publicly available.

Article 18   Dispute Settlement

If a dispute arises concerning the interpretation or application of this Protocol, the parties to the dispute shall, at the request of any one of them, consult among themselves as soon as possible with a view to having the dispute resolved by negotiation, inquiry, mediation, conciliation, arbitration, judicial settlement or other peaceful means to which the parties to the dispute agree.

Article 19   Choice of Dispute Settlement Procedure

1. Each Party, when signing, ratifying, accepting, approving or acceding to this Protocol, or at any time thereafter, may choose, by written declaration, one or both of the following means for the settlement of disputes concerning the interpretation or application of Articles 7, 8 and 15 and, except to the extent that an Annex provides otherwise, the provisions of any Annex and, insofar as it relates to these Articles and provisions, Article 13:

    (a) the International Court of Justice;
    (b) the Arbitral Tribunal.

2. A declaration made under paragraph 1 above shall not affect the operation of Article 18 and Article 20 (2).

3. A Party which has not made a declaration under paragraph 1 above or in respect of which a declaration is no longer in force shall be deemed to have accepted the competence of the Arbitral Tribunal.

4. If the parties to a dispute have accepted the same means for the settlement of a dispute, the dispute may be submitted only to that procedure, unless the parties otherwise agree.

5. If the parties to a dispute have not accepted the same means for the settlement of a dispute, or if they have both accepted both means, the dispute may be submitted only to the Arbitral Tribunal, unless the parties otherwise agree.

6. A declaration made under paragraph 1 above shall remain in force until it expires in accordance with its terms or until three months after written notice of revocation has been deposited with the Depositary.

7. A new declaration, a notice of revocation or the expiry of a declaration shall not in any way affect proceedings pending before the International Court of Justice or the Arbitral Tribunal, unless the parties to the dispute otherwise agree.

8. Declarations and notices referred to in this Article shall be deposited with the Depositary who shall transmit copies thereof to all Parties.

Article 20   **Dispute Settlement Procedure**

1. If the parties to a dispute concerning the interpretation or application of Articles 7, 8 or 15 or, except to the extent that an Annex provides otherwise, the provisions of any Annex or, insofar as it relates to these Articles and provisions, Article 13, have not agreed on a means for resolving it within 12 months of the request for consultation pursuant to Article 18, the dispute shall be referred, at the request of any party to the dispute, for settlement in accordance with the procedure determined by Article 19 (4) and (5).

2. The Arbitral Tribunal shall not be competent to decide or rule upon any matter within the scope of Article IV of the Antarctic Treaty [the freezing of territorial claims]. In addition, nothing in this Protocol shall be interpreted as conferring competence or jurisdiction on the International Court of Justice or any other tribunal established for the purpose of settling disputes between Parties to decide or otherwise rule upon any matter within the scope of Article IV of the Antarctic Treaty.

Article 21   **Signature**

This Protocol shall be open for signature at Madrid on the 4th of October 1991 and thereafter at Washington until the 3rd of October 1992 by any State which is a Contracting Party to the Antarctic Treaty.

Article 22   **Ratification, Acceptance, Approval or Accession**

1. This Protocol is subject to ratification, acceptance or approval by signatory States.

2. After the 3rd of October 1992 this Protocol shall be open for accession by any State which is a Contracting Party to the Antarctic Treaty.

3. Instruments of ratification, acceptance, approval or accession shall be deposited with the Government of the United States of America, hereby designated as the Depositary.

4. After the date on which this Protocol has entered into force, the Antarctic Treaty Consultative Parties shall not act upon a notification regarding the entitlement of a Contracting Party to the Antarctic Treaty to appoint representatives to participate in Antarctic Treaty Consultative Meetings in accordance with Article IX (2) of the Antarctic Treaty unless that Contracting Party has first ratified, accepted, approved or acceded to this Protocol.

Article 23   **Entry into Force**

1. This Protocol shall enter into force on the thirtieth day following the date of deposit of instruments of ratification, acceptance, approval or accession by all States which are Antarctic Treaty Consultative Parties at the date on which this Protocol is adopted.

2. For each Contracting Party to the Antarctic Treaty which, subsequent to the date of entry into force of this Protocol, deposits an instrument of ratification, acceptance, approval or accession, this Protocol shall enter into force on the thirtieth day following such deposit.

Article 24   **Reservations**

Reservations to this Protocol shall not be permitted.

Article 25   **Modification or Amendment**

1. Without prejudice to the provisions of Article 9 [amendment of annexes], this Protocol may be modified or amended at any time in accordance with the procedures set forth in Article XII (1) (a) and (b) of the Antarctic Treaty.

2. If, after the expiration of 50 years from the date of entry into force of this Protocol, any of the Antarctic Treaty Consultative Parties so requests by a communication addressed to the Depositary, a conference shall be held as soon as practicable to review the operation of this Protocol.

3. A modification or amendment proposed at any Review Conference called pursuant to paragraph 2 above shall be adopted by a majority of the Parties, including 3/4 of the States which are Antarctic Treaty Consultative Parties at the time of adoption of this Protocol.

4. A modification or amendment adopted pursuant to paragraph 3 above shall enter into force upon ratification, acceptance, approval or accession by 3/4 of the Antarctic Treaty Consultative Parties, including ratification, acceptance, approval or accession by all States which are Antarctic Treaty Consultative Parties at the time of adoption of this Protocol.

5.   (a) With respect to Article 7, the prohibition on Antarctic mineral resource activities contained therein shall continue unless there is in force a binding legal regime on Antarctic mineral resource activities that includes an agreed means for determining whether, and, if so, under which conditions, any such activities would be acceptable. This regime shall fully safeguard the interests of all States referred to in Article IV of the Antarctic Treaty and apply the principles thereof. Therefore, if a modification or amendment to Article 7 is proposed at a Review Conference referred to in paragraph 2 above, it shall include such a binding legal regime.

    (b) If any such modification or amendment has not entered into force within 3 years of the date of its adoption, any Party may at any time thereafter notify to the Depositary of its withdrawal from this Protocol, and such withdrawal shall take effect 2 years after receipt of the notification by the Depositary.

Article 26   Notifications by the Depositary

The Depositary shall notify all Contracting Parties to the Antarctic Treaty of the following:

    (a) signatures of this Protocol and the deposit of instruments of ratification, acceptance, approval or accession;
    (b) the date of entry into force of this Protocol and any additional Annex thereto;
    (c) the date of entry into force of any amendment or modification to this Protocol;
    (d) the deposit of declarations and notices pursuant to Article 19; and
    (e) any notification received pursuant to Article 25 (5) (b).

Article 27   Authentic Texts and Registration with the United Nations

1. This Protocol, done in the English, French, Russian and Spanish languages, each version being equally authentic, shall be deposited in the archives of the Government of the United States of America, which shall transmit duly certified copies thereof to all Contracting Parties to the Antarctic Treaty.

2. This Protocol shall be registered by the Depositary pursuant to Article 102 of the Charter of the United Nations.

Schedule to the Protocol: Arbitration ***

Annex I	**Environmental Impact Assessment * * ***
Annex II	**Conservation of Antarctic Fauna and Flora * * ***
Annex III	**Waste Disposal and Waste Management * * ***
Annex IV	**Prevention of Marine Pollution * * ***
Annex V	**Area Protection and Management * * ***

———————————————————

NON-LEGALLY BINDING AUTHORITATIVE STATEMENT OF PRINCIPLES FOR A GLOBAL CONSENSUS ON THE MANAGEMENT, CONSERVATION AND SUSTAINABLE DEVELOPMENT OF ALL TYPES OF FORESTS

U.N.Doc.A/conf.151/26 (Vol III) (1992);
31 I.L.M. 881(1992)
Signed: June 13, 1992

PREAMBLE

(a) The subject of forests is related to the entire range of environmental and development issues and opportunities, including the right to socio-economic development on a sustainable basis.

(b) The guiding objective of these principles is to contribute to the management, conservation and sustainable development of forests and to provide for their multiple and complementary functions and uses.

(c) Forestry issues and opportunities should be examined in a holistic and balanced manner within the overall context of environment and development, taking into consideration the multiple functions and uses of forests, including traditional uses, and the likely economic and social stress when these uses are constrained or restricted, as well as the potential for development that sustainable forest management can offer.

(d) These principles reflect a first global consensus on forests. In committing themselves to the prompt implementation of these principles, countries also decide to keep them under assessment for their adequacy with regard to further international cooperation on forest issues.

(e) These principles should apply to all types of forests, both natural and planted, in all geographical regions and climatic zones, including austral, boreal, subtemperate, temperate, subtropical and tropical.

(f) All types of forests embody complex and unique ecological precesses which are the basis for their present and potential capacity to provide resources to satisfy human needs as well as environmental values, and as such their sound management and conservation is of concern to the Governments of the countries to which they belong and are of value to local communities and to the environment as a whole.

(g) Forests are essential to economic development and the maintenance of all forms of life.

(h) Recognizing that the responsibility for forest management, conservation and sustainable development is in many States allocated among federal/national, state/provincial and local levels of government, each State, in accordance with its constitution and/or national legislation, should pursue these principles at the appropriate level of government.

PRINCIPLES/ELEMENTS

1.   (a) States have, in accordance with the Charter of the United Nations and the principles of international law, the sovereign right to exploit their own resources pursuant to their own environmental policies and have the responsibility to ensure that activities within their jurisdiction or control do not cause damage to the environment of other States or of areas beyond the limits of national jurisdiction.

(b) The agreed full incremental cost of achieving benefits associated with forest conservation and sustainable development requires increased international cooperation and should be equitably shared by the international community.

2.   (a) States have the sovereign and inalienable right to utilize, manage and develop their forests in accordance with their development needs and level of socio-economic development and on the basis of national policies consistent with sustainable development and legislation, including the conversion of such areas for other uses within the overall socio-economic development plan and based on rational land-use policies.

(b) Forest resources and forest lands should be sustainably managed to meet the social, economic, ecological, cultural and spiritual human needs of present and future generations. These needs are for forest products and services, such as wood and wood products, water, food, fodder, medicine, fuel, shelter, employment, recreation, habitats for wildlife, landscape diversity, carbon sinks and reservoirs, and for other forest products. Appropriate measures should be taken to protect forests against harmful effects of pollution, including air-born pollution, fires, pests and diseases in order to maintain their full multiple value.

(c) The provision of timely, reliable and accurate information on forests and forest ecosystems is essential for public understanding and informed decision-making and should be ensured.

(d) Governments should promote and provide opportunities for the participation of interested parties, including local communities and indigenous people, industries, labour, non-governmental organizations and individuals, forest dwellers and women, in the development, implementation and planning of national forest policies.

3. (a) National policies and strategies should provide a framework for increased efforts, including the development and strengthening of institutions and programmes for the management, conservation and sustainable development of forests and forest lands.

(b) International institutional arrangements, building on those organizations and mechanisms already in existence, as appropriate, should facilitate international cooperation in the field of forests.

(c) All aspects of environmental protection and social and economic development as they relate to forests and forest lands should be integrated and comprehensive.

4. The vital role of all types of forests in maintaining the ecological processes and balance at the local, national, regional and global levels through, inter alia, their role in protecting fragile ecosystems, watersheds and freshwater resources and as rich storehouses of biodiversity and biological resources and sources of genetic material for biotechnology products, as well as photosynthesis, should be recognized.

5. (a) National forest policies should recognize and duly support the identity, culture and the rights of indigenous people, their communities and other communities and forest dwellers. Appropriate conditions should be promoted for these groups to enable them to have an economic stake in forest use, perform economic activities, and achieve and maintain cultural identity and social organization, as well as adequate levels of livelihood and well-being, through, inter alia, those land tenure arrangements which serve as incentives for the sustainable management of forests.

(b) The full participation of women in all aspects of the management, conservation and sustainable development of forests should be actively promoted.

6. (a) All types of forests play an important role in meeting energy requirements through the provision of a renewable source of bio-energy, particularly in developing countries, and the demands for fuelwood for household and industrial needs should be met through sustainable forest management, afforestation and reforestation. To this end, the potential contribution of plantations of both indigenous and introduced species for the provision of both fuel and industrial wood should be recognized.

(b) National policies and programmes should take into account the relationship, where it exists, between the conservation, management and sustainable development of forests and all aspects related to the production, consumption, recycling and/or final disposal of forest products.

(c) Decisions taken on the management, conservation and sustainable development of forest resources should benefit, to the extent practicable, from a comprehensive assessment of economic and non-economic values of forest goods and services and of the environmental costs and benefits. The development and improvement of methodologies for such evaluations should be promoted.

(d) The role of planted forests and permanent agricultural crops as sustainable and environmentally sound sources of renewable energy and industrial raw material should be recognized, enhanced and promoted. Their contribution to the maintenance of ecological processes, to offsetting pressure on primary/old-growth forest and to providing regional employment and development with the adequate involvement of local inhabitants should be recognized and enhanced.

(e) Natural forests also constitute a source of goods and services, and their conservation, sustainable management and use should be promoted.

7. (a) Efforts should be made to promote a supportive international economic climate conducive to sustained and environmentally sound development of forests in all countries, which include, inter alia, the promotion of sustainable patterns of production and consumption, the eradication of poverty and the promotion of food security.

(b) Specific financial resources should be provided to developing countries with significant forest areas which establish programmes for the conservation of forests including protected natural forest areas. These resources should be directed notably to economic sectors which would stimulate economic and social substitution activities.

8.   (a) Efforts should be undertaken towards the greening of the world. All countries, notably developed countries, should take positive and transparent action towards reforestation, afforestation and forest conservation, as appropriate.

(b) Efforts to maintain and increase forest cover and forest productivity should be undertaken in ecologically, economically and socially sound ways through the rehabilitation, reforestation and re-establishment of trees and forests on unproductive, degraded and deforested lands, as well as through the management of existing forest resources.

(c) The implementation of national policies and programmes aimed at forest management, conservation and sustainable development, particularly in developing countries, should be supported by international financial and technical cooperation, including through the private sector, where appropriate.

(d) Sustainable forest management and use should be carried out in accordance with national development policies and priorities and on the basis of environmentally sound national guidelines. In the formulation of such guidelines, account should be taken, as appropriate and if applicable, of relevant internationally agreed methodologies and criteria.

(e) Forest management should be integrated with management of adjacent areas so as to maintain ecological balance and sustainable productivity.

(f) National policies and/or legislation aimed at management, conservation and sustainable development of forests should include the protection of ecologically viable representative or unique examples of forests, including primary/old-growth forests, cultural, spiritual, historical, religious and other unique and valued forests of national importance.

(g) Access to biological resources, including genetic material, shall be with due regard to the sovereign rights of the countries where the forests are located and to the sharing on mutually agreed terms of technology and profits from biotechnology products that are derived from these resources.

(h) National policies should ensure that environmental impact assessments should be carried out where actions are likely to have significant adverse impacts on important forest resources, and where such actions are subject to a decision of a competent national authority.

9.   (a) The efforts of developing countries to strengthen the management, conservation and sustainable development of their forest resources should be supported by the international community, taking into account the importance of redressing external indebtedness, particularly where aggravated by the net transfer of resources to developed countries, as well as the problem of achieving at least the replacement value of forests through improved market access for forest products, especially processed products. In this respect, special attention should also be given to the countries undergoing the process of transition to market economies.

(b) The problems that hinder efforts to attain the conservation and sustainable use of forest resources and that stem from the lack of alternative options available to local communities, in particular the urban poor and poor rural populations who are economically and socially dependent on forests and forest resources, should be addressed by Governments and the international community.

(c) National policy formulation with respect to all types of forests should take account of the pressures and demands imposed on forest ecosystems and resources from influencing factors outside the forest sector, and intersectoral means of dealing with these pressures and demands should be sought.

10.   New and additional financial resources should be provided to developing countries to enable them to sustainably manage, conserve and develop their forest resources, including through afforestation, reforestation and combating deforestation and forest and land degradation.

11.   In order to enable, in particular, developing countries to enhance their endogenous capacity and to better manage, conserve and develop their forest resources, the access to and transfer of environmentally sound technologies and corresponding know-how on favourable terms, including on concessional and preferential terms, as

mutually agreed, in accordance with the relevant provisions of Agenda 21, should be promoted, facilitated and financed, as appropriate.

12.   (a) Scientific research, forest inventories and assessments carried out by national institutions which take into account, where relevant, biological, physical, social and economic variables, as well as technological development and its application in the field of sustainable forest management, conservation and development, should be strengthened through effective modalities, including international cooperation. In this context, attention should also be given to research and development of sustainably harvested non-wood products.

(b) National and, where appropriate, regional and international institutional capabilities in education, training, science, technology, economics, anthropology and social aspects of forests and forest management are essential to the conservation and sustainable development of forests and should be strengthened.

(c) International exchange of information on the results of forest and forest management research and development should be enhanced and broadened, as appropriate, making full use of education and training institutions, including those in the private sector.

(d) Appropriate indigenous capacity and local knowledge regarding the conservation and sustainable development of forests should, through institutional and financial support and in collaboration with the people in the local communities concerned, be recognized, respected, recorded, developed and, as appropriate, introduced in the implementation of programmes. Benefits arising from the utilization of indigenous knowledge should therefore be equitably shared with such people.

13.   (a) Trade in forest products should be based on non-discriminatory and multilaterally agreed rules and procedures consistent with international trade law and practices. In this context, open and free international trade in forest products should be facilitated.

(b) Reduction or removal of tariff barriers and impediments to the provision of better market access and better prices for higher value-added forest products and their local processing should be encouraged to enable producer countries to better conserve and manage their renewable forest resources.

(c) Incorporation of environmental costs and benefits into market forces and mechanisms, in order to achieve forest conservation and sustainable development, should be encouraged both domestically and internationally.

(d) Forest conservation and sustainable development policies should be integrated with economic, trade and other relevant policies.

(e) Fiscal, trade, industrial, transportation and other policies and practices that may lead to forest degradation should be avoided.   Adequate policies, aimed at management, conservation and sustainable development of forests, including, where appropriate, incentives, should be encouraged.

14.   Unilateral measures, incompatible with international obligations or agreements, to restrict and/or ban international trade in timber or other forest products should be removed or avoided, in order to attain long-term sustainable forest management.

15.   Pollutants, particularly air-borne pollutants, including those responsible for acidic deposition, that are harmful to the health of forest ecosystems at the local, national, regional and global levels should be controlled.

UNITED NATIONS CONVENTION TO COMBAT DESERTIFICATION IN COUNTRIES EXPERIENCING SERIOUS DROUGHT AND/OR DESERTIFICATION, PARTICULARLY IN AFRICA
(including Regional Implementation Annex for Africa)

1954 U.N.T.S. 3
Signed: October 14, 1994
Entered into Force: December 26, 1996
Secretariat Homepage: http://www.unccd.ch/

The Parties to this Convention,

Affirming that human beings in affected or threatened areas are at the centre of concerns to combat desertification and mitigate the effects of drought,

Reflecting the urgent concern of the international community, including States and international organizations, about the adverse impacts of desertification and drought,

Aware that arid, semi-arid and dry sub-humid areas together account for a significant proportion of the Earth's land area and are the habitat and source of livelihood for a large segment of its population,

Acknowledging that desertification and drought are problems of global dimension in that they affect all regions of the world and that joint action of the international community is needed to combat desertification and/or mitigate the effects of drought,

Noting the high concentration of developing countries, notably the least developed countries, among those experiencing serious drought and/or desertification, and the particularly tragic consequences of these phenomena in Africa,

Noting also that desertification is caused by complex interactions among physical, biological, political, social, cultural and economic factors,

Considering the impact of trade and relevant aspects of international economic relations on the ability of affected countries to combat desertification adequately,

Conscious that sustainable economic growth, social development and poverty eradication are priorities of affected developing countries, particularly in Africa, and are essential to meeting sustainability objectives,

Mindful that desertification and drought affect sustainable development through their interrelationships with important social problems such as poverty, poor health and nutrition, lack of food security, and those arising from migration, displacement of persons and demographic dynamics,

Appreciating the significance of the past efforts and experience of States and international organizations in combating desertification and mitigating the effects of drought, particularly in implementing the Plan of Action to Combat Desertification which was adopted at the United Nations Conference on Desertification in 1977,

Realizing that, despite efforts in the past, progress in combating desertification and mitigating the effects of drought has not met expectations and that a new and more effective approach is needed at all levels within the framework of sustainable development,

Recognizing the validity and relevance of decisions adopted at the United Nations Conference on Environment and Development, particularly of Agenda 21 and its chapter 12, which provide a basis for combating desertification,

Reaffirming in this light the commitments of developed countries as contained in paragraph 13 of chapter 33 of Agenda 21,

Recalling General Assembly resolution 47/188, particularly the priority in it prescribed for Africa, and all other relevant United Nations resolutions, decisions and programmes on desertification and drought, as well as relevant declarations by African countries and those from other regions,

Reaffirming the Rio Declaration on Environment and Development which states, in its Principle 2, that States have, in accordance with the Charter of the United Nations and the principles of international law, the sovereign right to exploit their own resources pursuant to their own environmental and developmental policies, and the responsibility to ensure that activities within their jurisdiction or control do not cause damage to the environment of other States or of areas beyond the limits of national jurisdiction,

Recognizing that national Governments play a critical role in combating desertification and mitigating the effects of drought and that progress in that respect depends on local implementation of action programmes in affected areas,

Recognizing also the importance and necessity of international cooperation and partnership in combating desertification and mitigating the effects of drought,

Recognizing further the importance of the provision to affected developing countries, particularly in Africa, of effective means, inter alia substantial financial resources, including new and additional funding, and access to technology, without which it will be difficult for them to implement fully their commitments under this Convention,

Expressing concern over the impact of desertification and drought on affected countries in Central Asia and the Transcaucasus,

Stressing the important role played by women in regions affected by desertification and/or drought, particularly in rural areas of developing countries, and the importance of ensuring the full participation of both men and women at all levels in programmes to combat desertification and mitigate the effects of drought,

Emphasizing the special role of non-governmental organizations and other major groups in programmes to combat desertification and mitigate the effects of drought,

Bearing in mind the relationship between desertification and other environmental problems of global dimension facing the international and national communities,

Bearing also in mind the contribution that combating desertification can make to achieving the objectives of the United Nations Framework Convention on Climate Change, the Convention on Biological Diversity and other related environmental conventions,

Believing that strategies to combat desertification and mitigate the effects of drought will be most effective if they are based on sound systematic observation and rigorous scientific knowledge and if they are continuously re-evaluated,

Recognizing the urgent need to improve the effectiveness and coordination of international cooperation to facilitate the implementation of national plans and priorities,

Determined to take appropriate action in combating desertification and mitigating the effects of drought for the benefit of present and future generations,

Have agreed as follows:

PART I   INTRODUCTION

Article 1   Use of terms

For the purposes of this Convention:

(a) "desertification" means land degradation in arid, semi-arid and dry sub-humid areas resulting from various factors, including climatic variations and human activities;

(b) "combating desertification" includes activities which are part of the integrated development of land in arid, semi-arid and dry sub-humid areas for sustainable development which are aimed at:

(i) prevention and/or reduction of land degradation;

(ii) rehabilitation of partly degraded land; and

(iii) reclamation of desertified land;

(c) "drought" means the naturally occurring phenomenon that exists when precipitation has been significantly below normal recorded levels, causing serious hydrological imbalances that adversely affect land resource production systems;

(d) "mitigating the effects of drought" means activities related to the prediction of drought and intended to reduce the vulnerability of society and natural systems to drought as it relates to combating desertification;

(e) "land" means the terrestrial bio-productive system that comprises soil, vegetation, other biota, and the ecological and hydrological processes that operate within the system;

(f) "land degradation" means reduction or loss, in arid, semi-arid and dry sub-humid areas, of the biological or economic productivity and complexity of rainfed cropland, irrigated cropland, or range, pasture, forest and woodlands resulting from land uses or from a process or combination of processes, including processes arising from human activities and habitation patterns, such as:

(i) soil erosion caused by wind and/or water;

(ii) deterioration of the physical, chemical and biological or economic properties of soil; and

(iii) long-term loss of natural vegetation;

(g) "arid, semi-arid and dry sub-humid areas" means areas, other than polar and sub-polar regions, in which the ratio of annual precipitation to potential evapotranspiration falls within the range from 0.05 to 0.65;

(h) "affected areas" means arid, semi-arid and/or dry sub-humid areas affected or threatened by desertification;

(i) "affected countries" means countries whose lands include, in whole or in part, affected areas;

(j) "regional economic integration organization" means an organization constituted by sovereign States of a given region which has competence in respect of matters governed by this Convention and has been duly authorized, in accordance with its internal procedures, to sign, ratify, accept, approve or accede to this Convention;

(k) "developed country Parties" means developed country Parties and regional economic integration organizations constituted by developed countries.

Article 2   Objective

1. The objective of this Convention is to combat desertification and mitigate the effects of drought in countries experiencing serious drought and/or desertification, particularly in Africa, through effective action at all levels, supported by international cooperation and partnership arrangements, in the framework of an integrated approach which is consistent with Agenda 21, with a view to contributing to the achievement of sustainable development in affected areas.

2. Achieving this objective will involve long-term integrated strategies that focus simultaneously, in affected areas, on improved productivity of land, and the rehabilitation, conservation and sustainable management of land and water resources, leading to improved living conditions, in particular at the community level.

Article 3   Principles

In order to achieve the objective of this Convention and to implement its provisions, the Parties shall be guided, inter alia, by the following:

(a) the Parties should ensure that decisions on the design and implementation of programmes to combat desertification and/or mitigate the effects of drought are taken with the participation of populations and local communities and that an enabling environment is created at higher levels to facilitate action at national and local levels;

(b) the Parties should, in a spirit of international solidarity and partnership, improve cooperation and coordination at subregional, regional and international levels, and better focus financial, human, organizational and technical resources where they are needed;

(c) the Parties should develop, in a spirit of partnership, cooperation among all levels of government, communities, non-governmental organizations and landholders to establish a better understanding of the nature and value of land and scarce water resources in affected areas and to work towards their sustainable use; and

(d) the Parties should take into full consideration the special needs and circumstances of affected developing country Parties, particularly the least developed among them.

PART II GENERAL PROVISIONS

Article 4 General obligations

1. The Parties shall implement their obligations under this Convention, individually or jointly, either through existing or prospective bilateral and multilateral arrangements or a combination thereof, as appropriate, emphasizing the need to coordinate efforts and develop a coherent long-term strategy at all levels.

2. In pursuing the objective of this Convention, the Parties shall:

(a) adopt an integrated approach addressing the physical, biological and socio-economic aspects of the processes of desertification and drought;

(b) give due attention, within the relevant international and regional bodies, to the situation of affected developing country Parties with regard to international trade, marketing arrangements and debt with a view to establishing an enabling international economic environment conducive to the promotion of sustainable development;

(c) integrate strategies for poverty eradication into efforts to combat desertification and mitigate the effects of drought;

(d) promote cooperation among affected country Parties in the fields of environmental protection and the conservation of land and water resources, as they relate to desertification and drought;

(e) strengthen subregional, regional and international cooperation;

(f) cooperate within relevant intergovernmental organizations;

(g) determine institutional mechanisms, if appropriate, keeping in mind the need to avoid duplication; and

(h) promote the use of existing bilateral and multilateral financial mechanisms and arrangements that mobilize and channel substantial financial resources to affected developing country Parties in combating desertification and mitigating the effects of drought.

3. Affected developing country Parties are eligible for assistance in the implementation of the Convention.

Article 5 Obligations of affected country Parties

In addition to their obligations pursuant to article 4, affected country Parties undertake to:

(a) give due priority to combating desertification and mitigating the effects of drought, and allocate adequate resources in accordance with their circumstances and capabilities;

(b) establish strategies and priorities, within the framework of sustainable development plans and/or policies, to combat desertification and mitigate the effects of drought;

(c) address the underlying causes of desertification and pay special attention to the socio- economic factors contributing to desertification processes;

(d) promote awareness and facilitate the participation of local populations, particularly women and youth, with the support of non-governmental organizations, in efforts to combat desertification and mitigate the effects of drought; and

(e) provide an enabling environment by strengthening, as appropriate, relevant existing legislation and, where they do not exist, enacting new laws and establishing long-term policies and action programmes.

Article 6 Obligations of developed country Parties

In addition to their general obligations pursuant to article 4, developed country Parties undertake to:

(a) actively support, as agreed, individually or jointly, the efforts of affected developing country Parties, particularly those in Africa, and the least developed countries, to combat desertification and mitigate the effects of drought;

(b) provide substantial financial resources and other forms of support to assist affected developing country Parties, particularly those in Africa, effectively to develop and implement their own long-term plans and strategies to combat desertification and mitigate the effects of drought;

(c) promote the mobilization of new and additional funding pursuant to article 20, paragraph 2 (b);

(d) encourage the mobilization of funding from the private sector and other non-governmental sources; and

(e) promote and facilitate access by affected country Parties, particularly affected developing country Parties, to appropriate technology, knowledge and know-how.

Article 7   Priority for Africa

In implementing this Convention, the Parties shall give priority to affected African country Parties, in the light of the particular situation prevailing in that region, while not neglecting affected developing country Parties in other regions.

**Article 8   Relationship with other
                                      conventions**

1. The Parties shall encourage the coordination of activities carried out under this Convention and, if they are Parties to them, under other relevant international agreements, particularly the United Nations Framework Convention on Climate Change and the Convention on Biological Diversity, in order to derive maximum benefit from activities under each agreement while avoiding duplication of effort. The Parties shall encourage the conduct of joint programmes, particularly in the fields of research, training, systematic observation and information collection and exchange, to the extent that such activities may contribute to achieving the objectives of the agreements concerned.

2. The provisions of this Convention shall not affect the rights and obligations of any Party deriving from a bilateral, regional or international agreement into which it has entered prior to the entry into force of this Convention for it.

**PART III   ACTION PROGRAMMES, SCIENTIFIC AND
                                      TECHNICAL COOPERATION AND
                                      SUPPORTING MEASURES**

Section 1:   Action programmes

Article 9   Basic approach

1. In carrying out their obligations pursuant to article 5, affected developing country Parties and any other affected country Party in the framework of its regional implementation annex or, otherwise, that has notified the Permanent Secretariat in writing of its intention to prepare a national action programme, shall, as appropriate, prepare, make public and implement national action programmes, utilizing and building, to the extent possible, on existing relevant successful plans and programmes, and subregional and regional action programmes, as the central element of the strategy to combat desertification and mitigate the effects of drought. Such programmes shall be updated through a continuing participatory process on the basis of lessons from field action, as well as the results of research. The preparation of national action programmes shall be closely interlinked with other efforts to formulate national policies for sustainable development.

2. In the provision by developed country Parties of different forms of assistance under the terms of article 6, priority shall be given to supporting, as agreed, national, subregional and regional action programmes of affected developing country Parties, particularly those in Africa, either directly or through relevant multilateral organizations or both.

3. The Parties shall encourage organs, funds and programmes of the United Nations system and other relevant intergovernmental organizations, academic institutions, the scientific community and non-governmental organizations in a position to cooperate, in accordance with their mandates and capabilities, to support the elaboration, implementation and follow-up of action programmes.

Article 10   National action programmes

1. The purpose of national action programmes is to identify the factors contributing to desertification and practical measures necessary to combat desertification and mitigate the effects of drought.

2. National action programmes shall specify the respective roles of government, local communities and land users and the resources available and needed. They shall, inter alia:
          (a) incorporate long-term strategies to combat desertification and mitigate the effects of drought, emphasize implementation and be integrated with national policies for sustainable development;

(b) allow for modifications to be made in response to changing circumstances and be sufficiently flexible at the local level to cope with different socio-economic, biological and geo-physical conditions;

(c) give particular attention to the implementation of preventive measures for lands that are not yet degraded or which are only slightly degraded;

(d) enhance national climatological, meteorological and hydrological capabilities and the means to provide for drought early warning;

(e) promote policies and strengthen institutional frameworks which develop cooperation and coordination, in a spirit of partnership, between the donor community, governments at all levels, local populations and community groups, and facilitate access by local populations to appropriate information and technology;

(f) provide for effective participation at the local, national and regional levels of non-governmental organizations and local populations, both women and men, particularly resource users, including farmers and pastoralists and their representative organizations, in policy planning, decision-making, and implementation and review of national action programmes; and

(g) require regular review of, and progress reports on, their implementation.

3. National action programmes may include, inter alia, some or all of the following measures to prepare for and mitigate the effects of drought:

(a) establishment and/or strengthening, as appropriate, of early warning systems, including local and national facilities and joint systems at the subregional and regional levels, and mechanisms for assisting environmentally displaced persons;

(b) strengthening of drought preparedness and management, including drought contingency plans at the local, national, subregional and regional levels, which take into consideration seasonal to interannual climate predictions;

(c) establishment and/or strengthening, as appropriate, of food security systems, including storage and marketing facilities, particularly in rural areas;

(d) establishment of alternative livelihood projects that could provide incomes in drought prone areas; and

(e) development of sustainable irrigation programmes for both crops and livestock.

4. Taking into account the circumstances and requirements specific to each affected country Party, national action programmes include, as appropriate, inter alia, measures in some or all of the following priority fields as they relate to combating desertification and mitigating the effects of drought in affected areas and to their populations: promotion of alternative livelihoods and improvement of national economic environments with a view to strengthening programmes aimed at the eradication of poverty and at ensuring food security; demographic dynamics; sustainable management of natural resources; sustainable agricultural practices; development and efficient use of various energy sources; institutional and legal frameworks; strengthening of capabilities for assessment and systematic observation, including hydrological and meteorological services, and capacity building, education and public awareness.

Article 11   **Subregional and regional action programmes**

Affected country Parties shall consult and cooperate to prepare, as appropriate, in accordance with relevant regional implementation annexes, subregional and/or regional action programmes to harmonize, complement and increase the efficiency of national programmes. The provisions of article 10 shall apply mutatis mutandis to subregional and regional programmes. Such cooperation may include agreed joint programmes for the sustainable management of transboundary natural resources, scientific and technical cooperation, and strengthening of relevant institutions.

Article 12   **International cooperation**

Affected country Parties, in collaboration with other Parties and the international community, should cooperate to ensure the promotion of an enabling international environment in the implementation of the Convention. Such cooperation should also cover fields of technology transfer as well as scientific research and development, information collection and dissemination and financial resources.

| Article 13 | Support for the elaboration and implementation of action programmes |

1. Measures to support action programmes pursuant to article 9 include, inter alia:

(a) financial cooperation to provide predictability for action programmes, allowing for necessary long-term planning;

(b) elaboration and use of cooperation mechanisms which better enable support at the local level, including action through non-governmental organizations, in order to promote the replicability of successful pilot programme activities where relevant;

(c) increased flexibility in project design, funding and implementation in keeping with the experimental, iterative approach indicated for participatory action at the local community level; and

(d) as appropriate, administrative and budgetary procedures that increase the efficiency of cooperation and of support programmes.

2. In providing such support to affected developing country Parties, priority shall be given to African country Parties and to least developed country Parties.

| Article 14 | Coordination in the elaboration and implementation of action programmes |

1. The Parties shall work closely together, directly and through relevant intergovernmental organizations, in the elaboration and implementation of action programmes.

2. The Parties shall develop operational mechanisms, particularly at the national and field levels, to ensure the fullest possible coordination among developed country Parties, developing country Parties and relevant intergovernmental and non-governmental organizations, in order to avoid duplication, harmonize interventions and approaches, and maximize the impact of assistance. In affected developing country Parties, priority will be given to coordinating activities related to international cooperation in order to maximize the efficient use of resources, to ensure responsive assistance, and to facilitate the implementation of national action programmes and priorities under this Convention.

| Article 15 | Regional implementation annexes |

Elements for incorporation in action programmes shall be selected and adapted to the socio-economic, geographical and climatic factors applicable to affected country Parties or regions, as well as to their level of development. Guidelines for the preparation of action programmes and their exact focus and content for particular subregions and regions are set out in the regional implementation annexes.

| Section 2: | Scientific and technical cooperation |

| Article 16 | Information collection, analysis and exchange |

The Parties agree, according to their respective capabilities, to integrate and coordinate the collection, analysis and exchange of relevant short term and long term data and information to ensure systematic observation of land degradation in affected areas and to understand better and assess the processes and effects of drought and desertification. This would help accomplish, inter alia, early warning and advance planning for periods of adverse climatic variation in a form suited for practical application by users at all levels, including especially local populations. To this end, they shall, as appropriate:

(a) facilitate and strengthen the functioning of the global network of institutions and facilities for the collection, analysis and exchange of information, as well as for systematic observation at all levels, which shall, inter alia:

(i) aim to use compatible standards and systems;

(ii) encompass relevant data and stations, including in remote areas;

(iii) use and disseminate modern technology for data collection, transmission and assessment on land degradation; and

(iv) link national, subregional and regional data and information centres more closely with global information sources;

(b) ensure that the collection, analysis and exchange of information address the needs of local communities and those of decision makers, with a view to resolving specific problems, and that local communities are involved in these activities;

(c) support and further develop bilateral and multilateral programmes and projects aimed at defining, conducting, assessing and financing the collection, analysis and exchange of data and information, including, inter alia, integrated sets of physical, biological, social and economic indicators;

(d) make full use of the expertise of competent intergovernmental and non-governmental organizations, particularly to disseminate relevant information and experiences among target groups in different regions;

(e) give full weight to the collection, analysis and exchange of socio-economic data, and their integration with physical and biological data;

(f) exchange and make fully, openly and promptly available information from all publicly available sources relevant to combating desertification and mitigating the effects of drought; and

(g) subject to their respective national legislation and/or policies, exchange information on local and traditional knowledge, ensuring adequate protection for it and providing appropriate return from the benefits derived from it, on an equitable basis and on mutually agreed terms, to the local populations concerned.

Article 17   Research and development

1. The Parties undertake, according to their respective capabilities, to promote technical and scientific cooperation in the fields of combating desertification and mitigating the effects of drought through appropriate national, subregional, regional and international institutions. To this end, they shall support research activities that:

(a) contribute to increased knowledge of the processes leading to desertification and drought and the impact of, and distinction between, causal factors, both natural and human, with a view to combating desertification and mitigating the effects of drought, and achieving improved productivity as well as sustainable use and management of resources;

(b) respond to well defined objectives, address the specific needs of local populations and lead to the identification and implementation of solutions that improve the living standards of people in affected areas;

(c) protect, integrate, enhance and validate traditional and local knowledge, know-how and practices, ensuring, subject to their respective national legislation and/or policies, that the owners of that knowledge will directly benefit on an equitable basis and on mutually agreed terms from any commercial utilization of it or from any technological development derived from that knowledge;

(d) develop and strengthen national, subregional and regional research capabilities in affected developing country Parties, particularly in Africa, including the development of local skills and the strengthening of appropriate capacities, especially in countries with a weak research base, giving particular attention to multidisciplinary and participative socio- economic research;

(e) take into account, where relevant, the relationship between poverty, migration caused by environmental factors, and desertification;

(f) promote the conduct of joint research programmes between national, subregional, regional and international research organizations, in both the public and private sectors, for the development of improved, affordable and accessible technologies for sustainable development through effective participation of local populations and communities; and

(g) enhance the availability of water resources in affected areas, by means of, inter alia, cloud-seeding.

2. Research priorities for particular regions and subregions, reflecting different local conditions, should be included in action programmes. The Conference of the Parties shall review research priorities periodically on the advice of the Committee on Science and Technology.

Article 18   Transfer, acquisition, adaptation and development of technology

1. The Parties undertake, as mutually agreed and in accordance with their respective national legislation and/or policies, to promote, finance and/or facilitate the financing of the transfer, acquisition, adaptation and development of environmentally sound, economically viable and socially acceptable technologies relevant to combating desertification and/or mitigating the effects of drought, with a view to contributing to the achievement of sustainable development in affected areas. Such cooperation shall be conducted bilaterally or multilaterally, as appropriate,

making full use of the expertise of intergovernmental and non-governmental organizations. The Parties shall, in particular:

(a) fully utilize relevant existing national, subregional, regional and international information systems and clearing-houses for the dissemination of information on available technologies, their sources, their environmental risks and the broad terms under which they may be acquired;

(b) facilitate access, in particular by affected developing country Parties, on favourable terms, including on concessional and preferential terms, as mutually agreed, taking into account the need to protect intellectual property rights, to technologies most suitable to practical application for specific needs of local populations, paying special attention to the social, cultural, economic and environmental impact of such technology;

(c) facilitate technology cooperation among affected country Parties through financial assistance or other appropriate means;

(d) extend technology cooperation with affected developing country Parties, including, where relevant, joint ventures, especially to sectors which foster alternative livelihoods; and

(e) take appropriate measures to create domestic market conditions and incentives, fiscal or otherwise, conducive to the development, transfer, acquisition and adaptation of suitable technology, knowledge, know-how and practices, including measures to ensure adequate and effective protection of intellectual property rights.

2. The Parties shall, according to their respective capabilities, and subject to their respective national legislation and/or policies, protect, promote and use in particular relevant traditional and local technology, knowledge, know-how and practices and, to that end, they undertake to:

(a) make inventories of such technology, knowledge, know-how and practices and their potential uses with the participation of local populations, and disseminate such information, where appropriate, in cooperation with relevant intergovernmental and non-governmental organizations;

(b) ensure that such technology, knowledge, know-how and practices are adequately protected and that local populations benefit directly, on an equitable basis and as mutually agreed, from any commercial utilization of them or from any technological development derived therefrom;

(c) encourage and actively support the improvement and dissemination of such technology, knowledge, know-how and practices or of the development of new technology based on them; and

(d) facilitate, as appropriate, the adaptation of such technology, knowledge, know-how and practices to wideuse and integrate them with modern technology, as appropriate.

Section 3: Supporting measures

Article 19   Capacity building, education and public awareness

1. The Parties recognize the significance of capacity building -- that is to say, institution building, training and development of relevant local and national capacities -- in efforts to combat desertification and mitigate the effects of drought. They shall promote, as appropriate, capacity- building:

(a) through the full participation at all levels of local people, particularly at the local level, especially women and youth, with the cooperation of non-governmental and local organizations;

(b) by strengthening training and research capacity at the national level in the field of desertification and drought;

(c) by establishing and/or strengthening support and extension services to disseminate relevant technology methods and techniques more effectively, and by training field agents and members of rural organizations in participatory approaches for the conservation and sustainable use of natural resources;

(d) by fostering the use and dissemination of the knowledge, know-how and practices of local people in technical cooperation programmes, wherever possible;

(e) by adapting, where necessary, relevant environmentally sound technology and traditional methods of agriculture and pastoralism to modern socio-economic conditions;

(f) by providing appropriate training and technology in the use of alternative energy sources, particularly renewable energy resources, aimed particularly at reducing dependence on wood for fuel;

(g) through cooperation, as mutually agreed, to strengthen the capacity of affected developing country Parties to develop and implement programmes in the field of collection, analysis and exchange of information pursuant to article16;

(h) through innovative ways of promoting alternative livelihoods, including training in new skills;

(i) by training of decision makers, managers, and personnel who are responsible for the collection and analysis of data for the dissemination and use of early warning information on drought conditions and for food production;

(j) through more effective operation of existing national institutions and legal frameworks and, where necessary, creation of new ones, along with strengthening of strategic planning and management; and

(k) by means of exchange visitor programmes to enhance capacity building in affected country Parties through a long-term, interactive process of learning and study.

2. Affected developing country Parties shall conduct, in cooperation with other Parties and competent intergovernmental and non-governmental organizations, as appropriate, an interdisciplinary review of available capacity and facilities at the local and national levels, and the potential for strengthening them.

3. The Parties shall cooperate with each other and through competent intergovernmental organizations, as well as with non-governmental organizations, in undertaking and supporting public awareness and educational programmes in both affected and, where relevant, unaffected country Parties to promote understanding of the causes and effects of desertification and drought and of the importance of meeting the objective of this Convention. To that end, they shall:

(a) organize awareness campaigns for the general public;

(b) promote, on a permanent basis, access by the public to relevant information, and wide public participation in education and awareness activities;

(c) encourage the establishment of associations that contribute to public awareness;

(d) develop and exchange educational and public awareness material, where possible in local languages, exchange and second experts to train personnel of affected developing country Parties in carrying out relevant education and awareness programmes, and fully utilize relevant educational material available in competent international bodies;

(e) assess educational needs in affected areas, elaborate appropriate school curricula and expand, as needed, educational and adult literacy programmes and opportunities for all, in particular for girls and women, on the identification, conservation and sustainable use and management of the natural resources of affected areas; and

(f) develop interdisciplinary participatory programmes integrating desertification and drought awareness into educational systems and in non-formal, adult, distance and practical educational programmes.

4. The Conference of the Parties shall establish and/or strengthen networks of regional education and training centres to combat desertification and mitigate the effects of drought. These networks shall be coordinated by an institution created or designated for that purpose, in order to train scientific, technical and management personnel and to strengthen existing institutions responsible for education and training in affected country Parties, where appropriate, with a view to harmonizing programmes and to organizing exchanges of experience among them. These networks shall cooperate closely with relevant intergovernmental and non-governmental organizations to avoid duplication of effort.

Article 20   Financial resources

1. Given the central importance of financing to the achievement of the objective of the Convention, the Parties, taking into account their capabilities, shall make every effort to ensure that adequate financial resources are available for programmes to combat desertification and mitigate the effects of drought.

2. In this connection, developed country Parties, while giving priority to affected African country Parties without neglecting affected developing country Parties in other regions, in accordance with article 7, undertake to:

(a) mobilize substantial financial resources, including grants and concessional loans, in order to support the implementation of programmes to combat desertification and mitigate the effects of drought;

(b) promote the mobilization of adequate, timely and predictable financial resources, including new and additional funding from the Global Environment Facility of the agreed incremental costs of those activities concerning desertification that relate to its four focal areas, in conformity with the relevant provisions of the Instrument establishing the Global Environment Facility;

(c) facilitate through international cooperation the transfer of technology, knowledge and know-how; and

(d) explore, in cooperation with affected developing country Parties, innovative methods and incentives for mobilizing and channeling resources, including those of foundations, non- governmental organizations and other private sector entities, particularly debt swaps and other innovative means which increase financing by reducing the external debt burden of affected developing country Parties, particularly those in Africa.

3. Affected developing country Parties, taking into account their capabilities, undertake to mobilize adequate financial resources for the implementation of their national action programmes.

4. In mobilizing financial resources, the Parties shall seek full use and continued qualitative improvement of all national, bilateral and multilateral funding sources and mechanisms, using consortia, joint programmes and parallel financing, and shall seek to involve private sector funding sources and mechanisms, including those of non-governmental organizations. To this end, the Parties shall fully utilize the operational mechanisms developed pursuant to article 14.

5. In order to mobilize the financial resources necessary for affected developing country Parties to combat desertification and mitigate the effects of drought, the Parties shall:

(a) rationalize and strengthen the management of resources already allocated for combating desertification and mitigating the effects of drought by using them more effectively and efficiently, assessing their successes and shortcomings, removing hindrances to their effective use and, where necessary, reorienting programmes in light of the integrated long- term approach adopted pursuant to this Convention;

(b) give due priority and attention within the governing bodies of multilateral financial institutions, facilities and funds, including regional development banks and funds, to supporting affected developing country Parties, particularly those in Africa, in activities which advance implementation of the Convention, notably action programmes they undertake in the framework of regional implementation annexes; and

(c) examine ways in which regional and subregional cooperation can be strengthened to support efforts undertaken at the national level.

6. Other Parties are encouraged to provide, on a voluntary basis, knowledge, know-how and techniques related to desertification and/or financial resources to affected developing country Parties.

7. The full implementation by affected developing country Parties, particularly those in Africa, of their obligations under the Convention will be greatly assisted by the fulfillment by developed country Parties of their obligations under the Convention, including in particular those regarding financial resources and transfer of technology. In fulfilling their obligations, developed country Parties should take fully into account that economic and social development and poverty eradication are the first priorities of affected developing country Parties, particularly those in Africa.

Article 21   Financial mechanisms

1. The Conference of the Parties shall promote the availability of financial mechanisms and shall encourage such mechanisms to seek to maximize the availability of funding for affected developing country Parties, particularly those in Africa, to implement the Convention. To this end, the Conference of the Parties shall consider for adoption inter alia approaches and policies that:

(a) facilitate the provision of necessary funding at the national, subregional, regional and global levels for activities pursuant to relevant provisions of the Convention;

(b) promote multiple-source funding approaches, mechanisms and arrangements and their assessment, consistent with article 20;

(c) provide on a regular basis, to interested Parties and relevant intergovernmental and non- governmental organizations, information on available sources of funds and on funding patterns in order to facilitate coordination among them;

(d) facilitate the establishment, as appropriate, of mechanisms, such as national desertification funds, including those involving the participation of non-governmental organizations, to channel financial resources rapidly and efficiently to the local level in affected developing country Parties; and

(e) strengthen existing funds and financial mechanisms at the subregional and regional levels, particularly in Africa, to support more effectively the implementation of the Convention.

2. The Conference of the Parties shall also encourage the provision, through various mechanisms within the United Nations system and through multilateral financial institutions, of support at the national, subregional and regional levels to activities that enable developing country Parties to meet their obligations under the Convention.

3. Affected developing country Parties shall utilize, and where necessary, establish and/or strengthen, national coordinating mechanisms, integrated in national development programmes, that would ensure the efficient use of all

available financial resources. They shall also utilize participatory processes involving non-governmental organizations, local groups and the private sector, in raising funds, in elaborating as well as implementing programmes and in assuring access to funding by groups at the local level. These actions can be enhanced by improved coordination and flexible programming on the part of those providing assistance.

4. In order to increase the effectiveness and efficiency of existing financial mechanisms, a Global Mechanism to promote actions leading to the mobilization and channeling of substantial financial resources, including for the transfer of technology, on a grant basis, and/or on concessional or other terms, to affected developing country Parties, is hereby established. This Global Mechanism shall function under the authority and guidance of the Conference of the Parties and be accountable to it.

5. The Conference of the Parties shall identify, at its first ordinary session, an organization to house the Global Mechanism. The Conference of the Parties and the organization it has identified shall agree upon modalities for this Global Mechanism to ensure inter alia that such Mechanism:

(a) identifies and draws up an inventory of relevant bilateral and multilateral cooperation programmes that are available to implement the Convention;

(b) provides advice, on request, to Parties on innovative methods of financing and sources of financial assistance and on improving the coordination of cooperation activities at the national level;

(c) provides interested Parties and relevant intergovernmental and non-governmental organizations with information on available sources of funds and on funding patterns in order to facilitate coordination among them; and

(d) reports to the Conference of the Parties, beginning at its second ordinary session, on its activities.

6. The Conference of the Parties shall, at its first session, make appropriate arrangements with the organization it has identified to house the Global Mechanism for the administrative operations of such Mechanism, drawing to the extent possible on existing budgetary and human resources.

7. The Conference of the Parties shall, at its third ordinary session, review the policies, operational modalities and activities of the Global Mechanism accountable to it pursuant to paragraph 4, taking into account the provisions of article 7. On the basis of this review, it shall consider and take appropriate action.

PART IV   INSTITUTIONS

Article 22   Conference of the Parties

1. A Conference of the Parties is hereby established.

2. The Conference of the Parties is the supreme body of the Convention. It shall make, within its mandate, the decisions necessary to promote its effective implementation. In particular, it shall:

(a) regularly review the implementation of the Convention and the functioning of its institutional arrangements in the light of the experience gained at the national, subregional, regional and international levels and on the basis of the evolution of scientific and technological knowledge;

(b) promote and facilitate the exchange of information on measures adopted by the Parties, and determine the form and timetable for transmitting the information to be submitted pursuant to article 26, review the reports and make recommendations on them;

(c) establish such subsidiary bodies as are deemed necessary for the implementation of the Convention;

(d) review reports submitted by its subsidiary bodies and provide guidance to them;

(e) agree upon and adopt, by consensus, rules of procedure and financial rules for itself and any subsidiary bodies;

(f) adopt amendments to the Convention pursuant to articles 30 and 31;

(g) approve a programme and budget for its activities, including those of its subsidiary bodies, and undertake necessary arrangements for their financing;

(h) as appropriate, seek the cooperation of, and utilize the services of and information provided by, competent bodies or agencies, whether national or international, intergovernmental or non-governmental;

(i) promote and strengthen the relationship with other relevant conventions while avoiding duplication of effort; and

(j) exercise such other functions as may be necessary for the achievement of the objective of the Convention.

3. The Conference of the Parties shall, at its first session, adopt its own rules of procedure, by consensus, which shall include decision-making procedures for matters not already covered by decision-making procedures stipulated in the Convention. Such procedures may include specified majorities required for the adoption of particular decisions.

4. The first session of the Conference of the Parties shall be convened by the interim secretariat referred to in article 35 and shall take place not later than one year after the date of entry into force of the Convention. Unless otherwise decided by the Conference of the Parties, the second, third and fourth ordinary sessions shall be held yearly, and thereafter, ordinary sessions shall be held every two years.

5. Extraordinary sessions of the Conference of the Parties shall be held at such other times as may be decided either by the Conference of the Parties in ordinary session or at the written request of any Party, provided that, within three months of the request being communicated to the Parties by the Permanent Secretariat, it is supported by at least one third of the Parties.

6. At each ordinary session, the Conference of the Parties shall elect a Bureau. The structure and functions of the Bureau shall be determined in the rules of procedure. In appointing the Bureau, due regard shall be paid to the need to ensure equitable geographical distribution and adequate representation of affected country Parties, particularly those in Africa.

7. The United Nations, its specialized agencies and any State member thereof or observers thereto not Party to the Convention, may be represented at sessions of the Conference of the Parties as observers. Any body or agency, whether national or international, governmental or non-governmental, which is qualified in matters covered by the Convention, and which has informed the Permanent Secretariat of its wish to be represented at a session of the Conference of the Parties as an observer, may be so admitted unless at least one third of the Parties present object. The admission and participation of observers shall be subject to the rules of procedure adopted by the Conference of the Parties.

8. The Conference of the Parties may request competent national and international organizations which have relevant expertise to provide it with information relevant to article 16, paragraph (g), article 17, paragraph 1 (c) and article 18, paragraph 2(b).

Article 23   Permanent Secretariat

1. A Permanent Secretariat is hereby established.

2. The functions of the Permanent Secretariat shall be:
>   (a) to make arrangements for sessions of the Conference of the Parties and its subsidiary bodies established under the Convention and to provide them with services as required;
>   (b) to compile and transmit reports submitted to it;
>   (c) to facilitate assistance to affected developing country Parties, on request, particularly those in Africa, in the compilation and communication of information required under the Convention;
>   (d) to coordinate its activities with the secretariats of other relevant international bodies and conventions;
>   (e) to enter, under the guidance of the Conference of the Parties, into such administrative and contractual arrangements as may be required for the effective discharge of its functions;
>   (f) to prepare reports on the execution of its functions under this Convention and present them to the Conference of the Parties; and
>   (g) to perform such other secretariat functions as may be determined by the Conference of the Parties.

3. The Conference of the Parties, at its first session, shall designate a Permanent Secretariat and make arrangements for its functioning.

Article 24   Committee on Science and Technology

1. A Committee on Science and Technology is hereby established as a subsidiary body of the Conference of the Parties to provide it with information and advice on scientific and technological matters relating to combating desertification and mitigating the effects of drought. The Committee shall meet in conjunction with the ordinary

sessions of the Conference of the Parties and shall be multidisciplinary and open to the participation of all Parties. It shall be composed of government representatives competent in the relevant fields of expertise. The Conference of the Parties shall decide, at its first session, on the terms of reference of the Committee.

2. The Conference of the Parties shall establish and maintain a roster of independent experts with expertise and experience in the relevant fields. The roster shall be based on nominations received in writing from the Parties, taking into account the need for a multidisciplinary approach and broad geographical representation.

3. The Conference of the Parties may, as necessary, appoint ad hoc panels to provide it, through the Committee, with information and advice on specific issues regarding the state of the art in fields of science and technology relevant to combating desertification and mitigating the effects of drought. These panels shall be composed of experts whose names are taken from the roster, taking into account the need for a multidisciplinary approach and broad geographical representation. These experts shall have scientific backgrounds and field experience and shall be appointed by the Conference of the Parties on the recommendation of the Committee. The Conference of the Parties shall decide on the terms of reference and the modalities of work of these panels.

Article 25   **Networking of institutions, agencies and bodies**

1. The Committee on Science and Technology shall, under the supervision of the Conference of the Parties, make provision for the undertaking of a survey and evaluation of the relevant existing networks, institutions, agencies and bodies willing to become units of a network. Such a network shall support the implementation of the Convention.

2. On the basis of the results of the survey and evaluation referred to in paragraph 1, the Committee on Science and Technology shall make recommendations to the Conference of the Parties on ways and means to facilitate and strengthen networking of the units at the local, national and other levels, with a view to ensuring that the thematic needs set out in articles 16 to 19 are addressed.

3. Taking into account these recommendations, the Conference of the Parties shall:
    (a) identify those national, subregional, regional and international units that are most appropriate for networking, and recommend operational procedures, and a time frame, for them; and
    (b) identify the units best suited to facilitating and strengthening such networking at all levels.

PART V   **PROCEDURES**

Article 26   **Communication of information**

1. Each Party shall communicate to the Conference of the Parties for consideration at its ordinary sessions, through the Permanent Secretariat, reports on the measures which it has taken for the implementation of the Convention. The Conference of the Parties shall determine the timetable for submission and the format of such reports.

2. Affected country Parties shall provide a description of the strategies established pursuant to article 5 and of any relevant information on their implementation.

3. Affected country Parties which implement action programmes pursuant to articles 9 to 15 shall provide a detailed description of the programmes and of their implementation.

4. Any group of affected country Parties may make a joint communication on measures taken at the subregional and/or regional levels in the framework of action programmes.

5. Developed country Parties shall report on measures taken to assist in the preparation and implementation of action programmes, including information on the financial resources they have provided, or are providing, under the Convention.

6. Information communicated pursuant to paragraphs 1 to 4 shall be transmitted by the Permanent Secretariat as soon as possible to the Conference of the Parties and to any relevant subsidiary body.

7. The Conference of the Parties shall facilitate the provision to affected developing countries, particularly those in Africa, on request, of technical and financial support in compiling and communicating information in accordance with this article, as well as identifying the technical and financial needs associated with action programmes.

| Article 27 | Measures to resolve questions on implementation |

The Conference of the Parties shall consider and adopt procedures and institutional mechanisms for the resolution of questions that may arise with regard to the implementation of the Convention.

| Article 28 | Settlement of disputes |

1. Parties shall settle any dispute between them concerning the interpretation or application of the Convention through negotiation or other peaceful means of their own choice.

2. When ratifying, accepting, approving, or acceding to the Convention, or at any time thereafter, a Party which is not a regional economic integration organization may declare in a written instrument submitted to the Depositary that, in respect of any dispute concerning the interpretation or application of the Convention, it recognizes one or both of the following means of dispute settlement as compulsory in relation to any Party accepting the same obligation:

(a) arbitration in accordance with procedures adopted by the Conference of the Parties in an annex as soon as practicable;

(b) submission of the dispute to the International Court of Justice.

3. A Party which is a regional economic integration organization may make a declaration with like effect in relation to arbitration in accordance with the procedure referred to in paragraph 2 (a).

4. A declaration made pursuant to paragraph 2 shall remain in force until it expires in accordance with its terms or until three months after written notice of its revocation has been deposited with the Depositary.

5. The expiry of a declaration, a notice of revocation or a new declaration shall not in any way affect proceedings pending before an arbitral tribunal or the International Court of Justice unless the Parties to the dispute otherwise agree.

6. If the Parties to a dispute have not accepted the same or any procedure pursuant to paragraph 2 and if they have not been able to settle their dispute within twelve months following notification by one Party to another that a dispute exists between them, the dispute shall be submitted to conciliation at the request of any Party to the dispute, in accordance with procedures adopted by the Conference of the Parties in an annex as soon as practicable.

| Article 29 | Status of annexes |

1. Annexes form an integral part of the Convention and, unless expressly provided otherwise, a reference to the Convention also constitutes a reference to its annexes.

2. The Parties shall interpret the provisions of the annexes in a manner that is in conformity with their rights and obligations under the articles of this Convention.

| Article 30 | Amendments to the Convention |

1. Any Party may propose amendments to the Convention.

2. Amendments to the Convention shall be adopted at an ordinary session of the Conference of the Parties. The text of any proposed amendment shall be communicated to the Parties by the Permanent Secretariat at least six months before the meeting at which it is proposed for adoption. The Permanent Secretariat shall also communicate proposed amendments to the signatories to the Convention.

3. The Parties shall make every effort to reach agreement on any proposed amendment to the Convention by consensus. If all efforts at consensus have been exhausted and no agreement reached, the amendment shall, as a last

resort, be adopted by a two-thirds majority vote of the Parties present and voting at the meeting. The adopted amendment shall be communicated by the Permanent Secretariat to the Depositary, who shall circulate it to all Parties for their ratification, acceptance, approval or accession.

4. Instruments of ratification, acceptance, approval or accession in respect of an amendment shall be deposited with the Depositary. An amendment adopted pursuant to paragraph 3 shall enter into force for those Parties having accepted it on the ninetieth day after the date of receipt by the Depositary of an instrument of ratification, acceptance, approval or accession by at least two thirds of the Parties to the Convention which were Parties at the time of the adoption of the amendment.

5. The amendment shall enter into force for any other Party on the ninetieth day after the date on which that Party deposits with the Depositary its instrument of ratification, acceptance or approval of, or accession to the said amendment.

6. For the purposes of this article and article 31, "Parties present and voting" means Parties present and casting an affirmative or negative vote.

Article 31   Adoption and amendment of annexes

1. Any additional annex to the Convention and any amendment to an annex shall be proposed and adopted in accordance with the procedure for amendment of the Convention set forth in article 30, provided that, in adopting an additional regional implementation annex or amendment to any regional implementation annex, the majority provided for in that article shall include a two-thirds majority vote of the Parties of the region concerned present and voting. The adoption or amendment of an annex shall be communicated by the Depositary to all Parties.

2. An annex, other than an additional regional implementation annex, or an amendment to an annex, other than an amendment to any regional implementation annex, that has been adopted in accordance with paragraph 1, shall enter into force for all Parties to the Convention six months after the date of communication by the Depositary to such Parties of the adoption of such annex or amendment, except for those Parties that have notified the Depositary in writing within that period of their non- acceptance of such annex or amendment. Such annex or amendment shall enter into force for Parties which withdraw their notification of non-acceptance on the ninetieth day after the date on which withdrawal of such notification has been received by the Depositary.

3. An additional regional implementation annex or amendment to any regional implementation annex that has been adopted in accordance with paragraph 1, shall enter into force for all Parties to the Convention six months after the date of the communication by the Depositary to such Parties of the adoption of such annex or amendment, except with respect to:

    (a) any Party that has notified the Depositary in writing, within such six month period, of its non-acceptance of that additional regional implementation annex or of the amendment to the regional implementation annex, in which case such annex or amendment shall enter into force for Parties which withdraw their notification of non-acceptance on the ninetieth day after the date on which withdrawal of such notification has been received by the Depositary; and

    (b) any Party that has made a declaration with respect to additional regional implementation annexes or amendments to regional implementation annexes in accordance with article 34, paragraph 4, in which case any such annex or amendment shall enter into force for such a Party on the ninetieth day after the date of deposit with the Depositary of its instrument of ratification, acceptance, approval or accession with respect to such annex or amendment.

4. If the adoption of an annex or an amendment to an annex involves an amendment to the Convention, that annex or amendment to an annex shall not enter into force until such time as the amendment to the Convention enters into force.

Article 32   Right to vote

1. Except as provided for in paragraph 2, each Party to the Convention shall have one vote.

2. Regional economic integration organizations, in matters within their competence, shall exercise their right to vote with a number of votes equal to the number of their member States that are Parties to the Convention. Such an organization shall not exercise its right to vote if any of its member States exercises its right, and vice versa.

PART VI   FINAL PROVISIONS

Article 33   Signature

This Convention shall be opened for signature at Paris, on 14-15 October 1994, by States Members of the United Nations or any of its specialized agencies or that are Parties to the Statute of the International Court of Justice and by regional economic integration organizations. It shall remain open for signature, thereafter, at the United Nations Headquarters in New York until 13 October 1995.

Article 34   Ratification, acceptance, approval and accession

1. The Convention shall be subject to ratification, acceptance, approval or accession by States and by regional economic integration organizations. It shall be open for accession from the day after the date on which the Convention is closed for signature. Instruments of ratification, acceptance, approval or accession shall be deposited with the Depositary.

2. Any regional economic integration organization which becomes a Party to the Convention without any of its member States being a Party to the Convention shall be bound by all the obligations under the Convention. Where one or more member States of such an organization are also Party to the Convention, the organization and its member States shall decide on their respective responsibilities for the performance of their obligations under the Convention. In such cases, the organization and the member States shall not be entitled to exercise rights under the Convention concurrently.

3. In their instruments of ratification, acceptance, approval or accession, regional economic integration organizations shall declare the extent of their competence with respect to the matters governed by the Convention. They shall also promptly inform the Depositary, who shall in turn inform the Parties, of any substantial modification in the extent of their competence.

4. In its instrument of ratification, acceptance, approval or accession, any Party may declare that, with respect to it, any additional regional implementation annex or any amendment to any regional implementation annex shall enter into force only upon the deposit of its instrument of ratification, acceptance, approval or accession with respect thereto.

Article 35   Interim arrangements

The secretariat functions referred to in article 23 will be carried out on an interim basis by the secretariat established by the General Assembly of the United Nations in its resolution 47/188 of 22 December 1992, until the completion of the first session of the Conference of the Parties.

Article 36   Entry into force

1. The Convention shall enter into force on the ninetieth day after the date of deposit of the fiftieth instrument of ratification, acceptance, approval or accession.

2. For each State or regional economic integration organization ratifying, accepting, approving or acceding to the Convention after the deposit of the fiftieth instrument of ratification, acceptance, approval or accession, the Convention shall enter into force on the ninetieth day after the date of deposit by such State or regional economic integration organization of its instrument of ratification, acceptance, approval or accession.

3. For the purposes of paragraphs 1 and 2, any instrument deposited by a regional economic integration organization shall not be counted as additional to those deposited by States members of the organization.

Article 37   Reservations

No reservations may be made to this Convention.

Article 38   Withdrawal

1. At any time after three years from the date on which the Convention has entered into force for a Party, that Party may withdraw from the Convention by giving written notification to the Depositary.

2. Any such withdrawal shall take effect upon expiry of one year from the date of receipt by the Depositary of the notification of withdrawal, or on such later date as may be specified in the notification of withdrawal.

Article 39   Depositary

The Secretary-General of the United Nations shall be the Depositary of the Convention.

Article 40   Authentic texts

The original of the present Convention, of which the Arabic, Chinese, English, French, Russian and Spanish texts are equally authentic, shall be deposited with the Secretary-General of the United Nations.

IN WITNESS WHEREOF the undersigned, being duly authorized to that effect, have signed the present Convention.

DONE AT Paris, this 17th day of June one thousand nine hundred and ninety-four.

ANNEX I   REGIONAL IMPLEMENTATION ANNEX FOR AFRICA

Article 1   Scope

This Annex applies to Africa, in relation to each Party and in conformity with the Convention, in particular its article 7, for the purpose of combating desertification and/or mitigating the effects of drought in its arid, semi-arid and dry sub-humid areas.

Article 2   Purpose

The purpose of this Annex, at the national, subregional and regional levels in Africa and in the light of its particular conditions, is to:
          (a) identify measures and arrangements, including the nature and processes of assistance provided by developed country Parties, in accordance with the relevant provisions of the Convention;
          (b) provide for the efficient and practical implementation of the Convention to address conditions specific to Africa; and
          (c) promote processes and activities relating to combating desertification and/or mitigating the effects of drought within the arid, semi-arid and dry sub-humid areas of Africa.

Article 3   Particular conditions of the
                   African region

In carrying out their obligations under the Convention, the Parties shall, in the implementation of this Annex, adopt a basic approach that takes into consideration the following particular conditions of Africa:
          (a) the high proportion of arid, semi-arid and dry sub-humid areas;
          (b) the substantial number of countries and populations adversely affected by desertification and by the frequent recurrence of severe drought;
          (c) the large number of affected countries that are landlocked;

(d) the widespread poverty prevalent in most affected countries, the large number of least developed countries among them, and their need for significant amounts of external assistance, in the form of grants and loans on concessional terms, to pursue their development objectives;

(e) the difficult socio-economic conditions, exacerbated by deteriorating and fluctuating terms of trade, external indebtedness and political instability, which induce internal, regional and international migrations;

(f) the heavy reliance of populations on natural resources for subsistence which, compounded by the effects of demographic trends and factors, a weak technological base and unsustainable production practices, contributes to serious resource degradation;

(g) the insufficient institutional and legal frameworks, the weak infrastructural base and the insufficient scientific, technical and educational capacity, leading to substantial capacity building requirements; and

(h) the central role of actions to combat desertification and/or mitigate the effects of drought in the national development priorities of affected African countries.

| Article 4 | Commitments and obligations of African country Parties |

1. In accordance with their respective capabilities, African country Parties undertake to:

(a) adopt the combating of desertification and/or the mitigation of the effects of drought as a central strategy in their efforts to eradicate poverty;

(b) promote regional cooperation and integration, in a spirit of solidarity and partnership based on mutual interest, in programmes and activities to combat desertification and/or mitigate the effects of drought;

(c) rationalize and strengthen existing institutions concerned with desertification and drought and involve other existing institutions, as appropriate, in order to make them more effective and to ensure more efficient use of resources;

(d) promote the exchange of information on appropriate technology, knowledge, know-how and practices between and among them; and

(e) develop contingency plans for mitigating the effects of drought in areas degraded by desertification and/or drought.

2. Pursuant to the general and specific obligations set out in articles 4 and 5 of the Convention, affected African country Parties shall aim to:

(a) make appropriate financial allocations from their national budgets consistent with national conditions and capabilities and reflecting the new priority Africa has accorded to the phenomenon of desertification and/or drought;

(b) sustain and strengthen reforms currently in progress toward greater decentralization and resource tenure as well as reinforce participation of local populations and communities; and

(c) identify and mobilize new and additional national financial resources, and expand, as a matter of priority, existing national capabilities and facilities to mobilize domestic financial resources.

| Article 5 | Commitments and obligations of developed country Parties |

1. In fulfilling their obligations pursuant to articles 4, 6 and 7 of the Convention, developed country Parties shall give priority to affected African country Parties and, in this context, shall:

(a) assist them to combat desertification and/or mitigate the effects of drought by, inter alia, providing and/or facilitating access to financial and/or other resources, and promoting, financing and/or facilitating the financing of the transfer, adaptation and access to appropriate environmental technologies and know-how, as mutually agreed and in accordance with national policies, taking into account their adoption of poverty eradication as a central strategy;

(b) continue to allocate significant resources and/or increase resources to combat desertification and/or mitigate the effects of drought; and

(c) assist them in strengthening capacities to enable them to improve their institutional frameworks, as well as their scientific and technical capabilities, information collection and analysis, and research and development for the purpose of combating desertification and/or mitigating the effects of drought.

2. Other country Parties may provide, on a voluntary basis, technology, knowledge and know-how relating to desertification and/or financial resources, to affected African country Parties. The transfer of such knowledge, know-how and techniques is facilitated by international cooperation.

Article 6   **Strategic planning framework for
sustainable development**

1. National action programmes shall be a central and integral part of a broader process of formulating national policies for the sustainable development of affected African country Parties.

2. A consultative and participatory process involving appropriate levels of government, local populations, communities and non-governmental organizations shall be undertaken to provide guidance on a strategy with flexible planning to allow maximum participation from local populations and communities. As appropriate, bilateral and multilateral assistance agencies may be involved in this process at the request of an affected African country Party.

Article 7   **Timetable for preparation of
action programmes**

Pending entry into force of this Convention, the African country Parties, in cooperation with other members of the international community, as appropriate, shall, to the extent possible, provisionally apply those provisions of the Convention relating to the preparation of national, subregional and regional action programmes.

Article 8   **Content of national action
programmes**

1. Consistent with article 10 of the Convention, the overall strategy of national action programmes shall emphasize integrated local development programmes for affected areas, based on participatory mechanisms and on integration of strategies for poverty eradication into efforts to combat desertification and mitigate the effects of drought. The programmes shall aim at strengthening the capacity of local authorities and ensuring the active involvement of local populations, communities and groups, with emphasis on education and training, mobilization of non-governmental organizations with proven expertise and strengthening of decentralized governmental structures.

2. National action programmes shall, as appropriate, include the following general features:
         (a) the use, in developing and implementing national action programmes, of past experiences in combating desertification and/or mitigating the effects of drought, taking into account social, economic and ecological conditions;
         (b) the identification of factors contributing to desertification and/or drought and the resources and capacities available and required, and the setting up of appropriate policies and institutional and other responses and measures necessary to combat those phenomena and/or mitigate their effects; and
         (c) the increase in participation of local populations and communities, including women, farmers and pastoralists, and delegation to them of more responsibility for management.

3. National action programmes shall also, as appropriate, include the following:
         (a) measures to improve the economic environment with a view to eradicating poverty:
                 (i) increasing incomes and employment opportunities, especially for the poorest members of the community, by:
                 - developing markets for farm and livestock products;
                 - creating financial instruments suited to local needs;
                 - encouraging diversification in agriculture and the setting-up of agricultural enterprises; and
                 - developing economic activities of a para-agricultural or non- agricultural type;
                 (ii) improving the long-term prospects of rural economies by the creation of:
                 - incentives for productive investment and access to the means of production; and
                 - price and tax policies and commercial practices that promote growth;
                 (iii) defining and applying population and migration policies to reduce population pressure on land; and
                 (iv) promoting the use of drought resistant crops and the application of integrated dry- land farming systems for food security purposes;
         (b) measures to conserve natural resources:
                 (i) ensuring integrated and sustainable management of natural resources, including:
                 - agricultural land and pastoral land;

- vegetation cover and wildlife;
- forests;
- water resources; and
- biological diversity;

(ii) training with regard to, and strengthening, public awareness and environmental education campaigns and disseminating knowledge of techniques relating to the sustainable management of natural resources; and

(iii) ensuring the development and efficient use of diverse energy sources, the promotion of alternative sources of energy, particularly solar energy, wind energy and bio-gas, and specific arrangements for the transfer, acquisition and adaptation of relevant technology to alleviate the pressure on fragile natural resources;

(c) measures to improve institutional organization:

(i) defining the roles and responsibilities of central government and local authorities within the framework of a land use planning policy;

(ii) encouraging a policy of active decentralization, devolving responsibility for management and decision-making to local authorities, and encouraging initiatives and the assumption of responsibility by local communities and the establishment of local structures; and

(iii) adjusting, as appropriate, the institutional and regulatory framework of natural resource management to provide security of land tenure for local populations;

(d) measures to improve knowledge of desertification:

(i) promoting research and the collection, processing and exchange of information on the scientific, technical and socio-economic aspects of desertification;

(ii) improving national capabilities in research and in the collection, processing, exchange and analysis of information so as to increase understanding and to translate the results of the analysis into operational terms; and

(iii) encouraging the medium and long term study of:

- socio-economic and cultural trends in affected areas;
- qualitative and quantitative trends in natural resources; and
- the interaction between climate and desertification; and

(e) measures to monitor and assess the effects of drought:

(i) developing strategies to evaluate the impacts of natural climate variability on regional drought and desertification and/or to utilize predictions of climate variability on seasonal to interannual time scales in efforts to mitigate the effects of drought;

(ii) improving early warning and response capacity, efficiently managing emergency relief and food aid, and improving food stocking and distribution systems, cattle protection schemes and public works and alternative livelihoods for drought prone areas; and

(iii) monitoring and assessing ecological degradation to provide reliable and timely information on the process and dynamics of resource degradation in order to facilitate better policy formulations and responses.

| **Article 9** | **Preparation of national action programmes and implementation and evaluation indicators** |

Each affected African country Party shall designate an appropriate national coordinating body to function as a catalyst in the preparation, implementation and evaluation of its national action programme. This coordinating body shall, in the light of article 3 and as appropriate:

(a) undertake an identification and review of actions, beginning with a locally driven consultation process, involving local populations and communities and with the cooperation of local administrative authorities, developed country Parties and intergovernmental and non-governmental organizations, on the basis of initial consultations of those concerned at the national level;

(b) identify and analyze the constraints, needs and gaps affecting development and sustainable land use and recommend practical measures to avoid duplication by making full use of relevant ongoing efforts and promote implementation of results;

(c) facilitate, design and formulate project activities based on interactive, flexible approaches in order to ensure active participation of the population in affected areas, to minimize the negative impact of such activities, and to identify and prioritize requirements for financial assistance and technical cooperation;

(d) establish pertinent, quantifiable and readily verifiable indicators to ensure the assessment and evaluation of national action programmes, which encompass actions in the short, medium and long terms, and of the implementation of such programmes; and

(e) prepare progress reports on the implementation of the national action programmes.

Article 10	**Organizational framework of subregional action programmes**

1. Pursuant to article 4 of the Convention, African country Parties shall cooperate in the preparation and implementation of subregional action programmes for central, eastern, northern, southern and western Africa and, in that regard, may delegate the following responsibilities to relevant subregional intergovernmental organizations:

(a) acting as focal points for preparatory activities and coordinating the implementation of the subregional action programmes;

(b) assisting in the preparation and implementation of national action programmes;

(c) facilitating the exchange of information, experience and know-how as well as providing advice on the review of national legislation; and

(d) any other responsibilities relating to the implementation of subregional action programmes.

2. Specialized subregional institutions may provide support, upon request, and/or be entrusted with the responsibility to coordinate activities in their respective fields of competence.

Article 11	**Content and preparation of subregional action programmes**

Subregional action programmes shall focus on issues that are better addressed at the subregional level. They shall establish, where necessary, mechanisms for the management of shared natural resources. Such mechanisms shall effectively handle transboundary problems associated with desertification and/or drought and shall provide support for the harmonious implementation of national action programmes. Priority areas for subregional action programmes shall, as appropriate, focus on:

(a) joint programmes for the sustainable management of transboundary natural resources through bilateral and multilateral mechanisms, as appropriate;

(b) coordination of programmes to develop alternative energy sources;

(c) cooperation in the management and control of pests as well as of plant and animal diseases;

(d) capacity building, education and public awareness activities that are better carried out or supported at the subregional level;

(e) scientific and technical cooperation, particularly in the climatological, meteorological and hydrological fields, including networking for data collection and assessment, information sharing and project monitoring, and coordination and prioritization of research and development activities;

(f) early warning systems and joint planning for mitigating the effects of drought, including measures to address the problems resulting from environmentally induced migrations;

(g) exploration of ways of sharing experiences, particularly regarding participation of local populations and communities, and creation of an enabling environment for improved land use management and for use of appropriate technologies;

(h) strengthening of the capacity of subregional organizations to coordinate and provide technical services, as well as establishment, reorientation and strengthening of subregional centres and institutions; and

(i) development of policies in fields, such as trade, which have impact upon affected areas and populations, including policies for the coordination of regional marketing regimes and for common infrastructure.

Article 12	**Organizational framework of the regional action programme**

1. Pursuant to article 11 of the Convention, African country Parties shall jointly determine the procedures for preparing and implementing the regional action programme.

2. The Parties may provide appropriate support to relevant African regional institutions and organizations to enable them to assist African country Parties to fulfill their responsibilities under the Convention.

Article 13   **Content of the regional action**
                    programme

The regional action programme includes measures relating to combating desertification and/or mitigating the effects of drought in the following priority areas, as appropriate:

(a) development of regional cooperation and coordination of sub-regional action programmes for building regional consensus on key policy areas, including through regular consultations of sub-regional organizations;

(b) promotion of capacity building in activities which are better implemented at the regional level;

(c) the seeking of solutions with the international community to global economic and social issues that have an impact on affected areas taking into account article 4, paragraph 2 (b) of the Convention;

(d) promotion among the affected country Parties of Africa and its subregions, as well as with other affected regions, of exchange of information and appropriate techniques, technical know-how and relevant experience; promotion of scientific and technological cooperation particularly in the fields of climatology, meteorology, hydrology, water resource development and alternative energy sources; coordination of sub-regional and regional research activities; and identification of regional priorities for research and development;

(e) coordination of networks for systematic observation and assessment and information exchange, as well as their integration into world wide networks; and

(f) coordination of and reinforcement of sub-regional and regional early warning systems and drought contingency plans.

Article 14   **Financial resources**

1. Pursuant to article 20 of the Convention and article 4, paragraph 2, affected African country Parties shall endeavour to provide a macroeconomic framework conducive to the mobilization of financial resources and shall develop policies and establish procedures to channel resources more effectively to local development programmes, including through non-governmental organizations, as appropriate.

2. Pursuant to article 21, paragraphs 4 and 5 of the Convention, the Parties agree to establish an inventory of sources of funding at the national, subregional, regional and international levels to ensure the rational use of existing resources and to identify gaps in resource allocation, to facilitate implementation of the action programmes. The inventory shall be regularly reviewed and updated.

3. Consistent with article 7 of the Convention, the developed country Parties shall continue to allocate significant resources and/or increased resources as well as other forms of assistance to affected African country Parties on the basis of partnership agreements and arrangements referred to in article 18, giving, inter alia, due attention to matters related to debt, international trade and marketing arrangements in accordance with article 4, paragraph 2 (b) of the Convention.

Article 15   **Financial Mechanisms**

1. Consistent with article 7 of the Convention underscoring the priority to affected African country Parties and considering the particular situation prevailing in this region, the Parties shall pay special attention to the implementation in Africa of the provisions of article 21, paragraph 1 (d) and (e) of the Convention, notably by:

(a) facilitating the establishment of mechanisms, such as national desertification funds, to channel financial resources to the local level; and

(b) strengthening existing funds and financial mechanisms at the subregional and regional levels.

2. Consistent with articles 20 and 21 of the Convention, the Parties which are also members of the governing bodies of relevant regional and subregional financial institutions, including the African Development Bank and the African Development Fund, shall promote efforts to give due priority and attention to the activities of those institutions that advance the implementation of this Annex.

3. The Parties shall streamline, to the extent possible, procedures for channelling funds to affected African country Parties.

Article 16   **Technical assistance and cooperation**

The Parties undertake, in accordance with their respective capabilities, to rationalize technical assistance to, and cooperation with, African country Parties with a view to increasing project and programme effectiveness by, inter alia:

       (a) limiting the costs of support measures and backstopping, especially overhead costs; in any case, such costs shall only represent an appropriately low percentage of the total cost of the project so as to maximize project efficiency;

       (b) giving preference to the utilization of competent national experts or, where necessary, competent experts from within the subregion and/or region, in project design, preparation and implementation, and to the building of local expertise where it does not exist; and

       (c) effectively managing and coordinating, as well as efficiently utilizing, technical assistance to be provided.

Article 17   **Transfer, acquisition, adaptation and access to environmentally sound technology**

In implementing article 18 of the Convention relating to transfer, acquisition, adaptation and development of technology, the Parties undertake to give priority to African country Parties and, as necessary, to develop with them new models of partnership and cooperation with a view to strengthening capacity building in the fields of scientific research and development and information collection and dissemination to enable them to implement their strategies to combat desertification and mitigate the effects of drought.

Article 18   **Coordination and partnership agreements**

1. African country Parties shall coordinate the preparation, negotiation and implementation of national, subregional and regional action programmes. They may involve, as appropriate, other Parties and relevant intergovernmental and non-governmental organizations in this process.

2. The objectives of such coordination shall be to ensure that financial and technical cooperation is consistent with the Convention and to provide the necessary continuity in the use and administration of resources.

3. African country Parties shall organize consultative processes at the national, subregional and regional levels. These consultative processes may:

       (a) serve as a forum to negotiate and conclude partnership agreements based on national, subregional and regional action programmes; and

       (b) specify the contribution of African country Parties and other members of the consultative groups to the programmes and identify priorities and agreements on implementation and evaluation indicators, as well as funding arrangements for implementation.

4. The Permanent Secretariat may, at the request of African country Parties, pursuant to article 23 of the Convention, facilitate the convocation of such consultative processes by:

       (a) providing advice on the organization of effective consultative arrangements, drawing on experiences from other such arrangements;

       (b) providing information to relevant bilateral and multilateral agencies concerning consultative meetings or processes, and encouraging their active involvement; and

       (c) providing other information that may be relevant in establishing or improving consultative arrangements.

5. The subregional and regional coordinating bodies shall, inter alia:

       (a) recommend appropriate adjustments to partnership agreements;

       (b) monitor, assess and report on the implementation of the agreed subregional and regional programmes; and

       (c) aim to ensure efficient communication and cooperation among African country Parties.

6. Participation in the consultative groups shall, as appropriate, be open to Governments, interested groups and donors, relevant organs, funds and programmes of the United Nations system, relevant subregional and regional organizations, and representatives of relevant non-governmental organizations. Participants of each consultative group shall determine the modalities of its management and operation.

7. Pursuant to article 14 of the Convention, developed country Parties are encouraged to develop, on their own initiative, an informal process of consultation and coordination among themselves, at the national, subregional and regional levels, and, at the request of an affected African country Party or of an appropriate subregional or regional organization, to participate in a national, subregional or regional consultative process that would evaluate and respond to assistance needs in order to facilitate implementation.

Article 19   Follow-up arrangements

Follow-up of this Annex shall be carried out by African country Parties in accordance with the Convention as follows:

(a) at the national level, by a mechanism the composition of which should be determined by each affected African country Party and which shall include representatives of local communities and shall function under the supervision of the national coordinating body referred to in article 9;

(b) at the subregional level, by a multidisciplinary scientific and technical consultative committee, the composition and modalities of operation of which shall be determined by the African country Parties of the subregion concerned; and

(c) at the regional level, by mechanisms defined in accordance with the relevant provisions of the Treaty establishing the African Economic Community, and by an African Scientific and Technical Advisory Committee.

ANNEX II	**REGIONAL IMPLEMENTATION ANNEX FOR ASIA * * ***
ANNEX III	**REGIONAL IMPLEMENTATION ANNEX FOR LATIN AMERICA AND THE CARIBBEAN * * ***
ANNEX IV	**REGIONAL IMPLEMENTATION ANNEX FOR THE NORTHERN MEDITERRANEAN* * ***

NORTH AMERICAN AGREEMENT ON ENVIRONMENTAL COOPERATION BETWEEN THE GOVERNMENT OF CANADA, THE GOVERNMENT OF THE UNITED MEXICAN STATES AND THE GOVERNMENT OF THE UNITED STATES OF AMERICA
(annexes not included)

32 ILM 1480 (1993)
Signed: September 9 and 14, 1993 (Washington); September 12 and 14, 1993 (Ottawa); September 8 and 14, 1993 (Mexico City)
Entered into Force: January 1, 1994
Secretariat Homepage: http://www.cec.org/

The Government of Canada, the Government of the United Mexican States and the Government of the United States of America:

Convinced of the importance of the conservation, protection and enhancement of the environment in their territories and the essential role of cooperation in these areas in achieving sustainable development for the well-being of present and future generations;

Reaffirming the sovereign right of States to exploit their own resources pursuant to their own environmental and development policies and their responsibility to ensure that activities within their jurisdiction or control do not cause damage to the environment of other States or of areas beyond the limits of national jurisdiction;

Recognizing the interrelationship of their environments;

Acknowledging the growing economic and social links between them, including the North American Free Trade Agreement (NAFTA);

Reconfirming the importance of the environmental goals and objectives of the NAFTA, including enhanced levels of environmental protection;

Emphasizing the importance of public participation in conserving, protecting and enhancing the environment;

Noting the existence of differences in their respective natural endowments, climatic and geographical conditions, and economic, technological and infrastructural capabilities;

Reaffirming the Stockholm Declaration on the Human Environment of 1972 and the Rio Declaration on Environment and Development of 1992;

Recalling their tradition of environmental cooperation and expressing their desire to support and build on international environmental agreements and existing policies and laws, in order to promote cooperation between them; and

Convinced of the benefits to be derived from a framework, including a Commission, to facilitate effective cooperation on the conservation, protection and enhancement of the environment in their territories;

Have agreed as follows:

PART I   OBJECTIVES

Article 1   Objectives

The objectives of this Agreement are to:

(a)   foster the protection and improvement of the environment in the territories of the Parties for the well-being of present and future generations;

(b)   promote sustainable development based on cooperation and mutually supportive environmental and economic policies;

(c)   increase cooperation between the Parties to better conserve, protect, and enhance the environment, including wild flora and fauna;

(d)   support the environmental goals and objectives of the NAFTA;

(e)   avoid creating trade distortions or new trade barriers;

(f)   strengthen cooperation on the development and improvement of environmental laws, regulations, procedures, policies and practices;

(g)   enhance compliance with, and enforcement of, environmental laws and regulations;

(h)   promote transparency and public participation in the development of environmental laws, regulations and policies;

(i)   promote economically efficient and effective environmental measures; and

(j)   promote pollution prevention policies and practices.

PART II   OBLIGATIONS

Article 2   General Commitments

1.   Each Party shall, with respect to its territory:

(a)   periodically prepare and make publicly available reports on the state of the environment;

(b)   develop and review environmental emergency preparedness measures;

(c)   promote education in environmental matters, including environmental law;

(d)   further scientific research and technology development in respect of environmental matters;

(e)   assess, as appropriate, environmental impacts; and

(f)   promote the use of economic instruments for the efficient achievement of environmental goals.

2.   Each Party shall consider implementing in its law any recommendation developed by the Council under Article 10(5)(b).

3.   Each Party shall consider prohibiting the export to the territories of the other Parties of a pesticide or toxic substance whose use is prohibited within the Party's territory. When a Party adopts a measure prohibiting or severely restricting the use of a pesticide or toxic substance in its territory, it shall notify the other Parties of the measure, either directly or through an appropriate international organization.

Article 3   Levels of Protection

Recognizing the right of each Party to establish its own levels of domestic environmental protection and environmental development policies and priorities, and to adopt or modify accordingly its environmental laws and regulations, each Party shall ensure that its laws and regulations provide for high levels of environmental protection and shall strive to continue to improve those laws and regulations.

Article 4   Publication

1.   Each Party shall ensure that its laws, regulations, procedures and administrative rulings of general application respecting any matter covered by this Agreement are promptly published or otherwise made available in such a manner as to enable interested persons and Parties to become acquainted with them.

2.   To the extent possible, each Party shall:

(a)   publish in advance any such measure that it proposes to adopt; and

(b)   provide interested persons and Parties a reasonable opportunity to comment on such proposed measures.

Article 5   Government Enforcement Action

1.   With the aim of achieving high levels of environmental protection and compliance with its environmental laws and regulations, each Party shall effectively enforce its environmental laws and regulations through appropriate governmental action, subject to Article 37, such as:

(a)   appointing and training inspectors;

(b)   monitoring compliance and investigating suspected violations, including through on-site inspections;

(c)   seeking assurances of voluntary compliance and compliance agreements;

(d) publicly releasing non-compliance information;
(e) issuing bulletins or other periodic statements on enforcement procedures;
(f) promoting environmental audits;
(g) requiring record keeping and reporting;
(h) providing or encouraging mediation and arbitration services;
(i) using licenses, permits or authorizations;
(j) initiating, in a timely manner, judicial, quasi-judicial or administrative proceedings to seek appropriate sanctions or remedies for violations of its environmental laws and regulations;
(k) providing for search, seizure or detention; or
(l) issuing administrative orders, including orders of a preventative, curative or emergency nature.

2. Each party shall ensure that judicial, quasi-judicial or administrative enforcement proceedings are available under its law to sanction or remedy violations of its environmental laws and regulations.

3. Sanctions and remedies provided for a violation of a Party's environmental laws and regulations shall, as appropriate:
(a) take into consideration the nature and gravity of the violation, any economic benefit derived from the violation by the violator, the economic condition of the violator, and other relevant factors; and
(b) include compliance agreements, fines, imprisonment, injunctions, the closure of facilities, and the cost of containing or cleaning up pollution.

Article 6 Private Access to Remedies

1. Each Party shall ensure that interested persons may request the Party's competent authorities to investigate alleged violations of its environmental laws and regulations and shall give such requests due consideration in accordance with law.

2. Each Party shall ensure that persons with a legally recognized interest under its law in a particular matter have appropriate access to administrative, quasi-judicial or judicial proceedings for the enforcement of the Party's environmental laws and regulations.

3. Private access to remedies shall include rights, in accordance with the Party's law, such as:
(a) to sue another person under that Party's jurisdiction for damages;
(b) to seek sanctions or remedies such as monetary penalties, emergency closures or orders to mitigate the consequences of violations of its environmental laws and regulations;
(c) to request the competent authorities to take appropriate action to enforce that Party's environmental laws and regulations in order to protect the environment or to avoid environmental harm; or
(d) to seek injunctions where a person suffers, or may suffer, loss, damage or injury as a result of conduct by another person under that Party's jurisdiction contrary to that Party's environmental laws and regulations or from tortious conduct.

Article 7 Procedural Guarantees

1. Each Party shall ensure that its administrative, quasi-judicial and judicial proceedings referred to in Articles 5(2) and 6(2) are fair, open and equitable, and to this end shall provide that such proceedings:
(a) comply with due process of law;
(b) are open to the public, except where the administration of justice otherwise requires;
(c) entitle the parties to the proceedings to support or defend their respective positions and to present information or evidence; and
(d) are not unnecessarily complicated and do not entail unreasonable charges or time limits or unwarranted delays.

2. Each Party shall provide that final decisions on the merits of the case in such proceedings are:
(a) in writing and preferably state the reasons on which the decisions are based;
(b) made available without undue delay to the parties to the proceedings and, consistent with its law, to the public; and
(c) based on information or evidence in respect of which the parties were offered the opportunity to be heard.

3.   Each Party shall provide, as appropriate, that parties to such proceedings have the right, in accordance with its law, to seek review and, where warranted, correction of final decisions issued in such proceedings.

4.   Each Party shall ensure that tribunals that conduct or review such proceedings are impartial and independent and do not have any substantial interest in the outcome of the matter.

PART III   COMMISSION FOR ENVIRONMENTAL COOPERATION

Article 8   The Commission

1.   The Parties hereby establish the Commission for Environmental Cooperation.

2.   The Commission shall comprise a Council, a Secretariat and a Joint Public Advisory Committee.

Section A   The Council

Article 9   Council Structure and Procedures

1.   The Council shall comprise cabinet-level or equivalent representatives of the Parties, or their designees.

2.   The Council shall establish its rules and procedures.

3.   The Council shall convene:
    (a)   at least once a year in regular session; and
    (b)   in special session at the request of any Party.

Regular sessions shall be chaired successively by each Party.

4.   The Council shall hold public meetings in the course of all regular sessions. Other meetings held in the course of regular or special sessions shall be public where the Council so decides.

5.   The Council may:
    (a)   establish, and assign responsibilities to, ad hoc or standing committees, working groups or expert groups;
    (b)   seek the advice of non-governmental organizations or persons, including independent experts; and
    (c)   take such other action in the exercise of its functions as the Parties may agree.

6.   All decisions and recommendations of the Council shall be taken by consensus, except as the Council may otherwise decide or as otherwise provided in this Agreement.

7.   All decisions and recommendations of the Council shall be made public, except as the Council may otherwise decide or as otherwise provided in this Agreement.

Article 10   Council Functions

1.   The Council shall be the governing body of the Commission and shall:
    (a)   serve as a forum for the discussion of environmental matters within the scope of this Agreement;
    (b)   oversee the implementation and develop recommendations on the further elaboration of this Agreement and, to this end, the Council shall, within four years after the date of entry into force of this Agreement, review its operation and effectiveness in the light of experience;
    (c)   oversee the Secretariat;
    (d)   address questions and differences that may arise between the Parties regarding the interpretation or application of this Agreement;
    (e)   approve the annual program and budget of the Commission; and
    (f)   promote and facilitate cooperation between the Parties with respect to environmental matters.

2.   The Council may consider, and develop recommendations regarding:

(a)   comparability of techniques and methodologies for data gathering and analysis, data management and electronic data communications on matters covered by this Agreement;

(b)   pollution prevention techniques and strategies;

(c)   approaches and common indicators for reporting on the state of the environment;

(d)   the use of economic instruments for the pursuit of domestic and internationally agreed environmental objectives;

(e)   scientific research and technology development in respect of environmental matters;

(f)   promotion of public awareness regarding the environment;

(g)   transboundary and border environmental issues, such as the long-range transport of air and marine pollutants;

(h)   exotic species that may be harmful;

(i)   the conservation and protection of wild flora and fauna and their habitat, and specially protected natural areas;

(j)   the protection of endangered and threatened species;

(k)   environmental emergency preparedness and response activities;

(l)   environmental matters as they relate to economic development;

(m)   the environmental implications of goods throughout their life cycles;

(n)   human resource training and development in the environmental field;

(o)   the exchange of environmental scientists and officials;

(p)   approaches to environmental compliance and enforcement;

(q)   ecologically sensitive national accounts;

(r)   eco-labeling; and

(s)   other matters as it may decide.

3.   The Council shall strengthen cooperation on the development and continuing improvement of environmental laws and regulations, including by:

(a)   promoting the exchange of information on criteria and methodologies used in establishing domestic environmental standards; and

(b)   without reducing levels of environmental protection, establishing a process for developing recommendations on greater compatibility of environmental technical regulations, standards and conformity assessment procedures in a manner consistent with the NAFTA.

4.   The Council shall encourage:

(a)   effective enforcement by each Party of its environmental laws and regulations;

(b)   compliance with those laws and regulations; and

(c)   technical cooperation between the Parties.

5.   The Council shall promote and, as appropriate, develop recommendations regarding:

(a)   public access to information concerning the environment that is held by public authorities of each Party, including information on hazardous materials and activities in its communities, and opportunity to participate in decision-making processes related to such public access; and

(b)   appropriate limits for specific pollutants, taking into account differences in ecosystems.

6.   The Council shall cooperate with the NAFTA Free Trade Commission to achieve the environmental goals and objectives of the NAFTA by:

(a)   acting as a point of inquiry and receipt for comments from non-governmental organizations and persons concerning those goals and objectives;

(b)   providing assistance in consultations under Article 1114 of the NAFTA where a Party considers that another Party is waiving or derogating from, or offering to waive or otherwise derogate from, an environmental measure as an encouragement to establish, acquire, expand or retain an investment of an investor, with a view to avoiding any such encouragement;

(c)   contributing to the prevention or resolution of environment-related trade disputes by:

(i)   seeking to avoid disputes between the Parties,

(ii)   making recommendations to the Free Trade Commission with respect to the avoidance of such disputes, and

(iii)   identifying experts able to provide information or technical advice to NAFTA committees, working groups and other NAFTA bodies;

(d)   considering on an ongoing basis the environmental effects of the NAFTA; and

(e)   otherwise assisting the Free Trade Commission in environment-related matters.

7.   Recognizing the significant bilateral nature of many transboundary environmental issues, the Council shall, with a view to agreement between the Parties pursuant to this Article within three years on obligations, consider and develop recommendations with respect to:

(a)   assessing the environmental impact of proposed projects subject to decisions by a competent government authority and likely to cause significant adverse transboundary effects, including a full evaluation of comments provided by other Parties and persons of other Parties;

(b)   notification, provision of relevant information and consultation between Parties with respect to such projects; and

(c)   mitigation of the potential adverse effects of such projects.

8.   The Council shall encourage the establishment by each Party of appropriate administrative procedures pursuant to its environmental laws to permit another Party to seek the reduction, elimination or mitigation of transboundary pollution on a reciprocal basis.

9.   The Council shall consider and, as appropriate, develop recommendations on the provision by a Party, on a reciprocal basis, of access to and rights and remedies before its courts and administrative agencies for persons in another Party's territory who have suffered or are likely to suffer damage or injury caused by pollution originating in its territory as if the damage or injury were suffered in its territory.

Section B   The Secretariat

Article 11   Secretariat Structure and Procedures

1.   The Secretariat shall be headed by an Executive Director, who shall be chosen by the Council for a three-year term, which may be renewed by the Council for one additional three year term. The position of Executive Director shall rotate consecutively between nationals of each Party. The Council may remove the Executive Director solely for cause.

2.   The Executive Director shall appoint and supervise the staff of the Secretariat, regulate their powers and duties and fix their remuneration in accordance with general standards to be established by the Council. The general standards shall provide that:

(a)   staff shall be appointed and retained, and their conditions of employment shall be determined, strictly on the basis of efficiency, competence and integrity;

(b)   in appointing staff, the Executive Director shall take into account lists of candidates prepared by the Parties and by the Joint Public Advisory Committee;

(c)   due regard shall be paid to the importance of recruiting an equitable proportion of the professional staff from among the nationals of each Party; and

(d)   the Executive Director shall inform the Council of all appointments.

3.   The Council may decide, by a two-thirds vote, to reject any appointment that does not meet the general standards. Any such decision shall be made and held in confidence.

4.   In the performance of their duties, the Executive Director and the staff shall not seek or receive instructions from any government or any other authority external to the Council. Each Party shall respect the international character of the responsibilities of the Executive Director and the staff and shall not seek to influence them in the discharge of their responsibilities.

5.   The Secretariat shall provide technical, administrative and operational support to the Council and to committees and groups established by the Council, and such other support as the Council may direct.

6.   The Executive Director shall submit for the approval of the Council the annual program and budget of the Commission, including provision for proposed cooperative activities and for the Secretariat to respond to contingencies.

7.   The Secretariat shall, as appropriate, provide the Parties and the public information on where they may receive technical advice and expertise with respect to environmental matters.

8.   The Secretariat shall safeguard:

(a)   from disclosure information it receives that could identify a non-governmental organization or person making a submission if the person or organization so requests or the Secretariat otherwise considers it appropriate; and

(b)   from public disclosure any information it receives from any non-governmental organization or person where the information is designated by that non-governmental organization or person as confidential or proprietary.

Article 12   Annual Report of the Commission

1.   The Secretariat shall prepare an annual report of the Commission in accordance with instructions from the Council. The Secretariat shall submit a draft of the report for review by the Council. The final report shall be released publicly.

2.   The report shall cover:

(a)   activities and expenses of the Commission during the previous year;

(b)   the approved program and budget of the Commission for the subsequent year;

(c)   the actions taken by each Party in connection with its obligations under this Agreement, including data on the Party's environmental enforcement activities;

(d)   relevant views and information submitted by non-governmental organizations and persons, including summary data regarding submissions, and any other relevant information the Council deems appropriate;

(e)   recommendations made on any matter within the scope of this Agreement; and

(f)   any other matter that the Council instructs the Secretariat to include.

3.   The report shall periodically address the state of the environment in the territories of the Parties.

Article 13   Secretariat Reports

1.   The Secretariat may prepare a report for the Council on any matter within the scope of the annual program. Should the Secretariat wish to prepare a report on any other environmental matter related to the cooperative functions of this Agreement, it shall notify the Council and may proceed unless, within 30 days of such notification, the Council objects by a two-thirds vote to the preparation of the report. Such other environmental matters shall not include issues related to whether a Party has failed to enforce its environmental laws and regulations. Where the Secretariat does not have specific expertise in the matter under review, it shall obtain the assistance of one or more independent experts of recognized experience in the matter to assist in the preparation of the report.

2.   In preparing such a report, the Secretariat may draw upon any relevant technical, scientific or other information, including information:

(a)   that is publicly available;

(b)   submitted by interested non-governmental organizations and persons;

(c)   submitted by the Joint Public Advisory Committee;

(d)   furnished by a Party;

(e)   gathered through public consultations, such as conferences, seminars and symposia; or

(f)   developed by the Secretariat, or by independent experts engaged pursuant to paragraph 1.

3.   The Secretariat shall submit its report to the Council, which shall make it publicly available, normally within 60 days following its submission, unless the Council otherwise decides.

Article 14   Submissions on Enforcement
Matters

1.   The Secretariat may consider a submission from any non-governmental organization or person asserting that a Party is failing to effectively enforce its environmental law, if the Secretariat finds that the submission:

(a)   is in writing in a language designated by that Party in a notification to the Secretariat;

(b)   clearly identifies the person or organization making the submission;

(c)   provides sufficient information to allow the Secretariat to review the submission, including any documentary evidence on which the submission may be based;

(d)   appears to be aimed at promoting enforcement rather than at harassing industry;

(e)   indicates that the matter has been communicated in writing to the relevant authorities of the Party and indicates the Party's response, if any; and

(f)   is filed by a person or organization residing or established in the territory of a Party.

2.   Where the Secretariat determines that a submission meets the criteria set out in paragraph 1, the Secretariat shall determine whether the submission merits requesting a response from the Party. In deciding whether to request a response, the Secretariat shall be guided by whether:

(a)   the submission alleges harm to the person or organization making the submission;

(b)   the submission, alone or in combination with other submissions, raises matters whose further study in this process would advance the goals of this Agreement;

(c)   private remedies available under the Party's law have been pursued; and

(d)   the submission is drawn exclusively from mass media reports.

Where the Secretariat makes such a request, it shall forward to the Party a copy of the submission and any supporting information provided with the submission.

3.   The Party shall advise the Secretariat within 30 days or, in exceptional circumstances and on notification to the Secretariat, within 60 days of delivery of the request:

(a)   whether the matter is the subject of a pending judicial or administrative proceeding, in which case the Secretariat shall proceed no further; and

(b)   of any other information that the Party wishes to submit, such as

i)   whether the matter was previously the subject of a judicial or administrative proceeding, and

ii)   whether private remedies in connection with the matter are available to the person or organization making the submission and whether they have been pursued.

Article 15   Factual Record

1.   If the Secretariat considers that the submission, in the light of any response provided by the Party, warrants developing a factual record, the Secretariat shall so inform the Council and provide its reasons.

2.   The Secretariat shall prepare a factual record if the Council, by a two-thirds vote, instructs it to do so.

3.   The preparation of a factual record by the Secretariat pursuant to this Article shall be without prejudice to any further steps that may be taken with respect to any submission.

4.   In preparing a factual record, the Secretariat shall consider any information furnished by a Party and may consider any relevant technical, scientific or other information:

(a)   that is publicly available;

(b)   submitted by interested non-governmental organizations or persons;

(c)   submitted by the Joint Public Advisory Committee; or

(d)   developed by the Secretariat or by independent experts.

5.   The Secretariat shall submit a draft factual record to the Council. Any Party may provide comments on the accuracy of the draft within 45 days thereafter.

6.   The Secretariat shall incorporate, as appropriate, any such comments in the final factual record and submit it to the Council.

7.   The Council may, by a two-thirds vote, make the final factual record publicly available, normally within 60 days following its submission.

Section C   Advisory Committees

Article 16   Joint Public Advisory Committee

1.   The Joint Public Advisory Committee shall comprise 15 members, unless the Council otherwise decides. Each Party or, if the Party so decides, its National Advisory Committee convened under Article 17, shall appoint an equal number of members.

2.   The Council shall establish the rules of procedure for the Joint Public Advisory Committee, which shall choose its own chair.

3.   The Joint Public Advisory Committee shall convene at least once a year at the time of the regular session of the Council and at such other times as the Council, or the Committee's chair with the consent of a majority of its members, may decide.

4.   The Joint Public Advisory Committee may provide advice to the Council on any matter within the scope of this Agreement, including on any documents provided to it under paragraph 6, and on the implementation and further elaboration of this Agreement, and may perform such other functions as the Council may direct.

5.   The Joint Public Advisory Committee may provide relevant technical, scientific or other information to the Secretariat, including for purposes of developing a factual record under Article 15. The Secretariat shall forward to the Council copies of any such information.

6.   The Secretariat shall provide to the Joint Public Advisory Committee at the time they are submitted to the Council copies of the proposed annual program and budget of the Commission, the draft annual report, and any report the Secretariat prepares pursuant to Article 13.

7.   The Council may, by a two-thirds vote, make a factual record available to the Joint Public Advisory Committee.

Article 17   National Advisory Committees

Each Party may convene a national advisory committee, comprising members of its public, including representatives of non-governmental organizations and persons, to advise it on the implementation and further elaboration of this Agreement.

Article 18   Governmental Committees

Each Party may convene a governmental committee, which may comprise or include representatives of federal and state or provincial governments, to advise it on the implementation and further elaboration of this Agreement.

Section D   Official Languages

Article 19   Official Languages

The official languages of the Commission shall be English, French and Spanish. All annual reports under Article 12, reports submitted to the Council under Article 13, factual records submitted to the Council under Article 15(6) and panel reports under Part Five shall be available in each official language at the time they are made public. The Council shall establish rules and procedures regarding interpretation and translation.

PART IV   COOPERATION AND PROVISION OF INFORMATION

Article 20   Cooperation

1.   The Parties shall at all times endeavor to agree on the interpretation and application of this Agreement, and shall make every attempt through cooperation and consultations to resolve any matter that might affect its operation.

2.   To the maximum extent possible, each Party shall notify any other Party with an interest in the matter of any proposed or actual environmental measure that the Party considers might materially affect the operation of this Agreement or otherwise substantially affect that other Party's interests under this Agreement.

3.   On request of any other Party, a Party shall promptly provide information and respond to questions pertaining to any such actual or proposed environmental measure, whether or not that other Party has been previously notified of that measure.

4.   Any Party may notify any other Party of, and provide to that Party, any credible information regarding possible violations of its environmental law, specific and sufficient to allow the other Party to inquire into the matter. The notified Party shall take appropriate steps in accordance with its law to so inquire and to respond to the other Party.

Article 21   Provision of Information

1.   On request of the Council or the Secretariat, each Party shall, in accordance with its law, provide such information as the Council or the Secretariat may require, including:

     (a)   promptly making available any information in its possession required for the preparation of a report or factual record, including compliance and enforcement data; and
     (b)   taking all reasonable steps to make available any other such information requested.

2.   If a Party considers that a request for information from the Secretariat is excessive or otherwise unduly burdensome, it may so notify the Council. The Secretariat shall revise the scope of its request to comply with any limitations established by the Council by a two-thirds vote.

3.   If a Party does not make available information requested by the Secretariat, as may be limited pursuant to paragraph 2, it shall promptly advise the Secretariat of its reasons in writing.

PART V   CONSULTATION AND RESOLUTION OF DISPUTES

Article 22   Consultations

1.   Any Party may request in writing consultations with any other Party regarding whether there has been a persistent pattern of failure by that other Party to effectively enforce its environmental law.

2.   The requesting Party shall deliver the request to the other Parties and to the Secretariat.

3.   Unless the Council otherwise provides in its rules and procedures established under Article 9(2), a third Party that considers it has a substantial interest in the matter shall be entitled to participate in the consultations on delivery of written notice to the other Parties and to the Secretariat.

4.   The consulting Parties shall make every attempt to arrive at a mutually satisfactory resolution of the matter through consultations under this Article.

Article 23   Initiation of Procedures

1.   If the consulting Parties fail to resolve the matter pursuant to Article 22 within 60 days of delivery of a request for consultations, or such other period as the consulting Parties may agree, any such Party may request in writing a special session of the Council.

2.   The requesting Party shall state in the request the matter complained of and shall deliver the request to the other Parties and to the Secretariat.

3.   Unless it decides otherwise, the Council shall convene within 20 days of delivery of the request and shall endeavor to resolve the dispute promptly.

4.   The Council may:

    (a)   call on such technical advisers or create such working groups or expert groups as it deems necessary,
    (b)   have recourse to good offices, conciliation, mediation or such other dispute resolution procedures, or
    (c)   make recommendations,

as may assist the consulting Parties to reach a mutually satisfactory resolution of the dispute.   Any such recommendations shall be made public if the Council, by a two-thirds vote, so decides.

5.   Where the Council decides that a matter is more properly covered by another agreement or arrangement to which the consulting Parties are party, it shall refer the matter to those Parties for appropriate action in accordance with such other agreement or arrangement.

Article 24   Request for an Arbitral Panel

1.   If the matter has not been resolved within 60 days after the Council has convened pursuant to Article 23, the Council shall, on the written request of any consulting Party and by a two-thirds vote, convene an arbitral panel to consider the matter where the alleged persistent pattern of failure by the Party complained against to effectively enforce its environmental law relates to a situation involving workplaces, firms, companies or sectors that produce goods or provide services:

    (a)   traded between the territories of the Parties; or

    (b)   that compete, in the territory of the Party complained against, with goods or services produced or provided by persons of another Party.

2.   A third Party that considers it has a substantial interest in the matter shall be entitled to join as a complaining Party on delivery of written notice of its intention to participate to the disputing Parties and the Secretariat.   The notice shall be delivered at the earliest possible time, and in any event no later than seven days after the date of the vote of the Council to convene a panel.

3.   Unless otherwise agreed by the disputing Parties, the panel shall be established and perform its functions in a manner consistent with the provisions of this Part.

Article 25   Roster

1.   The Council shall establish and maintain a roster of up to 45 individuals who are willing and able to serve as panelists.   The roster members shall be appointed by consensus for terms of three years, and may be reappointed.

2.   Roster members shall:

    (a)   have expertise or experience in environmental law or its enforcement, or in the resolution of disputes arising under international agreements, or other relevant scientific, technical or professional expertise or experience;
    (b)   be chosen strictly on the basis of objectivity, reliability and sound judgment;
    (c)   be independent of, and not be affiliated with or take instructions from, any Party, the Secretariat or the Joint Public Advisory Committee; and
    (d)   comply with a code of conduct to be established by the Council.

Article 26   Qualifications of Panelists

1.   All panelists shall meet the qualifications set out in Article 25(2).

2.   Individuals may not serve as panelists for a dispute in which:

    (a)   they have participated pursuant to Article 23(4); or
    (b)   they have, or a person or organization with which they are affiliated has, an interest, as set out in the code of conduct established under Article 25(2)(d).

Article 27   Panel Selection

1.   Where there are two disputing Parties, the following procedures shall apply:

    (a)   The panel shall comprise five members.

    (b)   The disputing Parties shall endeavor to agree on the chair of the panel within 15 days after the Council votes to convene the panel. If the disputing Parties are unable to agree on the chair within this period, the disputing Party chosen by lot shall select within five days a chair who is not a citizen of that Party.

    (c)   Within 15 days of selection of the chair, each disputing Party shall select two panelists who are citizens of the other disputing Party.

    (d)   If a disputing Party fails to select its panelists within such period, such panelists shall be selected by lot from among the roster members who are citizens of the other disputing Party.

2.   Where there are more than two disputing Parties, the following procedures shall apply:

    (a)   The panel shall comprise five members.

    (b)   The disputing Parties shall endeavor to agree on the chair of the panel within 15 days after the Council votes to convene the panel. If the disputing parties are unable to agree on the chair within this period, the Party or Parties on the side of the dispute chosen by lot shall select within 10 days a chair who is not a citizen of such Party or Parties.

    (c)   Within 30 days of selection of the chair, the Party complained against shall select two panelists, one of whom is a citizen of a complaining Party, and the other of whom is a citizen of another complaining Party. The complaining Parties shall select two panelists who are citizens of the Party complained against.

    (d)   If any disputing Party fails to select a panelist within such a period, such panelist shall be selected by lot in accordance with the citizenship criteria of subparagraph (c).

3.   Panelists shall normally be selected from the roster. Any disputing Party may exercise a peremptory challenge against any individual not on the roster who is proposed as a panelist by a disputing Party within 30 days after the individual has been proposed.

4.   If a disputing Party believes that a panelist is in violation of the code of conduct, the disputing Parties shall consult and, if they agree, the panelist shall be removed and a new panelist shall be selected in accordance with this Article.

Article 28   Rules of Procedure

1.   The Council shall establish Model Rules of Procedure. The procedures shall provide:

    (a)   a right to at least one hearing before the panel;

    (b)   the opportunity to make initial and rebuttal written submissions; and

    (c)   that no panel may disclose which panelists are associated with majority or minority opinions.

2.   Unless the disputing Parties otherwise agree, panels convened under this Part shall be established and conduct their proceedings in accordance with the Model Rules of Procedure.

3.   Unless the disputing Parties otherwise agree within 20 days after the Council votes to convene the panel, the terms of reference shall be:

"To examine, in light of the relevant provisions of the Agreement, including those contained in Part Five, whether there has been a persistent pattern of failure by the Party complained against to effectively enforce its environmental law, and to make findings, determinations and recommendations in accordance with Article 31(2)."

Article 29   Third Party Participation

A party that is not a disputing Party, on delivery of a written notice to the disputing Parties and to the Secretariat, shall be entitled to attend all hearings, to make written and oral submissions to the panel and to receive written submissions of the disputing Parties.

Article 30   Role of Experts

On request of a disputing Party, or on its own initiative, the panel may seek information and technical advice from any person or body that it deems appropriate, provided that the disputing Parties so agree and subject to such terms and conditions as such Parties may agree.

Article 31   Initial Report

1.   Unless the disputing Parties otherwise agree, the panel shall base its report on the submissions and arguments of the Parties and on any information before it pursuant to Article 30.

2.   Unless the disputing Parties otherwise agree, the panel shall, within 180 days after the last panelist is selected, present to the disputing Parties an initial report containing:

   (a)   findings of fact;
   (b)   its determination as to whether there has been a persistent pattern of failure by the Party complained against to effectively enforce its environmental law, or any other determination requested in the terms of reference; and
   (c)   in the event the panel makes an affirmative determination under subparagraph (b), its recommendations, if any, for the resolution of the dispute, which normally shall be that the Party complained against adopt and implement an action plan sufficient to remedy the pattern of non-enforcement.

3.   Panelists may furnish separate opinions on matters not unanimously agreed.

4.   A disputing party may submit written comments to the panel on its initial report within 30 days of presentation of the report.

5.   In such an event, and after considering such written comments, the panel, on its own initiative or on the request of any disputing Party, may:

   (a)   request the views of any participating Party,
   (b)   reconsider its report; and
   (c)   make any further examination that it considers appropriate.

Article 32   Final Report

1.   The panel shall present to the disputing Parties a final report, including any separate opinions on matters not unanimously agreed, within 60 days of presentation of the initial report, unless the disputing Parties otherwise agree.

2.   The disputing Parties shall transmit to the Council the final report of the panel, as well as any written views that a disputing Party desires to be appended, on a confidential basis within 15 days after it is presented to them.

3.   The final report of the panel shall be published five days after it is transmitted to the Council.

Article 33   Implementation of Final Report

If, in its final report, a panel determines that there has been a persistent pattern of failure by the Party complained against to effectively enforce its environmental law, the disputing Parties may agree on a mutually satisfactory action plan, which normally shall conform with the determinations and recommendations of the panel.   The disputing Parties shall promptly notify the Secretariat and the Council of any agreed resolution of the dispute.

Article 34   Review of Implementation

1.   If, in its final report, a panel determines that there has been a persistent pattern of failure by the Party complained against to effectively enforce its environmental law, and:

   (a)   the disputing Parties have not agreed on an action plan under Article 33 within 60 days of the date of the final report, or

(b)   the disputing Parties cannot agree on whether the Party complained against is fully implementing
       (i)   an action plan agreed under Article 33,
       (ii)   an action plan deemed to have been established by a panel under paragraph 2, or
       (iii) an action plan approved or established by a panel under paragraph 4,

any disputing Party may request that the panel be reconvened. The requesting Party shall deliver the request in writing to the other Parties and to the Secretariat. The Council shall reconvene the panel on delivery of the request to the Secretariat.

2.   No Party may make a request under paragraph 1(a) earlier than 60 days, or later than 120 days, after the date of the final report. If the disputing Parties have not agreed to an action plan and if no request was made under paragraph 1(a), the last action plan, if any, submitted by the Party complained against to the complaining Party or Parties within 60 days of the date of the final report, or such other period as the disputing Parties may agree, shall be deemed to have been established by the panel 120 days after the date of the final report.

3.   A request under paragraph 1(b) may be made no earlier than 180 days after an action plan has been:

(a)   agreed under Article 33;
(b)   deemed to have been established by a panel under paragraph 2; or
(c)   approved or established by a panel under paragraph 4;

and only during the term of any such action plan.

4.   Where a panel has been reconvened under paragraph 1(a), it:

(a)   shall determine whether any action plan proposed by the Party complained against is sufficient to remedy the pattern of non-enforcement and
       (i)   if so, shall approve the plan, or
       (ii)   if not, shall establish such a plan consistent with the law of the Party complained against, and
(b)   may, where warranted, impose a monetary enforcement assessment in accordance with Annex 34,

within 90 days after the panel has been reconvened or such other period as the disputing Parties may agree.

5.   Where a panel has been reconvened under paragraph 1(b), it shall determine either that:

(a)   the Party complained against is fully implementing the action plan, in which case the panel may not impose a monetary enforcement assessment, or
(b)   the Party complained against is not fully implementing the action plan, in which case the panel shall impose a monetary enforcement assessment in accordance with Annex 34,

within 60 days after it has been reconvened or such other period as the disputing Parties may agree.

6.   A panel reconvened under this Article shall provide that the Party complained against shall fully implement any action plan referred to in paragraph 4(a)(ii) or 5(b), and pay any monetary enforcement assessment imposed under paragraph 4(b) or 5(b), and any such provision shall be final.

Article 35   Further Proceeding

A complaining Party, may at any time beginning 180 days after a panel determination under Article 34(5)(b), request in writing that a panel be reconvened to determine whether the Party complained against is fully implementing the action plan. On delivery of the request to the other Parties and the Secretariat, the Council shall reconvene the panel. The panel shall make the determination within 60 days after it has been reconvened or such other period as the disputing Parties may agree.

Article 36   Suspension of Benefits

1.   Subject to Annex 36A, where a Party fails to pay a monetary enforcement assessment within 180 days after it is imposed by a panel:

(a)   under Article 34(4)(b), or

(b)   under Article 34(5)(b), except where benefits may be suspended under paragraph 2(a),

any complaining Party or Parties may suspend, in accordance with Annex 36B, the application to the Party complained against of NAFTA benefits in an amount no greater than that sufficient to collect the monetary enforcement assessment.

2.   Subject to Annex 36A, where a panel has made a determination under Article 34(5)(b) and the panel:

(a)   has previously imposed a monetary enforcement assessment under Article 34 (4)(b) or established an action plan under Article 34(4)(a)(ii); or

(b)   has subsequently determined under Article 35 that a Party is not fully implementing an action plan;

the complaining Party or Parties may, in accordance with Annex 36B, suspend annually the application to the Party complained against of NAFTA benefits in an amount no greater than the monetary enforcement assessment imposed by the panel under Article 34(5)(b).

3.   Where more than one complaining Party suspends benefits under paragraph 1 or 2, the combined suspension shall be no greater than the amount of the monetary enforcement assessment.

4.   Where a Party has suspended benefits under paragraph 1 or 2, the Council shall, on the delivery of a written request by the Party complained against to the other Parties and the Secretariat, reconvene the panel to determine whether the monetary enforcement assessment has been paid or collected, or whether the Party complained against is fully implementing the action plan, as the case may be. The panel shall submit its report within 45 days after it has been reconvened. If the panel determines that the assessment has been paid or collected, or that the Party complained against is fully implementing the action plan, the suspension of benefits under paragraph 1 or 2, as the case may be, shall be terminated.

5.   On the written request of the Party complained against, delivered to the other Parties and the Secretariat, the Council shall reconvene the panel to determine whether the suspension of benefits by the complaining Party or Parties pursuant to paragraph 1 or 2 is manifestly excessive. Within 45 days of the request, the panel shall present a report to the disputing Parties containing its determination.

PART VI   GENERAL PROVISIONS

Article 37   Enforcement Principle

Nothing in this Agreement shall be construed to empower a Party's authorities to undertake environmental law enforcement activities in the territory of another Party.

Article 38   Private Rights

No Party may provide for a right of action under its law against any other Party on the ground that another Party has acted in a manner inconsistent with this Agreement.

Article 39   Protection of Information

1. Nothing in this Agreement shall be construed to require a Party to make available or allow access to information:

(a)   the disclosure of which would impede its environmental law enforcement; or

(b)   that is protected from disclosure by its law governing business or proprietary information, personal privacy or the confidentiality of governmental decision making.

2. If a Party provides confidential or proprietary information to another Party, the Council, the Secretariat or the Joint Public Advisory Committee, the recipient shall treat the information on the same basis as the Party providing the information.

3.   Confidential or proprietary information provided by a Party to a panel under this Agreement shall be treated in accordance with the rules of procedure established under Article 28.

Article 40   Relation to Other Environmental Agreements

Nothing in this Agreement shall be construed to affect the existing rights and obligations of the Parties under other international environmental agreements, including conservation agreements, to which such Parties are party.

Article 41   Extent of Obligations

Annex 41 applies to the Parties specified in that Annex.

Article 42   National Security

Nothing in this Agreement shall be construed:

   (a)   to require any Party to make available or provide access to information the disclosure of which it determines to be contrary to its essential security interests; or
   (b)   to prevent any Party from taking any actions that it considers necessary for the protection of its essential security interests relating to
       (i)   arms, ammunition and implements of war, or
       (ii)   the implementation of national policies or international agreements respecting the non-proliferation of nuclear weapons or other nuclear explosive devices.

Article 43   Funding of the Commission

Each Party shall contribute an equal share of the annual budget of the Commission, subject to the availability of appropriated funds in accordance with the Party's legal procedures. No Party shall be obligated to pay more than any other Party in respect of an annual budget.

Article 44   Privileges and Immunities

The Executive Director and staff of the Secretariat shall enjoy in the territory of each Party such privileges and immunities as are necessary for the exercise of their functions.

Article 45   Definitions

1.   For purposes of this Agreement:

A Party has not failed to "effectively enforce its environmental law" or to comply with Article 5(1) in a particular case where the action or inaction in question by agencies or officials of that Party:

   (a)   reflects a reasonable exercise of their discretion in respect of investigatory, prosecutorial, regulatory or compliance matters; or
   (b)   results from bona fide decisions to allocate resources to enforcement in respect of other environmental matters determined to have higher priorities;

"non-governmental organization" means any scientific, professional, business, non-profit, or public interest organization or association which is neither affiliated with, nor under the direction of, a government;

"persistent pattern" means a sustained or recurring course of action or inaction beginning after the date of entry into force of this Agreement;

"province" means a province of Canada, and includes the Yukon Territory and the Northwest Territories and their successors; and "territory" means for a Party the territory of that Party as set out in Annex 45.

2.   For purposes of Article 14(1) and Part Five:

(a)   "environmental law" means any statute or regulation of a Party, or provision thereof, the primary purpose of which is the protection of the environment, or the prevention of a danger to human life or health, through

(i)   the prevention, abatement or control of the release, discharge, or emission of pollutants or environmental contaminants,

(ii)   the control of environmentally hazardous or toxic chemicals, substances, materials and wastes, and the dissemination of information related thereto, or

(iii)   the protection of wild flora or fauna, including endangered species, their habitat, and specially protected natural areas

in the Party's territory, but does not include any statute or regulation, or provision thereof, directly related to worker safety or health.

(b)   For greater certainty, the term "environmental law" does not include any statute or regulation, or provision thereof, the primary purpose of which is managing the commercial harvest exploitation, or subsistence or aboriginal harvesting, of natural resources.

(c)   The primary purpose of a particular statutory or regulatory provision for purposes of subparagraphs (a) and (b) shall be determined by reference to its primary purpose, rather than to the primary purpose of the statute or regulation of which it is part.

3.   For purposes of Article 14(3), "judicial or administrative proceeding" means:

(a)   a domestic judicial, quasi-judicial or administrative action pursued by the Party in a timely fashion and in accordance with its law. Such actions comprise: mediation; arbitration; the process of issuing a license, permit, or authorization; seeking an assurance of voluntary compliance or a compliance agreement; seeking sanctions or remedies in an administrative or judicial forum; and the process of issuing an administrative order; and

(b)   an international dispute resolution proceeding to which the Party is party.

PART VII   FINAL PROVISIONS

Article 46   Annexes

The Annexes to this Agreement constitute an integral part of the Agreement.

Article 47   Entry into Force

This Agreement shall enter into force on January 1, 1994, immediately after entry into force of the NAFTA, on an exchange of written notifications certifying the completion of necessary legal procedures.

Article 48   Amendments

1.   The Parties may agree on any modification of or addition to this Agreement.

2.   When so agreed, and approved in accordance with the applicable legal procedures of each Party, a modification or addition shall constitute an integral part of this Agreement.

Article 49   Accession

Any country or group of countries may accede to this Agreement subject to such terms and conditions as may be agreed between such country or countries and the Council and following approval in accordance with the applicable legal procedures of each country.

Article 50   Withdrawal

A Party may withdraw from this Agreement six months after it provides written notice of withdrawal to the other Parties. If a Party withdraws, the Agreement shall remain in force for the remaining Parties.

Article 51   Authentic Texts

The English, French, and Spanish texts of this Agreement are equally authentic.

IN WITNESS WHEREOF, the undersigned, being duly authorized by the respective Governments, have signed this Agreement.

———————————————————

The General Agreement on Tariffs and Trade, 1947

55 U.N.T.S. 187
Signed: October 30, 1947
Entered into Force: January 1, 1948 (through the Protocol of Provisional Application to the General Agreement on Tariffs and Trade, 55 U.N.T.S. 308)

Secretariat Homepage: http://www.wto.org/

The Governments ...:

Recognizing that their relations in the field of trade and economic endeavour should be conducted with a view to raising standards of living, ensuring full employment and a large and steadily growing volume of real income and effective demand, developing the full use of the resources of the world and expanding the production and exchange of goods,

Being desirous of contributing to these objectives by entering into reciprocal and mutually advantageous arrangements directed to the substantial reduction of tariffs and other barriers to trade and to the elimination of discriminatory treatment in international commerce,

Have through their Representatives agreed as follows:

PART I

Article I   General Most Favoured-Nation Treatment

1. With respect to customs duties and charges of any kind imposed on or in connection with importation or exportation or imposed on the international transfer of payments for imports or exports, and with respect to the method of levying such duties and charges, and with respect to all rules and formalities in connection with importation and exportation, and with respect to all matters referred to in paragraphs 2 and 4 of Article III, any advantage, favour, privilege or immunity granted by any contracting party to any product originating in or destined for any other country shall be accorded immediately and unconditionally to the like product originating in or destined for the territories of all other contracting parties.

2. The provisions of paragraph 1 of this Article shall not require the elimination of any preferences in respect of import duties or charges which do not exceed the levels provided for in paragraph 4 of this Article and which fall within the following descriptions:

      (a) Preferences in force exclusively between two or more of the territories listed in Annex A, subject to the conditions set forth therein;

      (b) Preferences in force exclusively between two or more territories which on July 1, 1939, were connected by common sovereignty or relations of protection or suzerainty and which are listed in Annexes B, C and D, subject to the conditions set forth therein;

      (c) Preferences in force exclusively between the United States of America and the Republic of Cuba;

      (d) Preferences in force exclusively between neighbouring countries listed in Annexes E and F.

3. The provisions of paragraph 1 shall not apply to preferences between the countries formerly a part of the Ottoman Empire and detached from it on July 24, 1923, provided such preferences are approved under paragraph 5 of Article XXV, which shall be applied in this respect in the light of paragraph 1 of Article XXIX.

4. The margin of preference on any product in respect of which a preference is permitted under paragraph 2 of this Article but is not specifically set forth as a maximum margin of preference in the appropriate Schedule annexed to this Agreement shall not exceed:

      (a) in respect of duties or charges on any product described in such Schedule, the difference between the most-favoured-nation and preferential rates provided for therein; if no preferential rate is provided for, the preferential rate shall for the purposes of this paragraph be taken to be that in force on April 10, 1947, and, if no most-favoured-nation rate is provided for, the margin shall not exceed the difference between the most-favoured-nation and preferential rates existing on April 10, 1947;

(b) in respect of duties or charges on any product not described in the appropriate Schedule, the difference between the most-favoured nation and preferential rates existing on April 10, 1947.

In the case of the contracting parties named in Annex G, the date of April 10, 1947, referred to in sub-paragraphs (a) and (b) of this paragraph shall be replaced by the respective dates set forth in that Annex.

* * *

Article III   National Treatment on Internal Taxation and Regulation

1. The contracting parties recognize that internal taxes and other internal charges, and laws, regulations and requirements affecting the internal sale, offering for sale, purchase, transportation, distribution or use of products, and internal quantitative regulations requiring the mixture, processing or use of products in specified amounts or proportions, should not be applied to imported or domestic products so as to afford protection to domestic production.

2. The products of the territory of any contracting party imported into the territory of any other contracting party shall not be subject, directly or indirectly, to internal taxes or other internal charges of any kind in excess of those applied, directly or indirectly, to like domestic products. Moreover, no contracting party shall otherwise apply internal taxes or other internal charges to imported or domestic products in a manner contrary to the principles set forth in paragraph 1.

3. With respect to any existing internal tax which is inconsistent with the provisions of paragraph 2, but which is specifically authorized under a trade agreement, in force on April 10, 1947, in which the import duty on the taxed product is bound against increase, the contracting party imposing the tax shall be free to postpone the application of the provisions of paragraph 2 to such tax until such time as it can obtain release from the obligations of such trade agreement in order to permit the increase of such duty to the extent necessary to compensate for the elimination of the protective element of the tax.

4. The products of the territory of any contracting party imported into the territory of any other contracting party shall be accorded treatment no less favourable than that accorded to like products of national origin in respect of all laws, regulations and requirements affecting their internal sale, offering for sale, purchase, transportation, distribution or use. The provisions of this paragraph shall not prevent the application of differential internal transportation charges which are based exclusively on the economic operation of the means of transport and not on the nationality of the product.

5. No contracting party shall establish or maintain any internal quantitative regulation relating to the mixture, processing or use of products in specified amounts or proportions which requires, directly or indirectly, that any specified amount or proportion of any product which is the subject of the regulation must be supplied from domestic sources. Moreover, no contracting party shall otherwise apply internal quantitative regulations in a manner contrary to the principles set forth in paragraph 1.

6. The provisions of paragraph 5 shall not apply to any internal quantitative regulation in force in the territory of any contracting party on July 1, 1939, April 10, 1947, or March 24, 1948, at the option of that contracting party; Provided that any such regulation which is contrary to the provisions of paragraph 5 shall not be modified to the detriment of imports and shall be treated as a customs duty for the purpose of negotiation.

7. No internal quantitative regulation relating to the mixture, processing or use of products in specified amounts or proportions shall be applied in such a manner as to allocate any such amount or proportion among external sources of supply.

8.   (a) The provisions of this Article shall not apply to laws, regulations or requirements governing the procurement by governmental agencies of products purchased for governmental purposes and not with a view to commercial resale or with a view to use in the production of goods for commercial sale.

(b) The provisions of this Article shall not prevent the payment of subsidies exclusively to domestic producers, including payments to domestic producers derived from the proceeds of internal taxes or charges applied consistently with the provisions of this Article and subsidies effected through governmental purchases of domestic products.

9. The contracting parties recognize that internal maximum price control measures, even though conforming to the other provisions of this Article, can have effects prejudicial to the interests of contracting parties supplying imported products. Accordingly, contracting parties applying such measures shall take account of the interests of exporting contracting parties with a view to avoiding to the fullest practicable extent such prejudicial effects.

10. The provisions of this Article shall not prevent any contracting party from establishing or maintaining internal quantitative regulations relating to exposed cinematograph films and meeting the requirements of Article IV.

* * *

Article VI   Anti-dumping and Countervailing Duties

1. The contracting parties recognize that dumping, by which products of one country are introduced into the commerce of another country at less than the normal value of the products, is to be condemned if it causes or threatens material injury to an established industry in the territory of a contracting party or materially retards the establishment of a domestic industry. For the purposes of this Article, a product is to be considered as being introduced into the commerce of an importing country at less than its normal value, if the price of the product exported from one country to another

    (a) is less than the comparable price, in the ordinary course of trade, for the like product when destined for consumption in the exporting country, or,

    (b) in the absence of such domestic price, is less than either

        (i) the highest comparable price for the like product for export to any third country in the ordinary course of trade, or

        (ii) the cost of production of the product in the country of origin plus a reasonable addition for selling cost and profit.

Due allowance shall be made in each case for differences in conditions and terms of sale, for differences in taxation, and for other differences affecting price comparability.

2. In order to offset or prevent dumping, a contracting party may levy on any dumped product an anti-dumping duty not greater in amount than the margin of dumping in respect of such product. For the purposes of this Article, the margin of dumping is the price difference determined in accordance with the provisions of paragraph1.

3. No countervailing duty shall be levied on any product of the territory of any contracting party imported into the territory of another contracting party in excess of an amount equal to the estimated bounty or subsidy determined to have been granted, directly or indirectly, on the manufacture, production or export of such product in the country of origin or exportation, including any special subsidy to the transportation of a particular product. The term "countervailing duty" shall be understood to mean a special duty levied for the purpose of offsetting any bounty or subsidy bestowed, directly or indirectly, upon the manufacture, production or export of any merchandise.

4. No product of the territory of any contracting party imported into the territory of any other contracting party shall be subject to anti-dumping or countervailing duty by reason of the exemption of such product from duties or taxes borne by the like product when destined for consumption in the country of origin or exportation, or by reason of the refund of such duties or taxes.

5. No product of the territory of any contracting party imported into the territory of any other contracting party shall be subject to both anti-dumping and countervailing duties to compensate for the same situation of dumping or export subsidization.

6.   (a) No contracting party shall levy any anti-dumping or countervailing duty on the importation of any product of the territory of another contracting party unless it determines that the effect of the dumping or subsidization, as the case may be, is such as to cause or threaten material injury to an established domestic industry, or is such as to retard materially the establishment of a domestic industry.

      (b) The contracting parties may waive the requirement of subparagraph (a) of this paragraph so as to permit a contracting party to levy an anti-dumping or countervailing duty on the importation of any product for the purpose of offsetting dumping or subsidization which causes or threatens material injury to an industry in the territory of another contracting party exporting the product concerned to the territory of the importing contracting party. The contracting parties shall waive the requirements of sub-paragraph (a) of this paragraph, so as to permit the levying of a countervailing duty, in cases in which they find that a subsidy is causing or threatening material injury to an industry in the territory of another contracting party exporting the product concerned to the territory of the importing contracting party.

(c) In exceptional circumstances, however, where delay might cause damage which would be difficult to repair, a contracting party may levy a countervailing duty for the purpose referred to in sub-paragraph (b) of this paragraph without the prior approval of the contracting parties; Provided that such action shall be reported immediately to the contracting parties and that the countervailing duty shall be withdrawn promptly if the contracting parties disapprove.

7. A system for the stabilization of the domestic price or of the return to domestic producers of a primary commodity, independently of the movements of export prices, which results at times in the sale of the commodity for export at a price lower than the comparable price charged for the like commodity to buyers in the domestic market, shall be presumed not to result in material injury within the meaning of paragraph 6 if it is determined by consultation among the contracting parties substantially interested in the commodity concerned that:

(a) the system has also resulted in the sale of the commodity for export at a price higher than the comparable price charged for the like commodity to buyers in the domestic market, and

(b) the system is so operated, either because of the effective regulation of production, or otherwise, as not to stimulate exports unduly or otherwise seriously prejudice the interests of other contracting parties.

* * *

Article XI   General Elimination of Quantitative Restrictions

1. No prohibitions or restrictions other than duties, taxes or other charges, whether made effective through quotas, import or export licenses or other measures, shall be instituted or maintained by any contracting party on the importation of any product of the territory of any other contracting party or on the exportation or sale for export of any product destined for the territory of any other contracting party.

2. The provisions of paragraph I of this Article shall not extend to the following:

(a) Export prohibitions or restrictions temporarily applied to prevent or relieve critical shortages of foodstuffs or other products essential to the exporting contracting party;

(b) Import and export prohibitions or restrictions necessary to the application of standards or regulations for the classification, grading or marketing of commodities in international trade;

(c) Import restrictions on any agricultural or fisheries product, imported in any form, necessary to the enforcement of governmental measures which operate:

(i) to restrict the quantities of the like domestic product permitted to be marketed or produced, or, if there is no substantial domestic production of the like product, of a domestic product for which the imported product can be directly substituted; or

(ii) to remove a temporary surplus of the like domestic product, or, if there is no substantial domestic production of the like product, of a domestic product for which the imported product can be directly substituted, by making the surplus available to certain groups of domestic consumers free of charge or at prices below the current market level; or

(iii) to restrict the quantities permitted to be produced of any animal product the production of which is directly dependent, wholly or mainly, on the imported commodity, if the domestic production of that commodity is relatively negligible.

Any contracting party applying restrictions on the importation of any product pursuant to sub-paragraph (c) of this paragraph shall give public notice of the total quantity or value of the product permitted to be imported during a specified future period and of any change in such quantity or value. Moreover, any restrictions applied under (i) above shall not be such as will reduce the total of imports relative to the total of domestic production, as compared with the proportion which might reasonably be expected to rule between the two in the absence of restrictions. In determining this proportion, the contracting party shall pay due regard to the proportion prevailing during a previous representative period and to any special factors which may have affected or may be affecting the trade in the product concerned.

* * *

Article XX   General Exceptions

Subject to the requirement that such measures are not applied in a manner which would constitute a means of arbitrary or unjustifiable discrimination between countries where the same conditions prevail, or a disguised restriction on international trade, nothing in this Agreement shall be construed to prevent the adoption or enforcement by any contracting party of measures:

(a) necessary to protect public morals;

(b) necessary to protect human, animal or plant life or health;

(c) relating to the importation or exportation of gold or silver;

(d) necessary to secure compliance with laws or regulations which are not inconsistent with the provisions of this Agreement, including those relating to customs enforcement, the enforcement of monopolies operated under paragraph 4 of Article II and Article XVII, the protection of patents, trade marks and copyrights, and the prevention of deceptive practices;

(e) relating to the products of prison labour;

(f) imposed for the protection of national treasures of artistic, historic or archaeological value;

(g) relating to the conservation of exhaustible natural resources if such measures are made effective in conjunction with restrictions on domestic production or consumption;

(h) undertaken in pursuance of obligations under any intergovernmental commodity agreement which conforms to criteria submitted to the contracting parties and not disapproved by them or which is itself so submitted and not so disapproved;

(i) involving restrictions on exports of domestic materials necessary to ensure essential quantities of such materials to a domestic processing industry during periods when the domestic price of such materials is held below the world price as part of a governmental stabilization plan; *Provided* that such restrictions shall not operate to increase the exports of or the protection afforded to such domestic industry, and shall not depart from the provisions of this Agreement relating to non-discrimination;

(j) essential to the acquisition or distribution of products in general or local short supply; *Provided* that any such measures shall be consistent with the principle that all contracting parties are entitled to an equitable share of the international supply of such products, and that any such measures, which are inconsistent with the other provisions of this Agreement shall be discontinued as soon as the conditions giving rise to them have ceased to exist. The contracting parties shall review the need for this sub-paragraph not later than 30 June 1960.

* * *

———————————————————